D1141843

PRINCIPLES OF AUDITING

Third Edition

PRINCIPLES OF AUDITING
An Introduction to International Standards on Auditing

Rick Hayes, Hans Gortemaker and Philip Wallage

 Prentice Hall
FINANCIAL TIMES

An imprint of **Pearson Education**
Harlow, England • London • New York • Boston • San Francisco • Toronto • Sydney • Singapore • Hong Kong
Tokyo • Seoul • Taipei • New Delhi • Cape Town • Madrid • Mexico City • Amsterdam • Munich • Paris • Milan

Pearson Education Limited

Edinburgh Gate
Harlow CM20 2JE
United Kingdom
Tel: +44 (0)1279 623623
Web: www.pearson.com/uk

———————————

First published by McGraw-Hill Publishing Company 1999 (print)
Second edition published by Pearson Education Limited 2005 (print and electronic)
Third edition published 2014 (print and electronic)

ISBN: 978-0-273-76817-3 (print)
       978-0-273-76949-1 (PDF)
       978-0-273-78065-6 (eText)

British Library Cataloguing-in-Publication Data
A catalogue record for the print edition is available from the British Library

Library of Congress Cataloging-in-Publication Data
A catalog record for the print edition is available from the Library of Congress

10 9 8 7 6 5 4 3 2
16 15 14

Print edition typeset in 10.5/12.5 Minion Pro by 73
Printed by Ashford Colour Press Ltd., Gosport

NOTE THAT ANY PAGE CROSS REFERENCES REFER TO THE PRINT EDITION

Contents

6 Main Audit Concepts and Planning the Audit (ISA 300, 315, 320)   181

7 Internal Control and Control Risk   234

8 Analytical Procedures   282

9   Auditor's Response to Assessed Risk (ISA 330, ISA 500)   332

10   Audit Evidence   363

13 Overview of a Group Audit   507

14 Other Assurance and Non-Assurance Engagements   571

15 Corporate Governance and the Role of the Auditor   611

Companion Website

For open-access **student resources** specifically written to complement this textbook and support your learning, please visit **www.pearsoned.co.uk/hayes**

Lecturer Resources

For password-protected online resources tailored to support the use of this textbook in teaching, please visit **www.pearsoned.co.uk/hayes**

List of Illustrations

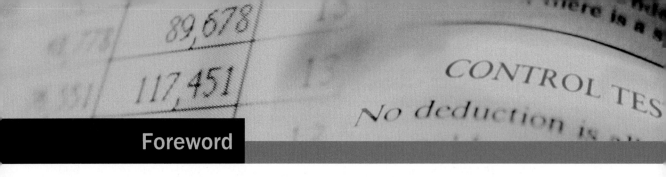

'The world has grown into a global marketplace at an exceedingly fast pace in recent years…changes in one part of the world can have significant effects on other parts.' Had I not used quotation marks, one could easily read this statement as a reference to the global financial crisis that shocked the world in the recent past. Rather, this is the observation of my predecessor Prof. Robert Roussey, with which he started his Foreword to the first edition of this book, Principles of Auditing, in 1999. Robert continued by describing how this global marketplace had triggered the emergence of International Accounting Standards (now IFRS) and International Standards on Auditing (ISAs), and stated, 'In the late 1990s, these international standards are on the brink of becoming the global standards of the future.'

Indeed, that is what they have become – and so have the 'Clarified' International Standards on Auditing. In his Foreword to the second edition of this book in 2005, my immediate predecessor, John Kellas, started with, 'In the last few years the auditing environment has changed dramatically. The failure of Enron was perhaps the biggest single catalyst for change….The International Auditing and Assurance Standards Board (IAASB), the independent standards-setter that operates under the auspices of the International Federation of Accountants (IFAC), has sought to respond effectively to the new environment.' Under John's leadership, the IAASB has completely rewritten the ISAs to make them more understandable and better fit for use. All 36 ISAs and International Standard on Quality Control (ISQC) 1 now clearly distinguish the auditor's objectives, the requirements of the standards, and the standard's application and other explanatory material. Many contain considerations specific to audits of smaller entities and of public sector entities, and as part of this 'clarification' effort many ISAs were also thoroughly revised for their content. As a result, there are now more robust requirements in key areas, such as risk assessment (e.g., estimates and related parties), materiality and its use in evaluating misstatements, audit evidence (e.g., confirmations and representations), using the work of others (e.g., group audits and experts), and communications and reporting.

This impressive exercise was essentially completed when I succeeded John as Chairman in January 2009. The full suite of the Clarified ISAs and ISQC 1 became effective for audits of financial statements for periods beginning or after 15 December 2009. Have they become the 'global standards' as Chairman Roussey had anticipated? Yes, they have. The authors show in Chapter 1, per April 2013, which 86 countries in various regions of the world had committed to using the Clarified ISAs. An impressive list (just think of the many translations needed!). And now, in December 2013, we already count 92 countries, and anticipate more additions in 2014. Further, the 24 larger international networks of accounting firms have committed to using the Clarified ISAs in their global audit methodologies. The Supreme Audit Institutions (SAIs) are also using the Clarified ISAs through a special public sector version called ISSAIs. So it is fair to say that there is one global language for auditing, both for the private and the public sector. And this is warmly supported by the International Organization of Securities Commissions (IOSCO), by banking and insurance regulators, and by global institutions like the World Bank, UNCTAD and IMF.

But…adoption and commitment to the use of standards is one thing. Implementation, including a thorough understanding and proper application of the standards, is another. This requires education, training, monitoring and enforcement. That is why I am delighted that Professors Rick Hayes, Hans Gortemaker and Philip Wallage have completed this third edition of 'Principles of Auditing – An Introduction to International Standards on Auditing.'

As a co-author on the previous editions, I know how much effort that takes. But it is urgently needed, as I learn time and again in my many outreach activities across the world.

This indeed is a global marketplace, and a marketplace with dramatic and ongoing changes, and practitioners and students need to update themselves about such changes. The Clarified ISAs are one striking example, but the IAASB issues other standards as well. I am pleased to see that this edition addresses those standards in a special chapter about other assurance and non-assurance engagements. This includes our recently revised standards on review engagements and compilation engagements, which are of particular relevance for services to smaller entities that are exempted from mandatory audits in many countries. The IAASB has also issued new assurance standards, such as International Standard on Assurance Engagements (ISAE) 3410 addressing greenhouse gas statements, a landmark standard in the area of sustainability-related assurance services, containing a number of interesting features, such as new definitions, a tabular presentation of requirements for reasonable and limited assurance engagements, guidance highlighting the importance of multidisciplinary teams, and illustrative assurance reports.

Will the changes stop here? A rhetorical question, of course. It is very likely that we will see expanded audit reports in the future, to better inform users of financial statements about significant audit matters. We may see the further emergence of Integrated Reporting, and assurance standards thereon. The IAASB may decide to update – again – the ISAs for key areas such as professional skepticism, risk assessment, group audits, quality control, and may enhance the ISAs further in relation to audits of financial institutions. But that will take time, and the authors rightly decided not to wait for that.

We hear critical comments with regard to the relevance and effectiveness of audit and assurance, in light of the financial crisis and findings from audit inspections across the world. However, underlying these comments are the positive expectations that many have of the contributions that auditors can make to this global, dynamic marketplace, and, in turn, to financial stability and trust. That is the public interest that all of us want to serve.

I wish this book a global uptake, and the readers much success with their professional endeavors.

Professor Arnold Schilder
Chairman, International Auditing and Assurance Standards Board

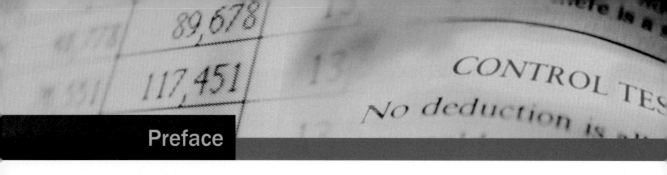

Auditing is not like financial or managerial accounting. Accounting is a system where an objective representation of reality is recorded and summarized. Auditing is a set of procedures and techniques by which that representation is 'agreed' to specific criteria. So, accounting endeavors to record economic values, categorize them, and then summarize them in a report. Using a set of proscribed procedures (audit standards), and given specific criteria (financial accounting standards), auditing analyses whether that representation is properly recorded, categorized and reported.

You are studying auditing to further your professional goals, if you are like most people reading this book. In addition to your university or college degree you would like to get a professional credential (such as CPA, CA, RA, CFE, WP, GR, CMA, etc.), or you have heard, correctly, that auditing is a 'high demand' profession. In other words, you would like some practical knowledge which will help you in your career. To fulfill your goals is our wish.

This textbook is written from the view of the professional auditor. Theory and academic concerns are covered. The emphasis is on the professional standards promulgated by the International Auditing and Assurance Standards Board (IAASB) and the practical day-to-day experience of international auditing firms. The authors of both the current and previous editions were all extremely successful professional auditors even before writing this book. The authors are also university professors who have taught hundreds of students from around the world, so this textbook is from the point of view of the international student.

Auditing is not just about accounting issues. Auditors don't just look at financial data, but also at controls, non-numerical data, and how an enterprise is governed. All sorts of enterprises are audited – profit oriented, not for profit, government, private and public. Auditors may be independent of the enterprise, a valuable internal analyst or working for the government. Audit-trained accountants are also hired to do forensic analysis. Today, as fraudulent schemes become ever larger and more harmful, it is auditors who are an important line of defence. Auditors' detailed analytical skills have created jobs in areas as diverse as marketing and divorce consulting.

Even before we co-authors began to write the first edition of this book over 25 years ago, we all agreed that our only concern was to produce a high-quality audit text for the international student. This meant that it had to be fully up to date, use outstanding material, have a sound balance of audit theory and real practice, and be based on international auditing and assurance standards. We see the world from a truly global, cross-cultural perspective.

We co-authors have a special place in our hearts for our students. We believe that it is our duty to convey our joy as auditors and audit teachers to you.

Acknowledgements

As always, this book was not the work of the co-authors alone, but also of the many professionals who helped us shape our ideas and give depth to the knowledge contained here.

First we would like to thank our team in the Netherlands who helped us in a professional, critical way, reviewing all chapters and providing many suggestions and improvements. We would like to thank Albert Bosch, Jeanine van Gestel (both from the VU University Amsterdam) and peter de Wolff (University of Amsterdam). Without their assistance the book in front of you would not have been there.

As in the previous editions, we also would like to acknowledge Lucas Hoogduin (KPMG) who contributed by writing the Appendix to Chapter 8.

Last but not Least we would like to thank to our former co-author Arnold Schilder (IAASB) for writing the Foreword.

To make this book we have used relevant material from other books. We would like to thank these publishers and professional organizations: American Accounting Association, American Institute of Certified Public Accountants, International Auditing and Assurance Standards Board, Internationl Ethics Standard Board of Accountants, International Federation of Accountants, European Union, US Securities and Exchange Commission, US Public Company Accounting Oversight Board, UK Financial Reporting Council and The Netherlands Institute of Accountants.

We would like to also thank the students in Hayes' auditing class at California State University, Los Angeles who gave us very helpful comments.

And, of course, who can do any massive undertaking without the support of their families. We take the Hayeses, Gortemakers and Wallages.

Acknowledgements

We would also to like to express our gratitude to the following academics who provide invaluable feedback on this book at various stages during its development:

- Laura Ipacs - Central European Business School
- Jane Nellist - University of Derby
- Zhiqi Wang - Bath Spa Uni

We are grateful to the following for permission to reproduce copyright material:

Figures

Illustration 4.1 after *Handbook of International Quality Control, Auditing Review, Other Assurance, and Related Services Pronouncements, Volume I,* International Federation of Accountants (2012); Illustrations 6.2 and 6.5 from *Auditing Organizations Through a Strategic-Systems Lens: The KPMG Business Measurement Process,* KPMG (Bell, T., *et al.* 1997) p. 27 and p. 41; Illustration 6.11 from *Auditing Procedures Study Audits of Small Business,* AICPA (1985) p. 44; Illustration 6.15 from *Other People's Money: A Study in the Social Psychology of Embezzlement,* Patterson Smith (Cressey, D. 1973) p. 30; Illustration 8.A.1 from CaseWare IDEA; Illustrations 9.3 and 13.2 after *Handbook of International Quality Control, Auditing Review, Other Assurance, and Related Services Pronouncements, Volume I,* International Federation of Accountants (2012) paragraph A111 and page 609, International Auditing and Assurance Standards Board (IAASB), Copyright © July 2012 by the International Federation of Accountants (IFAC). All rights reserved. Used with permission of IFAC.

Table

Table on page 485 from *Handbook of International Quality Control, Auditing Review, Other Assurance, and Related Services Pronouncements, Volume I,* International Federation of Accountants (2012) ISA 705, paragraph A1, International Auditing and Assurance Standards Board (IAASB), Copyright © July 2012 by the International Federation of Accountants (IFAC). All rights reserved. Used with permission of IFAC.

Text

Concept and a Company 1.2 on page 28 from 'The History of Deloitte', www .Deloitte.com; Concept and a Company 1.3 on page 29 from 'The History of Ernst & Young', www.ey.com; Concept and a Company 1.5 on page 30 from 'The History of PricewaterhouseCoopers', www.pwcglobal.com; Exam board questions on pages 70, 277 and 451 adapted from AICPA EPA exam questions, Copyright © 2000 & 1985 by American Institute of Certified Accountants, All rights reserved. Used with permission;

Illustrations 3.3 and 3.4 from *Handbook of the Code of Ethics for Professional Accountants*, International Federation of Accountants (2013), The International Ethics Standards Board (IESBA), Copyright © May 2013 by the International Federation of Accountants (IFAC). All rights reserved. Used with permission of IFAC; Exam board questions on pages 177, 276, 311 and 360 adapted from CICA exam questions, Canadian Institute of Chartered Accountants, Questions used in this publication are printed (or adapted) with permission from the *Uniform Evaluation Report* published by Chartered Professional Accountants of Canada (CPA Canada), Toronto, Canada. Any changes to the original material are the sole responsibility of the author (and/or publisher) and have not been reviewed or endorsed by CPA Canada; Illustrations 7.4, 7.5 and 7.8 from *Internal Control – Integrated Framework*, Committee of Sponsoring Organizations of the Treadway Commission (COSO) (1992), Copyright 1992. All rights reserved. Used with permission from the American Institute of Certified Public Accountants; Exam board questions on pages 329 and 330 from American Institute of Certified Public Accountants, Copyright © 2000 & 1985 by American Institute of Certified Accountants. All rights reserved. Used with permission; Illustrations 11.10, 12.7, 14.2, 14.3, 14.10 and 14.11 from *Handbook of International Quality Control, Auditing Review, Other Assurance, and Related Services Pronouncements, Volume I*, International Federation of Accountants (2012) Paragraph A2, p. 553; Appendix 3; pp. 762–764; p. 800; Appendix 2; Appendix 2 illustrations 1 and 2, International Auditing and Assurance Standards Board (IAASB), Copyright © July 2012 by the International Federation of Accountants (IFAC). All rights reserved. Used with permission of IFAC; Illustration 12.1 from Certification of Chief Executive Officer, Andrew Gould, 03/03/2004, US Securities and Exchange Commission; Illustration 12.3 from p. 49, 27/03/2012, US Securities and Exchange Commission; Illustration 14.6 from *Auditing Standard No. 5 – An Audit of Internal Control Over Financial Reporting That Is Integrated with An Audit of Financial Statements*, Public Company Accounting Oversight Board (2007) paragraph 87; Illustration 14.8 from Philips Annual Report 2012, with permission from Koninklijke Philips N.V. and KPMG; Illustration 14.9 from *International Standard on Assurance Engagements 3410: Assurance Engagements on Greenhouse Gas Statements*, International Federation of Accountants pp. 270–272, Copyright © July 2012 by the International Federation of Accountants (IFAC). All rights reserved. Used with permission of IFAC.

In some instances we have been unable to trace the owners of copyright material, and we would appreciate any information that would enable us to do so.

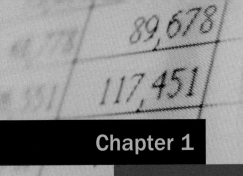

Chapter 1

INTERNATIONAL AUDITING OVERVIEW

1.1 Learning Objectives

After studying this chapter, you should be able to:

1 Relate some of the early history of auditing.

2 Discuss some of the audit expectations of the general public.

3 Identify organisations that affect international accounting and auditing.

4 Name the standards set by International Auditing and Assurance Standards Board.

5 Give an overview of the IFAC International Standards on Auditing (ISA).

6 Understand the basic definition of auditing in an international context.

7 Distinguish between audit risk and business risk

8 Differentiate the different types of audits.

9 Distinguish between the types of auditors and their training, licensing and authority.

10 Name and categorise the key management assertions.

11 Give the components of the audit process model.

12 Describe how international accountancy firms are organised and the responsibilities of auditors at the various levels of the organisation.

1.2 Auditing through World History

Auditing predates the Christian era. Anthropologists have found records of auditing activity dating back to early Mesopotamian times (around 3000 BC). There was also auditing activity in ancient China, Greece and Rome. The Latin meaning of the word 'auditor' was a 'hearer or listener' because in Rome auditors heard taxpayers, such as farmers, give their public statements regarding the results of their business and the tax duty due.

■ Scribes of Ancient Times

Auditors existed in ancient China and Egypt. They were supervisors of the accounts of the Chinese Emperor and the Egyptian Pharaoh. The government accounting system of the Zhao (1046–221 BC) dynasty in China included an elaborate budgetary process and audits of all government departments. From the dawn of the dynastic era in Egypt (3000 BC) the scribes (accountants) were among the most esteemed in society and the scribal occupation was one of the most prestigious occupations.

Egyptian Pharaohs were very severe with their auditors. Each royal storehouse used two auditors. One counted the goods when they came in the door and the second counted the goods after they were stored. The supervisor looked at both accounts. If there was a difference, the auditors were both killed.

Bookkeeping as a support mechanism for the determination of profit or wealth, or as a decision support system for achieving profit maximisation, was basically unknown in ancient cultures like the Mesopotamian, Egyptian, Greek or Roman. Auditing in English-speaking countries dates to AD 1130. Then, although they had highly developed economic systems, registration of economic facts or events was limited to the recording of single transactions whose sole purpose was to support the short-term memory of the trading partner.

Rational maximisation of wealth or profit did not fit into the systems of these cultures. Wealth was not a function of keen entrepreneurship or of smart cost–benefit trade-offs. It was merely a reward for one's loyalty to the government or for living in accordance with religious and moral principles and rules.

■ Profit Maximisation and Double Entry

The attitude of profit maximisation emerged at the end of the Middle Ages, with the emergence of large merchant houses in Italy. Trading was no longer the domain of the individual commercial traveller; it was now coordinated centrally at the luxurious desks of the large merchant houses in Venice, Florence or Pisa. As a result, communication became vital. Not unexpectedly, therefore, the system of double entry bookkeeping was first described in Italy, in Luca Pacioli's Summa de Arithmetica dated 20 November 1494.

The practice of modern auditing dates back to the beginning of the modern corporation at the dawn of the Industrial Revolution. In 1853, the Society of Accountants was founded in Edinburgh. Several other institutes emerged in Great Britain, merging in 1880 into the Institute of Chartered Accountants in England and Wales. This nationwide institute was a predecessor to institutes that emerged all over the Western world at the end of the nineteenth century, for example, in the USA (in 1886) or in the Netherlands (in 1895).

Further developments of the separation between provision of capital and management and in the complexity of companies, along with the occurrence of several financial scandals (e.g. City of Glasgow Bank, 1883; Afrikaansche Handels-vereeniging, 1879),[1] have led to a steady growth of the audit profession and regulation. The British Companies Acts (1845–62) were models for US auditing. The first US authoritative auditing pronouncement was issued in 1917.

■ Economic Conditions for Audit Reports

At the same time, companies across the world experienced growth in technology, improvement in communications and transportation, and the exploitation of expanding worldwide markets. As a result, the demands of owner-managed enterprises for capital rapidly exceeded the combined resources of the owners' savings and the wealth-creating potential of the enterprises themselves. It became necessary for industry to tap the savings of the community as a whole. The result has been the growth of sophisticated securities markets and credit-granting institutions serving the financial needs of large national, and increasingly international, corporations.

The flow of investor funds to the corporations and the whole process of allocation of financial resources through the securities markets have become dependent to a very large extent on financial reports made by company management. One of the most important characteristics of these corporations is the fact that their ownership is almost totally separated from their management. Management has control over the accounting systems. They are not only responsible for the financial reports to investors, but they also have the authority to determine the way in which the information is presented.

1.3 The Auditor, Corporations and Financial Information

Investors and creditors may have different objectives than management (e.g. management prefers higher salaries and benefits (expenses), whereas investors wish higher profits and dividends). Investors and creditors must depend on fair reporting of the financial statements. To give them confidence in the financial statements, an auditor[2] provides an independent and expert opinion on the fairness of the reports, called an audit opinion.

■ The Importance of Auditing

It can be said that the function of auditing is to lend credibility to the financial statements. The financial statements are the responsibility of management and the auditor's responsibility is to lend them credibility. By the audit process, the auditor enhances the usefulness and the value of the financial statements, but he also increases the credibility of other non-audited information released by management.[3]

■ The Expectations of Auditors

The importance of the company as a potential generator of wealth is increasingly understood, and so is the impact that a company's activities have on society and the environment. This has led to the expectation by investors that more information than just financial statements should be provided about a company. Public expectations go further and include questions such as:

- Is the company a going concern?[4]
- Is it free of fraud?
- Is it managed properly?
- Is there integrity in its database?
- Do directors have proper and adequate information to make decisions?
- Are there adequate controls?
- What effect do the company's products and by-products have on the environment?
- Can an 'unfortunate mistake' bring this company to its knees?

These are matters of corporate governance[5] as well as reporting and are all concerns of the auditor.

The auditors are very important to the directors of these corporations. As Sir Adrian Cadbury commented:[6]

> The external auditors are not part of the company team, but the chairmen (members of a corporate board of directors) have a direct interest in assuring themselves of the effectiveness of the audit approach within their companies. No chairman appreciates surprises, least of all in financial matters. The relationship between auditors and managers should be one where the auditors work with the appropriate people in the company, but do so on a strictly objective and professional basis, never losing sight of the fact that they are there on the shareholders' behalf. Chairmen need auditors who will stand up to management when necessary and who will unhesitatingly raise any doubts about the people or procedures with the audit committee. Weak auditors expose chairmen to hazards.

■ Auditing Expertise

Ordinarily, considerable expertise is needed to perform the auditing function. The auditor must be as competent in financial accounting as the most competent of his clients. He must be an expert in deciding what evidence is necessary to satisfy the assertions of the financial statements.

With the explosion in the use of information technology the auditor needs sufficient expertise, coupled with the knowledge of his client's affairs, to enable him to obtain and interpret all the evidence needed to provide reasonable assurance[7] that the financial statements are fairly presented. The new auditing environment will demand new skills of auditors if they are to be reporters and assessors of governance and measurements. They must have a questioning mind and be able to analyse and critically assess evidence.

■ Future of Auditing

In the future, as is the case today, the annual report, financial statements, notes and auditors' reports will be required. In addition to these, however, there will also be a director's report on corporate governance[8] (including effectiveness of internal control systems,[9] going concern, and adherence to best practice), and presumably an environmental management report.[10] These new reports come from the widespread concern about corporate governance resulting from major accounting scandals in the beginning of the twenty-first century (see Chapter 2 for further discussion). Auditing is spreading to audit of non-financial, textual and electronic data such as emails, phone messages, social media, human resources, intellectual capital, brand valuation and management, and other intangibles.[11]

Professor P. Percy outlined a perspective on the auditor's future.[12] He predicted that auditors will account for information not only in financial but also non-financial terms. Furthermore, only retrospective, but more and more prospective information will be in the annual report. The public desire will be for external and internal assessors on the board of directors. External assessors will appraise the integrity of information and business conduct, and internal assessors will appraise the efficiency and effectiveness of systems and their adequacy. Independent directors or assessors working on behalf of the shareholders within the board will ensure proper governance is being observed. (See Chapter 14 for further discussion of assurance services.)

1.4 International Accounting and Auditing Standards

■ International Financial Reporting Standards (IFRS)

Financial accounting standards are unique and separate from audit standards. By its nature, auditing requires that the real-world evidence of financial transactions be compared to financial standards. The standards to which an international auditor compares financial statements are generally standards in the reporting country (e.g. FAS in the USA, or national standards in European Union (EU) Member States which are based on EU Directives). In the future, companies and auditors in many additional countries will use International Financial Reporting Standards (IFRS), formerly called International Accounting Standards (IAS), which are set by the International Accounting Standards Board (IASB).

In March 2001, the IASC Foundation was formed as a not-for-profit corporation. The IASC Foundation is the parent entity of the International Accounting Standards Board, an independent accounting standard setter based in London, UK. In April 2001, the International Accounting Standards Board (IASB) assumed accounting standard setting responsibilities from its predecessor body, the International Accounting Standards Committee. Standards issued by the IASB are called International Financial Reporting Standards (IFRS). The EU has agreed to apply most of the IFRS.

The EU, formed in 1970, has issued a series of accounting standards for Member States. The European Commission (EC) achieves its law objectives through two instruments: Directives which must be incorporated into the laws of Member States; and Regulations, which become law throughout the EU without the need to pass through national legislatures.

Although all the EU Directives influence international accounting, the Eighth Company Law Directive is especially applicable to auditing. The Eighth Directive sets the minimum requirements for accounting training and experience for the community.

■ Auditing Standards Become International

As international accounting standards acquired more authority, logic dictated a set of international auditing standards collateral to them. Auditing standards were required by multinational corporations that wanted consistent auditing throughout the world.

With a set of international standards adopted for the world, international investors can be more confident in financial statements prepared in another country. The non-domestic auditor's opinion will lend as much credibility as a domestic auditor's opinion.

Developing Nations Adopt International Auditing Standards

International auditing standards encourage and assist developing nations to adopt codified sets of national auditing standards. The evolution of domestic accounting standards in developing nations can be expected to flow from the work of the IASB. Many developing countries rely to a large extent on foreign investment. Foreign investors are more likely to channel funds into a developing country if they have confidence in the accounting and auditing standards in that country. Audit has played a very important role in maintaining state financial and economic order, promoting the development of China's socialist economy and strengthening the construction of clean governments. The promulgation of the 1994 Audit Law symbolises that auditing in China has entered a new phase of development.[13] It is expected that many developing nations will adopt IASs.

■ IAASB Auditing Standards

The International Auditing and Assurance Standards Board (IAASB) is an independent standards board supported by the IFAC. Their objective is to improve the degree of uniformity of auditing practices and related services throughout the world by issuing pronouncements on a variety of audit and attest functions. The IAASB consists of a full-time chairman and 17 volunteer members from around the world. The board is balanced between practitioners in public practice with significant experience in the field of auditing and other assurance services and individuals who are not in public practice; in addition, at least three members are nominated by the public. Members are appointed by the IFAC Board based on recommendations from the IFAC Nominating Committee and are approved by the Public Interest Oversight Board (PIOB). In addition, there are a small number of observer members who have speaking rights at IAASB meetings but no voting rights. The IAASB is supported by a technical staff which has a wide range of standard-setting experience. [14]

IAASB issues several sets of standards to be applied to international auditing and assurance services. IAASB Standards contain basic principles and essential procedures together with related guidance in the form of explanatory and other material. IAASB issues:

- International Standards on Auditing (ISAs) as the standards to be applied by auditors in reporting on historical financial information;
- International Standards on Assurance Engagements (ISAEs) as the quality control standards to be applied by practitioners in assurance engagements dealing with information other than historical financial information;
- International Standards on Quality Control (ISQCs) as the standards to be applied for all services falling under the standards of the IAASB;
- International Standards on Related Services (ISRSs) as the standards to be applied on related services, as it considers appropriate; and
- International Standards on Review Engagements (ISREs) as the standards to be applied to the review of historical financial information.

Public Interest Oversight

The Public Interest Oversight Board (PIOB) oversees the public interest activities of IFAC. The objective of the PIOB is to increase confidence of investors and others that such activities, including the setting of standards by the IAASB, are properly responsive to the public interest. PIOB members are nominated by international institutions and regulatory bodies.

Role of the IAASB CAG

The IAASB Consultative Advisory Group (CAG} is comprised of representatives of regulators, business and international organizations, and users and preparers of financial statements who are interested in the development and maintenance of high-quality international standards for auditing, quality control, review, other assurance, and related services. Through active consultation, the IAASB receives valuable public interest input from the CAG on its agenda, project timetable, priorities and technical issues.

The International Auditing and Assurance Standards Board aims for voluntary international acceptance of its guidelines. Therefore, the International Standards on Auditing (ISAs) are not intended to override national regulations or pronouncements relating to audits of financial information. These ISAs are not yet authoritative in the way that pronouncements of, say, the Public Company Accounting Oversight Board (PCAOB) are to determine Generally Accepted Audit Standards (GAAS) in the USA. ISAs were made mandatory in Europe in 2005, and other regions in the world including the USA followed[15].

As of April 2013, the following countries are already using the Clarified ISAs:

- **Europe (33)**: Albania, Armenia, Belgium, Bulgaria, Croatia, Cyprus, Czech Republic, Denmark, Estonia, Finland, France (Experts Comptables), Georgia, Greece, Hungary, Iceland, Ireland, Kosovo, Latvia, Lithuania, Luxembourg, Malta, Moldova, Netherlands, Norway, Romania, Serbia, Slovakia, Slovenia, Sweden, Switzerland, Turkey, Ukraine, United Kingdom.
- **Americas (17)**: Argentina, Bahamas, Barbados, Brazil, Canada, Cayman Islands, Chile, Costa Rica, El Salvador, Guyana, Jamaica, Mexico, Panama, Puerto Rico (private companies), Trinidad and Tobago, Uruguay, USA (private companies).
- **Asia Pacific (18)**: Australia, Bangladesh, China, Hong Kong, India, Indonesia, Japan, Kazakhstan, Malaysia, Mongolia, Nepal, New Zealand, Pakistan, Philippines, Singapore, South Korea, Sri Lanka, Thailand.
- **Africa/Middle East (18)**: Botswana, Ghana, Kenya, Lebanon, Lesotho, Malawi, Mauritius, Namibia, Rwanda, Sierra Leone, South Africa, Swaziland, Tanzania, Tunisia, Uganda, United Arab Emirates (Abu Dhabi and Dubai), Zambia, Zimbabwe.

■ International Standards on Auditing (ISA)

International Standards on Auditing (ISAs) are developed by the International Federation of Accountants (IFAC) through its International Auditing and Assurance Standards Board (IAASB). The efforts of IFAC, founded in 1977, are directed towards developing international technical, ethical and educational guidelines for auditors, and reciprocal recognition of practitioners' qualifications. The membership of IFAC member bodies represents several million accountants in public and private practice, education, academe and government service.

There are several important groups within IFAC. The IFAC Council is responsible for overall governance of IFAC. The IFAC Board oversees the management of the organisation, takes action to enhance the transparency of certain IFAC activities, and overseas expansion of its size to include more member bodies. The standard-setting activities of the IFAC are carried out by the International Auditing and Assurance Standards Board (IAASB), the Ethics Committee, the Education Committee, and the Public Sector Committee with an interest in governmental financial reporting.

ISAs as Harmonisation Standards

International Standards on Auditing (ISAs) are the standards that are of most interest to auditors because they are the standards for the most frequent work of auditors, that is, financial statement audits and special purpose engagements. Although not all countries require ISAs, they will be used as the basic standards throughout this book because they represent the highest and best international representation of generally accepted auditing standards (GAAS).

ISAs are harmonisation standards, the application of which promotes consistent auditing across the world. The practice and theory of international auditing includes, in addition to knowledge of ISAs, consideration of quality control standards, allocating materiality, performing the audit, coordinating international reports and personnel, etc.

A listing of the International Standards on Auditing is given in Illustration 1.1.

ILLUSTRATION 1.1

List Of 2013 International Standards on Auditing

INTERNATIONAL STANDARDS ON QUALITY CONTROL (ISQCs)

International Standard on Quality Control (ISQC) 1, Quality Control for Firms that Perform Audits and Reviews of Financial Statements, and Other Assurance and Related Services Engagements

AUDITS OF HISTORICAL FINANCIAL INFORMATION

200–299 General Principles and Responsibilities

ISA 200 Overall Objectives of the Independent Auditor and the Conduct of an Audit in Accordance with International Standards on Auditing
ISA 210 Agreeing the Terms of Audit Engagements
ISA 220 Quality Control for an Audit of Financial Statements
ISA 230 Audit Documentation
ISA 240 The Auditor's Responsibilities Relating to Fraud in an Audit of Financial Statements
ISA 250 Consideration of Laws and Regulations in an Audit of Financial Statements
ISA 260 Communication with Those Charged with Governance
ISA 265 Communicating Deficiencies in Internal Control to Those Charged with Governance and Management

Illustration 1.1 (continued)

300–499 Risk Assessment and Response to Assessed Risks

ISA 300 Planning an Audit of Financial Statements
ISA 315 Identifying and Assessing the Risks of Material Misstatement through Understanding the Entity and Its Environment
ISA 320 Materiality in Planning and Performing an Audit
ISA 330 The Auditor's Responses to Assessed Risks
ISA 402 Audit Considerations Relating to an Entity Using a Service Organisation
ISA 450 Evaluation of Misstatements Identified during the Audit

500–599 Audit Evidence

ISA 500 Audit Evidence
ISA 501 Audit Evidence – Specific Considerations for Selected Items
ISA 505 External Confirmations
ISA 510 Initial Audit Engagements – Opening Balances
ISA 520 Analytical Procedures
ISA 530 Audit Sampling
ISA 540 Auditing Accounting Estimates, Including Fair Value Accounting Estimates, and Related Disclosures
ISA 550 Related Parties
ISA 560 Subsequent Events
ISA 570 Going Concern
ISA 580 Written Representations

600–699 Using the Work of Others

ISA 600 Special Considerations – Audits of Group Financial Statements (Including the Work of Component Auditors)
ISA 610 Using the Work of Internal Auditors
ISA 620 Using the Work of an Auditor's Expert

700–799 Audit Conclusions and Reporting

ISA 700 Forming an Opinion and Reporting on Financial Statements
ISA 705 Modifications to the Opinion in the Independent Auditor's Report
ISA 706 Emphasis of Matter Paragraphs and Other Matter Paragraphs in the Independent Auditor's Report
ISA 710 Comparative Information – Corresponding Figures and Comparative Financial Statements
ISA 720 The Auditor's Responsibilities Relating to Other Information in Documents Containing Audited Financial Statements

800–899 Specialised Areas

ISA 800 Special Considerations – Audits of Financial Statements Prepared in Accordance with Special Purpose Frameworks
ISA 805 Special Considerations – Audits of Single Financial Statements and Specific Elements Accounts or Items of a Financial Statement
ISA 810 Engagements to Report on Summary Financial Statements

International Auditing Practice Notes

IAPN 1000 Special Considerations in Auditing Financial Instruments

1.5 An Audit Defined

International auditing education starts with a thorough understanding of what we mean by an audit. There is no definition of an audit, *per se*, in the International Standards on Auditing. ISA 200, however, describes an audit of financial statements,[16] which we will discuss shortly.

A general definition of auditing is:[17]

> An audit is a systematic process of objectively obtaining and evaluating evidence regarding assertions about economic actions and events to ascertain the degree of correspondence between these assertions and established criteria, and communicating the results to interested users.

■ Components of the Audit Definition

An audit is a **systematic** approach. The audit follows a structured, documented plan (audit plan). In the process of the audit, accounting records are analysed by the auditors using a variety of generally accepted techniques. The audit must be planned and structured in such a way that those carrying out the audit can fully examine and analyse all-important evidence.

An audit is conducted **objectively**. An audit is an independent, objective and expert examination and evaluation of evidence. Auditors are fair and do not allow prejudice or bias to override their objectivity. They maintain an impartial attitude.

The auditor **obtains** and **evaluates evidence**. The auditor assesses the reliability and sufficiency of the information contained in the underlying accounting records and other source data by:

■ studying and evaluating accounting systems and internal controls on which he wishes to rely and testing those internal controls to determine the nature, extent and timing of other auditing procedures; and

■ carrying out such other tests, inquiries and other verification procedures of accounting transactions and account balances, as he considers appropriate in the particular circumstances.

The evidence obtained and evaluated by the auditor concerns **assertions** about economic actions and events. The basis of evidence-gathering objectives, what the evidence must prove, are the assertions of management. Assertions are representations by management, explicit or otherwise, that are embodied in the financial statements. One assertion of management about economic actions is that all the assets reported on the balance sheet actually exist at the balance sheet date. The assets are real, not fictitious. This is the existence assertion. Furthermore, management asserts that the company owns all these assets. They do not belong to anyone else. This is the rights and obligations assertion.

The auditor **ascertains the degree of correspondence** between assertions and established criteria. The audit programme tests most assertions by examining the physical evidence of documents, confirmation, inquiry, and observation. The auditor examines the evidence for the assertion presentation and disclosure to determine if the accounts are described in accordance with the applicable financial reporting framework, such as IFRS, local standards or regulations and laws.

The goal, or objective, of the audit is **communicating the results to interested users**. The audit is conducted with the aim of expressing an informed and credible opinion in a written report. If the item audited is the financial statements, the auditors must state that in their opinion the statements 'give a true and fair view' or 'present fairly, in all material respects' the financial position of the company. The purpose of the independent expert opinion is to lend credibility to the financial statements. The communication of the auditor's opinion is called attestation, or the attest function. In an audit this attestation is called the 'audit report' (see Chapter 12).

◼ General Principles Governing an Audit of Financial Statements[18]

Although a public auditor can also examine non-financial information, such as compliance with company policies or environmental regulations, the majority of audit work is concerned with the financial statements. The financial statements audited under international standards are the balance sheets, income statements and cash flow statements and the notes thereto.

Requirements of a Financial Statement Audit

ISA 200 sets out several requirements relating to an audit of financial statements.[19] The auditor is required to comply with relevant ethical requirements, including those pertaining to independence, relating to financial statement audit engagements The auditor shall plan and perform an audit with professional scepticism[20] recognising that circumstances may exist that cause the financial statements to be materially misstated.[21] The auditor shall exercise professional judgement[22] in planning and performing an audit of financial statements. To obtain reasonable assurance, the auditor must obtain sufficient appropriate audit evidence[23] to reduce audit risk to an acceptably low level and thereby enable the auditor to draw reasonable conclusions on which to base the auditor's opinion.

Objective, Purpose and Characteristics of a Financial Statement Audit

In conducting an audit of financial statements, the overall objectives of the auditor are:[24]

◼ to obtain reasonable assurance about whether the financial statements as a whole are free from material misstatement, whether due to fraud or error, thereby enabling the auditor to express an opinion on whether the financial statements are prepared, in all material respects, in accordance with an applicable financial reporting framework; and
◼ to report on the financial statements, and communicate as required by the ISAs, in accordance with the auditor's findings.

The purpose of an audit is to enhance the degree of confidence of intended users in the financial statements. This is achieved by the expression of an opinion by the auditor on whether the financial statements are prepared, in all material respects, in accordance with an applicable financial reporting framework (such as IFRS or generally accepted accounting principles). In the case of most general purpose frameworks, that opinion is on whether the financial statements are presented fairly, in all material respects, or give a true and fair view in accordance with the specific framework. An audit conducted in accordance with ISAs and relevant ethical requirements enables the auditor to form that opinion.

The financial statements subject to audit are prepared by management of the entity with oversight from those charged with governance. ISAs do not impose responsibilities on management or those charged with governance and do not override laws and regulations that govern their responsibilities. However, an audit in accordance with ISAs is conducted on the premise that management and, where appropriate, those charged with governance have acknowledged certain responsibilities that are fundamental to the conduct of the audit. The audit of the financial statements does not relieve management or those charged with governance of their responsibilities.

The concept of **materiality**[25] is applied by the auditor both in planning and performing the audit, and in evaluating the effect of identified misstatements on the audit and the financial statements. Misstatements, including omissions, are considered to be material if, individually or in the aggregate, they could reasonably be expected to influence the economic decisions of users taken on the basis of the financial statements. Judgements about materiality are made in the light of surrounding circumstances, and are affected by the auditor's perception of the financial information needs of users of the financial statements, and by the size or nature of a misstatement, or a combination of both. The auditor's opinion deals with the financial statements as a whole and therefore the auditor is not responsible for the detection of misstatements that are not material to the financial statements as a whole.

The ISAs require that the auditor exercise professional judgement and maintain professional scepticism throughout the planning and performance of the audit and, among other things:

- Identify and assess risks of material misstatement, whether due to fraud or error, based on an understanding of the entity and its environment, including the entity's internal control.
- Obtain sufficient appropriate audit evidence about whether material misstatements exist, through designing and implementing appropriate responses to the assessed risks.
- Form an opinion on the financial statements based on conclusions drawn from the audit evidence obtained.

The form of opinion expressed by the auditor will depend upon the applicable financial reporting framework and any applicable law or regulation. The auditor may also have certain other communication and reporting responsibilities to users, management, those charged with governance, or parties outside the entity.

Limitations of the Audit

There are certain inherent limitations in an audit that affect the auditor's ability to detect material misstatements. These limitations result from such factors as the use of testing, the inherent limitations of any accounting and internal control system and the fact that most audit evidence is persuasive rather than conclusive. Furthermore, the work performed by an auditor to form an opinion is permeated by judgement. Judgement is required to determine the nature and extent of audit evidence and the drawing of conclusions based on the audit evidence gathered. Because of these factors, an audit is no guarantee that the financial statements are free of material misstatement.

Risk in Financial Statements, Transactions, Account Balances and Disclosures

In order to design audit procedures to determine whether financial statements are materially misstated, the auditor considers the risk at two levels. One level of risk is that the overall financial statements may be misstated. The second risk is misstatement in relation to classes of transactions, account balances and disclosures.

The risk of material misstatement at the overall financial statement level often relate to the entity's **control environment**[26] (although these risks may also relate to other factors, such as declining economic conditions). This overall risk may be especially relevant to the auditor's consideration of fraud. The auditor also considers the risk of material misstatement at the class of transactions, account balance and disclosure level. These considerations directly assist in determining the nature, timing and extent of further audit procedures.

While the auditor is responsible for forming and expressing an opinion on the financial statements, the responsibility for preparing and presenting the financial statements is that of the management of the entity. However, the audit of the financial statements does not relieve management of its responsibilities.

1.6 Types of Audit

Audits are typically classified into three types: audits of financial statements, operational audits and compliance audits.

■ Audits of Financial Statements

Audits of financial statements examine financial statements to determine if they give a true and fair view or fairly present the financial statements in conformity with specified criteria. The criteria may be International Financial Reporting Standards (IFRS), generally accepted accounting principles (GAAP) as in the USA, national company laws as in Northern Europe, or the tax code in South America. This book primarily discusses audits of financial statements.

■ Operational Audits

An **operational audit** is a study of a specific unit of an organisation for the purpose of measuring its performance. Operational audits review all or part of the organisation's operating procedures to evaluate effectiveness and efficiency of the operation. Effectiveness is a measure of whether an organisation achieves its goals and objectives. Efficiency shows how well an organisation uses its resources to achieve its goals. Operational reviews may not be limited to accounting. They may include the evaluation of organisational structure, marketing, production methods, computer operations or whatever area the organisation feels evaluation is needed. Recommendations are normally made to management for improving operations.

The operations of the receiving department of a manufacturing company, for example, may be evaluated in terms of its effectiveness. Performance is also judged in terms of efficiency on how well it uses the resources available to the department. Because the criteria for effectiveness and efficiency are not as clearly established as accepted accounting principles and laws, an operational audit tends to require more subjective judgement than audits of financial statements or compliance audits.

■ Compliance Audits

A compliance audit is a review of an organisation's procedures to determine whether the organisation is following specific procedures, rules or regulations set out by some higher authority. A compliance audit measures the compliance of an entity with established criteria. The performance of a compliance audit is dependent upon the existence of verifiable data and of recognised criteria or standards, such as established laws and regulations, or an organisation's policies and procedures. Accounting personnel, for example, may be evaluated to determine if they are following the procedures prescribed by the company controller. Other personnel may be evaluated to determine if they follow policies and procedures established by management. Results of compliance audits are generally reported to management within the organisational unit being audited.

Compliance audits are usually associated with government auditors – for example, the tax authority, the government internal auditing arm, or audit of a bank by banking regulators. An example of a compliance audit is an audit of a bank to determine if they comply with capital reserve requirements. Another example would be an audit of taxpayers to see if they comply with national tax law, for example, the audit of an income tax return by an auditor of the government tax agency such as the Internal Revenue Service (IRS) in the USA.

Compliance audits are quite common in not-for-profit organisations funded at least in part by government. Many government entities and non-profit organisations that receive financial assistance from the federal government must arrange for compliance audits. Such audits are designed to determine whether the financial assistance is spent in accordance with applicable laws and regulations.

Illustration 1.2 summarises the three types of audit.

Each of these types of audit has a specialist auditor, namely the independent auditor, internal auditor and governmental auditor. The independent auditor is mainly concerned with financial statement audits, the internal auditor concentrates on operational audits, and the governmental auditor is most likely to determine compliance. However, given information technology developments, the different processes are becoming more and more integrated, and as a consequence the split between these categories may become theoretical.

ILLUSTRATION 1.2

Types of Audit

Audits of financial statements	Operational audits	Compliance audits
Examine financial statements, determine if they give a true and fair view or fairly present the financial position, results and cash flows.	A study of a specific unit of an organisation for the purpose of measuring its performance.	A review of an organisation's procedures and financial records performed to determine whether the organisation is following specific procedures, rules or regulations set out by some higher authority.

1.7 Types of Auditor

There are two basic types of auditor: independent external auditors and internal auditors. Governmental auditors take both the functions of internal and external auditor. The independent auditor and his qualifications will be discussed in the next section.

■ Internal Auditors

Many large companies and organisations maintain an internal auditing staff. Internal auditors are employed by individual companies to investigate and appraise the effectiveness of company operations for management. Much of their attention is often given to the appraisal of internal controls. A large part of their work consists of operational audits; in addition, they may conduct compliance audits. In many countries internal auditors are heavily involved in financial audits. In these circumstances the external auditor should review the work performed by the internal auditor.

The internal audit department reports directly to the president or board of directors. An internal auditor must be independent of the department heads and other executives whose work he reviews. Internal auditors, however, can never be independent in the same sense as the independent auditors because they are employees of the company they are examining.

Internal auditors have two primary effects on a financial statement audit:

1 Their existence and work may affect the nature, timing and extent of audit procedures.
2 External auditors may use internal auditors to provide direct assistance in performing the audit. If this is the case the external auditor must assess internal auditor competence (education, experience, professional certification, etc.) and objectivity (organisational status within the company).

Concept and a Company 1.1

WorldCom Internal Auditor Discovers Misstatements

Concept	The work of internal auditors in review of financial statements.
Story	To illustrate the importance of internal auditors to companies we can look at what happened at WorldCom (now called MCI). Everyone knows about Enron. It was the $9 billion fraud that was perpetrated at WorldCom, at the time the Number 2 long-distance telephone carrier in the USA, that formed the motivation to pass the first US accounting law since 1934. At the time the fraud was disclosed, US President George W. Bush said, 'I'm deeply concerned … There is a need for renewed corporate responsibility in America' (Wolffe 2002). One month later Bush signed the Sarbanes–Oxley Act. The fraud that created the largest bankruptcy in US history and resulted in the payment of the largest fine ever imposed by the Securities and Exchange Commission ($500 million (Larson and Michaels 2003)) involved transferring on the corporate books some $9 billion of telephone line leases and other expenses to capital investments, an asset. This allowed the

▶

WorldCom Internal Auditor Discovers Misstatements (continued)

expenses to be spread over 40 years. The accounting effect was to increase four crucial financial numbers: operating profit, cash flow from operations, total assets and retained earnings. This, in turn, increased WorldCom's share price and made those who exercised low-cost stock options rich. Chief Executive Officer (CEO) Bernard Ebbers made $35 million in June 1999, Chief Financial Officer Scott D. Sullivan made $18 million in August 2000, and chairman of the audit committee, Max Bobbitt, made $1.8 million in 1999 (Romeo and Norris 2002).

Cynthia Cooper, vice president for internal auditing, was the one who discovered the fraud at WorldCom and reported it to the board of directors. She may be the only internal auditor in history to be named *Time* magazine's person of the year (2002).

The story begins when a worried executive in the wireless division told Cooper in March 2002 that corporate accounting had taken $400 million out of his reserve account and used it to boost WorldCom's income. Cooper went to Arthur Andersen, the CPA firm. They told her it was not a problem. When she didn't relent, CFO Sullivan told Cooper that everything was fine and she should back off. Cooper, concerned that her job might be in jeopardy, cleaned out personal items from her office. Cooper told *Time* magazine, 'when someone is hostile, my instinct is to find out why' (Ripley, 2002).

As the weeks went on, Cooper directed her team members to widen their net. Having watched the Enron implosion and Andersen's role in it, she was worried they could not necessarily rely on the accounting firm's audits. So they decided to do part of Andersen's job over again. She and her team began working late into the night, keeping their project secret. And they had no allies. At one point, one of Cooper's employees bought a CD burner and started copying data, concerned that the information might be destroyed before they could finish.

In late May, Cooper and her group discovered a gaping hole in the books. In public reports the company had categorised billions of dollars as capital expenditures in 2001, meaning the costs could be stretched out over a number of years into the future. But in fact the expenditures were for regular fees WorldCom paid to local telephone companies to complete calls and therefore were not capital outlays but operating costs, which should be expensed in full each year. The trick allowed WorldCom to turn a $662 million loss into a $2.4 billion profit in 2001.

On 11 June, Sullivan called Cooper and gave her ten minutes to come to his office and describe what her team was up to, says a source involved with the case. She did, and Sullivan asked her to delay the audit. She told him that would not happen. The next day, Cooper told the head of the audit committee about her findings. On 25 June, after firing Sullivan, the board revealed the fraud to the public.

Nowadays, the SEC has its own Office of the Whistleblower, which was formed as a part of the Dodd–Frank Act (2010). See **http://www.sec.gov/whistleblower** for more information.

Discussion Questions	■ What advantages does an internal auditor have over an external auditor in discovering fraud? ■ And what disadvantages?
References	Larsen, Peter and Adrian Michaels, 2003, 'MCI Fined $500m Over Fraud Charges', *Financial Times*, p. 1, 20 May. Ripley, Amanda, 2002, 'The Night Detective', *Time*, Vol. No. 160, 27, p. 58, 30 December. Romeo, Simon and Floyd Norris, 2002, 'New Bookkeeping Problems Disclosed by WorldCom', *New York Times*, pp. A1–C8, 2 July. Spiegel, Peter, 2003, 'WorldCom Finance Chief "Tried to Delay Inquiry"', *Financial Times*, p. 1, 9 July. Wolffe, Richard, 2002, 'Bush Condemns New Scandal as Outrageous', *Financial Times*, p. 1, 27 June.

■ The Independent External Auditor: Training, Licensing and Authority

Independent auditors have primary responsibility to the performance of the audit function on published financial statements of publicly traded companies and non-public companies. Some countries have several classes of auditors who have different functions. Independent auditors are typically certified either by a professional organisation or a government agency.

The source of authority for the attest function comes from national commercial or company law in most countries, but in some cases (e.g. the USA and Canada) the individual provinces or states exercise considerable control over who the auditor is and how he becomes qualified. All CPAs in the USA are licensed by the individual states. Most countries have strong professional accountant organisations which may also influence who becomes an auditor.

Certified designations for auditors in different countries are listed in Illustration 1.3.

ILLUSTRATION 1.3

Auditor Certification Designations Around the World

Certified Public Accountants (CPA)	Australia, Belize, El Salvador, Guatemala, Hong Kong, Israel, Japan, Kenya (CPA (K)), Korea, Malaysia, Malawi, Myanmar, Philippines, Singapore, Taiwan, Western Samoa and the USA.
Chartered Accountants (CA)	Australia (ACA), Bahamas, Bermuda, Botswana, Canada, Cayman Islands, Channel Islands, Cyprus, Fiji, Guyana, Hungary, India, Jamaica, Nigeria, Trinidad, New Zealand, Papua New Guinea, Saudi Arabia, South Africa (CA-SA), Swaziland (CA (SD)), United Arab Emirates, the UK and Zimbabwe.
Contador Publico (CP)	Argentina, Brazil (Contador), Chile, Columbia (CP Titulado), Costa Rica (CP Autorizado -CPA), Dominican Republic (CPA), Ecuador (CPA), Mexico, Panama (CPA) and Peru.
Expert Comptable	France (or Commissaire aux comptes), Luxembourg and Senegal.
Auditors	Bahrain, Czech Republic, Qatar and Solomon Islands.
Other titles	Registeraccountants (RA) and Accountants Administratie-Consulenten (AC) in the Netherlands and Netherlands Antilles; Wirtschaftsprufer in Austria and Germany; Statautoriseret Revisor in Denmark and Norway; Dottore Commercialista in Italy; Revisor Official de Contas (ROC) in Portugal; Auktoriserad Revisor (AR) in Sweden; Wirtschaftsprufer and Expert Comptable in Switzerland; Reviseur d'Entreprises in Belgium; KHT or CGR in Finland; Soma Orkoton Logiston (SOL) in Greece; Licenciado en Contaduria Publico in Venezuela; Akuntan Publik in Indonesia; Loggilturendurskodandi in Iceland; Licensed Accountant (LA) in Iraq; Technician Superior in Lebanon; and Sworn Financial Advisor (SFA) in Turkey.

Licensing Requirements

The auditor is someone who is trained in an academic programme and who meets certain licensing requirements. Countries may have requirements for minimum age, citizenship, university degree and completion of a qualifying examination. The Eighth European Union (EU) Directive[27] has a minimum experience requirement of three years, whereas the USA only requires one or two years. It is common for people in the USA and Canada to become professional accountants in their early twenties, but in Germany and Japan many people do not attain their credentials until their mid-thirties.

The EU Eighth Company Law Directive sets minimum qualifications for statutory auditors. This directive specifies that an individual must attain at least entrance-level qualifications at university level, engage in a programme of theoretical instruction, receive at least three years' practical training and pass an examination of professional competence. Furthermore, the Eighth Directive puts an obligation on Member States to ensure that statutory audits are carried out with professional integrity and that there are appropriate safeguards in national law to protect the independence of auditors.

1.8 Setting Audit Objectives Based on Management Assertions

Conceptually, where does the audit start? It starts with the financial statements prepared by the client and the claims that the client makes about these numbers. These claims by management are called 'assertions'. Assertions are representations by management, explicit or otherwise, that are embodied in the financial statements, as used by the auditor to consider the different types of potential misstatements that may occur. For example, management claims (asserts) that sales exist, i.e. sales are not fiction created by management. Management claims that the expenses and liabilities are complete, i.e. they did not leave out any expenses to make net income look better. Management claims that they have disclosed all that should be disclosed. Inventory is properly valued and it belongs to the company, not some other company that put it there on consignment. And so on.

The Auditor's Process

Where it is management's responsibility to prepare the financial statements, it is the auditor's job to verify whether the financial statements are true and fair. Put differently, it is the auditor's job to validate management's assertions. In order to do so, the auditor will identify audit objectives, which can be regarded as the auditor's counterpart of management assertions. The auditor will define audit objectives for existence of sales, completeness of expenses, presentation and disclosure (based on IFRS) and valuation and rights and obligations of inventory. The auditor will develop these specific audit objectives for which they must test for evidence as proof.

After the identification of accounts, classes of transactions and the related management assertions and audit objectives, the auditor will determine the nature, amount and timing of the audit procedures to be carried out. In order to do so, he will perform risk analysis for each audit objective, i.e. he will determine the susceptibility of account balances and transactions to misstatement.

Further, the auditor will have to determine the exactness with which he will perform his audit. It is reasonable to suppose that the auditor will accept a greater tolerance in the audit of a large, multinational enterprise than in the audit of a small, local company. This raises the issue of materiality and of tolerable misstatement[28] in the audit process.

In designing an audit programme for a specific account, the auditor starts by developing general objectives from the financial statement assertions of management. Then, specific objectives are developed for each account under audit, and finally, audit procedures are designed to accomplish each specific audit objective.

■ Management Assertions and Audit Objectives

Audit procedures are designed to obtain evidence about the assertions of management that are embodied in the financial statements. Management assertions are implied or expressed representations by management about classes of transactions (e.g. sales transactions) and related accounts (e.g. revenue, accounts receivable) in the financial statements. When the auditors have gathered sufficient evidence to support each management assertion, they have sufficient evidence to support the audit opinion.

An example of a management assertion is that 'the company's financial statements are prepared based on international accounting standards'. This assertion is one of presentation and disclosure. The auditor must obtain sufficient evidence that this assertion is materially true. He must gather evidence that accounts are classified correctly and the proper disclosures have been made based on international standards.

Assertions Categorised

According to ISA 500, financial statement assertions are assertions by management, explicit or otherwise, that are embodied in the financial statements. They can be categorised as follows:[29]

(1) Assertions about classes of transactions and events for the period under audit

- **Occurrence** – transaction and events that have been recorded have occurred and pertain to the entity. For example, management asserts that a recorded sales transaction was actually made during the year under audit.
- **Completeness** – all transactions and events that should have been recorded have been recorded. For example, management asserts that all expense transactions are recorded, none were excluded.
- **Accuracy** – amounts and other data relating to recorded transactions and events have been recorded appropriately. For example, management asserts that sales invoices were properly extended and the total amounts that were thus calculated were input into the system exactly.
- **Cut-off** – transactions and events have been recorded in the correct accounting period. For example, management asserts that expenses for the period are recorded in that period and not in the next accounting period.
- **Classification** – transactions and events have been recorded in the proper accounts. For example, management asserts that expenses are not recorded as assets.

(2) Assertions about account balances at the period end

- **Existence** – assets, liabilities and equity interests exist. For example, management asserts that inventory in the amount given exists, ready for sale, at the balance sheet date.

ILLUSTRATION 1.4

Financial Statement Assertions, Definitions and Procedures for Auditing Receivables

Assertion	Definition	Procedures
Existence	Assets, liabilities and equity interests exist.	✓ Confirm customer account balances ✓ Inspect shipping documents
Rights and obligations	The entity holds or controls the rights to assets, and liabilities are the obligations of the entity.	✓ Inquire about factoring of receivables ✓ Inspect cash receipts
Occurrence	Transaction and events that have been recorded have occurred and pertain to the entity.	✓ Inspect notes receivable ✓ Inspect sales invoices
Completeness	All transactions, events, assets, liabilities and equity interests that should have been recorded have been recorded.	✓ Perform analytical procedures ✓ Inspect inter-company sales invoices
Valuation and allocation	Assets, liabilities, and equity interests are included in the financial statements at appropriate amounts and any resulting valuation or allocation adjustments are appropriately recorded.	✓ Reconcile subsidiary ledger to general ledger ✓ Age receivables to test adequacy of allowance for doubtful accounts
Accuracy	Amounts and other data relating to recorded transactions and events have been recorded appropriately.	✓ Recalculate sales invoices ✓ Reperform sales transactions
Classification	Transactions and events have been recorded in the proper accounts.	✓ Inquire about revenue recognition policies
Cut-off	Transactions and events have been recorded in the correct accounting period.	✓ Inspect next period bank statements for cash receipts ✓ Inspect credit memos for sales returns
Presentation and disclosure	An item is disclosed, classified, and described in accordance with acceptable accounting reporting framework.	✓ Review disclosures for compliance with IFRS and applicable regulation ✓ Inspect loan documents for pledging or discounting of accounts receivable

- **Rights and obligations** – the entity holds or controls the rights to assets, and liabilities are the obligations of the entity. For example, management asserts that the company has the legal rights to ownership of the equipment they use and that they have an obligation to pay the notes that finance the equipment.
- **Completeness** – all assets, liabilities and equity interests that should have been recorded have been recorded. For example, management asserts that all liabilities are recorded and included in the financial statements, that no liabilities were 'off the books'.
- **Valuation and allocation** – assets, liabilities, and equity interests are included in the financial statements at appropriate amounts and any resulting valuation or allocation adjustments are appropriately recorded. For example, management asserts that their accounts receivable are stated at face value, less an allowance for doubtful accounts.

(3) Assertions about presentation and disclosure

- **Occurrence and rights and obligations** – disclosed events, transactions, and other matters have occurred and pertain to the entity. For example, management asserts that events that did not occur have not been included in the disclosures.
- **Completeness** – all disclosures that should have been included in the financial statements have been included. For example, management asserts that all disclosures that are required by IFRS are made.
- **Classification and understandability** – financial information is appropriately presented and described, and disclosures are clearly expressed. For example, management asserts that all long-term liabilities listed on the balance sheet mature after one operating cycle or one year and that any special conditions pertaining to the liabilities are clearly disclosed.
- **Accuracy and valuation** – financial and other information are disclosed fairly and at appropriate amounts. For example, management asserts that account balances are not materially misstated.

Illustration 1.4 gives some management assertions/audit objectives, their definitions and an example of the type of audit procedures that may be required for that assertion based on the audit of marketable securities.

1.9 The Audit Process Model

In the international environment today, the professional auditor audits financial statements, internal control, compliance with policies, compliance with laws and regulations, and codes of best practice. However, no matter what subject matter the audit is designed to evaluate, the audit process is a well-defined methodology to help the auditor accumulate sufficient competent evidence.

■ Empirical Scientific Cycle and the Audit

The audit process may be compared to the empirical scientific cycle.[30] The empirical scientific cycle is a systematic process of experimenting that starts with a research question, then a plan for an empirical test of the question is made, the test is done, feedback is analysed, and the scientist makes a judgement. The scientist's opinion is that the experimental hypothesis is false or not false, or perhaps that the test is inconclusive.

Although the numerous judgments made during a financial audit (about audit approach, sampling, audit risk, etc.) make it more of an art than a science, the audit process follows a systematic process. The audit process begins with a client's request for an audit of financial statements, which is followed by a plan of the audit and tests of evidence, culminating in a judgement or opinion. The auditor's judgement is whether the financial statements are unmodified (unqualified)[31] as to their fairness, qualified[32] or disclaimed.[33]

A scientist poses a question; this is similar to the client asking an auditor to audit a set of financial statements. A plan is drawn up for the experiment (an audit plan). The scientist tests his theory and evaluates the evidence and an auditor tests the assertions made in the financial statements. The scientist writes up a report on the experiment and an auditor writes a report on the representational quality of the financial statements based on the underlying accounting evidence.

Assessing risk is the core of the audit. The rest of the audit is designed to provide a response to these identified risks. In this book, we will provide a 'business risk' orientated approach. Business risks result from significant conditions, events, circumstances, actions, or inactions that could adversely affect a company's ability to execute its strategies, for example, changes in customer demand, government regulations, etc. Most business risks will eventually have financial consequences and, therefore, an effect on the financial statements. As such, the auditors are required to discuss business risks as part of the planning process

Standard Audit Process Model in Four Phases

In this book, a four-phase standard audit process model is used, based on the scientific empirical cycle. The phases of the audit are:

1 client acceptance (pre-planning)
2 planning and design of an audit approach
3 tests for evidence
4 completion of the audit and issuance of an audit report.

Illustration 1.5 shows the four-phase audit process model and its major sub-components.

■ Phase I: Client Acceptance

An audit firm carries out audits for both existing clients and new clients. For existing clients, there is not much activity involved in accepting the client for another year's audit. The audit firm is familiar with the company and has a great deal of information for making an acceptable decision. However, in the case that it is concluded that the auditor's business risk is unacceptably high (client is a fraudster or acts illegally) the auditor reconsiders continuation of the agreement. Accountancy firms have strict procedures for reconsidering high-risk engagements.

When prospective clients approach the audit firm with a request to bid on their financial audits, audit firms must investigate the business background, financial statements, and industry of the client. The firm must also convince the client to accept them. The process of client acceptance involves evaluation of the client's background, selecting personnel for the audit, and evaluating the need and requirements for using the work of other professionals.

(The client acceptance phase of the auditing methodology is discussed in detail in Chapter 5 'Client Acceptance'.)

ILLUSTRATION 1.5

Audit Process Model

Phase I: Client Acceptance

Objective: Determine both acceptance of a client and acceptance by a client. Decide on acquiring a new client or continuation of relationship with an existing one and the type and amount of staff required.

Procedures: (1) Evaluate the client's background and reasons for the audit
(2) Determine whether the auditor is able to meet the ethical requirements regarding the client
(3) Determine need for other professionals
(4) Communicate with predecessor auditor
(5) Prepare client proposal
(6) Select staff to perform the audit
(7) Obtain an engagement letter

Phase II: Planning

Objective: Determine the amount and type of evidence and review required to give the auditor assurance that there is no material misstatement of the financial statements.

Procedures: (1) Perform audit procedures to understand the entity and its environment, including the entity's internal controls
(2) Assess the risks of material misstatements of the financial statements
(3) Determine materiality
(4) Prepare the planning memorandum and audit programme, containing the auditor's response to the identified risks

Phase III: Testing and Evidence

Objective: Test for evidence supporting internal controls and the fairness of the financial statements.

Procedures: (1) Tests of controls
(2) Substantive tests of transactions
(3) Analytical procedures
(4) Tests of details of balances
(5) Search for unrecorded liabilities

Phase IV: Evaluation and Reporting

Objective: Complete the audit procedures and issue an opinion.

Procedures: (1) Evaluate governance evidence
(2) Perform procedures to identify subsequent events
(3) Review financial statements and other report material
(4) Perform wrap-up procedures
(5) Prepare Matters for Attention of Partners
(6) Report to the board of directors
(7) Prepare audit report

■ Phase II: Planning

The audit firm must plan its work to enable it to conduct an effective audit in an efficient and timely manner. Plans should be based on knowledge of the client's business. Plans are developed after obtaining a basic understanding of the business background, **control environment, control activities (procedures)**,[34] the client's accounting system, and after performing **analytical procedures**.[35] The second part of the planning process is to determine the riskiness of the engagement and set materiality levels. Finally, the auditor prepares an **audit plan (programme)**[36] which outlines the nature, timing and extent of audit procedures required to gather evidence.

One of the most widely accepted concepts on auditing is the importance of the client's **internal control structure**[37] to reliable financial information. If the client has adequate internal control for proving reliable data and safeguarding assets and records, the amount of audit evidence required, and planned for, is significantly less than where internal controls are inadequate. Therefore, assessing internal controls is a very important part of the planning process.

An entity's internal control structure includes five basic categories of policies and procedures. Management designs and implements this in order to provide reasonable assurance that its control objectives will be met. These components of internal control are:[38]

1 the control environment
2 risk assessment
3 control procedures
4 information and communication
5 monitoring.

Planning concepts are discussed in Chapter 6 'Main Audit Concepts and Planning the Audit', Chapter 7 'Internal Control and Control Risk', Chapter 8 'Analytical Procedures' and Chapter 9 'Auditor's Response to Assessed Risk'. Illustration 1.6 shows a diagrammatic view of the result of planning – devising the audit programme from an understanding of the company, internal control analysis, and analysis of assertions.

■ Phase III: Testing and Evidence

The audit should be performed and the report prepared with due professional care by persons who have adequate training, experience and competence in auditing. The auditor should also be independent of the audit and keep the results of the audit confidential, as required by international ethics. 'Due professional care' means that the auditor is a professional responsible for fulfilling his duties diligently and carefully. Due care includes the completeness of the working papers, the sufficiency of the audit evidence and the appropriateness of the audit report.

The testing and evidence-gathering phase of the audit requires first testing any controls that the auditor expects to rely upon. Once the controls are tested, the auditor must decide on additional, substantive, tests. The understanding of controls is needed to determine what kind of tests (the nature), when they should be done (timing), and what the number (extent) of the tests should be.

Gathering Evidence

The auditor should obtain sufficient appropriate audit evidence through the performance of control and **substantive procedures**[39] to enable him to draw reasonable conclusions on

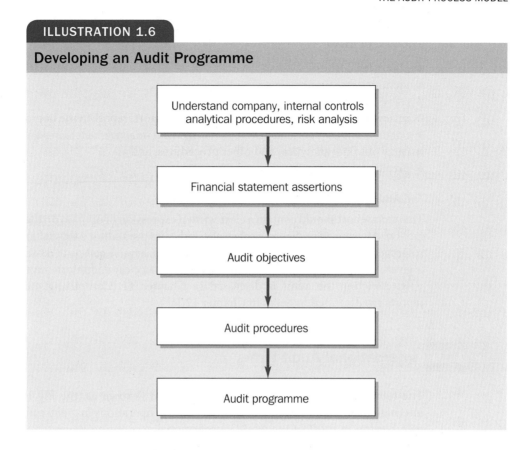

ILLUSTRATION 1.6

Developing an Audit Programme

which to base his audit opinion. **Tests of controls**[40] are tests designed to obtain reasonable assurance that financial information system controls are in place and effective. Substantive procedures are designed to obtain evidence as to the completeness, accuracy, and validity of the data produced by the accounting system. They are of three types: tests of details of transactions, account balances, and analysis of significant ratios and trends. (Audit evidence is discussed in Chapter 8 'Analytical Procedures', Chapter 9 'Auditor's Response to Assessed Risk' and Chapter 10 'Audit Evidence'.)

■ Phase IV: Evaluation and Reporting

The auditor should review and assess the conclusions drawn from audit evidence on which he will base his opinion on the financial information. This review and assessment involves forming an overall conclusion as to whether:

- the financial information has been prepared using acceptable accounting policies, consistently applied;
- the financial information complies with relevant regulations and statutory requirements;
- the view presented by the financial information as a whole is consistent with the auditor's knowledge of the business of the entity; and
- there is adequate disclosure of all material matters relevant to the proper presentation of the financial information.

The auditor must perform final audit procedures before the audit report can be written. The auditor must:

■ obtain legal letters,
■ identify subsequent events,
■ carry out an overall review,
■ review all material that goes into the annual report, report to the board of directors,
■ obtain a written representation from management (management representations letter),[41]
■ carry out final analytical and other procedures, and
■ prepare matters for attention of partners.[42]

The Audit Opinion

The audit report should contain a clear written expression of opinion on the financial information. An unmodified (unqualified) opinion indicates the auditor's satisfaction in all material respects with the matters. When a qualified opinion, adverse opinion or disclaimer of opinion[43] is given, the audit report should state the reasons in a clear and informative manner.

(Completing the audit is discussed in Chapter 11 'Completing the Audit'. Audit reports are discussed in detail in Chapter 12.)

1.10   International Audit Firms

The four largest accountancy firms in the world (known as 'the Big Four') influence international auditing because of their day-to-day operations in many countries and their membership in most of the world's professional accounting organisations. All of these firms have revenues of billions of dollars. The Big Four are: Deloitte, Ernst & Young, KPMG, and PricewaterhouseCoopers.

In the earliest days of multinational accountancy firms, the organisational form of audit firms was a partnership or professional corporation. This legal form still predominates, but legal forms vary around the world between countries as well as between firms. Recently the limited liability forms of organisation, such as Limited Liability Partnership (LLP), have come into widespread use.

■ Professional Staff

The partners hire professional staff to assist them in their work. The organisational hierarchy in a typical international auditing firm (shown in Illustration 1.7) includes partners, managers, supervisors, seniors or in-charge auditors, and staff accountants. A new employee usually starts as a staff accountant and spends several years at each classification before eventually achieving partner status.

In the remainder of this section the allocation of personnel to an audit is discussed. However, it must be remembered that human resource models will vary between auditing firms. The following describes the common threads of work.

Staff Accountants (or Junior Assistants then Senior)

The first position when someone enters the public accounting profession is that of staff accountant (also called assistant or junior accountant). The staff accountant often performs the more detailed routine audit tasks.

ILLUSTRATION 1.7

The Organisational Hierarchy of a Typical International Auditing Firm

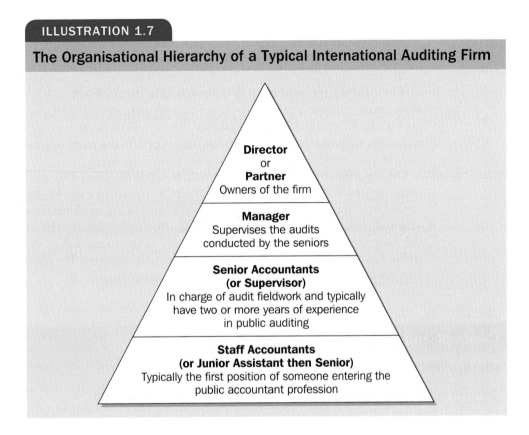

Director or **Partner**
Owners of the firm

Manager
Supervises the audits conducted by the seniors

Senior Accountants (or Supervisor)
In charge of audit fieldwork and typically have two or more years of experience in public auditing

Staff Accountants (or Junior Assistant then Senior)
Typically the first position of someone entering the public accountant profession

Senior Accountants (or Supervisor)

The senior ('in-charge') auditor or 'supervisor' is in charge of audit fieldwork and typically has two or more years' experience in public auditing. The senior takes a major part in planning the audit and is primarily responsible for conducting the audit engagement at the client's place of business. Planning and supervision of more complex audits may involve the partner or director in planning and the manager in supervising the engagement.

The senior supervises the work of the audit staff, reviews working papers and time budgets, and assists in drafting the audit report. The senior maintains a continuous record of staff hours in each phase of the audit examination and maintains professional standards of fieldwork. This work is subject to review and approval by the manager and partner.

Managers

The manager supervises the audits conducted by the seniors. The manager helps the seniors plan their audit programmes, reviews working papers periodically, and provides other guidance. The manager is responsible for determining the audit procedures applicable to specific audits and for maintaining uniform standards of fieldwork. Often managers have the responsibility of compiling and collecting the firm's billings to the audit client. The manager, who typically has at least five years' experience, needs a broad and current knowledge of tax laws, accounting standards and government regulations. A manager is likely to specialise in accounting requirements of a specific industry.

Partners/Directors

Partners are the owners of the auditing firm. The change in legal structure means that in some countries those formerly known as partners are directors. They are heavily involved in the planning of the audit, evaluation of the results and determination of the audit opinion. The degree to which they are involved in the audit will vary between firms and assignments because firms have to ensure that partners allocate their time in an appropriate way. Partners will delegate as much of the work as possible to experienced managers and seniors. Moreover, the larger the accountancy firm the more variation there is likely to be in practice depending on the nature of the engagement.

Other partner or director duties include maintaining contacts with clients, resolving controversies that may arise, and attendance at the client's stockholders' meetings to answer any questions regarding the financial statements or the auditor's report. They may also recruit new staff members, review audit working papers, supervise staff and sign the audit reports, depending on the complexity of the engagements. Partners may specialise in a particular area such as tax laws or a specific industry. The partner is the person who must make the final decisions involving complex judgments.

Concept and a Company 1.2

History of Deloitte

Concept	**Founding fathers and international mergers of Big Four audit firms.**
Story	In 1990 Deloitte Touche Tohmatsu was created following a number of earlier mergers. In 2003 the names of Touche and Tohmatsu were dropped, leaving Deloitte as the firm's full name. Deloitte was established by three founders: William Welch Deloitte, George Touche and Admiral Nobuzo Tohmatsu.

In 1845, at the age of 25, W.W. Deloitte opened his own office opposite the Bankruptcy Court in Basinghall Street, London. At that time three Companies Acts created joint-stock companies, laying the foundation for modern company structures. Deloitte made his name with the industry of the day – the railways – and in 1849 the Great Western Railway appointed Deloitte the first independent auditor in that industry. He discovered frauds on the Great North Railway, invented a system for railway accounts that protected investors from mismanagement of funds, and was to become the grand old man of the profession. As president of the newly created Institute of Chartered Accountants, Deloitte found a site for its headquarters in 1888. In 1893 he opened offices in the USA.

Financial disasters in the new and booming investment trust business in the England gave George Touche his business opportunity. His reputation for flair, integrity, and expertise brought him a huge amount of work setting these trusts on the straight and narrow. A similar flair for saving doomed businesses from disaster and restructuring them led to the formation of George A. Touche & Co. in 1899. In 1900, along with John Niven, the son of his original Edinburgh accounting mentor, Touche set up the firm of Touche, Niven & Co. in New York. Offices spread across the USA and Canada and were soon attracting clients like R.H. Macy, a large US nationwide department store. In the UK, General Electric Company was an important client and still is. Meanwhile Touche himself took his reputation for probity and ran for public election in England and became MP for North Islington, England, in 1910, and was knighted in 1917. He died in 1935.

After Tohmatsu qualified as a certified public accountant at the age of 57 in 1952, he became a partner in a foreign-affiliated accounting firm and a director of a private corporation. In 1967, he became president of the Japanese Institute of Certified Public Accountants. In the 1960s, the Japanese government wanted to see national audit corporations established, and Tohmatsu asked Iwao Tomita, a former student and a graduate of the Wharton School in Chicago, to respond to that challenge. In May of 1968, Tohmatsu & Co. (formerly Tohmatsu Awoki & Co.) was incorporated.

Discussion Question	■ What events and circumstances contributed to the growth and international scope of Deloitte's operations?
References	http://www.Deloitte.com.

Concept and a Company 1.3

A History of Ernst & Young

Concept	Founding fathers and international mergers of Big Four audit firms.
Story	The founders of Ernst & Young were Arthur Young who had an interest in investments and banking which led to the foundation in 1906 of Arthur Young & Co. in Chicago, USA, and A.C. Ernst, who was a bookkeeper while still in high school, joined his brother and started Ernst & Ernst in 1903.
	Ernst pioneered the idea that accounting information could be used to make business decisions – the forerunner of management consulting. He also was the first to advertise professional services. Young was profoundly interested in the development of young professionals. In the 1920s he originated a staff school; in the 1930s, his firm was the first to recruit from university campuses.
	Both firms were quick to enter the global marketplace. As early as 1924, they allied with prominent British firms – Young with Broads Paterson & Co. and Ernst with Whinney Smith & Whinney. In 1979, Ernst's original agreement led to the formation of Ernst & Whinney. These alliances were the first of many for both firms throughout the world – and they are the roots of the global firm today.
	Young and Ernst, never having met, both died in 1948 within only a few days of each other. In 1989, the firms they started combined to create Ernst & Young.
Discussion Questions	■ What is the impact today of Ernst's innovation of advertising professional services? ■ What do you think Young's staff school taught to professional accountants in 1920? ■ What do you think Ernst & Young teach today in their staff school?
References	www.ey.com.

Concept and a Company 1.4

History of KPMG

Concept	Founding fathers and international mergers of Big Four audit firms.
Story	KPMG was formed in 1987 with the merger of Peat Marwick International (PMI) and Klynveld Main Goerdeler (KMG) and their individual member firms. Spanning three centuries, the organisation's history can be traced through the names of its principal founding members – whose initials form the name 'KPMG.'

K stands for Klynveld. Piet Klijnveld founded the accounting firm Klynveld Kraayenhof & Co. in Amsterdam in 1917.
P is for Peat. William Barclay Peat founded the accounting firm William Barclay Peat & Co. in London in 1870.
M stands for Marwick. James Marwick founded the accounting firm Marwick, Mitchell & Co. with Roger Mitchell in New York City in 1897.
G is for Goerdeler. Dr Reinhardt Goerdeler was for many years chairman of Deutsche Treuhand-Gesellschaft and later chairman of KPMG. He is credited with laying much of the groundwork for the KMG merger.

In 1911, William Barclay Peat & Co. and Marwick Mitchell & Co. joined forces to form what would later be known as Peat Marwick International (PMI), a worldwide network of accounting and consulting firms. William Barclay Peat & Co. was founded in 1870 in London; Marwick Mitchell & Co. was founded in 1897 in New York City.

Klynveld Kraayenhof & Co. was founded in Amsterdam in 1917. In 1979, Klynveld Kraayenhof & Co. joined forces with Deutsche Treuhand-Gesellschaft and the international professional services firm McLintock Main Lafrentz & Co. to form Klynveld Main Goerdeler (KMG). Goerdeler was Dr Reinhard Goerdeler, the chairman of Deutsche Treuhand-Gesellschaft.

In 1987, PMI and KMG and their member firms joined forces. Today, all member firms throughout the world carry the KPMG name exclusively or include it in their national firm names. |
| Discussion Question | ■ What types of problem could result from combining four firms from different nations with different cultures into a working environment? |
| References | http://www.KPMG.nl. |

Concept and a Company 1.5

History of PricewaterhouseCoopers

Concept	Founding fathers and international mergers of Big Four audit firms.
Story	A merger in 1998 of Coopers & Lybrand and Price Waterhouse created PricewaterhouseCoopers. These two firms have historical roots going back some 150 years.

PricewaterhouseCoopers employs about 125,000 people in more than 142 countries throughout the world.

In 1849, Samuel Lowell Price started an accounting business in London. In 1865, William H. Holyland and Edwin Waterhouse joined him in partnership, and by 1874 the company name changes to Price, Waterhouse & Co. (or PW for short). In 1873, the firm conducted their first US project. The growing US practice lead to the establishment of permanent PW presence in the Western hemisphere, which began with the opening of the office in New York City in 1890. By the turn of the century, it had a register of clients that covered a wide range of industrial and commercial fields in most sections of the USA. Branch offices began to open throughout the USA and then in other parts of the world. In 1982 Price Waterhouse World Firm was formed.

In 1854, William Cooper established his own practice in London, which seven years later became Cooper Brothers. The firm's history in the USA began in 1898, when Robert H. Montgomery, William M. Lybrand, Adam A. Ross Jr, and his brother T. Edward Ross formed Lybrand Ross Brothers and Montgomery in Philadelphia. During the early twentieth century their offices spread around the country and then in Europe.

From 1953, the firm experienced a major transformation from a medium-size company, focused on auditing and primarily national in scope, into a multinational player with a growing mix of consulting services. The boldest step was a 1957 merger between Cooper Brothers & Co. (UK), McDonald, Currie and Co. (Canada), and Lybrand, Ross Bros, & Montgomery (US), forming Coopers & Lybrand, which had 79 offices in 19 countries. In 1990, Coopers & Lybrand merged with Deloitte Haskins & Sells in a number of countries around the world. Finally, in 1998 Price Waterhouse and Coopers & Lybrand merged worldwide to become PricewaterhouseCoopers, and the trading name of the firm was shortened to PwC in 2010.

Discussion Question	■ Why did the Western hemisphere operations of Price and Coopers grow rapidly in the twentieth century?
References	http://www.columbia.edu/cu/libraries/indiv/rare/guides/PWC/main. http://www.pwcglobal.com.

1.11   Summary

Anthropologists have found records of auditing activity dating back to early Babylonian times (around 3000 BC). There was also auditing activity in ancient China, Greece and Rome. Auditors existed in ancient China and Egypt. They were supervisors of the accounts of the Chinese Emperor and the Egyptian Pharaoh. From the dawn of the dynastic era in Egypt (3000 BC) the scribes (accountants) were among the most esteemed in society and the scribal occupation was one of the most prestigious occupations. The practice of modern auditing dates back to the beginning of the modern corporation at the dawn of the Industrial Revolution. In 1853, the Society of Accountants was founded in Edinburgh. Several other institutes emerged in Great Britain, merging in 1880 into the Institute of Chartered Accountants in England and Wales.

Auditors today are responsible for adding credibility to international corporate financial statements and annual reports. In addition to financial information, an auditor may be required to attest to the representational quality of non-financial information such as footnote disclosures, management's report, the directors' report, codes of best practice and internal controls. By the audit process, the auditor enhances the usefulness and the value of the financial statements, but he also increases the credibility of other non-audited information released by management.

Organisations that affect international auditing today are primarily the International Accounting Standards Board (IASB) and the International Federation of Accountants (IFAC), which set the International Standards on Auditing (ISAs). Increasingly, oversight bodies, such as the Public Company Accounting Oversight Board (PCAOB) and the Public Interest Oversight Board (PIOB), and national regulators emerge.

The International Auditing and Assurances Standards Board (IAASB) of the International Federation of Accountants (IFAC) issues international auditing standards (International Standards on Auditing (ISAs)). IAASB issues several sets of standards to be applied to international auditing and assurance services. IAASB issues:

1 International Standards on Auditing (ISAs) as the standards to be applied by auditors in reporting on historical financial information.
2 International Standards on Assurance Engagements (ISAEs) as the standards to be applied by practitioners in assurance engagements dealing with information other than historical financial information.
3 International Standards on Quality Control (ISQCs) as the quality control standards to be applied for all services falling under the Standards of the IAASB.
4 International Standards on Related Services (ISRSs) as the standards to be applied on related services, as it considers appropriate.

An audit may be defined as a systematic process of objectively obtaining and evaluating evidence regarding assertions about economic actions and events to ascertain the degree of correspondence between these assertions and established criteria and communicating the results to interested users.

Although an auditor may examine more than financial information such as company policies and the environment, the majority of audit work concerns financial statements. The financial statements audited under international standards are the income statement, balance sheet, statement of cash flows and attached disclosures.

ISA 200 sets out several requirements relating to an audit of financial statements. The auditor is required to comply with relevant ethical requirements, including those pertaining to independence, relating to financial statement audit engagements The auditor shall plan and perform an audit with professional scepticism recognising that circumstances may exist that cause the financial statements to be materially misstated. The auditor shall exercise professional judgement in planning and performing an audit of financial statements. To obtain reasonable assurance, the auditor must obtain sufficient appropriate audit evidence to reduce audit risk to an acceptably low level and thereby enable the auditor to draw reasonable conclusions on which to base the auditor's opinion.

Audits are classified into three types: audits of financial statements, operational audits and compliance audits. Audits of financial statements examine financial statements to determine if they give a true and fair view or fairly present the financial statements in conformity with specified criteria. An operational audit is a study of a specific unit of an organisation for the purpose of measuring its performance. A compliance audit is a review of an organisation's procedures to determine whether the organisation is following specific procedures, rules or regulations set out by some higher authority. A compliance audit measures the compliance of an entity with established criteria.

There are two basic types of auditor: independent external auditors and internal auditors. Governmental auditors take both the functions of internal and external auditor. Internal auditors are employed by individual companies to investigate and appraise the effectiveness of company operations for management. Much of their attention is often given to the appraisal of internal controls. A large part of their work consists of operational audits; in addition, they may conduct compliance audits. Independent auditors have primary responsibility to the performance of the audit function on published financial statements of publicly traded companies and non-public companies. Some countries have several classes of auditors who have different functions. Independent auditors are typically certified either by a professional organisation or a government agency.

Assertions are representations by management, explicit or otherwise, that are embodied in the financial statements, as used by the auditor to consider the different types of potential misstatements that may occur. Management assertions are implied or expressed representations by management about classes of transactions (e.g. sales transactions) and related accounts (e.g. revenue, accounts receivable) in the financial statements. When the auditors have gathered sufficient evidence to support each management assertion, they have sufficient evidence to support the audit opinion.

Management makes representations and assertions about the financial statements. Their assertions are about classes of transactions and related accounts in the financial statements and are used to set objectives for obtaining audit evidence. The assertions about financial statements fall into three categories:

1 assertions about classes of transactions and events for the period under audit;
2 assertions about account balances at the period end;
3 assertions about presentation and disclosure.

The individual assertions are occurrence, completeness, accuracy, cut-off, classification, existence, rights and obligations, valuation and allocation, and understandability. The auditor must systematically check these 'management assertions' because they form the basis of the audit process.

The audit process is a well-defined methodology to help the auditor accumulate sufficient competent evidence. In this book a four-phase standard audit process model is: (1) client acceptance (pre-planning); (2) planning and design of an audit approach; (3) tests for evidence; and (4) completion of the audit and issuance of an audit report. This four-phase audit process model discussed in this chapter is the basis for most audits and forms a structure for this book.

The four largest accountancy firms in the world (known as 'the Big Four') influence international auditing because of their day-to-day operations in many countries and their membership in most of the world's professional accounting organisations. Each of these firms has revenues of billions of dollars. The Big Four are: Deloitte, Ernst & Young, KPMG, and PricewaterhouseCoopers.

The organisational hierarchy in a typical international auditing firm includes partners, managers, supervisors, seniors or in-charge auditors, and staff accountants. A new employee usually starts as a staff accountant and spends several years at each classification before eventually achieving partner status.

1.12   Questions, Exercises and Cases

QUESTIONS

1.2   Auditing through World History

1–1   Identify and briefly discuss factors that have created the demand for international auditing.

1–2   What characteristics of the Industrial Revolution were essential for the enhanced development of the audit profession?

1.3   The Auditor, Corporations and Financial Information

1–3   Evaluate this quote: 'Every international business, large or small, should have an annual audit by an independent auditor.' Why should an auditor review the financial statements of a company each year?

1.4   International Accounting and Auditing Standards

1–4   How do International Financial Reporting Standards (IFRS) differ from International Standards on Auditing (ISA)?

1–5   Why is the adoption of International Auditing Standards important for developing nations?

1.5   An Audit Defined

1–6   What is the objective of an audit?

1–7   What is the general definition of an audit? Briefly discuss the key component parts of the definition.

1–8   Explain the concept of materiality.

1–9   Discuss the two levels of risk an auditor must consider when designing audit procedures.

1.6   Types of Audit

1–10   How many types of audits are there? Name each and briefly define them?

1–11   What are the differences and similarities in audits of financial statements, compliance audits and operational audits?

1.7   Types of Auditor

1–12   What are the three types of auditor? Briefly define them.

1.8   Setting Audit Objectives Based on Management Assertions

1–13   What are the financial statement assertions made by management according to ISA 500?

1–14   What is the existence assertion? The rights and obligation assertion? The completeness assertion?

1.9   The Audit Process Model

1–15   How can one compare the empirical scientific cycle to the financial audit process?

1–16   What are the four phases of an audit process model? Briefly describe each.

1–17   Based on the Evaluation and Judgement phase (IV) of the audit process model the overall conclusions are formed on what judgements?

1.10   International Audit Firms

1–18   List the four basic positions within the organisational structure of an audit firm and describe the duties of each position.

1–19   Name the Big Four international audit firms and give a brief history of each.

PROBLEMS AND EXERCISES

1.2 Auditing through World History

1-20 In this chapter, the history of auditing has been briefly described from an international perspective. Identify the major differences with the developments specific for your country and try to explain these based on differences in the economic system or development.

1.3 The Auditor, Corporations and Financial Information

1-21 Expectations Gap. The general public thinks that an auditor guarantees the accuracy of financial statements. Is this true? Why? What other things does the public believe about audited financial statements?

1.4 International Accounting and Auditing Standards

1-22 International Auditing Standards. The London, Tokyo and New York Stock Exchange, among others, require an annual audit of the financial statements of companies whose securities are listed on it. What are the possible reasons for this?

1-23 Describe the International Federation of Accountants (IFAC). Discuss the function of the groups within IFAC.

1.5 An Audit Defined

1-24 Objectives of an Audit. Tracy Keulen, the sole owner of a small bakery, has been told that the business should have financial statements reported on by an independent Registeraccountant (RA). Keulen, having some bookkeeping experience, has personally prepared the company's financial statements and does not understand why such statements should be examined by an RA. Keulen discussed the matter with Petra Dassen, an RA, and asked Dassen to explain why an audit is considered important.

Required:
A.   Describe the objectives of the independent audit.
B.   Identify five ways in which an independent audit may be beneficial to Keulen.

1-25 Based on ISA 200, what are the general principles governing an audit of financial statements? Discuss ethics and professional scepticism.

1.6 Types of Audit

1-26 Operational Audits. List four examples of specific operational audits that could be conducted by an internal audit in a manufacturing company. Describe how you would conduct each

1-27 Auditing Tasks. Each of the following represents tasks that auditors frequently perform:
1   Compilation of quarterly financial statements for a small business that does not have any accounting personnel capable of preparing financial statements.
2   Review of tax return of corporate president to determine whether she has included all taxable income.
3   Review of the activities of the receiving department of a large manufacturing company, with special attention to the efficiency of the materials inspection.
4   Evaluation of a company's computer system to determine whether the computer is being used effectively.
5   Examination on a surprise basis of Topanga Bank. Emphasis placed on verification of cash and loans receivable and observation of the California banking code.

6 Examination of vacation records to determine whether employees followed company policy of two weeks' paid vacation annually.

7 Audit of a small college to determine that the college had followed requirements of a bond indenture agreement.

8 Examination of financial statements for use by stockholders when there is an internal audit staff.

9 Audit of a German government agency to determine if the agency has followed policies of the German government.

10 Audit of annual financial statements to be filed with the SEC.

11 Examination of a French government grant to a private company to determine whether it would have been feasible to accomplish the same objective at less cost elsewhere.

12 Audit of a statement of cash receipts and disbursements to be used by a creditor.

Required:

For each of the above, identify the most likely type of auditor (independent, government or internal) and the most likely type of audit (financial, compliance or operational).

1–28 Internal and External Audit. Khaled Al-Zubari, an executive recruiter, is a member of the Board of Directors of Mantilla Corporation. At a recent board meeting, called to discuss the financial plan for 20X4, Mr Al-Zubari discovered two planned expenditures for auditing. In the Controller's Department budget he found an internal audit activity, and in the Treasurer's budget he found an estimate for the 20X4 annual audit by the company's external auditing firm. Mr Al-Zubari could not understand the need for two different expenditures for auditing. Since the fee for the annual external audit was less than the cost of the internal audit activity, he proposed eliminating the internal audit function.

Required:

A. Explain to Mr Al-Zubari the different purposes served by the two audit activities.

B. What benefits does the audit firm doing an audit of financial statements derive from the existence of an internal audit function? (CMA adapted)

1.7 Types of Auditor

1–29 Independent External Auditor. Give reasons why the following organisations should have annual audits by an independent external auditor:

(a) The US Federal Reserve Board

(b) A retail company traded on the London Stock Exchange

(c) Walt Disney Company

(d) Amnesty International

(e) A small grocery store in Ponta Grossa, Brazil

(f) A local Baptist church in Lubbock, Texas, USA.

1.8 Setting Audit Objectives Based on Management Assertions

1–30 Management Assertions and Audit Objectives. The following are management assertions (1 through 9) and audit objectives applied to the audit of accounts payable ((a) through (h)).

Management Assertion:

1 Existence

2 Rights and obligations

3 Occurrence

4 Completeness

5 Valuation and allocation

6 Accuracy

7   Cut-off
8   Classification
9   Understandability

Specific Audit Objective:

(a) Existing accounts payable are included in the accounts payable balance on the balance sheet date.
(b) Accounts payable are recorded in the proper account.
(c) Acquisition transactions in the acquisition and payment cycle are recorded in the proper period.
(d) Accounts payable representing the accounts payable balance on the balance sheet date agree with related subsidiary ledger amounts, and the total is correctly added and agrees with the general ledger.
(e) Accounts in the acquisition and payment cycle are properly disclosed according to IASs.
(f) Accounts payable representing the accounts payable balance on the balance sheet date are valued at the correct amount.
(g) Accounts payable exist.
(h) Any allowances for accounts payable discounts are taken.

Required:

A.   Explain the differences among management assertions and specific audit objectives and their relationships to each other.
B.   For each specific audit objective, identify the appropriate management assertion.

1.9   The Audit Process Model

1-31   Audit Process Model. What are the four Phases of an Audit? Discuss each. Determine which is the most important of the four and explain why.

1-32   Audit Process Model. Based on the standard Audit Process Model, trace the procedures an auditor would use to audit a retail clothing business (continuing client) from the initial client contact to the audit opinion.

1.10   International Audit Firms

1-33   Auditor Responsibility. Four friends who are auditing students have a discussion. Jon says that the primary responsibility for the adequacy of disclosure in the financial statements and footnotes rests with the auditor in charge of the audit fieldwork. Mai-ling says that the partner in charge of the engagement has the primary responsibility. Abdul says the staff person who draughts the statements and footnotes has the primary responsibility. Yalanda contends that it is the client's responsibility.

Required:

Which student is correct and why?

CASES

1–34 Audit Objectives and Financial Statement Accounts. Look at the financial statements of a major public company. Pick three accounts and discuss the financial statement assertions that might be associated with those accounts. For example, the financial statement assertions might be associated with 'Accrued Product Liability' are valuation, existence, completeness and understandability. Valuation relates to product liability because a judgement (estimate) must be made regarding the expected cost of defective products.

1–35 International Standards on Auditing (ISA). Download the latest version of *Handbook of International Quality Control, Auditing Review, Other Assurance, And Related Services Pronouncements* from the IFAC website **http://www.ifac.org/auditing-assurance**. Pick one ISA and discuss how that standard would influence the work of an auditor.

1–36 Qualifications of Auditors. From the library get a copy of the EC Eighth Company Law Directive which is about the qualifications and work of auditors.

Required:
Based on the Eighth Directive, answer the following questions.
A. How many years of work experience must an auditor have before he can receive an auditing credential?
B. How many years of education must an auditor have before certification?
C. Name some of the requirements for the work of auditors.

1–37 Due Professional Care. Discuss lawsuits resulting from negligence of 'due professional care'.

Required:
A. Consult the library, a database like Lexis-Nexis or the internet for lawsuits resulting from negligence of 'due professional care'. Discuss at least two.
B. Describe briefly the courts final conclusion and results from the court decision.
(Written by Thai Silver and Shirlene Xicotencatl)

1.13 Notes

1 The Afrikaansche Handels-vereeniging was a company controlled by a very reputable citizen of Rotterdam, the Netherlands. He managed to conceal important losses of his company to bankers, creditors and stockholders by providing false balance sheets.

2 As important audit terms are first introduced in a chapter they are set in colored type. If you see a word in color, the definition will be given in the glossary. 'Auditor' is used to refer to the person or persons conducting the audit, usually the engagement partner or other members of the engagement team, or, as applicable, the firm. Where an ISA expressly intends that a requirement or responsibility be fulfilled by the engagement partner, the term 'engagement partner' rather than 'auditor' is used. 'Engagement partner' and 'firm' are to be read as referring to their public sector equivalents where relevant.

3 Such non-financial information might include footnote disclosures, the management's report, the report of the directors, or even the whole annual report.

4 Going concern assumption – under the going concern assumption, an entity is ordinarily viewed as continuing in business for the foreseeable future with neither the intention nor the necessity of liquidation, ceasing trading, or seeking protection from creditors pursuant to laws or regulations. Accordingly, assets and liabilities are recorded on the basis that the entity will be able to realise its assets and discharge its liabilities in the normal course of business.

5 Governance – describes the role of person(s) or organisation(s) with responsibility for overseeing the strategic direction of the entity and obligations related to the accountability of the entity. Those charged with governance ordinarily are accountable for ensuring that the entity achieves its objectives, financial reporting, and reporting to interested parties. Those charged with governance include management only when it performs such functions.

6 Cadbury, Adrian, 1995, *The Company Chairman*, 2nd edn, Prentice Hall, Hemel Hempstead, England, p. 116.

7 Reasonable assurance – in the context of audit engagements, and in quality control is a high, but not absolute, level of assurance. In an audit engagement, the auditor provides a high, but not absolute, level of assurance, expressed positively in the audit report as reasonable assurance, that the information subject to audit is free of material misstatement.

8 Required of companies listed on the London Stock Exchange. Recommended in 1992 by the Committee on the Financial Aspects of Corporate Governance (the Cadbury Report). At the heart of the Cadbury Report is a Code of Best Practice designed to achieve the necessary high standards of corporate behaviour.

9 The Committee of Sponsoring Organizations of the Treadway Commission (COSO) recommended a management report on internal control in 1992. In 1989, one public company in four reported in some way on internal controls. For Fortune 500 companies, the number was about 60 per cent. Now internal control is required for all companies listed on the US Stock Exchange or otherwise reporting to the SEC under the Sarbanes-Oxley Act.

10 See: International Standards Organization (ISO), 2009, Environmental Management, The ISO 14000 family of International Standards, **http://www.iso.org/iso/theiso14000family_2009.pdf**.

11 See, for example, Admiraal, Michel and Turksema Rudi, 2009, 'Reporting on Non-financial Information', *International Journal of Government Auditing*, July, **http://www.intosaijournal.org/technicalarticles/technicaljul2009b.html** AND Tison, Jacques, 2013, 'Non-financial performance and reporting', **http://www.pwc.be/en/non-financial-performance-reporting/index.jhtml**.

12 Percy J.P., 1995, 'The Relevance of Research in the Development of Interpersonal Skills for Accountants', FEE/IFAC 1995 International Accountancy Conference, 12 May 1995, Amsterdam and Breukelen, the Netherlands.

13 See National Audit Office of the People's Republic of China, 2011, 'Performance Report of National Audit Office of the People's Republic of China (2011)', **http://www.cnao.gov.cn/main/articleshow_ArtID_1258.htm**; and Standing Committee of the National People's Congress on Amending the Audit Law of the People's Republic of China, 2006, **http://www.cnao.gov.cn/main/articleshow_ArtID_952.htm**.

14 See IAASB website factsheet currently
at https://www.ifac.org/sites/default/files/uploads/IAASB/IAASB%20FactSheet.pdf

15 SEC, 2003, Study Report: Study Pursuant to Section 108(d) of the Sarbanes–Oxley Act of 2002 on the Adoption by the United States Financial Reporting System of a Principles-Based Accounting System, Securities and Exchange Commission, 25 July: **http://www.sec.gov/news/studies/ principlesbasedstand.htm**.

16 International Auditing and Assurance Standards Board (IAASB), 2012, International Standard on Auditing 200 (ISA 200) 'Overall Objectives of the Independent Auditor and the Conduct of an Audit in Accordance with International Standards on Auditing', paragraphs 1–9. International Federation of Accountants, New York, *Handbook of International Quality Control, Auditing Review, Other Assurance, and Related Services Pronouncements*, 2012 edn, Volume 1, International Federation of Accountants, New york.

17 American Accounting Association, 1973, *A Statement of Basic Auditing Concepts*, Studies in Accounting Research (6), American Accounting Association, Sarasota, Florida, p. 2.

18 This section paraphrases ISA 200, op. cit. paragraphs 3–9.

19 ISA 200, op. cit. paragraphs 14–17.

20 Professional scepticism – an attitude that includes a questioning mind, being alert to conditions which may indicate possible misstatement due to error or fraud, and a critical assessment of evidence (discussed in more detail in Chapter 4).

21 Material misstatement – a significant mistake in financial information which would arise from errors and fraud if it could influence the economic decisions of users taken on the basis of the financial statements.

22 Professional judgement – the application of relevant training, knowledge and experience, within the context provided by auditing, accounting and ethical standards, in making informed decisions about the courses of action that are appropriate in the circumstances of the audit engagement. (Discussed in more detail in Chapter 4.)

23 Sufficient appropriate audit evidence – *sufficiency* is the measure of the quantity (amount) of audit evidence. *Appropriateness* is the measure of the quality of audit evidence and its relevance to a particular assertion and its reliability. (We will discuss evidence at some length in Chapters 9 and 10.)

24 ISA 200, op. cit. paragraph 11.

25 Materiality – information is material if its omission or misstatement could influence the economic decisions of users taken on the basis of the financial statements. Materiality depends on the size of the item or error judged in the particular circumstances of its omission or misstatement. Thus, materiality provides a threshold or cut-off point rather than being a primary qualitative characteristic which information must have if it is to be useful. (We discuss materiality in greater depth in Chapter 6.)

26 Control environment – includes the governance and management functions and the attitudes, awareness and actions of those charged with governance and management concerning the entity's internal control and its importance in the entity. The control environment is a component of internal control.

27 Council of European Communities, Eighth Council Directive of 10 April 1994, Article 24, *Official Journal of the European Communities*, No. L 126, 1994.

28 Tolerable misstatement – a monetary amount set by the auditor in respect of which the auditor seeks to obtain an appropriate level of assurance that the monetary amount set by the auditor is not exceeded by the actual misstatement in the population.

29 International Auditing and Assurance Standards Board (IAASB), 2012, International Standard on Auditing 315 (ISA 315) 'Identifying and Assessing the Risks of Material Misstatement through Understanding the Entity and Its Environment', paragraph A111. *Handbook of International Quality Control, Auditing Review, Other Assurance, and Related Services Pronouncements*, 2012 edn, Volume 1, International Federation of Accountants, New York.

30 Wallage Philip, 1993, 'Internationalizing Audit: A Study of Audit Approaches in the Netherlands', *European Accounting Review*, 1993, No. 3, pp. 555–578.

31 Unmodified (unqualified opinion) – an audit opinion expressed when the auditor concludes that the financial statements give a true and fair view (or are presented fairly, in all material respects) in accordance with the identified financial reporting framework.

32 Qualified opinion – a qualified opinion is expressed when the auditor concludes that an unqualified opinion cannot be expressed but that the effect of any disagreement with management, or limitation on scope, is not so material and pervasive as to require an adverse opinion or a disclaimer of opinion.

33 Disclaimer of opinion – a disclaimer of opinion is expressed when the possible effect of a limitation on scope is so material and pervasive that the auditor has not been able to obtain sufficient appropriate audit evidence and accordingly is unable to express an opinion on the financial statements.

34 Control activities – those policies and procedures that help ensure that management directives are carried out. Control activities are a component of internal control.

35 Analytical procedures – evaluations of financial information through analysis of plausible relationships among both financial and non-financial data. Analytical procedures also encompass such investigation as is necessary of identified fluctuations or relationships that are inconsistent with other relevant information or that differ from expected values by a significant amount.

36 Audit plan – a work plan that reflects the design and performance of all audit procedures, consisting of a detailed approach for the nature, timing and extent of audit procedures to be performed (including the performance of risk assessment procedures) and the rationale for their selection. The audit plan begins by planning risk assessment procedures and once these procedures have been performed it is updated and changed to reflect the further audit procedures needed to respond to the results of the risk assessments. Also called audit programme.

37 Internal control structure – the set of policies and procedures designed to provide management with reasonable assurance that the goals and objectives it believes are important will be met.

38 Committee of Sponsoring Organizations of the Treadway Commission (COSO), 1992, Chapter 1 'Definition' *Internal Control Integrated Framework – Framework*, American Institute of Certified Public Accountants, Jersey City, New Jersey, 1992.

39 Substantive procedure – an audit procedure designed to detect material misstatements at the assertion level. Substantive procedures comprise:
(a) Tests of details (of classes of transactions, account balances, and disclosures); and
(b) Substantive analytical procedures.

40 Tests of controls – an audit procedure designed to evaluate the operating effectiveness of controls in preventing, or detecting and correcting, material misstatements at the assertion level.

41 Written representation – a written statement by management provided to the auditor to confirm certain matters or to support other audit evidence. Written representations in this context do not include financial statements, the assertions therein, or supporting books and records.

42 Matters for attention of partners (MAP) – a report by audit managers to be reviewed by a partner or director detailing the audit decisions reached by managers or partners and the reasons for those decisions.

43 Disclaimer of opinion – a disclaimer of opinion is expressed when the possible effect of a limitation on scope is so material and pervasive that the auditor has not been able to obtain sufficient appropriate audit evidence and accordingly is unable to express an opinion on the financial statements.

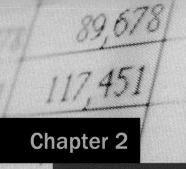

Chapter 2

THE AUDIT MARKET

2.1 Learning Objectives

After studying this chapter, you should be able to:

1 Distinguish between different theories of audit services including agency theory.

2 Understand drivers for audit regulation.

3 Understand the role of public oversight.

4 Distinguish between different audit firms.

5 Identify some current developments in the audit market.

6 Portray the series of industry codes of conduct and guidance.

2.2 Introduction

The emergence of today's auditors happened during the Industrial Revolution that started in Great Britain around 1780. This revolution led to the emergence of large industrial companies with complex bureaucratic structures and, gradually, the need to look for external funds in order to finance further expansion: the separation between capital provision and management. Both developments resulted in demand for the services of specialists in bookkeeping and in auditing internal and external financial representations. The institutionalisation of the audit profession was then merely a matter of time.

■ Management Controls Operations and Communications

Management has control over the accounting systems and internal controls of the enterprises that auditors audit. Management is not only responsible for the financial and internal control reports to investors, but also has the authority to determine the precise nature of the representations that go into those reports. However, management can scarcely be expected to take an impartial view of this process.

■ Communications to Stakeholders – the Financial Statements

The financial statements measure the financial and non-financial performance and financial position of the organisation that management manages. Internal controls determine what and how management objectives are met. They have an important influence on management's salaries, on the value of managers' shareholdings in the enterprise and even on their continued employment with the company. To increase the confidence of investors, creditors and other interested parties in these financial statements, the investors are provided with an independent and expert opinion on the fairness of the reports. An auditor provides this opinion.

2.3 Theories on the Demand and Supply of Audit Services

The demand for audit services may be explained by several different theories. Some theories like the **Theory of Inspired Confidence** and **Agency Theory** have been well researched and reported on. Other theories based on public perceptions such as the **Policeman Theory** and the **Lending Credibility Theory** serve more as a point of reference than as a researched construct.

These four audit theories are shown in Illustration 2.1.

■ The Policeman Theory

Is an auditor responsible for discovering fraud, like a policeman? Think of this idea as the Policeman Theory. Up until the 1940s it was widely held that an auditor's job was to focus on arithmetical accuracy and on prevention and detection of fraud. However, from the 1940s until the turn of the century there was a shift of auditing to mean verification of truth and fairness of the financial statements. Recent financial statement

ILLUSTRATION 2.1

An Illustration of Four Theories to Explain Audit Supply and Demand

Policeman Theory

An auditor's job is to focus on arithmetical accuracy and on the prevention and detection of fraud.

Lending Credibility Theory

Audited financial statements are used by management to enhance the stakeholders' faith in management's stewardship.

Theory of Inspired Confidence

The demand for audit services is the direct consequence of the participation of outside stakeholders (third parties) in the company. These stakeholders demand accountability from the management, in return for their contribution to the company. Since information provided by management might be biased, because of a possible divergence between the interests of management and outside stakeholders, an audit of this information is required.

Agency Theory

A company is viewed as the result of more or less formal contracts, in which several groups make some kind of contribution to the company, given a certain price. A reputable auditor is appointed not only in the interest of third parties, but also in the interest of management.

frauds such as those at Société Générale, Satyam, Ahold, Enron, etc. have resulted in careful reconsideration of this theory. There now is an ongoing public debate on the auditor's responsibility for detection and disclosure of **fraud** returning us to the basic public perceptions on which this theory derives.

■ The Lending Credibility Theory

Another public perception is that the primary function of auditing is the addition of credibility to the financial statements. We may think of this as the Lending Credibility Theory. Audited financial statements are used by management to enhance the stakeholders' faith in management's stewardship. If **stakeholders** such as stockholders, government, or creditors have to make their judgments based on the information they receive, they must have faith that this is a fair representation of the economic value and performances of the organisation. In audit research terms an audit reduces the 'information asymmetry', management knows more than the stakeholders.

■ The Theory of Inspired Confidence

This theory was developed in the late 1920s by the Dutch professor Theodore Limperg.[1] In contrast to the preceding theories, Limperg's theory addresses both the demand and the supply of audit services. According to Limperg, the demand for audit services is the direct consequence of the participation of outside stakeholders (third parties) in the company. These stakeholders demand accountability from the management, in return for their contribution to the company. Since information provided by management might be biased, because of a possible divergence between the interests of management and outside stakeholders, an audit of this information is required. With regard to the level of audit assurance that the auditor should provide (the supply side), Limperg adopts a normative approach. The auditor should act in such a way that he does not disappoint the expectations of a 'rational outsider', while, on the other hand, he should not arouse greater expectations in his report than his examination justifies. So, given the possibilities of audit technology, the auditor should do enough to meet reasonable public expectations.

■ Agency Theory

In the agency theory, originally proposed by Watts and Zimmerman,[2] a reputable auditor – an auditor who is perceived to meet expectations – is appointed not only in the interest of third parties, but also in the interest of management. A company is viewed as the result of more or less formal 'contracts', in which several groups make some kind of contribution to the company, given a certain 'price'. Company management tries to get these contributions under optimum conditions for management: low interest rates from bankers, high share prices for stockholders, and low wages for employees.

In these relationships, management is seen as the 'agent,' trying to obtain contributions from 'principals' such as bankers, stockholders and employees. Costs of an agency relationship are monitoring costs (the cost of monitoring the agents), bonding costs (the costs, incurred by an agent, of insuring that agents will not take adverse actions against the principals), and residual loss (effective loss that results despite the bonding and monitoring costs incurred).

Information Asymmetry within the Agency Theory

Several types of complexities arise in these agent–principal relationships, such as information asymmetry. The agent (management) has a considerable advantage over the principals regarding information about the company. Basically, management knows more about the company's ability to repay loans than the banker does, and it knows better than the stockholders what the actual profit is, or whether it enjoys excessive bonuses. Furthermore, management knows better than the employees whether the company's financial condition is such that everybody will still be employed next year. However, management needs the principals to look favourably on them, because they ultimately depend on principals for running the business that management supervises.

In order for the principals (who buy shares in the company, loan the company money, or work for them) to have faith in the information given by management, it must be reliable. This means that there is an incentive for both managers and outside investors to engage reputable auditors.

Supply Side of Agency Theory

Agency theory can also be used to explain the supply side[3] of the audit market. The contribution of an audit to third parties is basically determined by the probability that the auditor will detect errors in the financial statements (or other irregularities, such as fraud or illegal acts) and the auditor's willingness to report these errors (e.g. by qualifying the auditor's report), even against the wish of the auditee (auditor independence). Costs as a result of reputation damage have been demonstrated in several empirical studies, which showed that audit firms, having suffered a public rebuke, were confronted with a decline in their market share.

2.4   Audit Regulation: International Perspective

In the previous section, the demand and the supply side of the audit market has been described. In most countries, this demand has long been on a voluntary basis, i.e. it was left to the companies to decide whether they had their financial statements audited or not. As for the supply side, the provision of audit services has been left open to the free market in some countries, without any official legal requirements for auditors. Although regulation and legislation differ, both the demand and the supply of audit services are currently regulated to some degree in most countries. Recent accounting and finance research suggests that national legal environments are among the key determinants of financial market development, corporate ownership structures, corporate policies, and the properties of accounting information around the world.[4]

In most countries, audits are now legally required for some types of companies. For example, in the USA and the European Union, large, and in some cases medium-sized enterprises, are required by law to provide audited financial statements. The European Union audit rules apply to all companies within the individual Member States that are required to be audited. The requirements may vary from state to state. The major bourses (including NYSE, NASDAQ, London Stock Exchange, Tokyo NIKKEI, and Frankfurt DAX) have listing rules that require all listed companies to have their annual report (including financial statements) audited.

The supply of audit services is currently also regulated in most countries. In the European Union, statutory audits, i.e. audits required by law, can only be performed by auditors who have met specific technical requirements with regard to education and experience. Laws in other countries require audits of companies issuing public equity or debt, companies receiving government money, and companies in certain industries (like banking and utilities).

■ US Sarbanes–Oxley Act

Sparked by the Enron and WorldCom debacles and other widely publicised corporate and accounting scandals, the **Sarbanes–Oxley Act of 2002** was passed almost unanimously by Congress and signed into law by President George W. Bush on 30 July 2002. The Act, described by President Bush as incorporating 'the most far-reaching reforms of American business practices since the time of Franklin Delano Roosevelt,' was intended to establish investor confidence by improving the quality of corporate disclosure and financial reporting, strengthen the independence of accounting firms, and increase the role and responsibility of corporate officers and directors for financial statements and corporate disclosures.

The Sarbanes–Oxley Act of 2002 required the US Securities and Exchange Commission (SEC) to create a Public Company Accounting Oversight Board (PCAOB). The Board oversees and investigates the audits and auditors of public companies, and sanctions both firms and individuals for violations of laws, regulations and rules. The Board, at this point, has decided the generally accepted auditing standards (GAAS) set by the American Institute of Certified Public Accountants (AICPA) will only be used temporarily.[5]

■ European Union Regulation

Several European Union Directives on the annual accounts and consolidated accounts of financial and insurance corporations require that the annual accounts or consolidated accounts be audited by certified auditors. The conditions for the approval of qualified auditors were laid down in the Eighth Council Directive 84/253/EEC of 10 April 1984.[6]

EU Directive 2006/43/EC[7] aims at high-level – though not full – harmonisation of statutory audit requirements. The objectives of this Directive are requiring the application of a single set of international auditing standards, the updating of the educational requirements, the definition of professional ethics, and the technical implementation of the cooperation between competent authorities of EU Member States and the authorities of third countries.

Member states of the EU are given authorisation by Directive 2006/43 (1) to register all auditors and audit firms and make such information accessible to the public; (2) adopt an International Auditing Practice Statement on a case-by-case basis; (3) adopt a common audit report for the audit of annual accounts or consolidated accounts prepared on the basis of approved international accounting standards; (4) decide if individual auditors have a common quality assurance policy; and (5) organise an effective system of public oversight for statutory auditors and audit firms on the basis of home country control.

For Statutory auditors and audit firms, Directive 2006/43 required independence when carrying out statutory audits. Statutory auditors and audit firms are responsible for carrying out their work with due care and thus should be liable for the financial damage caused by a lack of the care owed. In order to reinforce the independence of auditors, the key audit partner(s) should rotate management of the audit.

Recently, Michel Barnier, EU Minister of Internal Market and Services, has suggested three areas of audit regulation that are essential: (1) the independence of the profession; (2) opening up the audit market; and (3) creating a more integrated European market and stepping up its supervision.[8] He said that the EU's first concern is the quality and credibility of auditing. Further, the independence of auditors is 'the condition sine qua non for their reports being fully trusted'. He feels that there is a need to restrict – or even prohibit – non-audit services being provided by audit firms to audited clients and that common EU rules in this area are needed. He proposed the concept of 'pure audit firms' (i.e. firms not allowed to provide services other than auditing), which would have the benefit of opening up these non-audit markets to a whole range of smaller audit firms that have no chance faced with the predominance of the major audit firms. Barnier put it this way: 'I am not happy that the audit market is so dominated by four firms whilst there are at least as many other firms wanting to break into this market in Europe.' Barnier believes 'It is unacceptable that an auditor has to pass additional examinations in each country where he wishes to work'. He suggests some solutions, for example the automatic recognition of firms already licensed in other Member States, the award of a European quality label demonstrating the holder's ability to audit large companies, or by harmonising auditing standards at the European Union level.

Other World Regulation

Regulation in other parts of the world is summarised in Illustration 2.2.

2.5 Independent Oversight

There is a recent growth in accounting oversight boards – government or professional committees to review the work of auditors and take an active part in setting and enforcing standards. The global oversight organisation is the International Forum of Independent Audit Regulators (IFIAR). Similar boards are in Australia (Financial Reporting Council), the UK (the Review Board), the Netherlands Authority for the Financial Markets (AFM), France Autorité des marchés financiers (AMF) and the USA (the Public Company Accounting Oversight Board). The similar boards are described in Illustration 2.2.

The **International Forum of Independent Audit Regulators** (IFIAR), whose membership includes the audit regulators from 37 countries (including USA, most of Europe, Africa, Asia, and the Middle East), was established on 15 September 2006, based on the following activities:

- to share knowledge of the audit market environment and practical experience of independent audit regulatory activity;
- to promote collaboration in regulatory activity; and
- to provide a focus for contacts with other international organisations which have an interest in audit quality.

Core principles of IFIAR cover the following:[9]

- comprehensive and well defined accounting and auditing principles and standards that are generally accepted;
- legal requirements for the preparation and publication of financial statements according to those principles and standards;
- an enforcement system for preparers of financial statements to ensure compliance with accounting standards (e.g. fines, shareholder redress, or penalties on responsible managers for non-compliance);

ILLUSTRATION 2.2

Specific Country Oversight Boards

In **Australia**, the Corporate Law Economic Reform Program Act 1999 established the **Financial Reporting Council (FRC)**, with the responsibility for the broad oversight of the accounting standard-setting process for the private, public and not-for-profit sectors. The FRC has an obligation to monitor the development of international accounting standards and accounting standards that apply in major international financial centres. It sets the broad strategic direction for the Australian Accounting Standards Board (AASB), approves and monitors its priorities and business plan, and oversees its operations.

The **Review Board** in the **United Kingdom** is funded by the Accountancy Foundation Limited. The Review Board's task is to monitor the operation of the regulatory system to confirm that it is fully meeting the public interest. In carrying out this function the Review Board's remit covers the work of the three associated bodies – the Ethics Standards Board, the Auditing Practices Board, and the Investigation and Discipline Board. It also has limited scrutiny over the UK accounting professional bodies' authority for investigation and discipline, monitoring, training, qualification, and registration of their members from the accounting profession.[1]

Netherlands Authority for the Financial Markets (AFM) has been responsible for supervising the operation of the financial markets since 1 March 2002. This means that AFM supervises the conduct of the entire financial market sector: savings, investment, insurance and loans. AFM is the successor of the STE (Securities Board of the Netherlands/Stichting Toezicht Effectenverkeer), which supervised all of the participants in the securities trade. AFM is responsible for supervision of financial institutions and financial markets.

In **France** the **Autorité des marchés financiers (AMF)** monitors the information disclosed by listed corporates, paying particular attention to quality and transparency. It investigates special topics on an ongoing basis such as enhancing the competitiveness of the Paris financial centre, replacing the traditional French concept of public issuance of securities (*appel public à l'épargne*) with the European notion of 'public offer', and the security and attractiveness of markets for small and mid-sized companies.

In the **United States of America**, the **Public Company Accounting Oversight Board** (PCAOB) was created by the Sarbanes–Oxley Act of 2002. The PCAOB is empowered to regularly inspect registered accounting firms' operations and will investigate potential violations of securities laws, standards, consistency and conduct. Accounting firms headquartered outside the USA that 'prepare and furnish' an audit report involving US firms registered with the SEC are subject to the authority of the PCAOB. The PCAOB is very influential as all corporations, no matter in what country they are headquartered, are subject to PCAOB audit standards if that company is traded on a US exchange (such as New York Stock Exchange, NASDAC, etc.)

[1] Comment: The Auditing Practices Board Limited (APB) was originally established in 1991 as a committee of the Consultative Committee of Accountancy Bodies, to take responsibility within the United Kingdom and Republic of Ireland for setting standards of auditing with the objective of enhancing public confidence in the audit process and the quality and relevance of audit services in the public interest. In 2002 APB was re-established under the auspices of The Accountancy Foundation and, following a UK government review, it has been transferred to the Financial Reporting Council (FRC). Its objective has remained the same, but its responsibilities have been extended to include responsibility for setting standards for auditors' integrity, objectivity and independence.

- corporate governance arrangements and practices that support high-quality corporate reporting and auditing practice; and
- effective educational and training arrangements for accountants and auditors.

2.6   Audit Firms

In previous sections we have extensively discussed the demand side of the audit market. But what about the supply side? How is it structured? Usually, audit firms are classified into two distinct categories:

- the Big Four firms; and
- the Non-Big Four firms.

The Big Four Firms

These firms resulted partially from several major mergers in the late 1980s. This group is made up of Deloitte, Ernst & Young, KPMG and PricewaterhouseCoopers (PwC). These audit firms have a global network of affiliated firms. Actually, there were the Big Five firms after a series of mergers, including Arthur Andersen. However, as a result of the Enron accounting scandal, the market lost its confidence in Arthur Andersen and this firm had to forfeit its business in 2002 after almost 90 years of having been a highly respected firm (see Concept and a Company 2.2). This case study demonstrates how important it is for auditors to fully respond to the inspired confidence of their stakeholders. (We discuss these ethics issues in Chapter 3.)

Although most of these firms are still structured as national partnerships with national instead of international profit sharing, these national member firms participate in an international head office, in which global technologies, procedures, and directives are developed. In addition to sharing the methodology, the networks are also used for the coordination of international audit engagements. The group auditor of a worldwide operating company uses the services of auditors of the member firms in the countries where the client has subsidiaries. As a result of the developments in communications technology, the effectiveness of these networks and the efficiency of the coordination of international engagements have increased significantly.

For the Big Four firms, audit and accounting services represent approximately half of the firms' total fee income.

The Non-Big Four Firms

These firms can hardly be treated as a homogeneous group. At one extreme there are a very large number of small local firms, with only a handful of professionals. At the other extreme there are a small number of second-tier firms, which also have an international network, although not quite as extensive as the Big Four network. In between, there are a large number of medium-sized national or regional audit firms with several offices. As of 2011 the second-tier firms in the United States included

Grant Thornton; BDO Seidman; McGladrey & Pullen; Moss Adams; and Myer, Hoffman & McCann.

Concept and a Company 2.1

The Basic Theory

Concept	Auditor's search for materiality.
Story	There was once a group of very famous accountants and auditors who joined together as a mutual study group. They determined that they could find the basic truths of auditing. They read all manner of philosophical, scientific and religious works and discussed those theories amongst themselves. They felt that knowledge of the pure truths of auditing would form a basis for discovering the core truths of business and, indeed, life itself.

They studied the great works of accounting for many years, but felt that they were getting nowhere. Finally, they decided to take leave of their day jobs and search the world to find the answer. They sought the advice of great teachers all over the world. They would ask each great teacher to recommend one who was even wiser. Thus, they collected these recommendations until their search pointed to one man – a teacher of teachers.

The group journeyed to an isolated area in the great desert wastes of Africa. There they met the great man and, paying their respects, they told him of their heart-felt desire and long suffering to find the pure truths of auditing. He said, 'I cannot give you the answers. These you must find yourself.' He instructed them to collect all the world's accounting knowledge, encompassing everything from the Sarbanes–Oxley Act 2002 back to cuneiform tablets of 3400 BCE. Then they were to condense all that knowledge to ten volumes.

The group went away and gathered and summarised knowledge for all the ages. After years of work, they again sat at the feet of the teacher of teachers and presented their ten volumes. The sage picked up the volumes and thumbed through them. He handed the volumes back to the group and then said, 'Go and make this into one volume.'

After years of toil, the group, whose membership was now thinning appreciably, returned with their one volume of the world's audit truths. The teacher of teachers said, 'Make this into one sentence.'

Taking on this almost impossible task, the remaining members of the group locked themselves into a cave and ate nothing but soup made of nettles to sustain them until they came up with the one true answer. When they returned to the guru with this sentence, he smiled and said to them, 'You got it.' This was the sentence:

'There is no such thing as a free lunch.'

Discussion Questions	■ Why can we expect that a fraud that works now may not work in the future?
	■ Why can a company not continue to grow indefinitely at 15 per cent per year?
	■ Why can a management that make up fictitious sales not profit in the long run?
	■ Why does every form of earnings manipulation have its cost?
	■ Based on this one sentence, how would you justify the existence of ethics?
References	The great audit works.

2.7 Legal Liability

There are many stakeholders who rely on audited financial statements: the client (with which there is a privity relationship), and third parties such as actual and potential stockholders, vendors, bankers and other creditors, employees, customers, and the government (like the tax authorities). Legal liability of the auditor to each stakeholder varies from country to country, district to district. This liability can generally be classified as based on one or more of the following: common law, civil liability under statutory law, criminal liability under statutory law, and liability as members of professional accounting organisations.

■ Liability under Common Law

Liability for auditors under common law generally falls in two categories: liabilities to clients and third party liability.

Liability to Clients

A typical civil lawsuit filed by a client involves a claim that the auditor did not discover financial statement fraud or employee fraud (defalcation) because the auditors showed negligence[10] in the conduct of an audit. The legal action can be for breach of contract[11] or, more likely, a tort[12] action for negligence. Tort actions are the most common, for generally they generate larger monetary judgements than breach of contract.

Liabilities to Third Parties

Third parties include all stakeholders in an audit other than the audit client. An audit firm may be liable to third parties such as banks that have incurred a loss due to reliance on misleading financial statements.

Ultramares

The most famous US audit case in third party liabilities happened in the 1931 *Ultramares–Touche* case (*Ultramares Corporation* v *Touche et al.*).[13] In this case, the court held that although the accountants were negligent in not finding that a material amount of accounts receivable had been falsified when careful investigation would have shown the amount to be fraudulent, they were not liable to a third party bank because the creditors were not a primary beneficiary, or known party, with whom the auditor was informed before conducting the audit. This precedent is called the Ultramares doctrine, that **ordinary negligence** (the failure to use reasonable care) is not sufficient for a liability to a third party because of lack of **privity of contract**[14] between the third party and the auditor.

Caparo

The 1990 *Caparo* case (*Caparo Industries, PLC* v *Dickman and Others*)[15] is a leading English tort law case on the test for a duty of care of an auditor. The decision arose in the context of a negligent preparation of accounts for a company. Prior to the decision, if a statement (like an audit opinion) was made negligently, then the person making the statement will be liable for any loss which results. The question in Caparo was the scope of the assumption of responsibility, and what the limits of liability ought to be.

The House of Lords, following the Court of Appeal, set out a 'threefold test'. In order for an obligation (duty of care)[16] to arise in negligence: (1) harm must be reasonably foreseeable as a result of the defendant's conduct; (2) the parties must be in a relationship of proximity; and (3) it must be fair, just and reasonable to impose liability. In the case of annual financial statements, this purpose was to give the shareholders the information necessary to enable them to question the past management of the company, to exercise their voting rights and to influence future policy and management.

German Liability

In Germany, auditors have an unlimited liability to the client if there is an intentional violation of duties, but the liability is capped by law at €1,000,000 to €4,000,000, depending on circumstances, for negligent violation of duties. Liability to third parties as described by the Tort Law (§823–826 BGB) is restricted to certain prerequisites such as intent and violation of morality. There is also liability to third parties under Contract Law, which has less restrictive prerequisites than Tort Law.

■ Civil Liability under Statutory Law

Most countries have laws that affect the civil liabilities of auditors. Securities laws, for example, may impose strict standards on professional accountants. In the USA, the Securities Act of 1933 not only created the Securities and Exchange Commission (SEC), it established the first statutory civil recovery rules for third parties against auditors. Original purchasers of securities of a firm newly registered to make a public offering have recourse against the auditor for up to the original purchase price if the financial statements are false or misleading.

Anyone who purchased securities described in the SEC registration statement (S1) may sue the auditor for material misrepresentations or omissions in financial statements published in the S1. The auditor has the burden of demonstrating that reasonable investigation was conducted or all that the loss of the purchaser of securities (plaintiff) was caused by factors other than the misleading financial statements. If the auditor cannot prove this, the plaintiff wins the case.

The United States Sarbanes–Oxley Act of 2002 also prescribes civil penalties for CFOs and CEOs. If there is a material restatement of a company's reported financial results due to the material noncompliance of the company, as a result of misconduct, the CEO and CFO must reimburse the company for any bonus or incentive or equity-based compensation received within the 12 months following the filing with the financial statements subsequently required to be restated.[17] Financial statements filed with the SEC by any public company must be certified by CEOs and CFOs. If all financials do not fairly present the true condition of the company, CEOs and CFOs may receive fines up to $1 million or up to $5 million for fraud.[18]

■ Criminal Liability under Statutory Law

A professional auditor may be held criminally liable under the laws of a country or district that make it a criminal offence to defraud another person through knowingly being involved with false financial statements.

US Securities and Exchange Act of 1934 and Sarbanes–Oxley Act of 2002

The Securities and Exchange Act of 1934 in the USA requires every company with securities traded on national and over-the-counter exchanges to submit audited financial statements annually (10-K) as well as other reports for quarterly financials (10-Q), unusual events (8-K) and other events. The Act also sets out (Rule 10b-5) criminal liability conditions if the auditor employs any device, scheme or artifice to defraud or make any untrue statement of a material fact or omits to state a material fact, i.e. the auditor intentionally or recklessly misrepresents information for third party use. The SEC also has authority to sanction or suspend an auditor from doing audits for SEC-registered companies.[19]

Several court cases have been subjected to an application of the Act's criminal liability section. In *United States* v *Natelli* (1975) two auditors were convicted of criminal liability for certifying financial statements of National Student Marketing Corporation that contained inadequate disclosures pertaining to accounts receivable. In *United States* v *Weiner* (1975) three auditors were convicted of securities fraud in connection with their audit of Equity Funding Corporation of America. The fraud the company perpetrated was so massive and the audit work so sub-standard that the court concluded that the auditors must have been aware of the fraud. Management revealed to the audit partner that the prior years' financials were misstated and the partner agreed to say nothing in *ESM Government Securities* v *Alexander Grant & Co.* (1986). The partner was convicted of criminal charges for his role in sustaining the fraud and was sentenced to a 12-year prison term.

The Sarbanes–Oxley Act of 2002 attaches criminal penalties to CEOs, CFOs and auditors. To knowingly destroy, create, manipulate documents and/or impede or obstruct federal investigations is considered a felony, and violators will be subject to fines or up to 20 years' imprisonment, or both[20]. All audit reports or related workpapers must be kept by the auditor for 7 years. Failure to do this may result in 10 years' imprisonment.[21] CFOs and CEOs who falsely certify financial statements or internal controls are subject to 10 years' imprisonment. Wilful false certification may result in a maximum of 20 years' imprisonment.[22]

Concept and a Company 2.2

Arthur Andersen and Obstruction of Justice

Concept	Auditor statutory legal liability – illegal acts.
Story	Arthur Andersen, LLP, one of the former Big Five audit firms with 2,311 public company clients and 28,000 US employees, was found guilty of 'obstruction of justice'. The obstruction of justice statute, 18 USC s 1512(b), makes it a crime for anyone to 'corruptly persuade' 'another person' to destroy documents 'with intent to impair' the use of the documents 'in an official proceeding'. The US District Court for the Southern District of Texas sentenced Andersen to pay a $500,000 fine and serve five years of probation (WSJ, 2002).
	The charge resulted from Andersen's destruction of thousands of documents and email messages relating to work performed for Enron. The court found that Andersen illegally destroyed the documents with the intent of thwarting an investigation by the US Securities

and Exchange Commission. On 15 June 2002, the tenth day of deliberations, the jury met for only 30 minutes, and then delivered its fatal verdict. This was the first time a major accounting firm had ever been convicted of a criminal charge (Manor, 2002).

Andersen contended that the document destruction was done in the standard course of business and was not illegal. The prosecution introduced evidence that Andersen billed Enron about $720,000 for consultation services relating to 'SEC Inquiry' at the same time the firm was destroying documents relating to the Enron audit. The Department of Justice said that the Andersen billing records presented strong evidence that the firm knew about the SEC investigation at the same time they were shredding documents that might have been subpoenaed in that investigation. This establishes that many people at Andersen who were involved in the document destruction had direct, personal knowledge of the investigation (Fowler, 2002).

The document destruction was precipitated by a memo from Nancy Temple in Andersen's legal department which stated that, under the Andersen document retention policy, superseded drafts of memos should be discarded. David Duncan, the Andersen lead audit partner on the Enron account, ordered employees to adhere to the firm's guidelines on 'document retention' and destroy irrelevant documents. In the trial, prosecution produced a binder of handwritten notes from Temple, taken from numerous conference calls with Andersen executives, to show that the attorney realised that the SEC would probably open an investigation into Enron (Beltran *et al.*, 2002).

Andersen appealed the judgment on several grounds. Andersen complained that the judge allowed the government to tell jurors about SEC actions against Andersen for faulty audits of Waste Management and Sunbeam, thereby prejudicing the jury. They also said that the judge gave improper instructions to the jury. The jury gave a message to the judge asking for guidance on making their decision. The question they asked was: 'If each of us believes that one Andersen agent acted knowingly and with a corrupt intent, is it for all of us to believe it was the same agent? Can one believe it was agent A, another believe it was agent B, and another believe it agent C?' (*Houston Chronicle*, 2003).

Over strenuous objections from the prosecution, Judge Harmon returned a message to the jury, telling them they could find Andersen guilty of obstructing justice even if they could not agree on which employee committed the crime (McNulty, 2002).

However, in May 2005 the Supreme Court reversed the previous conviction of Andersen. This was a symbolic victory for Andersen, as by then the firm was already nearly out of business due to the previous conviction. In a statement, Andersen said they were 'very pleased with the Supreme Court's decision, which acknowledges the fundamental injustice that has been done to Arthur Andersen and its former personnel and retirees.' As an audit firm, Andersen was not back in business as its reputation as an independent, high-quality auditor was pretty much gone.

Discussion Questions	▪ Should the whole audit firm be charged with an offence by a few of its auditors? ▪ In what ways can auditor working papers (correspondence, plans and audit notes) be beneficial to an investigation of company fraudulent practices?

References	Beltran, L., J. Rogers and P. Viles, 2002, 'U.S. Closes in Andersen Trial,' *CNNMoney*, 5 June. Fowler, Tom, 2002, 'Soul Searching Led to Plea, Duncan Says,' *Houston Chronicle*, 16 May. Manor, R., 2002, 'Andersen Finally Admits Demise,' *Chicago Tribune*, 17 June. McNulty, S., 2002, 'Andersen Guilty in Enron Obstruction Case,' *Financial Times*, 16 June. WSJ, 2002, 'Andersen Sentenced To 5 Years Probation,' *Wall Street Journal*, 17 October.

Concept and a Company 2.3

Trafigura and the Illegal Dumping of Toxic Waste

Concept	Auditor's responsibilities regarding laws and regulation – illegal acts.
Story	TrafiguraBeheer BV is a Dutch multinational commodity trading company founded in 1993 and trading in base metals and energy, including oil.

On 2 July 2006, the *Probo Koala*, a ship leased by the company, entered a port in Amsterdam to unload several hundred tonnes of toxic waste. Amsterdam Port Services BV, the company that had been contracted to take the waste, raised their price to process the waste twenty-fold soon after determining the waste was more toxic than previously understood. So, after baulking at a competitor's 1000 euro per cubic metre disposal charge near Amsterdam, Trafigura decided to have the ship take back the waste and have it processed en route to different offloading sites, which all refused it until Abidjan, Côte d'Ivoire, one of Africa's largest seaports. According to Trafigura the waste was then handed over to a local newly formed dumping company, Compagnie Tommy, which illegally dumped the waste instead of processing it. Many people there became sick due to exposure to the waste, and investigations were begun to determine whether it was intentionally dumped by Trafigura. Trafigura stated in a press statement that their tests showed the waste not to be as toxic as had been claimed, and that they were unsure why so many people had become ill from exposure to it. The *New York Times* reported on 3 October 2006 that the dumping of the waste by Compagnie Tommy was indeed illegal.

On 13 February 2007, to release its jailed executives in response to the deaths of ten people and the various illnesses of over 100,000 people attributed to the waste, Trafigura paid €152 million to Côte d'Ivoire in compensation. The payment also exonerated Trafigura from further legal proceedings in Côte d'Ivoire.

On 16 November 2012 Trafigura and the Dutch authorities agreed to a settlement. The settlement obliges Trafigura to pay the existing €1 million fine and in addition the company must also pay Dutch authorities a further €300,000 in compensation – the money it saved by dumping the toxic waste in Abidjan rather than having it properly disposed of in the Netherlands. The Dutch also agreed to stop the personal court case against Trafigura's chairman, Claude Dauphin, in exchange for a €67,000 fine.

Discussion Questions	■ Do you think the auditor of TrafiguraBeheer BV should have discovered the illegal activities of TrafiguraBeheer BV, given the attention in the international press during 2006 and early 2007? ■ Do you think the financial statements of TrafiguraBeheer BV for the year ending 31 December 2006 are materially incorrect, if the contingent liability of €152 million is not included in these financial statements?
References	http://en.wikipedia.org/wiki/Trafigura.

■ Liabilities as Members of Professional Accounting Organisations

Nearly all national audit professions have some sort of disciplinary court. In most countries, anyone can lodge a complaint against an auditor, regardless of one's involvement with the auditor. The disciplinary court typically consists of representatives of the audit and legal professions, and sometimes representatives of the general public. Having heard the arguments of the plaintiff and the defendant, the court makes its judgment and determines the sanction – if any – against the auditor. The sanction may vary. It may be:

- a fine;
- a reprimand (either oral or written);
- a suspension for a limited period of time (e.g. six months); or
- a lifetime ban from the profession.

In some countries, the trials of these disciplinary courts are public. In most countries, the verdicts are made public, in particular if the verdict is either a suspension or a lifetime ban. Appeal against the verdict of the disciplinary court is usually possible. Suppose the auditor is condemned by the disciplinary court for an audit failure. Is that enough for a civil suit against an auditor? No. In order to hold the auditor legally liable successfully in a civil suit, the following conditions have to be met:

- An audit failure/neglect has to be proven (*negligence* issue). A verdict by the disciplinary court is often the basis for meeting this condition.
- The auditor should owe a duty of care to the plaintiff (**due professional care** issue).
- The plaintiff has to prove a causal relationship between his losses and the alleged audit failure (causation issue).
- The plaintiff must quantify his losses (quantum issue).

■ Suggested Solutions to Auditor Liability

In the last two decades, several auditor litigation cases have resulted in multi-million dollar claims to be paid by auditors. For example, some Big Four audit firms made settlements with the US government for more than US $500 million, because of audit failures regarding several US hedge funds and financial institutions. Insurance against litigation is now common for audit firms (and in some countries like The Netherlands mandatory). Even though the premium rates for these insurance policies have risen dramatically over the last decade, these policies only cover damage to a certain amount. Claims paid above this 'cap' are not covered and have to be paid by the audit firm itself.

It is widely acknowledged that the financial risks resulting from litigation for audit firms and partners might be a threat to the viability of the audit profession. European Union Internal Market and Services Commissioner Charlie McCreevy has said: 'We have concluded that unlimited liability combined with insufficient insurance cover is no longer tenable. It is a potentially huge problem for our capital markets and for auditors working on an international scale. The current conditions are not only preventing the entry of new players in the international audit market, but are also threatening existing firms. In a context of high concentration and limited choice of audit firms, this situation could lead to damaging consequences for European capital markets'.[23]

In order to reduce these risks several measures are considered:

- A limit or **cap** on claims (a maximum settlement amount) is known in advance and limits settlements. Liability is now capped in Austria, Belgium, Germany, Greece and Slovenia.
- In some countries, a system of **proportionate liability** is under study. In such a system, an audit firm is not liable for the entire loss incurred by plaintiffs (as is the case

under joint and several liability), but only to the extent to which the loss is attributable to the auditor. The US has a system of proportionate liability, but only under the federal acts.

■ To make insurance of all liability risks compulsory using new legislation was one of the recommendations of a EU commission.

■ Exclude certain activities with a higher risk profile from the auditors' liability. A mechanism to achieve this outcome would be to introduce so-called safe harbour provisions by legislation.

■ In order to protect the personal wealth of audit partners, some audit firms are structured as a limited liability partnership (e.g. in the UK).

2.8 Some Developments in the Audit Market

In our discussion of audit theories, the Policeman Theory was mentioned and its inability to explain the historic shift (from around 1940 to 2002) from prevention and detection of fraud to verification of truth and fairness of the financial statements. The development of the auditor's duties, linked to changes in the audit market, is still an object of public debate, often referred to as the audit expectation gap debate. This gap results from the fact that users of audit services have expectations regarding the duties of auditors that exceed the current practice in the profession.

Auditors' Duties and the Expectations of Audit Services Users

The users of audit services can broadly be classified as auditees (the board of directors of the company) and third parties (shareholders, bankers, creditors, employees, customers, and other groups). Each of these groups has its own set of expectations with regard to an auditor's duties. Expectations were found with regard to the following duties of auditors in giving an opinion on the:

■ fairness of financial statements;
■ company's ability to continue as a going concern;
■ company's internal control system;
■ occurrence of fraud;
■ occurrence of illegal acts.

Current developments in each of these duties will be described in the remainder of this section.

■ Opinion on the Fairness of Financial Statements

Giving an opinion on the fairness of the financial statements is generally regarded as the auditor's core business. Most of the national and international auditing guidelines are concerned with this particular duty. Expectation gap studies demonstrate that public expectations are high. Basically, it seems that a large part of the financial community (users of audit services) expects that financial statements with an unmodified (unqualified) audit opinion are completely free from error. Companies like Enron, Parmalat and WorldCom which reported fraudulent financial statements had financial statements that did not fairly reflect the underlying financial condition of those companies. The inherent limitations of auditing, expressed in materiality and audit risk (see Chapter 6 'Main Audit Concepts and Planning the Audit') are not entirely accepted and/or understood by all groups of users.

Standard on Auditing (ISA) 705[24] deals with the auditor's responsibility to issue an appropriate report in circumstances when, in forming an opinion in accordance with ISA 700,[25] the auditor concludes that a modification to the auditor's opinion on the financial statements is necessary. ISA 700 requires the auditor, in order to form an opinion on the financial statements, to conclude as to whether reasonable assurance has been obtained about whether the financial statements as a whole are free from material misstatement.

■ Opinion on the Company's Ability to Continue as a Going Concern

Perhaps the most disturbing events for the public's trust in the audit profession are cases where an unmodified (unqualified) audit report has been issued shortly before a company's bankruptcy. Under ISA 570[26] and most national regulations, auditors need to determine whether the audited entity is able to continue as a going concern. Although warning the financial statement users of any threatening financial distress is appropriate, the disclosure of a possible future bankruptcy – especially when the future course of events is hard to predict – may prove to be a self-fulfilling prophecy which deprives management of its means to save the company.

■ Opinion on the Company's Internal Control System

The issue of testing and reporting on the quality of a company's internal control system has been recognised as one of the focal issues in auditing. ISA 315[27] states that 'the objective of the auditor is to identify and assess the risks of material misstatement ... through understanding the entity and its environment, including the entity's internal control.' ISAE 3000[28] states that 'the assurance report should be in writing and should contain a clear expression of the practitioner's conclusion about the subject matter information.' Furthermore, the United States Sarbanes–Oxley Act of 2002 requires that company officers certify that internal controls are effective and requires that an independent auditor verify management's analysis.[29] US Public Company Accounting Oversight Board (PCAOB) has promulgated Audit Standard No. 5[30] that addresses internal control audits.

Expectation gap surveys show high expectations of the auditor's role in testing whether a satisfactory system of internal control is being operated. These expectations are likely to be met in current audit environments.

Barings Bank Example

Barings Bank is an example of a company whose breakdown in internal controls, specifically segregation of duties, led to the ultimate destruction of the company.[31] In 1995 Nicholas Leeson, manager of the Singapore Branch of Barings, not only made investments in the Nikkei exchange index derivatives, but also was able to authorise and account for his investment (account settling). This ultimately led to the multi-billion dollar collapse of Barings and a jail sentence for Leeson.

Reporting on Effectiveness of Internal Control

There has been much discussion in Europe, Canada and the USA about reporting on the effectiveness and functioning of internal controls. The Sarbanes–Oxley Act requires auditors to report on internal control[32] and the AICPA Auditing Standards Board (ASB) released an exposure draft on Internal Control Reporting. Support for reporting lies in the belief that users of financial information have a legitimate interest in the condition of the controls over the accounting system and management's response to the suggestions of the auditors for correction of weaknesses. Those who argue against reporting on controls say that such reporting increases the cost of audits, increase auditor (and director) liability and is not relevant information.

Section 404 of the Sarbanes–Oxley Act requires each annual report of a company to contain an 'internal control report' which should:

1 state the responsibility of management for establishing and maintaining an adequate internal control structure and procedures for financial reporting;
2 contain an assessment, as of the end of the fiscal year, of the effectiveness of the internal control structure and procedures for financial reporting;
3 contain an 'attestation' to management's assessment by the company's independent, outside auditors; and
4 contain an attestation by an independent auditor to any difference between management's required assertions and the audit evidence on internal controls.

The Combined Code of the Committee on Corporate Governance,[33] which represents the Code of Best Practice of the London Stock Exchange, states in Principle D.2 that: 'The board should maintain a sound system of internal control to safeguard shareholders' investment and the company's assets.' Provision D.2.1 states that: 'The directors should, at least annually, conduct a review of the effectiveness of the group's system of internal control and should report to shareholders that they have done so. The review should cover all controls, including financial, operational and compliance controls and risk management.'

■ Opinion on the Occurrence of Fraud

The audit expectation gap is frequently associated with the **fraud** issue. Both governments and the financial community expect the auditor to find existing fraud cases and report them. The fact that this part of the expectation gap has attracted so much attention is partly attributable to the evolution of auditing. As stated in our brief description of the history of auditing, the detection of fraud has been one of the profession's cornerstones.

Famous Frauds

The largest non-financial statement fraud of all time was the ponzi scheme of Bernard Madoff, who ran a $60 billion fraudulent hedge fund.[34] Major companies that issued fraudulent financial statements in the twenty-first century included: US companies Enron, WorldCom, Xerox, Tyco, Health South, Bristol Myers, Citibank, KMart and NextCard; European firms Ahold, Parmalat and Comroad; Japanese bank Resona; and Australian insurance company HIH. Famous frauds before Enron include: Lincoln

Savings and Loan, Penn Square, Sunbeam, Regina, ZZZZ Best, Crazy Eddy, Waste Management, and Mattel. These cases are discussed in 'Concept and a Company' cases throughout this book.

Object of an Audit One Hundred Years Ago

In their review of the historical development of the audit profession's views regarding the issue of fraud, Humphrey *et al.* (1991)[35] cite from Dicksee's 1900 edition *of Auditing – A Practical Manual for Auditors*, which states:

> The object of an audit may be said to be threefold:
>
> 1 The detection of fraud.
> 2 The detection of technical errors.
> 3 The detection of errors of principle.
>
> The detection of fraud is a most important portion of the auditor's duties. Auditors, therefore, should assiduously cultivate this branch of their activities.

Fraud – A Responsibility Not Assumed

Gradually, the auditor's responsibilities began to change, with fraud no longer being a key priority. Some researchers have demonstrated this by the changing priority of the fraud issue in Montgomery's *Auditing*. In its first three editions, fraud was labelled as a chief audit objective but its priority was gradually eroded until, in the 1957 Eighth Edition, it was described as 'a responsibility not assumed'.

What was the reason of this development 'away from fraud?' Several reasons have been given for this phenomenon, but the most important reasons are:

■ the acceptance that the audit of the financial statements on behalf of the third parties is an art of its own and justifies the existence of auditors; and
■ the acceptance that an investigation aimed at finding any kind of fraud is extremely laborious, expensive and not practical, considering the increases in size and complexity of the companies, as well as their improved self or internal controls.

Fraud Back in the Spotlight

However, this 'total' rejection of responsibility for fraud, which is evident from this historical outline, gave way to renewed discussion in the 1970s, 1980s, and 1990s. Under public pressure to investigate the reasonableness of the auditors' position regarding fraud, the profession was forced to reconsider its total rejection stance that culminated in the installation of several committees such as the Cohen Commission (1978), the Treadway Commission (1987) and the Dingell Committee (1988) in the USA, and the Davison and Benson Committees (1985) in the UK.

The current position of the audit profession is described in ISA 240.[36] According to ISA 240, the primary responsibility for the prevention and detection of fraud and error rests with both those charged with the governance and the management of an entity. Fraud may involve sophisticated and carefully organised schemes designed to conceal it, such as forgery, deliberate failure to record transactions, or intentional misrepresentations being made to the auditor. The auditor is responsible for obtaining reasonable assurance the financial statements are free from material statement, whether caused by fraud or error.

Concept and a Company 2.4

Trading Fraud Early on at Enron

Concept	Investigation of fraudulent acts.

Story

The first sign of fraud at Enron goes back to a trading division called Enron Oil in January 1987.

David Woyek, the head of Enron's internal audit department, received a call from Apple Bank in New York. He was told that wire transfers amounting to about $5 million had been flowing in from a bank in the Channel Islands, and over $2 million went into an account of Tom Masteroeni, treasurer of Enron Oil. The Apple Bank account could not be found anywhere on Enron's books. Masteroeni admitted that he had diverted funds to his account, but insisted that it was a profit-sharing tactic and that he always intended to repay the money. After a preliminary investigation, Woyek's deputy, John Beard, wrote on his working papers 'misstatement of records, deliberate manipulation of records, impact on financials for the year ending 12/31/86' (McLean and Elkin, 2003).

Louis Borget, CEO of Enron Oil, explained that the Apple account was used to move profits from one quarter to another for Enron management. From 1985, the oil trader had been doing deals with companies Isla, Southwest, Petropol and other entities that allowed Enron Oil to generate the loss on one contract then have the loss cancelled out by a second contract to generate a gain of the same amount. Borget described Enron Oil as 'the swing entry to meet objectives each month.' Woyek wrote in a memo the process was a creation of 'fictitious losses' (McLean and Elkin, 2003). The management of Enron Oil were not even reprimanded. Instead, Borget received a thank you note saying, 'keep making millions for us.'

The internal auditors continued their investigation. They consulted directories of trading organisations, but could not find Isla, Southwest, or Petropol. They discovered other irregularities in the Apple account amounting to hundreds of thousands of dollars. Before they completed their fieldwork, management told them to stop and let the work be done by Enron's outside auditor, Arthur Andersen.

Andersen presented their findings to the Enron audit committee of the board of directors some months later. They told the board that they 'were unable to verify ownership or any other details' regarding Enron Oil's supposed trading partners. They also found that Enron Oil was supposed to have strict controls on trading – their open position was never supposed to exceed 8 million barrels, and when the losses reached $4 million, the traders were required to liquidate their position. Andersen could not test the controls because Borget and Masteroeni destroyed daily position reports.

But even so, Andersen would not give an opinion on these unusual transactions or whether the profit shifting had a material impact on the financial statements. Andersen claimed that it was beyond their professional competence and that they would rely on Enron itself to make that determination. Andersen got a letter from Rich Kidder, Enron CEO, and another Enron lawyer saying, 'the unusual transactions would not have a material effect on the financial statements and that no disclosure of these transactions is necessary.'

In October 1997, it was discovered that the management at Enron Oil had been losing on their trades and they were $1.5 billion short. Enron fired Borget and Masteroeni and brought in traders who were able to reduce the position to an $85 million charge which Enron announced for the third quarter of 1987 (Bryce, 2002).

Discussion Questions	■ Was Andersen fulfilling its responsibility to consider fraud and risk? ■ Whose responsibility is it to determine the materiality of fraud on the financial statements: Enron management or Andersen?
References	Bryce, Robert, 2002, *Pipe Dreams: Greed, Ego and the Death of Enron*, Public Affairs, New York. McLean, Bethany and Peter Elkind, 2003, *The Smartest Guys in The Room: The Amazing Rise and Scandalous Fall of Enron*, Portfolio, New York.

Fraud in Planning, Evaluating, and Reporting

This section only discusses fraud and illegal acts from a historical perspective and the demand for auditing. (Auditing aspects such as ISA 240 and ISA 250 are discussed in Chapter 6.)

ISA 210 establishes requirements and provides guidance on determining the acceptability of the applicable financial reporting framework.[37] ISA 800[38] deals with special considerations when financial statements are prepared in accordance with a special purpose framework (not being a full set of financial statements).

ISA 200[39] states that it is necessary for the auditor to direct audit effort to areas most expected to contain risks of material misstatement, whether due to fraud or error, with correspondingly less effort directed at other areas. ISA 240,[40] the fraud standard, describes specific audit procedures to respond to assessed risk due to fraud. The auditor plans and performs an audit with an attitude of professional scepticism, recognising that conditions or events may be found that indicate that fraud or error may exist in accordance with ISA.

Opinion on the Occurrence of Illegal Acts

Closely related to the subject of fraud is the auditor's reaction to the occurrence of illegal acts in a company. Both ISA 250[41] and most national regulators state that the auditor's responsibility in this area is restricted to designing and executing the audit in such a way that there is a reasonable expectation of detecting material illegal acts which have a direct impact on the form and content of the financial statements. In reporting illegal acts most national regulators require the auditor to assess the potential impact on the financial statements and determine the consequences of the uncertainty or error in the financial statements for the nature of the opinion.

Apart from reporting the acts through the report, the professional regulations in some countries require the auditor to inform members of the audit committee or board of directors. Informing third parties is not allowed, except for some very special, narrowly defined circumstances.

Most expectation gap studies reveal that respondents expect the auditor to detect and report illegal acts that have a significant impact on the financial statements. With regard to the auditor's responsibility for detecting and reporting other types of illegal acts, the answers found in expectation gap studies were inconclusive.

2.9 **Examples of Landmark Studies and Legislation that Influenced the International Audit Market**

Partly as a response to some of the expectation gap issues, there have been two landmark studies (the COSO Report[42] and the Cadbury Report[43] which lead to the Combined Code[44] and the Turnbull Report)[45] and most recently responses have been legislated into the US accounting profession by the Sarbanes–Oxley Act of 2002.[46]

■ The COSO Report

The COSO report was published by the Committee of Sponsoring Organizations of the Treadway Commission. The COSO report envisaged (see Illustration 2.3):

■ harmonising the definitions regarding internal control and its components;
■ helping management in assessing the quality of internal control;

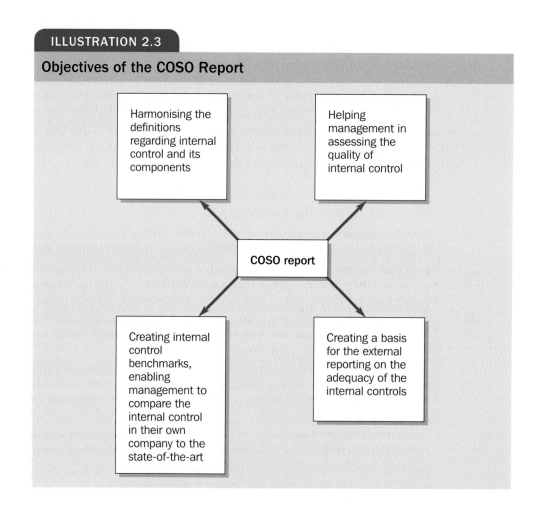

ILLUSTRATION 2.3

Objectives of the COSO Report

- creating internal control benchmarks, enabling management to compare the internal control in their own company to the state-of-the-art; and
- creating a basis for the external reporting on the adequacy of the internal controls.

Although all of these objectives might have an influence on the audit service, the latter subject is particularly relevant, because it might lead to certification by the auditor of management's assertions regarding the quality of a company's internal control system. (The COSO report is discussed extensively in Chapter 7 'Internal Control and Control Risk'.)

■ The Cadbury Report, Combined Code and Turnbull Report

Cadbury Report

The Cadbury Report was published in the UK by the Committee on the Financial Aspects of Corporate Governance. Cadbury deals with the responsibilities and duties of the executive and non-executive members of the board of directors. The report suggests that companies listed on the London Stock Exchange should adhere to a Code of Best Practice, in which these responsibilities and duties are listed. In June 1998 the London Stock Exchange published a new Listing Rule together with related Principles of Good Governance and Code of Best Practice (called 'the Combined Code'). The Combined Code combines the recommendations of the so-called Cadbury, Greenbury and Hampel committees on corporate governance.

In the published financial statements, the board should declare the adherence to this code and should explicitly assume responsibility for the financial statements. In addition, the Cadbury Report suggested that the board should report that it tested the adequacy of the company's internal control as well as the company's ability to continue as a going concern. Amongst the changes in Combined Code versus the Cadbury Best Practices, perhaps the greatest is the extension of the requirement to report on the review of internal controls beyond financial controls. The Cadbury Report originally suggested reporting on all controls, but had subsequently modified its stance to include only financial controls.

Turnbull Report/Combined Code

Internal Control: Guidance for Directors on the Combined Code, called the 'Turnbull Report' after Nigel Turnbull, Chairman of the Committee which wrote the Report, provides guidance to assist London Stock Exchange listed companies to implement the requirements in the Combined Code relating to internal control. The Report states that the board of directors should set appropriate policies on internal control and seek regular assurance that the internal control system is functioning effectively in managing risks in the manner that the board has approved.

■ The Sarbanes–Oxley Act of 2002

The accounting scandals begun by the Enron collapse and extending to such giant companies as WorldCom, Xerox and Tyco, caused a backlash in the USA, resulting in legislation being signed into law by the US President in July 2002. The Sarbanes–Oxley Act is the first accounting law passed by the US since the Securities and Exchange Act of 1934.

New Requirements for Audit Firms and Audit Committees

The Act has new requirements for audit firms and **audit committees**. Auditors must report to the audit committee,[47] not management. The lead audit partner and audit review partner must be rotated every five years. A second partner must review and approve audit reports. It is a felony with penalties of up to ten years in jail to wilfully fail to maintain 'all audit or review work papers' for at least five years. Destruction of documents carries penalties of up to 20 years in jail. The Act lists eight types of services that are 'unlawful' if provided to a publicly held company by its auditor: bookkeeping, information systems design and implementation, appraisals or valuation services, actuarial services, internal audits, management and human resources services, broker/dealer and investment banking, and legal or expert services related to audit service. The Public Company Accounting Oversight Board (PCAOB), created by the Act, may also determine by regulation other services it wishes to prohibit. Non-audit services not banned by the Act must be pre-approved by the audit committee. Management must assess and make representations about the effectiveness of the internal control structure and their auditor will be required to attest to the assessment and describe the tests used.

2.10   Summary

The Industrial Revolution, which started in Great Britain around 1780, resulted in demand for the services of specialists in bookkeeping and in auditing internal and external financial representations. The institutionalisation of the audit profession followed shortly thereafter.

The demand for audit services may be explained by several different theories. Some theories like the Theory of Inspired Confidence and Agency Theory have been well researched and reported on. Other theories based on public perceptions such as the Policeman Theory and the Lending Credibility Theory serves more as a point of reference than a researched construct.

Although regulation and legislation differ, both the demand and the supply of audit services are currently regulated to some degree in most countries. Recent accounting and finance research suggests that national legal environments are among the key determinants of financial market development, corporate ownership structures, corporate policies, and the properties of accounting information around the world.

The supply of audit services is regulated in most countries. In the European Union, statutory audits, i.e. audits required by law, can only be performed by auditors who have met specific technical requirements with regard to education and experience under the Eighth Council Directive and Directive 2006/43. The United States changed the demand and supply for audit services by enacting the Sarbanes–Oxley Act.

There is a recent growth in accounting oversight boards – government or professional committees to review the work of auditors and take an active part in setting and enforcing standards. The global oversight organisation is the International Forum of Independent Audit Regulators (IFIAR). Similar boards are in Australia (Financial Reporting Council), the UK (The Review Board), the Netherlands Authority for the Financial Markets (AFM), France Autorité des marchés financiers (AMF) and the USA (the Public Company Accounting Oversight Board.

Audit firms are classified into two distinct categories: Big Four firms and non-Big Four firms. Big Four firms participate in an international head office, in which global technologies, procedures and directives are developed. The non-Big Four firms include a range of firms from small local firms, with only a handful of professionals, to second-tier firms that also have an international network.

There are many stakeholders who rely on audited financial statements: the client (with which there is a privity relationship), actual and potential stockholders, vendors, bankers and other creditors, employees, customers and the government. Legal liability of the auditor to each stakeholder varies from country to country, district to district. This liability can generally be classified as based on one or more of the following: common law, civil liability under statutory law, criminal liability under statutory law, and liability for members of professional accounting organisations. Auditor liability is a serious issue for auditor to which several solutions have been discussed: a cap or limit on claims, proportionate liability, compulsory liability insurance, exclusion of certain audit activities from auditor liability, and change audit firm legal structure to a limited liability partnership.

The development of the auditor's duties, linked to changes in the audit market, is still an object of public debate, often referred to as the audit expectation gap debate. This gap results from the fact that users of audit services have expectations regarding the duties of auditors that exceed the current practice in the profession. Expectations gap arises in following duties of auditors in giving an opinion on the: fairness of financial statements; the company's ability to continue as a going concern; company's internal control system; occurrence of fraud; and occurrence of illegal acts.

In response to the controversies there have been in two landmark studies (the COSO Report and the Cadbury Report which lead to the Combined Code and the Turnbull Report) and most recently have been legislated into the US accounting profession by the Sarbanes–Oxley Act of 2002.

2.11 Questions, Exercises and Cases

QUESTIONS

2.2 Introduction

2-1 What areas that an auditor audits are the responsibility of management?

2.3 Theories on the Demand and Supply of Audit Services

2-2 What are the most important theories on the demand of audit services?

2-3 Give a brief description of the agency theory as applied to both the demand and the supply of audit services.

2.4 Audit Regulation: International Perspective

2-4 Describe the major US and European regulations discussed in this section.

2.5 Independent Oversight

2-5 Give the names of four national accounting oversight boards – government or professional committees to review the work of auditors and take an active part in setting and enforcing standards.

2-6 Describe the activities off the International Forum of Independent Audit Regulators (IFIAR).

2.6 Audit Firms

2-7 What are the names of the Big Four firms?

2-8 What is meant by second-tier firms?

2.7 Legal Liability

2-9 What are four major sources of auditors' legal liability? Briefly discuss them.

2-10 What measures are possibilities to reduce auditors' unlimited legal liability?

2.8 Some Developments in the Audit Market

2-11 Discuss the following statement: 'Auditors perform extensive tests on a company's internal control system, in order to determine whether they can rely on that system in the course of their audit. Therefore, auditors can express an opinion on the adequacy of the audited company's internal control system.'

2-12 Describe the historical shift in the audit profession's attitude towards the auditor's responsibilities regarding fraud.

2.9 Examples of Landmark Studies and Legislation that Influenced the International Audit Market

2-13 Discuss the potential impact of the Cadbury Report, Combined Code and COSO report on the audit profession.

2-14 Discuss the following statement: 'Auditors should not be allowed to combine an audit for one client with advisory services to that client.'

PROBLEMS AND EXERCISES

2.3 Theories on the Demand and Supply of Audit Services

2-15 Agency Theory. Identify principals and agents in the cases mentioned below. Describe the contributions and 'prices' associated with these relationships, identify potential risks for the principal and give suggestions for limiting these risks:
A. The Pasadena Bank lends money to the Alhambra Construction Company.
B. Employee Mario Auditorio considers leaving his current job and starting a new career with Instituto Milanese.
C. Manager Yu-Chang receives an annual bonus, based on last year's profit of company Shang-Zu.
D. Supplier 'Vite et Juste' delivers goods to company 'Merci'. Payment is due 60 days after the date of the invoice.

2.4 Audit Regulation: International Perspective

2-16 Comment on the following statements:
A. In most countries audits are legally required for every type of company.
B. The PCAOB sanctions firms but not individuals for violations of laws, regulations, and rules.
C. The European Eighth Directive objective is to register all auditors and audit firms and make such information accessible to the public.
D. Three areas of audit regulation that are essential are (1) the independence of the profession; (2) opening up the audit market, and (3) creating a more integrated European market and stepping up its supervision.

2.5 Independent Oversight

2-17 Comment on the following statements
A. The core principles of IFAR are comprehensive.
B. The FRC has broad oversight for setting accounting standards in the public and private sectors.
C. The Review Board is responsible for training the members of UK accounting professional bodies.

2.6 Audit Firms

2-18 How do the markets for the Big Four differ from second-tier firms? Describe a typical audit client for each group including average revenue, global nature, number of employees, government regulation and governance mechanism.

2.7 Legal Liability

2-19 Legal Liability to Third Parties. Suppose you are a judge in the following civil case.
Plaintiff Sue Bank, a banker, accuses auditor Big Zero of having performed a negligent audit in the financial statements of company 'Trouble'. Five months after the financial statements (with an unqualified opinion) were published, 'Trouble' filed for bankruptcy, leaving the bank with unrecovered loans amounting to $ 20 million.

Required:
Describe the relevant issues to be addressed in this case.

2.8 Some Developments in the Audit Market

2-20 Auditors Opinion on the Occurrence of Fraud. Sundback, CGR, is the auditor for Upseerin Manufacturing, a privately owned company in Espoo, Finland, which has a 30 June fiscal year. Upseerin arranged for a substantial bank loan which was dependent upon the bank receiving, by 30 September, audited financial statements which showed a current ratio of at least 2 to 1. On 25 September, just before the audit report was to be issued, Sundback received an anonymous letter on Upseerin's stationery indicating that a 5-year lease by Upseerin, as lessee, of a factory building which was accounted for in the financial statements as an operating lease was in fact a capital lease. The letter stated that there was a secret written agreement with the lessor modifying the lease and creating a capital lease.

Sundback confronted the president of Upseerin who admitted that a secret agreement existed but said it was necessary to treat the lease as an operating lease to meet the current ratio requirement of the pending loan and that nobody would ever discover the secret agreement with the lessor. The president said that if Sundback did not issue her report by 30 September, Upseerin would sue Sundback for substantial damages which would result from not getting the loan. Under this pressure and because the work papers contained a copy of the 5-year lease agreement which supported the operating lease treatment, Sundback issued her report with an unqualified opinion on 29 September.

In spite of the fact the loan was received, Upseerin went bankrupt within 2 years. The bank is suing Sundback to recover its losses on the loan and the lessor is suing Sundback to recover uncollected rents.

Required:
Answer the following, setting forth reasons for any conclusions stated.
A. Is Sundback liable to the bank?
B. Is Sundback liable to the lessor?
[adapted from AICPA EPA exam question, copyright © 2000 & 1985 by American Institute of Certified Accountants]

2-21 Opinion on the Occurrence of Illegal Acts. Ostling, Auktoriserad Revisor, accepted an engagement to audit the financial statements of Sandnes Company of Göteborg, Sweden. Ostling's discussions with Sandnes's new management and the predecessor auditor indicated the possibility that Sandnes's financial statements may be misstated due to the possible occurrence of errors, irregularities and illegal acts.

Required:
A. Identify and describe Ostling's responsibilities to detect Sandnes's errors and irregularities. Do not identify specific audit procedures.
B. Identify and describe Ostling's responsibilities to report Sandnes's errors and irregularities.
C. Describe Ostling's responsibilities to detect Sandnes's material illegal acts. Do not identify specific audit procedures.
[AICPA, adapted]

2.9 Examples of Landmark Studies and Legislation that Influenced the International Audit Market

2-22 Compare the COSO Report, Combined Code and the Sarbanes–Oxley Act on what each says about the following:
A. Corporate governance
B. Audit firms
C. Internal controls

CASE

2-23 Legal Responsibilities of Auditors. Pick five countries. Assume that you are the head of an international commission to determine legal responsibilities of accountants in various countries. Use your university library and the Internet to research accounting in these five countries.

Required:

A. List the country, concept of independence and functions generally not allowed.
B. List the ethical standards, enforcement, legal liabilities and responsibility for the detection of fraud.
C. Using the library, Lexis-Nexis, or Internet find one recent legal case in each country that impacts auditor independence or resulted from fraud. Summarise each case.
D. Write a brief comparing the recent legal case and auditor ethical standards in each country.

2.12 Notes

1 Limperg, Th., 1932, *Theory of Inspired Confidence*, University of Amsterdam, Amsterdam, 1932/1933.

2 See Watts, R.L. and Zimmerman J.L., 1978, 'Towards a Positive Theory of the Determination of Accounting Standards', *The Accounting Review,* January, pp. 112–134; and Watts, R.L. and Zimmerman J.L., 1979, 'The Demand for and Supply of Accounting Theories: The Market for Excuses,' *The Accounting Review,* April, pp. 273–305.

3 The supply side of the audit market is concerned with the determination of the level of audit labour and independence.

4 See Ball, R., Kothari, S. and Robin, A. 2000, 'The Effect of International Institutional Factors on Properties of Accounting Earnings', *Journal of Accounting and Economics,* 29 (February), pp 1–52; and Shleifer, A. and Vishny, R. 1997, 'A Survey of Corporate Governance', *Journal of Finance,* 52 (July), pp. 737–783.

5 As of November 2013 there were 15 permanent audit standards by PCAOB.

6 European Union, 1984,. Eighth Council Directive, 10 April 1984

7 European Union, 2006, Directive 2006/43/EC of the European Parliament and of the Council. 'On Statutory Audits of Annual Accounts and Consolidated Accounts, Amending Council Directives 78/660/EEC and 83/349/EEC and Repealing Council Directive 84/253/EEC17', May 2006.

8 Barnier, Michel, 2011, Speech, 'Audit – F.E.E.', 30 June 2011.

9 International Forum of Independent Audit Regulators, 2006, 'Core Principles for Independent Audit Regulators',

10 Negligence (ordinary negligence) is the failure to use reasonable care. The doing of something which a reasonably prudent person would not do, or the failure to do something which a reasonably prudent person would do under like circumstances (the 'Lectric Law Library, Lectlaw.com).

11 Breach of contract means failing to perform any term of a contract, written or oral, without a legitimate legal excuse. This may include not completing a job, not paying in full or on time, failure to deliver all the goods, substituting inferior or significantly different goods, not providing a bond when required, being late without excuse, or any act which shows the party will not complete the work ('anticipatory breach'). Breach of contract is one of the most common causes of law suits for damages and/or court-ordered 'specific performance' of the contract (**http://legal-dictionary .thefreedictionary.com**).

12 Tort is French for wrong, a civil wrong, or wrongful act, whether intentional or accidental, from which injury occurs to another. Torts include all negligence cases as well as intentional wrongs which result in harm. Therefore, tort law is one of the major areas of law (along with contract, real property and criminal law), and results in more civil litigation than any other category. Some intentional torts may also be crimes, such as assault, battery, wrongful death, fraud, conversion (a euphemism for theft) and trespass on property, and form the basis for a lawsuit for damages by the injured party. Defamation, including intentionally telling harmful untruths about another, either by print or broadcast (libel) or orally (slander), is a tort and used to be a crime as well (**http:// legal-dictionary.thefreedictionary.com**).

13 255 NY 170, 174 NE 441 (1931); see also Knapp, Michael C., 2010, *Contemporary Auditing: Real Issues and Cases,* 8th edn.

14 Privity of contract is the relation which subsists between two contracting parties.

15 *Caparo Industries PLC* v *Dickman and Others,* 1990, 1 All ER 568. See Cooper, B.J. and Barkoczy, M.L. 1994, 'Third Party Liability: The Auditor's Lament', *Managerial Auditing Journal,* Bradford, Vol. 9. Iss. 5. p. 31.

16 In tort law, a duty of care is a legal obligation imposed on an individual requiring that they adhere to a standard of reasonable care while performing any acts that could foreseeably harm others. It is the first element that must be established to proceed with an action in negligence. The claimant must be able to show a duty of care imposed by law which the defendant has breached. In turn, breaching a duty may subject an individual to liability.

17 Congress of the United States, 2002, Sarbanes–Oxley Act of 2002, s 304, 'Forfeiture of certain bonuses and profits', Washington, DC.

18 Ibid, s 906, paragraph 1350, 'Failure of corporate officers to certify financial reports.'

19 Rule 3(e) of the SEC's Rules of Practice states: 'The commission can deny, temporarily or permanently, the privilege of appearing or practicing before it in any way to any person who is found by the commission … (1) not to possess the requisite qualifications to represent others, or (2) to be lacking in character of integrity or to have engaged in unethical or improper professional conduct.'

20 Congress of the United States, 2002, Sarbanes–Oxley Act of 2002, s 805, paragraph 1519, 'Destruction, alteration or falsification of records in Federal investigations and bankruptcy', Washington, DC.

21 Ibid, s 801, paragraph 1520, 'Destruction of corporate audit records'.

22 Ibid, s 906, paragraph 1350, 'Failure of corporate officers to certify financial reports'.

23 European Union, 2008, press release 'Auditing: Commission issues Recommendation on limiting audit firms' liability (see MEMO/08/366)', 6 June 2008, Brussels: **http://europa.eu/rapid/ pressReleasesAction.do?reference=IP/08/897&format=HTML&aged=0&language=EN&guiLang uage=fr**.

24 International Auditing and Assurance Standards Board (IAASB), 2012, International Standard on Auditing 705 (ISA 705) 'Modifications to the Opinion in the Independent Auditor's Report', *Handbook of International Quality Control, Auditing, Review, Other Assurance, and Related Services Pronouncements,* 2012 edn, Volume 1, International Federation of Accountants, New York.

25 Ibid, ISA 700 'Forming an Opinion and Reporting on Financial Statements'.

26 Ibid. 570 (ISA 570) 'Going Concern'.

27 Ibid. ISA 315 'Identifying and Assessing the Risks of Material Misstatement Through Understanding The Entity And Its Environment'.

28 International Auditing and Assurance Standards Board (IAASB), 2012, International Standard on Assurance Engagements (ISAE) 3000 'Assurance Engagements Other Than Audits or Reviews of Historical Financial Information', Paragraph 46, *Handbook of International Quality Control, Auditing, Review, Other Assurance, and Related Services Pronouncements,* 2012 edn, Volume 2, International Federation of Accountants, New York.

29 Congress of the United States, 2002, Sarbanes–Oxley Act of 2002, s 404 'Management Assessment of Internal Controls', Washington, DC.

30 PCAOB, 2007, Audit Standard No. 5, 'An Audit of Internal Control Over Financial Reporting That Is Integrated with An Audit of Financial Statements', Public Company Accounting Oversight Board.

31 A movie was made in 1999 about this event called *Rogue Trader* (Warner Brothers).

32 PCAOB, 2007, Audit Standard No. 5, op. cit., Sec. 405.

33 The Committee on Corporate Governance, 1998, the Combined Code, London Stock Exchange, London, January.

34 US Securities and Exchange Commission Office of Investigations, 2009, 'Investigation of Failure of the SEC to Uncover Bernard Madoff's Ponzi Scheme', Report No. OIG-509, April 31, 2009, Washington, DC.

35 Humphrey, C., Turley, S. and Moizer, P., 1991, 'Protecting Against Detection: The Case of Auditors and Fraud', unpublished paper, University of Manchester.

36 International Auditing and Assurance Standards Board (IAASB), 2012, International Standard on Auditing 240 (ISA 240) 'The Auditor's Responsibilities Relating to Fraud in an Audit of Financial Statements', *Handbook of International Quality Control, Auditing Review, Other Assurance, and Related Services Pronouncements,* 2012 edn, Volume 1, International Federation of Accountants, New York.

37 Ibid, ISA 210 'Agreeing the Terms of Audit Engagements'.

38 Ibid, ISA 800 'Special Considerations – Audits of Financial Statements Prepared in Accordance with Special Purpose Frameworks'.

39 Ibid, ISA 200 'Overall Objectives of the Independent Auditor and the Conduct of an Audit in Accordance with International Standards on Auditing', Appendix A49.

40 Ibid, ISA 240 'The Auditor's Responsibilities Relating to Fraud in an Audit of Financial Statements', paragraphs 30–33 and appendix.

41 Ibid, ISA 250 'Consideration of Laws and Regulations in an Audit of Financial Statements'.

42 Committee of Sponsoring Organizations of the Treadway Commission (COSO), 1992, *Internal Control – Integrated Framework,* American Institute of Certified Public Accountants.

43 Committee on the Financial Aspects of Corporate Governance, *Report of the Committee on the Financial Aspects of Corporate Governance* (the Cadbury Report), Gee and Co. Ltd, London, December 1992.

44 KPMG Review, 1999, *The Combined Code: A Practical Guide,* KPMG, UK, January.

45 Internal Control Working Party, 1999, *Internal Control: Guidance for Directors on the Combined Code,* published by the Institute of Chartered Accountants in England and Wales, London, September.

46 107th US Congress, 2002, Sarbanes–Oxley Act of 2002, Public Law 107–204, Senate and House of Representatives of the United States of America in Congress Assembled, Washington, DC, 30 July.

47 An audit committee is selected members of the company's outside directors who take an active role in overseeing the company's accounting and auditing policies and practices.

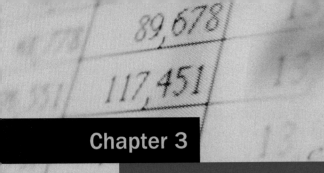

Chapter 3

ETHICS FOR PROFESSIONAL ACCOUNTANTS

3.1 Learning Objectives

After studying this chapter, you should be able to:

1 Explain the three general subject areas of ethics.

2 Explain what ethics means to an accountant.

3 State the purpose for a professional code of ethics.

4 Give the three parts of the IESBA Code and what each part covers.

5 Explain purpose and content of the IESBA Code of Ethics for Professional Accountants.

6 Identify and discuss the fundamental principles of ethics as described by the IESBA Code of Ethics.

7 Discuss what threats to the fundamental principles are.

8 List and define the four categories of threats to the fundamental principles.

9 Define safeguards and give some examples.

10 Recite the different areas of ethical concern listed as headings in the IESBA Code.

11 Explain the concept of independence and identify the principles-based approach for resolving the attendant issues.

12 Differentiate between 'independence of mind' and 'independence in appearance'.

13 Describe non-audit services prohibited by the Code of Ethics.

14 Discuss the responsibilities of an accountant in public practice in dealing with ethical conflicts that apply to his clients and colleagues.

15 State the topics of guidance that are particularly relevant to professional accountants working in industry, commerce, the public sector or education.

16 Summarise the possible disciplinary actions for violation of ethics codes.

3.2 | What Are Ethics?

Ethics represent a set of moral principles, rules of conduct, or values. Ethics are a discipline dealing with values relating to human conduct, with respect to the rightness and wrongness of certain actions and to the goodness and badness of the motives and ends of such actions.[1] Ethics apply when an individual has to make a decision from various alternatives regarding moral principles. All individuals and societies possess a sense of ethics in that they have some sort of agreement as to what right and wrong are, although this can be influenced by cultural differences. Ethical questions you can think of are: 'Do I always have to keep my promise?' and 'Do I need to put my own interest aside in favour of others?' Illustration 3.1 incorporates the characteristics most people associate with ethical behaviour.[2]

ILLUSTRATION 3.1

Ethical Principles

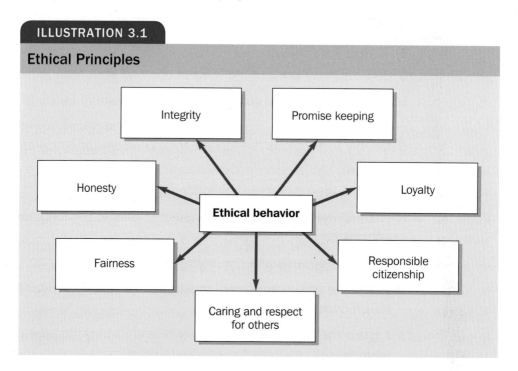

Ethical behaviour is necessary for society to function in an orderly manner. The need for ethics in society is sufficiently important that many commonly held ethical values are incorporated into laws. However, a considerable portion of the ethical values of a society such as integrity, loyalty, and pursuit of excellence cannot be incorporated into law. By establishing a code of ethics, a profession assumes self-discipline beyond the requirements of the law.

■ History of Ethics

Philosophers today usually divide ethical theories into three general subject areas: metaethics, normative ethics, and applied ethics.

Metaethics investigates where our ethical principles come from, and what they mean. Are they merely social inventions? Do they involve more than expressions of our individual emotions? Metaethical answers to these questions focus on the issues of universal truths, the will of God, the role of reason in ethical judgments, and the meaning of ethical terms themselves.

Normative ethics takes on a more practical task, which is to arrive at moral standards that regulate right and wrong conduct. This may involve articulating the good habits that we should acquire, the duties that we should follow, or the consequences of our behaviour on others.

Finally, applied ethics involves examining specific controversial issues, such as abortion, infanticide, animal rights, environmental concerns, homosexuality, capital punishment, or nuclear war.

By using the conceptual tools of metaethics and normative ethics, discussions in applied ethics try to resolve these controversial issues. The lines of distinction between metaethics, normative ethics, and applied ethics are often blurry. For example, the issue of abortion is an applied ethical topic since it involves a specific type of controversial behaviour. But it also depends on more general normative principles, such as the right of self-rule and the right to life, which are litmus tests for determining the morality of that procedure. The issue also rests on metaethical issues such as, 'where do rights come from?' and 'what kinds of beings have rights?'[3]

Normative ethics involves arriving at moral standards that regulate right and wrong conduct. In a sense, it is a search for an ideal litmus test of proper behaviour. The Golden Rule is a classic example of a normative principle: We should do to others what we would want others to do to us. Since I do not want my neighbour to steal my car, then it is wrong for me to steal her car. Since I would want people to feed me if I was starving, then I should help feed starving people. Using this same reasoning, I can theoretically determine whether any possible action is right or wrong. So, based on the Golden Rule, it would also be wrong for me to lie to, harass, victimise, assault or kill others. The Golden Rule is an example of a normative theory that establishes a single principle against which we judge all actions. Other normative theories focus on a set of foundational principles, or a set of good character traits.[4]

■ Ethics in the Accounting Profession

The attitude and behaviour of professional accountants in providing auditing and assurance services[5] have an impact on the economic well-being of their community and country. Accountants can remain in this advantageous position only by continuing to provide the public with these unique services at a level that demonstrates that the public confidence is well founded.

The distinguishing mark of the profession is acceptance of its responsibility to the public. Therefore the standards of the accountancy profession are heavily determined by the public interest. One could say in accountancy 'the public and the auditees are our clients and our main product is credibility'.

■ Objectives of Accountancy

It is in this context that the International Ethics Standards Board of Accountants (IESBA) Code of Ethics for Professional Accountants[6] states that it is an auditor's responsibility to act in the public interest – it is a distinguishing mark of the accountancy profession. The professional auditors' responsibility is not to satisfy only their client or employer, but to consider the public interest.

To achieve these objectives, the Code of Ethics suggests several fundamental principles for professional accountants and for those who are undertaking reporting assignments, which is discussed in the balance of this chapter.

3.3 The International Ethics Standards Board of Accountants (IESBA) Code of Ethics for Professional Accountants

The ethical guidance is set out by International Ethics Standards Board for Accountants (IESBA) which reports its recommendations to the IFAC Board after research and appropriate exposure of draft guidance. The guidance is incorporated into the *Handbook of the Code of Ethics for Professional Accountants* (the Code). The Code is intended to serve as a model on which to base national ethical guidance. It sets standards of conduct for professional accountants and states the fundamental principles that should be observed by professional accountants in order to achieve common objectives.

The Code is divided into three parts:

■ Part A establishes the fundamental principles of professional ethics for professional accountants and provides a conceptual framework that is applied to:
   ❑ identify threats to compliance with the fundamental principles;
   ❑ evaluate the significance of the threats identified; and
   ❑ employ safeguards, when necessary, to eliminate the threats or reduce them to an acceptable level.
■ Parts B and C describe how the conceptual framework applies in certain situations.[7] They provide examples of safeguards that may be appropriate to address threats to compliance with the fundamental principles. They also describe situations where safeguards are not available to address the threats. Part B applies to professional accountants in public practice.
■ Part C applies to professional accountants in business. Professional accountants in public practice may also find Part C relevant to their particular circumstances. We will not discuss Part C in detail in this chapter.

The process of establishing ethical principles is complicated. In France and Japan, the ethical code is a matter of law. In the USA, Singapore, Mexico and the UK, the standards are developed and regulated by professional bodies. The IESBA *Handbook of the Code of Ethics for Professional Accountants* offers fundamental principles that are of a general nature which may be threatened and safeguards that may be applied.

■ Conceptual Framework Approach

Rather than a list of rules that must be obeyed to be an ethical accountant, the so-called 'rule based' approach which holds sway in many countries, the IESBA and IFAC have chosen to use a 'conceptual framework' approach. A conceptual framework requires a professional accountant to identify, evaluate and address threats to compliance with the fundamental principles, rather than merely comply with a set of specific rules which may be arbitrary.

When an accountant identifies threats to compliance with the fundamental principles and determines that they are not at an acceptable level, he/she shall determine whether appropriate safeguards are available and can be applied to eliminate the threats or reduce them to an acceptable level.[8] What is a threat may depend on the auditor's perspective. The auditor should always consider the situation conservatively. If you put a safeguard in place that you believe will reduce the impact of a threat on a fundamental principle to an acceptable level, then the fundamental is not impaired. If you believe that a threat impairs the fundamental principle, then you should consider that no safeguard will repair that impairment.

There are five fundamental principles of ethics applicable to *all* accountants, as they are stated in part A of the Code. They are:

- Integrity – to be straightforward and honest in all professional and business relationships.
- Objectivity – to not allow bias, conflict of interest or undue influence of others to override professional or business judgements.
- Professional Competence and Due Care – to maintain professional knowledge and skill at the level required to ensure that a client or employer receives competent professional services based on current developments in practice, legislation and techniques, and act diligently and in accordance with applicable technical and professional standards.
- Confidentiality – to respect the confidentiality of information acquired as a result of professional and business relationships and, therefore, not disclose any such information to third parties without proper and specific authority, unless there is a legal or professional right or duty to disclose, nor use the information for the personal advantage of the professional accountant or third parties.
- Professional Behaviour – to comply with relevant laws and regulations and avoid any action that discredits the profession.

3.4 Part A – General Application of the IESBA Code of Ethics for Professional Accountants

The IESBA guideline offers further discussion on these five fundamental principles. Each concept is the topic of subsequent Sections (110–150) in the Code.

Integrity (Sec. 110)

The principle of integrity imposes an obligation on all professional accountants to be straightforward and honest in all professional and business relationships. Integrity also implies fair dealing and truthfulness.

A professional accountant must avoid reports and other information if she believes that the material contained is false or misleading, it includes information that was not verified, or leaves out information that makes the report misleading.

■ Objectivity (Sec. 120)

The principle of objectivity imposes an obligation on all professional accountants not to compromise their professional or business judgement because of bias, conflict of interest or the undue influence of others.

An accountant or auditor may be exposed to situations that may impair their objectivity. They should not perform a professional service if a circumstance or relationship biases or unduly influences the accountant's professional judgement.

But how does the auditor know if she is biased? A wealth of evidence suggests that judgements are often clouded by a number of cognitive and motivational biases. Individuals consistently rate themselves above average across a variety of domains, take credit for their successes but explain away their failures, assume they are more likely than their peers to experience the good things in life and avoid the bad, and tend to detect more support for their favoured beliefs than is objectively warranted.[9] Although the Code of Ethics does not address this, in the auditing sense bias is associated with money and personal association, e.g. if possible gains of wealth, prospects of a better income, or personal relationships as with family or friends are involved, this may bias the auditor's work. There exist religious and cultural biases that may also affect an auditor's work and these biases have been well studied. Psychologists at Harvard, the University of Virginia and the University of Washington created 'Project Implicit' to develop Hidden Bias Tests – to measure unconscious bias primarily of this sort.[10]

■ Professional Competence and Due Care (Sec. 130)

The principle of professional competence and due care requires that the professional accountant maintain her professional skill and knowledge to that of a competent professional. This means that the professional accountant understands and implements technical and professional standards when doing their work.

Professional competence may be divided into two separate phases: (a) Attainment of professional competence; and (b) Maintenance of professional competence. Professional competence requires a high standard of general education followed by specific education, training, examination in relevant subjects, and work experience. The maintenance of professional competence requires a continuing awareness and an understanding of relevant technical, professional and business developments through continuing professional education. Diligence is the responsibility to act in accordance with the requirements of an assignment, carefully, thoroughly and on a timely basis.

■ Confidentiality (Sec. 140)

Professional accountants have an obligation to respect the confidentiality of information about a client's (or employer's) affairs acquired in the course of professional services. The principle of confidentiality requires that the professional accountant refrain from disclosing, without the agreement of the client or employer or legal requirement, confidential information gained while performing their duties. Furthermore, the professional accountant should not use this confidential information to their own personal advantage.

Accountants should respect the confidentiality of information acquired during the course of performing professional services, including in a social environment. The auditor should be alert to the possibility of inadvertent disclosure, particularly to a close business associate or a close or immediate family member. There exists a responsibility to keep the information discovered in the course of an assurance service confidential and thus continues even after the accountant–client or the accountant–employer relationship ends. Accountants must also ensure that, in addition to themselves, staff and outside advisers under their control understand and follow the principle of confidentiality.

Permitted Disclosure of Confidential Information

Confidential information may be disclosed when disclosure is authorised by the client, required by law, or where there is a professional duty or right to disclose (such as in a peer review quality control programme). When disclosure is authorised by the employer or client, the accountants should consider the interests of all the parties, including third parties, that might be affected.

Concept and a Company 3.1

Confidentiality of Information – Ernst & Young and Doxis

Concept	Professional accountants have an obligation to respect the confidentiality of information about a client's (or employer's) affairs acquired in the course of professional services.
Story	In 1997, Ernst & Young Netherlands acquired Doxis. Doxis is a small consultancy firm that focuses on streamlining information processes and documentation management. In 2009, the company had a turnover of about €10 million.

In February 2010, Ernst & Young Netherlands agreed to sell Doxis to one of the two directors, Max Beekhuis. According to Ernst & Young Netherlands CFO Mike Hartkoorn, there were insufficient synergy and cross-selling opportunities for both companies. Doxis was sold for an undisclosed fee and the other director, Monique Vermeulen, left Doxis.

At the end of 2010 Ernst & Young had discovered that their CFO Mike Hartkoorn had acted as a funder of Max Beekhuis, the director that had purchased Doxis. In fact, Mike Hartkoorn had also acquired 50 per cent of the shares of the company that belonged to Max Beekhuis, which was used to purchase Doxis. When Ernst & Young discovered this, Mike Hartkoorn was forced to resign.

In a law suit in August 2011, the other Doxis director (Monique Vermeulen) requested that Ernst & Young hand over all relevant documentation regarding the management buy-out of Doxis. The judge granted the request. Also, it turned out Doxis was sold for €500,000, although it had equity of approximately €5 million. Monique Vermeulen claimed

	Confidentiality of Information – Ernst & Young and Doxis (continued)
	she would have bought Doxis if the price was €500,000. Ernst & Young later claimed the price of Doxis had dropped due to a lack of interested buyers.
	On 1 May 2011 Mike Hartkoorn joined Witlox Van Den Boomen, a small audit firm in the Netherlands. On their website, a profile of Mike Hartkoorn is published, including the following description: '... As a consultant he has frequently been involved in negotiations in the context of buying and selling of businesses.'
Discussion Questions	■ Should the board of Ernst & Young have informed the other director of Doxis when they found out about the doubtful involvement by their CFO? Or would that also be a violation of confidentiality of information?
References	http://www.accountancynieuws.nl/actueel/accountancymarkt/ernst-young-doet-dochter-doxis-van-de-hand.90567.lynkx. http://www.accountancynieuws.nl/actueel/accountancymarkt/ernst-young-dwong-cfo-tot-vertrek-vanwege.103027.lynkx. http://www.accountancynieuws.nl/actueel/accountancymarkt/ernst-young-moet-stukken-over-doxis-aan-voormalig.103164.lynkx. http://www.wvdb.nl/diensten/onze-adviseurs/bedrijfsadviseurs.html?member=267.

Examples of Disclosure

One example of when disclosure to client information is required by law is when the accountant produces documents or gives evidence in legal proceedings. Another example is disclosure of infringements of the law to appropriate public authorities. In the USA, accountants may be required to give evidence in court and in the Netherlands and UK auditors may be required to disclose fraud to government-appointed authorities.

There is also a professional duty to disclose information, when not prohibited by law, in the following circumstances:

■ In response to an inquiry from regulatory bodies
■ To participate in a quality control review of a peer auditing firm or professional body
■ In compliance with ethics requirement or technical accounting standards

Confidentiality of information is part of statute or common law and therefore requirements of confidentiality will depend on the law of the home country of each accountant.

■ Professional Behaviour (Sec. 150)

The principle of professional behavior means compliance with relevant laws and regulations and avoidance of any action that may discredit the accounting or auditing profession. Acts that discredit the profession are those that a reasonable and well informed third party upon consideration of the facts and circumstances at the time, would conclude that the act adversely affects the reputation of the profession.

For example, in marketing and promoting themselves and their work, professionals should be honest and truthful and not: (a) make exaggerated claims for the services they are able to offer, the qualifications they possess, or experience they have gained; or (b) make disparaging references or unsubstantiated comparisons to the work of others.

■ Threats to the Fundamental Principles and Safeguards

Compliance with the fundamental principles may potentially be threatened by a broad range of circumstances and relationships. The nature and significance of the threats may differ depending on whether the audit client is a public interest entity, to an assurance client that is not an audit client, or to a non-assurance client. The conceptual framework of the IESBA Code discusses ways to identify threats to fundamental principles, determine the significance of those threats, and, if they are significant, identify and apply safeguards to reduce or eliminate the threats.

Threats fall into one or more of the following categories:

- self-interest
- self-review
- advocacy
- familiarity
- intimidation.

Self-interest Threat

A 'self-interest threat' occurs when an auditor could benefit from a financial interest in, or other self-interest conflict with, an assurance client. Examples of circumstances that create self-interest threats for a professional accountant in public practice include:

- A member of the assurance team having a direct financial interest in the assurance client.
- A firm having undue dependence on total fees from a client.
- A member of the assurance team having a significant close business relationship with an assurance client.
- A firm being concerned about the possibility of losing a significant client.
- A member of the audit team entering into employment negotiations with the audit client.
- A firm entering into a contingent fee arrangement relating to an assurance engagement.
- A professional accountant discovering a significant error when evaluating the results of a previous professional service performed by a member of the professional accountant's firm.

Self-review threat

A 'self-review threat' occurs when (1) results of a previous engagement needs to be re-evaluated in reaching conclusions on the present assurance engagement or (2) when a member of the assurance team previously was an employee of the client (especially a director or officer) in a position to exert significant influence over the subject matter[11] of the assurance engagement. Examples of circumstances that create self-review threats for a professional accountant in public practice include:

- A firm issuing an assurance report on the effectiveness of the operation of financial systems after designing or implementing the systems.
- A firm having prepared the original data used to generate records that are the subject matter of the assurance engagement.
- A member of the assurance team being, or having recently been, a director or officer of the client.

- A member of the assurance team being, or having recently been, employed by the client in a position to exert significant influence over the subject matter of the engagement.
- The firm performing a service for an assurance client that directly affects the subject matter information of the assurance engagement.

Advocacy Threat

An 'advocacy threat' occurs when a member of the assurance team promotes, or seems to promote, an assurance client's position or opinion. That is, the auditor subordinates his judgement to that of the client. Examples of circumstances that may create this threat include:

- selling, underwriting or otherwise promoting financial securities or shares of an assurance client;
- acting as the client's advocate in a legal proceeding.

Familiarity Threat

A 'familiarity threat' occurs when an auditor becomes too sympathetic to the client's interests because he has a close relationship with an assurance client, its directors, officers or employees. Examples of circumstances that may create this threat include:

- A member of the engagement team having an immediate family member or close family member who is a director or officer of the assurance client.
- A member of the engagement team having a close family member who is an employee of the assurance client and in a position to significantly influence the subject matter of the assurance engagement.
- A director or officer of the client or an employee in a position to exert significant influence over the subject matter of the engagement having recently served as the engagement partner
- A professional accountant accepting gifts or preferential treatment from a client, unless the value is trivial or inconsequential.
- Senior personnel having a long association with the assurance client.
- In some countries, 'immediate family member' may mean the engagement member's spouse and dependent. In other countries immediate family member may be the engagement member's child, or her spouse, her parent or grandparent, parent-in-law, brother, sister, or brother-in-law or sister-in-law of the client. For example, a CPA firm that prepares a tax return for a client who is an immediate family member, for example, a spouse or a sister, and gives a tax deduction in which adequate evidence for the deduction is not provided, could be in violation of independency law.

Intimidation Threat

An 'intimidation threat' occurs when a member of the assurance team may be deterred from acting objectively and exercising professional scepticism by threats, actual or perceived, from the directors, officers or employees of an assurance client. Examples of circumstances that create intimidation threats for a professional accountant in public practice include:

- A firm being threatened with dismissal from a client engagement.
- An audit client indicating that it will not award a planned non-assurance contract to the firm if the firm continues to disagree with the client's accounting treatment for a particular transaction.

- A firm being threatened with litigation by the client.
- A firm being pressured to reduce inappropriately the extent of work performed in order to reduce fees.
- A professional accountant feeling pressured to agree with the judgement of a client employee because the employee has more expertise on the matter in question.
- A professional accountant being informed by a partner of the firm that a planned promotion will not occur unless the accountant agrees with an audit client's inappropriate accounting treatment.

■ Safeguards

When threats are identified, other than those that are clearly insignificant, appropriate safeguards should be identified and applied to eliminate the threats or reduce them to an acceptable level. If elimination or reduction is not possible the auditor should decline or terminate the engagement. When deciding what safeguards should be applied one must consider what would be unacceptable to an informed third party having knowledge of all relevant information.

Safeguards fall into two broad categories:

1 safeguards created by the profession, legislation or regulation; and
2 safeguards in the work environment.

Safeguards Created by the Profession, Legislation or Regulation: Examples

Safeguards created by the profession, legislation or regulation may include: educational, training and experience requirements to become a certified member of the profession; continuing education requirements; professional accounting, auditing and ethics standards and monitoring and disciplinary processes; peer review of quality control; and professional rules or legislation governing the independence requirements of the firm.

Safeguards within the Work Environment: Examples

In the work environment, the relevant safeguards will vary depending on the circumstances.

Work environment safeguards comprise firm-wide safeguards and engagement-specific safeguards. Examples of firm-wide safeguards in the work environment include:

- Leadership of the firm that stresses the importance of compliance with the fundamental principles and requires that members of an assurance team act in the public interest.
- Policies and procedures to implement and monitor quality control of engagements.
- Documented policies regarding the need to identify threats to compliance with the fundamental principles, evaluate the significance of those threats, and apply safeguards to eliminate or reduce the threats to an acceptable level or when to terminate or decline the relevant engagement.
- Policies and procedures that will enable the identification of interests or relationships between the firm or members of engagement teams and clients.
- Policies and procedures to monitor and, if necessary, manage the reliance on revenue received from a single client.
- Using different partners and engagement teams with separate reporting lines for the provision of non-assurance services to an assurance client.

- Policies and procedures to prohibit individuals who are not members of an engagement team from inappropriately influencing the outcome of the engagement.
- Timely communication of, appropriate training, and education on a firm's policies and procedures, including any changes to them, to all staff.
- Designating a member of senior management to be responsible for overseeing the adequate functioning of the firm's quality control system.
- Advising all staff of assurance clients from which independence is required.
- A disciplinary mechanism to promote compliance with policies and procedures.
- Published policies and procedures to encourage and empower staff to communicate to senior levels within the firm any issue relating to compliance with the fundamental principles.

Safeguards within the firm's own systems and procedures may also include engagement-specific safeguards such as:

- Using an additional professional accountant not on the assurance team to review the work done.
- Consulting an outside third party (e.g. a committee of independent directors or a professional regulatory body).
- Rotation of senior assurance team personnel.
- Communicating to the audit committee the nature of services provided and fees charged.
- Involving another audit firm to perform or re-perform part of the assurance engagement.

Depending on the nature of the engagement, the engagement team may be able to rely on safeguards that the client has implemented. However, it is not possible to rely solely on such safeguards to reduce threats. The audit client (auditee) may be biased or restrictive in what safeguards they implement or the safeguards may not be followed in the ordinary course of events.

3.5 Part B – Ethics Applicable to Professional Accountants in Public Practice

Whereas the ethics guidance discussed above (Part A of the Code) is applicable to all professional accountants, Part B of IESBA's Code of Ethics is only applicable to accountants in public practice. Part B describes how the conceptual framework contained in Part A applies in certain situations to professional accountants in public practice. A **professional accountant in public practice** is a professional accountant, irrespective of functional classification (for example, audit, tax or consulting) in a firm that provides professional services. This term is also used to refer to a firm of professional accountants in public practice.

Ethical guidance for accountants in public practice is offered in the areas of: professional appointment, conflicts of interest, second opinions, fees and other remuneration, marketing professional services, gifts and hospitality, custody of client assets, objectivity and independence.

Concept and a Company 3.2

Lincoln Savings & Loan – Employment of a Former Auditor

Concept	Independence in Fact and Appearance.

Story Upon completion of the 1987 Arthur Young (later Ernst & Young) audit of Lincoln Savings & Loan Association (Lincoln) which resulted in an unqualified opinion, the engagement audit partner, Jack Atchison, resigned from Arthur Young and was hired by Lincoln's parent American Continental Corporation (ACC) for approximately $930,000 annual salary. His prior annual earnings as a partner at Arthur Young was approximately $225,000 (Knapp, 2001).

Charles Keating Jr syphoned money out of Lincoln Savings and Loan for his own benefit from the day he acquired Lincoln in 1984 until the Federal Home Loan Bank Board (FHLBB) seized control on 14 April 1989. At the time of the seizure nearly two-thirds of Lincoln's asset portfolio was invested in high-risk land ventures and Keating had used fraudulent accounting methods to create net income. In the end, Lincoln's demise involved investors' losses of $200 million and its closure cost US taxpayers $3.4 billion in guaranteed deposit insurance and legal costs, making it the most costly savings and loan failure in US history. For their part in the Lincoln failure, Ernst & Young paid the California State Board of Accountancy (the state agency which registers California CPAs) $1.5 million in 1991 to settle negligence complaints and in 1992 paid the US Government $400 million to settle four lawsuits (Knapp, 2001).

In the court case of *Lincoln S&L* v *Wall*, it was suggested that Atchison might have known about the financial statement problems during his audit of Lincoln. ACC was in dire need of obtaining $10 million because of an agreement with the Bank Board to infuse an additional $10 million into Lincoln. Thus, Lincoln was actually the source of its own $10 million cash infusion. Ernst & Young LLC learnt of these facts from Jack Atchison after Atchison had become a top official at Lincoln (USDC – DC, 1990)

At the time Atchison made his move, the practice of 'changing sides' was not against the AICPA's ethics standards; however, the Securities and Exchange Commission (SEC) stated that Atchison's should certainly be examined by the accounting profession's standard setting authorities as to the impact such a practice has on an accountant's independence. Furthermore, they stated that it would seem that a 'cooling-off period' of one to two years would not be unreasonable before the client can employ a senior official on an audit (SEC, 1990).

Ultimately, the Sarbanes–Oxley Act of 2002 required a cooling-off period of one year after a company's last audit before clients can hire as an officer any member of the audit team.

Discussion Questions
■ What impact does employment of former independent auditors by an audit client have on that auditor's independence during the audit?
■ Were Atchison's actions ethical?

References Knapp, M., 2001, 'Lincoln Savings and Loan Association', *Contemporary Auditing Real Issues & Cases*, South Western College Publishing, Cincinnati, Ohio, pp. 57–70.

SEC, 1990, Final rule release 33-7919, *Final Rule: Revision of the Commission's Auditor Independence Requirements*, Securities and Exchange Commission, February, 5.

USDC – DC, 1990, *Lincoln Savings & Loan Association* v *Wall*, 'Consolidated Civil Action Nos. 89-1318, 89-1323', 743 F. Supp. 901; 1990 US Dist. LEXIS 11178, United States District Court for the District of Columbia, 22 August 1990; Decided, 22 August 1990, Filed.

■ Professional Appointment (Sec. 210)

Before an auditor in public practice takes on a new client relationship they should make a determination of whether acceptance of the client would create any threats to compliance with the fundamental principles of ethics.

The fundamental principle of professional competence and due care imposes an obligation on a professional accountant in public practice to provide only those services that they are competent to perform. Competence is important in engagement acceptance and the acceptance of the client themselves. Before accepting a specific client engagement, the auditor must determine whether acceptance would create any threats to compliance with the fundamental principles. A self-interest threat to professional competence and due care is created if the engagement team does not possess, or cannot acquire, the competencies necessary to properly carry out the engagement. When evaluating whether to accept the client, the auditor should consider that potential threats to integrity or professional behaviour may be created from questionable issues associated with that client (its owners, management or activities), client involvement in illegal activities (such as money laundering), or dishonesty or questionable financial reporting practices.

Basic safeguards against client acceptance and engagement acceptance threats include obtaining knowledge of the client and its governance and business activities or securing the client's commitment to improve corporate governance practices or internal controls. Examples of such safeguards include the following (some safeguards are also discussed in ISA 220[12] on quality control).

■ Acquiring an appropriate understanding of the nature of the client's business, the complexity of its operations, the specific requirements of the engagement and the purpose, nature and scope of the work to be performed.
■ Acquiring knowledge of relevant industries, subject matters and relevant regulatory or reporting requirements.
■ Assigning sufficient staff with the necessary competencies.
■ Using experts where necessary. (When an auditor in public practice intends to rely on the advice or work of an expert they should consider reputation, expertise, resources available and applicable ethical standards.) See ISA 620.[13]
■ Accept specific engagements only when they can be performed competently.

Replacing an Existing Auditor

An auditor who is asked to replace another auditor, or who is considering a new engagement for a company currently audited by another auditor must consider whether there are any reasons, professional or otherwise, for not accepting the engagement. There may be a threat to professional competence and due care if an auditor accepts the engagement before knowing all the pertinent facts. Determining possible reasons for not accepting a new client may require direct communication with the existing auditor to establish the facts and circumstances regarding the proposed change in auditors.

Safeguards to deal with a threat to due professional care include:

■ When requested by a prospective client to submit a proposal to perform the audit, stating in the tender that, before accepting the engagement, contact with the existing auditor[14] will be made.

- Asking the existing auditor to provide known information on any facts or circumstances that, in the existing accountant's opinion, the proposed auditor needs to be aware of before deciding whether to accept the engagement; or obtaining necessary information from other sources.
- A professional accountant in public practice will generally need to obtain the client's permission, preferably in writing, to initiate discussion with an existing accountant. The existing accountant should provide information to the proposed auditor honestly and unambiguously. If the proposed accountant for whatever reason is unable to communicate with the existing accountant, the proposed accountant should take reasonable steps to obtain information such as through inquiries of third parties or background investigations of senior management or those charged with governance of the client.

■ Conflicts of Interest (Sec. 220)

An auditor should develop procedures to identify circumstances that would lead to a conflict of interest and apply safeguards when necessary to eliminate the threats. For example, a threat to objectivity may be created when a professional accountant in public practice competes directly with a client or has a joint venture or similar arrangement with a major competitor of a client. If a conflict of interest may exist, application of one of the following safeguards is appropriate:

- notifying the client of the audit firm's activities that may represent a conflict of interest; or
- notifying all known relevant parties that the professional accountant in public practice is acting for two or more parties in respect of a matter where their respective interests are in conflict and obtaining their consent to so act; or
- notifying the client that the professional accountant in public practice does not act exclusively for any one client in the provision of proposed services (for example, in a particular market sector or with respect to a specific service).

The professional accountant shall also determine whether to apply one or more of the following additional safeguards:

- The use of separate engagement teams.
- Procedures to prevent access to information (for example, strict physical separation of such teams, confidential and secure data filing).
- The use of confidentiality agreements signed by employees and partner of the firm.
- Regular review of the application of safeguards by a senior individual not involved with relevant client engagements.

When there is a conflict of interest threat to the fundamental ethics principles that cannot be reduced to an acceptable level by employing safeguards, the auditor should not accept the engagement or, if already engaged, resign from the assurance engagement.

■ Second Opinions (Sec. 230)

Sometimes a professional accountant in public practice is asked to provide a second opinion on the application of accounting, auditing, reporting or other standards or principles to specific circumstances on behalf of a company that is not an existing client.

This may create threats to compliance with the fundamental principles. For example, there may be a threat to professional competence and due care in circumstances where the second opinion is not based on the same set of facts that were made available to the existing accountant or is based on inadequate evidence. When asked to provide such an opinion, the auditor should consider any threats that may arise and apply safeguards. Examples of possible safeguards include seeking client permission to contact the existing accountant, describing the limitations surrounding any opinion in communications with the client, and providing the existing accountant with a copy of the opinion.

■ Fees and Other Types of Remuneration (Sec. 240)

When negotiating to provide services to an assurance client, a professional accountant in public practice may quote whatever fee is deemed appropriate. The fact that one professional accountant in public practice may quote a fee lower than another is not in itself unethical. Nevertheless, there may be threats to compliance with the fundamental principles arising from the level of fees quoted. For example, a self-interest threat to professional competence and due care is created if the fee quoted is so low that it may be difficult to perform the engagement in accordance with applicable technical and professional standards for that price. Examples of safeguards against possible threats would include making the client aware of the terms of the engagement and the basis of the fees.

Contingent fees are widely used for certain types of non-assurance engagements. However, they may create threats to compliance with the fundamental principles in certain circumstances. They may create a self-interest threat to objectivity. The existence and significance of such threats will depend on a number of factors including nature of the engagement, fee range, and the basis for determining the fee.

Accepting a referral fee or commission relating to a client creates a self-interest threat to objectivity and professional competence and due care. For example, safeguards must be set up for a fee received for referring a continuing client to another accountant or other expert or receiving a commission from a third party (for example, a software vendor) in connection with the sale of goods or services to a client. Similarly, safeguards must be made for payments by a professional accountant in public practice such as a referral fee to obtain a client.

Examples of safeguards for receiving and paying fees include: disclosing to the client any arrangements either to pay a referral fee to another professional accountant for the work referred or to receive a referral fee for referring the client to another. Another safeguard would be to obtain advance agreement from the client for commission arrangements.

A professional accountant in public practice may purchase all or part of another accounting firm on the basis that payments will be made to individuals formerly owning the firm or to their heirs or estates. Such payments are not regarded as commissions or referral.

■ Marketing Professional Services (Sec. 250)

When a professional accountant in public practice solicits new work through advertising or other forms of marketing, there may be a threat to compliance with the fundamental principles. For example, a self-interest threat to compliance with the principle of professional behaviour is created if services, achievements, or products are marketed in a way that is inconsistent with that principle. The accountant shall be honest and truthful, and not make exaggerated claims for services offered, qualifications possessed, or experience gained; or make disparaging references or unsubstantiated comparisons to the work of another.

■ Gifts and Hospitality (Sec. 260)

An offer of gifts and hospitality from a client to a professional accountant in public practice, or an immediate or close family member may create threats to compliance with the fundamental principles. For example, a self-interest or familiarity threat to objectivity may be created if a gift from a client is accepted; an intimidation threat to objectivity may result from the possibility of such offers being made public. However, if a reasonable and informed third party, weighing all the specific facts and circumstances would consider specific gifts or hospitality trivial and inconsequential, the offers would be considered part of the normal course of business which was not intended to influence the auditor's decision making.

■ Custody of Client Assets (Sec. 270)

Unless permitted to do so by law, the professional accountant in public practice should not have custody of client money or assets. If asset custody is permitted by law, the accountant should comply with legal duties required by regulation. The holding of client assets creates threats to compliance with the fundamental principles; for example, there is a self-interest threat to professional behaviour and may be a self-interest threat to objectivity arising from holding client assets. An accountant entrusted with money (or other assets) belonging to others must:

- Keep other's assets separately from personal or accounting firm assets.
- Use such assets only for the purpose for which they are intended.
- At all times be ready to account for those assets and any income, dividends or gains generated to any persons entitled to such accounting.
- Comply with all relevant laws and regulations relevant to the holding of and accounting for such assets.
- Make appropriate inquiries about the source of such assets and consider legal and regulatory obligations.

■ Objectivity – All Services (Sec. 280)

Are there threats to compliance with the fundamental principle of objectivity resulting from having interests in, or relationships with, a client or its directors, officers or employees? For example, a familiarity threat to objectivity may be created from a family or close personal or business relationship. A professional accountant in public practice must determine when providing any professional service whether there are such threats and act accordingly with safeguards. Examples of such safeguards include:

- Withdrawing from the engagement team.
- Supervisory procedures.
- Terminating the financial or business relationship giving rise to the threat.
- Discussing the issue with higher levels of management within the firm.
- Discussing the issue with those charged with governance of the client.

A public practice accountant who provides assurance services must be independent of the assurance client. Both independence of mind and independence in appearance are necessary if the auditor is to express an unbiased opinion without conflict of interest or undue influence.

3.6 Independence – Audit and Review Engagements (Section 290)

The independence of the auditor from the firm that he is auditing is one of the basic requirements to keep public confidence in the reliability of the audit report. Independence adds credibility to the audit report on which investors, creditors, employees, government and other stakeholders depend to make decisions about a company. The benefits of safeguarding an auditor's independence extend so far as to the overall efficiency of the capital markets.

Across the world, national rules on auditors' independence differ in several respects such as: the scope of persons to whom independence rules should apply; the kind of financial, business or other relationships that an auditor may have with an audit client; the type of non-audit services that can and cannot be provided to an audit client; and the safeguards which should be used. The European Commission has issued independence standards to be applied throughout the European Union (EU). The USA enacted the Sarbanes–Oxley Act of 2002, which describes independence requirements of US auditors.

The European Commission Council Directive 84/253/EEC (EU Eighth Company Law Directive), gives discretionary power to Member States to determine the conditions of independence for a statutory auditor. Article 24 states[15] that Member States shall prescribe that auditors shall not carry out **statutory audits**[16] if they are not independent in accordance with the law of the Member State which requires the audit.

To provide each EU country with a common understanding of this independence requirement, the European Union Committee on Auditing developed a set of fundamental principles set out in a Commission Recommendation called *Statutory Auditors' Independence in the EU: A Set of Fundamental Principles*.[17] The principles based approach was considered 'preferable to one based on detailed rules because it creates a robust structure within which statutory auditors have to justify their actions.'[18]

The EU framework, which parallels the threat and safeguard approach of IESBA, is based on the requirement that an auditor must be independent from his audit client both in mind and appearance. The auditor should not audit a client if there are any financial, businesses, employment or other relationships between them that a 'reasonable and informed third party' would conclude compromised independence.

US based firms and firms that audit US publicly traded firms must adhere to the regulations of the Sarbanes–Oxley Act,[19] Title II, *Auditor Independence*, as interpreted by the Public Company Accounting Oversight Board (PCAOB).[20] The Independence sections and the prohibited services are listed in Illustration 3.2.

Under PCAOB rules all non-audit services to clients, which are not specifically prohibited, must be pre-approved by the Audit Committee and disclosed to the shareholders. Audit partners must be rotated every five years. Clients cannot hire as an officer any member of the audit team within one year after their last audit. Determination of independence of auditors who audit non-publicly traded firms is left up to the regulatory authorities of the 50 states of the USA.

ILLUSTRATION 3.2

Independence in the Sarbanes–Oxley Act of 2002

TITLE II – AUDITOR INDEPENDENCE
Sec. 201. Services outside the scope of practice of auditors.
Sec. 202. Pre-approval requirements.
Sec. 203. Audit partner rotation.
Sec. 204. Auditor reports to audit committees.
Sec. 205. Conforming amendments.
Sec. 206. Conflicts of interest.
Sec. 207. Study of mandatory rotation of registered public accounting firms.
Sec. 208. Commission authority.
Sec. 209. Considerations by appropriate State regulatory authorities.

Prohibited non-audit service contemporaneously with the audit include:
(1) bookkeeping or other services related to the accounting records or financial statements of the audit client;
(2) financial information systems design and implementation;
(3) appraisal or valuation services, fairness opinions, or contribution-in-kind reports;
(4) actuarial services;
(5) internal audit outsourcing services;
(6) management functions or human resources;
(7) broker or dealer, investment adviser, or investment banking services;
(8) legal services and expert services unrelated to the audit; and
(9) any other service that the Board determines, by regulation, is impermissible.

Europe is currently taking the lead in this global discussion of auditor independence strongly expressed by Michel Barnier, the European internal market and services commissioner. Mr Barnier has said, 'Just like beauty, quality and independence are in the eye of the beholder, therefore perception of audit quality and of auditor independence is paramount.'[21] He is proposing the questions: Why do companies with serious shortcomings receive a clean audit report? How great is the pressure on an auditor to not lose a company that has been a client for decades? How independent is an audit when there are other commercial interests and the auditor could be auditing work performed by other departments of his firm? He suggests that mandatory rotation of audit firms, restrictions on the provision of non-audit services, and the prohibition to provide any non-audit services for audit firms of a very substantial size would address these questions linked to independence. He has proposed several audit reforms in his European Commission Green Paper.[22]

■ Independence as Discussed in the IESBA Code (Section 290)

The IESBA Code of Ethics for Professional Accountants, Section 290, addresses the independence requirements for audit engagements and review engagements. Independence requirements for assurance engagements that are not audit or review engagements are addressed in Section 291, not covered in this chapter. The Code discusses independence in assurance services in terms of a principles-based, conceptual approach that takes into account threats to independence, accepted safeguards and the public interest.

Concepts-based Approach

IFAC strongly believes that a high-quality principles based approach to independence will best serve the public interest by eliciting thoughtful auditor assessment of the particular circumstances of each engagement.[23] However, the Code gives related guidance and explanatory material as well. The section on independence (Section 290) discusses the application of the conceptual approach to specific situations such as financial interest, loans, fees and others listed in Illustration 3.3.

ILLUSTRATION 3.3

Code of Ethics Section 290 on Independence

SECTION 290 INDEPENDENCE – AUDIT AND REVIEW ENGAGEMENTS CONTENTS

Paragraph

Structure of Section	290.1
A Conceptual Framework Approach to Independence	290.4
Networks and Network Firms	290.13
Public Interest Entities	290.25
Related Entities	290.27
Those Charged with Governance	290.28
Documentation	290.29
Engagement Period	290.30
Mergers and Acquisitions	290.33
Other Considerations	290.39
Application of the Conceptual Framework Approach to Independence	290.100
Financial Interests	290.102
Loans and Guarantees	290.118
Business Relationships	290.124
Family and Personal Relationships	290.127
Employment with an Audit Client	290.134
Temporary Staff Assignments	290.142
Recent Service with an Audit Client	290.143
Serving as a Director or Officer of an Audit Client	290.146
Long Association of Senior Personnel (Including Partner Rotation) with an Audit Client	290.150
Provision of Non-assurance Services to Audit Clients	290.156
Management Responsibilities	290.162
Preparing Accounting Records and Financial Statements	290.167
Valuation Services	290.175
Taxation Services	290.181
Internal Audit Services	290.195
IT Systems Services	290.201
Litigation Support Services	290.207
Legal Services	290.209
Recruiting Services	290.214
Corporate Finance Services	290.216
Fees	290.220
Fees – Relative Size	290.220
Fees – Overdue	290.223
Contingent Fees	290.224
Compensation and Evaluation Policies	290.228
Gifts and Hospitality	290.230
Actual or Threatened Litigation	290.231
Reports that Include a Restriction on Use and Distribution	290.500

Accountants must not only maintain an independent attitude in fulfilling their responsibilities, but the users of financial statements must have confidence in that independence. These two objectives are frequently identified as 'independence of mind' and 'independence in appearance'. Independence of mind (historically referred to as independence in fact) exists when the accountant is able to maintain an unbiased attitude throughout the audit, so being objective and impartial, whereas independence in appearance is the result of others' interpretations of this independence.

The conceptual framework involves two views of independence to which the auditor must comply: (1) independence of mind and (2) independence in appearance. Independence of mind is a state of mind that allows to draw conclusions that are unaffected by influences that compromise professional judgment. Independence in mind allows the professional accountant to act with integrity, objectivity, and professional scepticism. Independence in appearance involves avoidance of significant circumstances that a reasonable an informed third party, considering all the facts and circumstances, might conclude that the professional accountant's integrity, objectivity or professional scepticism has been compromised.

The Ethics Code discusses independence in assurance services in terms of a principles-based approach that takes into account threats to independence, accepted safeguards and the public interest. The Section states principles that members of assurance teams should use to identify threats to independence (self-interest, self-review, advocacy, familiarity and intimidation threats), evaluate the significance of those threats, and, if the threats are other than clearly insignificant, identify and apply safeguards created by the profession, legislation or regulation, safeguards within the assurance client, and safeguards within the firm's own systems and procedures to eliminate the threats or reduce them to an acceptable level.

A professional accountant shall use professional judgement in applying this conceptual framework to:

- identify threats to independence;
- evaluate the significance of the threats identified; and
- apply safeguards, when necessary, to eliminate the threats or reduce them to an acceptable level.

Independence for audit and review services and possible threats and safeguards are given in detail in Section 290, the largest section of the Code. See Illustration 3.3. Review and audit independence is discussed on the topics of conceptual framework, network firms, public interest entities, documentation, engagement period, financial interests, loans and guarantees, business relationships, family and personal relationships, employment with an audit client, temporary staff assignments, recent service with an audit client, serving as director or officer of an audit client, long association of senior personnel with audit clients, and other topics not covered in this chapter, including mergers and acquisitions and related entities. The sub-section on non-assurance services discusses safeguards and threats of non-assurance services to the audit client including the following topics: management responsibilities, preparing accounting records and financial statements, taxation services, internal audit services, IT systems services, litigation support services, legal services, recruiting services, and valuation and corporate finance services. The independence section ends with a discussion of general topics including fees, compensation and evaluation policies, gifts and hospitality, actual or threatened litigation, and restricted reports (not discussed in this chapter).

The Code emphasizes that during audit engagements it is in the public interest and required that members of audit teams must be independent of audit clients.

If a firm is a **network firm**,[24] the firm must be independent of the audit clients of the other firms within the network. The independence requirements that apply to a network firm apply to any entity, such as a consulting practice or professional law practice, which meets the definition of a network firm irrespective of whether the entity itself meets the definition of a firm.

■ Documentation of Independence (290.29)

The auditor has to document conclusions regarding compliance with independence requirements as well as the discussions that support these conclusions. Accordingly:

- when safeguards are required, the auditor shall document the nature of the threat and the safeguards in place or applied that reduce the threat to an acceptable level; and
- when a threat required significant analysis to determine whether safeguards were necessary and the conclusion was that they were not because the threat was already at an acceptable level, the professional accountant shall document the nature of the threat and the rationale for the conclusion.

■ Engagement Period (290.30)

Independence from the audit client is required both during the engagement period and the period covered by the financial statements.[25] The engagement period starts when the audit team begins to perform audit services. The engagement period ends when the audit report is issued. When the engagement is of a recurring nature, it ends at the later of the notification by either party that the professional relationship has terminated or the issuance of the final audit report. During or after the period covered by the financial statements the audit firm must consider threats to independence created by financial or business relationships with the audit client or previous services provided to the audit client.

Auditors should consider threats if a non-assurance service that would not be permitted during the period of the audit engagement was provided to the audit client before the audit. Safeguards include:

- not including personnel who provided the non-assurance service as members of the audit team;
- having a professional accountant review the audit and non-assurance work as appropriate; or
- engaging another accounting firm to evaluate the results of the non-assurance service or having another firm re-perform the non-assurance service to the extent necessary to enable it to take responsibility for the service.

■ Application of the Conceptual Framework Approach to Independence (290.100)

The final paragraphs of Part B (paragraphs 290.102 to 290.231) of the IESBA Code describe specific circumstances and relationships that create or may create threats to independence. The paragraphs describe the potential threats and the types of safeguards that may be appropriate to eliminate the threats or reduce them to an acceptable level and identify certain situations where no safeguards could reduce the threats to an acceptable level. Here we will not cover all the examples discussed in these paragraphs, but cover the most common safeguards concerning financial interests, loans, guarantees and business relationship. To determine whether a material interest exists the combined net worth of the individual and the individual's immediate family members may be taken into account.

■ Financial Interests (290.102)

The self-interest threat created when an auditor, her firm, or a member of her immediate family has direct or material indirect financial interest in an audit client is such that no safeguards could reduce it to an acceptable level. None of the following shall have a direct financial interest or a material indirect financial interest in the client: a member of the audit team; a member of that individual's immediate family; or the firm. If other partners and managerial employees who provide non-audit services to the audit client, or their immediate family members, hold a direct financial interest or a material indirect financial interest in the audit client, the self-interest threat created would be so significant that no safeguards could reduce the threat to an acceptable level.

A loan, or a guarantee of a loan, to a member of the audit team, or a member of that individual's immediate family, or the firm from an audit client that is a bank, a similar institution, or non-bank entity (except if the non-bank loan is immaterial) may create a threat to independence. The loan or guarantee must not be made except under normal lending procedures, terms and conditions, otherwise a self-interest threat would be created that would be so significant that no safeguards could be sufficient. If the loan or guarantee is made under normal lending procedures, terms and conditions safeguards such as having the work reviewed by a professional accountant from a network firm that is neither involved with the audit nor received the loan.

■ Business, Family and Personal Relationships (290.124–290.150)

A close business relationship between a firm, or a member of the audit team, or a member of that individual's immediate family, and the audit client or its management, arises from a commercial relationship or common financial interest and may create self-interest or intimidation threats. Unless the financial interest is immaterial and the business relationship is insignificant, the business relationship must not be entered into because *no* safeguards would be sufficient and the individual with the relationship must be removed from the audit team. Examples of close business relationships include:

- Having a financial interest in a joint venture with either the client or a controlling owner, director, officer or other individual who performs senior managerial activities for that client.
- Arrangements to combine one or more services or products of the firm with one or more services or products of the client and to market the package with reference to both parties.
- Distribution or marketing arrangements under which the firm distributes or markets the client's products or services, or the client distributes or markets the firm's products or services.

Family and personal relationships between a member of the audit team and a director or officer or certain employees (depending on their role) of the audit client may create self-interest, familiarity or intimidation threats. If an immediate family member of a member of the audit team is a director or officer of the audit client, or an employee in a position to exert significant influence over the preparation of the client's accounting records or the financial statements or was in such a position during any period covered by the engagement the threats can only be reduced to an acceptable level by removing that individual from the audit team.

If a director or officer of the audit client, or a significant employee, has been a member of the audit team or partner of the firm, familiarity or intimidation threats may be created. The threat would be so significant that no safeguards could reduce the threat to an acceptable level unless: the individual is not entitled to any benefits or payments from the audit firm and any amount owed to the individual is not material to the firm; and that individual does not continue to participate in the audit firm's business activities. Furthermore, a self-interest threat is created when a member of the audit team participates in the audit engagement while knowing that the member of the audit team will, or may, join the client some time in the future.

The lending of staff by a firm to an audit client may create a self-review threat. Such assistance may be given, but only for a short period of time, and the firm's personnel shall not be involved in providing non-assurance services not permitted under Section B of the IESBA Code or assuming management responsibilities.

Familiarity and self-interest threats are created by using the same senior personnel on an audit engagement over a long period of time. Examples of such safeguards include:

- rotating the senior personnel off the audit team;
- having a professional accountant who was not a member of the audit team review the work of the senior personnel; or
- regular independent internal or external quality reviews of the engagement.

In respect of an audit of a public interest entity, an individual shall not be a key audit partner for more than seven years. After such time, the individual shall not be a member of the engagement team or be a key audit partner for the client for two years.

■ Provision of Non-assurance Services to Audit Clients (290.156–290.216)

Firms have traditionally provided to their audit clients a range of non-assurance services that are consistent with their skills and expertise. Providing non-assurance services may, however, create threats to the independence of the firm or members of the audit team. The threats created are most often self-review, self-interest and advocacy threats. Providing certain non-assurance services to an audit client may create a threat to independence so significant that no safeguards could reduce the threat to an acceptable level.

If a firm were to assume a **management responsibility**[26] for an audit client, the threats created would be so significant that no safeguards could reduce the threats to an acceptable level. For example, deciding which recommendations of the firm to implement will create self-review and self-interest threats. Further, assuming a management responsibility creates a familiarity threat because the firm becomes too closely aligned with the views and interests of management. Therefore, the firm shall not assume a management responsibility for an audit client.

Providing an audit client with **accounting and bookkeeping services**, such as preparing accounting records or financial statements, creates a self-review threat when the audit firm subsequently audits the financial statements. Except in emergency situations,[27] an audit firm shall not provide to an audit client that is a public interest entity accounting and bookkeeping services, including payroll services, or prepare financial statements or financial information which forms the basis of the financial statements. However, the firm may provide some services related to the preparation of accounting records and financial statements to an audit client that is not a public interest entity. Examples of such services include:

- Providing payroll services based on client-originated data.
- Recording transactions for which the client has determined or approved the appropriate account classification.
- Posting transactions coded by the client to the general ledger.
- Posting client-approved entries to the trial balance.
- Preparing financial statements based on information in the trial balance.

Tax return preparation services involve assisting clients with their tax reporting obligations by drafting and completing information, including the amount of tax due (usually on standardised forms) required to be submitted to the applicable tax authorities. The tax returns are subject to whatever review or approval process the tax authority deems appropriate. Accordingly, providing such service does not generally create a threat to independence if management takes responsibility for the returns including any significant judgments made.

Tax planning or other tax advisory services such as advising the client how to structure its affairs in a tax efficient manner or advising on the application of a new tax law or regulation may create a self-review threat where the advice will affect matters to be reflected in the financial statements. For example, where the effectiveness of the tax advice depends on a particular accounting treatment or presentation in the financial statements and the audit team has reasonable doubt as to the appropriateness of the related accounting treatment and the outcome or consequences of the tax advice will have a material effect on the financial statements, the self-review threat would be so significant that no safeguards could reduce the threat to an acceptable level.

The existence and significance of any threat will depend on a number of factors. For example, providing tax advisory services where the advice is clearly supported by tax authority or other precedent does not generally create a threat to independence. If safeguards are required, they may include:

- using professionals who are not members of the audit team to perform the service;
- having a tax professional, who was not involved in providing the tax service, advise the audit team on the service and review the financial statement treatment;
- obtaining advice on the service from an external tax professional; or
- obtaining pre-clearance or advice from the tax authorities.

An advocacy or self-review threat may be created when the firm represents an audit client in the resolution of a **tax dispute**. Where the taxation services involve acting as an advocate for an audit client before a public tribunal or court in the resolution of a tax matter and the amounts involved are material to the financial statements the advocacy threat created would be so significant that no safeguards could eliminate or reduce the threat to an acceptable level. Therefore, the firm shall not perform this type of service for an audit client.

The provision of **internal audit services** to an audit client creates a self-review threat to independence if the firm uses the internal audit work in the course of a subsequent external audit. Performing a significant part of the client's internal audit activities increases the possibility that firm personnel providing internal audit services will assume a management responsibility. Assuming management responsibility when providing internal audit services to an audit client creates a threat that would be so significant that no safeguards could reduce the threat to an acceptable level.

To avoid assuming a management responsibility, the firm shall only provide internal audit services to an audit client if it is satisfied that:

- Client senior management takes responsibility at all times for internal audit activities and acknowledges responsibility for designing, implementing and maintaining internal control.
- Client management reviews, assesses and approves the scope, risk and frequency of the internal audit services.
- The client's management evaluates and determines which recommendations resulting from internal audit services to implement and manages the implementation process.
- The client's management reports to those charged with governance the significant findings and recommendations resulting from the internal audit services.

In the case of an audit client that is a **public interest entity**, a firm shall not provide internal audit services that relate to:

- a significant part of the internal controls over financial reporting;
- financial accounting systems that generate information that is significant to the client's accounting records or financial statements; or
- amounts or disclosures that are material to the financial statements on which the audit firm will express an opinion.

Providing **IT systems services** may create a self-review threat depending on the nature of the services and the IT systems. Providing services to an audit client involving the design or implementation of IT systems that form a significant part of the internal control over financial reporting or generate accounting records or financial statements creates a self-review threat. For a non-public interest entity other IT systems services may not create a threat to independence if the audit firm's personnel do not assume management responsibility, but safeguards must be put in place.

Performing **valuation services** or **litigation support services** for an audit client may create a self-review threat. The existence and significance of any threat will depend on several factors such as whether the services will have a material effect on the financial statements, the active participation of the client's in determining and approving the methodology and other significant matters of judgement, the degree of subjectivity inherent in the service, the extent and clarity of the disclosures in the financial statements.

Legal services that support an audit client in executing a transaction (for example, contract support, legal advice, legal due diligence and restructuring) may create self-review threats. Acting in an advocacy role for an audit client in resolving a dispute or litigation when the amounts involved are material to the financial statements on which the firm will express an opinion would create advocacy and self-review threats so significant that no safeguards could reduce the threat to an acceptable level. Therefore, the firm shall not perform this type of service for an audit client. However, when the amounts involved are not material to the financial statements, the audit firm may provide the service if safeguards are in place.

Providing **recruiting services** to an audit client may create self-interest, familiarity or intimidation threats. The audit firm may generally provide such services as reviewing the professional qualifications of a number of applicants and providing advice on their suitability for the post. In addition, the firm may interview candidates and advice on a candidate's competence for financial accounting, administrative or control positions. The audit firm cannot provide search services or reference checks for a director, officer or senior management who has influence over the accounting records or financial statements.

Advocacy and self-review threats may be created if the auditor provides the audit client **corporate finance services** such as assisting in developing corporate strategies, identifying possible targets for the audit client to acquire, advising on disposal transactions, assisting finance raising transactions, or providing structuring advice, If the effectiveness of corporate finance advice depends on a particular accounting treatment or presentation in the financial statements and the audit team has reasonable doubt as to the appropriateness and the consequences of the corporate finance advice, and the treatment will have a material effect on the financial statements, the self-review threat would be so significant that no safeguards could reduce the threat to an acceptable level. Providing corporate finance services involving promoting, dealing in, or underwriting an audit client's shares would create an advocacy or self-review threat that no safeguards could reduce to an acceptable level.

■ Fees (290.220–290.224)

Professional fees should be a fair reflection of the value of the professional service performed for the client, taking into account the skill and knowledge required, the level of training and experience of the persons performing the services, the time necessary for the services and the degree of responsibility that performing those services entails. The IESBA Ethics Code discusses threats to independence in pricing auditing services in terms of size, whether fees are overdue and contingent fees.

When the total fees from an audit client represent a **large proportion of the total fees** of the firm expressing the audit opinion, the dependence on that client and concern about losing the client creates a self-interest or intimidation threat. These threats are also created when the fees generated from one audit client represent a large proportion of the revenue from an individual partner's clients or a large proportion of the revenue of an individual office of the audit firm. Safeguards should be applied to eliminate the threat or reduce it to an acceptable level. Examples of such safeguards include: reducing the dependency on the client; internal or external quality control reviews; or consulting a third party to review key audit judgements.

The ethics code lists a specific situation of a single client's fees as a proportion of total fees. If an audit client is a public interest entity and, for two consecutive years, the total fees from the client represent more than 15 per cent of the total fees received by the audit firm, the firm must disclose to the audit client that fact and discuss which safeguards (such as those in Ethics Code paragraph 290.222) it will apply.

The Code warns that a self-interest threat may be created if fees due from an assurance client for professional services **remain unpaid for a long time**, especially if a significant part is not paid before the issue of the assurance report for the following year. Generally the payment of such fees should be required before the report is issued. The firm should also consider whether the overdue fees might be regarded as being equivalent to a loan to the client and whether, because of the significance of the overdue fees, it is appropriate for the firm to be reappointed.

Contingent fees are fees (except those established by courts) calculated on a predetermined basis relating to the outcome of a transaction or the result of the services performed by the firm. A contingent fee charged directly or indirectly by an audit firm for an audit or non-assurance engagement creates a self-interest threat that is so significant that no safeguards could reduce the threat to an acceptable level. Some non-assurance engagements may be acceptable under certain safeguards.[28]

Fees are distinct from reimbursement of expenses. Out-of-pocket expenses, in particular travelling expenses, attributable directly to the professional services performed for a particular client would normally be charged in addition to the professional fees.

■ Compensation and Evaluation Policies (290.228)

A self-interest threat is created when a member of the audit team or a key audit partner is evaluated on or compensated for selling non-assurance services to that audit client. The significance of the threat must be evaluated and, if the threat is not at an acceptable level, the firm shall either revise the compensation plan or evaluation process for that individual or apply safeguards to eliminate the threat or reduce it to an acceptable level. Examples of such safeguards include: removing such members from the audit team; or having a professional accountant review the work of the audit team member.

Concept and a Company 3.3

Independence of the External Auditor – Rentokil and KPMG UK

Concept	Auditor independence – auditors should be aware of significant threats to independence that may arise and the appropriate safeguards to apply in an attempt to eliminate those threats.
Story	On 31 July 2009 KPMG UK raised the eyebrows of competitors in the UK and elsewhere in the world with their agreement with Rentokil Initial. Rentokil hired KPMG as their new external auditor, replacing PwC. However, KPMG also replaced Deloitte, who handled much of the internal audit, along with Rentokil's own internal audit team. Other audit firms questioned whether the combination of offering external and internal audit services could be provided by the same firm, without the creation of conflicting interests and threatening independence.
	'The arrangement is controversial, since the Enron and WorldCom accounting scandals have resulted in new rules largely designed to split external and internal audit roles to avoid auditors becoming too tied to their clients', the *Financial Times* wrote.

Oliver Tant, the head of audit for KPMG UK, argued the arrangement was ethically sound. According to Tant, 'the internal audit work does not replace, conflict with, or undermine the independence of the external audit – it simply extends our understanding of the business and its controls and hence the breadth and depth of insight we can offer'. Tant said the arrangement did not merge internal and external audit functions.

In the US under SOX legislation, external auditors are not allowed to combine internal audit services and external audit services to the same client.

This combo deal was favourable for Rentokil, as the new deal saved about £1 million per year in total (internal and external) audit fees.

Discussion Questions	■ To what extent would providing both internal and external audit services to an audit client be considered a threat to independence? ■ What safeguards could KPMG have put in place to compensate for this threat?
References	http://www.ft.com/cms/s/0/ae47504a-7fc4-11de-85dc-00144feabdc0.html#axzz2Ms9NDegv. http://www.accountancyage.com/aa/news/1749104/kpmg-audit-head-defends-controversial-rentokil-role.

■ Gifts and Hospitality (290.230)

Accepting gifts or hospitality from an audit client may create self-interest and familiarity threats. If a firm or a member of the audit team accepts gifts or hospitality, unless the value is trivial and inconsequential, the threats created would be so significant that no safeguards could reduce the threats to an acceptable level.

■ Actual or Threatened Litigation (290.231)

When litigation takes place, or appears likely, between the audit firm or a member of the audit team and the audit client, self-interest and intimidation threats are created. The relationship between client management and the members of the audit team must be characterised by complete candour and full disclosure regarding all aspects of a client's business operations. When the firm and the client's management are placed in adversarial positions by actual or threatened litigation, affecting management's willingness to make complete disclosures, self-interest and intimidation threats are created. The significance of the threats shall be evaluated and safeguards applied when necessary to eliminate the threats or reduce them to an acceptable level. Examples of such safeguards include: removing the individual involved in litigation from the audit or having a professional review the work performed. If such safeguards do not reduce the threats to an acceptable level, the only appropriate action is to withdraw from, or decline, the audit engagement.

■ Independence Requirements for Assurance Engagements that Are not Audit or Review Engagements (Section 291)

The IESBA Code of Ethics for Professional Accountants Section 291 (see Illustration 3.4 for contents) addresses independence requirements for assurance engagements that are not audit or review engagements. If the assurance client is also an audit or review

ILLUSTRATION 3.4

Section 291: Independence – Other Assurance Engagements

CONTENTS

Paragraph

client, the requirements in the prior section of this chapter (and Ethics Code Section 290) also apply to the firm, network firms and members of the audit or review team. We will not explore the non-financial statement audit or review assurance ethics in this book.

3.7 Part C – Professional Accountants in Business

Part C of the IESBA Code describes how the conceptual framework contained in Part A applies in certain situations to professional accountants in business. Part C also addresses circumstances in which compliance with the fundamental principles may be compromised under the topics of potential conflicts, preparation and reporting information, acting with sufficient expertise, financial interests, and inducements. Part C does not contain discussion of independence. This is because accountants in business do not provide assurance in any form and do not play a role in the society at large. Also, because accountants in business are employees it is difficult to require independence from the organisation that is the source of their income.

A professional accountant in business may be a salaried employee, a partner, director, an owner manager, a volunteer or another working for one or more employing organisation. Professional accountants in business may be responsible for the preparation and reporting of financial and other information or for providing effective financial management and competent advice on a variety of business-related matters. The accountant has a responsibility to further the legitimate aims of the accountant's employing organisation. A professional accountant in business is expected to encourage an ethics-based culture in an employing organisation that emphasises the importance that senior management places on ethical behaviour. **A professional accountant in business shall not knowingly engage in any business, occupation, or activity that impairs or might impair integrity, objectivity or the good reputation of the profession and as a result would be incompatible with the fundamental principles.**[29]

As we discussed in the Part A section of this chapter, compliance with the fundamental principles may potentially be threatened by a broad range of circumstances and relationships. Threats fall into one or more of the following categories: self-interest, self-review, advocacy, familiarity and intimidation.

Self-interest threats are perhaps the most frequent for a professional accountant in business:

■ Holding a financial interest in, or receiving a loan or guarantee from the employing organisation.
■ Participating in incentive compensation arrangements offered by the employing organisation.
■ Inappropriate personal use of corporate assets.
■ Concern over employment security.
■ Commercial pressure from outside the employing organisation.

Some examples of circumstances leading to self-review and advocacy threats for a professional accountant in business can be mentioned. Determining the appropriate accounting treatment for a business combination after performing the feasibility study that supported the acquisition decision creates a self-review threat. Any false or misleading statements made when furthering the goals and objectives of their employing organisations creates an advocacy threat.

Examples of circumstances that may create familiarity threats for professional accountants in business include:

■ Being responsible for the employing organisation's financial reporting when an immediate or close family member employed by the entity makes decisions that affect the entity's financial reporting.
■ Long association with business contacts influencing business decisions.
■ Accepting a gift or preferential treatment, unless the value is trivial and inconsequential.

Examples of circumstances that may create intimidation threats for a professional accountant in business include:

■ Threat of dismissal or replacement of the accountant or a close or immediate family member over a disagreement about the application of an accounting principle or the way in which financial information is to be reported.

■ A dominant personality attempting to influence the decision making process, for example with regard to the awarding of contracts or the application of an accounting principle.

As previously discussed in the Part A section of this chapter, safeguards that may eliminate or reduce threats to an acceptable level fall into two broad categories: (1) safeguards created by the profession, legislation or regulation; and (2) safeguards in the work environment. Safeguards in the work environment for the professional accountant include:

■ The employing organisation's systems of corporate oversight or other oversight structures.
■ The employing organisation's ethics and conduct programmes.
■ Recruitment procedures in the employing organisation emphasising the importance of employing high calibre competent staff.
■ Strong internal controls.
■ Appropriate disciplinary processes.
■ Leadership that stresses the importance of ethical behaviour and the expectation that employees will act in an ethical manner.
■ Policies and procedures to implement and monitor the quality of employee performance.
■ Timely communication of the employing organisation's policies and procedures, including any changes to them, to all employees and appropriate training and education on such policies and procedures.
■ Policies and procedures to empower and encourage employees to communicate to senior levels within the employing organisation any ethical issues that concern them without fear of retribution.
■ Consultation with another appropriate professional accountant.

In those extreme situations where all available safeguards have been exhausted and it is not possible to reduce the threat to an acceptable level, a professional accountant in business may conclude that it is appropriate to resign from the employing organisation.

■ Potential Conflicts (Sec. 310)

Although, this section is written for accountants in business it may also be particularly interesting for accountants in public practice because understanding conflicts in the work place may give the public accountant a perspective on the quality of the accounting numbers. There may be times when a professional accountant's responsibilities to an employing organisation and professional obligations to comply with the fundamental principles are in conflict. Pressure may come from the employing organisation to act contrary to law or regulation or to technical or professional standards. Pressure may be exerted to facilitate unethical or illegal earnings management strategies, to lie or otherwise intentionally mislead others, in particular auditors or regulators, to be associated with an employer report (financial statements, tax compliance, securities reports, etc.) that materially misrepresents the facts.

Safeguards applied should be applied to eliminate or reduce these threats to an acceptable level, for example:

■ Obtaining advice, where appropriate, from within the employing organisation, an independent professional adviser or a relevant professional body.

■ Using a formal dispute resolution process within the employing organisation.
■ Seeking legal advice.

■ Other Sections of Part C (Sections 320, 330, 340 and 350)

There are other sections in Part C which address specific aspects of the work of professional accountants in business. These sections include discussion of preparation and reporting of information (Sec. 320), acting with sufficient expertise (Sec. 330), financial interests (Sec. 340) and inducements (Sec. 350). We will not discuss these sections in this chapter.

Concept and a Company 3.4

Accountant Falsifies Accounts for Bosses at WorldCom

Concept	Ethics and the employed accountant – caving in to pressure from your bosses.
Story	On 10 October 2002 the US attorney's office announced that Betty Vinson, former Director of Management Reporting at WorldCom, had pleaded guilty to two criminal counts of conspiracy and securities fraud, charges that carry a maximum sentence of 15 years in prison. One year later, 10 October 2003, she was charged with breaking Oklahoma securities laws by entering false information on company documents – a charge that potentially carries a ten-year prison sentence (English, 2003).

Over the course of six quarters Vinson made illegal entries to bolster WorldCom's profits at the request of her superiors. Each time she worried. Each time she hoped it was the last time. At the end of 18 months she had helped falsify at least $3.7 billion in profits (Lacter, 2003).

In 1996, Ms Vinson got a job in the international accounting division at WorldCom making $50,000 a year. Ms Vinson developed a reputation for being hardworking and diligent. Within two years Ms Vinson was promoted to be a senior manager in WorldCom's corporate accounting division where she helped compile quarterly results and analysed the company's operating expenses and loss reserves. Ten employees reported to her (Pulliam, 2003).

Work began to change in mid-2000. WorldCom had a looming problem: its huge line costs – fees paid to lease portions of other companies' telephone networks – were rising as a percentage of the company's revenue. Chief Executive Bernard Ebers and Chief Financial Officer Scott Sullivan informed Wall Street in July that the company's results for the second half of the year would fall below expectations.

A scramble ensued to try to reduce expenses on the company's financial statements enough to meet Wall Street's expectations for the quarter. But the accounting department was able to scrape together only $50 million, far from the hundreds of millions it would take to hit the company's profit target. In October, her boss told Vinson to dip into a reserve account set aside to cover line costs and other items for WorldCom's telecommunications unit and use $828 million to reduce expenses, thereby increasing profits (Pulliam, 2003).

Ms Vinson was shocked by her bosses' proposal and the huge sum involved. She worried that the adjustment wasn't proper. She agreed to go along. But afterwards Ms Vinson suffered pangs of guilt. On 26 October, the same day the company publicly reported its

Accountant Falsifies Accounts for Bosses at WorldCom (continued)

third-quarter results, she told her colleagues who were also involved that she was planning to resign. A few suggested that they, too, would quit.

CFO Sullivan heard of the mutiny in accounting and called Vinson and other employees into his office. He explained that he was trying to fix the company's financial problems. Think of it as an aircraft carrier, he said; we have planes in the air. Let's get the planes landed. Once they are landed, if you still want to leave, then leave. But not while the planes are in the air. Mr Sullivan assured them that nothing they had done was illegal and that he would assume all responsibility. He noted that the accounting switch wouldn't be repeated (Pulliam, 2003).

That night, she told her husband about the meeting and her worries over the accounting. Mr Vinson urged her to quit. But in the end, she decided not to quit. She was the family's chief support, earning more than her husband. She, her husband and daughter depended on her health insurance. She was anxious about entering the job market as a middle-aged worker.

By the end of the first quarter of 2001, it was clear Ms Vinson could find no large pools of reserves to transfer to solve the profit shortfall. Sullivan suggested that rather than count line costs as part of operating expenses in the quarterly report, they would shift $771 million in line costs to capital-expenditure accounts which would result in decreased expenses and increased assets and retained earnings. Accounting rules make it clear that line costs are to be counted as operating leases, not capital assets.

Ms Vinson felt trapped. That night she reviewed her options with her husband and decided to put together a resumé and begin looking for a job. Nevertheless, she made the entries transferring the $771 million, backdating the entries to February by changing the dates in the computer for the quarter. She faced the same dilemma in the second, third and fourth quarters of 2001. Each subsequent quarter she made more fraudulent entries (Pulliam, 2003).

Ms Vinson began waking up in the middle of the night, unable to go back to sleep because of her anxiety. Her family and friends began to notice she was losing weight and her face took on a slightly gaunt look. At work she withdrew from co-workers, afraid she might let something slip. In early 2002, she received a promotion, from senior manager to director, along with a raise that brought her annual salary to about $80,000 (Pulliam, 2003).

In March 2002 the SEC made requests for information from WorldCom and Cynthia Cooper, head of internal auditing (see Chapter 1), started asking questions. Ms Vinson and two other accountants hired an attorney and told their story to federal officials from the FBI, SEC and US attorney, hoping to get immunity from prosecution for their testimony.

On 1 August 2002, Ms Vinson received a call from her attorney telling her that the prosecutors in New York would probably indict her. In the end, they viewed the information Ms Vinson had supplied at the meeting with federal officials as more of a confession than a tip-off to wrongdoing. Within hours, WorldCom fired her because of the expected indictment. The only thing she was allowed to take with her was a plant from her desk (Pulliam, 2003).

Two of her colleagues pleaded guilty to securities fraud. Unable to afford the legal bill that would result from a lengthy trial, Betty Vinson decided to negotiate a guilty plea as well.

Discussion Questions	■ Was Betty Vinson justified in her actions because they were at the request of her superiors? Why?
	■ If you were in Ms Vinson's situation, what would you have done?
References	English, S., 2003, 'City – WorldCom Boss on Fraud Charges', *The Daily Telegraph*, 4 September.
	Lacter, M., 2003, 'Looking the Other Way (Comment) (Editorial)', *Los Angeles Business Journal*, 30 June.
	Pulliam, S., 2003, 'Over the Line: A Staffer Ordered To Commit Fraud Baulked, Then Caved – Pushed by WorldCom Bosses, Accountant Betty Vinson Helped Cook the Books – A Confession at the Marriott', *The Wall Street Journal*, 23 June, p. 1.

3.8 Enforcement of Ethical Requirements

The effectiveness of enforcing ethical standards varies from country to country. In many countries an auditor who violates the ethical standard may be disciplined by law or by the professional organisation. The penalties range from a reprimand to expulsion or fine. In the USA expulsion from a state society or the American Institute of Certified Public Accountants (AICPA) does not mean that the expelled member cannot practice public accounting because only the state boards of public accountancy have the authority to revoke a license. As illustrated in the case of Arthur Andersen,[30] if a company is convicted of a felony, the US Security and Exchange Commission (SEC) prohibits them from auditing publicly traded companies. In other countries, such as Japan, France and Germany, government often takes a formal role in the enforcement of the standards.

International Ethics Standards Board of Accountants (IESBA) has no authority to require disciplinary action for violation of the Code of Ethics. IESBA relies on legislation or the constitution of professional bodies in each country.

Disciplinary action ordinarily arises from such issues as: failure to observe the required standard of professional care, skills or competence; non-compliance with rules of ethics; and discreditable or dishonourable conduct. Sanctions commonly imposed by disciplinary bodies include: reprimand, fine, payment of costs, withdrawal of practising rights, suspension, and expulsion from membership. Other sanctions can include a warning, the refund of the fee charged to the client, additional education, and the work to be completed by another member at the disciplined member's expense.

3.9 Summary

The attitude and behaviour of professional accountants in providing auditing and assurance services have an impact on the economic well-being of their community and country. Accountants can remain in this advantageous position only by continuing to provide the public with these unique services at a level that demonstrates that the public confidence is well-founded. The standards of the accountancy profession are heavily determined by the public interest. Therefore, a professional accountant's responsibility is not exclusively to satisfy the needs of an individual client or employer.

The International Ethics Standards Board of Accountants (IESBA) Ethics Code is divided into three parts:

■ Part A establishes the fundamental principles of professional ethics for all professional accountants and provides a conceptual framework that is applied to: identify threats to compliance with the fundamental principles; evaluate the significance of the threats identified; and apply safeguards, when necessary, to eliminate the threats or reduce them to an acceptable level.
■ Parts B and C describe how the conceptual framework applies in certain situations. They provide examples of safeguards that may be appropriate to address threats to compliance with the fundamental principles. They also describe situations where safeguards are not available to address the threats. Part B applies only to those professional accountants in public practice; and Part C applies to employed professional accountants.

Rather than a list of rules that must be obeyed to be an ethical accountant, the so-called 'rule-based' approach which holds sway in many countries, the IESBA and IFAC have chosen to use a 'conceptual framework' approach. A conceptual framework requires a professional accountant to identify, evaluate and address threats to compliance with the fundamental principles, rather than merely comply with a set of specific rules which may be arbitrary.

The fundamental principles of ethics are described in Part A of the Code. They are: integrity, objectivity, professional competence and due care, confidentiality and professional behaviour. Part A of the Code offers further discussion on these principles. Each concept is the topic of subsequent Sections (110–150) in the Code.

Compliance with the fundamental principles may potentially be threatened by a broad range of circumstances and relationships. The nature and significance of the threats may differ depending on whether the audit client is a public interest entity, to an assurance client that is not an audit client, or to a non-assurance client. The conceptual framework of the IESBA Code discusses ways to identify threats to fundamental principles, determine the significance of those threats, and, if they are significant, identify and apply safeguards to reduce or eliminate the threats. Threats fall into one or more of the following categories: self-interest; self-review; advocacy; familiarity; and intimidation.

When threats are identified, other than those that are clearly insignificant, appropriate safeguards should be identified and applied to eliminate the threats or reduce them to an acceptable level. If elimination or reduction is not possible the auditor should decline or terminate the engagement. When deciding what safeguards should be applied one must consider what would be unacceptable to an informed third party having knowledge of all relevant information. Safeguards fall into two broad categories: (1) safeguards created by the profession, legislation or regulation; and (2) safeguards in the work environment.

Whereas the ethics guidance discussed above is applicable to all professional accountants. Part B of IESBA's Code of Ethics is only applicable to accountants in public practice. A professional accountant in public practice is a professional accountant, irrespective of functional classification (for example, audit, tax or consulting) in a firm that provides professional services. Part B describes how the conceptual framework contained in Part A applies in certain situations to professional accountants in public practice. Ethical guidance for accountants in public practice is offered in the areas of: professional appointment, conflicts of interest, second opinions, fees and other remuneration, marketing professional services, gifts and hospitality, custody of client assets, objectivity, and independence for both audit and review engagements and other assurance engagements.

An auditor who is asked to replace another auditor, or who is considering a new engagement for a company currently audited by another auditor, must consider whether there are any reasons, professional or otherwise, for not accepting the engagement. Determining possible reasons for not accepting a new client may require direct communication with the existing auditor to establish the facts and circumstances regarding the proposed change in auditors.

Across the world, national rules on auditors' independence differ in several respects such as: the scope of persons to whom independence rules should apply; the kind of financial, business or other relationships that an auditor may have with an audit client; the type of non-audit services that can and cannot be provided to an audit client; and the safeguards which should be used. The European Commission has issued independence standards to be applied throughout the EU. The USA enacted the Sarbanes–Oxley Act of 2002 that describes independence requirements of US auditors.

The IESBA Code of Ethics for Professional Accountants, Part B Section 290, addresses the independence requirements for audit engagements and review engagements. Independence requirements for assurance engagements that are not audit or review engagements are addressed in Section 291. The Code discusses independence in assurance services in terms of a principles-based, conceptual approach that takes into account threats to independence, accepted safeguards and the public interest.

Accountants must not only maintain an independent attitude in fulfilling their responsibilities, but the users of financial statements must have confidence in that independence. These two objectives are frequently identified as 'independence of mind' and 'independence in appearance.' Independence of mind (historically referred to as independence in fact) exists when the accountant is able to maintain an unbiased attitude throughout the audit, so being objective and impartial, whereas independence in appearance is the result of others' interpretations of this independence. The Ethics Code defines the two views. Independence of mind is the state of mind that permits the expression of a conclusion without being affected by influences that compromise professional judgement, thereby allowing an individual to act with integrity and exercise objectivity and professional scepticism. Independence in appearance is the avoidance of facts and circumstances that are so significant that a reasonable and informed third party would be likely to conclude, weighing all the specific facts and circumstances, that a firm's, or a member of the audit team's, integrity, objectivity or professional scepticism has been compromised.

The Ethics Code discusses independence in assurance services in terms of a principles-based approach that takes into account threats to independence, accepted safeguards and the public interest. The section states principles that members of assurance teams should use to identify threats to independence (self-interest, self-review, advocacy, familiarity and intimidation threats), evaluate the significance of those threats, and, if the threats are other than clearly insignificant, identify and apply safeguards created by the profession, legislation or regulation, safeguards within the assurance client, and safeguards within the firm's own systems and procedures to eliminate the threats or reduce them to an acceptable level.

Independence for audit and review services and possible threats and safeguards are given in detail in Section 290, the largest section of the Code. Review and audit independence is discussed in on the topics of conceptual framework, network firms, public interest entities, documentation, engagement period, financial interests, loans and guarantees, business relationships, family and personal relationships, employment with an audit client, temporary staff assignments, recent service with an audit client, serving as director or officer of an audit client, long association of senior personnel with audit clients, and other topics not covered in this chapter, including mergers and acquisitions and related entities. Non-assurance services discuss safeguards and threats of no-assurance services to the audit client including the following topics: management responsibilities, preparing accounting records and financial statements, taxation services, internal audit services, IT systems services, valuation and litigation support services, legal services, recruiting services, and corporate finance services. The independence section ends with a discussion of general topics including fees, compensation and evaluation policies, gifts and hospitality, actual or threatened litigation, and restricted reports (not discussed in this chapter).

Part C of the IESBA Code describes how the conceptual framework contained in Part A applies in certain situations to professional accountants in business. A professional accountant in business may be a salaried employee, a partner, director, an owner manager, a volunteer or another working for one or more employing organisation. Professional accountants in business may be responsible for the preparation and reporting of financial and other information or for providing effective financial management and competent advice on a variety of business-related matters. The accountant has a responsibility to further the legitimate aims of the accountant's employing organisation. A professional accountant in business is expected to encourage an ethics-based culture in an employing organisation that emphasises the importance that senior management places on ethical behaviour.

The effectiveness of enforcing ethical standards varies from country to country. In many countries an auditor who violates the ethical standard may be disciplined by law or by the professional organisation. The penalties range from a reprimand to expulsion or fine. In the USA expulsion from a state society or the American Institute of Certified Public Accountants (AICPA) does not mean that the expelled member cannot practise public accounting because only the state boards of public accountancy have the authority to revoke a licence. As illustrated in the case of Arthur Andersen, if a company is convicted of a felony, the US Security and Exchange Commission (SEC) prohibits them from auditing publicly traded companies. In other countries, such as Japan, France and Germany, government often takes a formal role in the enforcement of the standards.

3.10 Questions, Exercises and Cases

QUESTIONS

3.2 What Are Ethics?

3-1 What is ethics?

3-2 What ethical principles incorporate characteristics used by society as good moral behaviour?

3-3 According to the IESBA ethics code, what is the ethics objective of the accountancy profession?

3.3 The International Ethics Standards Board of Accountants (IESBA) Code of Ethics for Professional Accountants

3-4 Describe each of the three parts of the IESBA Ethics Code.

3-5 Name and define the five fundamental principles of ethics applicable to *all* accountants.

3.4 Part A – General Application of the IESBA Code of Ethics for Professional Accountants

3-6 What are the Fundamental Principles an accountant must observe to achieve the objectives of the accounting profession according the to IFAC ethics guidelines? Briefly discuss them.

3-7 Confidential client information may generally be disclosed only with the permission of the client. What are the exceptions to this rule?

3-8 Can an accountant claim that the returns he prepares are always acceptable to the taxing authorities? Why?

3-9 Name and define the basic categories of threats.

3-10 Safeguards fall into two broad categories. What are the categories? Give examples of each.

3.5 Part B – Ethics Applicable to Professional Accountants in Public Practice

3-11 Give an example of a threat and corresponding safeguard for each of the following activities of a professional accountant in public practice.
A. Professional appointment
B. Conflicts of interest
C. Second opinions
D. Fees and other types of remuneration
E. Marketing professional services
F. Gifts and hospitality
G. Custody of client assets
H. Objectivity – all services

3-12 What are contingent fees? Give two examples and explain why accountants in public practice should or should not take them.

3-13 An auditor who is asked to replace another auditor, or who is considering a new engagement for a company currently audited by another auditor must consider what safeguards are appropriate. Discuss which safeguards would apply to such circumstances.

3.6 Independence – Audit and Review Engagements (Section 290)

3-14 Discuss the differences between the European Commission Council Directive on independence and the Sarbanes–Oxley Act's view of auditor independence.

3-15 What is the difference between 'independence in mind' and 'independence in appearance'? State two activities that may not affect independence in fact but are likely to affect independence in appearance.

3-16 Describe two threats and related safeguards associated with each of the following independence activities (Code Section):

A. Documentation of independence (290.29)
B. Engagement Period (290.30)
C. Financial interests (290.102)
D. Business, family and personal relationships (290.124–290.150)
E. Provision of non-assurance services to audit clients (290.156–290.216)
F. Fees (290.220–290.224)
G. Compensation and evaluation policies (290.228)
H. Gifts and hospitality (290.230)
I. Actual or threatened litigation (290.231)

3-17 Name some forms of financial involvement with a client that may affect independence.

3.7 Part C – Professional Accountants in Business

3-18 What self-interest threats are perhaps the most frequent for a professional accountant in business?

3-19 What should an employed accountant do if they feel they are being asked to do something that is contradictory to accounting standards?

3.8 Enforcement of Ethical Requirements

3-20 Can IESBA discipline an accountant for violation of the Code of Ethics? What sanctions are commonly imposed by disciplinary bodies?

PROBLEMS AND EXERCISES

3.2 What Are Ethics?

3-21 **Ethics Guidelines.** Why is there a need for an ethics guideline for professional accountants? Explain. In what ways should the ethics code for accountants be different from that of other groups such as physicians or attorneys?

3.3 The International Ethics Standards Board of Accountants (IESBA) Code of Ethics for Professional Accountants

3-22 Discuss the differences between a conceptual framework and a rules-based approach to ethics.

3.4 Part A – General Application of the IESBA Code of Ethics for Professional Accountants

3-23 **Violations of Code of Ethics.** For each of the following situations involving relations between auditors and the companies they audit indicate whether it violates IESBA's Code of Ethics for Professional Accountants and the rationale for the applicable guideline.

A. Yaping Lei, CPA, discloses confidential information in a peer review of the firm's quality control procedures.
B. Frank Smith, CPA, prepares and submits a tax return to the Internal Revenue Service which he believes omits income his client receives from trading goods on eBay.com.
C. El-Hussein El-Masery, CA, is auditing a company in Nigeria that has offered to send him and his wife on a holiday in Hawaii for two weeks.
D. Tabula Gonzales, CP, says in an interview in the local paper that Emilio Rios, CP, misleads his clients about the quality of his audit work.

3.5 Part B – Ethics Applicable to Professional Accountants in Public Practice

3-24 Professional Accountants in Public Practice. Galati and Brambila formed a corporation called Financial Fitness Systems, each woman taking 50 per cent of the authorised common stock. Galati is a Dottore Commercialista (CONSOB), a public accountant, and Brambila is an insurance underwriter. The corporation provides auditing and tax services under Galati's direction and insurance services under Branbila's direction. The opening of the corporation's office was announced by a 15 cm, 2-column announcement in the local newspaper.

One of the corporation's first audit clients was the Galore Company. Galore had total assets of €923,820,000 and total liabilities of €415,719,000. In the course of her examination, Galati found that Galore's building with a book value of €369,528,000 was pledged as security for a ten-year term note in the amount of €307,940,000. Galore's statements did not mention that the building was pledged as security for the ten-year term note. However, as the failure to disclose the lien did not affect either the value of the assets or the amount of the liabilities and her examination was satisfactory in all other respects, Galati rendered an unqualified opinion on Galore's financial statements. About two months after the date of her opinion, Galati learnt that an insurance company was planning to loan Galore €230,955,000 in the form of a first mortgage note on the building. Galati had Brambila notify the insurance company of the fact that Galore's building was pledged as security for the term note.

Shortly after the events described above, Galati was charged with a violation of professional ethics.

Required:
Identify and discuss the ethical implications of those acts by Galati that were threats according to IESBA's Code of Ethics for Professional Accountants.

3.6 Independence Requirements

3-25 Independence in Fact and Appearance. Auditors must not only appear to be independent; they must also be independent in fact.

Required:
A. Explain the concept of auditor's independence as it applies to third-party reliance upon financial statements.
B. (1) What determines whether or not an auditor is independent in fact?
   (2) What determines whether or not an auditor appears to be independent?
C. Explain how an auditor may be independent in fact but not appear to be independent.
D. Would an accountant in public practice be considered independent for a review of the financial statement of (1) a church in which the accountant is serving as treasurer without compensation? (2) A club for which the accountant's spouse is serving as a treasurer-bookkeeper if the accountant is not to receive a fee for the review.

3-26 Independence and Gifts. Samantha Seekineau, Soma Orkoton Logiston (SOL), is in charge of the audit of Olympic Fashions. Five young assistant accountants are working with Seekineau on the engagement, and several are avid wind-surfers. Olympic Fashions owns two villas on Mikonos, which it uses to entertain clients. The comptroller of Olympic Fashions has told Seekineau that she and her audit staff are welcome to use the villas at no charge any time they are not already in use. How should Seekineau respond to this offer? Explain.

3.7 Part C – Professional Accountants in Business

3-27 Jemmy Le, CPA, worked for BarrelOn corporation, a manufacturer of wine and beverage oak barrels. He has been a good employee, so when he got married the CEO of BarrelOn loaned him the down payment for a house. Instead of a bonus last year, the company gave Mr Le a compensation arrangement that is based on the profits of the company. The company also gave Mr Le a Lexus RX350 for business use which makes a good ride when he goes skiing on vacation. Part of the reason for Mr Le's success is the influence of his step-brother who is on the board of directors.

Required:
Describe any threats that Mr Le's working relationship may have and what safeguards may be put in place to compensate.

CASES

3-28 **Ethical Issues.** The following situation involves Kevin Smith, staff accountant with the local CPA firm of Hobb, Mary, and Khang (HM&K). The bookkeeper of Mirage Manufacturing Company resigned three months ago and has not yet been replaced. As a result, Mirage's transactions have not been recorded and the books are not up to date. Mirage must prepare interim financial statements to comply with terms of a loan agreement, but cannot do so until the books are posted. To help them with this matter, Mirage turns to HM&K, their independent auditors. Mirage wants Kevin Smith to update their books because Kevin had audited them last year.

Required:
A. Identify the ethical issues that are involved.
B. Discuss whether there has or has not been any violation of ethical conduct.

3.11 Notes

1 Other definitions of ethics are (1) the discipline dealing with what is good and bad and with moral duty and obligation – Merriam-Webster Dictionary, (2) the moral correctness of specified conduct – for instance, the ethics of euthanasia, or (3) the branch of knowledge that deals with moral principles – Wikipedia.

2 Developed by the Josephson Institute for the Advancement of Ethics, a US not-for-profit foundation to encourage ethical conduct of professionals in the fields of government, law, medicine, business, accounting and journalism.

3 Internet Encyclopedia of Philosophy: **http://www.iep.utm.edu/ethics**.

4 Ibid.

5 An assurance service or assurance engagement is an engagement in which a practitioner expresses a conclusion designed to enhance the degree of confidence of the intended users other than the responsible party about the outcome of the evaluation or measurement of a subject matter against criteria.

6 International Ethics Standards Board of Accountants (IESBA), 2010, Introduction – Objectives, para. 100.1, *Handbook of the Code of Ethics for Professional Accountants 2010 Edition*, International Federation of Accountants, New York.

7 The Dutch version (or translation) of the Code of Ethics distinguishes between Part B1 and Part B2, making a distinction between accountants (auditors) in public practice and internal accountants (auditors) as opposed to Part B and C. Other translations may have similar distinctions. The original code does not make this distinction.

8 This book and the Code of Ethics (implicitly) assume a scalability of threats to the fundamental principles. One can challenge whether this is possible regarding fundamental principles.

9 Ehrliner, J., Thomas Gilovich and Lee Ross, 2005, 'Peering into the Bias Blind Spot: People's Assessments of Bias in Themselves and Others', p. 2, *Personality and Social Psychology Bulletin*, 31, pp. 1–13.

10 Project Implicit website: **https://implicit.harvard.edu/implicit/**.

11 A subject matter of an assurance is the topic about which the assurance is conducted.

12 International Auditing and Assurance Standards Board (IAASB), 2012, International Standard on Auditing 220 (ISA 220) 'Quality Control For An Audit Of Financial Statements', *Handbook of International Quality Control, Auditing, Review, Other Assurance, and Related Services Pronouncements*, 2012 edn., Volume 1, International Federation of Accountants, New York.

13 International Auditing and Assurance Standards Board (IAASB), 2012, International Standard on Auditing 620 (ISA 620) 'Using the Work of an Auditor's Expert', *Handbook of International Quality Control, Auditing, Review, Other Assurance, and Related Services Pronouncements*, 2012 edn, Volume 1, International Federation of Accountants, New York.

14 Existing auditor is the auditor who is currently holding an audit or assurance services appointment with the prospective client.

15 Council of European Communities, Eighth Council Directive of 10 April 1994, Article 24, *Official Journal of the European Communities*, No. L126, 12.5.1984, pp. 20–26.

16 Statutory audits are audits established by law.

17 European Union Committee on Auditing, 2002, Commission Recommendation, Statutory Auditors' Independence in the EU: A Set of Fundamental Principles, 2002/590/EC, *Official Journal of the European Communities*, 19.7.2002, pp. L191/22–L191/97.

18 Ibid., Commission Recommendation, para. 11.

19 The Senate and House of Representatives of the United States of America, Sarbanes–Oxley Act of 2002, Public Law, 107–204, 30 July 2002.

20 SEC, 2003, *Final Rule: Strengthening the Commission's Requirements Regarding Auditor Independence*; Rel. Nos. 33-8183, 34-47265; 35-27642; IC-25915; IA-2103; File No. S7-49-02, Securities and Exchange Commission, January 28.

21 Barnier, Michel, 2012, 'Audit Reform: Michel Barnier', The Parliament.com: **http://www.theparliament .com/latest-news/article/newsarticle/audit-reform-michel-barnier/**/#.Un70K-mKpQE

22 European Commission, 2010, Green Paper, 'Audit Policy: Lessons from the Crisis', October, Brussels.

23 Pendergast, Marilyn A., 'Strengthening the Commission's Requirements Regarding Auditor Independence: file s7-49-02', International Federation of Accountants, New York, 10 January 2003.

24 A network firm is a firm or entity that belongs to a network. A network is a larger structure that is aimed at cooperation, and is clearly aimed at profit or cost-sharing or shares common ownership, control or management, common quality control policies and procedures, common business strategy, the use of a common brand name, or a significant part of professional resources.

25 IESBA Code of Ethics for Professional Accountants, paragraph 290.30.

26 IESBA Code of Ethics for Professional Accountants, paragraphs 290.162–164 describe what management responsibilities might be.

27 IESBA Code of Ethics for Professional Accountants, paragraph 290.174 describes emergency situations.

28 IESBA Code of Ethics for Professional Accountants, paragraph 290.227.

29 IESBA Code of Ethics for Professional Accountants, paragraph 300.6.

30 Arthur Andersen was one of the largest auditing firms in the world (one of the Big Five) when they were convicted by the US Department of Justice of obstruction of justice (a felony) when in 2001, the Houston, Texas, branch shredded documents relating to their audit client, Enron Corporation. (See Concept and a Company 2.2 in Chapter 2.)

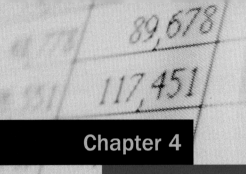

Chapter 4

AN AUDITOR'S SERVICES

4.1 Learning Objectives

After studying this chapter, you should be able to:

1 Understand the general definition of assurance services.

2 Identify the assurance and non-assurance services normally performed by auditors.

3 Explain what an assurance engagement entails.

4 Describe the five elements exhibited by all assurance engagements.

5 Know the various subject matters that can be covered in an assurance engagement.

6 Distinguish between the different suitable criteria applicable to an assurance service.

7 Understand what distinguishes a review from a compilation.

8 Understand the place of professional judgement in audits.

9 Describe professional scepticism.

10 Give the inherent limitations of an audit.

11 Discuss the requirements of International Standard on Quality Control #1.

4.2 International Framework for Auditor Services

Auditor services are work that an audit firm performs for their clients. Except for consulting services, the work that auditors do is under the guidance of engagement standards set by the International Auditing and Assurance Standards Board (IAASB). All auditor services standards have as their basis the IESBA Code of Ethics (see Chapter 3) and International Standards on Quality Control (ISQC). In this chapter we discuss the basic requirements of assurance engagements, audits of historical financial information, professional judgement, professional scepticism, inherent limitation and quality control. We will give details on other assurance engagements including sustainability, internal controls and review engagements and non-assurance engagements (such as compilation in Chapter 14). Consulting services engagements will not be discussed in this book.

■ IAASB'S Technical Pronouncements

Illustration 4.1 shows the general structure of IAASB'S technical pronouncements.

Code of Ethics and ISQC

All auditor services standards have as their basis the Code of Ethics for Professional Accountants (the IESBA Code) issued by the International Ethics Standards Board of Accountants (IESBA) (discussed in Chapter 3 Ethics for Professional Accountants) and International Standard on Quality Control 1[1] (ISQC # 1) (see Chapter 1 'International

---

ILLUSTRATION 4.1

Assurance Engagements and Related Services

Scope of services addressed by the IAASB			
Assurance engagements		**Non-assurance engagements**	
Audit and review of historical financial information	**Other assurance engagements**	**Agreed-upon procedures**	**Other engagements**
Financial statements / Other financial reports			
ISA 200-2999	**ISAE 3000-3999**	**ISRS 4400**	

Auditing Overview'). The Code has been employed by IFAC from the early days. Quality control standards are currently being created by the IAASB.

Two Audit Services Frameworks – 'Assurance' and 'Related Services'

Some engagement standards are based on 'International Framework for Assurance Engagements' (assurance engagements), and others result from the 'Related Services Framework' (related services engagements). Three sets of standards (ISAs, ISREs and ISAEs) share the **assurance engagement** framework and one standard set (ISRS) is based on the related services framework. ISAs, ISREs, ISAEs and ISRSs are collectively referred to as the IAASB's Engagement Standards.

IAASB's Engagement Standards

The IAASB engagement standards encompass the following:[2]

- International Standards on Auditing (ISAs) are to be applied in the audit of historical financial information.
- International Standards on Review Engagements (ISREs) are to be applied in the **review** of historical financial information.
- International Standards on Assurance Engagements (ISAEs) are to be applied in assurance engagements other than audits or reviews of historical financial information.
- International Standards on Related Services (ISRSs) are to be applied to **compilation engagements**, engagements to apply **agreed upon procedures** to information, and other related services engagements as specified by the IAASB.

Assurance Engagements for Audits and Reviews for Historical Financial Information (ISAs and ISREs)

International Standards on Auditing (ISA) 200 'Overall Objectives of the Independent Auditor and the Conduct of an Audit in Accordance With International Standards on Auditing' describes the main concepts applicable to audit, review or **special purpose** frameworks. Financial statement audit standards are described in ISA 200–799. Special purpose frameworks and other examinations of historical financial information are given in ISA 800-899. Review standards are ISREs 2000–2699.

Assurance Engagements Other than Audits or Reviews of Historical Financial Information (ISAEs)

International Standards on Assurance Engagements (ISAE) 3000 'Assurance Engagements Other than Audits or Reviews of Historical Financial Information' describes concepts applicable to assurance services whose subject matter is not related to historical financial information. (These audit services will be discussed in Chapter 14 'Other Assurance and Non-Assurance Engagements'.)

The ISAE standards are divided into two parts:

1 ISAEs 3000–3399 which are topics that apply to all assurance engagements.
2 ISAEs 3400–3699 which are subject specific standards, for example standards relating to examination of **prospective financial information.**

The subject matter of ISAEs 3400–3699 now includes examination of prospective financial information (ISAE 3400) and assurance reports on controls at a service organisation

(ISAE 3402). However, in future it might include non-financial information (e.g. corporate governance, statistical, environmental), systems and processes (e.g. internal control (such as that required under the Sarbanes-Oxley Act), corporate governance, environmental management systems), and behaviour (corporate governance, compliance, and human resources practices). Right now, because IAASB does not set these standards, reports of social, environmental and economic assurance engagements are commonly based on a whole variety of established criteria, for example the Global Reporting Initiative (GRI) Sustainability Reporting Guidelines.[3] (These audit services will be discussed in Chapter 14 'Other Assurance and Non-Assurance Engagements'.)

Other Engagements Performed by Auditors

Not all engagements performed by auditors are assurance engagements. Other engagements frequently performed by auditors that do not meet the definition of an assurance engagement and which are therefore not covered by the framework for assurance engagements include:

- engagements covered by International Standards for Related Services (ISRSs);
- the preparation of tax returns where no conclusion conveying assurance is expressed;
- consulting engagements such as tax consulting, or engagements in which a practitioner is engaged to testify as an expert witness in accounting, auditing, taxation or other matters, given stipulated facts.

Related Services Framework (ISRSs)

Engagements covered by International Standards on Related Services ISRS are based on the 'Related Services Framework' – a framework that is still in the development stage at the IAASB. Standards under this framework (ISRSs) are applied currently to two audit services: engagements to perform agreed-upon procedures regarding financial information (ISRS 4400) and compilation engagements (ISRS 4410). Compilations offer no assurance whatsoever. On agreed-upon procedures no assurance is expressed. Instead, users of the report assess for themselves the procedures and findings reported by the auditor and draw their own conclusions from the auditor's audit procedures in a very limited 'agreed upon' area with a proscribed set of users. (These audit services will be discussed in Chapter 14 'Other Assurance and Non-Assurance Engagements'.)

Guidance and Practical Assistance Provided by Practice Statements (IAPS, IAEPs, IRSPSs)

The IAASB'S Standards contain basic principles and essential procedures together with related guidance in the form of explanatory and other material, including appendices. International Auditing Practice Notes (IAPNs), represented by IAPN 1000–1100, are issued to provide interpretive guidance and practical assistance to auditors in implementing ISAs for audit, review and special purpose engagements. Although there are currently no practice notes for assurance engagements or related services, in the planning stage are International Assurance Engagement Practice Notes (IAEPNs), provide interpretive guidance for ISAEs, and International Related Services Practice Notes (IRSPNs) will provide assistance for auditors implementing ISRSs.

4.3 Elements of an Assurance Engagement

'Assurance engagement' means an engagement in which a practitioner expresses a conclusion designed to enhance the degree of confidence of the intended users[4] (other than the responsible party)[5] about the outcome of the evaluation or measurement of a subject matter[6] against criteria.[7]

The outcome of the evaluation or measurement of a subject matter is the information that results from applying the criteria to the subject matter. For example, an assertion about the effectiveness of internal control (outcome) results from applying a framework for evaluating the effectiveness of internal control, such as COSO[8] or CoCo[9] (criteria) to internal control, a process (subject matter)). The assurance framework uses the term 'subject matter information' to mean the outcome of the evaluation or measurement of a subject matter. It is the subject matter information about which the practitioner gathers evidence to provide a reasonable basis for expressing a conclusion in an assurance report.

The subject matter of an assurance engagement is the topic about which the assurance engagement is conducted. Subject matter could be financial statements, statistical information, non-financial performance indicators, capacity of a facility, etc. The subject matter could also be systems and processes (e.g. internal controls, environment, IT systems) or behaviour (e.g. corporate governance, compliance with regulation, human resource practices). The assurance engagement evaluates whether the subject matter conforms to suitable criteria that will meet the needs of an intended user.

■ Assurance Engagement Defined

Under International Framework for Assurance Engagements, there are two types of assurance engagement: a *reasonable assurance engagement* and a *limited assurance engagement*. The objective of a reasonable assurance engagement is a reduction in assurance engagement risk to an acceptably low level based on the circumstances of the engagement[10] as the basis for a positive form of expression of the practitioner's conclusion. The objective of a limited assurance engagement is a reduction in assurance engagement risk to a level that is acceptable in the circumstances of the engagement, but where that risk is greater than for a reasonable assurance engagement, as the basis for a negative form of expression of the practitioner's conclusion.

■ Five Elements Exhibited by all Assurance Engagements

The International Framework for Assurance Engagements describes five elements[11] that all assurance engagements exhibit:

1 a three-party relationship involving a practitioner, a responsible party, and the intended users;
2 an appropriate subject matter;
3 suitable criteria;
4 sufficient appropriate evidence; and
5 A written assurance report in the form appropriate to a reasonable assurance engagement or a limited assurance engagement.

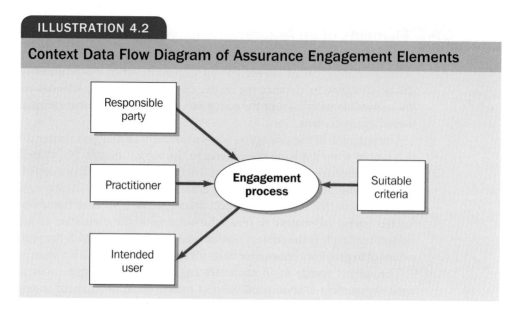

ILLUSTRATION 4.2

Context Data Flow Diagram of Assurance Engagement Elements

Illustration 4.2 is a context data flow diagram of the engagement process. Illustration 4.3 shows a more in depth (zero level) data flow diagram of the relations between the five elements during an engagement process.

■ Three-Party Relationship – Practitioner, Responsible Party and User

Assurance engagements always involve three separate parties: a practitioner, a responsible party, and the intended users. The practitioner (e.g. auditor, accountant, expert) gathers evidence to provide a conclusion to the intended users about whether a subject matter (e.g. financial statements) conforms, in all material respects, to identified criteria.

The responsible party is the person (or persons) – usually management or the board of directors – who in a direct reporting engagement is responsible for the subject matter. In an assertion-based engagement, the responsible party is responsible for the subject matter information (the assertion), and may be responsible for the subject matter.[12]

The responsible party may or may not be the party who engages the practitioner (the engaging party). The responsible party ordinarily provides the practitioner with a written representation that evaluates or measures the subject matter against the identified criteria.

The intended users are the person, persons or class of persons for whom the practitioner prepares the assurance report. The responsible party can be one of the intended users, but not the only one. Whenever practical, the assurance report is addressed to all the intended users. Also, whenever practical, intended users are involved with the practitioner and the responsible party in determining the requirements of the engagement. However, the practitioner is responsible for determining the nature, timing and extent of procedures and is required to pursue any matter he becomes aware of that leads him to believe that a material modification should be made to the subject matter information.

As you can see from Illustration 4.3, the responsible party selects criteria (e.g. the tax code), determines the subject matter (financial statements) and engages the practitioner

ILLUSTRATION 4.3

Data Flow Diagram Assurance Engagement Elements and Engagement Sub-Processes

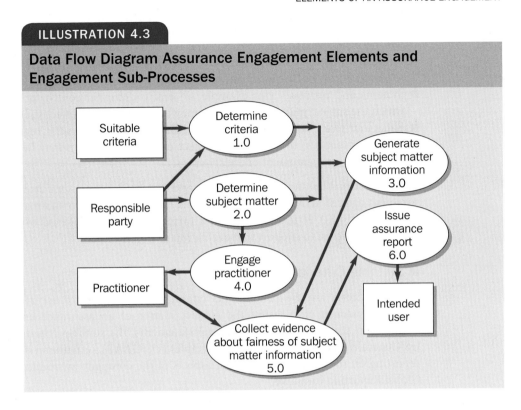

(public accountant). The subject matter and criteria taken together generates the subject matter information. For example, the tax code criteria and financial statements subject matter combine to make the company income tax returns. In an audit, the criteria could be IFRS, the subject matter is financial performance and position of the company, and subject matter information would be the income statement and balance sheet. In preparing internal control assurances, the criteria could be the COSO criteria, subject matter internal controls, and the subject matter information could be a measure of effectiveness of internal control.

The practitioner determines if the criteria are suitable, collects evidence about the subject matter information and issues an assurance report. For example, the auditor determines if the proper income tax codes are being used, evaluates the income tax information provided by the company by seeking evidence that the information is complete and all transactions from which the data were derived exist. Put another way – a responsible party **measures**, the auditor **re-measures**.

■ Subject Matter

The subject matter, and subject matter information, of an assurance engagement can take many forms, such as:

■ Financial performance or conditions (for example, historical or prospective financial position, financial performance and cash flows) for which the subject matter information may be the recognition, measurement, presentation and disclosure represented in financial statements.

■ Non-financial performance or conditions (for example, performance of an entity) for which the subject matter information may be key indicators of efficiency and effectiveness.

■ Physical characteristics (for example, capacity of a facility) for which the subject matter information may be a specifications document.

■ Systems and processes (for example, an entity's internal control or IT system) for which the subject matter information may be a statement of effectiveness.

■ Behaviour (for example, corporate governance, compliance with regulation, human resource practices) for which the subject matter information may be a statement of compliance or a statement of effectiveness.

The subject matter must be identifiable and capable of consistent evaluation or measurement against identified, suitable criteria (such as International Financial Reporting Standards (IFRS)). It must also be in a form that can be subjected to procedures for gathering evidence to support that evaluation or measurement.

■ Suitable Criteria

Suitable criteria are the benchmarks (standards, objectives, or set of rules) used to evaluate evidence or measure the subject matter of an assurance engagement. For example, in the preparation of financial statements, the suitable criteria may be IFRS, US Generally Accepted Accounting Principles (US GAAP), or national standards. When reporting on social or environmental aspects of the company an auditor might use the Global Reporting Initiative.

Several standards may guide the report, depending on the assurance service. When using accounting criteria to report on internal control, the criteria may be an established internal control framework, such as the COSO report criteria, or individual control objectives specifically designed for the engagement. When reporting on compliance, the criteria may be the applicable law, regulation or contract, or an agreed level of performance (for instance, the number of times a company's board of directors is expected to meet in a year). Without the frame of reference provided by suitable criteria, any conclusion is open to individual interpretation and misunderstanding.

The Characteristics for Assessing Suitable Criteria

An auditor cannot evaluate or measure a subject matter on the basis of his own expectations, judgments and individual experience. That would not constitute suitable criteria. The characteristics for assessing whether criteria are suitable are as follows:[13]

■ **Relevance:** relevant criteria contribute to conclusions that meet the objectives of the engagement, and assist decision making by the intended users.

■ **Completeness:** criteria are sufficiently complete when relevant factors that could affect the conclusions in the context of the engagement objectives are not omitted. Complete criteria include, where relevant, benchmarks for presentation and disclosure of the subject matter.

■ **Reliability:** reliable criteria result in reasonably consistent evaluation or measurement including, where relevant, presentation and disclosure of the subject matter, when used in similar circumstances by similarly qualified practitioners.

■ **Neutrality:** neutral criteria that contribute to conclusions are free from bias.

■ **Understandability:** understandable criteria are clear and comprehensive and are not subject to significantly different interpretation.

Criteria Established or Specifically Developed

Criteria can be either established or specifically developed. Established criteria are those embodied in laws or regulations, or issued by recognised bodies of experts that follow due process. Examples of established criteria are GAAP, IFRS, the national tax code, etc. Specifically developed criteria are those identified for the purpose of the engagement and which are consistent with the engagement objective. Examples of specifically developed criteria are criteria generally understood by the intended users (e.g. the criterion for measuring time in hours and minutes is generally understood); or criteria available only to specific intended users (e.g. the terms of a contract, or criteria issued by an industry association that are available only to those in the industry). Criteria need to be available to the intended users to allow them to understand how the subject matter has been evaluated or measured.

Concept and a Company 4.1

A 'Clean Audit' for HealthSouth

Concept	What is an assurance service? What is an audit-related service?
Story	Ernst & Young (E&Y) were the independent auditors of HealthSouth between 2000 and 2002. They also conducted janitorial inspections of the company's facilities. These inspections were called 'pristine audits.' E&Y advised HealthSouth to classify the payments for 'pristine audits' as 'audit-related fees'.

HealthSouth, headquartered in Birmingham, Alabama, USA, is the largest provider of outpatient surgery, diagnostic and rehabilitative healthcare services in the USA with approximately 1,800 worldwide facilities in the USA, Australia, Puerto Rico and the UK. Its former CEO, Richard M. Scrushy, was under an 85-count federal indictment, accused of conspiracy, securities fraud, mail and wire fraud, and money laundering (SEC, 2003).

A US government indictment charged that between 1996 and 2002 HealthSouth managers, at the insistence of Scrushy, inflated profits by $2.74 billion. Scrushy certified the HealthSouth financial statements when he knew that they were materially false and misleading. On 4 November 2003, he became the first CEO of a major company to be indicted for violating the Sarbanes–Oxley Act, which holds executives personally accountable for their companies' financial reporting (*Business Week*, 2003).

Six months elapsed from the start of the SEC's investigation to the filing of its fraud suit against Scrushy in March 2003. It took just seven weeks, from 19 March to 5 May, for the US Justice Department to accumulate 11 guilty pleas from Scrushy aides. All five CFOs in the company's history have admitted to cooking the books (Helyar, 2003).

Pristine Audits

Scrushy devised a facilities inspection programme called 'Pristine Audits' and hired E&Y to do the work. The primary purpose of the inspections was to check the cleanliness and physical appearance of HealthSouth's surgical and rehabilitation facilities. Under the programme, E&Y made unannounced visits to each facility once a year, using dozens of junior-level accountants who were trained for the inspections at HealthSouth's headquarters. For the most part E&Y used audit personnel who were not members of the HealthSouth audit-engagement team to conduct the pristine audits.

▶

A 'Clean Audit' for HealthSouth (continued)

The accountants carried out the reviews using as criteria a 50-point checklist designed by Mr Scrushy. The checklist included procedures such as seeing if magazines in waiting rooms were orderly, the toilets and ceilings were free of stains, and the trash receptacles all had liners. Other items on the checklist included: check the walls, furniture, floors and whirlpool areas for stains; check that the heating and cooling vents 'are free of dust accumulation'; that the 'floors are free of trash'; and that the 'overall appearance is sanitary'. A small portion of the checklist pertained to money matters, though none of it pertained to accounting. Assignments included checking if petty-cash drawers were secure and company equipment was properly tagged. The checklists did not cover insurance-billing procedures or the quality of the medical treatment (Weil, 2003a).

Describing the pristine audits, Mr Scrushy told an investor group: 'We believe one of the reasons that we have done so well has to do with the fact that we do audit all of our facilities, 100 per cent, annually. And we use an outside audit firm, our auditors, Ernst & Young. They visit all our facilities, 100 per cent.' On its website, HealthSouth said the pristine audit 'administered independently by Ernst & Young LLP ... ensures that all of our patients enjoy a truly pristine experience during their time at HealthSouth. The average score was 98 per cent, with more than half of our facilities scoring a perfect 100 per cent.'

In 2002 E&Y ended their relationship with HealthSouth, and HealthSouth discontinued the pristine audits.

E&Y Fees Charged HealthSouth

HealthSouth's April 2001 proxy (form DEF14A), filed with the SEC, said the company paid E&Y $1.03 million to audit its 2000 financial statements and $2.65 million of 'all other fees'. The proxy said the other fees included $2.58 million of 'audit-related fees', and $66,107 of 'non-audit-related fees'. In its April 2002 proxy, HealthSouth said it paid E&Y $1.16 million for its 2001 audit and $2.51 million for 'all other fees'. The proxy said the other fees included $2.39 million for 'audit-related fees' and $121,580 for 'non-audit-related fees'.

Neither proxy described in any detail the audit-related or non-audit-related services for which E&Y was paid. Andrew Brimmer, a HealthSouth spokesman, was quoted as saying the 'audit-related-fee' figures for each year included about $1.3 million for the pristine audits. Mr Brimmer said HealthSouth paid E&Y $5.4 million for 2002, including $1.1 million for financial-statement audit services and $1.4 million for the pristine audits (Weil, 2003a).

Pristine Audits as 'Audit-Related Fees'

A March 2002 E&Y report to HealthSouth's Board of Directors included an attachment that summarised E&Y's fees and provided a suggested 'Proxy Disclosure Format'. The attachment classified the pristine audits as 'audit-related services' and the fees for them as 'audit-related fees' (Weil, 2003a).

David Howarth, a spokesman for E&Y is quoted as saying: 'The audit-related category is not limited to services related to the financial statement audit per se. At the time of HealthSouth's disclosures, there were no SEC rules that defined audit-related services. Describing operational audit procedures as audit-related services was reasonable.' Howarth claimed that SEC ruled that audit-related fees would include assurance services traditionally performed by the independent auditor, including 'internal-control reviews'. He maintained the pristine audit was an internal control review. 'Under the new SEC rules adopted in response to the Sarbanes–Oxley Act, these (internal control review) fees are specifically mentioned as ones that should be included in audit-related fees' (Weil, 2003b).

After the Weil (2003b) article appeared, Scott A. Taub, the Deputy Chief Accountant of the SEC wrote a letter to E&Y partner Ed Caulson. Taub wrote: 'The Commission's current rules state that registrants are to 'disclose, under the caption *Audit-Related Fees*, the aggregate fees billed in each of the last two fiscal years for assurance and related services by the principal accountant that are reasonably related to the performance of the audit or review of the registrant's financial statements. It is clear from a reading of the release text and related rules that the Commission's intent is that only fees for services that are reasonably related to the performance of an audit or review of the financial statements and that traditionally have been performed by the independent accountant should be classified as audit-related' (emphasis added) (Taub, 2003).

Discussion Questions	■ What criteria would the pristine audits have to meet to be considered an audit engagement? ■ What criteria would the pristine audits have to meet to be considered 'audit-related'? ■ Can the pristine audits be considered an assurance service? How does the pristine audit meet the five criteria required to qualify an engagement as an assurance service?
References	*Business Week*, 2003, 'Sarbanes-Oxley's First', p. 52, 17 November. Helyar, J., 2003, 'The Insatiable King Richard; He Started as a Nobody. He Became a Hotshot CEO. He tried to be a Country Star. Then it All Came Crashing Down. The Bizarre Rise and Fall of HealthSouth's Richard Scrushy', *Fortune*, p. 76. 7 July. SEC, 2003, Litigation Release 18044, 'SEC Charges HealthSouth Corp. CEO Richard Scrushy with $1.4 Billion Accounting Fraud', US Security and Exchange Commission, 20 March. Taub, S., 2003, *Letter to Ed Coulson, Partner Ernst & Young*, Office of Chief Accountant, US Security and Exchange Commission, 8 July. Weil, J., 2003a, 'What Ernst Did for HealthSouth – Proxy Document Says Company Performed Janitorial Inspections Misclassified as Audit-Related', *Wall Street Journal*, 11 June. Weil, J., 2003b, 'HealthSouth and Ernst Renew Flap Over Fee Disclosures', *Wall Street Journal*, 1 July.

■ Evidence

The practitioner plans and performs an assurance engagement with an attitude of professional scepticism to obtain sufficient appropriate evidence about whether the subject matter information is free of material misstatement. The practitioner considers materiality, assurance engagement risk, and the quantity and quality of available evidence when planning and performing the engagement, in particular when determining the nature, timing and extent of evidence-gathering procedures.

Sufficiency, Appropriateness, Reliability and Materiality of Evidence

Sufficiency is the measure of the quantity of evidence. Appropriateness is the measure of the quality of evidence; that is, its relevance and its reliability. The quantity of evidence needed is affected by the risk of the subject matter information being materially misstated (the greater the risk, the more evidence is likely to be required) and also by the quality of such evidence (the higher the quality, the less may be required). The reliability of evidence is influenced by its source and by its nature, and is dependent on the individual circumstances under which it is obtained (which will be discussed in Chapter 10).[14]

129

Materiality is relevant when the auditor determines the nature, timing and extent of evidence-gathering procedures, and when assessing whether the subject matter information is free of misstatement. Materiality is considered in the context of quantitative and qualitative factors, such as relative magnitude and the nature and extent of the effect of these factors on the evaluation of the subject matter.

Ordinarily, available evidence will be persuasive rather than conclusive. The quantity or quality of evidence available is affected by:

- The characteristics of the subject matter. For example, when the subject matter is future oriented, less objective evidence might be expected to exist than when the subject matter is historical.
- Circumstances of the engagement other than the characteristics of the subject matter, when evidence that could reasonably be expected to exist is not available because of, for example, the timing of the practitioner's appointment, an entity's document retention policy, or a restriction imposed by the responsible party.

(Evidence is discussed further in Chapter 10 'Audit Evidence'.)

■ Assurance Report

The auditor provides a written report containing a conclusion that conveys the assurance obtained from the subject matter information. ISAs, ISREs and ISAEs establish basic elements for assurance reports. Also, the auditor considers other reporting responsibilities, including communicating with those charged with governance when appropriate.

In an assertion-based engagement, the practitioner's conclusion can be worded either:

- in terms of the responsible party's assertion (for example: 'In our opinion the responsible party's assertion that internal control is effective, in all material respects, based on XYZ criteria, is fairly stated'); or
- directly in terms of the subject matter and the criteria (for example: 'In our opinion internal control is effective, in all material respects, based on XYZ criteria').

Reasonable and Limited Assurance Engagements

An auditor may conduct a reasonable assurance or a limited assurance engagement with different conclusions.

In a reasonable assurance engagement, the practitioner expresses the conclusion in the positive form, for example: 'In our opinion internal control is effective, in all material respects, based on XYZ criteria.' This form of expression conveys 'reasonable assurance'. Having performed evidence gathering procedures that were reasonable given the characteristics of the subject matter, the auditor has obtained **sufficient appropriate evidence** to reduce assurance engagement risk to an acceptably low level. In most assurance services the audit conclusion is expressed in the positive form (see Chapter 12 'Audit Reports and Communications'). The opinion on an audit of financial statements and a report on internal controls for the Sarbanes–Oxley Act are both examples of opinions with positive assurance.

In a limited assurance engagement, the practitioner expresses the conclusion in the negative form, for example, 'Based on our work described in this report, nothing has come to our attention that causes us to believe that internal control is not effective, in all material respects, based on XYZ criteria.' This form of expression conveys a level of 'limited assurance' that is proportional to the level of the practitioner's evidence-gathering procedures given the characteristics of the subject matter and other engagement circumstances. In a review of historical financial statements (under International Standards for Review Engagements (ISRE)), the conclusion is expressed in the negative form, for example, 'nothing has come to our attention that causes us to believe that [subject matter] does not conform, in all material respects, with [criteria].' This form of expression conveys 'limited assurance', which indicates that the auditor has obtained sufficient appropriate evidence to reduce assurance engagement risk to a moderate level. Prospective financial reports give a disclaimer that 'actual results are likely to be different from forecast (projection).' (See Chapter 14, 'Other Assurance and Non-Assurance Engagements'.)

The differences between reasonable assurance and limited assurance are given in Illustration 4.4.[15]

Expression of Other than Unqualified (Unmodified) Assurance Opinion

A practitioner does not express an unqualified (unmodified) conclusion for either type of assurance engagement when the following material circumstances exist:

- There is a limitation on the scope of the practitioner's work. The practitioner expresses a qualified conclusion or a disclaimer of conclusion depending on how material or pervasive the limitation is. In some cases the practitioner considers withdrawing from the engagement.
- In those cases where:
  - ❑ the practitioner's conclusion is worded in terms of the responsible party's (e.g. management) assertion, and that assertion is not fairly stated, in all material respects; or
  - ❑ the practitioner's conclusion is worded directly in terms of the subject matter and the criteria, and the subject matter information is materially misstated.
- When it is discovered after the engagement has been accepted, that the criteria are unsuitable or the subject matter is not appropriate for an assurance engagement.

ILLUSTRATION 4.4

COMPARISON OF REASONABLE AND LIMITED ASSURANCE ENGAGEMENTS (ISAE 3000)

Type of engagement	Evidence-gathering procedures	The assurance report
Reasonable assurance engagement	Sufficient appropriate evidence is obtained as part of a systematic engagement process	Description of the engagement circumstances, and a positive form of expression of the conclusion
Limited assurance engagement	Sufficient appropriate evidence is obtained as part of a systematic engagement process, but in which procedures are deliberately limited relative to a reasonable assurance engagement	Description of the engagement circumstances, and a negative form of expression of the conclusion

The assurance report may be in 'short-form' or 'long-form'. 'Short-form' reports ordinarily include only the basic elements identified in appropriate ISAs and International Standards on Assurance Engagements (ISAEs). 'Long-form' not only gives the auditor's conclusion on compliance ISAs and ISAEs, but also reports in detail the terms of the engagement, the criteria being used, findings relating to particular aspects of the engagement and related recommendations.

4.4 General Considerations in an Assurance Engagement

The assurance engagement calls for planning, gathering evidence and reporting. The extent of planning, the sufficiency of evidence, acceptable engagement risk, and the level of assurance of the opinion will depend on the type of assurance engagement. An assurance engagement based on historical financial information requires more intensive planning and evidence gathering than a related services engagement. The auditor should reduce assurance engagement risk to an acceptably low level in the case of a historical financial information engagement. It is also possible to conduct an assurance engagement that provides a reasonable level of assurance on a subject matter other than historical financial information (e.g. the subject matter of a sustainability report or internal control report).

■ Assurance Report Basic Elements

International Standards on Assurance Engagements 3000 (ISAE 3000) 'Assurance Engagements Other Than Audits or Reviews of Historical Financial Information' discusses preparing an assurance report for audits other than financial statement audits (covered in Chapter 12) and reviews (covered in Chapter 14). In preparing the audit report the practitioner should conclude whether sufficient appropriate evidence has been obtained to support the conclusion expressed in the assurance report. The assurance report should be in writing and should contain a clear expression of the practitioner's conclusion about the subject matter information. The ISAE does not require a standardised format for reporting on all assurance engagements, but rather identifies the basic elements required to be included in the assurance report.[16]

The standard elements of the report include the title, addressee, the identification of the subject matter information, identification of the criteria, identification of the responsible party and their responsibilities, the practitioner's responsibilities, a statement that the engagement was performed in accordance with ISAEs, summary of the work performed, practitioner's conclusion, assurance report date, practitioner's name and specific location, and, if appropriate, a description of any significant inherent limitations, or a statement restricting the use to certain intended users. Illustration 4.5 gives the basic elements of the assurance report.

A **title** that clearly indicates the report is an independent assurance report.[17] An appropriate title helps to identify the nature of the assurance report, and to distinguish it from reports issued by others.

An **addressee** identifies the party or parties to whom the assurance report is directed. Whenever practical, the assurance report is addressed to all the intended users, but in some cases there may be other intended users.

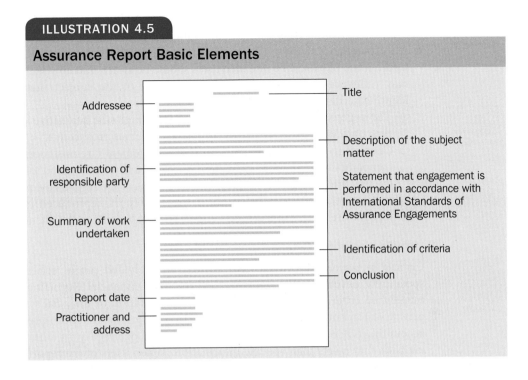

ILLUSTRATION 4.5

Assurance Report Basic Elements

A statement to identify **the responsible party** and to describe the responsible party's and the practitioner's responsibilities: this informs the intended users that the responsible party is responsible for the subject matter in the case of a direct reporting engagement, or the subject matter information in the case of an assertion-based engagement, and that the practitioner's role is to independently express a conclusion about the subject matter information.

Where there is a subject matter specific ISAE, that ISAE may require that the assurance report refers specifically to being performed **in accordance with that specific ISAE**.

The **name of the firm** or the practitioner, and a **specific location**, which ordinarily is the city where the practitioner maintains the office that has responsibility for the engagement: this informs the intended users of the individual or firm assuming responsibility for the engagement.

Subject Matter

In the body of the report is a description of the subject matter, for example, identification of the subject matter and explanation of the subject matter characteristics. The subject matter description gives the name of the entity to which the subject matter relates and the period of time covered. Are characteristics of the subject matter qualitative, quantitative, objective, subjective, historical or prospective? Are there inherent limitations such as the imprecision of the measurement techniques being applied?

An identification and description of the subject matter information and the subject matter includes, for example:

■ The point in time or period of time to which the evaluation or measurement of the subject matter relates.

- The name of the entity or component of the entity (such as a subsidiary company or transactions in the sales cycle) to which the subject matter relates.
- An explanation of those characteristics of the subject matter or the subject matter information of which the intended users should be aware, and how such characteristics may influence the precision of the evaluation of the subject matter against the identified criteria. For example:
  - The degree to which the subject matter information is qualitative versus quantitative, objective versus subjective, or historical versus prospective.
  - Changes in the subject matter or other engagement circumstances that affect the comparability of the subject matter information from one period to the next. When the practitioner's conclusion is worded in terms of the responsible party's assertion, that assertion is appended to the assurance report, reproduced in the assurance report or referenced therein to a source that is available to the intended users.

Identification of the Criteria

Criteria by which the evidence is measured or evaluated can be either established or specifically developed. To illustrate, International Financial Reporting Standards are established criteria for the preparation and presentation of financial statements in the private sector, but specific users may decide to specify some other comprehensive basis of accounting (OCBOA) such as cash accounting, rules of a regulatory authority, or income tax basis that meets their specific information. When users of the report have agreed to criteria other than established criteria, then the assurance report states that it is only for the use of identified users and for the purposes they have specified.

The assurance report identifies the criteria so the intended users can understand the basis for the auditor's conclusion. Disclosure of the source of the criteria, measurement methods used and significant interpretations made are important for that understanding. The auditor may consider disclosing the source of the criteria (e.g. laws, regulations, recognised bodies of experts, measurement methods used, and any significant interpretations made in applying the criteria).

A Summary of the Work Performed

The summary will help the intended users understand the nature of the assurance conveyed by the assurance report. ISA 700 'Forming an Opinion and Reporting on Financial Statements'[18] and ISRE 2400 'Engagements to Review Financial Statements' provide a guide to the appropriate type of summary. Where no specific ISAE provides guidance on evidence-gathering procedures for a particular subject matter, the summary might include a more detailed description of the work performed.

Because in a limited assurance engagement an appreciation of the nature, timing and extent of evidence-gathering procedures performed is essential to understanding the assurance conveyed by a conclusion expressed in the negative form. The limited assurance summary is more detailed than for a reasonable assurance engagement and identifies the limitations on the nature, timing and extent of evidence-gathering procedures. The summary for a limited assurance engagements states that the evidence-gathering procedures are more limited than for a reasonable assurance engagement, and therefore less assurance is obtained than in a reasonable assurance engagement.

Special Statements in an Assurance Report

Special statements should be in the assurance report concerning inherent limitations, a statement restricting use because subject matter criteria has limited availability.

A description of any significant, inherent limitation associated with the evaluation or measurement of the subject matter against the criteria is necessary in the assurance report. For example, in an assurance report related to the effectiveness of internal control, it may be appropriate to note that the historic evaluation of effectiveness is not relevant to future periods due to the risk that internal control may become inadequate because of changes in conditions, or that the degree of compliance with policies or procedures may deteriorate.

When the criteria used to evaluate or measure the subject matter are available only to specific intended users, or are relevant only to a specific purpose, a statement restricting the use of the assurance report to those intended users or that purpose. Furthermore, when the assurance report is intended only for specific intended users or a specific purpose this would be stated in the assurance report.

Practitioner's Conclusion

The practitioner's conclusion is expressed in positive form, negative form or as a reservation or denial of conclusion.

In the case of an audit of financial statements or Sarbanes–Oxley internal control engagement, the conclusion should be expressed in the positive form. The practitioner's conclusion may, for example, be worded as follows: 'In our opinion internal control is effective, in all material respects, based on XYZ criteria' or 'In our opinion the responsible party's assertion that internal control is effective, in all material respects, based on XYZ criteria, is fairly stated.'

In the case of a review of financial statements, the conclusion should be expressed in the negative form. For example, 'Based on our work described in this report, nothing has come to our attention that causes us to believe that internal control is not effective, in all material respects, based on XYZ criteria' or 'Based on our work described in this report, nothing has come to our attention that causes us to believe that the responsible party's assertion that internal control is effective, in all material respects, based on XYZ criteria, is not fairly stated.'

The conclusion should clearly express a reservation in circumstances where some or all aspects of the subject matter do not conform, in all material respects, to the identified criteria; or the auditor is unable to obtain sufficient appropriate evidence.

When the subject matter information is made up of a number of different aspects, separate conclusions may be provided on each aspect. The conclusion should inform the intended user of the context to which the conclusion applies.

Qualified Conclusions, Adverse Conclusions and Disclaimers of Conclusion

The practitioner should not express unqualified conclusion when the following circumstances exist and, the effect of the matter is or may be material:

- There is a limitation on the scope of the practitioner's work, that is, either circumstances or the responsible party imposes restrictions that prevent him from obtaining sufficient appropriate audit evidence.

■ In those cases where the practitioner's conclusion is worded in terms of the responsible party's assertion which is not fairly stated; and the subject matter information is materially misstated, the practitioner should express a qualified or adverse conclusion; or when it is discovered, after the engagement has been accepted, that the criteria are unsuitable or the subject matter is not appropriate for an assurance engagement. The practitioner should express a qualified conclusion when the effect of a matter is not as material or pervasive as to require an adverse conclusion or a disclaimer of conclusion. A qualified conclusion is expressed as being 'except for' the effects of the matter to which the qualification relates.

Communications with the Audit Committee

The auditor communicates relevant matters arising from the assurance engagement with those charged with governance (such as the audit committee). Relevant matters of governance interest include only information that has come to the attention of the auditor as a result of performing the assurance engagement. He is not required to design procedures for the specific purpose of identifying matters of governance interest.

An auditor who, before the completion of an assurance engagement, is requested to change the engagement to a non-assurance engagement or from an audit-level engagement to a review-level engagement should consider if that is appropriate. He should not agree to a change where there is no reasonable justification for the change. Examples of a reasonable basis for requesting a change in the engagement are a change in circumstances that affects the intended users' requirements or a misunderstanding concerning the nature of the engagement.

4.5 Audits of Historical Financial Information

Audits, reviews and examination (special purpose engagements) of historical financial information are assurance engagements that have as their subject matter historical financial information.

■ Engagements to Audit Financial Statements

The overall objectives of an audit of financial statements is to obtain reasonable assurance about whether the financial statements as a whole are free from material misstatement, whether due to fraud or error, thereby enabling the auditor to express an opinion whether the financial statements are prepared, in all material respects, in accordance with an identified financial reporting framework. The auditor also must report on the financial statements, and communicate as required by the ISAs, in accordance with the auditor's findings. The expression of a conclusion by an auditor is designed to enhance the degree of confidence intended users can have about historical financial statements. The rest of this book is about financial statement audit engagements, so these will not be discussed here.

4.6 Professional Judgement, Professional Scepticism and Inherent Limitations

■ Professional Judgement

The introduction to *Handbook of International Quality Control, Auditing, Review, Other Assurance, and Related Services Pronouncements* states: 'The nature of the International Standards requires the professional accountant to exercise professional judgement[19] in applying them.'[20] Professional judgement is the application of relevant training, knowledge and experience, within the context provided by auditing, accounting and ethical standards, in making informed decisions about the courses of action that are appropriate in the circumstances of the audit engagement. The ISAs require that the auditor exercise professional judgment and maintain professional scepticism throughout the planning and performance of the audit.[21]

Professional judgement is required for the critical elements of auditing including criteria, independence of mind, sufficient appropriate audit evidence, determining and communicating significant deficiencies in internal control[22] and determination of whether an audit objective has been achieved. The assessment of risks is a matter of professional judgement, rather than a matter capable of precise measurement.[23] Professional judgement is required in determination of the level of supervision of the engagement team.[24]

To plan the audit and evaluate evidence, the auditor exercises professional judgement, for example, when:[25]

- Assessing risks of material misstatement of the financial statements.
- Determining materiality.[26]
- Considering the appropriateness of the selection and application of accounting policies, and the adequacy of financial statement disclosures.
- Identifying areas where special audit consideration may be necessary, for example related party transactions, the appropriateness of management's use of the going concern assumption or considering the business purpose of transactions.
- Developing expectations for use when performing analytical procedures.
- Responding to the assessed risks of material misstatement, including designing and performing further audit procedures to obtain sufficient appropriate audit evidence.
- Evaluating the sufficiency and appropriateness of audit evidence obtained, such as the appropriateness of assumptions and of management's oral and written representations.

Professional judgement is essential to the proper conduct of an audit. This is because interpretation of relevant ethical requirements and the ISAs and the informed decisions required throughout the audit cannot be made without the application of relevant knowledge and experience to the facts and circumstances. Professional judgement is necessary in particular regarding decisions about:[27]

- Materiality and audit risk.
- The nature, timing and extent of audit procedures used to meet the requirements of the ISAs and gather audit evidence.
- Evaluating whether sufficient appropriate audit evidence has been obtained and whether more needs to be done to achieve the objectives of the ISAs.

- The evaluation of management's judgements in applying the financial reporting framework.
- The drawing of conclusions based on the audit evidence obtained, for example assessing the reasonableness of the estimates made by management.
- Determination of what other matters arising from the audit significant to the oversight of the financial reporting process.[28]

The exercise of professional judgement in any particular case is based on the facts and circumstances that are known by the auditor. Consultation on difficult or contentious matters during the course of the audit, both within the engagement team and between the engagement team and others within or outside the firm, assist the auditor in making informed and reasonable judgements. Consultation uses appropriate research resources as well as the collective experience and technical expertise of the firm improves the application of professional judgement.[29]

Documenting Professional Judgement

Professional judgement needs to be exercised throughout the audit. It also needs to be appropriately documented. An important factor in determining the form, content and extent of audit documentation of significant matters is the extent of professional judgement exercised in performing the work and evaluating the results. Documentation of the professional judgements made, where significant, serves to explain the auditor's conclusions and to reinforce the quality of the judgement. The auditor is required to prepare audit documentation sufficient to enable an experienced auditor, having no previous connection with the audit, to understand the significant professional judgements made in reaching conclusions on significant matters arising during the audit.[30]

The auditor may consider it helpful to prepare and retain as part of the audit documentation a summary (sometimes known as a **completion memorandum**) that describes the significant matters identified during the audit and how they were addressed. The summary may facilitate effective and efficient reviews and inspections of the audit documentation, particularly for large and complex audits. Further, the preparation of such a summary may assist the auditor's consideration of the significant matters. It may also help the auditor to consider whether there is any individual relevant ISA objective that the auditor cannot achieve.

■ Professional Scepticism

The ISAs require[31] that the auditor's professional actions including planning and performing an assurance engagement must be carried out with an attitude of professional scepticism recognising that circumstances may exist that cause the subject matter information (financial statements, internal controls, etc.) to be materially misstated. **Professional scepticism** is an attitude that includes a questioning mind, being alert to conditions which may indicate possible misstatement due to error or fraud, and a critical assessment of audit evidence.[32] An attitude of professional scepticism means the practitioner makes a critical assessment, with a questioning mind, of the validity of evidence obtained and is alert to evidence that contradicts or brings into question the reliability of documents or representations by the management (responsible party). For example, an attitude of professional scepticism is necessary throughout the engagement process for the auditor to reduce the risk of overlooking suspicious circumstances, of over-generalising when drawing conclusions from observations, and of using faulty assumptions in determining the nature, timing and extent of evidence-gathering procedures and evaluating their results.

Professional scepticism is necessary to the critical assessment of audit evidence. This includes questioning contradictory audit evidence and the reliability of documents and responses to inquiries and other information obtained from management. It also includes consideration of the sufficiency and appropriateness of audit evidence obtained in the light of the circumstances, for example in the case where fraud risk factors exist. Professional scepticism includes being alert to audit evidence that contradicts other audit evidence obtained, information that brings into question the reliability of documents and responses to inquiries, conditions that may indicate possible fraud, and circumstances that suggest the need for audit procedures in addition to those required by the ISAs.

The auditor may accept records and documents as authentic unless he has reason to believe the information is not genuine. However, the auditor is required to consider the reliability of information to be used as audit evidence.[33] In cases of doubt about the reliability of information or indications of possible fraud, the ISAs require that the auditor investigate further and determine what modifications or additions to audit procedures are necessary to resolve the matter.[34]

Maintaining professional scepticism throughout the audit is necessary if the auditor is to reduce the risks of: overlooking unusual circumstances, over-generalising when drawing conclusions from audit observations, and using inappropriate assumptions in determining the nature, timing and extent of the audit procedures.

Professional scepticism should be documented to provide evidence of the auditor's exercise of professional scepticism in accordance with the ISAs. There is no single way in which the auditor's professional scepticism is documented but it may include, for instance, specific procedures performed to corroborate management's responses to the auditor's inquiries. As management is often in the best position to perpetrate fraud, professional scepticism may make it necessary to corroborate management responses to inquiries with other information suggesting fraud.

If related party relationships and transactions exist at the auditee, the auditor would be an increased emphasis on the importance of maintaining professional scepticism throughout the audit regarding the potential for material misstatement associated with related parties.

4.7 Quality Control (ISQC #1 and ISA 220)

Quality control is a very important consideration for auditors. International Standard on Quality Control #1 (ISQC #1)[35] applies to all firms of professional accountants in respect to audits and reviews, other assurance, and related services engagements. ISQC #1 gives the requirements designed to enable the accounting firm to meet the objective of quality control. In addition, it contains related guidance in the form of application and other explanatory material. ISA 220[36] deals with quality control procedures for audits of financial statements.

A major objective of the audit firm is to establish and maintain a system of quality control to provide it with reasonable assurance that the accounting firm and its personnel comply with professional standards, legal and regulatory requirements and that reports issued are appropriate in the circumstances. The audit firm must establish, maintain, document and communicate to their personnel a system of quality control that includes policies and procedures that address each of the following elements:

- Leadership responsibilities for quality within the firm.
- Relevant ethical requirements.
- Acceptance and continuance of client relationships and specific engagements.
- Human resources.
- Engagement performance.
- Monitoring.

■ Leadership Responsibilities for Quality within the Audit Firm

The audit firm must establish policies and procedures designed to promote an internal culture recognising that quality is essential in performing engagements.

Quality control policies and procedures require the firm's chief executive officer to assume ultimate responsibility for the firm's system of quality control. The firm's leadership and the examples it sets significantly influence the internal culture of the firm. Actions and messages should encourage a culture that recognises and rewards high-quality work. These actions and messages may be communicated by, for instance, training seminars, meetings, formal or informal dialogue, mission statements, newsletters or briefing memoranda. They may be incorporated in the firm's internal documentation and in partner and staff appraisal procedures.

The firm audit must establish policies and procedures such that any person assigned operational responsibility for the firm's system of quality control has sufficient and appropriate experience and ability, and the necessary authority, to assume that responsibility. Sufficient and appropriate experience and ability enables one responsible for the firm's system of quality control to identify and understand quality control issues and to develop appropriate policies and procedures. Necessary authority enables that person to implement those policies and procedures.

■ Relevant Ethical Requirements

The practitioner firm must establish policies and procedures designed to provide reasonable assurance that the firm and its personnel comply with relevant ethical requirements.

The IESBA Code establishes the fundamental principles of professional ethics (see Chapter 3).

Part B of the IESBA Code illustrates how the conceptual framework is to be applied in specific situations for public accountants. It provides examples of safeguards that may be appropriate to address threats to compliance with the fundamental principles. The fundamental principles are reinforced in particular by: the leadership of the firm, education and training, monitoring, and a process for dealing with non-compliance.

The audit firm should establish policies and procedures designed to provide it with reasonable assurance that the firm and its personnel maintain independence (see Chapter 3). These policies and procedures shall require: relevant information about client engagements, including the scope of services, to evaluate the overall impact on independence requirements; personnel to promptly notify the firm of threats to independence; and the accumulation and communication of relevant information to appropriate personnel. Policies should provide reasonable assurance that the firm is notified of breaches of independence requirements. At least annually, the firm must obtain written confirmation of compliance with its policies and procedures on independence from all firm personnel required to be independent by relevant ethical requirements.

The practitioner firm must establish policies and procedures setting out criteria for safeguards when using the same senior personnel on an assurance engagement over a long period of time. For audits of financial statements of listed entities, this generally requires the rotation of the engagement partner and the individuals responsible for engagement quality control review after a specified period. The IESBA Code (see Chapter 3) discusses the familiarity threat that may be created by using the same senior personnel on an assurance engagement over a long period of time and the safeguards that might be appropriate to address such threats. For financial statement audits of listed entities the IESBA Code requires the rotation of the key audit partner after a pre-defined period, normally no more than seven years. National requirements may establish shorter rotation periods. For example, rotation in five years is required in the United States.

■ Acceptance and Continuance of Client Relationships and Specific Engagements

The auditor must establish policies and procedures for the acceptance and continuance of client relationships designed to provide them with reasonable assurance that the firm is competent to perform the engagement and have the capabilities, including time and resources, to do so and can comply with relevant ethical requirements. Furthermore, policies should ensure that the auditor has considered the integrity of the client, and does not have information that would lead it to conclude that the client lacks integrity.

■ Human Resources

The audit firm must establish policies to ensure that it has sufficient personnel with the competence and capabilities to perform engagements in accordance with professional standards, legal and regulatory requirements. For instance, the audit firm must assign responsibility for each engagement to an engagement partner and establish policies and procedures requiring that the identity and role of the engagement partner are communicated to the client.

■ Engagement Performance

The firm must establish policies and procedures designed to ensure that engagements are performed in accordance with professional standards and legal and regulatory requirements. These policies and procedures must include matters relevant to promoting consistency in the quality of engagement performance, supervision responsibilities and review responsibilities. Specifically, the audit firm should establish policies and procedures regarding consultation and engagement quality control. For instance, the consultation policy should be designed to provide it with reasonable assurance that appropriate consultation takes place on difficult or contentious matters, sufficient resources are available, the scope and conclusions resulting from the consultations are documented, and conclusions are implemented

Policies and procedures requiring an engagement quality control review should be established. These policies would provide an objective evaluation of the significant judgements made by the engagement team and the conclusions reached in formulating the report. The engagement quality control report must not be dated until the completion of the engagement quality control review. The engagement quality control review must include review of the financial statements, subject matter information, engagement documentation relating to significant judgements made, evaluation of the conclusions reached in formulating the report, and a discussion of significant matters with the engagement partner. When the audit is of financial statements of listed entities, the firm must evaluate their independence and see that appropriate consultation has taken place on matters involving differences of opinion and difficult or contentious matters. Documentation should reflect the work performed and support the conclusions reached.

The engagement quality control review requires documentation that the procedures required by the firm's policies on engagement quality control review have been performed, the review has been completed on or before the date of the report, and contain a statement that the reviewer is not aware of any unresolved matters that would cause the reviewer to believe that the judgements the engagement team made and the conclusions it reached were not appropriate.

Documentation of the engagement quality control review requires assembly of engagement files. Engagement teams must complete the assembly of final engagement files on a timely basis after the engagement reports have been finalised. The audit team must have in place policies to maintain the confidentiality, safe custody, integrity, accessibility and retrievability of engagement documentation.

■ Monitoring

The audit firm establishes a monitoring process designed to provide reasonable assurance that their quality control policies and procedures are relevant, adequate and operating effectively. This monitoring process includes an evaluation of the firm's system of quality control including inspection of at least one completed engagement for each engagement partner and assignment of the monitoring process to a partner who is not performing the engagement. The firm also evaluates the effect of deficiencies noted as a result of the monitoring process and communicates to personnel deficiencies noted and recommendations for appropriate remedial action.

Recommendations for fixing deficiencies may include changing training and professional development; the quality control policies and procedures; and disciplinary action against those who fail to comply with the policies. For cases where the results of the monitoring procedures indicate that an assurance report is inappropriate or that procedures were omitted, the firm should determine what further action is appropriate and consider whether to obtain legal advice.

The results of the monitoring of quality control are communicated at least annually to engagement partners and other appropriate individuals including its managing board of partners. This communication should be detailed enough to enable the firm to take prompt and appropriate action. Information communicated includes a description of the monitoring procedures performed, the conclusions drawn, significant deficiencies and the actions taken to resolve them.

Handling complaints is an important part of quality control, therefore, the audit firm establishes policies to provide reasonable assurance that it deals appropriately with complaints and allegations that the work performed does not comply with professional standards, legal and regulatory requirements. Clearly defined channels for firm personnel to raise any concerns should be in place.

4.8 Summary

Auditor services are work that an audit firm performs for their clients. Except for consulting services, the work that auditors do is under the guidance of engagement standards set by the International Auditing and Assurance Standards Board (IAASB). Some engagement standards are based on 'International Framework for Assurance Engagements' (assurance engagements), and others result from the 'Related Services Framework' (related services engagements). Two sets of standards (ISAs and ISAEs) share the assurance engagement framework and one standard set (ISRS) is based on the related services framework. ISAs, ISAEs and ISRSs are collectively referred to as the IAASB's Engagement Standards. All auditor services standards have as their basis the IESBA Code of Ethics (see Chapter 3) and International Standards on Quality Control (ISQC).

The two sets of standards based on the assurance framework are ISA and ISAE. International Standards on Auditing 200 (ISA 200) 'Overall Objectives of The Independent Auditor and the Conduct of an Audit in Accordance with International Standards on Auditing' describes the main concepts applicable to audit, review or special purpose engagements. International Standards on Assurance Engagements 3000 (ISA 3000) 'Assurance Engagements on Subject Matters Other than Historical Financial Information' describes concepts applicable to assurance services whose subject matter is not related to historical financial information. Engagements covered by International Standards on Related Services (ISRS) are based on the 'Related Services Framework'. Standards under this framework (ISRS) are applied currently to two audit services: engagements to perform agreed-upon procedures regarding financial information (ISRS 4400) and compilations (ISRS 4410).

There are two types of assurance engagement: a reasonable assurance engagement and a limited assurance engagement. The objective of a reasonable assurance engagement is a reduction in assurance engagement risk to an acceptably low level based on the circumstances of the engagement as the basis for a positive form of expression of the practitioner's conclusion. The objective of a limited assurance engagement is a reduction in assurance engagement risk to a level that is acceptable in the circumstances of the engagement, but where that risk is greater than for a reasonable assurance engagement, as the basis for a negative form of expression of the practitioner's conclusion.

The International Framework for Assurance Engagements describes five elements that all assurance engagements exhibit: (1) a three-party relationship involving a practitioner, a responsible party and the intended users; (2) an appropriate subject matter; (3) suitable criteria; (4) sufficient appropriate evidence; and (5) a written assurance report in the form appropriate to a reasonable assurance engagement or a limited assurance engagement.

Assurance engagements always involve three separate parties: a practitioner, a responsible party and the intended users. A subject matter of an assurance is the topic about which the assurance is conducted. Subject matter could be financial statements, statistical information, non-financial performance indicators, systems and processes (e.g. internal controls, environment and IT systems) or behaviour (e.g. corporate governance, compliance with regulation, human resource practices). Suitable criteria, which can be either established or specifically developed, are the benchmarks (standards, objectives or set of rules) used to evaluate evidence or measure the subject matter of an assurance engagement. In general, the same evidence-gathering procedures, quality control and planning process apply to assurance services as applies to audits. The auditor provides a written report containing a conclusion that conveys the assurance obtained from the subject matter information.

In preparing the audit report the practitioner should conclude whether sufficient appropriate evidence has been obtained to support the conclusion expressed in the assurance report. The assurance report should be in writing and should contain a clear expression of the practitioner's conclusion about the subject matter information. ISAE does not require a standardised format for reporting on all assurance engagements, but rather identifies the basic elements required to be included in the assurance report. The standard elements of the report include the title, addressee, the identification of the subject matter information, identification of the criteria, identification of the responsible party and their responsibilities, the practitioner's responsibilities, a statement that the engagement was performed in accordance with ISAEs, summary of the work performed, practitioner's conclusion, assurance report date, and practitioner's name and specific location, and, if appropriate, a description of any significant inherent limitations, or a statement restricting the use to certain intended users.

The auditor communicates relevant matters arising from the assurance engagement with those charged with governance (such as the audit committee). Relevant matters of governance interest include only information that has come to the attention of the auditor as a result of performing the assurance engagement. He is not required to design procedures for the specific purpose of identifying matters of governance interest.

The nature of the International Standards requires the professional accountant to exercise professional judgement in applying them. Professional judgement is the application of relevant training, knowledge and experience, within the context provided by auditing, accounting and ethical standards, in making informed decisions about the courses of action that are appropriate in the circumstances of the audit engagement. The ISAs require that the auditor exercise professional judgement and maintain professional scepticism throughout the planning and performance of the audit.

The critical elements of auditing including criteria, independence of mind, sufficient appropriate audit evidence and determining and communicating significant deficiencies in internal control, and determination of whether an audit objective has been achieved, among other areas, requires professional judgement. The assessment of risks is a matter of professional judgement, rather than a matter capable of precise measurement. Professional judgement is required in determination of the level of supervision of the engagement team.

The ISAs require that the practitioner auditor's professional actions including planning and performing an assurance engagement must be carried out with an attitude of professional scepticism recognising that circumstances may exist that cause the subject matter information (financial statements, internal controls, etc.) to be materially misstated. Professional scepticism is an attitude that includes a questioning mind, being alert to conditions which may indicate possible misstatement due to error or fraud, and a critical assessment of audit evidence. An attitude of professional scepticism means the practitioner makes a critical assessment, with a questioning mind, of the validity of evidence obtained and is alert to evidence that contradicts or brings into question the reliability of documents or representations by the management (responsible party).

Quality control is a very important consideration for accounting practitioners. International Standard on Quality Control #1 (ISQC #1) applies to all firms of professional accountants in respect to audits and reviews, other assurance, and related services engagements. ISQC #1 gives the requirements designed to enable the firm to meet the objective of quality control. In addition, it contains related guidance in the form of application and other explanatory material. ISA 220 deals with quality control procedures for audits of financial statements.

A major objective of the audit firm is to establish and maintain a system of quality control to provide it with reasonable assurance that the firm and its personnel comply with professional standards, legal and regulatory requirements and that reports issued are appropriate in the circumstances. The audit firm must establish, maintain, document and communicate to their personnel a system of quality control that includes policies and procedures that address each of the following elements: (1) leadership responsibilities for quality within the firm; (2) relevant ethical requirements; (3) acceptance and continuance of client relationships and specific engagements; (4) human resources; (5) engagement performance; and (6) monitoring.

4.9 Questions, Exercises and Cases

QUESTIONS

4.2 International Framework for Auditor Services

4-1 Name IAASB's two engagement frameworks and the audit and practice standards that apply to these two frameworks

4-2 What are audit related services? List the major categories (except for consulting) of auditor's related services.

4.3 Elements of an Assurance Engagement

4-3 What is an assurance engagement? Name the five elements exhibited by all assurance engagements.

4-4 Define subject matter and subject matter information. Give some examples of common subject matter in assurance and related service engagements.

4-5 Discuss the difference between a reasonable assurance and a limited assurance engagement.

4.4 General Considerations in an Assurance Engagement

4-6 What are the basic elements required to be included in the assurance report according to International Standards on Assurance Engagements 3000 'Assurance Engagements Other Than Audits or Reviews of Historical Financial Information'?

4-7 Are the criteria given in the assurance report always based on established criteria? Explain.

4.5 Audits of Historical Financial Information

4-8 What are the assurance engagements that have as their subject matter historical financial information? Discuss the differences between these assurance engagements.

4.6 Professional Judgement, Professional Scepticism and Inherent Limitations

4-9 Define professional judgement and explain when it is used during an audit.

4-10 Define professional scepticism and explain when it is used during an audit.

4.7 Quality Control (ISQC #1 and ISA 220)

4-11 Explain the difference between the two standards that deal with quality control.

4-12 What areas must policies and procedures on quality control address?

4-13 Discuss quality control policies for engagement performance.

PROBLEMS AND EXERCISES

4.2 International Framework for Auditor Services

4-14 Summarise in your own words Illustration 4.1, the Structure of IAASB's Technical Pronouncements.

4-15 Halmtorvet, a Copenhagen, Denmark, company that manufactures security devices, has contacted Christian Jespersen, Statautoriseret Revisor, to submit a proposal to do a financial statement audit. Halmtorvet was a bit taken aback when they saw the cost of the financial statement audit, even though the fees were about average for an audit of a company Halmtorvet's size. Halmtorvet's board of directors determined that the company could not afford to pay that price.

Required:
A.   Discuss the alternatives to having a financial statement audit.
B.   What should Halmtorvet consider when choosing the assurance service?

4.3 Elements of an Assurance Engagement

4-16 Kolitar Corporation offers a unique service to telecommunication companies in South America. For a fee they will review the telecom's telephone transactions for calls from outside their country that might originate illegally from inside their country.

Required:
Use the five elements exhibited by all assurance engagements to prove that Kolitar's work is an assurance engagement.

4-17 Discuss the differences between assurance conclusions expressed in the positive (reasonable assurance) form versus the negative (limited assurance) form. Give examples of assurance engagements that generally use the positive form. The negative form.

4.4 General Considerations in an Assurance Engagement

4-18 Primo Promo, an advertising and public relations firm headquartered in Ljubljana, Slovenia, owned by Arnold Rikli III, wishes an assurance report in accordance with ISAEs on the prospective financial impact on local towns resulting from tourist attendance at castles such as Bled, Polhov Gradec, Brisra and other locations. The report will be used to solicit new advertising business in the local towns. Primo Promo have retained the public accounting firm of Cankarja, Kugy and Ormoz, Public Auditors, located in Piran, Slovenia. Cankarja, Kugy and Ormoz found, after examining local, Slovenian and international statistics that the castle tourist business should increase 23 per cent over the next ten years.

Required:
Write the assurance opinion for this audit.

4.6 Professional Judgement, Professional Scepticism and Inherent Limitations

4-19 In early 2012, JP Morgan Chase's Chief Investment Office (CIO), charged with managing $350 billion in excess deposits, placed a massive bet on a complex set of synthetic credit derivatives, lost at least $6.2 billion in the so-called 'London Whale' case.

The CIO's losses were the result of the so-called 'London Whale' trades executed by traders in its London office – trades so large in size that they roiled world credit markets. Initially dismissed by the bank's chief executive as a 'tempest in a teapot', the trading losses quickly doubled and then tripled despite a relatively benign credit environment. The magnitude of the losses shocked the investing public and drew attention to the CIO which was found, in addition to its conservative investments, to be bankrolling high stakes, high risk credit derivative trades that were unknown to its regulators.

The JP Morgan Chase whale trades demonstrate how inadequate derivative valuation practices enabled traders to hide substantial losses for months at a time; lax hedging practices obscured whether derivatives were being used to offset risk or take risk; risk limit breaches were routinely disregarded; risk evaluation models were manipulated to downplay risk; inadequate regulatory oversight was too easily dodged or stonewalled; and derivative trading and financial results were misrepresented to investors, regulators, policymakers, and the taxpaying public who, when banks lose big, may be required to finance multi-billion-dollar bailouts. (Reference: US Senate Permanent Subcommittee on Investigations, 15 March 2013, 'JP Morgan Chase Whale Trades: A Case History Of Derivatives Risks And Abuses'.)

Required:

Use the facts of this case to illustrate how the auditors would use professional judgement to discover the issues before they became public knowledge.

4–20 Use the same facts as given in 4.20 above on JP Morgan Chase's London Whale case.

Required:

Use the facts of this case to illustrate how the auditors would use professional scepticism to discover the issues when planning the audit of current investments.

4.7 Quality Control (ISQC #1 and ISA 220)

4–21 Quality Review. Charalambos Viachoutsicos is assigned the responsibility of setting up a quality review programme at his St Petersburg, Russia, audit firm, Levenchuk.

Required:
A. What should the verification procedures include? Who should perform the procedures?
B. What type of documentation is required?
C. What should be covered in the report on the quality review programme?
D. What organisational authority is required for the personnel who carry out the quality audit?
E. What qualifications should the personnel have?

CASES

4–22. Scott London, an ex-KPMG partner in Los Angeles, has been charged in a federal complaint with one count of conspiracy to commit securities fraud through insider trading. The complaint alleges that London provided confidential information about KPMG clients to Bryan Shaw, a close friend, over a period of several years and that Shaw used this information to make highly profitable securities trades that generated more than $1 million in illegal proceeds.

In some cases, London called Shaw two to three days before press releases of KPMG clients were issued and read him the details that would soon be made public. He also tipped him off to mergers and even strategised with Shaw on how to conceal his trading so that the two would not be caught.

From late 2010 and continuing until March 2013, London secretly passed 'highly sensitive and confidential information' to Shaw regarding forthcoming earnings announcements by certain KPMG clients, including Herbalife, Skechers, and Deckers Outdoor Corp., before that financial information was disclosed to the public. In exchange, Shaw gave London tens of thousands of dollars in cash, typically instructing London to meet him on a side street near Shaw's business in order to give him bags containing $100 bills wrapped in $10,000 bundles. (Reference: Walter Hamilton and Andrea Chang, 2013, 'Details emerge in case against ex-KPMG auditor Scott London', *Los Angeles Times*, 11 April). KPMG said it plans to reassess its internal safeguards.

Required:
Using the details in the Scott London story, answer these questions:
A. If KPMG contracted another Big Four firm to reassess its internal safeguards, what type of auditor service would this be? What IAASB framework would the outside auditors use?
B. If the audit services to reassess internal safeguards by another Big Four firm is an assurance service: (1) Who would be the practitioner, responsible party and intended user? (2) What would be the subject matter and subject matter information? (3) What criteria should be used? (4) What would constitute sufficient appropriate evidence?
C. What quality control procedure could KPMG put in place to assure that the risk of insider information coming from partners would be reduced to a reasonably low level?

4.10 Notes

1 International Auditing and Assurance Standards Board (IAASB), 2012, International Standard on Quality Control (ISQC) 1, 'Quality Controls for Firms that Perform Audits and Reviews of Financial Statements, and Other Assurance and Related Services Engagements', *Handbook of International Quality Control, Auditing Review, Other Assurance, and Related Services Pronouncements*, 2012 edn, Volume 1, International Federation of Accountants, New York.

2 International Auditing and Assurance Standards Board (IAASB), 2012, 'Preface to the International Standards on Quality Control, Auditing, Review, Other Assurance and Related Services', *Handbook of International Quality Control, Auditing Review, Other Assurance, and Related Services Pronouncements*, 2012 edn, Volume 1, International Federation of Accountants, New York.

3 Global Reporting Initiative, 2011, *Sustainability Reporting Guidelines Version 3.1*, GRI Secretariat: **https://www.globalreporting.org/resourcelibrary/G3.1-Sustainability-Reporting-Guidelines. pdf**, Amsterdam, Netherlands.

4 The intended users are the person, persons or class of persons for whom the practitioner prepares the assurance report. The responsible party can be one of the intended users, but not the only one.

5 The responsible party is the person (or persons) who: (a) in a direct reporting engagement, is responsible for the subject matter; or (b) in an assertion-based engagement, is responsible for the subject matter information (the assertion), and may be responsible for the subject matter.

6 The subject matter of an assurance engagement is the topic about which the assurance engagement is conducted. Subject matter could be financial statements, statistical information, non-financial performance indicators, capacity of a facility, etc.

7 Criteria are the benchmarks used to evaluate or measure the subject matter including, where relevant, benchmarks for presentation and disclosure. Criteria can be formal or less formal. There can be different criteria for the same subject matter. Suitable criteria are required for reasonably consistent evaluation or measurement of a subject matter within the context of professional judgement.

8 'Internal Control – Integrated Framework', The Committee of Sponsoring Organizations of the Treadway Commission.

9 'Guidance on Assessing Control – The CoCo Principles', Criteria of Control Board, The Canadian Institute of Chartered Accountants.

10 Engagement circumstances include the terms of the engagement, including whether it is a reasonable assurance engagement or a limited assurance engagement, the characteristics of the subject matter, the criteria to be used, the needs of the intended users, relevant characteristics of the responsible party and its environment, and other matters, for example events, transactions, conditions and practices, that may have a significant effect on the engagement.

11 International Auditing and Assurance Standards Board (IAASB), 2012, 'International Framework for Assurance Engagements', paragraph 20, *Handbook of International Quality Control, Auditing Review, Other Assurance, and Related Services Pronouncements*, 2012 edn, Volume 2, International Federation of Accountants, New York.

12 Ibid. See Paragraph 25 for examples of when the responsible party might be responsible for subject matter, subject matter information, or both.

13 Ibid. Paragraph 36.

14 Ibid. See Paragraphs 43–46 for details of what constitutes reliability of evidence.

15 Ibid. Appendix.

16 Assurance report content is described in paragraph 49 of International Auditing and Assurance Standards Board (IAASB), 2012, International Standards on Assurance Engagements 3000 (ISAE 3000) 'Assurance Engagements Other than Audits or Reviews of Historical Financial Information', *Handbook of International Quality Control, Auditing Review, Other Assurance, and Related Services Pronouncements*, 2012 edn, Volume 2, International Federation of Accountants, New York.

17 If a professional accountant not in public practice, for example an internal auditor, applies ISAEs, and (a) the Framework or ISAEs are referred to in the professional accountant's report; and (b) the professional accountant or other members of the assurance team and, when applicable, the

professional accountant's employer, are not independent of the entity in respect of which the assurance engagement is being performed, the lack of independence and the nature of the relationship(s) with the assurance client are prominently disclosed in the professional accountant's report. Also, that report does not include the word 'independent' in its title, and the purpose and users of the report are restricted.

18 There has been a good deal of change in this standard. ISA 700 'The Auditor's Report on Financial Statements' was withdrawn in December 2006, replaced by ISA 700 'The Independent Auditor's Report on a Complete Set of General Purpose Financial Statements', which was replaced by the present ISA 700 'Forming an Opinion and Reporting on Financial Statements'.

19 Professional judgement is the application of relevant training, knowledge and experience, within the context provided by auditing, accounting and ethical standards, in making informed decisions about the courses of action that are appropriate in the circumstances of the audit engagement.

20 'Preface to the International Standards on Quality Control, Auditing, Review, Other Assurance and Related Services', op. cit., paragraph 16. See note 2.

21 International Auditing and Assurance Standards Board (IAASB), 2012, International Standards on Auditing 200 (ISA 200) 'Overall Objectives of the Independent Auditor and the Conduct of an Audit in Accordance With International Standards on Auditing', paragraph 7, *Handbook of International Quality Control, Auditing Review, Other Assurance, and Related Services Pronouncements*, 2012 edn, Volume 1, International Federation of Accountants, New York.

22 International Auditing and Assurance Standards Board (IAASB), 2012, International Standards on Auditing 265 (ISA 265) 'Communicating Deficiencies in Internal Control to those Charged with Governance and Management', paragraph 5, *Handbook of International Quality Control, Auditing Review, Other Assurance, and Related Services Pronouncements*, 2012 edn, Volume 1, International Federation of Accountants, New York.

23 Ibid. ISA 200, paragraph A32.

24 International Auditing and Assurance Standards Board (IAASB), 2012, International Standard for Quality Control (ISQC) #1, 'Quality Control for Firms That Perform Audits and Reviews of Financial Statements, and Other Assurance and Related Services Engagements', paragraph A31, *Handbook of International Quality Control, Auditing Review, Other Assurance, and Related Services Pronouncements*, 2012 edn, Volume 1, International Federation of Accountants, New York.

25 International Auditing and Assurance Standards Board (IAASB), 2012, International Standards on Auditing 315 (ISA 315) 'Identifying and Assessing the Risks of Material Misstatement through Understanding the Entity and Its Environment', paragraph A1, *Handbook of International Quality Control, Auditing Review, Other Assurance, and Related Services Pronouncements*, 2012 edn, Volume 1, International Federation of Accountants, New York.

26 International Auditing and Assurance Standards Board (IAASB), 2012, International Standards on Auditing 320 (ISA 320) 'Materiality in Planning and Performing an Audit', *Handbook of International Quality Control, Auditing Review, Other Assurance, and Related Services Pronouncements*, 2012 edn, Volume 1, International Federation of Accountants, New York.

27 Ibid. ISA 200, paragraph A23.

28 International Auditing and Assurance Standards Board (IAASB), 2012, International Standards on Auditing 260 (ISA 260) 'Communication With Those Charged With Governance', paragraphs 16, 17 and A20, *Handbook of International Quality Control, Auditing Review, Other Assurance, and Related Services Pronouncements*, 2012 edn, Volume 1, International Federation of Accountants, New York.

29 Ibid. ISQC #1, paragraphs A36–A37.

30 International Auditing and Assurance Standards Board (IAASB), 2012, International Standards on Auditing 230 (ISA 230) 'Audit Documentation', paragraph 8, *Handbook of International Quality Control, Auditing Review, Other Assurance, and Related Services Pronouncements*, 2012 edn, Volume 1, International Federation of Accountants, New York.

31 Ibid. ISA 200, paragraphs 7, 15 and A18–A22.

32 Ibid. ISA 200, paragraphs 7, 15 and A18–A22.

33 International Auditing and Assurance Standards Board (IAASB), 2012, International Standards on Auditing 500 (ISA 500) 'Audit Evidence', paragraphs 7–8, *Handbook of International Quality Control, Auditing Review, Other Assurance, and Related Services Pronouncements*, 2012 edn, Volume 1, International Federation of Accountants, New York.

34 International Auditing and Assurance Standards Board (IAASB), 2012, International Standards on Auditing 240 (ISA 240) 'The Auditor's Responsibilities Relating to Fraud in an Audit of Financial Statements, paragraphs 10, 30, *Handbook of International Quality Control, Auditing Review, Other Assurance, and Related Services Pronouncements*, 2012 edn, Volume 1, International Federation of Accountants, New York.

35 International Auditing and Assurance Standards Board (IAASB), 2012, International Standard on Quality Control (ISQC) #1 'Quality Control for Firms That Perform Audits and Reviews of Financial Statements, and Other Assurance and Related Services Engagements', *Handbook of International Quality Control, Auditing Review, Other Assurance, and Related Services Pronouncements*, 2012 edn, Volume 1, International Federation of Accountants, New York.

36 International Auditing and Assurance Standards Board (IAASB), 2012, International Standards on Auditing 220 (ISA 220) 'Quality Control for an Audit of Financial Statements', *Handbook of International Quality Control, Auditing Review, Other Assurance, and Related Services Pronouncements*, 2012 edn, Volume 1, International Federation of Accountants, New York.

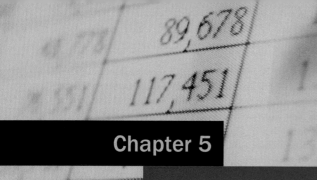

Chapter 5

CLIENT ACCEPTANCE

5.1 Learning Objectives

After studying this chapter, you should be able to:

1 Explain what is meant by client acceptance.

2 Describe the seven primary procedures involved in the client acceptance process.

3 Understand the main reasons for obtaining an understanding of client's business and industry.

4 Know the sources of client information and the methods for gathering the information.

5 Discuss the ethical and competency requirements of the audit team.

6 Know what is required in using the work of another auditor.

7 Understand the auditor's responsibility in using the work of an expert.

8 Describe the procedures for communicating with an existing (predecessor) auditor.

9 Know the contents of a client audit engagement proposal.

10 Express the differences between items covered in an audit engagement proposal to existing clients and one for new clients.

11 Explain on what basis audit fees are negotiated.

12 Understand what an audit engagement letter includes and why its contents are important.

13 Describe the differences between items covered in an audit engagement proposal to existing clients and one for new clients.

5.2 Client Acceptance: The First Step on the Journey to an Opinion

The client acceptance phase of the audit has two objectives:

1 Examination of the proposed client to determine if there is any reason to reject the engagement (acceptance of the client);
2 Convincing the client to hire the auditor (acceptance by the client).

The procedures towards acceptance of the client are: acquiring knowledge of the client's business; examination the audit firm's ethical requirements and technical competence; determining possible use of other professionals (including outside specialist) in the audit; communication with the **predecessor auditor**; preparation of client proposal; assignment of staff and the submission of the **terms of the engagement** in the form of an **audit engagement letter**. See Illustration 5.1.

ILLUSTRATION 5.1

Standard Audit Process Model – Phase I Client Acceptance

Objective	Determine both acceptance of a client and acceptance by a client. Decide on acquiring a new client or continuation of relationship with an existing one and the type and amount of staff required.
Procedures	1 Evaluate the client's background and reasons for the audit [sec. 5.3]. 2 Determine whether the auditor is able to meet the ethical requirements regarding the client [sec. 5.4]. 3 Determine need for other professionals [sec. 5.5]. 4 Communicate with predecessor auditor [sec. 5.6]. 5 Prepare client proposal [sec. 5.7]. 6 Select staff to perform the audit. 7 Obtain an engagement letter [sec. 5.8].

An auditor must exercise care in deciding which clients are acceptable. An accounting firm's legal and professional responsibilities are such that clients who lack integrity can cause serious and expensive problems. Some auditing firms refuse to accept clients in certain high-risk industries. For example, in the 1990s many large auditing firms in the USA and Northern Europe were very careful when accepting audit engagements of financial institutions after the legal judgments and fines resulting from audits of Lincoln Savings, Standard Charter Bank, and International Bank of Credit and Commerce (BCCI). At the beginning of the twenty-first century, there were great problems in the energy business (Enron, Dynergy, Pacific Gas and Electric, the State of California), the telecommunications industry (WorldCom, Global Crossing, Qwest), and healthcare (HealthSouth, ImClone), investment banks and hedge funds (Bear Sterns, Lehman Brothers, MF Global) and even in old-line industries such as retailing (K-mart, Ahold) and food products (Parmalat).

■ Audit Clients

The client–audit firm relationship is *not* a one-way street where the audit firm evaluates the client and then, judging the client 'acceptable', sends out an engagement letter closing the deal. The market for audit services is competitive and, like in any other business, there are highly desirable clients with whom any audit firm would like to have an audit relationship. Although not always the case, audit firms prepare and submit **engagement proposals** to many of their (potential) clients, especially the large ones.

■ Steps in the Client Acceptance Process

The next section in this chapter discusses the importance of obtaining a preliminary understanding of the client, in order to both evaluate the client's background and the risks associated with accepting the engagement. There must also be an understanding of the auditors' relationship to the client to enable the auditor to consider if the ethical and professional requirements (**independence**, competence, etc.) typical to the specific engagement can be met. That is the second step in the client acceptance process.

The balance of the chapter concerns acceptance by the client (called **responsible party** in assurance services terms). The audit firm must write and present to the client an engagement proposal (some auditors consider this a beauty contest). The chapter also discusses the components of a client engagement proposal for existing and new clients; and briefly discusses the International Organization for Standardization (ISO) quality control standard 9000 and how that applies to an auditing firm and its engagement services.

| 5.3 | Evaluate the Client's Background |

The auditor should obtain knowledge of the client's business that is sufficient to enable him to identify and understand the events, transactions, and practices that may have a significant effect on the financial statements or on the **audit report**. More specifically, the ISAs[1] put client acceptance in terms of identifying threats that may emerge in taking on clients, and suggest that safeguards be put in place to mitigate those risks. The main reasons for obtaining this understanding, from the auditors view, are (1) to evaluate the engagement risks associated with accepting the specific engagement and (2) to help the auditor in determining whether all professional and ethical requirements (including independence, competence, etc.) regarding this client can be met.

Auditors do not just obtain knowledge of the client preliminary to the engagement, during the client acceptance phase (Phase I of the audit process model). Once the engagement has been accepted, auditors will do a more extensive search for knowledge of the client, its business and industry in the planning phase (Phase II of the model – see Chapter 6 'Main Audit Concepts and Planning the Audit (ISA 300, 315, 320)').

Auditors may do a preliminary examination of both new and existing clients by visiting their premises, reviewing annual reports, having discussions with client's management and staff, and accessing public news and public information databases, usually via the Internet. If the client is an existing one, prior years' working papers should be reviewed. If the client is new, the auditor should consult prior auditors and increase the preliminary information search. (See Illustration 5.2.)

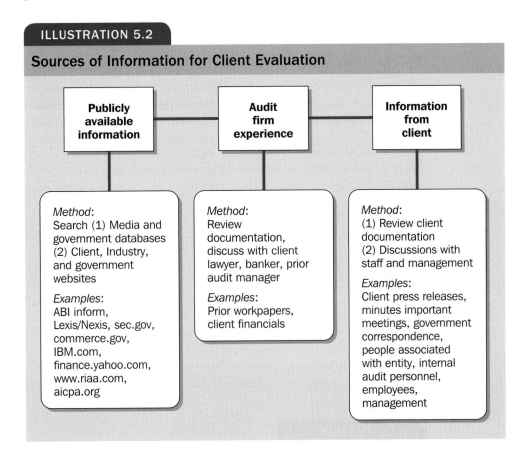

ILLUSTRATION 5.2

Sources of Information for Client Evaluation

Publicly available information	Audit firm experience	Information from client
Method: Search (1) Media and government databases (2) Client, Industry, and government websites	*Method*: Review documentation, discuss with client lawyer, banker, prior audit manager	*Method*: (1) Review client documentation (2) Discussions with staff and management
Examples: ABI inform, Lexis/Nexis, sec.gov, commerce.gov, IBM.com, finance.yahoo.com, www.riaa.com, aicpa.org	*Examples*: Prior workpapers, client financials	*Examples*: Client press releases, minutes important meetings, government correspondence, people associated with entity, internal audit personnel, employees, management

Auditors get their information about an audit client from three basic sources: their experience with the client, publicly available information, and from the client themselves. Methods used to assess the information vary from database search for public information to discussions with staff and management at the client entity. (See Illustration 5.2.)

■ Topics of Discussion

Discussions with client's management and staff are important to evaluate **governance, internal controls** and possible risks. These discussions might include such subjects as:

■ changes in management, organisational structure, and activities of the client;
■ current government regulations affecting the client;
■ current business developments affecting the client such as social, technical and economic factors;
■ current or impending financial difficulties or accounting problems;
■ susceptibility of the entity's financial statements to material misstatement due to error or fraud;
■ existence of **related parties**;

- new or closed premises and plant facilities;
- recent or impending changes in technology, types of products or services and production or distribution methods;
- changes in the accounting system and the system of internal control.

■ New Client Investigation

Before accepting a new client an audit firm will do a thorough investigation to determine if the client is acceptable and if the auditor can meet the ethical requirements of independence, specific competence, etc.

Sources of information outside those mentioned for both new and existing clients include interviews with local lawyers, other CPAs, banks and other businesses, although many of them may be bound by obligations of confidentiality, depending on local circumstances. Sometimes the auditor may hire a professional investigator or use its forensic accounting department to obtain information about the reputation and background of the key members of management. If there has not been a previous auditor, more extensive investigation may be undertaken.

■ Continuing Clients

Many auditing firms evaluate existing clients every year. In addition to the research discussed above, the auditor will consider any previous conflicts over scope of the audit, type of opinion and fees, pending litigation between the audit firm and client, and management integrity. (See Illustration 5.3.) These three factors strongly influence whether the relationship will continue. For continuing engagements, the auditor would update and re-evaluate information gathered from the prior years' working papers. The auditor

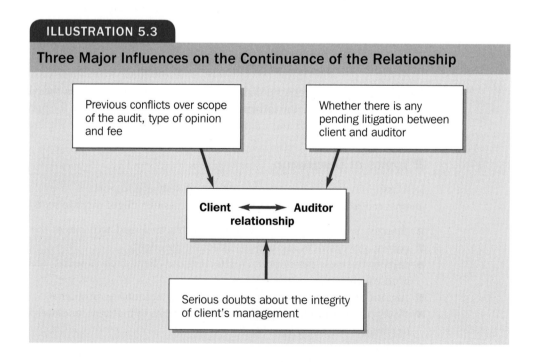

ILLUSTRATION 5.3

Three Major Influences on the Continuance of the Relationship

Previous conflicts over scope of the audit, type of opinion and fee

Whether there is any pending litigation between client and auditor

Client ⟷ Auditor relationship

Serious doubts about the integrity of client's management

should also perform procedures designed to identify significant changes that have taken place since the last audit.

The auditor may also choose not to continue conducting audits for a client because he feels excessive risk is involved. For example, there may be regulatory conflict between a governmental agency and a client which could result in financial failure of the client and perhaps ultimately lawsuits against the auditor. It may be that the auditor feels that the industry (such as financial services) offers more risk than is acceptable to the specific auditor.

Concept and a Company 5.1

Resona, the Auditor and Japan's Banking Industry

Concept	An auditor must consider company and industry background before accepting an audit client.

Story	'Auditors shouldn't be allowed to act like God,' said Hideyuki Aizawa, a senior member of Japan's major political party, the LDP. 'Resona should be the first and last time this happens.' Mr Aizawa's comments came in reaction to the government's decision to inject ¥2,000 billion ($17 billion, £10.4 billion) into Resona after auditors found that Japan's fifth largest bank was badly undercapitalised (Pilling, 2003).

The Resona filing was the first-ever test of emergency assistance under the Deposit Insurance Law. Resona had already received around ¥1,000 billion ($8.5 billion) from the government in two previous rounds of fund injections (*Nikkei Weekly*, 2003).

Auditor Says No

Shin Nihon, one of Japan's Big Four accounting firms, in effect forced Resona to seek government help by refusing to accept the bank's estimate of how much deferred tax assets it should be allowed to include as capital. This was after co-auditor Asahi & Co refused to sign off on the banks accounts. Shin Nihon's move stunned the Japanese business community, which had been accustomed to more lenient treatment from auditors.

Troubles at Resona

Resona Bank was created after the integration of Daiwa Bank and Asahi Bank, and began operating 3 March 2003. Neither bank wanted to merge, but both were forced to do so by the combined efforts of the Ministry of Finance and the Financial Services Agency, which were overseeing the consolidation of Japan's banking industry from 13 large lenders to five mega-lenders (Ibison, 2003).

Resona admitted that its capital-adequacy ratio (i.e. its capital divided by its assets, weighted by risk) had fallen to around 2 per cent, half the required minimum for domestic banks that do not have international operations.

Resona's Tier 1 capital comprised 70 per cent deferred tax assets (DTAs) according to Moody's Investors Service, the credit rating company. This compares with about 40 per cent at Japan's four other largest banks – Mizuho, SMFG, MTFG and UFJ – and is enormous compared with US regulations, which limit banks to using DTAs of just 10 per cent of their capital (Ibison, 2003).

Deferred tax assets are generated through the losses from taxable bad-loan write-offs by entities such as banks. The losses can be set off against future taxable income. Since the

Resona, the Auditor and Japan's Banking Industry (continued)

tax burden on the bank is effectively reduced, the deferred amount is counted towards the entity's shareholders' equity.

Combined with the dual pressures of a more strict calculation of its non-performing loans and exposure to a declining stock market, the circumstances for Resona's bailout were created. Their solvency was also affected by participation in government development schemes.

Japan's Banking Industry in Early 2004

Resona is an example of the problems that are occurring in the Japanese banking industry. Other major banks staved off a crisis in March 2003 by procuring more than 2 trillion yen in capital from the government, but by the end of 2003, they still needed to bolster their capital bases.

At that time Japan's seven biggest banks held around ¥6,510 billion ($60.5 billion) as deferred tax assets. Mizuho Holdings held over ¥1,500 billion in net deferred tax assets – accounting for over 41 per cent of its Tier 1 capital – even though it reduced them by 22 per cent in March and December 2003. Bank of Mitsubishi-Tokyo Group and Sumitomo Trust Bank have made similar-sized efforts to reduce their deferred tax assets, which at the beginning of 2004 accounted for 30 per cent and 26 per cent of their Tier 1 capital respectively. Mitsui-Sumitomo Banking Group, Mitsui Trust and UFJ Holdings made virtually no effort to reduce their deferred tax asset levels, cutting them by just single-digit percentage amounts. The most worrying was Mitsui Trust in early 2004, with deferred tax assets accounting for 77 per cent of its capital (*The Accountant*, 2003).

Discussion Questions	■ Assuming that another bank was in similar circumstances to Resona, what concerns would a replacement auditor have?
	■ What kind of industry risks would have been encountered by audit firms wishing to audit a Japanese bank in 2004?

References	*The Accountant*, 2003, 'Japan's Top Seven Banks Slash Deferred Tax Assets by 18 per cent', 31 December.
	Ibison, D., 2003, 'Unholy Japanese Alliance Ends in Tears', *Financial Times*, 19 May, p. 23.
	Nikkei Weekly, 2003, 'Resona Accepts 2 Trillion Yen Bailout', Nihon Keizai Shimbun, 19 May.
	Pilling, D., 2003, 'Japanese Bailout Prompts Political Backlash', *Financial Times*, 22 May.

5.4   Ability to Meet Ethical and Specific Competence Requirements

Based on the evaluation obtained regarding the background of the client, the auditor should determine whether all ethical requirements (as discussed in Chapter 3 'Ethics for Professional Accountants') can be met with regard to the specific engagement. Probably the most important procedure in this step of the engagement acceptance process is verification of the auditor's independence. Given the facts and circumstances identified in the client evaluation phase, a determination is made whether the auditor and the audit team collectively possess the specific competence required to deal with the issues that the auditor is likely to encounter in the audit.

This audit team evaluation is also important for Step 6 in the client acceptance process – selecting staff to perform the audit.

Concept and a Company 5.2

New Client Acceptance – Penn Square Bank

Concept	Evaluation of a client and the audit firm for client acceptance.
Story	In late November 1981, without prior warning, B.P 'Beep' Jennings, CEO of Penn Square Bank, notified Harold Russell, managing partner of audit firm Arthur Young Oklahoma City, that Peat Marwick would be the new auditor for the bank's 1981 financial statements. For the years ending 31 December 1976, through 31 December 1979, Penn received unqualified (clean) opinions from Arthur Young (predecessor of Ernst & Young). In 1980, Arthur Young issued a qualified opinion on Penn Square's financial statements stating that the auditors were unable to satisfy themselves 'as to the adequacy of the reserve for possible loan losses'.

Penn Square Bank – Loans to Wildcatters

Penn Square Bank, in Oklahoma City, USA, was named after a shopping mall and served small business and residents of the surrounding community until 1974 when the bank was acquired by Jennings. From that date onward, the bank expanded its deposit base by offering interest rate premiums on 'jumbo' bank certificates of deposit that carried interest rates 25 to 150 basis points above prevailing market rates.

The money deposited was loaned to the highest risk oil and gas speculators ('wildcatters'). Because of the rapid growth in their loan portfolio that doubled the bank's assets every two years from 1976 to 1982, they joint-ventured the loans with major metropolitan banks around the country. Penn Square performed all necessary administrative functions for these loans, including obtaining appraisals and engineering estimates of oil reserves.

Oil and gas prices worldwide plummeted in 1980. Many of the Penn Square-backed exploration ventures were aimed at recovering oil and gas from the deepest reservoirs. However, due to large exploration costs these were not economically feasible when the price of crude oil dropped.

Also in 1980, the bank's large profits and rapidly increasing high-risk loan volume caused an investigation by the US Office of the Comptroller of the Currency (OCC), federal bank examiners. The investigation uncovered numerous violations of banking laws by Penn Square, including insufficient liquidity, inadequate capital and poor loan documentation. In late 1980, the OCC forced the bank's directors to sign an 'administrative agreement' that required them to take remedial measures to correct these problems (Knapp, 2001).

Qualified Opinion – Management Not Pleased

Russell reported (US Congress, 1982) that there were loan considerations that led to the qualification of the 1980 audit opinion. The bank's loan documentation practices had deteriorated between 1979 and 1980. Many loans did not have current engineering reports documenting oil reserves. Other loans had engineering reports that did not include an opinion of the engineer or did not list the assumptions used in estimating the reserves. When Russell discussed these problems with client management they were 'not pleased'.

▶

New Client Acceptance – Penn Square Bank (continued)

Peat Marwick Steps In

Peat Marwick officials testified (US Congress, 1982) that their firm made the standard inquiries required of predecessor auditor Arthur Young. Arthur Young responded to these inquiries by stating that its relationship with Penn Square Bank had been 'free of significant problems'. However, Arthur Young did bring to Peat Marwick's attention the qualified opinion that it had issued on Penn Square's 1980 financial statements.

Jim Blanton, the managing partner of Peat Marwick's Oklahoma City office, told the US Congress committee (US Congress, 1982) that several members of his firm were well-acquainted with Penn Square's top executives. Peat Marwick disclosed that several Oklahoma City partners had previously obtained more than $2 million in loans and a $1 million line of credit from Penn Square. To resolve a possible independence problem an agreement reached between the two parties required Penn Square to 'fully participate out' (sell) the loans and the line of credit to other banks.

The results of the Peat Marwick 1981 Penn Square audit were an unqualified (clean) opinion. On 5 July 1982, bank examiners from the Federal Deposit Insurance Corporation (FDIC) locked the doors of the Penn Square Bank. The more than $2 billion in losses suffered by Penn Square, its affiliated banks, uninsured depositors, and the FDIC insurance fund made this bank failure the most costly in US history at the time.

Discussion Questions	■ When Penn Square Bank replaced Arthur Young in late 1980, what concerns should have been apparent to any proposed new auditor? ■ What independence issues were at stake for the new auditor Peat Marwick?
References	Knapp, M., 2001, 'Penn State Bank', *Contemporary Auditing Real Issues & Cases*, South Western College Publishing, Cincinnati, Ohio. US Congress, 1982, House Committee on Banking, Finance and Urban Affairs, *Penn Square Bank Failure, Part 1*, US Government Printing Office, Washington, DC.

■ Ethics Requirements

The auditor will ensure that the members of the auditor team as well as the entire audit firm meet the relevant ethics requirements (see Chapter 3 'Ethics for Professional Accountants'). This will require procedures to check personal financial investments of partners and employees and the business relationships with the potential audit client. He should review the non-audit services his audit firm are providing or have recently been providing to this potential client.

IEASB's *Handbook of Ethics for Professional Accountants* in a commentary on fees[2] suggests a self-interest threat may be created if fees due from an audit client remain unpaid for a long time, especially if a significant part is not paid before the issue of the audit report for the following year. Generally the firm is expected to require payment of these fees before the audit report is issued. If fees remain unpaid after the report has been issued, safeguards need to be applied. For instance, a possible safeguard is having an additional professional accountant who does not take part in the audit engagement provide advice or review the work performed.

■ Litigation and Independence

Another influence on the continuance of the relationship is whether there is any pending litigation between client and auditor. If the client is involved in litigation with the auditor, to continue to audit the client could jeopardise independence.[3] The commencement by a client or other third party of proceedings against the auditor would compromise independence. The commencement of litigation by the auditor alleging, for example, fraud or deceit by the officers of a company, or substandard performance of the client's audit by the accountant, would also impair independence. On the other side of the legal fence, acting as an advocate on behalf of an assurance client in litigation or in resolving disputes with third parties is an 'advocacy threat' to independence.[4]

■ Specific Competencies

The issue of specific competence needs consideration in the light of client evaluation in the previous step of the engagement process. On the basis of the specific circumstances of the client and its industry, the auditor should determine if the necessary expertise regarding the industry, specific GAAP issues, or certain non-audit skills are available to the audit team.

Audit team members must have a degree of technical training and proficiency required in the circumstances. There should be sufficient direction, supervision and review of work at all levels in order to provide reasonable assurance that the work performed meets appropriate standards of quality. There is a preference for year-to-year continuity in staffing.

Consideration of whether the firm has the competencies and resources to undertake a new engagement includes reviewing existing partner and staff competencies, for:[5]

■ knowledge of relevant industries or subject matters;
■ experience with relevant regulatory or reporting requirements, or the ability to gain the necessary skills and knowledge in an effective manner;
■ ability to complete the engagement within the reporting deadline; experts are available, if needed;
■ individuals meeting the criteria and eligibility requirements to perform engagement quality control review are available.

■ Partner Rotation

In some countries audit partners must be rotated every specified number of years. In the European Union Guidelines (see Chapter 3 'Ethics for Professional Accountants'), audit partners should rotate once every seven years. The Sarbanes–Oxley Act of the USA requires that audit partners rotate at least every five years.

■ Group Audit (ISA 600)

International Standard on Auditing 600 (ISA 600) 'Special Considerations – Audits of Group Financial Statements (Including the Work of Component Auditors)' provides practical assistance to auditors in the audit of group financial statements.[6]

Concept and a Company 5.3

SureBeam Not Sure of its Auditor

Concept	Client acceptance.
Story	SureBeam Corporation makes systems that irradiate food to remove harmful bacteria. Using SureBeam's system, a food company can scan a food product and break down the DNA chains of bacteria that can cause illnesses such as E. coli, Listeria Monocytogenes, Salmonella and Campylobacter (PR Newswire, 2003).
	In 2003, Big Four firm Deloitte & Touche was dismissed from its role as auditor for SureBeam Corporation after expressing concern over SureBeam's compliance with generally accepted accounting principles. Before they hired Deloitte, the company discharged Andersen and KPMG in the span of less than a year. As they were publicly traded, SureBeam needed audited financial statements (Wallmeyer, 2003).
	After Andersen was prohibited from auditing listed firms in 2002, SureBeam hired KPMG to carry on its audit work, but in June 2003 KPMG was fired for charging too much for the audit work. Deloitte was hired to replace KPMG (Freeman, 2004).
	After a preliminary examination of SureBeam's accounting records, Deloitte questioned SureBeam's accounting treatment of the sale of equipment to an international company in 2000. Millions of dollars of revenue were recognised on the sale, but the money was ultimately not recovered. According to SureBeam's chief executive officer, John C. Arme, Deloitte 'said they could not come to a conclusion as to whether accounting for that contract was proper.' Deloitte also questioned the accounting treatment of a barter transaction whereby SureBeam recognised revenue from the exchange of equipment for services with Texas A&M University (AcccountingWeb.com, 2003).
	Some of SureBeam's accounting practices have been questioned by the Securities and Exchange Commission, but no request for a change in the company's accounting methods occurred right up until they went bankrupt in 2004 (Freeman, 2004; Norris, 2003).
Discussion Questions	■ SureBeam has approached your audit firm to do their current audit. What client acceptance procedures should be carried out? What risks are involved in taking on this client?
References	AccountingWeb.com, 2003, 'Deloitte Relieved of Duties After Questioning Accounting Methods', AccountingWeb.com, 4 September.
	Freeman, M., 2004, 'Accounting Dispute Led to Demise of SureBeam', *San Diego Union-Tribune*, 14 January.
	Norris, F. 2003, 'Don't Like the Audit? Then Fire the Auditor; SureBeam Searches for Accountant No. 4', *International Herald Tribune*, 23 August, p.13.
	PR Newswire, 2003, 'SureBeam Corporation Appoints Peterson & Co., LLP as Independent Auditor', PR Newswire Association LLC, 3 December.
	Wallmeyer, A., 2003, 'SureBeam Says It Won't Meet Targets for Revenue and Profit', *Wall Street Journal* (Eastern edition), New York, NY, 17 September, p. A.22.

5.5   Use of Other Professionals in the Audit

The auditor may discover in doing the search for background information that another auditor will audit a portion of the client's financial statements or that an outside specialist such as IT, environmental or tax specialist, may be needed to properly audit the client. International standards dictate certain procedures in these cases.

■ Using the Work of another Auditor

Part of the search for background information includes considering if another auditor will be required to audit a component of the business such as a division in another country. If another auditor is auditing part of the financial statements, the auditor should consider the impact of using the work of another auditor on the combined financial statements.

The purpose of ISA 600,[7] the standard about the work of a group auditor, is to determine whether to act as the auditor of the group financial statements; and, if acting as the auditor of the group financial statements, to communicate clearly with **component auditors**[8] about the scope and timing of their work on financial information related to components and their findings; and to obtain sufficient appropriate audit evidence regarding the financial information of the **components**[9] to express an opinion. A component of a business is an entity or business activity for which group or component management prepares financial information that should be included in the group financial statements. The component auditor is an auditor who, at the request of the group engagement team, performs work on financial information related to a component for the group audit.

Group Auditor

The group auditor is responsible for expressing an audit opinion on whether the group financial statements give a true and fair view (or are presented fairly, in all material respects) in accordance with the applicable financial reporting framework. The group auditor is responsible for determining the work to be performed on the components' financial information and on the consolidation in order to obtain sufficient appropriate audit evidence to be able to express an opinion on the group financial statements. If the group auditor uses a component auditor to work on the audit, the group auditor determines the scope of work to be performed and communicates the plan to the component auditor. (See Chapter 13 'Overview of a Group Audit' for more details.)

Audit Responsibility

Unless national standards enable, and national law or regulation permits, the group auditor is to divide responsibility for the audit opinion on the group financial statements (referred to as 'division of responsibility') and the group auditor decides to do so, the group auditor should take sole responsibility for the audit opinion on the group financial statements. When the group auditor takes sole responsibility for the audit opinion on the group financial statements, the group auditor should not refer to the other auditor in the auditor's report on the group financial statements.[10]

National standards differ as to whether division of responsibility is allowed. No divided responsibility is allowed in Australia,[11] Japan[12] and the UK. The Canadian standards allow division of responsibility only when expressing an opinion with reservation.

The auditor may refer to his inability to rely on the work of the secondary auditor in his report if such a disclosure explains the reason for his or her reservation.

When the group auditor decides to use the work of another auditor, she should consider the professional qualifications, independence, professional competence and resources of the other auditor, and the quality control process of the other auditor's firm in the context of the work to be performed by the other auditor.

Documentation

The group auditor should document in the audit working papers the following matters:[13]

- An analysis of components, indicating those that are significant, and the type of work performed on the financial information of the components.
- The nature, timing and extent of the group engagement team's involvement in the work performed by the component auditors on significant components including the group engagement team's review of relevant parts of the component auditors' audit documentation and conclusion.
- Written communications between the group engagement team and the component auditors about the group engagement team's requirements.

When the group auditor concludes that the work of the component auditor cannot be used and the group auditor has not been able to perform sufficient additional procedures, the group auditor should express a qualified opinion because there is a limitation in the scope of the audit. In some countries, like the Netherlands, the group auditor may only refer to the use made of other auditors to motivate a qualified disclaimer of adverse audit opinion. This is to emphasise the undivided responsibility of the group auditor. In other countries (e.g. the USA) it is possible to assume divided responsibility, which is expressed by referring in the audit opinion to the fact that the financial statements include numbers that have been audited by another auditor, without affecting the unqualified nature of the opinion.

Using the Work of an Expert

The auditor's education and experience enable her to be knowledgeable about business matters in general, but she is not expected to have the expertise of a person trained for another profession such as an actuary or engineer. If the auditor requires special expertise, the auditor should consider hiring an expert to assist in gathering the necessary evidence.[14] ISA 620[15] defines an expert as an individual or organisation possessing expertise in a field other than accounting or auditing, whose work in that field is used by the auditor to assist the auditor in obtaining sufficient appropriate audit evidence. Situations where an auditor might use an expert are valuations of certain types of assets (land and building, complex financial instruments, works of art, precious stones, intangibles etc.), determination of physical condition of assets (e.g. estimation of oil and gas reserves), actuarial valuation, value of contracts in progress, specific IT expertise (e.g. in the audit of a telecommunications company), and legal opinions.

Expert's Competence, Objectivity

If an expert's work is to be used as audit evidence, the auditor should determine the expert's skills and competence by considering professional certifications, experience and reputation. The expert's objectivity should be evaluated. A broad range of circumstances may threaten objectivity, for example, self-interest threats, advocacy threats, familiarity threats, self-review threats, and intimidation threats. Safeguards may eliminate or reduce such threats (see Chapter 3). Interests and relationships that it may be relevant to discuss with the auditor's expert include financial interests, business and personal relationships.

Communications to Expert

The client should write instructions to the expert which cover:

- the nature, scope and objectives of the expert's work,
- the respective roles and responsibilities of the auditor and that expert;
- the nature, timing and extent of communication between the auditor and that expert, including the form of any report to be provided by that expert; and
- the need for the auditor's expert to observe confidentiality requirements.

When issuing an unqualified and unmodified auditor's report, the auditor should not refer to the work of the expert. Such a reference might be misunderstood to be a qualification of the auditor's opinion or division of responsibility, neither of which is intended. If, as a result of the work of an expert, the auditor decides to issue a modified auditor's report, in some circumstances when explaining the nature of the modification it may be appropriate to refer to the expert by name and the extent of his involvement. This disclosure requires the permission of the expert.

5.6 Communicating With the Predecessor (Existing) Auditor

If there is an existing auditor, the IESBA *Code of Ethics for Professional Accountants* (discussed in Chapter 3 'Ethics for Professional Accountants') suggests that, depending on the circumstance, the new auditor communicate directly with the predecessor auditor.[16] In cases when a new auditor will replace an existing auditor, the code of ethics advises the new, proposed auditor to communicate with the **existing accountant** (auditor).[17] The extent to which an existing accountant can discuss the affairs of the client with the **proposed accountant** will depend on receipt of the client's permission and the legal or ethical requirements relating to this disclosure. The purpose of this communication is to reduce or eliminate threats by getting information on any facts or circumstances that, in the existing accountant's opinion, the proposed accountant needs to be aware of before deciding whether to accept the engagement. This requirement is an important measure to prevent 'opinion shopping', or to notify the new auditor of the circumstances under which the predecessor auditor has ended the relationship with the client.

Request Permission of Client

As stated in the *Code of Ethics for Professional Accountants* (the Code), a professional accountant in public practice will generally need to obtain the client's permission, preferably in writing, to initiate discussion with an existing accountant (auditor). Once the permission of the client is obtained, the existing accountant shall comply with the request. Where the existing accountant (auditor) provides information, the auditor must provide it honestly and unambiguously. If the client denies the existing auditor permission to discuss its affairs with the proposed successor auditor or limits what the existing auditor may say, that fact should be disclosed to the proposed successor auditor.

When the predecessor (existing) auditor receives the communication of the newly proposed auditor, professional courtesy dictates that he should reply, preferably in writing, advising of any professional reasons why the proposed accountant should not accept the appointment. If the proposed accountant is unable to communicate with the existing accountant, the proposed accountant shall take reasonable steps to obtain information about any possible threats by other means, such as through inquiries of third parties or background investigations of senior management or those charged with governance of the client.

■ First Time Engagements

For first-time engagements, ISA 510 suggests:[18]

> In conducting an initial audit engagement, the objective of the auditor with respect to opening balances is to obtain sufficient appropriate audit evidence about whether: (a) Opening balances contain misstatements that materially affect the current period's financial statements; and (b) Appropriate accounting policies reflected in the opening balances have been consistently applied in the current period's financial statements, or changes made are appropriately accounted for, presented and disclosed in accordance with the applicable financial reporting framework.

Of course, one of the best ways to be assured that the opening balances and accounting policies are correct when the prior period financial statements were audited by another auditor, is to review the predecessor auditor's working papers. This should allow the new auditor to obtain sufficient appropriate evidence. The new auditor should also consider the professional competence and independence of the predecessor auditor. If the prior period's auditor's report was not the standard **unqualified opinion**, the new auditor should pay particular attention in the current period to the matter which resulted in the modification.

5.7 Acceptance by the Client – The Engagement Proposal

The auditor has determined that the client is acceptable from a risk and ethics perspective, and has concluded that the ethical requirements regarding the specific client engagement can be met. Then, typically, significant effort will be devoted to gaining the auditee as a client, given the competitive pressure that exists in the current audit environment (see Chapter 2 'The Audit Environment'). This requires a carefully prepared engagement proposal.

Aspects of the procedures for the engagement proposal may be found in ISA 210 'Agreeing the Terms of Audit Engagements.'[19] The auditor and the client should have a mutual understanding of the nature of the audit services to be performed, the timing of those services, the expected fees, audit team, audit approach, audit quality, use of client's internal auditors, and the transition needs.

References to the quality aspects of the client proposal may be found in ISO 9001,[20] which suggests that the auditing firm should define and document its policy and objectives for, and commitment to, quality. The auditor should ensure that this policy is understood, implemented, and maintained at all levels in the organisation.

There are two basic types of audit engagement proposals: those to continuing clients and those for new clients.

■ Continuing Client Audit Proposal

The continuing client proposal will differ between firms, but generally it discusses the following:

- ■ a review of how the auditing firm can add value, both to the company in general and to those directly responsible for the engagement of the auditor, for example the Audit Committee;
- ■ plans for further improvement in value added including discussion of present regulatory trends, audit scope, and any recent changes in the company that may affect the audit;
- ■ a description of the audit team and any changes in the audit team from the previous year;
- ■ a detailed fee proposal.

A Review of How the Auditing Firm Can Add Value

The introductory part of the client proposal is a discussion of how the proposing firm can benefit (*add value* to) the client firm. There is a discussion of the focus of the firm, its management philosophy, and quality control policies. The relationship with the client's internal audit department and accounting department may be discussed.

This section on plans for *further improvement in value added* might identify the client's requirements and discuss how the audit firm meets these requirements. The audit scope and materiality limits may also be discussed. Reliance on audit regulatory requirements – local, national and international – should also be discussed. The extent of reliance on the client's internal audit staff should be spelt out. Finally, it is important to review any changes in client company management, new projects undertaken, and the general regulatory environment. Especially important are those changes that affect the audit.

Audit Team

An important part of the proposal is a description of members of the audit team and summary of their work experience. Special emphasis may be placed on the members of the team returning from previous engagements. Selecting the audit team is Step 6 in the client acceptance process (see Illustration 5.1).

Fee Proposal

The detailed description of the proposed *fee* is traditionally a separate part of the proposal, presented as a separate document. The fee proposal may involve several levels of detail or a few depending on type. The core audit requires the most time and detail. It will show costs for operation audits including, perhaps, audits of subsidiaries and quarterly audits. Less level of detail would be required for statutory audits and potential future developments.

■ New Client Audit Proposal

A proposal to audit a new client is very important to audit firms because new clients are the primary growth engine for firms. Obtaining more prestigious clients is the desire of most firms. A proposal to a large, solid client may be very complex, requiring many hours of staff time to prepare, especially if it is a competitive situation. A sample table of contents for a new client proposal is shown in Illustration 5.4.

ILLUSTRATION 5.4

Sample Table of Contents of New Client Proposal

ABC Company Engagement Proposal

- Executive summary
- ABC Company business and audit expectations
- Strengths of Big One, LLP
- The audit team
- The audit approach
- ABC Company internal auditors
- ABC Company transition needs and management
- After service monitoring
- Fee details
- Appendix

Big One, LLP CPAs

The **executive summary** gives a brief summary of the proposal with special emphasis on client expectation, audit approach, firm selling points and coordination of the audit with staff internal auditors.

The general proposal may begin with a description of client business sectors, technology, financial strengths and divisions. The client's objectives as the basis of the audit strategy[21] could be outlined. It may point out audit requirements relating to securities exchange, environmental, governmental and other regulations, including items in the company's policies that go beyond existing statutory requirements.

Strengths of the audit firm may explore client service attitudes, technical competency, experience, desire to exceed expectations, and advice and assistance. This section might also emphasise report quality, continuity of audit teams, worldwide service, cost effectiveness of audits, and audit firm's quality standards.

The **audit team** section includes a description of members of the team and a summary of their work experience. This section might also detail how the team will communicate with management, the role of the team and supervisors, and team meetings and communications. Choosing the audit team is Step 6 in the client acceptance process and is generally done well ahead of writing the client proposal.

The **audit approach** is an important section because it allows a discussion of how the audit is tailored to this one, specific client. The section could explain audit emphasis or concentration on specific audit risks, the use of information technology on the audit, the involvement of other auditors or experts, and the number of locations or components reviewed. The section could address terms of the engagement, any statutory responsibilities, and internal control and client systems. The nature and timing of reports or other communications (e.g., audit opinion, review, special procedures, governmental reporting, oral and written reports to the audit committee) expected under the engagement is also important.

The client's **internal auditors' work**[22] must be relied upon to a certain extent in all audits. However, the external auditor has sole responsibility for the audit opinion expressed, and that responsibility is not reduced by the external auditor's use of the work of the internal auditors. This section may include reference to the internal auditors' work and production, supplier selection, and supplier failure. Other issues explored may include safeguarding of assets, internal controls, management information systems, systems security, adherence to corporate policy, due diligence reviews, and opportunities for improvement.

A discussion of the **transition needs of the company** in terms of accommodating the new auditor may be very important in convincing a new client to switch auditors. This section of the proposal might include a transition schedule detailing meetings with management and former auditors. Other areas addressed might include permanent file documentation, understanding of internal control, and benefits of the change.

After the audit is complete there are still opportunities for the auditor to offer service to the client. These after-service monitoring activities may include monitoring the audit performance, audit firm self-evaluation (usually at closing meetings), questionnaires for management to evaluate the audit performance, and written summaries of what was done in the audit (i.e. audit and satisfaction survey) can be given to the client.

An **appendix** might include further information about the audit team, an outline of the audit plan and a list of representative publications. The outline of the audit plan usually shows the degree of audit time required for fieldwork, confirmation of controls, validation of balances and transactions. In particular, the outline of the audit plan will provide an overview of the audit risks, and the auditor's suggested response to those risks, in the form of detailed audit procedures.

■ Establishing and Negotiating Audit Fees

According to the IESBA Code of Ethics,[23] when entering into negotiations regarding professional services, a professional accountant in public practice may quote whatever fee is deemed appropriate. Professional fees should be a fair reflection of the value of the professional services performed for the client, taking into account: the skill and knowledge required, the level of training and experience of the persons engaged in performing the professional services, the time required, and the degree of responsibility that performing those services entail. These factors can be influenced by the legal, social and economic conditions of each country.

Sometimes an auditing firm charges a lower fee when a client is first signed up. This is called 'low balling'. The fact that one professional accountant in public practice may quote a fee lower than another is not in itself unethical. Nevertheless, there may be threats to compliance with the fundamental principles arising from the level of fees quoted. For example, a self-interest threat to professional competence and due care is created if the fee quoted is so low that it may be difficult to perform the engagement in accordance with applicable technical and professional standards for that price.[24]

Contingent Fees[25]

A contingent (or contingency) fee is an arrangement whereby no fee will be charged unless a specified finding or result is obtained, or when the fee is otherwise contingent on the findings or results of these services. Fees charged on a percentage or similar basis are regarded as a contingent fee. Contingent fees are widely used for certain types of non-assurance engagements. They may, however, create threats to compliance with the fundamental principles in certain circumstances. They may create a self-interest threat to objectivity. The existence and significance of such threats will depend on factors including: the nature of the engagement, range of possible fee amounts, the basis for determining the fee, and whether the outcome will be reviewed by an independent third party. If the threats are significant, safeguards are applied such as: an advance written agreement with the client as to the basis of remuneration. Some countries do not allow auditors to charge contingent fees (they are prohibited by the US Securities and Exchange Commission, for example).

Commissions and Referral Fees

In certain circumstances, an auditor in public practice may receive a referral fee or commission relating to a client. For example, when she does not provide the specific service required, a fee may be received for referring a continuing client to another professional accountant in public practice or other expert. An auditor in public practice may receive a commission from a third party (for example, a software vendor) in connection with the sale of goods or services to a client. However, accepting such a referral fee or commission creates a self-interest threat to objectivity and professional competence and due care. If the threat is significant, safeguards should be applied to eliminate the threat or reduce it to an acceptable level. Examples of safeguards include: disclosing to the client any arrangements to pay or receive referral fees or obtaining advance agreement from the client for commission arrangements.

A professional accountant in public practice may also pay a referral fee to obtain a client, for example where the client continues as a client of another professional accountant in public practice but requires specialist services not offered by the existing accountant. The payment of such a referral fee also creates a self-interest threat to objectivity and professional competence and due care.

5.8 The Audit Engagement Letter

It is in the interests of both client and auditor that the auditor sends an engagement letter,[26] preferably before the commencement of the engagement, to help in avoiding misunderstandings with respect to the engagement. An engagement letter is an agreement between the accounting firm and the client for the conduct of the audit and related services. An auditor's engagement letter documents and confirms his acceptance of the appointment, the objective and scope of the audit, the extent of auditor responsibilities to the client, and the form of any reports.

The engagement letter may affect legal responsibilities to the client. In litigation, the auditor may use an engagement letter as a contract stating its scope, responsibilities, and limitations. The letter describes the auditor's purpose, that the audit entails study of internal control, the time schedule of the engagement, and fees.

Contents of the Engagement Letter

The form and content of the audit engagement letter may vary for each client, but they should be recorded in an audit engagement letter or other suitable form of written agreement and should include:[27]

- The objective of the audit of financial information.
- The responsibilities of the auditor.
- Management's responsibility.
- The applicable financial reporting framework.
- Reference to the expected form and content of any reports to be issued by the auditor and a statement that there may be circumstances in which a report may differ from its expected form and content.

The auditor may also wish to include in the letter:[28]

- Elaboration of the scope of the audit, including reference to applicable legislation, regulations, ISAs, and ethical and other pronouncements of professional bodies to which the auditor adheres.
- The form of any other communication of results of the audit engagement.
- The fact that because of the test nature and other inherent limitations of an audit, together with the inherent limitations of any system of internal control, there is an unavoidable risk that even some material misstatement may remain undiscovered.
- Arrangements regarding the planning and performance of the audit, including the composition of the audit team.
- The expectation that management will provide written representations.
- The agreement of management to make available to the auditor draft financial statements and any accompanying other information in time to allow the auditor to complete the audit in accordance with the proposed timetable.
- The agreement of management to inform the auditor of facts that may affect the financial statements, of which management may become aware during the period from the date of the auditor's report to the date the financial statements are issued.
- A request for the client to confirm the terms of the engagement by acknowledging receipt of the engagement letter.
- The basis on which fees are computed and any billing arrangements.

When relevant, the following points could also be made:

- Arrangements concerning the involvement of other auditors and experts in some aspects of the audit.
- Arrangements concerning the involvement of internal auditors and other client staff.
- Arrangements to be made with the predecessor auditor, if any, in the case of an initial audit.
- Any restriction of the auditor's liability.
- A reference to any further agreements between the auditor and the client.
- Any obligations to provide audit working papers to other parties.

On recurring audits, the auditor may decide not to send a new engagement letter each year. However, he should consider sending a letter in any of the following circumstances:

- where there is an indication that the client misunderstands the objective and scope of the audit;

171

- where the terms of the engagement are revised;
- where there has been a recent change in management;
- where the size or nature of the business has changed; and
- where there are legal requirements that an engagement letter be written.

If the auditor reviews both the parent and a subsidiary, branch or division of the company, he may consider sending a separate engagement letter to that component business. The factors that the auditor should consider are who appoints the auditor of the component, legal requirements, degree of ownership by parent and the extent of any work performed by the auditors.

Illustration 5.5 shows a sample engagement letter.[29]

ILLUSTRATION 5.5

Sample Audit Engagement Letter

The following is an example of an audit engagement letter for an audit of general purpose financial statements prepared in accordance with International Financial Reporting Standards. This letter is not authoritative but is intended only to be a guide that may be used in conjunction with the considerations outlined in ISA 210. It will need to be varied according to individual requirements and circumstances. It is drafted to refer to the audit of financial statements for a single reporting period and would require adaptation if intended or expected to apply to recurring audits (see paragraph 13 of ISA 210). It may be appropriate to seek legal advice that any proposed letter is suitable.

***

To the appropriate representative of management or those charged with governance of ABC Company:

[*The objective and scope of the audit.*]

You have requested that we audit the financial statements of ABC Company, which comprise the balance sheet as at 31 December 20X1, and the income statement, statement of changes in equity and cash flow statement for the year then ended, and a summary of significant accounting policies and other explanatory information. We are pleased to confirm our acceptance and our understanding of this audit engagement by means of this letter. Our audit will be conducted with the objective of our expressing an opinion on the financial statements.

[*The responsibilities of the auditor.*]

We will conduct our audit in accordance with International Standards on Auditing (ISAs). Those standards require that we comply with ethical requirements and plan and perform the audit to obtain reasonable assurance about whether the financial statements are free from material misstatement. An audit involves performing procedures to obtain audit evidence about the amounts and disclosures in the financial statements. The procedures selected depend on the auditor's judgement, including the assessment of the risks of material misstatement of the financial statements, whether due to fraud or error. An audit also includes evaluating the appropriateness of accounting policies used and the reasonableness of accounting estimates made by management, as well as evaluating the overall presentation of the financial statements.

Because of the inherent limitations of an audit, together with the inherent limitations of internal control, there is an unavoidable risk that some material misstatements may not be detected, even though the audit is properly planned and performed in accordance with ISAs.

In making our risk assessments, we consider internal control relevant to the entity's preparation of the financial statements in order to design audit procedures that are appropriate in the circumstances, but not for the purpose of expressing an opinion on the effectiveness of the entity's internal control. However, we will communicate to you in writing concerning any significant

Illustration 5.5 (continued)

deficiencies in internal control relevant to the audit of the financial statements that we have identified during the audit.

[*The responsibilities of management and identification of the applicable financial reporting framework (for purposes of this example it is assumed that the auditor has not determined that the law or regulation prescribes those responsibilities in appropriate terms; the descriptions in paragraph 6(b) of this ISA are therefore used).*]

Our audit will be conducted on the basis that [management and, where appropriate, those charged with governance] acknowledge and understand that they have responsibility:

a. For the preparation and fair presentation of the financial statements in accordance with International Financial Reporting Standards;

b. For such internal control as [management] determines is necessary to enable the preparation of financial statements that are free from material misstatement, whether due to fraud or error; and

c. To provide us with:

  (i) Access to all information of which [management] is aware that is relevant to the preparation of the financial statements such as records, documentation and other matters;

  (ii) Additional information that we may request from [management] for the purpose of the audit; and

  (iii) Unrestricted access to persons within the entity from whom we determine it necessary to obtain audit evidence.

As part of our audit process, we will request from [management and, where appropriate, those charged with governance], written confirmation concerning representations made to us in connection with the audit.

We look forward to full cooperation from your staff during our audit.

[*Other relevant information.*]

[*Insert other information, such as fee arrangements, billings and other specific terms, as appropriate.*]

[*Reporting.*]

[*Insert appropriate reference to the expected form and content of the auditor's report.*]

The form and content of our report may need to be amended in the light of our audit findings.

Please sign and return the attached copy of this letter to indicate your acknowledgement of, and agreement with, the arrangements for our audit of the financial statements including our respective responsibilities.

XYZ & Co.

Acknowledged and agreed on behalf of ABC Company by

(signed)

....

Name and Title

Date

Note: In some jurisdictions, the auditor may have responsibilities to report separately on the entity's internal control. In such circumstances, the auditor reports on that responsibility as required in that jurisdiction. The reference in the auditor's report on the financial statements to the fact that the auditor's consideration of internal control is not for the purpose of expressing an opinion on the effectiveness of the entity's internal control may not be appropriate in such circumstances.

■ Financial Reporting Framework

The form of opinion expressed by the auditor will depend upon the **applicable financial reporting framework**[30] and any applicable law or regulation. The auditor may also have certain other communication and reporting responsibilities to users, management, those charged with governance, or parties outside the entity, in relation to matters arising from the audit. These may be established by the ISAs or by applicable law or regulation.[31] ISA 200 describes how the financial reporting frameworks are acceptable for general purpose financial statements.[32]

5.9   Summary

The Client Acceptance phase of the audit has two objectives:

1 Examination of the proposed client to determine if there is any reason to reject the engagement (acceptance of the client and consideration whether the auditor is able to meet the ethical requirements vis-à-vis the particular client engagement).
2 Convincing the client to hire the auditor (acceptance by the client).

In the client acceptance phase of the audit, the auditor is primarily concerned with the riskiness of his client and the complexities that can be expected when an audit is performed. The audit firm is also interested in preparing a client proposal to convince the acceptable client to develop a relationship.

Components of acceptance of the client are: acquiring knowledge of the client's business; examination of the audit firm's ethical requirements and technical competence; possible use of other professionals (including outside specialists) in the audit; communication with the predecessor auditor; preparation of client proposal; assignment of staff; and the submission of the terms of the engagement in the form of an audit engagement letter.

The auditor should obtain knowledge of the client's business that is sufficient to enable him to identify and understand the events, transactions and practices that may have a significant effect on the financial statements or on the audit report. More specifically, the ISAs put client acceptance in terms of identifying threats that may emerge in taking on clients, and suggest that safeguards be put in place to mitigate those risks. There must also be an understanding of the auditors' relationship to the client to enable the auditor to consider if the ethical and professional requirements (independence, competence, etc.) typical to that specific engagement can be met. Given the facts and circumstances identified in the client evaluation phase, a determination is made whether the auditor and the audit team collectively possess the specific competence required to deal with the issues that the auditor is likely to encounter in the audit.

The auditor may discover in doing the search for background information that another auditor will audit a portion of the client's financial statements or that an outside specialist, such as IT, environmental or tax specialist, may be needed to properly audit the client. International standards dictate certain procedures in these cases. If the auditor uses a component auditor, he becomes the 'group auditor'. The group auditor is responsible for expressing an audit opinion on whether the group financial statements give a true and fair view (or are presented fairly, in all material respects) in accordance with the applicable financial reporting framework.

If there is an existing auditor, the IESBA *Code of Ethics for Professional Accountants* suggests that, depending on the circumstance, the new auditor communicate directly with the predecessor auditor. The extent to which an existing accountant can discuss the affairs of the client with the proposed accountant will depend on receipt of the client's permission and the legal or ethical requirements relating to this disclosure, receipt of the client's permission and the legal or ethical requirements relating to this disclosure. The purpose of this communication is to reduce or eliminate threats by getting information on any facts or circumstances that, in the existing accountant's opinion, the proposed accountant needs to be aware of before deciding whether to accept the engagement.

There are two basic types of audit engagement proposals:

1 those to continuing clients;
2 those to new clients.

The continuing client proposal discusses how the auditing firm can add value, plans for further improvement in the client relationship, and provides a description of the audit team and a detailed fee proposal. The new client proposal discusses business and audit expectations, audit firm strengths, audit team, audit approach, reliance on internal auditors, transition needs and management, after-service monitoring, and fee details.

It is in the interests of both client and auditor that the auditor sends an engagement letter, preferably before the commencement of the engagement, to help in avoiding misunderstandings with respect to the engagement. An engagement letter is an agreement between the accounting firm and the client for the conduct of the audit and related services. An auditor's engagement letter documents and confirms his acceptance of the appointment, the objective and scope of the audit, the extent of auditor responsibilities to the client, and the form of any reports. The form and content of the audit engagement letter may vary for each client, but they should be recorded in an audit engagement letter or other suitable form of written agreement and should include: the objective of the audit of financial information; the responsibilities of the auditor; management's responsibility; and the applicable financial reporting framework.

5.10 Questions, Exercises and Cases

QUESTIONS

5.2 Client Acceptance: The First Step on the Journey to an Opinion

5-1 What is the difference between acceptance of the client and acceptance by the client?

5.3 Evaluate the Client's Background

5-2 What are the major sources of client information auditors have available? Which source would prove the best for new businesses? Why?

5.4 Ability to Meet Ethical and Specific Competence Requirements

5-3 Consideration of whether the firm has the competencies and resources to undertake a new engagement includes reviewing existing partner and staff competencies. What competencies are these?

5.5 Use of Other Professionals in the Audit

5-4 What is a group auditor? What must he consider when the work of another auditor is used?

5-5 How is an 'expert' defined according to ISA 620? When should an auditor bring in an expert?

5.6 Communicating With the Predecessor (Existing) Auditor

5-6 To what extent can an existing auditor discuss the affairs of their client with a new auditor?

5.7 Acceptance by the Client – The Engagement Proposal

5-7 List four things an auditor must consider when establishing professional fees. What is meant by 'lowballing'?

5-8 Define a contingency fee. Why should a contingency fee not be used? What are the two exceptions for using contingency fees?

5-9 Briefly list the four items found in a continuing client audit proposal. List and define the items that may be found in an audit proposal for a new client.

5.8 The Audit Engagement Letter

5-10 What should be included in an engagement letter? What are some reasons a client might change the terms of the engagement?

5-11 Under what circumstances will an auditor send a new engagement letter each year to a continuing client?

5-12 List the ISAs used in this chapter and briefly define them.

PROBLEMS AND EXERCISES

5.3 Evaluate the Client's Background

5-13 Client Evaluation. The audit firm of F.A. Bloch and Co. has been approached by the following companies who wish to retain Bloch for audit work:

1 Interlewd, an internet company, whose website features explicit images of male nudes and which operates male strip clubs on the west coast of Australia.

2   Dreamtime, a company that operates gambling casino boats off shore and video game machines in major Australian cities.

3   Bernadette, an entertainment company, whose chief executive officer has been investigated by the Italian government for taking bribes, violating public securities laws, conspiring to commit bodily harm and issuing bad checks. The CEO has not been convicted of any of these charges. The board of directors claim that this happened many years ago, and since he has run several companies successfully.

Required:

A.   What procedures should F.A. Bloch and Co. use to investigate these potential clients?

B.   What would F.A. Bloch and Co. consider in determining whether to accept these clients?

5.4 Ability to Meet Ethical and Specific Competence Requirements

5-14 The audit firm of Guiseppe Mulciber, Dottore Commercialista, has been asked to bid on an annual audit of the financial statements of Mammon, a publicly traded gold jewellery manufacturer. The Mulciber firm has been performing assurance services for Mammon over the past there years. Almost everyone on the audit team has investments in stocks and mutual funds. Mammon and the Mulciber had disputes in the past about the extent of assurance services provided. One of the members of the proposed audit staff was an employee of Mammon until 14 months ago. Only one person on the proposed audit team had audited a jewellery manufacturer.

Required:

A.   What procedures would Mulciber conduct to determine independence of the firm and audit team?

B.   Does the Mulciber audit team have the proper competencies? Explain.

C.   What circumstances might disqualify Mulciber from serving as an auditor for Mammon?

5.5 Use of Other Professionals in the Audit

5-15 Use of Other Auditor. Rene Lodeve, Reviseur d'Entreprises, has been hired by BelleRei, N.V., a Liege, Belgium, company. Lodeve will audit all accounts except those of a subsidiary in Spain, which represents 15 per cent of the total sales of BelleRei, which is audited by an 'other accountant', Jeme Indigena.

Required:

A.   What procedures would Lodeve perform to determine whether Indigena has sufficient professional competence to perform the work?

B.   If Lodeve concludes that he cannot depend on the work of Indigena, and he cannot perform additional procedures, what sort of audit opinion should Lodeve give?

5.6 Communicating With the Predecessor (Existing) Auditor

5-16 Preparation and Planning. Roger Buckland was recently appointed auditor of Waterfield, Ltd, a public company. He had communicated with the company's previous auditor before accepting the audit. Buckland attended the company's shareholders meeting at which he was appointed but he has not yet visited the company's offices.

Required:

List the matters that Buckland should attend to between the time of his appointment and the commencement of his audit work in order to effectively plan the audit.

[*Uniform Evaluation Report* (Toronto: CPA Canada)]

5.7 Acceptance by the Client – The Engagement Proposal

5-17 Audit Proposal. Juao Castelo, Revisor Oficial de Contas (ROC), is required to write a client audit proposal for two clients, one continuing (Jinne) and one new (Autodafe).

Required:

A. Based on the proposal for a continuing client and a new client discussed in this chapter, list the contents of the proposal to Jinne and Autodafe.

B. What do the two proposals have in common? What is different?

C. Describe what is discussed in each section of the proposal to Autodafe.

5-18 Audit Fees. Ursula Chona, Contador Publico (CP Titulado), an auditor from Medellin, Columbia, was referred a client by a local attorney and she has agreed to accept the client for a financial statements audit. She must now determine what fee she will charge.

Required:

A. According to international ethics, the fee should be a fair reflection of effort, taking what conditions into account?

B. On what basis should the fee be calculated? Should out-of-pocket expenses be included or listed separately?

C. What are the circumstances under which Chona can ask for a contingency fee?

D. Can Chona pay a 'finder's fee' to the attorney who referred the client to her?

5.8 The Audit Engagement Letter

5-19 Engagement Letter. Stephen Hu, CPA, from Taipei, Taiwan, has just accepted a new client, Kiwan Xou. The company will be audited under the ISA and IAS standards. The client will be given an audit opinion and a management letter. The fees are based on hourly fees, will take 125 hours, and will involve one senior (TD 3,500 per hour), two staff auditors (TD 2,800 per hour), and a partner (TD 5,000 per hour). Out-of-pocket expense is estimated at TD 65,000. The payments will be 33 per cent at the beginning of the audit with the balance at the end of the audit.

Required:

Based on the above information, write an engagement letter to Kiwan Xou from Stephen Hu.

CASES

5-20 Description of the business: Compu Group Corporation designs, develops, manufactures and markets a wide range of personal computing products, including desktop personal computers, portable computers, network servers and peripheral products that store and manage data in network environments. The company markets its products primarily to business, home, government and education customers. The company operates in one principal industry segment across geographically diverse markets.

The company is subject to legal proceedings and claims which arise in the ordinary course of its business. Management does not believe that the outcome of any of those matters will have a material adverse effect on the company's consolidated financial position or operating results.

Required:

A. Based on the information presented, evaluate the company for acceptance. List criteria that must be reviewed in order to determine acceptability.

B. Make a checklist for areas covered

C. Outline your audit approach.

(Adopted from an idea by Phoong Ngo, Qiang Hsing and Chi-hui Lee)

5.11 Notes

1 ISEBA 210 and ISA 315. See IESBA, 2010, paragraph 210.7, *Handbook of the Code of Ethics for Professional Accountants*. And International Auditing and Assurance Standards Board (IAASB), 2012, International Standard on Auditing 315 (ISA 315) 'Identifying and Assessing the Risks of Material Misstatement through Understanding the Entity and Its Environment', paragraph 11, *Handbook of International Quality Control, Auditing, Review, Other Assurance and Related Services Pronouncements*, 2012 edn, Volume 1. Both International Federation of Accountants, New York.

2 International Ethics Standards Board of Accountants (IESBA), 2010, Section 290 'Independence – Audit and Review Engagements', para. 290.220, *Handbook of the Code of Ethics for Professional Accountants*, 2010 edn, International Federation of Accountants, New York.

3 See, for example, AICPA, 2011, *Code of Professional Conduct*, Section 08 101-6, 'Independence', para. 8, American Institute of Certified Public Accountants, New York, states: 'Independence may be impaired whenever the covered member and the covered member's client company or its management are in threatened or actual positions of material adverse interest by reason of threatened or actual litigation.'

4 IESBA, 2010, *Handbook of the Code of Ethics for Professional Accountants*, International Auditing, Assurance, and Ethics Pronouncements: Independence – Audit and Review Engagements Ethics, Section 290, para. 290.211, International Federation of Accountants, New York.

5 International Auditing and Assurance Standards Board (IAASB), 2012, International Standard on Quality Control #1 (ISQC #1) 'Quality Control for Audit, Assurance and Related Services Practices', paragraph A18, *Handbook of International Quality Control, Auditing, Review, Other Assurance and Related Services Pronouncements*, 2012 edn, Volume 1, International Federation of Accountants, New York,

6 International Auditing and Assurance Standards Board (IAASB), 2012, International Standard on Auditing 600 (ISA 600) 'Special Considerations – Audits of Group Financial Statements (Including the Work of Component Auditors)', *Handbook of International Quality Control, Auditing, Review, Other Assurance and Related Services Pronouncements*, 2012 edn, Volume 1, International Federation of Accountants, New York.

7 Ibid.

8 Component auditor is an auditor who, at the request of the group engagement team, performs work on financial information related to a component for the group audit.

9 A component of a business is an entity or business activity for which group or component management prepares financial information that should be included in the group financial statements. Component might refer to components of financial statements – the auditor may be requested to express an opinion on one or more components of a financial statement, for example accounts receivable, inventory, an employee's bonus calculation, or a provision for income taxes. This is described in ISA 800.

10 The group auditor will mention the related or other auditor if his work does not provide sufficient appropriate audit evidence and the reference to the other auditor is necessary for an adequate explanation of the circumstances. See para. A9 of ISA 600.

11 ISA 600, April 2006, *Using the work of another auditor*: 'The auditor should not refer to the work of another auditor in an audit report unless required by legislation or as part of a modification.'

12 The 'Implementation Guidance' (Auditing Standards Committee Statements) issued by the JICPA provides that while the principal auditor may use the work of the other auditor, the principal auditor should express an opinion based on his own judgement and does not make reference to the work of the other auditor in the auditor's report.

13 International Auditing and Assurance Standards Board (IAASB), 2012, International Standard on Auditing 600 (ISA 600) 'Special Considerations – Audits of Group Financial Statements (Including the Work of Component Auditors)', para. 50, *Handbook of International Quality Control, Auditing, Review, Other Assurance and Related Services Pronouncements*, 2012 edn, Volume 1, International Federation of Accountants, New York.

14 In the ISA context the expert is considered a specialist employed by the auditor, whereas in the USA and other countries the expert is considered to be an assistant rather than a specialist.

15 International Auditing and Assurance Standards Board (IAASB), 2012, International Standards on Auditing 620 (ISA 620) 'Using the Work of an Auditor's Expert', para. 6a, *Handbook of International Quality Control, Auditing, Review, Other Assurance and Related Services Pronouncements*, 2012 edn, Volume 1, International Federation of Accountants. New York.

16 IESBA, 2010, *Handbook of the Code of Ethics for Professional Accountants*, s 210, para. 210.10, International Federation of Accountants, New York.

17 Existing accountant (or auditor) is a professional accountant in public practice currently holding an audit appointment or carrying out accounting, taxation, consulting or similar professional services for a client.

18 International Auditing and Assurance Standards Board (IAASB), 2012, International Standards on Auditing 510 (ISA 510) 'Initial Audit Engagements – Opening Balances', para. 6, *Handbook of International Quality Control, Auditing, Review, Other Assurance and Related Services Pronouncements*, 2012 edn, Volume 1, International Federation of Accountants. New York.

19 International Auditing and Assurance Standards Board (IAASB), 2012, International Standards on Auditing 210 (ISA 210) 'Agreeing the Terms Audit Engagements', paras A11–A14, A21–A37, *Handbook of International Quality Control, Auditing, Review, Other Assurance and Related Services Pronouncements*, 2012 edn, Volume 1, International Federation of Accountants, New York.

20 International Standards Organization (ISO), 2000, ISO 9001:2000(E) 'Quality Management Systems – Requirements', ISO copyright office, Geneva.

21 Audit strategy is the design of an optimised audit approach that seeks to achieve the necessary audit assurance at the lowest cost within the constraints of the information available.

22 International Auditing and Assurance Standards Board (IAASB), 2012, International Standards on Auditing 610 (ISA 610) 'Using the Work of Internal Auditors', para. 4, *Handbook of International Quality Control, Auditing, Review, Other Assurance and Related Services Pronouncements*, 2012 edn, Volume 1, International Federation of Accountants, New York.

23 IESBA, 2010, *Handbook of the Code of Ethics for Professional Accountants*, para. 240, *Handbook of International Quality Control, Auditing, Review, Other Assurance and Related Services Pronouncements*, Part I, International Federation of Accountants, New York.

24 Ibid.

25 Ibid. Section 240 'Fees and Other Types of Remuneration' discusses fees including contingent fees and referral fees.

26 In the USA and other national contexts, an engagement letter is not required, although it is usually recommended.

27 International Auditing and Assurance Standards Board (IAASB), 2012, International Standards on Auditing 210 (ISA 210) 'Agreeing the Terms of Audit Engagements', para. 10, *Handbook of International Quality Control, Auditing, Review, Other Assurance and Related Services Pronouncements*, 2012 edn, Volume 1, International Federation of Accountants, New York.

28 Ibid. ISA 210, paras A23–A24.

29 Ibid. Appendix I 'Example of an Audit Engagement Letter'.

30 Applicable financial reporting framework is the financial reporting framework adopted by management and, where appropriate, those charged with governance in the preparation of the financial statements that is acceptable in view of the nature of the entity and the objective of the financial statements, or that is required by law or regulation.

31 See, for example, ISA 260 'Communication with Those Charged with Governance' and ISA 240, 'The Auditor's Responsibilities Relating to Fraud in an Audit of Financial Statements', para. 43.

32 International Auditing and Assurance Standards Board (IAASB), 2012, International Standards on Auditing 200 (ISA 200) 'Overall Objectives of the Independent Auditor and the Conduct of an Audit in Accordance With International Standards On Auditing', paras A3–A10, *Handbook of International Quality Control, Auditing, Review, Other Assurance and Related Services Pronouncements*, 2012 edn, Volume 1, International Federation of Accountants, New York.

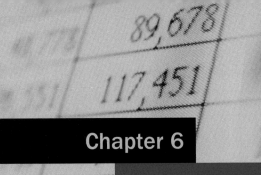
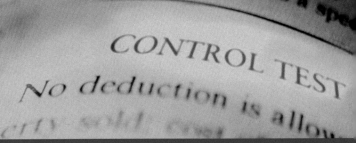

Chapter 6

MAIN AUDIT CONCEPTS AND PLANNING THE AUDIT (ISA 300, 315, 320)

After studying this chapter, you should be able to:

1 State what the general objective is in planning an audit.

2 Give the standard planning procedures.

3 Understand the knowledge of a client's business required to plan the audit.

4 Discuss the relevant aspects of understanding the entity and its environment.

5 Describe what is done during initial interviews, discussions and site visits with the client.

6 Know how legal obligations of the client are investigated.

7 Give examples of a management objective, the related strategy and the resultant business risk.

8 Identify the steps in the strategy-oriented framework for understanding the entity.

9 List the different types of risk that auditors must assess in planning.

10 Define each type of risk.

11 Understand what is meant by 'significant risk'.

12 Know the auditor's definition of 'materiality'.

13 Illustrate the conditions that determine materiality.

14 Understand the difference between financial statement fraud and misappropriation of assets.

15 Discuss the 'fraud triangle' factors that may lead to fraud.

16 Identify reponses to fraud assessment.

17 Grasp the role of the auditor's expert in the audit.

18 Be acquainted with the relationship between the external auditor and the auditee's internal auditor.

19 Be aware of the audit procedures when the entity uses third-party service organisations for activities that impact the financial statements.

20 Comprehend inherent risk and the procedures to assess it.

21 Be familiar with the planning memorandum and audit plan.

6.2   Planning Objective and Procedures

International Standards on Auditing 300 (ISA 300) 'Planning an Audit of Financial Statements' states:[1] 'the objective of the auditor is to plan the audit so that it will be performed in an effective manner ... The auditor shall establish an overall audit strategy that sets the scope, timing and direction of the audit, and that guides the development of the audit plan.'

■ Planning Objective and Procedures

In other words, the objective of planning is to determine timing and scope of the audit and the amount and type of evidence and review required to assure the auditor that there is no material misstatement of the financial statements. This is Phase II in the Audit Process Model (see Illustration 6.1).

The planning procedures are:

1 Perform audit procedures to understand the entity and its environment, including the entity's internal control.
2 Assess the risks of material misstatements of the financial statements.
3 Determine materiality.
4 Prepare the planning memorandum and audit programme containing the auditor's response to the identified risks.

This chapter will primarily deal with the first three steps of the planning procedures, with the exception of the internal control considerations, which will be dealt with later in the text (see Chapter 7 'Internal Control and Control Risk'). Step 4 of the planning procedures is also covered later (see Chapter 9 'Auditor's Response to Assessed Risk'). Before an audit programme can be written for the audit, the audit planning process should include procedures to: acquire an understanding of the entity and its

ILLUSTRATION 6.1

Audit Process Model

Phase I: Client Acceptance

Objective	Determine both acceptance of a client and acceptance by a client. Decide on acquiring a new client or continuation of relationship with an existing one and the type and amount of staff required.
Procedures	1 Evaluate the client's background and reasons for the audit 2 Determine whether the auditor is able to meet the ethical requirements regarding the client 3 Determine need for other professionals 4 Communicate with predecessor auditor 5 Prepare client proposal 6 Select staff to perform the audit 7 Obtain an engagement letter

Phase II: Planning the Audit

Objective	Determine the amount and type of evidence and review required to give the auditor assurance that there is no material misstatement of the financial statements.
Procedures	1 Perform audit procedures to understand the entity and its environment, including the entity's internal control 2 Assess the risks of material misstatements of the financial statements 3 Determine materiality 4 Prepare the planning memorandum and audit programme containing the auditor's response to the identified risks

Phase III: Testing and Evidence

Objective	Test for evidence supporting internal controls and the fairness of the financial statements.
Procedures	1 Tests of controls 2 Substantive tests of transactions 3 Analytical procedures 4 Tests of details of balances 5 Search for unrecorded liabilities

Phase IV: Evaluation and Reporting

Objective	Complete the audit procedures and issue an opinion.
Procedures	1 Evaluate governance evidence 2 Perform procedures to identify subsequent events 3 Review financial statements and other report material 4 Perform wrap-up procedures 5 Prepare Matters for Attention of Partners 6 Report to the board of directors 7 Prepare audit report

environment by reviewing financial (e.g. going concern, analytical procedures) and non-financial (e.g. industry, company, legal, related party, statutory) information; understand the accounting and internal control systems; and assess risk and materiality. Other issues such as the nature and timing of the engagement, involvement of other auditors, determination to use auditor's experts, staffing requirements, and reports usually receive preliminary attention at the client acceptance phase (Phase I in the model in Chapter 5 'Client Acceptance'), but might require follow-up in the planning phase and subsequent phases. The auditor determines the nature, timing and extent of audit procedures as well as the form of supervision and review, and incorporates that into an audit programme.

6.3 Understanding the Entity and its Environment

In the client acceptance phase (Phase I of the audit process model), the auditors review material that is readily available about the entity and the entity's environment (annual reports, public news, and public information databases). However, in the planning phase the auditor's understanding of the entity and its environment should grow significantly. As ISA 315[2] points out, this understanding is an essential aspect of carrying out an ISA audit. It establishes a frame of reference within which the auditor plans the audit and exercises professional judgement about assessing risks of material misstatement of the financial statements and responding to those risks.

■ Procedures to Obtain an Understanding

ISA 315 provides an overview of the procedures that the auditor should follow in order to obtain an understanding sufficient to assess the risks and consider these risks in designing the audit plans. The risk assessment procedures should, at a minimum, be a combination of the following:[3]

- **Inquiries of management** and others within the entity. It is important to have discussions with the client's management about their objectives and expectations, and plans for achieving these goals. The discussions may encompass short-term management objectives such as increasing profit, reducing investment in working capital, introducing new product lines, reducing taxes, or reducing selling and distribution expenses. Expectations should be explored concerning the company's external agents such as customers, suppliers, shareholders, financial institutions, government, etc. However, although management will typically be the most effective and efficient information source, it might be worthwhile to obtain information from others, in order to reduce the potential for bias.
- **Analytical procedures**. These may help the auditor in identifying unusual transactions or positions. Analytical procedures usually involve a comparison of company results to that of the industry. There are publications of major industry ratios and trends that might be helpful to the auditor doing analytical procedures (see Chapter 7 'Internal Control and Control Risk').

■ **Observation and inspection**. These procedures may cover a broad area, ranging from the observation of an entity's core activities, the reading of management reports or internal control manuals to the inspection of documents. A visit to, and tour of, the company premises will help the auditor develop a better understanding of the client's business and operations. Viewing the facilities helps to identify some internal control safeguards. Seeing the production process will help in assessing the inventory movement and the use of fixed assets. Observations of the orderliness, cleanliness, and physical layout of facilities and of the employees' routine functions and work habits can often tell the auditor more about the client than can be learnt from studying the accounting records. Knowledge of the physical facilities and plant layout may point to the right questions to ask during the planning phase, or getting the right answers to questions later in the audit. Knowing the layout will assist in planning how many audit staff members will be needed to participate in observing the physical inventory. On the site visit one may see signs of potential problems. Rust on equipment may indicate that plant assets have been idle. Excessive dust on raw materials or finished goods may indicate a problem of obsolescence. The auditors can see the physical extent of segregation of duties within the client organisation by observing the number of office employees.

Other Information Sources

In addition to these procedures, the auditor might consider obtaining information from others sources, for example, the entity's external legal counsel, or externally available data sources, including analysts' reports, industry journals, government statistics, surveys, texts, financial newspapers, etc. Professional organisations like the American Institute of Certified Public Accountants (AICPA) distribute industry audit guides and most industries have trade magazines and books describing their business. Most large audit firms also have industry groups following the developments in those industries and creating newsletters on industry-specific items.

■ Audit Team Discussion

Finally, ISA 315 requires a team-wide discussion of the susceptibility of the financial statements to material misstatement.[4] An important reason for this requirement is the consideration that the team members collectively have a broader access to people within the organisation and their insights. As they say, the most interesting information may typically be obtained in elevators and on the car park, and, again, there might be a better balance in the team's insights if the perspectives on the entity are not just confined to those conveyed by top management.

■ Continuing Client

If the client is a continuing one, prior year's working papers are reviewed and reliance can be placed on the observations from prior periods. The client's **permanent audit file** frequently contains information on company history and records of most important accounting policies in previous years. However, before relying on existing working papers, the auditor needs to make sure that there have been no significant changes in the relevant aspects of the client's entity or environment.

■ Understanding the Entity and its Environment

ISA 315 distinguishes the following relevant aspects in the understanding of the entity and its environment:[5]

- industry, regulatory and other external factors, including the applicable financial reporting framework;
- nature of the entity, including the entity's selection and application of accounting policies;
- the entity's selection and application of accounting policies, including the reasons for changes the appropriateness for its business and consistency with the applicable financial reporting framework.
- objectives and strategies, and the related business risks that may result in a material misstatement of the financial statements;
- measurement and review of the entity's financial performance.

Illustration 6.2 gives a global systems perspective of client business risk.[6]

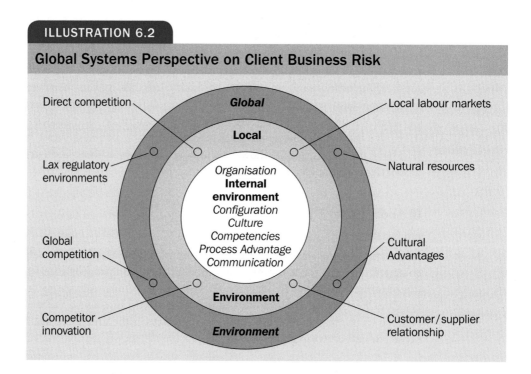

ILLUSTRATION 6.2

Global Systems Perspective on Client Business Risk

■ Industry, Regulatory and Other External Factors

It is important to understand the client's industry because their industry has specific risks created by the nature of the business, accounting conventions, and industry regulation. Understanding inherent risks common to all companies in a certain industry helps the auditor identify the inherent risks of the individual company. For example, the telecommunications industry has certain risks because it is globally competitive, technological changes may render certain assets obsolete at a quicker pace than anticipated, and tele-communication laws control a client's base and service fees. In other words, the industry gives rise to risks that may result in material misstatement of the financial statements of an individual company.

One of the relevant factors in this regard is the financial reporting framework (e.g. International Financial Reporting Standards (IFRS)) that is applicable to the jurisdiction in which the company operates. Other factors relevant to the industry understanding could be the competition, supplier and customer relationships, technological develop-ments and energy costs. The regulatory environment issues relevant to understanding the industry are: accounting principles (and their industry specific application), taxation, environmental requirements, and the laws and government policies affecting the indus-try. Industries are also affected by external factors such as general economic conditions, interest rates, and availability of capital and debt. A list of matters that an auditor might consider when obtaining an understanding of the industry, regulatory and other external factors affecting an entity is given in Illustration 6.3.

ILLUSTRATION 6.3

Industry, Regulatory and Other External Factors, Including the Applicable Financial Reporting Framework Auditors Should Consider

Industry conditions

- The market and competition, including demand, capacity and price competition
- Cyclical or seasonal activity
- Product technology relating to the entity's products
- Energy supply and cost

Regulatory environment

- Accounting principles and industry specific practices
- Regulatory framework for a regulated industry
- Legislation and regulation that significantly affect the entity's operations
    - Regulatory requirements
    - Direct supervisory activities
- Taxation (corporate and other)
- Government policies currently affecting the conduct of the entity's business
    - Monetary, including foreign exchange controls
    - Financial incentives (e.g. government aid programmes)
    - Tariffs, trade restrictions
- Environmental requirements affecting the industry and the entity's business

Other external factors currently affecting the entity's business

- General level of economic activity (e.g. recession, growth)
- Interest rates and availability of financing
- Inflation, currency revaluation

■ Nature of the entity

This aspect of the understanding phase deals with the entity's core, i.e. its operations, types of investments, its financing/ownership, and how management applies and discloses accounting policies.

■ Information acquired about **business operations** may include nature of revenue sources (retailer, manufacturer, and professional services); products and services (e.g. pricing policies, locations and quantities of inventory, profit margins, warranties, order book); market (exports, contracts, terms of payment, market share, franchises, licences, patents, composition of customer group), location of company facilities (warehouses, offices); employment (wage levels, supply, union contracts, pensions), key suppliers, and customers.

■ *Investments* that have reduced in value have been the downfall of as diverse a group of entities as Metallgesellschaft, a German manufacturer who lost a large amount on the derivatives market,[7] and Orange County, California, which was forced into bankruptcy by speculation on their municipal bonds.[8] Important transactions for which information should be gathered include: acquisitions, mergers and disposals of business divisions; use of derivative financial instruments; type of major investments by the company; capital investment activities (in plant and equipment, technology, etc.) and investment in non-consolidated entities such as joint ventures, **special purpose entities,**[9] and partnerships.

■ The entity's choice and application of **financial reporting policies** is one of the core considerations of the auditor, because this is the *criteria* on which the auditor gives his assurance. The auditor should review company accounting policies including revenue recognition, inventories, research and development, important expense categories, judgmental accounting valuations, and financial statement **presentation and disclosure.** Foreign currency assets, liabilities, and transactions require special attention.

A list of matters that an auditor might consider when obtaining an understanding of the nature of the entity is given in Illustration 6.4.[10]

There are models, such as in an Entity Level Business Model (see Illustration 6.5),[11] which allows an auditor to organise all information gathered about industry, company, strategic audit, and related party transactions. The entity level business model may be prepared to provide a pictorial summary of the entity's business to the entity's management, audit committee, board of directors, etc., or to facilitate communication within the engagement team.

Legal Documents

Many of these aspects of the nature of the entity can be affected by legal considerations. Therefore, it is important, at an early stage, to consider specific legal documents, including corporate charter and bylaws, minutes of the board of directors and stockholders' meetings, and contracts. Local standards may require disclosure of contracts in the financial statements. Examples are listed in Illustration 6.6.

ILLUSTRATION 6.4

CONSIDERATIONS WHEN OBTAINING AN UNDERSTANDING OF THE NATURE OF THE ENTITY

- **Business operations**
- **Investments and investment activities**
- **Financing and financing activities**
- **Financial reporting**

Business operations (derived from the Business Model) such as

- Products, services and markets, resources, value drivers
- Conduct of operations like production, sales, transport
- Joint ventures, alliances
- Governance structure, market position, locations
- Key customers, suppliers, employee arrangements

Investments and investment activities such as

- Mergers and acquisitions
- Investments and divestments in capital, loans, securities and assets
- Investments in non consolidated entities
- Market conditions and opportunities

Financing and financing activities such as

- Debt structure, solvency and liquidity policies
- Debt arrangements and convenants
- Ownership structure
- Use of derivatives
- Subsidiaries and contingent obligations

Financial reporting such as

- Accounting principles
- Industry and company specific standards and rules
- (Inter) national accounting standards, law, rules, guidance
- Revenue recognition practice
- Accounting for fair values, unusual or complex transactions

ILLUSTRATION 6.5

Entity Level Business Model

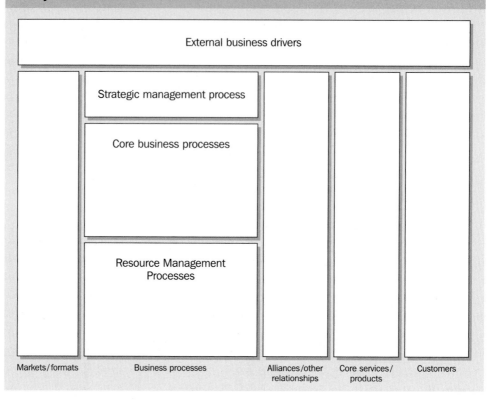

ILLUSTRATION 6.6

Examples of Legal Documents and Records to Consider in the Context of Understanding the Entity's Nature

Corporate charter – generally gives the name of the corporation, the date of incorporation, the kinds and amounts of capital stock the corporation is authorised to issue, and the types of business activities the corporation is authorised to conduct.

Bylaws – includes rules and procedures of the corporation including fiscal year, frequency of stockholder meetings, method of voting for board of directors, and the duties and powers of the corporate officer.

Corporate minutes – official record of the meetings of the board of directors and stockholders. Include authorisation of compensation of officers, new contracts, acquisition of fixed assets, loans and dividends payments.

Contracts – include long-term notes and payables, stock options, pension plans, contracts with vendors, government contracts, royalty agreements, union contracts, and leases.

Auditors are interested in all contracts. Contracts that are of particular interest to auditors are long-term notes and bonds payable, stock options, pension plans, contracts with vendors for future delivery of supplies, government contracts for completion and delivery of manufactured products, royalty agreements, union contracts, and leases. Contracts may affect the assessed inherent risk.

■ The Entity's Objectives, Strategies and Related Business Risks

The auditor will also consider the entity's objectives and strategies, and the related business risks that may affect the financial statements. The entity's objectives are the overall plans for the company as determined by those charged with governance[12] and management. Strategies are the operational approaches by which management intends to achieve its objectives. Significant conditions, events, circumstances or actions that could adversely affect the entity's ability to achieve its objectives and execute its strategies create business risks. The concept of business risks is broader than the concept of risks of material misstatements in the financial statements. However, most business risks will typically have a financial consequence, and hence will find their way into the financial statements.

One could compare a business entity to a living system. The communications network (formal and informal) is like a central nervous system where important direction is given from the brain to the body to perform work. In an organisation, management or those responsible for governance (e.g. the board of directors) formulate a strategy which, in turn, influences how employees perform work. Any living organism has a symbiotic relationship with the environment. Events such as severe weather may engender survival risks for an entity. Searching for food in the environment modifies the work an organism does and shapes its survival strategy. Similarly, in business organisations there exists a symbiotic alliance between the business processes of the organisation and external economic agents. Customers, suppliers, shareholders and the general public are external economic agents who impact on a company's profitability and ultimate survival. Financial statements are the communications that describe, on a monetary level, the company's dynamic interrelationship with external agents.

■ Strategic Framework

An interesting interpretation of this part of the 'understanding and risk assessment' phase is taken in a strategy-orientated framework,[13] which involves the following steps:

1 Understand the client's strategic advantage. What are the entity's plans? What market niches do they control?
2 Understand the risks that threaten the client's business objectives. What forces are challenging the entity's competitive advantages?
3 Understand the key processes and related competencies to realise strategic advantage. What advantages and competencies are needed to increase market share in their business area? What are the risks and safeguards?
4 Measure and benchmark process performance. What is the evidence that the expected value is being created by the strategy?
5 Document the understanding of the client's ability to create value and generate future cash flows using a client business model, process analysis, key performance indicators, and a business risk profile.

6 Use the comprehensive business knowledge decision frame to develop expectations about key **assertions** embodied in the overall financial statements.

7 Compare reported financial results to expectations and design additional audit test work to address any gaps between expectations.

This method uses the models given in Illustrations 6.2 and 6.5.

Illustration 6.7 shows what an auditor might consider in determining objectives, strategies and risks of the firm.

ILLUSTRATION 6.7

Considerations Concerning Entity Objectives, Strategies and Related Business Risks

Existence of objectives (i.e. how the entity addresses industry, regulatory and other external factors) relating to, for example, the following:

- Industry developments (potential related business risk – entity does not have the personnel or expertise to deal with the changes in the industry)
- New products and services (potential related business risk – increased product liability)
- Expansion of the business (potential related business risk – demand has not been accurately estimated)
- New accounting requirements (potential related business risk – incomplete or improper implementation, increased costs)
- Regulatory requirements (potential related business risk – increased legal exposure)
- Current and prospective financing requirements (potential related business risk – loss of financing due to inability to meet requirements)
- Use of IT (potential related business risk – systems and processes not compatible)
- Effects of implementing a strategy, particularly any effects that will lead to new accounting requirements (potential related business risk – incomplete or improper implementation)

■ Measurement and Review of the Entity's Financial Performance

In order to assess the risk of material misstatements in the financial statements, an auditor should examine internally generated information used by management and external (third party) evaluations of the company. Internal measures provide management with information about progress towards meeting the entity's objectives. Internal information may include key performance indicators, budgets, variance analysis, segment information, and divisional, departmental or other level performance reports, and comparisons of an entity's performance with that of competitors. External information, such as analysts' reports and credit rating agency reports, may be useful to the auditor. Internal or external performance measures may create pressures on management to misstate the financial statements. A deviation in the performance measures may indicate a risk of misstatement of related financial statement information.[14] See Illustration 6.8.

ILLUSTRATION 6.8

Measurement and Review of the Entity's Financial Performance

The following are internally-generated information used by management for analysing financial performance that an auditor might consider before performing analytical procedures during the planning phase:

- Key performance indicators (financial and non-financial) and key ratios, trends and operating statistics
- Employee performance measures and incentive compensation policies
- Use of forecasts, budgets variance analysis, segment information and divisional, departmental or other level performance reports
- Comparisons of an entity's performance with that of competitors
- Period-on-period financial performance (revenue growth, profitability, leverage)

Analytical procedures are so important to the audit, and so universally employed, that a separate chapter is needed to describe them (Chapter 9 'Analytical Procedures'). Analytical procedures[15] are performed at least once in an audit – near the end of the audit. ISA 520 states:[16] 'The objectives of the of auditor are … to design and perform analytical procedures near the end of the audit that assist the auditor when forming an overall conclusion as to whether the financial statements are consistent with the auditor's understanding of the entity.'

In addition, most practising accountants recommend analytical procedures also are applied during Phase I (planning) and Phase III (testing and evidence). However, in this section we will only discuss the analytical procedures in the planning stage. Illustration 6.9 summarises some important characteristics of analytical procedures performed at the three stages of an audit.

The auditor ordinarily applies analytical procedures at the planning stage to assist in understanding the business and in identifying areas of potential risk. Application of analytical procedures may indicate aspects of the business of which the auditor was unaware. Analytical procedures in planning the audit use information that is both financial and non-financial (e.g. the relationship between sales and square footage of selling space or volume of goods sold).

In order to better understand the client's business and industry, the auditor will calculate typical ratios and compare the company ratios to those of the industry. If the auditor is concerned about possible misstatements the ratios like repair and maintenance expenses can be compared to prior years and looked at for fluctuations. To learn about liquidity or going concern, one may compare the current or quick ratio to previous years and to the industry.

When analytical procedures identify significant fluctuations or relationships that are inconsistent with other relevant information or that deviate from predicted amounts, the auditor should increase procedures to obtain adequate explanations and appropriate corroborative evidence.

ILLUSTRATION 6.9

Important Characteristics of Analytical Procedures at Three Audit Stages

Stage of an audit	Required?	Purpose	Comment
Planning	No	To assist in planning the nature, timing and extent of other auditing procedures	Level of aggregation can vary and will have impact on effectiveness
Substantive testing	No	To obtain evidential matter about particular assertions related to account balances or classes of transactions	Effectiveness depends upon: ■ nature of assertion ■ plausibility and predictability of relations ■ reliability of data ■ precision of expectation
Overall review	Yes	To assist in assessing the conclusions reached and in the evaluation of the overall financial statement presentation	Includes reading financial statements to consider: ■ accuracy of evidence gathered for unusual or unexpected balances identified during planning or during course of audit ■ unusual or unexpected balances or relationships previously identified

■ Internal Control

As addressed before, internal control – the final aspect to consider in understanding the entity and its environment – will be dealt with separately later in the text (Chapter 7 'Internal Control and Control Risk'), given the complexity and extent of this topic. However, it should be borne in mind that the auditor needs to obtain a level of understanding of an entity's internal control that is sufficient for a proper understanding of the entity. A good understanding of internal control is required for an appropriate assessment of the risk of material misstatement in the financial statements.

6.4 Audit Risk Model

■ The Risk Assessment Process

Before risk can be assessed, the auditor must perform procedures to obtain an understanding of accounting and internal control systems (see Chapter 7 'Internal Control and Control Risk'). Audit procedures to obtain an understanding are referred to as 'risk assessment procedures'[17] because some of the results may be used by the auditor as audit evidence to support the assessments of the risks of material misstatement of the financial statements. The audit evidence obtained might also apply to transactions, account balances, disclosures, and the operating effectiveness of controls.

The auditor examines the risks of material misstatement at the financial statement level and at the financial statement assertion level for classes of transactions, account balances and disclosures. Risks that exist at the financial statement level are pervasive, i.e. they have a potential impact on a large number of items in the financial statements. An example is the risk that a company is unable to continue as a going concern. This risk would not just have an impact on one item of the financial statements, but would be of importance on the recognition and valuation of many items. Other risks are confined to one or only a few assertions in the financial statements, e.g. the risk of theft from a specific warehouse A could have an impact on the existence of the items recorded on account balance 'Inventory warehouse A'. 'Inventory' is the financial statement element and the related class of transaction would be 'Goods in' or 'Goods out'.

Assessment Tasks

To assess the risks of misstatement of the financial statements, the auditor performs four tasks:

1 Identify risks by developing an understanding of the entity and its environment, including relevant controls that relate to the risks. Analyse the strategic risks and the significant classes of transactions.
2 Relate the identified risks to what could go wrong in management's assertions about completeness, existence, valuation, occurrence, and measurement of transactions or assertions about rights, obligations, presentation, and disclosure.
3 Determine whether the risks are of a magnitude that could result in a material misstatement of the financial statements.
4 Consider the likelihood that the risks will result in a material misstatement of the financial statements and their impact on classes of transactions, account balances and disclosures.

Illustration 6.10 gives some guidance on how these four tasks can be documented in terms of strategic risk on significant classes of transactions.

■ Business Risk, Audit Risk and its Components

As discussed before, business risks result from significant conditions, events, circumstances, or actions that could adversely affect the entity's ability to achieve its objectives and execute its strategies. Even though such risks are likely to eventually have an impact on an entity's financial statements, not every business risk will translate directly in a risk of a material misstatement in the financial statements, which is often referred to as audit risk. For example, the fact that an engineering company has difficulty finding sufficient engineers is clearly a business risk, without there being an obvious direct link to an audit risk.

Audit Risk

Audit risk is the risk that the auditor gives an inappropriate audit opinion when the financial statements are materially misstated. Audit risk is a measure the reliability of the

ILLUSTRATION 6.10

Documentation Formats for Strategic Risk and Significant Classes of Transactions

Strategic risk(s)

W/P ref	Description	Significance		Potential FS effect (including assertion)
		Magnitude of impact	Likelihood of occurrence	
	[Enter description here]			

Significant classes of transactions

W/P ref	Description	FS assertion
	[Enter description here]	

information used by the accounting system is, i.e. how much reliance can be put on it. The higher the audit risk, the more evidence must be gathered in order for the auditor to obtain sufficient assurance as a basis for expressing an opinion on the financial statements.

Audit risk has three components: **inherent risk**, **control risk** and **detection risk**.[18] Even though the new ISAs make only scarce reference to these components, we believe that they are illustrative in understanding how the risk assessment process works. The three components are traditionally defined as follows:

1 **Inherent risk** is the susceptibility of an account balance or class of transactions to misstatements that could be material, individually or when aggregated with misstatements in other balances or classes, assuming that there were no related internal controls. The assessment of inherent risk is discussed in more detail later in this chapter.

2 **Control risk** is the risk that a misstatement that could occur in an account balance or class of transactions and that could be material – individually or when aggregated with misstatements in other balances or classes – will not be prevented or detected and corrected on a timely basis by accounting and internal control systems.

3 **Detection risk** is the risk that an auditor's **substantive procedures**[19] will not detect a misstatement that exists in an account balance or class of transactions that could be material, individually or when aggregated with misstatements in other balances or classes.

When inherent and control risks are high, acceptable detection risk needs to be low to reduce audit risk to an acceptably low level. For example, if the internal control structure is effective in preventing and/or detecting errors (i.e. control risk is low), the auditor is able to perform less effective substantive tests (detection risk is high). Alternatively, if the account balance is more susceptible to misstatement (inherent risk is higher), the auditor must apply more effective substantive testing procedures (detection risk is lower). In short, the higher the assessment of inherent and control risk, the more audit evidence the auditor should obtain from the performance of substantive procedures.

Concept and a Company 6.1

Business Risk and Significant Risk – Lehman Brothers and Ernst & Young

Concept	What is business risk? What is significant risk? When does a business turn out to become an audit risk?
Story	The financial market turmoil in 2007 and 2008 has led to the most severe financial crisis since the Great Depression and also had large repercussions on the real economy. The bursting of the US housing bubble forced banks to write down several hundred billion dollars in bad loans caused by mortgage delinquencies. At the same time, the stock market capitalisation of the major banks declined by more than twice as much.

Lehman Brothers Holdings Inc. was a global financial services firm. It was the fourth-largest investment bank in the US (behind Goldman Sachs, Morgan Stanley, and Merrill Lynch), doing business in investment banking, equity and fixed-income sales and trading (especially US Treasury securities), research, investment management, private equity and private banking, until it filed for bankruptcy on 15 September 2008.

Lehman borrowed significant amounts to fund its investing in the years leading to its bankruptcy in 2008, a process known as leveraging or gearing. A significant portion of this investing was in housing-related assets, making it vulnerable to a downturn in that market.

In March 2008, Lehman Brothers had survived the fallout (in which competitor Bear Stearns went bankrupt), but only narrowly. It subsequently made heavy use of the Fed's new Primary Dealer Credit Facility and had to issue new equity to strengthen its balance sheet. The inability to do so was a significant business risk for Lehman, resulting from the failure to mitigate other business risks.

In order to avoid this business failure, Lehman Brothers used an accounting procedure termed 'repo 105' to temporarily exchange $50 billion of assets into cash just before publishing its financial statements. This conclusion was drawn by Anton R. Valukas, a court-appointed examiner, in a report in which he published the results of a year-long investigation into the finances of Lehman Brothers.

Repo 105 is an accounting manoeuvre where a short-term loan is classified as a sale.

In December 2010, New York's attorney general, Cuomo filed a lawsuit in the New York Supreme Court claiming that Ernst & Young (E&Y), a Big Four firm, helped hide Lehman's 'fraudulent financial reporting'. As the auditor of Lehman Brothers, Ernst & Young approved the use of repo 105 transactions and approved the financial statements of Lehman Brothers.

▶

Business Risk and Significant Risk – Lehman Brothers and Ernst & Young (continued)

In a press release, Ernst & Young stated: 'Lehman's bankruptcy occurred in the midst of a global financial crisis triggered by dramatic increases in mortgage defaults, associated losses in mortgage and real estate portfolios, and a severe tightening of liquidity. Lehman's bankruptcy was preceded and followed by other bankruptcies, distressed mergers, restructurings, and government bailouts of all of the other major investment banks, as well as other major financial institutions. In short, Lehman's bankruptcy was not caused by any accounting issues.'

Discussion Questions	■ Do you believe it is possible that Lehman Brothers was able to borrow more money thanks to the use of repo 105 transactions? ■ Did Ernst & Young put too much emphasis on the form of repo 105 transactions and neglected the substance of repo 105 transactions? ■ Do you blame Lehman Brothers for trying almost anything to avoid bankruptcy?
References	Brunnermeier, M.K. (2008), 'Deciphering the Liquidity and Credit Crunch 2007–08', NBER Working Paper No. 14612, National Bureau of Economic Research, Cambridge, MA. http://en.wikipedia.org/wiki/Lehman_Brothers. http://www.accountingweb.com/topic/accounting-auditing/did-ernst-young-really-assist-financial-fraud.

Illustration 6.11 shows a symbolic graphic used by AICPA to illustrate how audit risk works. The potential pool of material errors is represented by the *tap*[20] at the top of the illustration. The *sieves*[21] represent the means by which the client and the auditor attempt to remove material errors from the financial statements. In Illustration 6.11,[22] the first sieve represents the internal control system. The client may install a system of internal accounting control to detect material errors and correct them. Ideally, the control system should detect any material errors before they enter the financial statements. However, there is some risk that errors will either pass undetected through the control system (perhaps as a result of a breakdown or weakness) or will bypass the control system altogether (e.g. where there are no controls in place such as an unusual exchange of non-monetary assets). The liquid falling through the sieve represents the errors not detected and the spillover represents those errors that bypass the control system. If the internal control system does not detect and correct the errors, they will be included in the financial statements. The auditor must design audit procedures that will provide reasonable assurance that material errors will be detected and removed from the financial statements. In Illustration 6.11, the second sieve represents the auditor's procedures. Despite internal controls and auditors' procedures to detect misstatement, there will always be the possibility that some misstatements will be undetected. This is audit risk.

Illustrations 6.12 and 6.13 show the relationship between inherent, control and detection risks.

There is an inverse relationship between detection risk and the combined level of inherent and control risks. For example, when inherent and control risks are high, acceptable levels of detection risk need to be low to reduce audit risk to an acceptably low

ILLUSTRATION 6.11

Components of Audit Risk

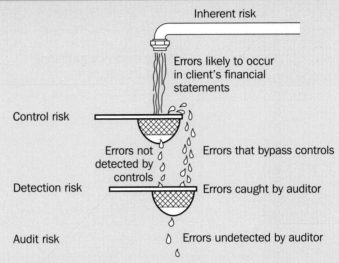

Source: AICPA, 'Auditing Procedures Study' in *Audits of Small Business*, AICPA, New York, 1985, p. 44, reproduced in Dan M. Guy, C. Wayne Alderman and Alan J. Winters, *Auditing*, Harcourt Brace Jovanovich, San Diego, California, 1996, p. 131.

ILLUSTRATION 6.12

Interrelationship of the Components of Audit Risk

The following table shows how the acceptable level of detection risk may vary based on assessments of inherent and control risks, based on the Appendix to International Standard on Auditing 400.

		Auditor's assessment of control risk		
		High	Medium	Low
Auditor's assessment of inherent risk	High	Lowest	Lower	Medium
	Medium	Lower	Medium	Higher
	Low	Medium	Higher	Highest

The darker shaded areas in this table relate to detection risk.

There is an inverse relationship between detection risk and the combined level of inherent and control risks. For example, when inherent and control risks are high, acceptable levels of detection risk need to be low to reduce audit risk to an acceptably low level. On the other hand, when inherent and control risks are low, an auditor can accept a higher detection risk and still reduce audit risk to an acceptably low level.

level. On the other hand, when inherent and control risks are low, an auditor can accept a higher detection risk and still reduce audit risk to an acceptably low level.

199

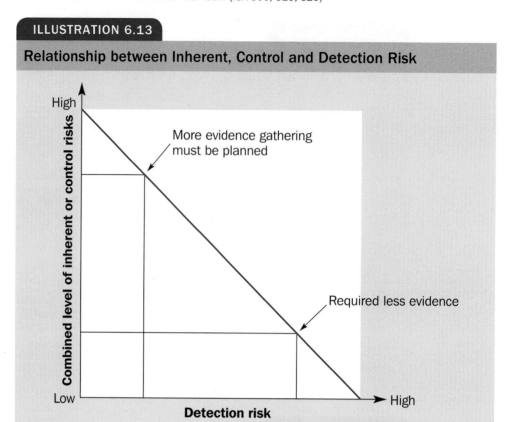

ILLUSTRATION 6.13

Relationship between Inherent, Control and Detection Risk

■ Significant Risks

Significant risks are audit risks that require special audit consideration. Significant risks generally relate to judgemental matters and significant non-routine transactions. Judgement is used, for example, in the development of significant accounting or fair value estimates. Non-routine transactions are transactions that are unusual, either due to size or nature, and that therefore occur infrequently. Risks of material misstatement may be greater for significant judgmental matters requiring accounting estimates or revenue recognition and for assumptions about the effects of future events (e.g. fair value) than for ordinary transactions.

Significant non-routine transactions may arise from management intervention in specifying the accounting treatment for a transaction, manual intervention for data collection and processing, complex calculations or accounting principles, transactions for which there is difficulty in implementing effective controls, and significant related party transactions. These risks are less likely to be subjected to routine control systems and so a more in-depth understanding helps the auditor develop an effective audit approach.

Special Audit Consideration

As part of risk assessment, the auditor may determine some of the risks identified are significant risks that require special audit consideration. Classification of a risk as requiring special consideration is important in the context of the auditor's response to the risk (see Chapter 7 'Internal Control and Control Risk'). In particular, it is even more important for significant than for non-significant risks that the auditor evaluates the design of the entity's controls, including relevant control procedures, and obtains contemporaneous evidence as to whether or not they have been implemented. Further, it is required that the auditor performs substantive procedures that are specifically responsive to the risks.

Is the Risk Significant?

Significant risks arise on most audits, but their determination is a matter for the auditor's professional judgement. In determining what a significant risk is the auditor considers a number of matters, including the following:[23]

- Whether the risk is a risk of fraud.
- The likelihood of the occurrence of the risk.
- Whether the risk is related to recent significant economic, accounting, or other developments and, therefore, requires specific attention.
- The complexity of transactions that may give rise to the risk.
- Whether the risk involves significant transactions with related parties.
- The degree of subjectivity in the measurement of financial information related to the risk.
- Whether the risk involves significant transactions that are outside the normal course of business for the entity, or that otherwise appear to be unusual given the auditor's understanding of the entity and its environment.

6.5 Materiality

Materiality is not specifically defined in the ISAs. ISA 320, instead, defines materiality in the context of an audit and as performance materiality. Although financial reporting frameworks may discuss materiality in different terms, in the context of an audit, they generally explain that:

1 Misstatements, including omissions, are considered to be material if they, individually or in the aggregate, could reasonably be expected to influence the economic decisions of users taken on the basis of the financial statements.
2 Judgements about materiality are made in light of surrounding circumstances, and are affected by the size or nature of a misstatement, or a combination of both.
3 Judgements about matters that are material to users of the financial statements are based on a consideration of the common financial information needs of users as a group. The possible effect of misstatements on specific individual users, whose needs may vary widely, is not considered.[24]

Performance materiality means the amount or amounts set by the auditor at less than materiality for the financial statements as a whole. This reduces to an appropriately low level the probability that the total of uncorrected and undetected misstatements exceeds materiality for the financial statements as a whole. If applicable, performance materiality also refers to the amounts set by the auditor at less than the materiality levels for particular classes of transactions, account balances or disclosures.[25]

The auditor's responsibility is to express an opinion on whether the financial statements are prepared, in all material respects, in accordance with financial accounting standards. Materiality is the degree of inaccuracy or imprecision that is still considered acceptable given the purpose of the financial statements.[26]

■ Materiality Level

Planning materiality is a concept that is used to design the audit such that the auditor can obtain reasonable assurance that any error of a relevant (material) size or nature will be identified. There are additional costs for an auditor to audit with a lower materiality. The lower the materiality, the more costly is the audit. If any error of whatever small size needs to be found in the audit, the auditor would spend significantly more time than when a certain level of imprecision (higher materiality level) is considered acceptable.

What is material is often difficult to determine in practice. However, four factors are generally considered: size of item; nature of item; the circumstances; and the cost and benefit of auditing the item.

■ Size of the Item

The most common application of materiality concerns the *size of the item* considered. A large dollar amount item omitted from the financial statements is generally material. Size must be considered in relative terms, for example as a percentage of the relevant base (net income, total assets, sales, etc.) rather than an absolute amount. The view that size is an essential determinant of materiality means that, for financial reporting purposes, materiality can only be judged in relation to items or errors which are quantifiable in monetary terms.

■ Nature of the Item

The *nature of an item* is a qualitative characteristic. An auditor cannot quantify the materiality decision in all cases; certain items may have significance even though the dollar amount may not be quite as large as the auditor would typically consider material. For example, a political bribe by an auditee, even though immaterial in size, may nevertheless be of such a sensitive nature and have such an effect on the company financial statement that users would need to be told. It has been suggested[27] that in making judgements about materiality, the following aspects of the nature of a misstatement should be considered:

■ the events or transactions giving rise to the misstatement;
■ the legality, sensitivity, normality and potential circumstances of the event or transaction;
■ the identity of any other parties involved; and
■ the accounts and disclosure notes affected.

■ Circumstances of Occurrence

The materiality of an error depends upon the *circumstances of its occurrence*. There are two types of relevant circumstances:

1 the users of the accounting information's economic decision-making process;
2 the context of the accounting information in which an item or error occurs.

Since materiality means the impact on the decisions of the user, the auditor must have knowledge of the likely users of the financial statements and those users' decisions process. If a company is being audited prior to listing on a national stock exchange or a large loan or merger, the users will be of one type. If statements of a closely held partnership are being audited, users will be of a different type.

For example, if the primary users of the financial statements are creditors, the auditor may assign a low materiality threshold to those items on financial statements that affect liquidity[28] such as current assets and current liabilities. On the other hand, if the primary users are investors or potential investors, the auditor may assign a low materiality threshold to income.

■ Reliability, Precision and Amount of Evidence

The auditor should consider materiality and its relationship with audit risk when conducting an audit, according to ISA 320.[29] What does this mean? In statistical sampling, there is a fixed relationship between:

■ the reliability of an assertion based on the sampling (in auditing this is determined by audit risk);
■ the precision of this statement (in auditing it is determined by materiality);
■ the amount of evidence that should be gathered in order to make this assertion.

Changes in one of these three items have implications for (one of) the other two.

Example: Three Assumptions in the Same Circumstance

A real-life example might illustrate this relationship between reliability, precision and amount of evidence. Suppose you are asked to make an assertion about the average taxable income of randomly selected people, shopping at the Kurfürstendamm in Berlin. Also suppose that gathering information regarding the taxable income of these people is costly. Consider the following three situations:

1 You are asked to make, with a high degree of reliability (you were asked to bet quite some money on the correctness of your assertion), the assertion that the average annual taxable income of ten people will be between minus and plus €300,000,000. Even though a high degree of reliability is requested (i.e. a lot is at stake for you), you will probably do little or no investigative work because you were allowed to make a very imprecise statement (i.e. a very high level of tolerance is allowed).

2 You are asked to make, with a low degree of reliability (you were asked to bet only a symbolic €1 on the correctness of your assertion), the assertion that the average annual taxable income of these random ten people will be between €0 and €70,000. Even though this time a high degree of precision is requested, you will probably only do little or no (costly) investigative work, since you were only asked to make your assertion with a low degree of reliability (not a lot at stake for you).

3 You are asked to make, with a high degree of reliability (again, you were asked to bet quite some money on the correctness of your assertion), the assertion that the average annual taxable income of these ten people will be between €0 and €70,000. Because of the high degree of reliability and precision requested (i.e. a lot is at stake for you and only a relatively low degree of tolerance is accepted in your statement), you will probably do extensive investigative work.

These examples might clarify how there is an inverse relationship between audit risk (as a measure of reliability) and materiality (as a measure of precision). (See also Illustration 6.14.)

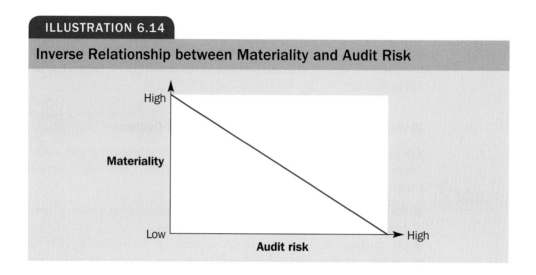

ILLUSTRATION 6.14

Inverse Relationship between Materiality and Audit Risk

What degree of imprecision or materiality is acceptable in auditing financial statements? In order to decide this, the imprecision tolerated should be related to the size of the audited company's business and its profitability. Try to determine how much error or misstatement auditors would be willing to tolerate and still render an opinion that the financial statements were not materially misleading in Case One and Case Two, following.

■ Materially Misstated or Not?

Case One

A few days before the end of 20X1, $1,000 expenditure for the repair of equipment was incorrectly charged to the equipment account in the balance sheet rather than to operating expenses in the income statement. As a result (ignoring depreciation), total assets should be stated at $1,589,000 instead of $1,590,000 and income before taxes should be stated at $107,000 instead of $108,000. Are the financial statements still fairly presented and not materially misleading?

Case Two

A few days before the end of 20X1, $50,000 expenditure for the repair of equipment was incorrectly charged to the equipment account rather than to operating expenses. As a result (ignoring depreciation), total assets should be stated at $1,490,000 rather than $1,540,000 and income before taxes should be stated at $58,000 rather than $108,000? Are the financial statements fairly presented and not materially misleading?

Analysis

In Case One the financial statements are fairly presented and not materially misstated because the $1,000 difference in assets and net income will not make a difference to the financial statement user, i.e. it is not material. Case Two is different. The financial statements are materially misstated, primarily because net income, an important basis of materiality, is overstated by 86 per cent. This overstatement of net income is something that could definitely change the decisions of a financial statement user, i.e. it is material.

■ Where to Set Materiality?

Considering all these materiality factors, then, at what amount should materiality be set? The international standards give no guidelines. In the USA only 10 per cent of authoritative accounting pronouncements contain specific materiality percentages, and only 6 per cent give judgement items.[30] In practice, however, every accounting firm has its own set of guidelines or 'rules of thumb' related to a financial statement base such as net income, total revenues, etc. Rules of thumb commonly used in practice include:

- 5 to 10 per cent of net income before taxes;
- 5 to 10 per cent of current assets;
- 5 to 10 per cent of current liabilities;
- 0.5 to 2 per cent of total assets;
- 0.5 to 2 per cent of total revenues;
- 1 to 5 per cent of total equity.

The appropriate financial statement base for computing materiality will vary based on the nature of the client's business. For example, if a company is near break-even, net income for the year will be much too small to use as the financial statement base. In that case the auditors will often choose another financial statement base or use an average of net income over a number of prior years.

Concept and a Company 6.2

Arthur Andersen, Waste Management and Materiality

Concept	What is material and how is materiality determined?
Story	In 1993 and early 1994, Arthur Andersen audited Waste Management's 1993 financial statements. By 1 February 1994, the engagement team quantified current and prior period misstatements totalling $128 million, which, if recorded, would have reduced net income before special items by 12 per cent.
	The engagement team prepared Proposed Adjusting Journal Entries (PAJEs) in that amount for Waste Management to record in 1993. A PAJE is an adjustment proposed by the auditor to the company during the audit that, if accepted by the company, would correct a misstatement in the books.

▶

Arthur Andersen, Waste Management and Materiality (continued)

The engagement team also identified 'accounting practices that gave rise to other known and likely misstatements' involving understatements of operating expenses for which no PAJEs were prepared. These misstatements included, among other things:

1 amounts for deferred costs of impaired projects that should have been written off;
2 land carrying values in excess of net realisable value;
3 improper purchase acquisition accruals in connection with the establishment of environmental remediation reserves (liabilities);
4 reversals of the environmental remediation reserves (liabilities) to income; and
5 unsupported changes to the salvage values of waste vehicles and containers.

The engagement team also knew of the company's capitalised interest methodology, which Andersen knew did not conform to GAAP but which it had determined was 'not materially inaccurate'.

Waste Management refused to record the PAJEs or to correct the accounting practices giving rise to the PAJEs and other misstatements and likely misstatements.

The engagement team informed Andersen's risk management partner of the PAJEs and questionable accounting practices. Andersen's Audit Objectives and Procedures Manual required that risk management partners consult with senior partners when cumulative PAJEs exceeded 8 per cent of net income from continuing operations. These partners reviewed and discussed the unrecorded PAJEs as well as 'continuing audit issues'. They determined that Andersen would nonetheless issue an unqualified audit report on Waste Management's 1993 financial statements.

Applying an analytical procedure for evaluating the materiality of audit findings referred to as the 'roll-forward' method, these partners determined that, because the majority of PAJEs concerned prior period misstatements, the impact of the PAJEs relating to current period misstatements on Waste Management's 1993 income statement was not material. They would issue an unqualified audit report. But they also warned Waste Management that Andersen expected the company to change its accounting practices and to reduce the cumulative amount of the PAJEs in the future.

Waste Management later paid US$457 million to settle a shareholder class-action suit. The SEC fined Waste Management's independent auditor, Arthur Andersen, US$7 million for its role.

Discussion Questions	■ What analysis do you think the engagement team did to determine the amount of the PAJEs?
	■ By what reasoning did the audit team determine the accounting practices that gave rise to other known and likely misstatements mentioned that did not need adjustment?
	■ What items do you think the senior partners discussed when determining that Andersen would issue an unqualified opinion?
	■ ISA 450 did not exist when this case occurred. If it had existed, did Arthur Andersen meet all requirements of ISA 450?

References   SEC, 2001, Release No. 44444, Accounting And Auditing Enforcement Release No. 1405, 'In the Matter of Arthur Andersen LLP Respondent', Securities and Exchange Commission, 19 June. http://en.wikipedia.org/wiki/Waste_Management,_Inc#Accounting_improprieties.

Concept and a Company 6.3

US SEC Response to WorldCom Illegal Acts

Concept	Liability under statutory law – involving auditors in the disciplinary process.
Story	WorldCom's illegal activities, which included providing falsified financial information to the public, led to the company's downfall in 2002.

WorldCom misled investors from at least as early as 1999 through the first quarter of 2002, and during that period, as a result of undisclosed and improper accounting, WorldCom materially overstated the income it reported on its financial statements by approximately $9 billion (SEC, *Litigation Release*, 2002).

WorldCom was ordered to hire a qualified consultant, acceptable to the SEC, to review the effectiveness of its material internal accounting control structure and policies, including those related to line costs, reserves and capital expenditures, as well as the effectiveness and propriety of WorldCom's processes, practices and policies to ensure that the company's financial data was accurately reported in its public financial statements. The company hired KPMG to launch a comprehensive audit of its financial statements for 2001 and 2002 (Ulick, 2002).

WorldCom was also ordered to provide reasonable training and education to certain officers and employees to minimise the possibility of future violations of federal securities laws.

The SEC proposed a settlement in its civil action against WorldCom Inc. in a federal district court. The proposed settlement was for WorldCom to pay a civil penalty of $1.5 billion. As a result of the company's pending bankruptcy case, the proposed settlement provides for satisfaction of the Commission's judgment by WorldCom's payment, after review and approval of the terms of the settlement by the bankruptcy court, of $500 million (SEC, *Litigation Release*, 2003).

Discussion Questions	■ What security procedures should WorldCom have taken overall in order to prevent these illegal acts from happening?
	■ What steps should innocent middle management have taken in order to stop or prevent top executives who performed the illegal acts?
	■ Should they have reported to officials at the first sign of improper accounting? Or should they have just quit the company immediately?

References	SEC, 2002, Litigation Release 17866, 'In *SEC* v *WorldCom*, Court Imposes Full Injunctive Relief, Orders Extensive Reviews of Corporate Governance Systems and Internal Accounting Controls', US Securities and Exchange Commission, November 2002.
	SEC, 2003, Litigation Release 18147, 'In WorldCom Case, SEC Files Proposed Settlement of Claim for Civil Penalty', US Securities and Exchange Commission, May 2003.
	Ulick, Jake, 2002, 'WorldCom's Financial Bomb', *CNN/Money*, 26 June.

6.6 Fraud and Irregularities

The audit standards define fraud as 'an intentional act by one or more individuals among management, those charged with governance, employees, or third parties, involving the use of deception to obtain an unjust or illegal advantage.' Many aspects of being an auditor require a close look-out for fraud. Professional scepticism requires that the auditor be alert to conditions which may indicate possible misstatement due to fraud. The auditor employs risk assessment procedures to uncover material misstatement, whether due to fraud or error, at the financial statement and assertion levels. And, of course, one must be mindful of fraud when giving an opinion. As the basis for the auditor's opinion, ISAs require the auditor to obtain reasonable assurance about whether the financial statements as a whole are free from material misstatement, whether due to fraud (or error).

The Audit Standard on fraud, ISA 240 'The Auditor's Responsibilities Relating to Fraud in an Audit of Financial Statements', deals with the auditor's responsibilities relating to fraud. Specifically, it expands on how risk assessment and response are to be applied in relation to risks of material misstatement due to fraud.

An auditor conducting an audit in accordance with ISAs is responsible for obtaining reasonable assurance that the financial statements taken as a whole are free from material misstatement, whether caused by fraud or error. Because of the inherent limitations of an audit, material misstatements of the financial statements may not be detected. As described in ISA 200 the potential effects of inherent limitations are particularly significant if misstatement results from fraud. The risk of not detecting fraud is higher than the risk of not detecting error because fraud may involve sophisticated and carefully organised schemes designed to conceal it (such as forgery, deliberate failure to record transactions). Concealment of fraud as a result of collusion may be even more difficult to detect. Collusion may cause the auditor to believe that audit evidence is persuasive when it is, in fact, false. Furthermore, because management is frequently in a position to manipulate accounting records or override controls, the risk of the auditor not detecting management fraud is greater than for employee fraud.

With regards to fraud, the objectives of the auditor are:[31]

- to identify and assess the risks of material misstatement of the financial statements due to fraud;
- to obtain sufficient appropriate audit evidence regarding the assessed risks of material misstatement due to fraud, through designing and implementing appropriate responses; and
- to respond appropriately to fraud or suspected fraud identified during the audit.

In this book we have noted several times how misstatements in the financial statements can arise from either fraud or error. The distinguishing factor between fraud and error is whether the underlying action that results in the misstatement is intentional or unintentional. Error is unintentional whereas fraud is intentional.

■ Fraudulent Financial Reporting and Misappropriation of Assets

Two types of intentional misstatements are relevant to the auditor: misstatements resulting from fraudulent financial reporting and misstatements resulting from misappropriation of assets.

Fraudulent financial reporting involves intentional misstatements including omissions of amounts or disclosures in financial statements to deceive financial statement users. Fraudulent financial reporting may be accomplished by the following:

- Manipulation, falsification (including forgery), or alteration of accounting records (e.g. recording fictitious journal entries, particularly close to the end of an accounting period) or the supporting documentation from which the financial statements are prepared.

- Misrepresentation in, or intentional omission from, the financial statements of events, transactions or other significant information (e.g. engaging in complex transactions that are structured to misrepresent the financial position or financial performance of the entity).
- Intentional misapplication of accounting principles relating to amounts, classification, manner of presentation or disclosure, such as inappropriately adjusting assumptions and changing judgements used to estimate account balances.

Fraudulent financial reporting can be caused by management's effort to manage earnings in order to deceive financial statement users as to the company's performance and profitability. Such earnings management may start with small actions such as inappropriate adjustment of assumptions or changes in judgements by management. Pressures to meet market expectations and the desire to maximise executive compensation may cause these actions to increase until they result in fraudulent financial reporting. On the other hand, management of some other entities may be motivated to reduce earnings by a material amount to minimise tax or to inflate earnings to secure bank financing.

Misappropriation of assets involves the theft of an entity's assets and is often perpetrated by employees in relatively small and immaterial amounts. However, it can also involve management who are usually more able to disguise or conceal misappropriations in ways that are difficult to detect. Misappropriation of assets is often accompanied by false or misleading records or documents in order to conceal the fact that the assets are missing or have been pledged without proper authorisation.

Misappropriation of assets can be accomplished in a variety of ways including:

- Embezzling receipts (for example, misappropriating collections on accounts receivable or diverting receipts in respect of written-off accounts to personal bank accounts).
- Stealing physical assets or intellectual property (for example, stealing inventory for personal use or for sale, stealing scrap for resale, colluding with a competitor by disclosing technological data in return for payment).
- Causing an entity to pay for goods and services not received (for example, payments to fictitious vendors, kickbacks paid by vendors to the entity's purchasing agents in return for inflating prices, payments to fictitious employees).
- Using an entity's assets for personal use (for example, using the entity's assets as collateral for a personal loan or a loan to a related party).

■ Fraud Triangle

To understand the risk of fraud, auditors often refer to the 'Fraud Triangle', first identified by sociologist Donald Cressey.[32] Fraud involves *incentive or pressure* to commit fraud, a perceived *opportunity* to do so and some *rationalisation* of the act. These three 'points' of the Fraud Triangle are factors which are present for fraud (see Illustration 6.15):

- *Incentive/pressure.* Pressure, such as a financial need, is the 'motive' for committing the fraud. Individuals may be under pressure to misappropriate assets because of a gambling problem or because the individuals are living beyond their means. Fraudulent financial reporting may be committed because management is under pressure, from sources outside or inside the entity, to achieve an expected (and perhaps unrealistic)

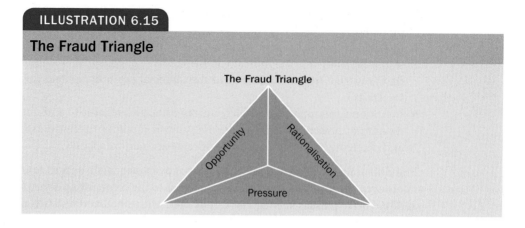

ILLUSTRATION 6.15

The Fraud Triangle

The Fraud Triangle

earnings target – particularly since the consequences to management for failing to meet financial goals can be significant.

- *Opportunity.* The person committing the fraud sees an internal control weakness and believes internal control can be overridden, for example, because the individual is in a position of trust or has knowledge of specific weaknesses in internal control. The individual, believing no one will notice if funds are taken, begins the fraud with a small amount of money. If no one notices, the amount will usually grow larger.
- *Rationalisation.* The person committing the fraud frequently rationalises the fraud. Rationalisations may include, 'I'll pay the money back', 'They will never miss the funds' or 'They don't pay me enough'.

In any organisation, the risk of fraud can be reduced. Even otherwise honest individuals can commit fraud in an environment that imposes sufficient pressure on them, so it is difficult to predict or reduce their personal pressures. Rationalisations seem to come naturally to most people. However, internal control procedures can particularly diminish the 'opportunity' point of the Fraud Triangle.

■ Procedures to Consider Regarding Fraud

When considering fraud during an audit, the auditor should be mindful of the need for professional scepticism, discuss the possibility of fraud with the engagement team, perform certain risk assessment procedures, identify the risks of material misstatement due to fraud, respond to those assessed risks and evaluate the audit evidence gathered.

We have discussed professional scepticism (see Chapter 4 'An Auditor's Services'). The auditor must maintain professional scepticism throughout the audit, recognising the possibility that a material misstatement due to fraud could exist, notwithstanding the auditor's past experience of the honesty and integrity of the entity's management and those charged with governance. If the auditor believes that a document may not be authentic or that terms in a document have been modified but not disclosed or where responses to inquiries of management are inconsistent, the auditor shall investigate the inconsistencies.

Discussion with Engagement Team and Risk Assessment Procedures

ISA 315 requires a discussion among the engagement team members and a determination by the engagement partner of which matters should be communicated to those team members not involved in this discussion.[33] This discussion shall place particular emphasis on how and where the entity's financial statements may be susceptible to material misstatement due to fraud, including how fraud might occur, setting aside beliefs that the management and those charged with governance are honest and have integrity.

Risk assessment procedures that may indicate fraud include inquiries of management regarding:

■ Management's assessment of the risk that the financial statements may be materially misstated due to fraud, including the nature, extent and frequency of such assessments.
■ Management's process for identifying and responding to the risks of fraud, including any specific risks of fraud that has been brought to management's attention, and classes of transactions, account balances or disclosures for which a risk of fraud is likely to exist;
■ Any management communication to those charged with governance regarding the risks of fraud in the entity; and, to employees regarding management views on business practices and ethical behaviour.
■ Whether management has knowledge of any actual, suspected or alleged fraud affecting the entity.

Internal auditors and the board of directors might also give insight. The auditor should make inquiries of internal auditors to determine whether they have knowledge of any actual, suspected or alleged fraud, and to obtain their views about the risks of fraud. The auditor shall obtain an understanding of how those charged with governance exercise oversight of management's processes for identifying and responding to the risks of fraud. The auditor must ask those charged with governance if they have knowledge of any actual, suspected or alleged fraud. These inquiries are made in part to corroborate the responses to the inquiries of management.

The auditor must understand whether the information obtained from the other risk assessment procedures (for instance, unusual or unexpected relationships identified when performing analytical procedures) indicates that one or more fraud risk factors are present.

ISA 315[34] states that the auditor shall identify and assess the risks of material misstatement due to fraud at the financial statement level, and at the assertion level for classes of transactions, account balances and disclosures. Revenue recognition manipulation is a frequent basis for fraud, so the auditor must evaluate which types of revenue, revenue transactions or assertions give rise to fraud risks.

Responses to Fraud Risk Assessment

According to ISA 330,[35] the auditor shall determine overall responses to address the assessed risks of material misstatement due to fraud at the financial statement level.

In determining overall responses to address the assessed risks of fraud at the financial statement level, the auditor must:

■ Assign and supervise audit staff taking into account the knowledge, skill and ability of each staff member.
■ Evaluate whether the company's accounting policies, especially those related to subjective measurements and complex transactions, may indicate fraudulent financial reporting resulting from management of earnings,
■ Incorporate an element of unpredictability in the selection of the nature, timing and extent of audit procedures.

Based on this general assessment of risk, the auditor must design and perform audit procedures to:

- Test the appropriateness of journal entries recorded in the general ledger and other adjustments made in the preparation of the financial statements; review journal entries or any adjustments made at the end of a reporting period; and test journal entries throughout the audit period. In audit procedures for such tests, the auditor should ask individuals involved in the financial reporting process about inappropriate or unusual activity relating to the processing of journal entries
- Review accounting estimates for biases and evaluate whether they represent a risk of material misstatement due to fraud. In performing this review, the auditor must evaluate whether management accounting estimates indicate a possible bias and perform a retrospective review of management judgements and assumptions related to significant accounting estimates made the prior year. If estimates or prior year statements show bias, the auditor must re-evaluate the accounting estimates.
- For significant transactions that are outside the normal course of business for the entity, or appear to be unusual, the auditor must evaluate whether the business rationale (or the lack thereof) for the transactions suggests they have been entered into for the purpose of fraudulent financial reporting or to conceal misappropriation of assets.

■ Evaluation of Audit Evidence and Documentation

Once procedures to determine fraud are complete the auditor must evaluate the audit evidence gathered, especially results of analytical procedures and misstatements possibly due to fraud.

The auditor must evaluate whether analytical procedures that are performed near the end of the audit indicate a previously unrecognised risk of material misstatement due to fraud. If a misstatement is found and it is indicative of fraud, the auditor must determine if the findings affect other aspects of the audit, particularly the reliability of management representations. An instance of fraud is unlikely to be an isolated occurrence.

If the auditor identifies a misstatement in which management (in particular, senior management) is involved, the auditor shall re-evaluate the initial assessment of the risks of material misstatement due to fraud. They may then modify the nature, timing and extent of audit procedures to respond.

Fraud related procedures must be documented in the audit work papers describing the entity and its environment, responses to assessed risk, and communications to management and the governance organisation,

The auditor must include in the audit documentation[36] of the entity and its environment and the assessment of the risks of material misstatement required by ISA 315[37] significant decisions reached from the engagement team discussion regarding the susceptibility of the financial statements to fraud. Also documented are the identified and assessed risks of material misstatement resulting from financial statement fraud.

In the documentation of the auditor's responses to the assessed risks of material misstatement required by ISA 330[38] the auditor must include the responses to the assessed risks of financial statement fraud and the nature, timing and extent of audit procedures undertaken and what those procedures revealed.

■ Discontinuance of the Engagement

If there is a misstatement resulting from fraud or suspected fraud, this might bring into question whether the auditor should continue performing the audit. Before she acts, the auditor should determine the professional and legal responsibilities applicable in the circumstances, including whether there is a requirement for her to report to management, those charged with governance, or regulatory authorities. Further, the auditor must consider whether it is appropriate to withdraw from the engagement. Before the auditor withdraws from the engagement she should discuss the possibility of, and the reasons for, withdrawal with management and those charged with governance. There may be professional or legal requirements to report withdrawal from the engagement.

Written Representations of Management and Entity Communications

Regardless of whether fraud is suspected, the written representations from management (see Chapter 11 'Completing the Audit') should require management to acknowledge their responsibility to prevent, detect and disclose any fraud. The auditor must obtain written representations from management stating that management acknowledges their responsibility for the design, implementation and maintenance of internal control to prevent and detect fraud. Management also states that they have disclosed to the auditor their knowledge of fraud, suspected fraud or allegations of fraud involving management or employees who have significant roles in internal control.

If the auditor has identified a fraud or has obtained information that indicates that a fraud may exist, it is her duty to communicate these matters to management. Unless all of those charged with governance are involved in managing the entity, the auditor will report to them any identified or suspected fraud involving management, employees who have significant roles in internal control, or others. The auditor will also discuss with them the nature, timing and extent of audit procedures necessary to complete the audit and any other matters related to fraud that are, in the auditor's judgement, relevant to their responsibilities.

If the auditor has identified or suspects a fraud, she must determine whether there is a responsibility to report it to third parties outside the entity (such as government regulators). Although the auditor's professional duty to maintain the confidentiality of client information may preclude such reporting, the auditor's legal responsibilities may override the duty of confidentiality in some circumstances.

6.7 Using the Work of Others (including ISA 610, ISA 620) and Considering Auditee Use of Service Organisations (ISA 402)

In the course of an audit engagement an auditor may rely on the work of the company's internal auditors, and in some cases they may hire an expert external to their firm to provide expertise[39] necessary for the audit but not available at the audit firm. The auditor may also find it necessary to review the work of any outsourced services which may impact the financial statement.

■ Using the Work of an Auditor's Expert

ISA 620 'Using the Work of an Auditor's Expert'[40] deals with the auditor's responsibilities relating to the work of an auditor's expert when that work is used to assist the auditor in obtaining sufficient appropriate audit evidence. An **auditor's expert** is an individual or organisation possessing expertise in a field other than accounting or auditing, whose work in that field is used by the auditor to assist the auditor in obtaining sufficient appropriate audit evidence. An auditor's expert may be either an auditor's internal expert (who is a partner or staff, including temporary staff, of the auditor's firm or a network firm), or an auditor's external expert.[41] It is important to note that the auditor has sole responsibility for the audit opinion expressed, and that responsibility is not reduced by the auditor's use of the work of an auditor's expert, but the auditor may accept that expert's findings or conclusions in the expert's field as appropriate audit evidence.

In using an expert the objective of the auditor are to determine whether to use the auditor's expert in the first place and, if using the expert's work, to determine whether that work is adequate.

The auditor must evaluate whether the auditor's expert has the necessary competence, capabilities and objectivity. Furthermore, the auditor must obtain a sufficient understanding of the expert's field of expertise to evaluate the adequacy their work. Evaluating the work of the auditor's expert means reviewing the relevance and reasonableness of their findings and its consistency with other audit evidence. If that expert's work involves use of significant assumptions and methods, the auditor must evaluate the relevance and reasonableness of that approach. If that expert's work involves the use of source data that is significant to that expert's work, the auditor considers the relevance, completeness and accuracy of that source data.

Auditor's Expert Agreement and Reports

The auditor must agree with the auditor's expert, in writing when appropriate, on the following matters: the nature, scope and objectives of that expert's work; the respective roles and responsibilities of the auditor and that expert; the nature, timing and extent of communication between the auditor and that expert, including the form of any report to be provided by that expert; and the need for the auditor's expert to observe confidentiality requirements.

The type of opinion determines if an auditor may or may not refer to the work of an auditor's expert. If the audit opinion is unmodified (unqualified), the auditor may *not* refer to the work of an auditor's expert unless required by law or regulation to do so. If such reference is required by law or regulation, the auditor shall indicate in the auditor's report that the reference does not reduce the auditor's responsibility for the auditor's opinion. If the audit opinion is for a modification (qualified, adverse or disclaimer), however, the auditor may reference to the work of an auditor's expert if such reference is relevant to an understanding of a modification. If reference is made to the expert, the auditor must indicate in the auditor's report that such reference does not reduce the auditor's responsibility for that opinion.

Using the Work of the Auditee's Internal Auditors

ISA 610[42] 'Using the Work of Internal Auditors' deals with the external auditor's responsibilities relating to the internal audit function when the external auditor has determined that the internal audit function is likely to be relevant to the audit. The **internal audit function** is an appraisal activity established or provided as a service to the entity. Its functions include, amongst other things, examining, evaluating and monitoring the adequacy and effectiveness of internal control. Irrespective of the degree of autonomy and objectivity of the auditee's internal auditors, they are not independent of the auditee as is required of the external auditor.[43] **Internal auditors** are those individuals who perform the activities of the internal audit function. Internal auditors may belong to an internal audit department or equivalent function.[44] Again, the external auditor has sole responsibility for the audit opinion expressed, and that responsibility is not reduced by the external auditor's use of the work of the internal auditors.

The external auditor must determine the adequacy, and the planned effect, of the work of the internal auditors on the nature, timing or extent of her audit procedures. To determine whether the work of the internal auditors is adequate, the external auditor has to evaluate the objectivity of the internal audit function, the technical competence of the internal auditors, whether the internal auditors use due professional care, and whether communication between the internal auditors and the external auditor is likely to be effective. In determining the planned effect of the internal auditors' work on the audit procedures, the external auditor must consider the nature and scope of specific work performed by the internal auditors, the related assessed risks of material misstatement the degree of subjectivity involved in the evaluation of the audit evidence gathered by the internal auditors.

To determine the adequacy of specific work performed by the internal auditors, the external auditor must evaluate whether the work was performed by internal auditors having adequate technical training and proficiency and was properly supervised, reviewed and documented. Was adequate audit evidence obtained to enable the internal auditors to draw reasonable conclusions? Were the conclusions reached appropriate and were any reports prepared by the internal auditors consistent with the results of the work performed? If there were any exceptions or unusual matters disclosed by the internal auditors, were they properly resolved?

If the external auditor uses specific work of the internal auditors, the external auditor must include in the audit documentation the conclusions reached regarding the evaluation of the adequacy of the work of the internal auditors and the audit procedures performed by the external auditor on that work.

■ Audit Considerations Relating to an Auditee Using a Service Organisation

ISA 402[45] 'Audit Considerations Relating to an Entity Using a Service Organisation' discusses the external auditor's responsibility to obtain sufficient appropriate audit evidence when an auditee uses the services of one or more service organisations. Specifically, it expands on how the auditor applies ISA 315 and ISA 330 in obtaining an understanding of the auditee sufficient to identify and assess the risks of material misstatement and in designing and performing further audit procedures responsive to those risks. A **service organisation** is a third-party organisation (or segment of a third-party organisation) that provides services to user entities that are part of those entities' information systems relevant to financial reporting.

Many entities outsource aspects of their business to organisations that provide services ranging from performing a specific task to replacing an entity's entire business units or functions. Services provided by a service organisation are relevant to the audit of financial statements when those services are part of the entity's information system. A service organisation's services are part of a user entity's information system if these services affect any of the following:

- The classes of transactions in the auditee's operations that are significant to their financial statements.
- The procedures, within both information technology (IT) and manual systems, by which the entity's transactions are initiated, recorded, processed, corrected, transferred to the general ledger and reported in the financial statements.
- The related accounting records supporting information and specific accounts in the user entity's financial statements.
- The financial reporting process used to prepare the user entity's financial statements, including significant accounting estimates and disclosures.
- Controls surrounding journal entries, including non-standard journal entries used to record non-recurring, unusual transactions or adjustments.

The objectives of the auditor when the auditee uses the services of a service organisation are to obtain an understanding of the nature and significance of the services provided by the service organisation and their effect on the user entity's internal control and to design and perform audit procedures responsive to those risks.

Obtaining an Understanding of the Use of Services of Service Organisations

To obtain an understanding of the auditee based on ISA 315[46] the auditor must obtain an understanding of how that entity uses the services of a service organisation in its operations, including understanding the nature of the services provided by the service organisation and their significance; the nature and materiality of the transactions, accounts or financial reporting processes affected by the service organisation; and the nature of the relationship between the auditee and the service organisation (including contractual agreements). Also in accordance with ISA 315[47] the auditor evaluates the design and implementation of relevant controls.

If the auditor is unable to get the data they need from the auditee, the auditor must obtain that understanding from one or more of the following procedures: obtaining a Type 1 or Type 2 report; contacting the service organisation, through the auditee, to obtain specific information; visiting the service organisation and performing procedures to provide information about the relevant controls at the service organisation; or using another auditor to perform procedures that will provide the necessary controls information at the service organisation.

Type 1 and Type 2 reports may be critical to understanding the service organisation. The **Type 1 report**, described as 'a report on the description and design of controls at a service organisation'[48] encompasses: (a) a description by management of the service organisation, the **service organisation's system**,[49] control objectives and related controls and (b) a report by the **service auditor**[50] conveying her opinion of the service organisation's system, control objectives and related controls and the suitability of the design of the controls to achieve the specified control objectives. The **Type 2 report**, called 'report on the description, design, and operating effectiveness of controls at a service organisation',[51] encompasses: (a) management's description of the service organisation, service organisation's system, control objectives and related controls, their design and implementation and, in some cases, their operating effectiveness throughout a specified period; (b) a report by the service auditor conveying her opinion on the description of the service organisation's system, control objectives and related controls, the suitability of the design of the controls to achieve the specified control objectives, and the operating effectiveness of the controls; and (c) a description of the service auditor's tests of the controls and the results thereof.

The auditor has to consider the sufficiency and appropriateness of the audit evidence provided by a Type 1 or Type 2 report. If the auditor plans to use a Type 1 or Type 2 report as audit evidence to support an understanding of controls at the service organisation, she should make sure it is for a date or for a period that is appropriate and determine whether controls identified by the service organisation are relevant to the auditee's business.

Sometimes a service organisation may use its own service organisation, called a subservice organisation, to provide services to the auditee. A **subservice organisation** is a service organisation used by another service organisation to perform some of the services provided to **user entities**[52] (the auditee) that are part of those user entities' information systems relevant to financial reporting. If the service organisation user's auditor plans to use a Type 1 or a Type 2 report that excludes the services provided by a subservice organisation and those services are relevant to the audit of the user entity's financial statements, the auditor must get a report on the subservice organisation, or carry out her own investigation.

6.8 Inherent Risk Assessment

The risk that the financial statements are materially misstated prior to the audit consists of two components, control risk, which we have discussed earlier in this chapter, and inherent risk. Inherent risk and control risk are the entity's risks which exist independently of the audit of the financial statements. **Inherent risk** is the susceptibility of an assertion about a class of transaction, account balance or disclosure to a misstatement that could be material, either individually or when aggregated with other misstatements, before consideration of any related controls.

The ISAs usually do not refer to inherent risk and control risk separately, but rather to a combined assessment of the 'risks of material misstatement'. However, the auditor may make separate or combined assessments of inherent and control risk depending on preferred audit methodologies and practical considerations. The assessment of the risks of material misstatement may be expressed in quantitative terms, such as in percentages, or in non-quantitative terms.

Inherent risk is higher for some assertions and related classes of transactions, account balances, and disclosures than for others. For example, it may be higher for complex calculations or for accounts consisting of amounts derived from accounting estimates that are subject to significant estimation uncertainty. External circumstances giving rise to business risks may also influence inherent risk. **Business risk** is a risk resulting from significant conditions, events, circumstances, actions or inactions that could adversely affect an entity's ability to achieve its objectives and execute its strategies, or from the setting of inappropriate objectives and strategies. For example, technological developments might make a particular product obsolete, thereby causing inventory to be more susceptible to overstatement. Factors in the entity and its environment that impact several or all of the classes of transactions, account balances, or disclosures may also influence the inherent risk. Such factors may include, for example, a lack of sufficient working capital to continue operations or a declining industry characterised by a large number of business failures.

An understanding of the business risks facing the entity increases the likelihood of identifying inherent risks, since most business risks will eventually have financial consequences and, therefore, an effect on the financial statements.

The procedures for assessing inherent risk are the same as those for general risk assessment covered in ISA 315, discussed earlier in this chapter. Specifically, inherent risk is a combination of industry, regulatory and other external factors. Also important for the auditor is to understand the risk inherent in the entity's operations, its ownership and governance structures, the types of investments being made and the way that the entity is structured and how it is financed. Inherent risks may come from the entity's objectives and strategies, and those related business risks.

6.9 Other Planning Activities

Other planning activities include planning discussions with those charged with governance (like the board of directors) and preparing the audit planning memorandum.

■ Discussions with Those Charged with Governance

As part of the planning process, it may be appropriate to have discussions with those charged with governance. The auditor should understand where the entity has an internal audit function, the extent to which the auditor will use the work of internal audit, and how the external and internal auditors can best work together in a constructive and complementary manner. Further, the auditor may seek the views of those charged with governance about the appropriate person(s) in the entity's governance structure with whom to communicate, the allocation of responsibilities between those charged with governance and management, the entity's objectives and strategies, and the related business risks that may result in material misstatements, significant communications with regulators and matters they believe warrant particular attention during the audit.

Discussion with those charged with governance will be helpful in planning audit procedures. The attitudes, awareness, and actions of those charged with governance concerning the entity's internal control and its importance in the entity, including how they oversee the effectiveness of internal control, and the detection or possibility of fraud will shape the assessment of control risk and planned procedures for fraud detection. The actions of those charged with governance in response to developments in accounting standards, corporate governance practices, exchange listing rules and related matters will determine how much accounting practices should be considered. Their responses to previous communications with the auditor will say a lot about whether prior year problems have been resolved.

■ Audit Planning Memorandum

The final step in the planning process is to prepare an audit planning memorandum and an audit plan. The audit planning memorandum summarises the overall audit strategy and contains the decisions regarding the overall scope, emphasis, and conduct of the audit, planned audit responses at the overall financial statement level, along with a summarisation of significant matters documented in the audit plan.

Typically, an audit planning memorandum would contain the following sections:

■ Background information describing the client company's structure, business and organisation. This should include significant matters affecting the client, cross-referenced as required to the audit files to enable a member of the audit team to gain an overview of the client.
■ The **objectives of the audit** showing whether it is an audit for stockholders, the national government filings, or some special purpose audit.
■ The **assessment of engagement risk** and potential follow-up on identified increased engagement risks, as identified during the client acceptance phase.
■ An identification of **other auditors or experts** that will be relied upon in the audit and a recap of the instructions provided to them.
■ An assessment of **materiality**.
■ **Inherent risks**, emerging from insight into the client's industry and business, specified for each important combination of financial statement account and audit objective.
■ **Conclusions regarding the control environment**, including the possible reliance on internal auditors.
■ Classification of the client's CIS environment and the **level of reliance on the client's CIS systems**.
■ An evaluation of the **quality of the accounting and internal control systems**, in particular an identification of internal control procedures mitigating the identified inherent risks.
■ Summary of the **audit approach** for addressing each account balance and related audit objective for which an inherent risk has been identified.
■ The **timing and scheduling of audit work**, including determining which procedures may be performed before the balance sheet date. Also considered is what audit work must be done on or after the balance sheet date. Dates are shown for such critical procedures as cash counts, accounts receivable confirmations and inventory observation.
■ **Audit budget**, detailed for each level of expertise available in the audit team.

The audit planning memorandum is normally completed before starting work at the client's offices. It is typically reviewed and approved by both the audit manager and the audit partner before the field work is commenced. It may be modified throughout the engagement as special problems are encountered and as the auditors' consideration of internal control leads to identification of areas requiring more or less audit work.

■ Audit Plan (Audit Programme)

Audit plan is the term used by the current ISAs, but in the prior standards the audit plan was referred to as the 'audit programme'. According the ISA 300,[53] 'Planning an audit involves establishing the overall audit strategy for the engagement and developing an audit plan.'

The audit plan (audit programme) sets out the nature, timing and extent of planned audit procedures required by ISA 315[54] and ISA 330[55] to implement the overall audit strategy into a comprehensive description of the work to be performed. It serves as a set of instructions to staff involved in the audit and as a means to control and record the proper execution of the work. Illustration 6.16 gives a detail of a sample audit plan for accounts receivable.

ILLUSTRATION 6.16

Sample Audit Plan (Audit Programme) – Accounts Receivable

Objectives:

1 Recorded sales are for shipments actually made to bona fide customers (existence).
2 Recorded sales are correctly billed for the amount of goods ordered (completeness and accuracy).
3 Cut-off is proper (completeness and existence).
4 All revenue from the sale of goods and performance of service are recorded accurately in the journal and ledger based on sales, credit authorisation and sales agreements (completeness, accuracy, measurement, and rights and obligations).
5 Trade accounts receivable represent uncollected sales or other charges to bona fide customers and are owned by the entity (existence, valuation and rights, and obligations).
6 All disclosures are in compliance with local and international standards (presentation and disclosure).

	Obj.	Done by	Refer
1 Vouch sales from shipping records to sales journal, authorisation, and sales invoices, including relevant data (e.g. party, price, description, quantity, and dates). Sample 100.			
2 Foot journals and trace to the general ledger and master file printout.			
3 Obtain a sample of shipping documents and compare dates on shipping documents to dates recorded in the journal.			
4 Select a sample of general ledger sales entries and trace them to the sales journals. Sample 200 throughout year.			
5 Observe if authorised price list is used to price the product.			
6 Sample sales invoices for agreement with price list.			
7 Confirm a sample of receivables and perform alternative procedures for non-responses.			
8 Vouch (match) a sample of recorded receivables to sales agreements.			
9 Trace a sample of credit sales invoices to accounts receivable billings.			
10 Compare a sample of shipping documents to related sales invoices.			
11 Investigate the credit ratings for delinquent and large receivables accounts.			
12 Obtain an aged trial balance of receivables, test its clerical accuracy and reconcile to the ledgers.			
13 Perform procedures to identify receivables from related parties.			

The audit plan includes the details of the planned audit procedures for material classes of transactions, account balances and disclosures. It includes risk-assessment procedures. The auditor uses the information obtained from the risk-assessment procedures to plan further audit procedures. As the auditor performs audit procedures outlined in the audit plan, the audit plan is updated and changed to reflect the further audit procedures considered necessary given the circumstances.

The demand for audit evidence can be derived from the planning stage. The combination of materiality (precision) and audit risk (reliability) determines, for each account balance and audit objective, how much evidence should be gathered. Audit procedures should be selected to ensure that the combined evidence provides adequate assurance. The greater the diversity between the audit procedures selected, the greater the combined assurance derived from them.

■ Audit Evidence

Audit evidence is available from a variety of different sources: procedures to obtain an understanding of the client's business and the internal controls, tests of controls, analytical procedures and detailed substantive testing (either substantive tests of transactions or tests of details of balances). How much the auditor can rely on the first two will determine the extent of the rest. If the auditor determines from the understanding of the business that inherent risk is low and from the understanding of internal controls that control risk is low, then less evidence is required from the substantive tests, as can be derived from the audit assurance model.

■ Audit Procedures

In planning the timing of audit work, crucial procedures should be performed first. Whenever possible, tailored audit plans, showing procedures to be performed, should be prepared in chronological order of execution. The outcome of certain audit procedures can require significant modification of the planned approach, and such procedures should be performed at the earliest opportunity.

Tests of controls and substantive procedures should cover the whole of the accounting period. Where the auditor intends to carry out audit work in advance of the period end (e.g. during an interim audit visit), he should plan whatever additional procedures are required at the final audit stage to ensure that the whole period is covered.

■ Documentation

The auditor should document the overall audit strategy and the audit plan, including reasons for significant changes made during the audit engagement. The auditor's documentation of reasons for significant changes to the overall audit strategy and audit plan includes the auditor's response to the events, conditions or results of audit procedures that resulted in such changes. The manner in which these matters are documented is for the auditor to determine based on professional judgement.

6.10   Summary

The objective of the auditor is to plan the audit so that it will be performed in an effective manner. The auditor shall establish an overall audit strategy that sets the scope, timing and direction of the audit, and that guides the development of the audit plan. The objective of planning is to determine the amount and type of evidence and review required to give the auditor assurance that there is no material misstatement of the financial statements.

The planning procedures are:

- perform audit procedures to understand the entity and its environment, including the entity's internal control;
- assess the risks of material misstatements of the financial statements;
- determine materiality;
- prepare the planning memorandum and audit programme, containing the auditor's response to the identified risks.

This chapter has covered the first three steps in the planning process, with the exception of the internal control considerations (which are dealt with in Chapter 7 'Internal Control and Control Risk').

ISA 315 provides an overview of the procedures that the auditor should follow in order to obtain an understanding sufficient to assess the risks and consider these risks in designing the audit plans. The risk assessment procedures should, at a minimum, be a combination of the following: inquiries of management, analytical procedures, and observation and inspection. In addition to these procedures, the auditor might consider obtaining information from others sources, for example, the entity's external legal counsel, or externally available data sources, including analysts' reports, industry journals, government statistics, surveys, texts, financial newspapers, etc. ISA 315 also requires an audit team-wide discussion of the susceptibility of the financial statements to material misstatement. If the client is a continuing one, prior year's working papers are reviewed and reliance can be placed on the observations from prior periods.

ISA 315 distinguishes the following relevant aspects in the understanding of the entity and its environment:

- industry, regulatory and other external factors, including the applicable financial reporting framework;
- nature of the entity, including the entity's selection and application of accounting policies;
- the entity's selection and application of accounting policies, including the reasons for changes the appropriateness for its business and consistency with the applicable financial reporting framework;
- objectives and strategies, and the related business risks that may result in a material misstatement of the financial statements;
- measurement and review of the entity's financial performance.

The understanding of a business environment requires a broad view. It is important to understand the client's industry because their industry has specific risks created by the nature of the business, accounting conventions, and industry regulation. Other factors relevant to the industry understanding could be the competition, supplier and customer relationships, technological developments and energy costs. One aspect of the understanding phase deals with the entity's core, i.e. its operations, types of investments, its financing/ownership and how management applies and discloses accounting policies. The auditor should review company accounting policies including revenue recognition, inventories, research and development, important expense categories, judgmental accounting valuations, and financial statement presentation and disclosure. Foreign currency assets, liabilities and transactions require special attention. In business organisations there exists a symbiotic alliance between the business processes of the organisation and external economic agents. Customers, suppliers, shareholders and the general public are external economic agents that impact on a company's profitability and ultimate survival. Financial statements are the communications that describe, on a monetary level, the company's dynamic interrelationship with external agents. In order to assess the risk of material misstatements in the financial statements, an auditor should examine internally generated information used by management and external (third-party) evaluations of the company.

Before risk can be assessed, the auditor must perform procedures to obtain an understanding of accounting and internal control systems. Audit procedures to obtain an understanding are referred to as 'risk assessment procedures' because some of the results may be used by the auditor as audit evidence to support the assessments of the risks of material misstatement of the financial statements. The audit evidence obtained might also apply to transactions, account balances, disclosures and the operating effectiveness of controls. Risks that exist at the financial statement level are pervasive, i.e. they have a potential impact on a large number of items in the financial statements.

Audit risk is the risk that the auditor gives an inappropriate audit opinion when the financial statements are materially misstated. The higher the audit risk, the more evidence must be gathered in order for the auditor to obtain sufficient assurance as a basis for expressing an opinion on the financial statements. Audit risk has three components: inherent risk, control risk and detection risk. Inherent risk is the susceptibility of an account balance or class of transactions to misstatements that could be material (individually or when aggregated with misstatements in other balances or classes), assuming that there were no related internal controls. Control risk is the risk that a material misstatement that could occur will not be prevented or detected and corrected on a timely basis by accounting and internal control systems. Detection risk is the risk that an auditor's substantive procedures will not detect a misstatement that exists in an account balance or class of transactions that could be material.

There is an inverse relationship between detection risk and the combined level of inherent and control risks. For example, when inherent and control risks are high, acceptable levels of detection risk need to be low to reduce audit risk to an acceptably low level. On the other hand, when inherent and control risks are low, an auditor can accept a higher detection risk and still reduce audit risk to an acceptably low level.

Significant risks are audit risks that require special audit consideration. Significant risks generally relate to judgmental matters and significant non-routine transactions. Judgement is used, for example, in the development of significant accounting or fair value estimates. Non-routine transactions are transactions that are unusual, either due to size or nature, and that therefore occur infrequently. Risks of material misstatement may be greater for significant judgemental matters requiring accounting estimates or revenue recognition and for assumptions about the effects of future events (e.g. fair value) than for ordinary transactions.

The auditor should consider materiality and its relationship with audit risk when conducting an audit. It is the auditor's responsibility to determine whether financial statements are materially misstated. The auditor considers materiality at both the overall financial statement level and in relation to individual account balances, classes of transactions, and disclosures.

The audit standards define fraud as 'an intentional act by one or more individuals among management, those charged with governance, employees, or third parties, involving the use of deception to obtain an unjust or illegal advantage.' Many aspects of being an auditor require a close look-out for fraud. Professional scepticism requires that the auditor be alert to conditions which may indicate possible misstatement due to fraud. The auditor employs risk assessment procedures to uncover material misstatement, whether due to fraud or error, at the financial statement and assertion levels. And, of course, one must be mindful of fraud when giving an opinion. As the basis for the auditor's opinion, ISAs require the auditor to obtain reasonable assurance about whether the financial statements as a whole are free from material misstatement, whether due to fraud (or error). Two types of intentional misstatements are relevant to the auditor: misstatements resulting from fraudulent financial reporting and misstatements resulting from misappropriation of assets.

To understand the risk of fraud, auditors often refer to the 'Fraud Triangle', first identified by sociologist Donald Cressey. Fraud involves incentive or pressure to commit fraud, a perceived opportunity to do so and some rationalisation of the act. These three 'points' of the Fraud Triangle are factors which are present for fraud. In any organisation, the risk of fraud can be reduced. Even otherwise honest individuals can commit fraud in an environment that imposes sufficient pressure on them, so it is difficult to predict or reduce their personal pressures. Rationalisations seem to come naturally to most people. However, internal control procedures can particularly diminish the 'opportunity' point of the Fraud Triangle.

According to ISA 330, the auditor shall determine and document responses to address the assessed risks of material misstatement due to fraud at the financial statement level. The auditor must include in the audit documentation of the entity and its environment and the assessment of the risks of material misstatement significant decisions reached from the engagement team discussion regarding the susceptibility of the financial statements to fraud.

In the course of an audit engagement an auditor may rely on the work of the company's internal auditors, and in some cases they may hire an expert external to their firm to provide expertise necessary for the audit but not available at the audit firm. The auditor may also find it necessary to review the work of any outsourced services which may impact the financial statement. ISA 620 'Using the Work of an Auditor's Expert' deals with the auditor's responsibilities relating to the work of an auditor's expert when that work is used to assist the auditor in obtaining sufficient appropriate audit evidence. An auditor's expert is an individual or organisation possessing expertise in a field other than accounting or auditing, whose work in that field is used by the auditor to assist the auditor in obtaining sufficient appropriate audit evidence. An auditor's expert may be either an auditor's internal expert (who is a partner or staff, including temporary staff, of the auditor's firm or a network firm), or an auditor's external expert. ISA 610 'Using the Work of Internal Auditors' deals with the external auditor's responsibilities relating to the internal audit function when the external auditor has determined that the internal audit function is likely to be relevant to the audit. Internal auditors are those individuals who perform the activities of the internal audit function. Internal auditors may belong to an internal audit department or equivalent function. ISA 402 'Audit Considerations Relating to an Entity Using a Service Organisation' discusses the external auditor's responsibility to obtain sufficient appropriate audit evidence when an auditee uses the services of one or more service organisations. A service organisation is a third-party organisation (or segment of a third-party organisation) that provides services to user entities that are part of those entities' information systems relevant to financial reporting.

As part of the planning process, it may be appropriate to have discussions with those charged with governance. The auditor should understand where the entity has an internal audit function, the extent to which the auditor will use the work of internal audit, and how the external and internal auditors can best work together in a constructive and complementary manner. Further, the auditor may seek the views of those charged with governance as to the appropriate person(s) in the entity's governance structure with whom to communicate, the allocation of responsibilities between those charged with governance and management, the entity's objectives and strategies, and the related business risks that may result in material misstatements, significant communications with regulators and matters they believe warrant particular attention during the audit.

The final step in the planning process is to prepare an audit planning memorandum and an audit plan. The audit planning memorandum summarises the overall audit strategy and contains the decisions regarding the overall scope, emphasis and conduct of the audit, planned audit responses at the overall financial statement level, along with a summarisation of significant matters documented in the audit plan.

6.11 Questions, Exercises and Cases

QUESTIONS

6.2 Planning Objective and Procedures

6-1 What is the objective of audit planning?

6-2 List the planning procedures.

6.3 Understanding the Entity and Its Environment

6-3 ISA 315 provides an overview of the procedures that the auditor should follow in order to obtain an understanding sufficient to assess the risks and consider these risks in designing the audit plans. Describe the procedures.

6-4 How can understanding a certain industry help an auditor?

6.4 Audit Risk Model

6-5 What are the definitions of the three audit risk components?

6-6 What components of the audit risk exist independently of the audit? What does an auditor do in this situation?

6-7 Distinguish between business risk and significant risk.

6.5 Materiality

6-8 How is materiality defined in the ISAs (specifically ISA 320)?

6-9 What four factors are generally considered in determining materiality? Briefly discuss them.

6-10 What guidelines or 'rules of thumb' related to a financial statement base such as net income, total revenues, etc. are commonly used in practice?

6.6 Fraud and Irregularities

6-11 Define fraud and give the ISA standard on fraud.

6-12 Describe the difference between financial statement fraud and misappropriation of assets

6.7 Using the Work of Others (including ISA 610, ISA 620) and Considering Auditee Use of Service Organisations (ISA 402)

6-13 Define auditor's expert. What must the auditor consider when evaluating the work of an auditor's expert?

6-14 Type 1 and Type 2 internal control reports from service organisations may be critical to understanding the service organisation. Discuss the difference between Type 1 and Type 2 reports.

PROBLEMS AND EXERCISES

6.2 Planning Objective and Procedures

6-15 Planning Procedures. Constantijn & Nianias, Soma Orkaton Logistons (SOLs), have been hired to audit Eidola Company, a biochemical company listed on the Athens Stock Exchange. Constantijn & Nianias is auditing the client for the first time in the current year as a result of a dispute between Eidola and the previous auditor over the proper booking of sales and accounts receivable for sales of inventory that has not been delivered but has for practical purposes been completed and sold.

Eidola has been grown from a small start-up to a highly successful company in the industry in the past seven years, primarily as a result of many successful mergers negotiated by George Panis, the president and chairman of the board. Although other biotech firms have had difficulty in recent years, Eidola continues to prosper, as shown by its constantly increasing earnings and growth. Bayer, the large German chemical company, has a special discount contract with them and represents 15 per cent of their sales. In the last year, however, the company's profits turned downward.

His board of directors that include many of his old university classmates generally supports Panis. The board, which meets twice annually, recently issued a policy on corporate ethics conduct. Panis says he owes much of his success to the hiring of aggressive young executives paid relatively low salaries combined with an unusually generous profit-sharing plan. The corporate structure is very informal, as Panis does not believe than any employee should have a title or a specific job description as it 'gives people airs'. Panis's only corporate objective is 'to make large profits so our stock price will increase and our shareholders will be happy'.

The management information system at Eidola is very limited and they lack sophisticated accounting records for a company that size. The information system will be updated this year. The personnel in the accounting department are competent but somewhat overworked and underpaid relative to the other employees, and therefore turnover is high. The most comprehensive records are for production and marketing because Panis believes these areas are more essential to operations than accounting. There are only four internal auditors and they spend the majority of their time taking inventories, which is time consuming because inventories are located at 11 facilities in four countries.

The financial statements for the current year include a profit 20 per cent less than the last year, but the auditors feel it should be a larger decrease because of the reduced volume and the disposal of a segment of the business, Kata-Karpos. The disposal of this segment was considered necessary because it had become increasingly unprofitable over the past three years. When it was acquired from Christopher Panis, George Panis's brother, it was considered profitable even though its largest customer was Kata-Klino, also owned by Christopher Panis.

Eidola is considered under-financed by market analysts. There is excessive current debt and management is reluctant to sell equity on the capital markets because increasing the number of shares will decrease share price. George Panis is now talking to several large companies in hopes of a merger.

Required:

A. Briefly discuss which matters Constantijn & Nianias, SOLs, should consider for each of the first three planning procedures.

B. What techniques should the auditors use to gather the needed information?

6.3 Understanding the Entity and Its Environment

6–16 Nature of the Entity. To get information about the core processes of the entity an auditor examines its business operations, investments, capital structure and financing activities, and financial reporting policies

Required:

A. Explain the problems an auditor may incur in each of these four areas.

B. What would be the characteristics of a company that had low risk in each of these areas?

C. You are assigned to evaluate on general economic and industry characteristics Eikon Elektronik, AS, a small, but fast-growing Turkish company that manufactures chip memories for personal computers. What business operations, investments, capital structure and financing activities, and financial reporting policies factors do you believe will be important in this evaluation?

6-17 Client Facilities Tour. When an auditor has accepted an engagement from a new client who is a manufacturer, it is customary for the auditor to tour the client's plant facilities. Discuss the ways in which the auditor's observations made during the course of the plant tour would be of help in planning and conducting the audit.
[AICPA adapted]

6.4 Audit Risk Model

6-18 Risk Analysis. Four tasks are required to assess the risk of misstatement. They are (1) identify risk by developing an understanding of the entity and its environment, (2) relate the risk to what could go wrong in management's assertion, (3) determine whether risks could result in material misstatement of the financial statements, and (4) consider that risks will result in material misstatement.

Required:
Using these tasks, analyse the following risks:
A. Cash receipts from sales in an office supply store are not recorded.
B. Investment in securities by the treasury department of a small manufacturing firm result in large losses.
C Financial statement disclosures do not comply with IASs.
D. Pollution equipment in a large international steel refinery does not comply with local pollution control laws.
E. Bank statements do not correlate with cash receipts and disbursements.

6.5 Materiality

6-19 Materiality and Risk. Dag Nilsson, Auktoriserad Revisor (AR), considers the audit risk at the financial statement level in the planning of the audit the financial statements of Lycksele Lappmark Bank (LLB) in Storuman, Sweden, for the year ended 31 December 20X5. Audit risk at the financial statement level is influenced by the risk of material misstatements, which may be indicated by a combination of factors related to management, the industry, and the entity. In assessing such factors, Nilsson has gathered the following information concerning LLB's environment.

LLB is a nationally insured bank and has been consistently more profitable than the industry average by making mortgages on properties in a prosperous rural area, which has experienced considerable growth in recent years. LLB packages its mortgages and sells them to large mortgage investment trusts. Despite recent volatility of interest rates, LLB has been able to continue selling its mortgages as a source of new lendable funds.

LLB's board of directors is controlled by Kjell Stensaker, the majority stockholder, who is also the chief executive officer (CEO). Management at the bank's branch offices has authority for directing and controlling LLB's operations and is compensated based on branch profitability. The internal auditor reports directly to Hakon Helvik, a minority stockholder, who is chairman of the board's audit committee.

The accounting department has experienced little turnover in personnel during the five years Nilsson has audited LLB. LLB's formula consistently underestimates the allowance for loan losses, but its controller has always been receptive to Nilsson's suggestions to increase the allowance during each engagement.

During 20X5, LLB opened a branch office in Ostersund, 300 km from its principal place of business. Although this branch is not yet profitable due to competition from several well-established regional banks, management believes that the branch will be profitable by 20X7.

Also during 20X5 LLB increased the efficiency of its accounting operations by installing a new computer system.

Required:

Based only on the information above, describe the factors that most likely would have an effect on the risk of material misstatement. Indicate whether each factor increases or decreases the risk. Use the format illustrated below:

Environmental factor	Effect on risk of material misstatements
Branch management has authority for directing and controlling operations	Increase

6.6 Fraud and Irregularities

6-20 In a California smart phone app company an employee discovered a flaw in the accounting system. The accounts payable clerk found she was able to change the names of vendors in the computer system to her name. She would create false invoices and create a cheque for the false invoice. The name on the cheque was changed to the name of the employee. After the cheque was printed, the name in the system could then be changed back to the appropriate vendor. The cheque register would show only the name of the vendor. The fraudulent employee had authorisation to sign cheques under $2,000. By writing small cheques, he was able to defraud the company of $90,000. An employee of another department was looking through the vendor list on her computer after the fraudulent employee had changed the vendor name to his name. A few entries later, the vendor name changed again. She wondered how this switch could occur and asked her supervisor. Soon after, the fraudulent employee was caught.

Required:

A. What kind of fraud is being committed – financial statement or misappropriation of assets? Discuss.

B. Discuss four safeguards that might have prevented this fraud.

CASES

6-21 Materiality. Via Internet get the latest balance sheet and income statement of Nokia, an international manufacturer of portable telephones headquartered in Finland. At the **www. Nokia.com** website click investors, click reports, click financial reports, finally click annual information or use the site search box using the terms Nokia's financial statements.

Required:

A. Use professional judgement in deciding on the initial judgement about materiality for the basis of net income, current assets, current liabilities and total assets. State materiality in both percentages of the basis and monetary amounts.

B. Assume materiality for this audit is 7 per cent of earnings from operations before income taxes. Furthermore, assume that every account in the financial statements may be misstated by 7 per cent and each misstatement is likely to result in an over-statement of earnings. Allocate materiality to these financial statements.

C. Now, assume that you have decided to allocate 80 per cent of your preliminary judge-ment (on the basis of earnings from operations before taxes) to accounts receivable, inventories and accounts payable. Other accounts on the balance sheet are low in inher-ent and control risk. How does this allocation of materiality impact evidence gathering?

D. After completing the audit you determine that your initial judgement about materiality for current assets, current liabilities and total assets has been met. The actual estimate of misstatements in earnings exceeds your preliminary judgement. What should you do?

6.12 Notes

1 International Auditing and Assurance Standards Board (IAASB), 2012, International Standard on Auditing 300 (ISA 300) 'Planning an Audit of Financial Statements', para. 4, *Handbook of International Quality Control, Auditing, Review, Other Assurance, and Related Services Pronouncements*, 2012 edn, Volume 1, International Federation of Accountants, New York.

2 International Auditing and Assurance Standards Board (IAASB), 2012, International Standard on Auditing 315 (ISA 315) 'Identifying and Assessing the Risks of Material Misstatement through Understanding the Entity and Its Environment', *Handbook of International Quality Control, Auditing, Review, Other Assurance, and Related Services Pronouncements*, 2012 edn, Volume 1, International Federation of Accountants, New York.

3 Ibid. ISA 315, para. 6.

4 Ibid. ISA 315, para. 10.

5 Ibid. ISA 315, para. 11.

6 Bell, T., *et al.*, 1997, *Auditing Organizations Through a Strategic-Systems Lens: The KPMG Business Measurement Process*, KPMG, p. 27.

7 See Degenan, J.D. *et al.*, 1995, 'Metallgesellschaft AG: A Case Study', *The FMT Review*, Illinois Institute of Technology; and Lowenstein, R., 1995, 'Is Corporate Hedging Really Speculation?', *Wall Street Journal*, 20 July.

8 See Jorion, P., 1995, *Big Bets Gone Bad: Derivatives and Bankruptcy in Orange County*, Academic Press, September.

9 Special Purpose Entity (SPE) is defined as an entity (e.g. corporation, partnership, trust, joint venture) created for a specific purpose or activity. SPEs may be used to transfer assets and liabilities from an entity – accounted for as a gain for that entity. Between 1993 and 2001, Enron created over 3,000 SPEs.

10 International Auditing and Assurance Standards Board (IAASB), 2012, International Standard on Auditing 315 (ISA 315) 'Identifying and Assessing the Risks of Material Misstatement through Understanding the Entity and Its Environment', para. A24, *Handbook of International Quality Control, Auditing, Review, Other Assurance, and Related Services Pronouncements*, 2012 edn, Volume 1, International Federation of Accountants, New York.

11 For an entity level model of a retail client, see Bell, T., *et al.*, 1997, *Auditing Organizations Through a Strategic-Systems Lens: The KPMG Business Measurement Process*, KPMG, p. 41.

12 Governance – the term 'governance' describes the role of persons entrusted with the supervision, control and direction of an entity. Those charged with governance ordinarily are accountable for ensuring that the entity achieves its objectives, financial reporting, and reporting to interested parties. Those charged with governance include management only when it performs such functions.

13 Bell, T., *et al.*, 1997, *Auditing Organizations Through a Strategic-Systems Lens: The KPMG Business Measurement Process*, KPMG, p. 31.

14 International Auditing and Assurance Standards Board (IAASB), 2012, International Standard on Auditing 315 (ISA 315) 'Identifying and Assessing the Risks of Material Misstatement through Understanding the Entity and Its Environment', para. A38, *Handbook of International Quality Control, Auditing, Review, Other Assurance, and Related Services Pronouncements*, 2012 edn, Volume 1, International Federation of Accountants, New York.

15 For the purposes of the ISAs, the term 'analytical procedures' means evaluations of financial information through analysis of plausible relationships among both financial and non-financial data. Analytical procedures also encompass such investigation as is necessary of identified fluctuations or relationships that are inconsistent with other relevant information or that differ from expected values by a significant amount. International Auditing and Assurance Standards Board (IAASB), 2012, International Standard on Auditing 520 (ISA 520) 'Analytical Procedures', para. 4, *Handbook of International Quality Control, Auditing, Review, Other Assurance, and Related Services Pronouncements*, 2012 edn, Volume 1, International Federation of Accountants, New York.

16 International Auditing and Assurance Standards Board (IAASB), 2012, International Standard on Auditing 520 (ISA 520) 'Analytical Procedures', para. 3, *Handbook of International Quality Control, Auditing, Review, Other Assurance, and Related Services Pronouncements*, 2012 edn, Volume 1, International Federation of Accountants, New York.

17 International Auditing and Assurance Standards Board (IAASB), 2012, International Standard on Auditing 315 (ISA 315) 'Identifying and Assessing the Risks of Material Misstatement through Understanding the Entity and Its Environment', para. 4(d), *Handbook of International Quality Control, Auditing, Review, Other Assurance, and Related Services Pronouncements*, 2012 edn, Volume 1, International Federation of Accountants, New York.

18 International Auditing and Assurance Standards Board (IAASB), 2012, Glossary of Terms, *Handbook of International Quality Control, Auditing, Review, Other Assurance, and Related Services Pronouncements*, 2012 edn, Volume 1, International Federation of Accountants, New York.

19 Ibid. Glossary. Substantive procedure – an audit procedure designed to detect material misstatements at the assertion level. Substantive procedures comprise: (a) tests of details (of classes of transactions, account balances and disclosures); and (b) substantive analytical procedures.

20 Tap – an apparatus used for controlling the flow of liquid or gas from a pipe: *Oxford Student's Dictionary*, 2003.

21 Sieve – utensil with wire network, used for separate small and large lumps, etc.: *Oxford Student's Dictionary*, 2003.

22 AICPA, 1985, Auditing Procedures Study *Audits of Small Business*, AICPA, New York, p. 44.

23 International Auditing and Assurance Standards Board (IAASB), 2012, International Standard on Auditing 315 (ISA 315) 'Identifying and Assessing the Risks of Material Misstatement through Understanding the Entity and Its Environment', para. 28, *Handbook of International Quality Control, Auditing, Review, Other Assurance, and Related Services Pronouncements*, 2012 edn, Volume 1, International Federation of Accountants, New York.

24 International Auditing and Assurance Standards Board (IAASB), 2012, International Standard on Auditing 320 (ISA 320) ' Materiality in Planning and Performing an Audit', para, 2. *Handbook of International Quality Control, Auditing, Review, Other Assurance, and Related Services Pronouncements*, 2012 edn, Volume 1, International Federation of Accountants, New York.

25 Ibid. ISA 320, para. 9.

26 Public Company Accounting Oversight Board (PCA0B) Audit Standard number 11, 2010, para. 2, gives yet another definition of materiality: in interpreting the federal securities laws, the Supreme Court of the United States has held that a fact is material if there is 'a substantial likelihood that the … fact would have been viewed by the reasonable investor as having significantly altered the "total mix" of information made available.' As the Supreme Court has noted, determinations of materiality require delicate assessments of the inferences a 'reasonable shareholder' would draw from a given set of facts and the significance of those inferences to him.

27 Financial Reporting and Auditing Group, *Of International Auditing, Assurance and Ethics Release FRAG 1/9, Materiality in Financial Reporting – A Discussion Paper*, para. 27, the Institute of Chartered Accountants in England and Wales, January 1995.

28 A liquid company has less risk of being able to meet debt than an illiquid one. Also, a liquid business generally has more financial flexibility to take on new investment opportunities.

29 International Auditing and Assurance Standards Board (IAASB), 2012, International Standard on Auditing 320 (ISA 320) 'Materiality in Planning and Performing an Audit', para. A1, *Handbook of International Quality Control, Auditing, Review, Other Assurance, and Related Services Pronouncements*, 2012 edn, Volume 1, International Federation of Accountants, New York.

30 Worthington, J.S., 1990, 'An Inventory of Materiality Guidelines in Accounting Literature', *CPA Journal Online*, New York Society of CPAs, July.

31 International Auditing and Assurance Standards Board (IAASB), 2012, International Standard on Auditing 240 (ISA 240) 'The Auditor's Responsibilities Relating to Fraud in an Audit of Financial Statements', para. 10, *Handbook of International Quality Control, Auditing, Review, Other Assurance, and Related Services Pronouncements*, 2012 edn, Volume 1, International Federation of Accountants, New York.

32 Cressey, Donald, 1973, *Other People's Money: A Study in the Social Psychology of Embezzlement*, p. 30, Montclair, NJ: Patterson Smith, ISBN 978-0-87585-202-7.

33 International Auditing and Assurance Standards Board (IAASB), 2012, International Standard on Auditing 315 (ISA 315) 'Identifying and Assessing the Risks of Material Misstatement through Understanding the Entity and Its Environment', para. 10, *Handbook of International Quality Control, Auditing, Review, Other Assurance, and Related Services Pronouncements*, 2012 edn, Volume 1, International Federation of Accountants, New York.

34 Ibid. ISA 315, para. 25.

35 International Auditing and Assurance Standards Board (IAASB), 2012, International Standard on Auditing 330 (ISA 330) 'The Auditor's Responses to Assessed Risks', para. 6, *Handbook of International Quality Control, Auditing, Review, Other Assurance, and Related Services Pronouncements*, 2012 edn, Volume 1, International Federation of Accountants, New York.

36 International Auditing and Assurance Standards Board (IAASB), 2012, International Standard on Auditing 230 (ISA 230) 'Audit Documentation', paras 8–11, *Handbook of International Quality Control, Auditing, Review, Other Assurance, and Related Services Pronouncements*, 2012 edn, Volume 1, International Federation of Accountants, New York.

37 Ibid. ISA 315, para. 32

38 Ibid. ISA 330, para. 28.

39 Expertise is skills, knowledge and experience in a particular field.

40 International Auditing and Assurance Standards Board (IAASB), 2012, International Standard on Auditing 620 (ISA 620) 'Using the Work of an Auditor's Expert', *Handbook of International Quality Control, Auditing, Review, Other Assurance, and Related Services Pronouncements*, 2012 edn, Volume 1, International Federation of Accountants, New York.

41 Ibid. ISA 620, para. 6(a).

42 International Auditing and Assurance Standards Board (IAASB), 2012, International Standard on Auditing 610 (ISA 610) 'Using the Work of Internal Auditors', *Handbook of International Quality Control, Auditing, Review, Other Assurance, and Related Services Pronouncements*, 2012 edn, Volume 1, International Federation of Accountants, New York.

43 Ibid. ISA 610, para. 7(a).

44 Ibid. ISA 610, para. 7(b).

45 International Auditing and Assurance Standards Board (IAASB), 2012, International Standard on Auditing 402 (ISA 402) 'Audit Considerations Relating to an Entity Using a Service Organization', *Handbook of International Quality Control, Auditing, Review, Other Assurance, and Related Services Pronouncements*, 2012 edn, Volume 1, International Federation of Accountants, New York.

46 Ibid. ISA 315, para. 11.

47 Ibid. ISA 315, para. 12.

48 Report on the description and design of controls at a service organisation (referred to in this ISA as a Type 1 report) – a report that comprises: '(1) A description, prepared by management of the service organization, of the service organization's system, control objectives and related controls that have been designed and implemented as at a specified date; and (2) A report by the service auditor with the objective of conveying reasonable assurance that includes the service auditor's opinion on the description of the service organization's system, control objectives and related controls and the suitability of the design of the controls to achieve the specified control objectives' – as defined in ISA 402, para. 8.

49 Service organisation's system – the policies and procedures designed, implemented and maintained by the service organisation to provide user entities with the services covered by the service auditor's report.

50 Service auditor – an auditor who, at the request of the service organisation, provides an assurance report on the controls of a service organisation.

51 Report on the description, design and operating effectiveness of controls at a service organisation (referred to in this ISA as a Type 2 report) – a report that comprises: '(1) A description, prepared by management of the service organization, of the service organization's system, control objectives and related controls, their design and implementation as at a specified date or throughout a specified

period and, in some cases, their operating effectiveness throughout a specified period; and (2) A report by the service auditor with the objective of conveying reasonable assurance that includes: (a) The service auditor's opinion on the description of the service organization's system, control objectives and related controls, the suitability of the design of the controls to achieve the specified control objectives, and the operating effectiveness of the controls; and (b) A description of the service auditor's tests of the controls and the results thereof' – as defined in ISA 402, para. 8.

52 User entity – an entity that uses a service organisation and whose financial statements are being audited.

53 International Auditing and Assurance Standards Board (IAASB), 2012, International Standard on Auditing 300 (ISA 300) 'Planning an Audit of Financial Statements', *Handbook of International Quality Control, Auditing, Review, Other Assurance, and Related Services Pronouncements*, 2012 edn, Volume 1, International Federation of Accountants, New York.

54 Ibid. ISA 315, 'Identifying and Assessing the Risks of Material Misstatement through Understanding the Entity and Its Environment'.

55 Ibid. ISA 330, 'The Auditor's Responses to Assessed Risks'.

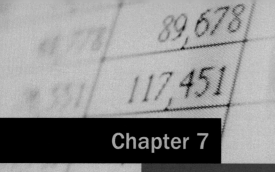

Chapter 7

INTERNAL CONTROL AND CONTROL RISK

7.1 Learning Objectives

After studying this chapter, you should be able to:

1 Understand the basic definition of internal control.

2 Discuss why internal controls are important to the auditor.

3 Characterise the differences between general and application IT controls and how to reduce IT risk.

4 Distinguish between the different components of internal control.

5 Describe the elements of the control environment.

6 Evaluate how management's objectives are related to risk assessment.

7 Explain the effects of information and communication on the internal control system.

8 Distinguish between the major types of control activities.

9 Give examples of major types of control procedures (activities).

10 Identify monitoring controls.

11 Distinguish between hard and soft controls and understand their control objectives.

12 Know what is meant by design of controls.

13 Follow what an auditor does in preliminary planning assessments of internal control risk.

7.2 Introduction

Internal control is not only essential to maintaining the accounting and financial records of an organisation, it is essential to managing the entity. Everyone from the external auditors to management to the board of directors to the stockholders of large public companies to government have an interest in internal controls. In many parts of the world, regulators have emphasised the importance of internal control by requiring management to make annual public statements about the effectiveness of internal controls.

Reinforcing internal controls is generally seen as one of the most important steps in avoiding negative surprises. Even a company that is considered 'in control' will face risks. Effective internal controls will ensure that risks are identified at an early stage. Company risk management procedures will identify ways to deal with these risks, to the extent possible.

As we discussed earlier (see Chapter 6), the consideration of internal control is an important part of Phase II (Planning) of the Audit Process Model. It was also stated that the first two steps in the planning procedures are:

1 perform audit procedures to understand the entity and its environment, including the entity's internal control; and
2 assess the risks of material misstatements of the financial statements.

For both steps, the consideration of internal control and **control risk** is essential.

This chapter will concentrate on the importance of internal control, on general concepts in internal control, and on its components (the control environment, risk assessment, control activities, information and communication, and monitoring). Assessment of control risk and the techniques for testing internal control as part of the audit will be discussed later (see Chapter 9).

7.3 Internal Control Defined

Internal control, according to the Committee of Sponsoring Organisations of the Treadway Commission (COSO), is a process, effected by an entity's board of directors, management and other personnel, designed to provide **reasonable assurance** regarding the achievement of objectives in the following categories: effectiveness and efficiency of operations, reliability of financial reporting, compliance with applicable laws and regulations, and safeguarding of assets against unauthorised acquisition, use or disposition.[1]

This definition reflects certain fundamental concepts:

- **Internal control is a 'process'.** Internal control is not one event or circumstance, but a series of actions that permeate an entity's activities. These actions are pervasive and are inherent in the way management runs the business.
- Internal control is **effected by people.** A board of directors, management, and other personnel in an entity effect internal control. The people of an organisation accomplish it, by what they do and say. People establish the entity's objectives and put control mechanisms in place.
- Internal control can be **expected to provide only reasonable assurance**, not absolute assurance, to an entity's management and board that the company's objectives are

achieved. ISA 315 makes clear that internal control, no matter how effective, can only provide an entity with reasonable assurance about achieving the entity's objectives. The likelihood of achievement is affected by limitations inherent in all internal control systems. These limitations include the realities that human judgement can be faulty, breakdowns may occur because of human failures such as simple error, and controls may be circumvented by collusion of two or more people. Finally, management has the ability to override the internal control system. For example, management may enter into side agreements[2] with customers that alter the terms and conditions of the entity's standard sales contract in ways that would preclude revenue recognition.

■ Internal control is geared to the **achievement of objectives** in one or more separate overlapping categories:

1 **operations** – relating to effective and efficient use of the entity's resources;
2 **financial reporting** – relating to preparation of reliable published financial statements;
3 **compliance** – relating to the entity's compliance with applicable laws and regulations;
4 **safeguarding of assets**.

The ISA audit standards defines internal control very similarly to COSO:

> Internal control is the process designed, implemented and maintained by those charged with governance, management and other personnel to provide reasonable assurance about the achievement of an entity's objectives with regard to reliability of financial reporting, effectiveness and efficiency of operations, and compliance with applicable laws and regulations. The term 'controls' refers to any aspects of one or more of the components of internal control.[3]

■ Components of Internal Control (see also Section 7.6)

The US Securities Exchange Commission (and other regulatory agencies around the world) rules require that management must base its evaluation of the effectiveness of the company's internal control over financial reporting on a suitable, recognised control framework established by a body or group that followed due-process procedures, including the broad distribution of the framework for public comment.[4] For example, the report of the Committee of Sponsoring Organizations of the Treadway Commission (known as the COSO report) provides such a framework, as does the report published by the Financial Reporting Council, 'Internal Control Revised Guidance for Directors on the Combined Code', October 2005 (known as the Turnbull Report). If the auditor is evaluating management's assessment of internal control, she should use the same suitable, recognised control framework to perform her audit of internal control over financial reporting as management uses for its annual evaluation of the effectiveness of the company's internal control over financial reporting.[5]

International standards require that the auditor obtain an understanding of internal control relevant to the audit.[6] ISA 315[7] distinguishes the following components of internal control:

■ the control environment;
■ the entity's risk assessment process;
■ the information system and related business processes relevant to financial reporting and communication;
■ control procedures;
■ monitoring of controls.

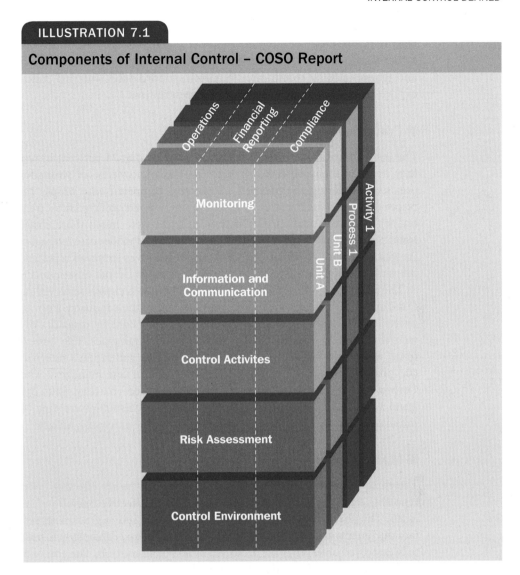

ILLUSTRATION 7.1

Components of Internal Control – COSO Report

Illustration 7.1 shows internal control components from the most recent COSO report.[8] (For a more detailed discussion of the components of internal control, see Section 7.6 of this chapter.)

The reason a company establishes a system of control is to help achieve its performance and profitability goals and prevent loss of resources by fraud and other means. Internal control can also help to ensure reliable financial reporting and compliance with laws and regulations. The entity's internal control system consists of many specific policies and procedures designed to provide management with reasonable assurance that the goals and objectives it believes important to the company will be met. Everyone in the organisation has responsibility for internal controls: management, board of directors, internal auditors, and other personnel. The chief executive officer is ultimately responsible and should assume ownership of the internal control system, providing leadership and direction to senior managers. Of particular significance are financial officers and their staff. The board of directors provides governance, guidance and oversight. A strong, active board is best able to identify and correct management attempts to override controls and ignore or stifle communications from subordinates. Internal control should be an explicit or implicit part of everyone's job description.

■ Fraud Surveys

The 2009 annual fraud survey by KPMG[9] showed that 74 per cent of respondents report they had personally observed or had first-hand knowledge of wrongdoing within their organisation during the previous 12 months, compared with 62 per cent of executives responding to a similar survey in 1998. Employee fraud occurred most frequently, although financial reporting and medical/insurance fraud were much more costly. KPMG's 2009 fraud survey reveals senior executive's perception that inadequate internal controls heighten the risks of fraud, as 66 per cent of the 204 executives surveyed reported that inadequate internal controls or compliance programmes allow fraud and misconduct to go unchecked.

The fraud survey also reported 65 per cent of the executives surveyed said they consider fraud and misconduct to be significant risks within their industry. Poor internal controls, override of internal controls, and inadequate oversight by directors over management were the top three reasons cited as to why frauds took place. The survey also found that fraud would most likely be discovered by their organisation's internal audit, legal, or compliance personnel, employee whistleblowers, or line managers. The Association of Certified Fraud Examiners survey,[10] which was based on actual fraud cases, showed that fraud was most likely to be discovered through whistleblowers' tips (43.3 per cent of initial detections vs. 3.3 per cent for detection by the external auditor).

■ Management Control Objectives

The three major categories of management objectives are effective operations, financial reporting and compliance. An important goal of effective operations is safeguarding of assets. The physical assets (e.g. cash), non-physical assets (e.g. accounts receivable), important documents and records (e.g. journals) of a company can be stolen, misused or accidentally destroyed unless they are protected by adequate controls. The goal of financial controls requires accurate information for internal decision because management has a legal and professional responsibility to be sure that information is prepared fairly in accordance with accounting standards. Organisations are required to comply with many laws and regulations including company law,[11] tax law and environmental protection regulations.

A company's management sets objectives and then implements controls to assure the achievement of these objectives. For example, management requires that all order dates and delivery dates for all products be recorded as a control to monitor the CEO's strategic objective of 'all deliveries on time'. But not all of these objectives and their corresponding controls are relevant to the audit of the entity's financial statements. Most objectives and controls of management have to do with efficiency of operations.

■ Financial Reporting Controls

The auditor is interested primarily in controls that relate to reliability of financial reporting – accounting and internal control systems. These controls pertain to the entity's objective of preparing financial statements for external purposes that give a true and fair view in accordance with the applicable financial accounting standards.

If the auditor is able to assess the quality of accounting and internal control systems and to verify their proper operation throughout the year under audit, the auditor might be able to rely heavily on these systems for sufficient audit evidence.

The rationale for relying on a company's accounting and internal control systems is twofold. First, reliance on accounting and control procedures will enhance the efficiency of the external audit. If inherent risks are mitigated by effective internal control procedures, less substantive testing is required to gather sufficient audit evidence. Further, by testing accounting and internal control procedures, the auditor is able to add value to the client by assessing the quality of the internal control system and giving recommendations for further improvement. In some countries a third rationale for relying on controls is the requirement that management, the external auditor or both report on controls.

The auditor's primary consideration is whether, and how, a specific control prevents, or detects and corrects, material misstatements in classes of transactions, account balances or disclosures.

■ Controls over Transactions

Emphasis by auditors is placed on understanding controls over classes of transactions rather than account balances or disclosures. The reason is that the accuracy of the output of the accounting system (account balances) is dependent upon the accuracy of the inputs and processing (transactions). If, for example, controls are adequate to ensure all billings, cash receipts, charge-offs, and returns and allowances are correct, then the ending balance in accounts receivable is likely to be correct. Disclosures are generally dependent on the account balances.

■ Management Information System, Operations and Compliance Controls

Auditors primarily rely on financial controls, but controls affecting internal management information, such as budgets and internal performance reports, controls relating to operations, and controls for compliance objectives may also be relevant to an audit. Auditors have significant responsibility for the discovery of management and employee fraud and, to a lesser degree, certain types of illegal acts, even though management has the primary responsibility for regarding fraud and illegal acts. Controls over non-financial data that the auditor uses in analytical procedures or controls over compliance with income tax laws may be relevant to an audit. The extensive use of general information system controls like restricted access (i.e. password controls) that limit access to the data are also relevant. Conversely, controls to prevent the excessive use of materials in production generally are not relevant to a financial statement audit, as the auditor provides a judgement on the true and fair view of the financial statements and not a judgement on the effectiveness or efficiency of operations.

■ Design and Implementation of Controls

To understand the entity's internal control the auditor will evaluate the design of a control and judge whether it has been implemented. He determines whether the control, individually or in combination with other controls, is capable of effectively preventing, or detecting and correcting, material misstatements.[12] Implementation of a control means that the control exists and that the entity is using it. There is little point in assessing the implementation of a control that is not effective, and so the design of a control is considered first. An improperly designed control may represent a significant deficiency in internal control. Further, if more controls are capable of effectively preventing, or detecting and correcting the same material misstatements, the auditor will test only the controls that are most efficient to test.

7.4 The Importance of Internal Control

Are management objectives important? Is achieving management objectives important? Is the mechanism for assuring that objectives are achieved important? If your answer was yes to these three questions, then it is obvious that internal controls are important. Why? Because internal controls are the best mechanism management has for seeing that their goals and objectives are achieved.

Whether formally or informally, management sets objectives that they expect their business to achieve. For example, profit making organisations have profit as a goal and not-for-profit entities wish to achieve their mission (like finding a cure for Alzheimer's disease). Of course management may have many objectives and sub-objectives and each entity will differ in what they consider important, but all must do something to make their objectives happen.

Management could just tell all the employees what their objectives are and ask everyone to make it happen. Of course, it is not likely that just asking everyone to help achieve the objectives will be a strong enough incentive. Management identifies the risk of not achieving their objectives. For instance, employees may not agree with the objectives and avoid helping achieve them. To minimise these risks, management designs and puts in place a set of rules, physical constraints and activities called 'internal controls' which, if they are implemented properly, will minimise the risks of not meeting objectives.

Controls that may be important to management are controls to assure efficient operations (such as controls to reduce waste from a manufacturing process), controls to hire and retain the best employees (such as employment tests, continuing education requirements, and supervisory review), and controls to keep the customers happy (such as good relationships maintained by salespeople). Management may also have controls to achieve objectives in compliance with laws (employee health and safety rules), safeguarding of assets (locks on the doors), and financial reporting (a good accounting system and knowledgeable accountants).

Internal controls that are important for the auditor are those that assure that the financial statements reflect the true economic condition of the entity such as control to ensure accuracy of input of data, access controls to make sure that the only the people who are authorised can access the accounting system, and segregation of duties controls so individuals are not tempted to commit fraud,

To understand why internal controls are important, it might be worthwhile to give an example of what would happen if controls were *not* in place. Let's take a simple example of a retail ice-cream shop. The ice cream seller has an unwritten objective of not having her equipment and supplies stolen. If she has not installed basic security measures such as locks on the doors and windows and perhaps an alarm, these objectives will not be met. Another obvious objective is to attract customers. If she does not have signs attached to the building letting customers know the business name and function (ice cream), she will lose many potential customers. If she does not track her supplies she is in danger of running out of product. She wants to make sure she complies with state and federal taxes so she is not in danger of being fined or held criminally liable. Without an accounting system and controls over accurate input into accounts, the next appointment she makes may be with an attorney to defend her on a tax charge.

7.5 IT Risk and Controls

The heart of any internal control system is the information technology (IT) upon which so much of the business processes rely. **General IT controls** are policies and procedures that relate to many applications and support the effective functioning of application controls by helping to ensure the continued proper operation of information systems. General IT controls commonly include controls over data centre and network operations; system software acquisition, change and maintenance; access security; back-up and recovery; and application system acquisition, development, and maintenance. A good example of a general control in accounting software is an error message if there is a problem in using the operating system (e.g. 'Please insert a CD-ROM in Drive E'). The **IT environment** is the policies and procedures that the entity implements and the IT infrastructure (hardware, operating systems, etc.) and application software that it uses to support business operations and achieve business strategies.

Controls in IT systems consist of a combination of automated or application controls (for example, controls embedded in computer programs) and manual controls. In manual systems, general controls are controls over proper authorisation of transactions and activities. Further, manual controls may be independent of IT, may use information produced by IT, or may be limited to monitoring the effective functioning of IT and of automated controls, and to handling exceptions. An entity's mix of manual and automated elements in internal control varies with the nature and complexity of the entity's use of IT.

Generally, IT benefits an entity's internal control by enabling them to consistently apply predefined business rules and perform complex calculations in processing large volumes of transactions or data; enhance the timeliness, availability, and accuracy of information; and facilitate the additional analysis of information. IT systems enhance the ability to monitor the performance of the entity's activities and its policies and procedures; reduce the risk that controls will be circumvented; and enhance the ability to achieve effective segregation of duties by implementing security controls in applications, databases, and operating systems.

Information processing control procedures are primarily of two types: application controls and general controls. **Application controls** are controls that apply to applications that initiate, record, process and report transactions (such as MS Office, SAP, QuickBooks), rather than the computer system in general. Examples of application controls are **edit checks** of input data, numerical **sequence checks**, and manual follow-up of exception reports. In manual systems applications controls may be referred to as adequate document and record controls.

There is a multitude of risks associated with IT, so auditors must expend a good deal of effort analysing these systems for issues that may affect the financial statements and the auditor's opinion.

■ Application Controls

There are several standard application controls. The chart of accounts is an important application control because it provides the framework for determining the information presented on to financial statements and budgets. The most widely applicable control device is the use of serial numbers on documents and input transactions. Serial numbers provide control over the number of documents issued. Cheques, tickets, sales invoices, purchase orders, stock certificates, and many other business papers use this control. Documents should be recorded immediately because long periods between transaction and recording increase the chance of misstatement. Systems manuals for computer accounting software should provide sufficient information to make the accounting functions clear.

■ General IT Controls

General IT controls assure that access to the computer system is limited to people who have a right to the information. Appropriate delegation of authority sets limits on what levels of risk are acceptable and these limits determine the discretion of the employees delegated to authorise the main types of business transactions. Authorisation may be general or specific. An example of general limits set by policy is product price lists, inventory reorder points and customer credit limits. Specific authorisation may be made on a case-by-case basis such as authorisation of reduction in the price of a dress with buttons missing in a retail-clothing store.

■ Computer Facility Controls

Computer facilities may have several types of controls. General controls such as access controls or application controls such as passwords allow only authorised people admittance to the computer software. A very important general control is back-up and recovery procedures, as anyone who has had a system go down without current records being adequately backed up will tell you. Physical controls such as locks on the doors to the computer room and locked cabinets for software and back-up tapes protect the tangible components of a computer system.

■ IT Risks

The auditor should be aware that IT poses specific risks to an entity's internal control including:

■ Reliance on systems or programs that are inaccurately processing data, processing inaccurate data, or both. For instance, individuals may inappropriately override such automated processes, by changing the amounts being automatically passed to the general ledger or to the financial reporting system. Furthermore, where IT is used to transfer information automatically, there may be little or no visible evidence of such intervention in the information systems.

- Unauthorised access to data that may result in destruction of data or improper changes to data, including the recording of unauthorised or non-existent transactions or inaccurate recording of transactions. Particular risks may arise where multiple users access a common database.
- The possibility of IT personnel gaining access privileges beyond those necessary to perform their assigned duties thereby breaking down segregation of duties. A frequent problem in audits of small to medium-sized businesses is that there is only one IT employee and he has unlimited access to all computer systems hardware and software, all security systems and all back-ups. A response to this risk is to have someone periodically review the security and access logs to monitor the IT employee's activity.
- Unauthorised changes to data in master files.
- Unauthorised changes to systems or programs.
- Failure to make necessary changes to systems or programs.
- Inappropriate manual intervention.
- Potential loss of data or inability to access data as required.
- Management's failure to commit sufficient resources to address IT security risks may adversely affect internal control by allowing improper changes to be made to computer programs or to data, or unauthorised transactions to be processed.
- Inconsistencies between the entity's IT strategy and its business strategies.
- Changes in the IT environment.

■ Input Risks

Risk exists at all levels of the information system, but especially related to input. Input should be only by those people and systems with authorised access. Data entry should be secure from unauthorised access. Input should be accurate (correct data is entered correctly), valid (transaction is approved or authorised), and complete (all valid transactions should be entered and captured by the system). Subsystems should process transactions completely (all data that should be transacted into the general ledger is there) and accurately (data that is entered is reflected in the general ledger). Lack of controls or insufficient controls on authorisation, data input and processing by subsystems increases risk.

7.6 Components of Internal Control

Internal control consists of five interrelated components:

1 control environment;
2 risk assessment process;
3 the information system, communication and related business processes;
4 control procedures;
5 monitoring of controls.

Illustration 7.2 gives more detail on each component including a description. Risk assessment should not be treated as a strictly separate component, for risk is assessed in all the other components – control environment risk, information system risk, risk of lack of control procedures, and risk from absence of adequate monitoring.

ILLUSTRATION 7.2

Components of Internal Control Structure

Components	Description of component	Component elements
Control environment	Actions, policies and procedures that reflect the overall attitude of top management, directors and owners of an entity about controls and its importance	■ Integrity and ethical values ■ Commitment to competence ■ Those charged with governance (board of directors or audit committee) ■ Management's philosophy and operating style ■ Organisational structure ■ Assignment of authority and responsibility ■ Human resource polices and practice
Management's risk assessment	Management's identification and analysis of risks relevant to the preparation of financial statements in accordance with IFRS	Management's assertions: existence, completeness, valuation, presentation and disclosure, measurement, occurrence
Accounting information systems and communication	Methods used to identify, assemble, classify, record and report an entity's transactions and to maintain accountability for related assets	Transaction-related audit objectives: existence, completeness, accuracy, classification, timing, posting and summarisation
Control activities (control procedures)	Policies and procedures that management established to meet its objectives for financial reporting	■ Adequate segregation of duties ■ Proper authorisation of transactions and activities (specific computer controls) ■ Adequate documents and records (general computer controls) ■ Physical control over assets and records ■ Independent checks on performance
Monitoring	Management's ongoing and periodic assessment of the effectiveness of the design and operation of an internal control structure to determine if it is operating as intended and modified when needed	Not applicable

7.7 Control Environment

The Control environment includes the governance and management functions and the attitudes, awareness and actions of those charged with governance and management concerning the entity's internal control and its importance in the entity. The control environment has a pervasive influence on the way business activities are structured, the way objectives are established, and the way risks are assessed. The control environment is influenced by the entity's history and culture. It influences the control consciousness of its people. Effectively controlled companies have top management with a positive and establish appropriate policies and procedures.

■ Cumulative Effect of Controls

When analysing the control environment, the auditor must think about the collective effect of various control environment elements. Strengths in one of the elements might mitigate weaknesses in another element. For example, an active and independent board of directors may influence the philosophy and operating style of senior management. Alternatively, human resource policies directed towards hiring competent accounting personnel might not mitigate a strong bias by top management to overstate earnings.

■ Organisation's Management

The attitude of an organisation's management, its management style, corporate culture, and values are the essence of an efficient control. If management believes control is important, others in the company will observe the control policies and procedures. If employees in the organisation feel control is not important to top management, it will not be important to them. The control environment consists of the actions, policies and procedures that reflect the overall attitudes of top management, directors and owners.

■ Elements of the Control Environment

There are a number of specific elements that that may be relevant when obtaining an understanding of the control environment and which may be used as indicators of the quality of the control environment of a particular organisation. These elements are:[13]

- communication and enforcement of integrity and ethical values;
- commitment to competence;
- participation by those charged with governance – attributes including independence from management, experience, extent of involvement and scrutiny of entity activities and appropriateness of their actions including the degree to which difficult questions are raised and pursued with management, and their interaction with internal and external auditors;
- management's philosophy and operating style – characteristics such as management's approach to taking and managing business risks, attitudes and actions towards financial reporting, attitudes towards information processing and accounting functions and personnel,
- organisational structure;
- assignment of authority and responsibility – matters such as how authority and responsibility for operating activities are assigned and how reporting relationships and authorisation hierarchies are established; and
- human resource policies and practices – policies and practices that relate to, for example, recruitment, orientation, training, evaluation, counselling, promotion, compensation and remedial actions.

■ Integrity and Ethical Values

The integrity and ethical values of the people who create, administer, and monitor controls determines their effectiveness. The communication of company integrity and ethical values to employees and reinforcement in practice affects the way in which employees view their work. Setting a good example is not enough. Top management should verbally communicate the entity's values and behavioural standards to employees.

Concept and a Company 7.1

Weaknesses in the Control Environment – The Case of Xerox (1997–2000)

Concept	A control environment in which there is motivation to misstate financial statements may lead to problems.
Story	Xerox is a US copy machine manufacturing company that saw its market share eroded in the USA in the 1990s because of foreign competition. The management, in order to cash in on a compensation scheme that would net them $35 million if Xerox's stock price rose to more than $60 per share, developed a scheme to artificially increase revenue.
	To settle charges that included fraud, the Securities and Exchange Commission (SEC) required that Xerox pay a $10 million civil penalty – at that time, the largest ever by a company for financial-reporting violations. The SEC also required that Xerox restate its financial statements for the years 1997 to 2000 (SEC, *Litigation release*, 2002).
	Most of the improper accounting – involving $2.8 billion in equipment revenue and $660 million in pre-tax earnings – resulted from improper accounting for revenue. On some sales, service revenue was immediately recognised, in violation of GAAP. The revenue associated with the servicing component of multi-year lease contracts was recognised during the first year, instead of recognised over the life of the lease. To increase revenue, Xerox increasingly booked more revenue associated with the equipment.
	Xerox also increased earnings by nearly $500 million by improperly setting aside various reserves, then gradually adding them back as gains to make up for profit shortfalls. In one instance Xerox changed its vacation policy by limiting the amount of time off employees could carry over from one period to the next, saving $120 million. But instead of taking the gain immediately as required by US GAAP, Xerox systematically and improperly released the money at a rate of $30 million per year (Bandler and Hechinger, 2002).
Discussion Questions	■ What impact does this weakness in the control environment have on Xerox, its auditors, its management and its shareholders?
	■ What audit procedures in this case should the auditor perform to reduce the risk of misstatement?
References	Bandler, J. and Hechinger, J., 2001, 'Fired Executive Questioned Xerox's Accounting Practices', *The Wall Street Journal*, 6 February.
	SEC, 2002, Litigation Release 17465, 'Xerox Settles SEC Enforcement Action Charging Company with Fraud', US Securities and Exchange Commission, 11 April.

Management can act to maximise control integrity and reduce misstatement. Management might remove incentives and temptations that prompt personnel to engage in fraudulent or unethical behaviour. Incentives for unethical behaviour include pressure to meet unrealistic performance targets, high performance-dependent rewards, and upper and lower cut-offs on bonus plans. Temptations for employees to engage in improper acts include: non-existent or ineffective controls; top management who are unaware of actions taken at lower organisational levels; ineffective board of directors; and insignificant penalties for improper behaviour.

Communication and enforcement of integrity and ethical values are essential elements which influence the effectiveness of the design, administration, and monitoring of internal controls. The auditor uses information gathered by performing risk assessment procedures to obtain an understanding of the design of controls as audit evidence to support the risk assessment. The effectiveness of controls cannot rise above the integrity and ethical values of the people who create, administer and monitor them. Integrity and ethical values are essential elements of the control environment that influence the design of other components.

■ Commitment to Competence

A company's control environment will be more effective if its culture is one in which quality and competence are openly valued. Competence is the knowledge and skills necessary to accomplish tasks that define the individual's job. Management needs to specify the competence levels for particular jobs and make sure those possessing the necessary training, experience, and intelligence perform the job.

■ Participation of Those Charged with Governance

The participation of those charged with governance, especially the entity's board of directors and audit committee, significantly influences the control environment and 'tone at the top'. The guidance and oversight responsibilities of an active and involved board of directors who possess an appropriate degree of management, technical and other expertise is critical to effective internal control.

Because the board must be prepared to question and scrutinise management's activities, present alternative views and have the courage to act in the face of obvious wrongdoing, it is necessary that the board contain at least a critical mass of independent (non-executive) directors.[14] For instance, the Sarbanes–Oxley Act requires that members of the audit committee be independent. In order to be considered to be independent, a member of an audit committee may not accept any consulting, advisory or other compensatory fee from the company they govern or be affiliated with any company subsidiary.[15]

The responsibilities of those charged with governance are of considerable importance for publicly traded companies. This is recognised in codes of practice such as the London Stock Exchange Combined Code and other regulations such as the Sarbanes–Oxley Act. The board of directors usually has a compensation committee charged with executive and management compensation. If the compensation is performance-related the board must counterbalance the pressures for management to manipulate financial reporting.

■ Auditor Evaluation of Those Charged with Governance

Important factors to consider in evaluating a board of directors, board of trustees, or comparable body is experience and stature of its members, extent of its involvement, scrutiny of activities and the appropriateness of its action. Another factor is the degree to which difficult questions are raised and pursued with management regarding plans or performance. Interaction of the audit committee with internal and external auditors, existence of a written audit committee charter and regularity of meetings are other factors affecting the control environment.

■ Management's Philosophy and Operating Style

Management's philosophy and operating style is their attitude about, and approach to, financial reporting, accounting issues, and to taking and managing business risk. A personal example set by top management and the board provides a clear signal to employees about the company's culture and about the importance of control. In particular, the chief executive plays a key role in determining whether subordinates decide to obey, bend or ignore company rules, and the kinds of business risks accepted.

Management philosophy may create significant risk. A key element of risk is dominance of management by a few individuals. Dick Fuld, the CEO of Lehman Brothers when it declared bankruptcy in 2008 leading the worse financial crisis in the United States since the Great Depression, was so domineering that against the advice of Lehman executives he turned down two offers to save the company (one from billionaire Warren Buffett). Auditors may consider key questions, such as: Does management take significant risk or are they risk adverse? What is management's attitude towards monitoring of business risk?

■ Organisational Structure

The entity's organisational structure provides the framework within which business activities are planned, executed, controlled and monitored. Important considerations are clarity of lines of authority and responsibility; the level at which policies and procedures are established; adherence to these policies and procedures; adequacy of supervision and monitoring of decentralised operations; and appropriateness of organisational structure for size and complexity of the entity. By understanding the entity's organisational structure, the auditor can discover the management and functional elements of the business and how control policies are carried out.

■ Assignment of Authority and Responsibility

How authority and responsibility are assigned throughout the organisation and the associated lines of reporting have an impact on controls. For example, a bank may require that two officers sign all cheques written for more than a certain amount. Computer users are only allowed to access certain parts of the accounting system. Responsibility and delegation of authority should be clearly assigned. How responsibility is distributed is usually spelt out in formal company policy manuals.

These manuals describe policies such as business practice, employee job responsibilities, duties and constraints (including written job descriptions). The auditor should consider whether management may have established a formal code of conduct but nevertheless acts in a manner that condones violations of that code or authorises exceptions to it.

ILLUSTRATION 7.3

Organisational Chart Segregation of Duties and Assignment of Authority and Responsibility

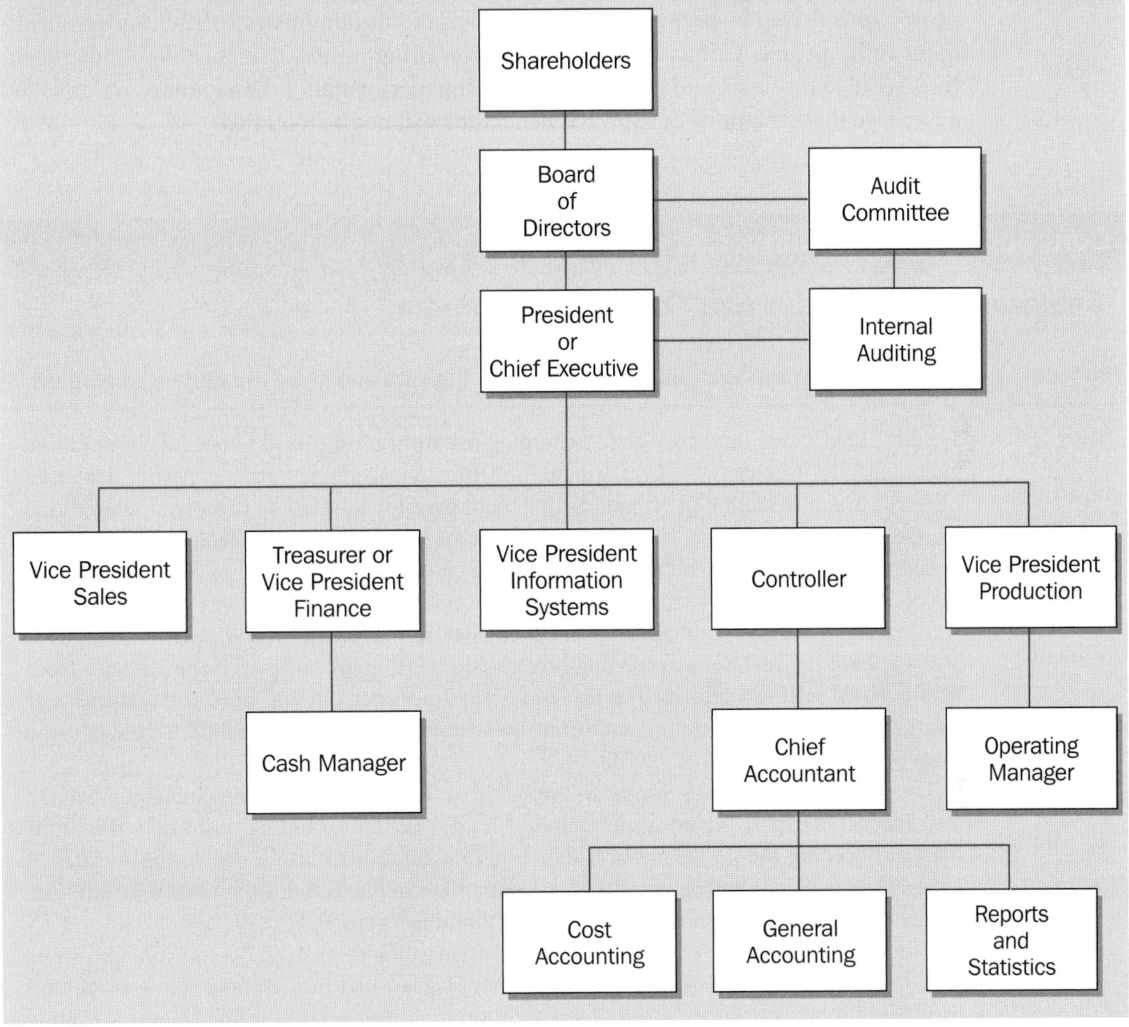

Illustration 7.3 gives a company organisation that demonstrates a good organisational segregation of duties and assignment of authority and responsibility of accounting personnel.

■ Human Resource Policies and Practices

The most important element of the control environment is personnel, which is why human resource policies and practices are essential. With trustworthy and competent employees, weaknesses in other controls can be compensated and reliable financial statements might still result. Honest, efficient people are able to perform at a high level even when there are few other controls to support them.

A company should take care in hiring, orientation, training, evaluation, counselling, promoting, compensating, and remedial actions. Recruiting practices that include formal, in-depth employment interviews and evidence of integrity and ethical behaviour result in hiring high-quality employees. Training improves employee technical skills and communicates their prospective roles in the enterprise. Rotation of personnel and promotions driven by periodic performance appraisals demonstrate the entity's commitment to its people. Competitive compensation programmes that include bonus incentives serve to motivate and reinforce outstanding performance. Disciplinary actions send a message that violations of expected behaviour will not be tolerated.

Concept and a Company 7.2

'Chainsaw Al', Sunbeam and Control Environment

Concept	'Tone at the top' sets the control environment. Big egos and greed can destroy a company.
Story	The SEC filed a civil injunctive action charging five former officers of Sunbeam Corporation, including CEO 'Chainsaw Al' Dunlap, and the former engagement partner of Arthur Andersen LLP with fraud, resulting in billions of dollars of investor losses. The complaint alleged that management of Sunbeam, a US manufacturer of small appliances, security devices and camping gear, engaged in a fraudulent scheme to create the illusion of a successful restructuring of Sunbeam and thus facilitate a sale of the company at an inflated price (SEC, 2001).

Sunbeam management employed a laundry list of fraudulent techniques, including creating 'cookie jar' revenues, recording revenue on contingent sales, accelerating sales from later periods into the present quarter, and using improper bill and hold transactions. For fiscal 1997, at least $60 million of Sunbeam's record setting $189 million earnings came from accounting fraud (SEC, 2001).

The biggest problem was Sunbeam's practice of overstating sales by recognising revenue in improper periods, including its 'bill and hold' practice of billing customers for products, but holding the goods for later delivery. One famous example was Sunbeam sales of $58 million worth of barbecue grills at cut-rate prices in December (giving stores until June to pay for them). Barbecue grills are ordinarily sold in summer.

When he became CEO of Sunbeam, a faltering manufacturer in an overcrowded business with low profit margins, Albert (Chainsaw Al) Dunlap had just orchestrated a successful turn-around of Scott Paper and had a reputation for ruthless cost cutting (hence the name 'chainsaw'). He was also a tireless self-promoter. When the Sunbeam board awarded him a three-year, $70 million contract, he boasted, 'You can't overpay a great executive. Don't you think I'm a bargain?' (Harrop, 1998).

At his first press conference Dunlap announced that he had already begun firing executives (Schifrin, 1996). Three months later, Dunlap said he would fire half of Sunbeam's 12,000 employees, sell or consolidate 39 of the company's 53 facilities, divest the company of several business lines, eliminate six regional headquarters in favour of a single office in Florida, and scrap 87 per cent of Sunbeam's products. In July 1996 when Dunlap became CEO, Sunbeam had already been through a bankruptcy and years of cost cutting. In October 1997, Dunlap hired Morgan Stanley to find potential suitors or takeover targets (*Weekly Corporate Growth Report*, 1998).

Dunlap believed in carrots and sticks. Dunlap preached sales at any cost and in any way. He gave people great incentives to perform and fired them when they did not. The need to overpower was also present in the executive suite. In fact, as a biographer puts it, 'working with Al Dunlap was a lot like going to war ... The pressure was brutal, the hours exhausting, and the casualties high ... At Sunbeam, Dunlap created a culture of misery, an environment of moral ambiguity, indifferent to everything except the stock price. He would throw papers or furniture, bang his hands on his desk, knock glasses of water off a table, and shout so ferociously that a manager's hair could lift from his head by the stream of air that rushed from Dunlap's screaming mouth' (Byrne, 1999).

The bullying and outrageous sales targets left Sunbeam with no idea of what its real inventory was. Divisional managers would report sales that met the targets, whether they had been effected or not. By early 1998, routine operational functions within the company were breaking down. Assembly lines were not working at peak efficiency. Supplies were not arriving on time. Maintenance was not being performed when it was needed. So goods were not getting shipped to the shops (Uren, 1998).

Discussion Questions	■ When Dunlap became CEO of Sunbeam in 1996, the share price shot up from $12.12 to $18.58 in a day. What aspect of Dunlap's management style could have caused this? ■ If you were auditing Sunbeam in 1996, what financial statement accounts do you believe would be susceptible to misstatement?
References	Byrne, J.A., 1999, *Chainsaw: The Notorious Career of Al Dunlap in the Era of Profit-at-Any-Price*, HarperCollins Publishing Inc., New York. Harrop, F., 1998, 'Dunlap Backers Had it Coming', *Rocky Mountain News*, 22 June, p. 35A. Schifrin, M., 1996, 'Chain Saw Al to the Rescue? (Corporate turn-around expert Albert Dunlap hired to help Sunbeam Corp.)', *Forbes*, Vol. 158, No. 5, 26 August, p. 42. SEC, 2001, Litigation News Release 2001–49, 'SEC Sues Former CEO, CFO, Other Top Former Officers of Sunbeam Corporation in Massive Financial Fraud', Securities and Exchange Commission, 15 May. Uren, D., 1998, 'Dunlap Style No Match for Tough Times', *The Australian*, 20 June, p. 57. 'Sunbeam to Acquire Coleman Co. for 1.3 Times Revenue', *Weekly Corporate Growth Report*, 9 March 1998.

■ Factors on Which to Assess Internal Control

Illustration 7.4 lists issues that might be focused on to assess the internal control environment, based on the COSO report.[16] These elements are cited as factors to consider when doing a control environment assessment to determine whether a positive control environment exists, but the absence or opposite of these factors indicate negative control environment. Elements of a negative control environment such as unethical management, management with low integrity, incompetent management, or governance promoting a 'cowboy culture' in the company increase the risk of financial misstatement. If the boards of directors seldom meet or are lax in their oversight responsibility, risk increases. Poor training, retention or morale of employees increases the risk that controls will not be implemented.

ILLUSTRATION 7.4

Factors on Which to Assess Internal Control Environment

Integrity and Ethical Values
(Communication and enforcement of integrity and ethical values)

- Existence and implementation of codes of conduct and other policies regarding acceptable business practice, conflicts of interest, or expected standards of ethical and moral behaviour.
- Dealings with employees, suppliers, customers, investors, creditors, insurers, competitors and auditors, etc. (e.g. whether management conducts business on a high ethical plane, and insists that others do so, or pays little attention to ethical issues).
- Pressure to meet unrealistic performance targets – particularly for short-term results – and extent to which compensation is based on achieving those performance targets.

Commitment to Competence

- Formal or informal job descriptions or other means of defining tasks that comprise particular jobs.
- Analysis of the knowledge and skills needed to perform jobs adequately.

Board of Directors or Audit Committee
(Participation by those charged with governance)

- An entity's control consciousness is influenced significantly by those charged with governance. Independence from management.
- Frequency and timeliness with which meetings are held with chief financial and/or accounting officers, internal auditors and external auditors.
- Sufficiency and timeliness with which information is provided to board or committee members, to allow monitoring of management's objectives and strategies, the entity's financial position and operating results, and terms of significant agreements.
- Sufficiency and timeliness with which the board or audit committee is apprised of sensitive information, investigation and improper acts (e.g. travel expenses of senior officers, significant litigation, investigations of regulatory agencies, defalcations, embezzlement or misuse of corporate assets, violations of insider trading rules, political payments, illegal payments).
- Oversight of the design and effective operation of whistle blower procedures and the process for reviewing the effectiveness of the entity's internal control.

Management's Philosophy and Operating Style

- Nature of business risks accepted, for example, whether management often enters into particularly high-risk ventures, or is extremely conservative in accepting risks.
- Frequency of interaction between senior management and operating management, particularly when operating from geographically removed locations.
- Attitudes and actions towards financial reporting, including disputes over application of accounting treatments (e.g. selection of conservative versus liberal accounting policies, whether accounting principles have been misapplied, important financial information not disclosed, or records manipulated or falsified).

Organisational Structure

- Appropriateness of the entity's organisational structure and its ability to provide the necessary information flow to manage its activities.
- Adequacy of definition of key managers' responsibilities and their understanding of these responsibilities.

Illustration 7.4 (continued)

Assignment of Authority and Responsibility

■ Assignment of responsibility and delegation of authority to deal with organisational goals and objectives, operating functions and regulatory requirements, including responsibility for information systems and authorisations for changes.
■ Appropriateness of control-related standards and procedures, including employee job descriptions.
■ Appropriate numbers of people, particularly with respect to data processing and accounting functions, with the requisite skill levels related to the size of the entity and nature and complexity of activities and systems.

Human Resource Policies and Practices

■ Extent to which policies and procedures for hiring, training, promoting, and compensating employees are in place.
■ Appropriateness of remedial action taken in response to departures from approved policies and procedures.
■ Adequacy of employee candidate background checks, particularly with regard to prior actions and activities considered to be unacceptable by the entity.
■ Adequacy of employee retention and promotion criteria and information-gathering techniques (e.g. performance evaluations) and relation to the code of conduct or other behavioural guidelines.

7.8 Risk Assessment

All components of internal control, from control environment to monitoring, should be assessed for risk. Managements risk assessment differs from, but is closely related to, the auditor's risk assessment discussed earlier (see Chapter 6). Management assesses risks as part of designing and operating the internal control system to minimise errors and irregularities. Auditors assess risks to decide the evidence needed in the audit. The two risk assessment approaches are related in that if management effectively assesses and responds to risks, the auditor will typically need to accumulate less audit evidence than when management fails to, because control risk is lower.

■ Internal and External Business Risk

Risks to the organisation may arise from external or internal factors. Externally, technological developments can affect the nature or timing of research and development, or lead to changes in procurement. Changing customer needs affect product development, pricing, warranties and service. New legislation and regulation can force changes in operating policies and strategies. Economic changes have an impact on decisions relating to financing, capital expenditures and expansion. Risks arising from internal factors might include a disruption of information systems processing; the quality of personnel and training; changes in management responsibilities; misappropriation opportunities because of the nature of the entity's activities or employee accessibility to assets; and an ineffective audit committee.

ILLUSTRATION 7.5

Risk Assessment Blank Evaluation Tool

Considerations	Comments Yes/No
Entity-Wide Objectives and Strategies	
1 Management has established entity-wide objectives.	1
2 Information on the entity-wide objectives is disseminated to employees and the board of directors.	2
3 Management obtains feedback from key managers, other employees, and the board signifying that communication to employees is effective.	3
Strategies	
4 Are strategies related to and consistent with entity-wide objectives?	4
5 The strategic plan supports the entity-wide objectives.	5
6 The strategic plan addresses high-level resource allocations and priorities.	6
Plans and Budgets	
7 Are business plans and budgets consistent with entity-wide objectives, strategic plans and current conditions?	7
8 Assumptions inherent in the plans and budgets reflect the entity's historical experience and current conditions.	8
9 Plans and budgets are at an appropriate level of detail for each management level.	9
Activity-Level Objectives	
Are objectives established for each of the following activities?	
10 Operations	10
11 Marketing and Sales	11
12 Service	12
13 Process Accounts Receivable	13
14 Procurement	14
15 Process Accounts Payable	15
16 Process Funds	16
17 Fixed Assets	17
18 Benefits and Retiree Information	18
19 Payroll	19
20 Product Costs	20
21 Tax Compliance	21
22 Financial and Management Reporting	22
23 Human Resources and Administrative Services	23
24 External Relations	24
25 Information Technology	25
26 Technology Development	26
27 Legal Affairs	27
28 Are those activity-level objectives consistent with each other?	28
29 Are activity-level objectives linked with entity-wide objectives and strategic plans?	29
30 Activity-level objectives are reviewed from time to time for continued relevance.	30
31 Are activity-level objectives complementary and reinforcing within activities?	31

■ Identify Risks of a Business

Many techniques have been developed to identify general risks to a business. The majority involves identifying and prioritising high-risk activities. One method[17] follows this procedure:

1 identify the essential resources of the business and determine which are most at risk;
2 identify possible liabilities that may arise;
3 review the risks that have arisen in the past;
4 consider any additional risks imposed by new objectives or new external factors;
5 seek to anticipate change by considering problems and opportunities on a continuing basis.

To illustrate, let us take as an example. Feats, an importer of apparel and footwear, established an objective of becoming an industry leader in high-quality fashion merchandise. Entity-wide risks are: supply sources (including quality, stability and number of foreign suppliers); currency rate fluctuations; timeliness of receiving shipments (including customs delays); availability, reliability and costs of shipping; and likelihood of trade embargoes caused by political instability. Other more generic business risks such as economic conditions, market acceptance, competitors and changes in regulations also have to be considered.

■ Conditions That May Increase Risk

Certain conditions may increase risk and, therefore, deserve special consideration. These conditions are: changed operating environment; new personnel; new or revamped information systems; rapid growth; new technology; new lines, products and activities; corporate restructuring; and foreign operations.

A sample blank risk assessment internal control questionnaire is shown in Illustration 7.5.[18]

7.9 Information Systems, Communication and Related Business Processes

Every enterprise must capture pertinent information related to both internal and external events and activities in both financial and non-financial forms. The information must be identified by management as relevant and then communicated to people who need it in a form and time frame that allows them to do their jobs.

The information relevant to financial reporting is recorded in the accounting system and is subjected to procedures that initiate, record, process and report entity transactions. The quality of information generated by the system affects management's ability to make appropriate decisions in controlling the entity's activities and preparing reliable financial reports.

Not just a matter of reporting, communication occurs in a broader sense, flowing down, across and up the organisation. All personnel must receive a clear message from top management that control responsibilities must be taken seriously. Employees must understand their own role in the internal control system, as well as how individual activities relate to the work of others, and how to report significant information to senior management. There also needs to be effective communication with external parties such as customers, suppliers and regulators.

■ Information System Includes

An organisation uses an array of information. The information systems used by companies include the accounting system; production system; budget information; personnel system; systems software; applications software for word-processing, calculating, presentations, communications and databases; and all the records and files generated by this software such as customer and vendor records. The information system also includes information about external events, activities, and conditions necessary to make informed business decisions and comply with external reporting.

Illustration 7.6 shows the typical input, subsystems and output of an information system.

ILLUSTRATION 7.6

Typical Input, Subsystems and Output of an Information System

Input

- accounting transactions
- correspondence
- personnel information
- customer and vendor information
- entity objectives and standards
- procedure manuals
- information about external events, activities and conditions

Subsystems

- accounting system
- customer and vendor records
- production system
- budget system
- personnel system
- computer systems software
- computer applications software (word processing, spreadsheet, presentation, communication, computer languages and database)

Output

- accounting reports
- budget reports
- production reports
- operating reports
- correspondence
- all the records and files generated by applications software

■ Financial Reporting Information System and Processes

For an audit, the auditor should obtain an understanding of the information system and the related business processes relevant to financial reporting in the following areas:[19]

- the classes of transactions in the entity's operations that are significant to the financial statements;
- the procedures, within both IT and manual systems, by which those transactions are initiated, recorded, processed and reported from their occurrence to their inclusion in the financial statements; this includes the correction of incorrect information and how information is transferred to the general ledger;
- the related accounting records, supporting information, and specific accounts in the financial statements and how they initiate, record, process and report transactions;
- how the information system captures events and conditions, other than transactions, that are significant to the financial statements;
- controls surrounding journal entries, including non-standard journal entries used to record non-recurring, unusual transactions or adjustments;
- the financial reporting process used to prepare the entity's financial statements, including significant accounting estimates and disclosures.

■ IT Transaction Procedures

The procedures by which transactions are initiated, recorded, processed and reported from their occurrence to their inclusion in the financial statements include entries of transaction totals into the general ledger (or equivalent records) and an understanding recurring and infrequent or unusual adjustments to the financial statements.

IT may be used to transfer information automatically from transaction processing systems to general ledger to financial reporting. The automated processes and controls in such systems may reduce the risk of inadvertent error but creates new risk. When IT is used to transfer information automatically, there may be little or no visible evidence of unauthorised intervention in the information systems if it occurs.

The auditor should also understand how the incorrect processing of transactions is resolved. For example, is there an automated **suspense file** and, if so, how are suspense items cleared out on a timely basis? How are system overrides or bypasses to controls accounted for?

IT risks were discussed earlier in this chapter.

■ Accounting System

For internal control and documentation purposes the auditor may view an **accounting system** as a series of steps by which economic events are captured by the enterprise, recorded and assembled in a normal ledger and ultimately reflected in the financial statements. Controls are needed to ensure that all the relevant economic events are captured by the accounting system, and that processes that modify and summarise financial information do not introduce errors.

To understand the accounting system sufficiently, the auditor should identify major classes of transactions in the client's operations and understand the accounting and financial reporting process thoroughly – from how the transactions are initiated to their inclusion in the financial statements. The auditor should identify significant accounting records, supporting documents and accounts in the financial statements. The critical points of interest for an auditor are where financial information *changes* along the path of recording and assembling a ledger.

■ Financial Reporting Process

The auditor should know how the company communicates significant matters relating to financial reporting. Open communication channels help ensure that exceptions are reported and acted on. When evaluating the communication system, the auditor will consider:

■ effectiveness with which employees' duties and control responsibilities are communicated;
■ establishment of channels of communication for people to report suspected improprieties;
■ receptivity of management to employee suggestions of ways to enhance productivity, quality or other similar improvements;
■ adequacy of communication across the organisation (e.g. between procurement and production activities), and the completeness and timeliness of information and its sufficiency to enable people to discharge their responsibilities effectively;
■ openness and effectiveness of channels with customers, suppliers, and other external parties for communicating information on changing customer needs;
■ timely and appropriate follow-up action by management resulting from communications received from customers, vendors, regulators or other external parties.

7.10   Control Activities (Control Procedures)

Control procedures (sometimes called 'control activities')[20] are policies and procedures that help ensure management directives are carried out. They help ensure that necessary actions are taken to address risks to the achievement of the entity's objectives for operations, financial reporting, or compliance. Generally, control procedures fall into five broad categories: authorisation, performance reviews, information processing, physical controls and segregation of duties.[21]

■ Two Elements of Control Procedures

Control procedures may be divided into two elements: a **policy** establishing what should be done and **procedures to effect that policy**. A policy, for example, might be that a securities dealer retail branch manager must monitor (conduct performance reviews of) customer trades. The control procedure to effect that policy is a review of a report of trade activities by the customer, performed in a timely manner and with attention given to the nature and volume of securities traded. Control procedures implement the control policies by specific routine tasks, performed at particular times by designated people, held accountable by adequate supervision and evidence of performance.

The categories of control activities given in ISA 315 are:

- performance reviews;
- information processing (accuracy, adequate documents, application controls);
- physical controls;
- segregation of duties;
- authorisation of transactions and activities, general controls.

The first four categories of control activities will be discussed in this section. Authorisation, not discussed in detail here, is the delegation of initiation of transactions and obligations on the company's behalf. Management should restrict authorisation of personnel to access assets and records. It includes general computer controls with limit access (user ID, passwords, etc.).

■ Performance Reviews

Performance reviews are independent checks on performance by a third party not directly involved in the activity. Sometimes called internal verification, these control activities include reviews and analyses of actual performance versus budgets, forecasts and prior period performance; relating different sets of data – operating or financial – to one another, together with analyses of the relationships and investigative and corrective actions; comparing internal data with external sources of information; and review of functional or activity performance. These reviews may also include reviews of actual performance versus budgets; surprise checks of procedures; periodic comparisons of accounting records and physical assets; and a review of functional or activity performance. An example of surprise check would be to pull the time cards at the beginning of a shift and see that everyone who is 'punched in' is present. A routine comparison of accounting records and physical assets is a bank reconciliation performed by a person independent of the accounting records and handling of cash. A review of functional or activity performance would be a bank's consumer loan manager's review of reports by branch, region, and loan type for loans.

■ Information Processing

Information processing control procedures (discussed in Section 7.5 of this chapter) are those controls that ensure accuracy of input and processing, adequacy of documents and records, and computer application controls. Application controls are controls that apply to applications that initiate, record, process and report transactions (such as MS Office, SAP, QuickBooks), rather than the computer system in general.

There are several standard application controls. The chart of accounts is an important application control because it provides the framework for determining the information presented on to financial statements and budgets. The most widely applicable control device is the use of serial numbers on documents and input transactions. Serial numbers provide control over the number of documents issued. Cheques, tickets, sales invoices, purchase orders, stock certificates and many other business papers use this control. Documents should be recorded immediately because long periods between transaction and recording increase the chance of misstatement. Systems manuals for computer accounting software should provide sufficient information to make the accounting functions clear.

Information system authorisation controls, called general controls, is considered an authorisation control rather than an information processing control. **General controls** are policies and procedures that relate to many applications and support the effective functioning of application controls by helping to ensure the continued proper operation of information systems. General controls include access controls like user ID, passwords and back-up and recovery procedures.

■ Information Processing of Transaction Records

A standard general information processing control is an entity's transaction records. The entity should maintain a set of records on which transactions are recorded and summarised. In a manual system these records include sales invoices, shipping documents, purchase orders, subsidiary records, journals, ledgers and employee time cards. In a computer system, these records are all represented in the **database** maintained by an accounting application program (such as QuickBooks, SAP and Oracle Financials).

These records must be adequate to provide good assurance that all assets are properly controlled and all transactions correctly recorded. Well-designed documents in a manual system and **preformatted** input screens in a computer system should be pre-numbered consecutively, prepared at the time a transaction takes place, simple enough to be clearly understood, designed for multiple uses to minimise the number of different forms, and constructed in a manner that encourages correct preparation.

■ Physical Controls

Physical controls are procedures to ensure the physical security of assets. Assets and records that are not adequately protected can be stolen, damaged, or lost. In highly computerised companies damaged data files could be costly or even impossible to replace. For these reasons, only individuals who are properly authorised should be allowed access to the company's assets. Direct physical access to assets may be controlled through physical precautions, for example: storerooms guard inventory against pilferage; locks, fences and guards protect other assets such as equipment; and fireproof safes and safety deposit vaults protect assets such as currency and securities.

■ Segregation of Duties

Segregation of duties seeks to prevent persons with access to readily realisable assets from being able to adjust the records that record and thereby control those assets. Duties are divided, or segregated, among different people to reduce the risks of error or inappropriate actions. For instance, responsibilities for authorising transactions, for recording them, and for handling the related assets (called custody of assets) are separated.

Segregation of duties entails three fundamental functions (acronym ARC) that must be separated and adequately supervised:

1 **Authorisation** is the delegation of initiation of transactions and obligations on the company's behalf.
2 **Recording** is the creation of documentary evidence of a transaction and its entry into the accounting records.
3 **Custody** is physical control over assets or records.

A separation of these three functions is an essential element of control. Let us use the example of wages. Authorisation is required for hiring of staff and is a function of the personnel department. The accounting department handles the recording of the time records and the payroll in the payroll journals. The receipt of pay cheques and issuance of them to the employees is handled by work supervisors.

Illustration 7.7 shows an overview of segregation of duties.

ILLUSTRATION 7.7

Overview of Segregation of Duties

Transaction type	Controls
Authorisation	Controls that ensure that only necessary transactions based on the entity's objectives are undertaken. They prevent unnecessary and fraudulent transactions. Examples: organisational chart, accounting procedures manual, chart of accounts, conflict of interest policy, signatures on cheques limited to that of president, etc.
Recording	Controls which ensure that all authorised transactions are allowed in the accounting records, they are properly entered, and are not deleted or amended without proper authorisation. Examples: entries in journals then ledgers, posting reference in journals, rotation of accounting personnel, listing of mail receipts, cash register tapes, reconciliation of bank statements, etc.
Custody	Controls that ensure that assets cannot be misused. Examples: pre-numbered forms, access to records (computer or manual) limited to authorised personnel, individuals handling cash do not keep the accounting records of cash, bonding of employees, locked storage, people responsible for assets should not be authorised to sell them, daily deposits of cash, etc.

Authorisation in Segregation of Duties

People who authorise transactions should not have control over the related asset. Jérôme Kerviel, a derivative trader, brought one of the world's largest banks, Société Générale, to its knees with fraud worth €4.9 billion in early 2008. 'Le rogue trader' made €50 billion of unauthorised trades and futures positions – more than SocGen's own stock market value. Kerviel tried to conceal the activity by creating losing trades intentionally so as to offset his early gains.[22] In 1995 another investment bank, Barings, a British bank founded in 1762 and the investment bank for the 'Louisiana purchase' from Napoleon by US President Thomas Jefferson's administration, was forced into insolvency by losses. Nicholas Leeson, the head derivatives trader of the Singapore branch, lost £827 million in speculative trading, mainly on the futures markets. He not only made investments in Nikkei exchange indexed derivatives, but also was able to authorise his own investments.[23] The authorisation of a transaction and the handling of the related asset by the same person increase the possibility of defalcation within the organisation.

Another example of when duties were not separated with a disastrous result was the bond trading loss in the New York Office of Daiwa Bank in 1995. Over 11 years, 30,000 unauthorised trades were made resulting in a $1.1 billion loss (an average of $400,000 in losses for every trading day). Daiwa allowed Toshihide Iguchi, a bond trader, to authorise sales, have custody of the bond assets and record these transactions.[24] Daiwa Bank paid fines of $340 million, and closed its American operations, after being sued by US authorities. Mr Iguchi was convicted and jailed for four years and paid $2.5 million in fines in 1996.[25] Four years later, in 2000, a court in Osaka, Japan ordered 11 senior executives at the bank to repay a total of $775 million in damages to their own bank.

Custody and Recording in Segregation of Duties

If an individual has custody of assets and also accounts for them, there is a high risk of that person disposing of the asset for personal gain and adjusting the records to cover the theft. The basic control imposed by double-entry bookkeeping means that in order to conceal the theft or fraudulent use of an asset, the perpetrator must be able to prevent the asset being recorded in the first place or to write it off. If the theft cannot be permanently written off, it may still be temporarily concealed by being carried forward in preparing inventory sheets, in performing the bank reconciliation, or in reconciling the debtor or creditor control accounts.

IT Segregation of Duties

Operations responsibility and record keeping and the information technology (IT) duties should be separate. Information systems are crucially important to control, so it is suggested that those duties be segregated for programmer, computer operator, librarian and data reviewer. A programmer wrote (or configured) the software. Giving the programmer access to input data creates temptation. The computer operator (who inputs the accounting data) should not be allowed to modify the program. A librarian maintains and is custodian of the records and files that should only be released to authorised personnel. The person who tests the efficiency of all aspects of the system should be independent of the other computer jobs.

Concept and a Company 7.3

Weaknesses in the Control Environment – The Case of Société Générale

Concept	A control environment in which the motivation to misstate financial statements may lead to problems.
Story	In 2000, Jérôme Kerviel graduated from University Lumière Lyon with a Master of Finance specialising in organisation and control of financial markets. Subsequently, he found employment with the bank Société Générale in the summer of 2000. He started out on the compliance department.
	In 2005 he was promoted to the bank's Delta One products team in Paris where he was a junior trader. Société Générale's Delta One business includes programme trading, exchange-traded funds, swaps, index futures and quantitative trading. Kerviel was assigned to arbitrage discrepancies between equity derivatives and cash equity prices.

In January 2008, Société Générale announced they had lost approximately €4.9 billion closing out positions over three days of trading beginning 21 January 2008, a period in which the market was experiencing a large drop in equity indices. Bank officials also claim that throughout 2007, Kerviel had been trading profitably in anticipation of falling market prices; however, they have accused him of exceeding his authority to engage in unauthorised trades totalling as much as €49.9 billion, a figure far higher than the bank's total market capitalisation. Bank officials claim that Kerviel tried to conceal the activity by creating losing trades intentionally so as to offset his early gains. So, Société Générale concluded these positions were fraudulent transactions created by Jérôme Kerviel.

On 24 January 2008, Société Générale filed a lawsuit against Kerviel. On 5 October 2010, he was found guilty and sentenced to at least three years' imprisonment and was ordered to pay back the damages Société Générale suffered (€4.9 billion). Kerviel appealed, claiming is supervisors knew what he was doing. However, on 24 October 2012, a Paris appeals court upheld the October 2010 sentence.

In an interview with German newspaper *Der Spiegel*, Kerviel said: 'In the process, I didn't make a penny, I didn't enrich myself personally and I didn't commit any fraud. I only wanted to be a good employee who generated as much profit as possible for his employer. I was merely a small cog in the machine – and now I'm suddenly supposedly the main person responsible for the financial crisis.' Also, he pointed out that 'having more controls and regulations goes against efforts to pursue consistently higher profits at a time when all banks want to maximise their return on equity.' In the same interview, Kerviel explained how it was possible for him to make trades of this size, since the maximum official risk exposure for that traders in Jérôme's department was €125 million. Kerviel stated: 'My supervisors had deactivated the system of alerts. If I had wanted to, I could have even invested €100 billion in a single day. My bosses removed all the safeguards off my computer.'

Earlier on 21 February 2008, the London *Sunday Times* reported that according to an independent report Société Générale had missed 75 warning signs on the activities of rogue trader Jérôme Kerviel. Risk control procedures were followed correctly, the report said, but compliance officers rarely went beyond routine checks and did not inform managers of anomalies, even when large sums were concerned. Nor were follow-up checks made on cancelled or modified transactions.

Discussion Questions	■ What controls were in place, but not operating? ■ If Jérôme Kerviel had managed to deactivate the system of alerts by himself, given his previous experience at the compliance department of the bank, do you believe he was the only person responsible for the loss?

References	Seib C., 2008, 'Société Générale Missed 75 Warnings on Trader Kerviel', *Sunday Times*, 21 February. http://en.wikipedia.org/wiki/J%C3%A9r%C3%B4me_Kerviel. http://en.wikipedia.org/wiki/2008_Soci%C3%A9t%C3%A9_G%C3%A9n%C3%A9rale_trading_loss. http://richardbrenneman.wordpress.com/2010÷11/19/jerome-kerviel-rogue-trader-or-the-perfect-patsy/. http://www.spiegel.de/international/business/rogue-trader-jerome-kerviel-i-was-merely-a-small-cog-in-the-machine-a-729155.html.

Control Procedures Risk

All control procedures should be analysed for risk. The main risk is that a control procedure is not in place to ensure a policy is carried out. In other words, a policy has been identified, but there are no control activities to support the policy. If there is no control activity in place to ensure the achievement and monitoring of that objective, it is considered a weakness in internal control. Risk is also increased if a control procedure is designed, but has not been operating. Also, because of changes in business, product or industry, there may be control activities in place that are no longer pertinent.

7.11 Monitoring of Controls

Internal control systems need to be monitored. Monitoring is a process that deals with ongoing assessment of the quality of internal control performance. The process involves assessing the design of controls and their operation on a timely basis and taking necessary corrective actions. By monitoring, management can determine that internal controls are operating as intended and that they are modified as appropriate for changes in conditions.

Ongoing monitoring information comes from several sources: exception reporting on control activities, reports by government regulators, feedback from employees, complaints from customers, and most importantly from internal auditor reports. For large companies, an internal audit department is essential to effective monitoring.[26] This feedback from the internal auditors may also help external auditors reduce evidence requirements.

Management's monitoring activities may include using information from communications from external parties such as customer complaints and regulator comments that may indicate problems or highlight areas in need of improvement. Two more examples of monitoring activities are management's review of **bank reconciliations**, and an internal auditors' evaluation of sales personnel's compliance with the company's human resource policies.

■ Internal Controls over Time

Internal control systems change over time. The way controls are applied may evolve. Some procedures can become less effective or perhaps are no longer performed. This can be due to the arrival of new personnel, the varying effectiveness of training and supervision, time and resource constraints, or additional pressures. Furthermore, circumstances for which the internal control system originally was designed also may change. Accordingly, management needs to determine whether the internal control system continues to be relevant and able to address new risks. This is the monitoring function.

■ Evaluation of Monitoring Activities

When evaluating the ongoing monitoring the following issues might be considered:[27]

- periodic comparisons of amounts recorded with the accounting system with physical assets;
- responsiveness to internal and external auditor recommendations on means to strengthen internal controls;

- extent to which training seminars, planning sessions, and other meetings provide management with information on the effective operation of controls;
- whether personnel are asked periodically to state whether they understand and comply with the entity's code of conduct and regularly perform critical control activities;
- effectiveness of internal audit activities;
- extent to which personnel, in carrying out their regular activities, obtain evidence as to whether the system of internal control continues to function.

Evaluations of all the components are taken together for an overall evaluation and a sample blank evaluation form is shown in Illustration 7.8.[28]

7.12 Hard and Soft Control

To minimise risks, management designs and sets in place a set of rules, physical constraints and activities called 'internal controls'. Due to the explicit, formal and tangible character of these controls, these controls are generally referred to as **hard controls**. However, the dynamic environment with its rapidly changing technology, increasing regulatory requirements and globalisation requires more than rigorous adherence to policy, procedures and protocols, which may be referred to as **soft controls**.

Social–Psychological Factors

The recent financial and economic crisis has exposed the more softer human factor, the so-called soft controls, in the inner workings of organisations as never before. Soft controls are the intangible factors in an organisation that influence the behaviour of managers and employees. Whereas soft controls are founded in the culture or climate of an organisation, the hard-controls are more explicit, formal and visible. The control environment includes soft controls like tone-at-the-top, risk-awareness, openness to raise issues and discuss ideas, trust and loyalty, stakeholder focus, and enforcement.

Based on scientific research, Muel Kaptein[29] distinguishes seven social–psychological factors which influence people's behaviour within organisations. These factors highly influence the effectiveness of internal control measures and procedures. The factors are as follows:

1 **Clarity** for directors, managers and employees as to what constitutes desirable and undesirable behaviour: the clearer the expectations, the better people know what they must do, how to perform the control and the more likely they are to act on it.
2 **Role-modelling** among administrators, management or immediate supervisors: the better the examples given in an organisation, the better people behave, while the worse the example, the worse the behaviour.
3 **Achievability** of goals, tasks and responsibilities set: the better equipped people in an organisation are, the better they are able to execute the control activities that are expected from them.
4 **Commitment** on the part of directors, managers and employees in the organisation: the more the organisation treats its people with respect and involves them in the organisation, the more these people will try to serve the interests of the organisation and reach the internal control objectives.

ILLUSTRATION 7.8

Overall Internal Control Evaluation Tool

This exhibit is a blank tool (work paper) for the evaluation of an entity's control environment. This form is to be filled in after the detailed forms such as that shown in Illustration 7.5 are complete.

Internal control components	Comments Yes/No
Control Environment	
1 Does management adequately convey the message that integrity cannot be compromised?	1
2 Does a positive control environment exist, whereby there is an attitude of control consciousness throughout the organisation and a positive 'tone at the top'?	2
3 Is the competence of the entity's people commensurate with their responsibilities?	3
4 Is management's operating style, the way it assigns authority and responsibility, and organises and develops its people appropriate?	4
5 Does the board provide the right level of attention?	5
Risk Assessment	
6 Are entity-wide objectives and supporting activity-level objectives established and linked?	6
7 Are the internal and external risks that influence the success or failure of the achievement of the objectives identified and assessed?	7
8 Are mechanisms in place to identify changes affecting the entity's ability to achieve its objectives?	8
9 Are policies and procedures modified as needed?	9
Control Activities	
10 Are control activities in place to ensure adherence to established policy and the carrying out of actions to address the related risks?	10
11 Are there appropriate control activities for each of the entity's activities?	11
Information and Communication	
12 Are information systems in place to identify and capture pertinent information – financial and non-financial, relating to external and internal events – and bring it to personnel in a form that enables them to carry out their responsibilities?	12
13 Does communication of relevant information take place?	13
14 Is information communicated clear with respect to expectations and responsibilities of individuals and groups, and reporting of results?	14
15 And does communication occur down, across and upwards in the entity, as well as between the entity and other parties?	15
Monitoring	
16 Are appropriate procedures in place to monitor on an ongoing basis, or to periodically evaluate the functioning of the other components of internal control?	16
17 Are deficiencies reported to the right people?	17
18 Are policies and procedures modified as needed?	18
Overall Conclusion	See attached

5 **Transparency of behaviour**: the better people observe their own and others' behaviour, and its effects, the more they take this into account and the better they are able to control and adjust their behaviour to the expectations of others.

6 **Openness** to discussion of viewpoints, emotions, dilemmas and transgressions: the lower the bar for people within the organisation to talk about moral or ethical issues regarding internal control, the more they will be likely to do this, and the more they will learn from one another.

7 **Enforcement** of behaviour, such as appreciation or even reward for desirable behaviour, sanctioning of undesirable behaviour and the extent to which people learn from mistakes, near misses, incidents, and accidents: the better the enforcement, the more people tend towards what will be rewarded and avoid what will be punished.

All these seven factors influence the way people examine their control activities. Therefore, these seven factors may be relevant for the auditor when obtaining an understanding of the control environment and may be used as indicators of the quality of the control environment of a particular organisation.

■ Testing Soft Controls

To gather sufficient evidence of the effective operation of soft controls, some of the traditional testing approaches and tools may not be appropriate. Instead, the auditor will need to think 'outside-the-box' to gather sufficient, competent evidential matter in such audits. Observations, self-assessments, surveys, workshops, or similar techniques may be better suited than traditional methods. Specifically:[30]

■ Employee surveys are frequently used in evaluating the success of management's efforts in establishing an effective control environment. These surveys provide useful measurements of the effectiveness of one or more control environment elements. Annual employee ethics compliance forms are another example.

■ The Chief Audit Executive should use his or her network within the organisation. The network is critical in discerning whether communication, tone at the top, management walking the talk, and effective supervision are present on a day-to-day basis.

■ Audit team discussion with the secretaries of executives can be a useful source of information about behaviour in the organisation.

■ The internal auditor's knowledge of the organisation's inner-workings is useful to further corroborate the effectiveness of soft controls.

■ The value of 'auditing by walking around' cannot be overstated. By being present, visible and observant across the organisation, auditors can identify those intangible clues that may lead to deeper assessments. Associates who trust they can provide concerns to auditors with an appropriate degree of anonymity are also valuable.

■ Past audit results over control activities and the reaction and remediation from management are also good indicators.

■ Internal auditors' participation in committees, taskforces, workgroups, and involvement in ethics and compliance programme implementation and assessments provide valuable insights over extended periods of time.

7.13   Design of Internal Controls

Today, careful evaluation of internal control design and how it is operating in practice is stimulated by regulatory requirements, such as the Sarbanes–Oxley Act[31] (in which internal control statements are required), and the SEC.[32] This internal control report contains a statement of management's responsibility for establishing and maintaining adequate control over financial reporting, and a description of the framework management uses to evaluate the effectiveness of controls. Management must give their assessment of the effectiveness of internal controls and the auditor is asked for an attestation report on management's assessment. (Reporting on internal controls is discussed in Chapter 14 'Other Assurance and Non-Assurance Engagements'.)

To gain an understanding of the entity's internal control, the auditor is required to evaluate the design of controls and determine whether they have been implemented. Evaluating the design of a control involves considering whether the control is capable of effectively preventing, or detecting and correcting, material misstatements.

Errors in design occur when crucial internal control activities are designed by individuals with limited knowledge of accounting. For instance, if an entity's IT personnel do not completely understand how an order entry system processes sales transactions, they may erroneously design changes to the system. On the other hand, good designs may be poorly implemented. An IT controls change may be correctly designed but misunderstood by individuals who translate the design into program code. IT controls may be designed to report transactions over a predetermined dollar amount to management, but individuals responsible for conducting the review may not understand the purpose of such reports and, accordingly, may fail to review them or investigate unusual items. For example, there may be an error in the design of a control. Equally, the operation of a control may not be effective, such as where information produced for the purposes of internal control is not effectively used because the individual responsible for reviewing the information does not understand its purpose or fails to take appropriate action.

■ Controls Addressing Significant Risk

It is especially important to evaluate the design of controls that address **significant risks** and controls for which substantive procedures alone is not sufficient. For significant risks, the auditor should evaluate the design of the entity's controls, including relevant control procedures. Implementation of a control means that the control exists and that the entity is using it. (We will discuss tests of implementation of controls in Chapter 8.)

■ Control Risk

Control risk is a function of the effectiveness of the design, implementation and maintenance of internal control by management to address identified risks that threaten the achievement of the entity's objectives relevant to preparation of the entity's financial statements.[33] Some control risk will always exist because of the inherent limitations of internal control. Internal control, no matter how well designed and operated, can provide only reasonable assurance of achieving the entity's objectives. Limitations inherent to internal control include the faultiness of human judgement in decision making and simple human failures such as errors or mistakes.

■ Assessing Control Design

There are no standard procedures for assessing the design of internal controls, but all controls are created to assure that an objective be met. When assessing control design, the auditor will start with the objective. Then he will ask himself what controls should and could be in place to assure that this objective is met and in what way these controls may be implemented. This is the design of the control.

■ Financial Statement Assertions and Controls

There are standard financial statement objectives, or assertions, that are assumed to be in place for a financial statement that fairly represents the underlying financial condition of the entity. For example, the assertion existence may be applied to sales, i.e. 'revenue exists'. The objective is that all sales that sum to the revenue account balance actually exist – each sales transaction composing the revenue meets the definition of 'revenue' and actually occurred (sales were not fictitious). Controls such as cash registers, restricted access for recording sales in the general ledger, and control activities such as segregation of duties and monitoring of unusual transactions should be designed and implemented to assure that the revenue account balance is correct. Inputting revenue transactions through the cash register is a design to assure revenue exists. In addition to using a cash register, an additional part of the design of the control is that all employees are trained to use the cash register.

■ Methods for Obtaining Controls Audit Evidence

Obtaining audit evidence about the design and implementation of relevant controls may involve:[34]

- **Inquiring of entity personnel.** Inquiries directed towards internal audit personnel may relate to their activities concerning the design and effectiveness of the entity's internal control. Ordinarily, only inquiring of entity personnel will not be sufficient to evaluate the design of a control or to determine whether a control has been implemented.
- **Observing and re-performing the application of a specific control.** The auditors may observe the application of the control or re-perform the application themselves.
- **Inspecting documents and reports.**
- **Tracing transactions through the information system** relevant to financial reporting.

■ Control Tests of Design

Tests of the operating effectiveness of controls may be performed on controls that the auditor has determined are suitably designed to prevent, or detect and correct, a material misstatement. Some control design risk assessment procedures may provide audit evidence and, consequently, serve as tests of controls. For instance, in obtaining an understanding of the control environment, the auditor may make inquiries about management's use of budgets, observe management's comparison of monthly budgeted and actual expenses, and inspect reports pertaining to the investigation of variances between budgeted and actual amounts. These procedures provide knowledge about the design of the entity's budgeting policies and may also provide audit evidence about the effectiveness of the operation of budgeting policies in preventing or detecting material misstatements.

The result of testing the design may reveal **deficiencies in internal control**,[35] which must be reported to management (ISA 265). Deficiency in internal control exists when: (a) a control is designed, implemented or operated in such a way that it is unable to prevent, or detect and correct, misstatements in the financial statements on a timely basis; or (b) a control necessary to prevent, or detect and correct, misstatements in the financial statements on a timely basis is missing. The auditor must communicate in writing significant deficiencies in internal control identified during the audit to those charged with governance on a timely basis.[36] The auditor must also communicate in writing to management on timely basis significant deficiencies in internal control that the auditor will communicate to those charged with governance, unless circumstances make it inappropriate.[37] The auditor is responsible for considering what the timing of the reporting on internal control deficiencies should be. It is possible the timely basis for reporting internal control deficiencies is before the year-end audit.

7.14   Preliminary Assessment of Control Risk

It is difficult for an auditor to prepare an audit plan if they do not get a preliminary idea of the risks that internal controls may not be operating. One needs to have a certain faith that the data in the accounts and transactions was initiated and processed accurately. It is the controls that give an auditor some assurance that the data is accurate. For example, the auditor has to have assurance that people who input the data were authorised to do so, did not have segregation of duties conflicts and were supervised or reviewed by another party.

When planning an audit, in order to assess control risk the auditor undertakes a number of tasks. First the auditor considers the results of previous audits that involved evaluating the operating effectiveness of internal control, including the nature of identified deficiencies and action taken to address them. The auditor will also discuss the possibility of audit risk with audit firm personnel responsible for performing other services to the entity. He will interview entity personnel to find evidence of management's commitment to the design, implementation and maintenance of sound internal control and the importance attached to internal control throughout the entity. The auditor might try to get a good idea of the volume of transactions, which may determine whether it is more efficient for the auditor to rely on internal control.

Knowledge of the industry and the environment might also help in determining control risk. There are obvious questions. For instance, what is the impact on controls of significant business developments affecting the entity, including changes in information technology and business processes, changes in key management, and acquisitions, mergers and divestments? Have controls adapted to significant industry developments such as changes in industry regulations and new reporting requirements? Were there changes in the financial reporting framework, such as changes in accounting standards? Are there other relevant developments, such as changes in the legal environment affecting the entity?

If the entity uses service organisations[38] the auditor may want to discover the control risks at the service organisation. He can get either a Type 1 or Type 2 report[39] which may assist the auditor in obtaining a preliminary understanding of the controls implemented at the service organisation.[40] (See Chapter 6 for more details.) If there is no report available or the report is too old, the auditor may perform procedures to update the information, such as discussing the changes at the service organisation with auditee personnel who would be in a position to know of such changes, reviewing current documentation and correspondence issued by the service organisation, or discussing the changes with service organisation personnel.

7.15 Summary

Internal control is not only essential to maintaining the accounting and financial records of an organisation, it is essential to managing the entity. For that reason everyone from the external auditors to management to the board of directors to the stockholders of large public companies to government has an interest in internal controls. In many parts of the world, regulators have emphasised the importance of internal control by requiring management to make annual public statements about the effectiveness of internal controls.

Internal control, according to the Committee of Sponsoring Organizations of the Treadway Commission (COSO), is a process, effected by an entity's board of directors, management and other personnel, designed to provide reasonable assurance regarding the achievement of objectives in the following categories: effectiveness and efficiency of operations, reliability of financial reporting, compliance with applicable laws and regulations, and safeguarding of assets against unauthorised acquisition, use or disposition.

The reason a company establishes a system of control is to help achieve its performance and profitability goals and prevent loss of resources by fraud and other means. Internal control can also help to ensure reliable financial reporting and compliance with laws and regulations. The entity's internal control system consists of many specific policies and procedures designed to provide management with reasonable assurance that the goals and objectives it believes important to the company will be met. Controls are especially important in preventing fraud, supporting management objectives, ensuring accuracy of transactions, and supporting assessment of the financial statements.

To understand the entity's internal controls the auditor will evaluate the design of a control and judge whether it has been implemented. He determines whether the control, individually or in combination with other controls, is capable of effectively preventing, or detecting and correcting, material misstatements.

Whether formally or informally, management sets objectives that they expect their business to achieve. For example, profit making organisations have profit as a goal and not-for-profit entities wish to achieve their mission (like finding a cure for Alzheimer's disease). Management identifies the risk of not achieving their objectives. To minimise these risks, management designs and puts in place a set of rules, physical constraints and activities called 'internal controls' which, if they are implemented properly, will minimise the risks of not meeting objectives.

The heart of any internal control system is the information technology (IT) upon which so much of the business processes rely. General IT controls are policies and procedures that relate to many applications and support the effective functioning of application controls by helping to ensure the continued proper operation of information systems. General IT controls commonly include controls over data centre and network operations; system software acquisition, change and maintenance; access security; and application system acquisition, development and maintenance.

The auditor should be aware that IT poses specific risks to an entity's internal control including reliance on systems or programs that are inaccurately processing data, processing inaccurate data, or both, unauthorised access to data that may result in destruction of data or improper changes to data; the possibility of IT personnel gaining access privileges beyond those necessary to perform their assigned duties thereby breaking down segregation of duties; unauthorised changes to data in master files; unauthorised changes to systems or programs, and other inappropriate actions.

The internal control components are: the control environment, risk assessment, control activities, information and communication, and monitoring.

The control environment means the overall attitude, awareness, and actions of directors and management regarding the internal control system and its importance in the entity. The control environment has a pervasive influence on the way business activities are structured, the way objectives are established, and the way risks are assessed. The control environment is influenced by the entity's history and culture. Effectively controlled companies set a positive 'tone at the top' and establish appropriate policies and procedures.

Elements of the control environment are: communication and enforcement of integrity and ethical values; commitment to competence; participation by those charged with governance; management's philosophy and operating style; organisational structure; assignment of authority and responsibility; and human resource policies and practices.

All components of internal control, from control environment to monitoring, should be assessed for risk. Certain conditions may increase risk and, therefore, deserve special consideration. These conditions are: changed operating environment; new personnel; new or revamped information systems; rapid growth; new technology; new lines, products and activities; corporate restructuring; and foreign operations.

Management's risk assessment differs from, but is closely related to, the auditor's risk assessment. Management assesses risks as part of designing and operating the internal control system to minimise errors and irregularities. Auditors assess risks to decide the evidence needed in the audit. The two risk assessment approaches are related in that if management effectively assesses and responds to risks, the auditor will typically need to accumulate less audit evidence than when management fails to, because control risk is lower.

Information is needed at all levels of the organisation: financial information; operating information; compliance information; and information about external events, activities, and conditions. This information must be identified, captured, and communicated in a form and time frame that enables people to carry out their responsibilities. The information system controls should be tested because there are general IT and input risks that the accounting system does not produce sufficient audit evidence.

Control procedures (sometimes called 'control activities') are policies and procedures that help ensure management directives are carried out. They help ensure that necessary actions are taken to address risks to the achievement of the entity's objectives for operations, financial reporting or compliance. Generally, control procedures fall into five broad categories: authorisation, performance reviews, information processing, physical controls and segregation of duties.

Internal control systems need to be monitored. Monitoring is a process that deals with ongoing assessment of the quality of internal control performance over time. The process involves assessing the design of controls and their operation on a timely basis and taking necessary corrective actions. By monitoring, management can determine that internal controls are operating as intended and that they are modified as appropriate for changes in conditions.

Due to the explicit, formal and tangible character of the controls management designs and puts in place in the form of a set of rules, physical constraints and activities, these controls are generally referred to as *hard* controls. However, the dynamic environment with the rapidly changing technology, increasing regulatory requirements and globalisation requires more than rigorous adherence to policy, procedures and protocols, which may be termed soft controls. Soft controls are the intangible factors in an organisation that influence the behaviour of managers and employees. Whereas soft controls are founded in the culture or climate of an organisation, the hard controls are more explicit, formal and visible. The control environment includes soft controls like tone-at-the-top, risk-awareness, openness to raise issues and discuss ideas, trust and loyalty, stakeholder focus and enforcement.

To gain an understanding of the entity's internal control, the auditor is required to evaluate the design of controls and determine whether they have been implemented. Evaluating the design of a control involves considering whether the control is capable of effectively preventing, or detecting and correcting, material misstatements. It is especially important to evaluate the design of controls that address significant risks and controls for which substantive procedures alone are not sufficient.

In the planning stage of an audit in order to assess control risk, the auditor undertakes a number of tasks. First the auditor considers the results of previous audits that involved evaluating the operating effectiveness of internal control, including the nature of identified deficiencies and action taken to address them. The auditor will also discuss the possibility of audit risk with audit firm personnel responsible for performing other services to the entity. He will interview entity personnel to find evidence of management's commitment to the design, implementation and maintenance of sound internal control and the importance attached to internal control throughout the entity. The auditor might try to get a good idea of the volume of transactions, which may determine whether it is more efficient for the auditor to rely on internal control.

7.16 Questions, Exercises and Cases

QUESTIONS

7.2 Introduction

7-1 What are the first two steps in the planning procedures?

7.3 Internal Control Defined

7-2 Define internal control. Discuss the fundamental concepts in the definition: process, people, reasonable assurance, and objectives.

7-3 Describe the four objectives of internal control.

7-4 Do corporations believe fraud to be a problem according to KPMG fraud survey reports? Explain.

7-5 Why is the auditor interested primarily in controls that relate to reliability of financial reporting, accounting and internal control systems?

7.4 The Importance of Internal Control

7-6 What importance would internal controls have for an audit firm?

7.5 IT Risk and Controls

7-7 IT controls may generally be grouped into two types. Define these two.

7-8 What things might an auditor consider when evaluating the information system of an entity?

7.6 Components of Internal Control

7-9 What are the five interrelated components of internal control? Briefly discuss them.

7.7 Control Environment

7-10 Define control environment. Why is it important to an entity?

7-11 Can evaluation of the control environment be a key element in determining the nature of the audit work? Why or why not?

7-12 What is meant by 'tone at the top'?

7.8 Risk Assessment

7-13 What is the difference between management risk assessment and auditor risk assessment?

7-14 Name and discuss one technique that has been developed to identify risk.

7.9 Information Systems, Communication and Related Business Processes

7-15 What is the accounting system designed to do? What should be documented about an accounting system as part of the procedures to understand the internal control system?

7.10 Control Activities (Control Procedures)

7-16 Into what five categories do control activities fall?

7-17 Discuss the Baring case and the Daiwa Bank case. How could similar problems be prevented in the future? What is your opinion of these cases?

7.12 Hard and Soft Control

7-18 Muel Kaptein distinguishes seven social–psychological factors which influence people's behaviour within organisations. Discuss.

7.13 Design of Internal Controls

7-19 Discuss the four methods of obtaining audit evidence about the design and implementation of relevant controls.

7.14 Preliminary Assessment of Control Risk

7-20 When planning an audit, in order to assess control risk the auditor undertakes a number of tasks. Discuss some of those tasks.

PROBLEMS AND EXERCISES

7.3 Internal Control Defined

7-21 Internal control is geared to the achievement of objectives in one or more separate overlapping categories.

Required:
A. Define these four categories of objectives.
B. For each objective give an example of internal control goals for three industries: retail, manufacturing and services.

7.4 The Importance of Internal Control

7-22 Obtain Understanding of Internal Control. Johannes Mullauer, Wirtschaftsprufer, who has been engaged to audit the financial statements of Ais, GmbH, is about to start obtaining an understanding of the internal control structure and is aware of the inherent limitations that should be considered.

Required:
A. What are the reasons for establishing objectives of internal control?
B. What are the reasonable assurances that are intended to be provided by the accounting internal control structure?
C. When considering the potential effectiveness of any internal control structure, what are the inherent limitations that should be recognised?
[AICPA adapted]

7.5 IT Risk and Controls

7-23 Discuss the following statements:
A. Information technology benefits an entity's internal control by enabling them to consistently apply predefined business rules and perform complex calculations in processing large volumes of transactions or data; enhance the timeliness, availability and accuracy of information; and facilitate the additional analysis of information.
B. IT systems enhance the ability to monitor the performance of the entity's activities and its policies and procedures; reduce the risk that controls will be circumvented; and enhance the ability to achieve effective segregation of duties by implementing security controls in applications, databases and operating systems.

7.6 Components of Internal Control

7-24 Components of Internal Control. Internal control consists of five interrelated components. These are derived from the way management runs a business, and are integrated with the management process.

Required:

A. Name and define the components of internal control.
B. How do the components of internal control affect each other?
C. Discuss the interrelationship of components using as an example a retail clothing store.

7.7 Control Environment

7–25 Assess Internal Control Environment. Using the COSO criteria for assessing internal control environment (Illustration 7.5) describe a company with an effective control environment.

7–26 Control Environment. Hasse Nilsson, Statautoriseret, is in charge of the audit of a new client, US Clothing Store. It is owned by three men, Messrs. Simpson, Andersson and Ding. Only one of the owners, Mr Simpson, is active in the business – the other two live and work in another city. Mr Simpson operated the business as a proprietorship until a few years ago, when he incorporated it and obtained additional capital for store improvements by selling to Ding and Andersson 24 per cent of his equity. In addition to Mr Simpson, the store employs three sales clerks and Miss Tearsson, the cashier-book-keeper. Miss Tearsson has worked for Mr Simpson for many years. Nilsson and the partner in his firm responsible for the US Clothing Store audit have agreed that one of the first things Nilsson should do when he starts work on the audit is to consider the internal control environment.

Required:

A. Why is it important to consider the internal control environment of even a small company such as US Clothing Store?
B. What particular features of the internal control environment would Nilsson inquire into in the circumstances described above?

[*Uniform Evaluation Report* (Toronto: CPA Canada)]

7.8 Risk Assessment

7–27 Risk Assessment. OK Yen, Ltd. is a Japanese electronics games and amusements company specialising in pachinko games. Pachinko parlours are a big industry in Japan, whose 18,000 pachinko parlours in 1996 accounted for a quarter of the country's civil sector and are thought to produce Japanese Yen (¥) 30 trillion per year in revenue – more than Japan's auto industry. Customers who play pachinko buy a supply of pinballs costing around ¥4 and cash in the balls they win back for prizes equivalent to ¥2.5 each. Although it is illegal to give cash to winners, the customers may go to nearby shops and sell their prizes for cash. Recently a new form of pachinko has been developed that gives very large prizes to winners, but decreases the chances of winning. Although the number of players has decreased over the last four years, the gross sales have doubled. Location of the stores is not crucial, so OK Yen can locate in low-rent areas.

Government authorities have recently given much attention to pachinko gaming. Operations featuring the game have been associated with the yacuza, the Japanese criminal organisation. Some people in Japan are concerned that pachinko is really addictive gambling. There are complaints to authorities over children being left to play on busy streets or locked up in parked automobiles while their parents go to play pachinko.

Required:

Following the five-step procedure outlined in the chapter, identify the risks associated with OK Yen's business.

7.9 Information Systems, Communication and Related Business Processes

7–28 Information and Communications. The firm of Hayes & Hu, Ltd, personal financial advisers in the Notting Hill section of London, has asked Joseph Smallman, Chartered

Accountant (CA), to recommend a computer information system. Hayes & Hu advises individuals on equity investments, manage finances for individuals whom are outside the country and develop family budgets.

Required:
A.   What type of inputs (information transactions) are Hayes & Hu likely to make?
B.   What information subsystems are Hayes & Hu likely to need?
C.   What sort of outputs in the form of reports and documents will Hayes & Hu require?

7.10 Control Activities (Control Procedures)

7-29 Separation of Duties. Aurello Pellegrini, Dottore Commercialista (CONSOB), is approached by his client who has just reorganised his medium-sized manufacturing company to make it more structured by giving responsibilities in related areas to one employee. The 'supervisor for customers' is responsible for both collection of accounts receivable and maintenance of accounts receivable records. The 'inventory coordinator' is responsible for purchasing, receiving and storing inventory. The 'payroll agent' handles all payroll matters including personnel records, keeping time cards, preparation of payrolls, and distribution of payroll cheques.

Required:
Consider each of these new positions and discuss the implications of their duties on the internal control system. Discuss what sorts of problems could arise if these positions are created.

7.11 Monitoring of Controls

7-30 Monitoring. Monitoring is done in two ways: through ongoing activities and individual evaluations.

Required:
A.   From what sources does ongoing monitoring come? What issues might be considered?
B.   When doing individual evaluations, what should the auditor consider?
C.   What type of reports on monitoring should management receive?

7.12 Hard and Soft Control

7-31 Ambazam, an airline shuttle service operating out of the Tampa, Florida, USA, airport wishes to analyse the necessary controls required for their operation. They pick up arrivals at the airport and deliver people to the airport from hotels in the Tampa area. They operate five shuttle vans and have 10 employees. Their owner, Julio Cruz's, objective is to respond quickly to calls, be courteous to customers, and keep hotel employees, who refer them to hotel guests, happy.

Required:
For each of the seven factors that influence the way people look at controls discuss how Mr Cruz could use these factors to set controls the assure employees, customers and hotel employees meet the objectives.

7.13 Design of Internal Controls

7-32 Control Design. Luxury Auto Leases, Inc. of New Mexico, USA, has offices in Tucumcari, Santa Fe and Albuquerque. Lisa Dockery, the company president, has an office in Santa Fe and visits the other offices periodically for internal audits.

Ms Dockery is concerned about the honesty of her employees. She contacted Back & Front, CPAs, and informed them that she wanted them to recommend a computer system that would prohibit employees from embezzling cash. She also told Back & Front that before starting her own business she managed a nationwide auto leasing company with over 200 offices and was familiar with their accounting and internal control systems. She suggested that Back & Front could base her requested system on the nationwide one.

Required:

A. How should Back & Front advise Ms Dockery regarding the installation of a system similar to the nationwide one? Explain.

B. What should Back & Front advise Ms Dockery regarding a system that will absolutely prevent theft? Discuss.

C. If Back & Front takes Luxury Auto Leasing as an audit client, what procedures should they perform to detect fraud? Would they guarantee that their audit could discover fraud? Why?

[adapted from AICPA EPA exam question, copyright © 2000 & 1985 by American Institute of Certified Accountants]

7.14 Preliminary Assessment of Control Risk

7-33 The audit firm of Abdel-Meguid, Okyere and Yildirim (AOY) is planning and audit of Dye Shipper Corporation of Cairo, a television documentary production company. AOY need to assess the control risk of Dye Shipper.

Required:

Describe how Abdel-Meguid, Okyere and Yildirim will systematically asses risk.

CASES

7-34 Internal Control Activities. An example of a lack of internal controls with a disastrous result was the bond trading loss in the New York Office of Daiwa Bank in 1995. Over 11 years 30,000 unauthorised trades were made resulting in a $1.1 billion loss (an average of $400,000 in losses for every trading day). Daiwa allowed Toshihide Iguchi, a bond trader, to authorise sales, have custody of the bond assets and record these transactions.

As a novice trader Iguchi misjudged the bond market, racking up a $200,000 loss. To raise cash to pay Daiwa's brokers, Iguchi would order Bankers Trust New York to sell bonds held in Daiwa's account. The statements from Banker's Trust came to Iguchi who forged duplicates, complete with bond numbers and maturity dates, to make it look as if Banker's Trust still held the bonds he had sold. When he confessed to his misdeeds, Daiwa thought their bond account was $4.6 billion when in fact only $3.5 billion was left.

Inadequate review of internal controls was also to blame. Daiwa's internal auditors had reviewed the New York branch several times since the fraud began, but Banker's Trust was never contacted for confirmation of Daiwa's bank statements. If they had, Iguchi's fraud would have been exposed. Diawa's external auditor never audited the New York branch.

Required:

A. What type of control procedures were ignored at Daiwa?

B. For each internal control procedure missing, what damage was caused?

C. What kind of controls could have been instituted that would have prevented the problems at Daiwa?

D. For each of the five internal control procedures discussed above, applying each to a bank trading operation, identify a specific error that is likely to be prevented if the procedure exists and is effective.

E. For each of the five internal control procedures discussed in this chapter, applying each to a bank trading operation, list a specific intentional or unintentional error that might result from the absence of the control.

7.17 Notes

1 Committee of Sponsoring Organizations of the Treadway Commission (COSO), 1992, Chapter 1 'Definition, *Internal Control – Integrated Framework*', American Institute of Certified Public Accountants, Jersey City, New Jersey, p. 9.

2 Side letters – agreements made outside the standard company contracts. These otherwise undisclosed agreements may be signed by senior officers, but not approved by the board of directors.

3 International Auditing and Assurance Standards Board (IAASB), 2012, Glossary of Terms, *Handbook of International Quality Control, Auditing Review, Other Assurance, and Related Services Pronouncements*, 2012 edn, Volume 1, International Federation of Accountants, New York.

4 Securities Exchange Act Rules 13a-15(c) and 15d-15(c), 17 CFR, § 240.13a-15(c) and 240.15d-15(c), Securities and Exchange Commission.

5 Public Company Accounting Oversight Board, 2007, Auditing Standard No. 5 'An Audit of Internal Control Over Financial Reporting That is Integrated with an Audit of Financial Statements': **http://pcaobus.org/Standards/Auditing/Pages/Auditing_Standard_5.aspx.**

6 International Auditing and Assurance Standards Board (IAASB), 2012, International Standard on Auditing 315 (ISA 315) 'Identifying and Assessing the Risks of Material Misstatement through Understanding the Entity and Its Environment', para. 12, *Handbook of International Quality Control, Auditing Review, Other Assurance, and Related Services Pronouncements*, 2012 edn, Volume 1, International Federation of Accountants, New York.

7 Ibid. ISA 315, paras 14–24.

8 Committee of Sponsoring Organizations of the Treadway Commission (COSO), 1992, *Internal Control – Integrated Framework*, American Institute of Certified Public Accountants, New Jersey.

9 KPMG, LLP, 2009, *Fraud Survey 2009*, KPMG Forensic, USA.

10 Association of Certified Fraud Examiners, 2012, *Report to the Nations on Occupational Fraud and Abuse*: **http://www.acfe.com/rttn.aspx.**

11 Examples of the laws requiring 'proper record-keeping systems' or 'proper accounting records' are the Foreign Corrupt Practices Act of 1977 in the USA and the UK Companies Act 1985.

12 International Auditing and Assurance Standards Board (IAASB), 2012, International Standard on Auditing 315 (ISA 315) 'Identifying and Assessing the Risks of Material Misstatement through Understanding the Entity and Its Environment', para. A66, *Handbook of International Quality Control, Auditing Review, Other Assurance, and Related Services Pronouncements*, 2012 edn, Volume 1, International Federation of Accountants, New York.

13 Ibid. ISA 315, para. A70.

14 All companies traded on the New York Stock Exchange are required to have an audit committee composed of outside (non-executive) directors. The Code of Best Practice of the London Stock Exchange emphasises that the independence and integrity of the board as a whole is enhanced by having non-executive (outside) directors and recommends their use on the audit committee.

15 107th US Congress, 2002, 'Sec. 301, Public Company Audit Committees', para. 3, Sarbanes–Oxley Act of 2002, Public Law 107–204, Senate and House of Representatives of the United States of America in Congress assembled, Washington, DC, 30 July.

16 The illustration is a combination of: (1) Committee of Sponsoring Organizations of the Treadway Commission (COSO), 1992, Chapter 2 'Control Environment', *Internal Control – Integrated Framework*, American Institute of Certified Public Accountants, Jersey City, New Jersey, pp. 31–32; and (2) International Auditing and Assurance Standards Board (IAASB), 2012, International Standard on Auditing 315 (ISA 315) 'Identifying and Assessing the Risks of Material Misstatement through Understanding the Entity and Its Environment', Appendix I, para. 2, *Handbook of International Quality Control, Auditing Review, Other Assurance, and Related Services Pronouncements*, 2012 edn, Volume 1, International Federation of Accountants, New York.

17 From: Internal Control Working Group, 1993, *Internal Control and Financial Reporting: Draft guidance for directors of listed companies registered in the UK in response to the recommendations of the Cadbury Committee*, Institute of Chartered Accountants in England and Wales, London, October, p. 19.

18 Based on the Committee of Sponsoring Organizations of the Treadway Commission (COSO), 1992, 'Blank Tools – Control Environment', *Internal Control – Evaluation Tools*, American Institute of Certified Public Accountants, Jersey City, New Jersey, pp. 31–32.

19 ISA 315, op. cit., para. 18.

20 There is sometimes confusion between 'control activities' and 'control procedures'; ISA and US Generally Accepted Auditing Standards do not define 'control activities', but defined 'control procedures' as the policies and procedures that management installs to meet objectives. The COSO Report uses the term 'control activities' and gives it virtually the same definition.

21 ISA 315, op. cit., para. A88.

22 Clark, Nicola and David Jolly, 2008, 'French Bank Says Rogue Trader Lost $7 Billion', *New York Times, 25 January*: **http://www.nytimes.com/2008/01/25/business/worldbusiness/25bank.html**; accessed 25 January 2008.

23 Bank of England, 1995, *Report of the Board of Banking Supervision Inquiry Into the Circumstances of the Collapse of Barings*, 18 July.

24 Mary Jo White, United States Attorney, 1996, *Complaint against Masaxiro Tsuda* (along with Daiwa Bank and Toshihide Iguchi), US Supreme Court Southern District Of New York.

25 Wall Street Journal, 1996, 'Daiwa Bank Ex-trader Fined and Sent to Prison', *The Wall Street Journal*, 17 December 1996, p. B5.

26 See for additional guidance International Auditing and Assurance Standards Board (IAASB), 2012, International Standard on Auditing 610 (ISA 610) 'Using the Work of Internal Auditors', *Handbook of International Quality Control, Auditing Review, Other Assurance, and Related Services Pronouncements*, 2012 edn, Volume 1, International Federation of Accountants, New York.

27 Committee of Sponsoring Organizations of the Treadway Commission (COSO), 1992, Chapter 6 'Monitoring', *Internal Control – Integrated Framework*, American Institute of Certified Public Accountants, Jersey City, New Jersey, pp. 73–74.

28 Based on the Committee of Sponsoring Organizations of the Treadway Commission (COSO), 1992, 'Blank Tools – Control Environment', *Internal Control – Evaluation Tools*, American Institute of Certified Public Accountants, New Jersey, pp. 31–32.

29 Kaptein, Muel, 2012, *Why Good People Sometimes Do Bad Things? 52 Reflections of Ethics at Work*: **http://papers.ssrn.com/sol3/papers.cfm?abstract_id=2117396**.

30 Based on Institute of Internal Auditors, 2012, 'Auditing the Control Environment', *IPPF – Practice Guide*, p. 9, April 2011, The Institute of Internal Auditors (IIA).

31 107th US Congress, 2002, 'Sec. 404 Management Assessment of Internal Controls', Sarbanes–Oxley Act of 2002, Public Law 107-204, Senate and House of Representatives of the United States of America in Congress assembled, Washington, DC, 30 July.

32 SEC, 2003, 'SEC Implements Internal Control Provisions of Sarbanes–Oxley Act; Adopts Investment Company R&D Safe Harbor', **http://www.sec.gov/news/press/2003-66.htm**, Washington, DC, 27 May.

33 International Auditing and Assurance Standards Board (IAASB), 2012, International Standard on Auditing 200 (ISA 200) 'Overall Objectives of the Independent Auditor and the Conduct of an Audit in Accordance with International Standards on Auditing', para. A39, *Handbook of International Quality Control, Auditing Review, Other Assurance, and Related Services Pronouncements*, 2012 edn, Volume 1, International Federation of Accountants, New York.

34 Ibid. ISA 315, para. A67.

35 Deficiency in internal control – this exists when: (a) a control is designed, implemented or operated in such a way that it is unable to prevent, or detect and correct, misstatements in the financial statements on a timely basis; or (b) a control necessary to prevent, or detect and correct, misstatements in the financial statements on a timely basis is missing.

36 International Auditing and Assurance Standards Board (IAASB), 2012, International Standard on Auditing 265 (ISA 265) 'Communicating Deficiencies in Internal Control to Those Charged with Governance and Management', para. 9, *Handbook of International Quality Control, Auditing Review, Other Assurance, and Related Services Pronouncements*, 2012 edn, Volume 1, International Federation of Accountants, New York.

37 Ibid. ISA 265, para. 10.

38 International Auditing and Assurance Standards Board (IAASB), 2012, International Standard on Auditing 402 (ISA 402) 'Audit Considerations Relating to an Entity Using a Service Organization', para. A23, *Handbook of International Quality Control, Auditing Review, Other Assurance, and Related Services Pronouncements*, 2012 edn, Volume 1, International Federation of Accountants, New York.

39 For US Audit standards on internal control reports from service organisations see: Auditing Standards Board, 1992, Statement of Auditing Standards (SAS) 70 'Reports on the Processing of Transactions by Service Organizations', para. 24, Content codified as AU 324, American Institute of Certified Public Accountants, New York.

40 International Auditing and Assurance Standards Board (IAASB), 2012, International Standard on Assurance Engagements 3402 (ISAE 3402) 'Assurance Reports on Controls at a Service Organization', *Handbook of International Quality Control, Auditing Review, Other Assurance, and Related Services Pronouncements*, 2012 edn, Volume 1, International Federation of Accountants, New York.

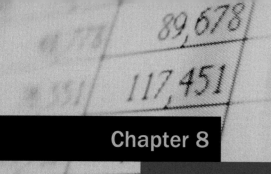

Chapter 8

ANALYTICAL PROCEDURES

8.1 Learning Objectives

After studying this chapter you should be able to:

1 Understand the general nature of analytical procedures.

2 Describe four general analytical procedures.

3 Explain how expectations are developed and what sources are used.

4 Clarify how the effectiveness of an analytical procedure is a function of the nature of the account and the reliability and other characteristics of the data.

5 Calculate the customary ratios that are used during the planning phase to determine accounts that may represent significant risks to the entity of liquidity, solvency, profitability and activity.

6 Understand some indications that the going concern assumption may be questioned.

7 Comprehend why and how analytical procedures may be used at each audit phase.

8 Grasp how analytical procedures are used in substantive procedures.

9 Describe some of the analytical procedures carried out by computer-aided audit techniques.

10 Illustrate data mining methods, techniques and algorithms used to analyse client data.

11 Portray the auditor's procedures when analytical procedures identify significant fluctuations that deviate from predicted amounts.

8.2 Introduction

Analytical procedures are evaluations of financial information through analysis of plausible relationships among both financial and non-financial data. Analytical procedures also encompass such investigation as is necessary of identified fluctuations or relationships that are inconsistent with other relevant information or that differ from expected values by a significant amount.[1] Put another way, analytical procedures entail the use of comparisons and relationships to determine whether account balances or other data appear reasonable. Such procedures allow the auditor to look at things in overview and answer the question: Do the numbers make sense?

■ Relationships Among Data

A basic premise of using analytical procedures is that there exist plausible relationships among data and these relationships can reasonably be expected to continue. Analytical procedures include the comparison of the entity's financial statements with prior period information, anticipated results such as budgets, and similar industry information. For instance, an entity's accounts receivable turnover ratio may be compared to that ratio for the industry or for a similar company.

Analytical procedures are used to determine relationships among financial information that would be expected to conform to predictable patterns based on the entity's experience, such as gross margin percentages, and between financial and non-financial information such as the relationship between payroll costs and the number of employees.

■ Types of Analytical Procedure

General analytical procedures include trend analysis, ratio analysis, statistical and data mining analysis, and reasonableness tests. Trend analysis is the analysis of changes in an account balance over time. Ratio analysis is the comparison of relationships between financial statement accounts, the comparison of an account with non-financial data, or the comparison of relationships between firms in an industry. Reasonableness testing is the analysis of account balances or changes in account balances within an accounting period in terms of their 'reasonableness' in light of expected relationships between accounts. Data mining is a set of computer-assisted techniques that use sophisticated statistical analysis, including artificial intelligence techniques, to examine large volumes of data with the objective of indicating hidden or unexpected information or patterns. For these tests auditors generally use computer-aided audit software (CAATs).

■ When to Use Analytical Procedures

The auditor shall design and perform analytical procedures near the end of the audit that assist the auditor when forming an overall conclusion as to whether the financial statements are consistent with the auditor's understanding of the entity according to ISA 520.[2]

In the overall review stage (at the end of the audit) the objective of analytical procedures is to assess the conclusions reached and evaluate the overall financial statement presentation. It may be used to detect material misstatements that other tests can overlook, such as fraud or understatement errors.

Analytical procedures may also be used in planning and applied to substantive testing. In the planning stage analytical procedures may be used to highlight risk areas to narrow the focus of planning the nature, timing, and extent of auditing procedures. In the substantive testing stage of the audit, analytical procedures are used to see 'the big picture', i.e. obtain evidence to identify misstatements in account balances and thus to reduce the risk of misstatements.

■ Computer Assisted Audit Techniques (CAATs)

The use of computer assisted audit techniques (CAATs) may enable more extensive testing of electronic transactions and account files. CAATs can be used to select sample transactions from key electronic files, to sort transactions with specific characteristics, or to test an entire population instead of a sample. CAATs generally include data manipulation, calculation, data selection, data analysis, identification of exceptions and unusual transactions, regression analysis and statistical analysis. CAATs are available on generalised audit software (GAS) which provides the auditors with the ability to access, manipulate, manage, analyse and report data in a variety of formats. Data mining software may also be used for analytical procedures.

When analytical procedures identify significant fluctuations or relationships that are inconsistent with other relevant information or that deviate from predicted amounts, the auditor should investigate and obtain adequate explanations and appropriate corroborative evidence. The investigation of unusual fluctuations and relationships ordinarily begins with inquiries of management followed by corroboration of management's responses and other audit procedures based on the results of these inquiries.

8.3 The Analytical Review Process

The process of planning, executing, and drawing conclusions from analytical procedures is called analytical review. There are several views, theoretical and practical, of the sub-processes involved in analytical review.

The theoretical view[3] is that the review process consists of four diagnostic processes:

1 mental representation,
2 hypothesis generation,
3 information search,
4 hypothesis evaluation.

In particular, auditors hypothesise causes and related probabilities, gather evidence to test the hypotheses, and ultimately select which hypotheses are most likely to cause the fluctuation.[4]

Concept and a Company 8.1

'Crazy Eddie – His prices are insane!'

Concept	Analytical procedures to test inventory.

Story In 1969, Eddie Antar, a 21-year-old high school dropout from Brooklyn, opened a consumer electronics store with 15 square metres of floor space in New York City. By 1987, Antar's firm, Crazy Eddie, Inc., had 43 retail outlets, sales exceeding $350 million, and outstanding common shares with a collective market value of $600 million.

Shortly after a hostile takeover of the company in November 1987, the firm's new owners discovered that Crazy Eddie's inventory was overstated by more than $65 million. Subsequent investigations by regulatory authorities would demonstrate that Crazy Eddie's profits had been intentionally overstated by Eddie Antar and several subordinates (Belsky and Furman, 1989).

Crazy Like a Fox

Antar acquired the nickname 'Crazy Eddie' because of his unique sales tactic. Whenever a customer would attempt to leave his store without purchasing something, Eddie would block the store's exit, sometimes locking the door until the individual agreed to buy something – anything. To entice a reluctant customer to make a purchase, Antar would lower the price until the customer finally gave in. From 1972, Doctor Jerry was the spokesperson for Crazy Eddie. He made a series of ear-piercing television commercials that featured him screaming 'Crazy Eddie – His prices are insane!' The company promised to refund the difference between the selling price of a product and any lower price for that same item that a customer found within 30 days of the purchase date (Knapp, 2001).

Inventory Overstated

Trouble was that in late 1986 the boom days had ended for the consumer electronics industry. To continue the growth of the company and keep the stock price up, Antar had to do something. Within the first six months after the company went public, Antar ordered a subordinate to overstate inventory by $2 million, resulting in the firm's gross profit being overstated by the same amount. The following year Antar ordered year-end inventory to be overstated by $9 million and accounts payable to be understated by $3 million (Belsky and Furman, 1989). Crazy Eddie employees overstated year-end inventory by preparing inventory count sheets for items that did not exist. To overstate accounts payable, bogus debit memos were prepared and entered in the company's accounting records.

The Audits

Crazy Eddie's auditor was Main Hurdman (later merged with Peat Marwick – now KPMG). Their audits were generally made difficult by management and employee collusion. There were several reported instances in which the auditors requested client documents, only to be told that those documents had been lost or inadvertently destroyed. Upon discovering which sites the auditors would be visiting to perform year-end inventory procedures, Antar would ship sufficient inventory to those stores or warehouses to conceal any shortages. Furthermore, personnel systematically destroyed incriminating documents to conceal inventory shortages from the auditors (Weiss, 1993).

285

'Crazy Eddie – His prices are insane!' (continued)

Main Hurdman has been criticised for charging only $85,000 for a complete SEC audit, but millions to install a computerised inventory system. This is even more interesting because Antar ordered his employees to stop using the sophisticated, computer-based inventory system designed by Main Hurdman. Instead, the accounting personnel were required to return to a manual inventory system previously used by the company. The absence of a computer-based inventory system made it much more difficult for the auditors to determine exactly how much inventory the firm had at any point in time (Weiss, 1993).

Crazy Eddie Comparative Income Statements 1984–87

	31 March 87	31 March 86	31 March 85	31 March 84
Net sales	$352,523	$262,268	$136,319	$137,285
Cost of goods sold	−0272,255	−194,371	−103,421	−106,934
Gross profit	80,268	67,897	32,898	30,351
Selling, G&A expense	−61,341	−42,975	−20,508	−22,560
Interest and other income	7,403	3,210	1,211	706
Interest expense	−5,233	−820	−438	−522
Income before taxes	$21,097	$27,312	$13,163	$7,975
Pension contribution	−500	−800	−600	−4,202
Income taxes	−10,001	−13,268	−6,734	
Net income	$10,596	$13,244	$5,829	$3,773
Net income per share	$0.34	$0.48	$0.24	$0.18

Crazy Eddie Comparative Balance Sheets 1984–87

	31 March 87	31 March 86	31 March 85	31 March 84
Current assets				
Cash	$9,347	$13,296	$22,273	$1,375
Short-term investments	121,957	26,840		
Receivables	10,846	2,246	2,740	2,604
Merchandise inventories	109,072	59,864	26,543	23,343
Prepaid expenses	10,639	2,363	645	514
Total current assets	261,861	104,609	52,201	27,836
Restricted cash		3,356	7,058	
Due from affiliates				5,739
Property, plant and equipment	26,401	7,172	3,696	1,845
Construction in process		6,253	1,154	
Other assets	6,596	5,560	1,419	1,149
Total assets	$294,858	$126,950	$65,528	$36,569
Current liabilities				
Accounts payable	$50,022	$51,723	$23,078	$20,106
Notes payable				2,900
Short-term debt	49,571	2,254	423	124
Unearned revenue	3,641	3,696	1,173	764
Accrued expenses	5,593	17,126	8,733	6,078
Total current liabilities	108,827	74,799	33,407	29,972

	31 March 87	31 March 86	31 March 85	31 March 84
Long-term debt	8,459	7,701	7,625	46
Convertible subordinated debentures	80,975			
Unearned revenue	3,337	1,829	635	327
Stockholders' equity				
Common stock	313	280	134	50
Additional paid-in capital	57,678	17,668	12,298	574
Retained earnings	35,269	24,673	11,429	5,600
Total stockholders' equity	93,260	42,621	23,861	6,224
Total liabilities and stockholders' equity	$294,858	$126,950	$65,528	$36,569

Discussion Questions

Review the Crazy Eddie comparative financial statements and discuss:

- What analytical procedures can be performed to determine if inventory is misstated?
- What indicators other than financial hinted that there might be problems?

References

Belsky, G. and Furman, P., 1989, 'Calculated Madness: The Rise and Fall of Crazy Eddie Antar', *Cram's New York Business*, 5 June, pp. 21–33.

Knapp, M., 2001, 'Crazy Eddie, Inc', *Contemporary Auditing Real Issues and Cases*, South Western College Publishing, Cincinnati, Ohio, pp. 71–82.

Weiss, M.I., 1993, 'Auditors: Be Watchdogs, Not Just Bean Counters', *Accounting Today*, 15 November, p. 41.

■ Four-Phase Process

Here we use a practitioner approach, the four-phase process most common in professional literature:[5]

- phase one – formulate expectations (expectations);
- phase two – compare the expected value to the recorded amount (identification);
- phase three – investigate possible explanations for a difference between expected and recorded values (investigation);
- phase four – evaluate the impact of the differences between expectation and recorded amounts on the audit and the financial statements (evaluation).

Illustration 8.1 shows the four-phase process and its inputs and outputs.

Phase One

According to ISA 520,[6] the auditor should 'evaluate the reliability of data from which the auditor's expectation of recorded amounts or ratios is developed, taking account of source, comparability, and nature and relevance of information available, and controls over preparation.' In phase one of the analytical review process, the auditor develops expectations of what amounts should appear in financial statement account balances based on prior year financial statements, budgets, industry information and non-financial information. Expectations are the auditor's estimations of recorded accounts or ratios. The auditor develops his expectation in such a way that a significant difference between it and the recorded amount will indicate a misstatement.

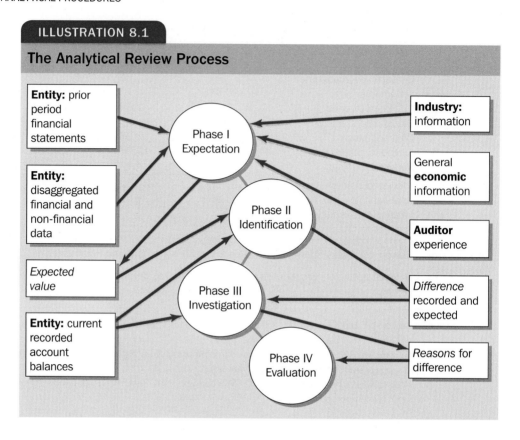

ILLUSTRATION 8.1

The Analytical Review Process

Forming an expectation is the most important phase of the analytical procedure process. The closer the auditor's expectation is to the correct balance or relationship, the more effective the procedure will be at identifying potential misstatements.

Expectations are formed from a variety of sources. Research[7] suggests that the use of industrial, economic, or environmental data can improve the predictive ability of analytical procedures. Other resources include industry data, data about similar businesses, and auditor experience. Expectations are also based on the entities prior financial statements, same store sales, non-financial data, budgets and public reports.

Before determining what analytical procedures to use the auditor must 'determine the suitability of particular substantive analytical procedures for given assertions, taking account of the assessed risks of material misstatement and tests of details, if any, for these assertions.'[8]

Phase Two

Phase two of the analytical review process (identification) is when the auditor compares his expected value with the recorded amount. Audit efficiency and effectiveness depend on competency in recognising error patterns in financial data and in hypothesising likely causes of those patterns to serve as a guide for further testing.

The auditor should determine the amount of any difference of recorded amounts from expected values that is acceptable without further investigation. The auditor must consider how large a difference between expected value and recorded amount he will accept. The threshold amount may very well relate to or derived from materiality. If the difference is less than the acceptable threshold, the auditor accepts the book value without further investigation. If the difference is greater, the next step is to investigate the difference.

Phase Three

In phase three of the analytical review process (investigation), the auditor undertakes an investigation of possible explanations for the expected/recorded amount difference. The difference between an auditor's expectation and the recorded book value of an account not subject to auditing procedures can be due to misstatements, inherent factors that affect the account being audited, and factors related to the reliability of data used to develop the expectation.

The greater the precision of the expectation, the more likely the difference between the auditor's expectation and the recorded value will be due to misstatements. Conversely, the less precise the expectation, the more likely the difference is due to factors related to inherent factors, and the reliability of data used to develop the expectation.

Inquiries and Corroboration of Differences

Where differences between expectation and recorded amounts are found, the first step is usually to ask management for an explanation. However, it is important that the auditor maintains his **professional scepticism** (see Chapter 4) when considering these answers and it is suggested that the auditor conduct other audit procedures to corroborate them. When analytical procedures are used in the planning phase, corroboration is not immediately required because the purpose of analytical procedures in planning is to chart the work to follow.

Phase Four

The final phase (phase four – evaluation) of the analytical review process involves evaluating the impact on the financial statements of the difference between the auditor's expected value and the recorded amount. It is usually not practical to identify factors that explain the exact amount of a difference investigated. The auditor attempts to quantify that portion of the difference for which plausible explanations can be obtained and, where appropriate, corroborated. If the amount that cannot be explained is sufficiently small, the auditor may conclude there is no material misstatement. *However, if the amount that cannot be explained exceeds the threshold (phase two), additional substantive procedures are required.*

8.4 Formulating Expectations

Expectations are developed by identifying plausible relationships that are reasonably expected to exist based on the auditor's understanding of the client and of his industry. These relationships may be determined by comparisons with the following sources:[9]

- comparable information for prior periods;
- anticipated results (such as budgets and forecasts, or auditor expectations);
- elements of financial information within the period;
- similar industry information;
- non-financial information.

The auditor can identify account balances that have changed significantly simply by comparing the current client data with prior period data. He may compare the current year's account balances with that of the preceding year; the current trial balance with similar detail for the preceding year; and ratios and percentage relationships between years. He compares current recorded account balances of the entity with results expected by the entity. For example, company budgets may be compared with actual results for indications of potential misstatements or the auditor calculates the expected balance for interest expense (notes payable monthly balance times average monthly interest rate) and compares this to recorded interest rates.

One of the standard bases of comparison is with like companies in the same industry. For example, the auditor compares the gross margin of the industry to the client's gross margin.

Analytical procedures may include consideration of relationships between financial information and relevant non-financial information, such as payroll costs to number of employees. Another example is the revenue of a hotel may be estimated by multiplying the average room rate times the number of rooms times the average occupancy percentage (e.g. $100 average rate × 20 rooms × 60 per cent average occupancy). Similarly revenues may be calculated for school tuition (average number of students enrolled times the average tuition cost), payroll, and cost of materials sold using non-financial factors.

Sources of Information and Precision of Expectations

The source of information on which the expectations are based (e.g. prior period statements, forecasts, industry information) determines, in part, the precision with which the auditor predicts an account balance. For example, information from other, similar stores in the same retail chain is more precise than general industry information. Recent years' financial statements are more precise a predictor of this year's balance than older financial statements. The desired precision of the expectation varies according to the purpose of the analytical procedure. Expectations developed at a detailed level generally have a greater chance of detecting misstatement of a given amount than do broad comparisons. Monthly amounts will generally be more effective than annual amounts and comparisons by location or line of business usually will be more effective than company-wide comparisons. Precision is more important for analytical procedures used as substantive tests than for those used in planning.

Nature of Account and Characteristics of Data

The effectiveness of an analytical procedure is a function of the **nature of the account** and the reliability and other **characteristics of the data**. In determining the nature of the account we consider whether the balance is based on estimates or accumulations of transactions, the number of transactions represented by the balance, and the control environment. Subjectively determined balances are more easily manipulated than accumulations of transactions. If the characteristic of the account is that it comprises millions of transactions (e.g. retail revenue), it should be more predictable than those comprising a few transactions (e.g. obsolete inventory). Fixed expenses (e.g. leases) are more predictable than variable expenses (e.g. shipping).

Other data characteristics such as the level of detail (aggregation) on which the auditor is able to base his expectation and the reliability of the data are key characteristics. In general, the more disaggregated the data, the more precise the expectation. For example, the use of monthly instead of annual data tends to improve the precision of the expectation. Preparing an expectation by division is also more precise than an expectation based on consolidated data. Accounting researchers conclude that disaggregated monthly, segment or product line balances are required to implement reliable attention-directing analytical procedures.

The more reliable the source of the data, the more precise the expectation will be. Reliability of data is determined based on the strength of the company's internal control, if the data source is objective or independent, and if data has been subject to auditing procedures or not. Stronger internal control over financial reporting and accounting systems produces more reliable data on the financial statements. The use of reliable non-financial data (e.g. store square footage or occupancy rates) and the use of data that has been subjected to auditing procedures improve the precision of the expectation based on that data.

8.5 General Analytical Procedures

The general analytical procedures are trend analysis, ratio analysis, statistical and data mining analysis, and reasonableness tests. Determining which type of analytical procedure is appropriate is a matter of professional judgement. A review of audit practice indicates that simple judgemental approaches (such as comparison and ratio analysis) are used more frequently than complex statistical approaches (such as time series modelling or regression analysis).[10] These tests are generally carried out using computer software (i.e. CAATs). Trend analysis, ratio analysis and reasonableness tests are discussed in this section. Statistical and data mining analysis is discussed in the following section on CAATs.

■ Trend Analysis

Trend analysis is the analysis of changes in an account balance or ratio over time. Trend analysis could compare last year's account balance to the current unaudited balance or balances in many time periods. Trend analysis works best when the account or relationship is fairly predictable (e.g. rent expense in a stable environment). It is less effective when the audited entity has experienced significant operating or accounting changes. The number of years used in the trend analysis is a function of the stability of operations. The more stable the operations over time, the more predictable the relations and the more appropriate the use of multiple time periods. Trend analysis at an aggregate level (e.g. on a consolidated basis) is relatively imprecise because a material misstatement is often small relative to the aggregate account balance. The most precise trend analysis would be on disaggregated data (e.g. by segment, product or location, and monthly or quarterly rather than on an annual basis).

■ Ratio Analysis

Ratio analysis is the comparison of relationships between financial statement accounts, the comparison of an account with non-financial data, or the comparison of relationships between firms in an industry. Another example of ratio analysis (which is sometimes referred to as common size analysis) is to set all the account balances as either a percentage of total assets or revenue.

Ratio analysis is most appropriate when the relationship between accounts is fairly predictable and stable (e.g. the relationship between sales and accounts receivable). Ratio analysis can be more effective than trend analysis because comparisons between the balance sheet and income statement can often reveal unusual fluctuations that an analysis of the individual accounts would not. Like trend analysis, ratio analysis at an aggregate level is relatively imprecise because a material misstatement is often small relative to the natural variations in the ratios.

Types of Ratio Analysis

There are five types of ratio analysis used in analytical procedures (see Illustration 8.2):

1. ratios that compare client and industry data;
2. ratios that compare client data with similar prior period data;
3. ratios that compare client data with client-determined expected results;
4. ratios that compare client data with auditor-determined expected results;
5. ratios that compare client data with expected results using non-financial data.

The Risk Management Association (RMA), Standard & Poors, Dun & Bradstreet, Ibis World and others publish standard ratios by industry.[11] Similar ratios for both industry and entity may be compared to indicate differences that might affect the auditor's judgement of the nature and extent of audit procedures. The ratios indicate entity liquidity, solvency, profitability and activity. See Illustration 8.3 for some standard ratios often used and compared.

ILLUSTRATION 8.2

Five Types of Ratio Analysis

Procedures	Examples
Ratios that compare client data with industry.	Standard ratios published by the industry by the Risk Management Association, Standard & Poors, Dun & Bradstreet and others.
Ratios that compare client data with similar prior period data.	Auditor compares the current year's account balances with that for the preceding year; current trial balances with similar detail for the preceding year; and ratios and percentage relationships between years.
Ratios that compare client data with client-determined expected results.	Client budgets may be compared with actual results for indications of potential misstatements.
Ratios that compare client data with auditor-determined expected results.	Auditor calculates the expected balance for interest expense and compares to recorded interest.
Ratios that compare client data with expected results using non-financial data.	Non-financial data may serve as a basis for expected results and comparison, the revenue of a hotel may be estimated by multiplying average room rate times the number of rooms times the average occupancy percentage.

ILLUSTRATION 8.3

Standard Client and Industry Ratios

Client and industry standard ratios	Calculation
Liquidity: (1) Current ratio (2) Quick ratio	(1) Current assets/Current liabilities (2) (Cash + Short-term securities + Accounts receivable)/ Current liabilities
Solvency: (1) Debt to equity (2) Times interest earned (3) Debt service coverage	(1) Long-term debt/Stockholders' equity (2) (Net income before interest and taxes)/Interest expense (3) (Net income before interest and depreciation)/Principal and interest payments
Profitability: (1) Net profit margin (2) Gross margin (3) Return on investment (4) Times interest earned	(1) Net profit/Revenue (2) (Revenue less cost of goods sold)/Revenue (3) Net income/Stockholders' equity (4) (Net income before interest and taxes)/Interest expense
Activity: (1) Receivable turnover (2) Inventory turnover (3) Asset turnover	(1) Revenue/Average accounts receivable (2) Cost of goods sold/Average inventory (3) Revenue/Total assets

■ Reasonableness Testing

Reasonableness testing is the analysis of account balances or changes in account balances within an accounting period in terms of their 'reasonableness' in light of expected relationships between accounts. This involves the development of an expectation based on financial data, non-financial data, or both. For example, using the number of employees hired and terminated, the timing of pay changes, and the effect of vacation and sick days, the model could predict the change in payroll expense from the previous year to the current balance within a fairly narrow dollar range.

In contrast to both trend and ratio analyses (which implicitly assume stable relationships), reasonableness tests use information to develop an explicit prediction of the account balance. The auditor develops assumptions for each of the key factors (e.g. industry and economic factors) to estimate the account balance. Considering the number of units sold, the unit price by product line, different pricing structures, and an understanding of industry trends during the period could explicitly form a reasonableness test for sales. This is in contrast to an implicit trend expectation for sales based on last year's sales. The latter expectation is appropriate only if there were no other factors affecting sales during the current year, which is not the usual situation.

■ Trend Analysis, Ratio Analysis and Reasonableness Tests Compared

Trend analysis, ratio analysis and reasonableness tests differ as to the number of independent predictive variables considered, use of external data, and statistical precision. Trend analysis is limited to a single predictor, that is, the prior periods' data for that account. Trend analysis, by relying on a single predictor, does not allow the use of potentially relevant operating data, as do the other types of procedures. Because ratio analysis employs two or more related financial or non-financial sources of information, the result is a more precise expectation. Reasonableness tests and regression analysis further improve the precision of the expectation by allowing potentially as many variables (financial and non-financial) as are relevant for forming the expectation. Reasonableness tests and regression analysis are able to use external data (e.g. general economic and industry data) directly in forming the expectation. The most statistically precise expectations are formed using statistical and data mining analysis.

■ Standard Client and Industry Ratios

At the planning stage of an audit, there are certain customary ratios that are always calculated to determine accounts that may represent significant risks to the entity of liquidity, solvency, profitability and activity. These ratios help to answer some key questions:

■ Is there a possible going concern problem (liquidity ratios)?
■ Is the entity's capital structure sustainable (solvency ratios)?
■ Is gross margin reasonable (profitability)?
■ Could inventory be overstated (activity)?

Illustration 8.3 (earlier) gives a list of these ratios.

■ Liquidity and Going Concern

Auditors must determine the possibility that the company is having liquidity problems – that is, is there a possibility that the company may no longer be a going concern? ISA 570[12] states that under the going concern assumption, an entity is viewed as continuing in business for the foreseeable future. General purpose financial statements are prepared on a going concern basis, unless management either intends to liquidate the entity or to cease operations, or has no realistic alternative but to do so. When the use of the going concern assumption is appropriate, assets and liabilities are recorded on the basis that the entity will be able to realise its assets and discharge its liabilities in the normal course of business.

Analytical procedures may point to indications of risk that the going concern assumption needs to be questioned. Illustration 8.4 shows the indications of risk that the going concern assumption may be questioned.[13] The significance of the indications in Illustration 8.4 can often be mitigated by other factors. For example, the effect of an entity being unable to make its normal debt repayments may be counterbalanced by management's plans to maintain adequate cash flows by alternative means, such as disposal of assets.

ILLUSTRATION 8.4

Indications that the Going Concern Assumption Might be Questioned

The following are examples of events or conditions that, individually or collectively, may cast significant doubt about the going concern assumption. This listing is not all-inclusive nor does the existence of one or more of the items always signify that a material uncertainty exists.

Financial

- Net liability or net current liability position.
- Fixed-term borrowings approaching maturity without realistic prospects of renewal or repayment, or excessive reliance on short-term borrowing to finance long-term assets.
- Indications of withdrawal of financial support by creditors.
- Negative operating cash flows indicated by historical or prospective financial statements.
- Adverse key financial ratios.
- Substantial operating losses or significant deterioration in the value of assets used to generate cash flows.
- Arrears or discontinuance of dividends.
- Inability to pay creditors on due dates.
- Difficulty in complying with the terms of loan agreements.
- Change from credit to cash-on-delivery transactions with suppliers.
- Inability to obtain financing for essential new product development or other essential investments.

Operating

- Management intentions to liquidate the entity or to cease operations.
- Loss of key management without replacement.
- Loss of a major market, key customer(s), franchise, licence or principal supplier(s).
- Labour difficulties.
- Shortages of important supplies. Labour difficulties or shortages of important supplies.
- Emergence of a highly successful competitor.

Other

- Non-compliance with capital or other statutory requirements.
- Pending legal proceedings against the entity that may, if successful, result in claims that are likely to be satisfied.
- Changes in law or regulation or government policy expected to adversely affect the entity.
- Uninsured or underinsured catastrophes when they occur.

Concept and a Company 8.2

Peregrine Systems – The 37th of December

Concept	Analytical procedures for revenue tests.
Story	The accounting irregularities that brought down Peregrine Systems, a San Diego, California, maker of software that large companies use to manage their technology resources, included inflated revenues of more than 60 per cent or some $509 million.

Peregrine had reported revenues of $1.34 billion for 2000 and 2001. Of that, $225 million was based on 'non-substantiated transactions' as the company booked revenues when it transferred goods to a software reseller, even when there were no firm commitments in place. Another $70 million of the fictitious revenue was from swap transactions and $100 million came from the premature booking of revenues from long-term instalment contracts. Peregrine had reported another $80 million of revenues that, for a variety of reasons, should not have been recorded until future years and that $34 million of revenues had been based on 'erroneous calculations or unsupported transactions' (Waters, 2003).

An SEC complaint, settled by Peregrine, alleged that the company improperly booked millions of dollars of revenue for purported software licence sales to resellers. These transactions were non-binding sales of Peregrine software with the understanding – reflected in secret side agreements – that the resellers were not obligated to pay Peregrine. Those involved in the scheme called this 'parking' the transaction. Peregrine personnel parked transactions when Peregrine was unable to complete direct sales it was negotiating (or hoping to negotiate) with end-users, but needed revenue to achieve its forecasts (SEC, 2003a).

Peregrine engaged in other deceptive practices to inflate the company's revenue, including entering into reciprocal transactions in which Peregrine essentially paid for its customers' purchases of Peregrine software. Peregrine routinely kept its books open after fiscal quarters ended, and improperly recorded as revenue, for the prior quarter, software transactions that were not consummated until after quarter end. Certain Peregrine officers characterised these transactions as having been completed on 'the 37th of December' (SEC, 2003a).

To conceal the revenue recognition scheme, Peregrine abused the receivable financing process. When Peregrine booked the non-binding contracts, and the customers predictably did not pay, the receivables ballooned on Peregrine's balance sheet. To make it appear that Peregrine was collecting its receivables more quickly than it was, Peregrine 'sold' receivables to banks and then removed them from the company's balance sheet. There were several problems with this. First, Peregrine had given the banks recourse and frequently paid or repurchased unpaid receivables from them. Peregrine should have accounted for the bank transactions as loans and left the receivables on its balance sheet. Secondly, the sold receivables were not valid because the customers were not obligated to pay. Thirdly, several of the sold invoices were fake, including one that purported to reflect a $19.58 million sale (SEC, 2003b).

The SEC complaint also alleged that, as part of the cover up, Peregrine personnel wrote off millions of dollars in uncollectible – primarily sham – receivables, to acquisition-related accounts in Peregrine's financial statements and books and records. These write-offs were improper because they had nothing to do with acquisitions (SEC, 2003a).

Chief Executive Officer Mathew C. Gless, it was alleged in an SEC civil suit, signed false SEC filings and false management representation letters to Peregrine's outside auditors, and responded falsely to an SEC Division of Corporation Finance Comment Letter that inquired about Peregrine's revenue recognition practice. According to the complaint, while Gless was aware of the ongoing fraud, he illegally sold 68,625 shares of Peregrine stock for approximately $4 million, based on material non-public information he possessed about Peregrine's true financial condition (SEC, 2003b).

Peregrine Comparative Balance Sheet 2000–2001 (in 000)

	31 March 01	31 March 00
ASSETS		
Cash and cash equivalents	$286,658	$33,511
Accounts receivable, net of allowance for doubtful accounts of $11,511 and $2,179, respectively	180,372	69,940
Other current assets	62,811	22,826
Total current assets	529,841	126,277
Property and equipment, net	82,717	29,537
Goodwill, net of accumulated amortisation of $334,178 and $54,406, respectively	1,192,855	233,504
Other intangible assets, investments and other, net of accumulated amortisation of $24,015 and $1,398, respectively	198,353	134,112
	$2,003,766	$523,430
LIABILITIES AND STOCKHOLDERS' EQUITY		
Current liabilities:		
Accounts payable	$36,024	$19,850
Accrued expenses	200,886	49,064
Current portion of deferred revenue	86,653	36,779
Current portion of long-term debt	1,731	74
Total current liabilities	325,294	105,767
Deferred revenue, net of current portion	8,299	4,556
Other long-term liabilities	17,197	
Long-term debt, net of current portion	884	1,257
Convertible subordinated notes	262,327	
Total liabilities	614,001	111,580
Stockholders' equity:		
Preferred stock, $0.001 par value, 5,000 shares authorised, no shares issued or outstanding		
Common stock, $0.001 par value, 500,000 shares authorised, 160,359 and 109,501 shares issued and outstanding, respectively	160	110
Additional paid-in capital	2,342,235	480,957
Accumulated deficit	−917,104	−64,863
Unearned portion of deferred compensation	−22,151	−678
Cumulative translation adjustment	−3,950	−666
Treasury stock, at cost	−9,425	−3,010
Total stockholders' equity	1,389,765	411,850
	$2,003,766	$523,430

Peregrine Systems Comparative Income Statement 1999–2001 (in 000)

Revenues:	31 March 01	31 March 00	31 March 99
Licences	$354,610	$168,467	$87,362
Services	210,073	84,833	50,701
Total revenues	564,683	253,300	138,063

Peregrine Systems – 37 December (continued)

Revenues:	31 March 01	31 March 00	31 March 99
Costs and expenses:			
Cost of licences	2,582	1,426	1,020
Cost of services	111,165	51,441	31,561
Amortisation of purchased technology	11,844	1,338	50
Sales and marketing	223,966	101,443	50,803
Research and development	61,957	28,517	13,919
General and administrative	48,420	19,871	10,482
Acquisition costs and other	918,156	57,920	43,967
Total costs and expenses	1,378,090	261,956	151,802
Loss from operations before interest (net) and income tax expense	−813,407	−8,656	−13,739
Interest income (expense), net	−538	38	664
Loss from operations before income tax expense	−813,945	−8,618	−13,075
Income tax expense	−38,296	−16,452	−10,295
Net loss	−$852,241	−$25,070	−$23,370
Net loss per share basic and diluted:			
Net loss per share	−$6.16	−$0.24	−$0.27
Shares used in computation	138,447	102,332	87,166

Source: US Securities and Exchange Commission, www.sec.gov.

Discussion Questions	■ Review the Peregrine financial statements and determine what analytical procedures could be used to predict the revenue recognition fraud. Are there other indicators that a revenue recognition fraud was under way?

References	SEC, 2003a, Litigation Release No. 18205A, Accounting and Auditing Enforcement Release No. 1808A, 'SEC Charges Peregrine Systems, Inc. with Financial Fraud and Agrees to Partial Settlement', US Securities and Exchange Commission, 30 June.
	SEC, 2003b, Litigation Release No. 18093, Accounting and Auditing Enforcement Release No. 1759, 'SEC Charges Former Peregrine CFO with Financial Fraud', US Securities and Exchange Commission, 16 April.
	Waters, R., 2003, 'Irregularities at Peregrine Lifted Revenues 60 Per Cent', *Financial Times*, 3 March, p. 19.

8.6 Analytical Procedures During Different Phases in the Audit Process

Analytical procedures are used: (a) to assist the auditor in planning the nature, timing and extent of audit procedures; (b) as substantive procedures; and (c) as an overall review of the financial statements in the final stage of the audit. The auditor is required to apply analytical procedures at overall review stages of the audit.

■ Planning

Analytical procedures performed in the planning stage (Stage II in the Audit Process Model, Illustration 5.1) are used to identify unusual changes in the financial statements, or the absence of expected changes, and specific risks. During the planning stage, analytical procedures are usually focused on account balances aggregated at the financial statement level and relationships. Application of analytical procedures at the planning stage indicates aspects of the business of which the auditor was unaware and will assist in determining the nature, timing and extent of other audit procedures. Surveys of auditors show that the most extensive use of analytical procedures has been in the planning and completion stages.[14]

■ Substantive Testing

During the substantive testing stage (Phase III of the Audit Process Model, Illustration 5.1), analytical procedures are performed to obtain assurance that financial statement account balances do not contain material misstatements. In substantive testing, analytical procedures focus on underlying factors that affect those account balances through the development of an expectation of how the recorded balance should look.

■ Overall Review

Analytical procedures performed during the overall review stage (Phase IV of the Audit Process Model, Illustration 5.1) are designed to assist the auditor in assessing that all significant fluctuations and other unusual items have been adequately explained and that the overall financial statement presentation makes sense based on the audit results and an understanding of the business.

According to ISA 520, 'The auditor shall design and perform analytical procedures near the end of the audit that assist the auditor when forming an overall conclusion as to whether the financial statements are consistent with the auditor's understanding of the entity.'[15] Analytical procedures at the review stage are intended to corroborate conclusions formed during the audit of individual components of the financial statements. Moreover, they assist in determining the reasonableness of the financial statements. They may also identify areas requiring further procedures.

■ Tests of Controls Over Information Used for Analytics

An important consideration in applying analytical procedures is tests of controls over the preparation of information used for analytics. When those controls are effective, the auditor will have more confidence in the reliability of the information and, therefore, in the results of analytical procedures.

The controls over non-financial information can often be tested in conjunction with tests of accounting-related controls. For example, a company's controls over the processing of sales invoices may include controls over the recording of unit sales; therefore, an auditor could test the controls over the recording of unit sales in conjunction with tests of the controls over the processing of sales invoices.

8.7 Analytical Procedures as Substantive Tests

Substantive procedures in the audit are designed to reduce **detection risk** relating to specific financial statement **assertions**. Substantive tests include tests of details (either **of balances** or **of transactions**) and analytical procedures. Auditors use analytical procedures to identify situations that require increased use of other procedures (i.e. tests of control, substantive audit procedures), but seldom to reduce audit effort.[16]

■ Analytical Procedures Instead of Tests of Details

There are a number of advantages of performing substantive analytical procedures instead of tests of details. One advantage is that the auditor may use his understanding of the client's business obtained during planning procedures. The key factors affecting business may be expected to reflect underlying financial data. Substantive analytical procedures often enable auditors to focus on a few key factors that affect the account balance. Substantive analytical procedures may be more efficient in performing understatement tests. For example, in a test for unrecorded sales, it may be easier to develop an expectation of sales and investigate any significant differences between the expectation and the recorded amount, than to sample statistically a reciprocal population and then perform tests of details.

In planning an audit that uses analytical procedures as substantive procedures, the auditor should:[17]

■ Determine the suitability of particular substantive analytical procedures for given assertions, considering the assessed risks of material misstatement.
■ Evaluate the reliability of data from which the auditor's expectation is developed, taking account of quality of controls, as well as the source, comparability and relevance of the information.
■ Evaluate whether the expectation is sufficiently precise to identify a misstatement that may cause the financial statements to be materially misstated.
■ Determine the amount of any difference of recorded amounts from expected values that is acceptable without further investigation.

■ Disadvantages of Analytical Procedures

Substantive analytical procedures have some disadvantages. They may be more time-consuming initially to design and might be less effective than performing tests of details of balances. Obtaining data used to develop an expectation and ensuring the reliability of that data at a disaggregated level can take a substantial amount of the time otherwise spent performing tests of details. Analytical procedures may be less effective when applied to the financial statements as a whole than when applied to financial information on individual sections of an operation or to financial statements of components of a the company.

Substantive analytical procedures will not necessarily deliver the desired results every year. In periods of instability and rapid change, it may be difficult to develop a sufficiently precise expectation of the recorded amount, and it may be more appropriate to apply tests of details. For example, if an economy reaches hyperinflation, it is unlikely that we will be able to develop meaningful expectations efficiently, except in limited circumstances.

■ Corroboration

When analytical procedures serve as substantive tests, the auditor should corroborate explanations for significant differences by obtaining sufficient audit evidence. For example, re-calculation of invoice extensions (quantity multiplied by price) may be corroborated by interviewing a salesperson about how invoices are filled out. This evidence needs to be of the same quality, as the evidence the auditor would expect to obtain to support tests of details.

To corroborate an explanation, one or more of the following techniques may be used:

- inquiries of persons outside the client's organisation including bankers, suppliers, customers, etc.;
- inquiries of independent persons inside the client's organisation (e.g. an explanation received from the Chief Financial Officer for an increase in advertising expenditures might be corroborated with the marketing director: it is normally inappropriate to corroborate explanations only by discussion with other accounting department personnel);
- evidence obtained from other auditing procedures;
- examination of supporting evidence. The auditor may examine supporting documentary evidence of transactions to corroborate explanations. For example, if an increase in cost of sales in one month was attributed to an unusually large sales contract, the auditor might examine supporting documentation, such as the sales contract and delivery dockets.

■ Substantive Analytical Procedures Examples

Fraudulent payments are often in large amounts. An analytical procedure to detect this is the use of a CAATs program (discussed in the next section) to stratify the payments by size and then extract all large payments. The auditor may sort the records by type of purchase, since the size of an expenditure is related to the typical cost of the product or service.

By analysing revenue over at least three years, the auditor can detect unexpected trends in revenues. Sales can also be analysed by type, activity, salesperson, month, or customer. The sales data can be stratified to determine if sales in a certain area or by a certain salesperson are made up of a few large or unusual transactions.

Benford's Law calculations may be done by a CAATs. Benford's Law determines the expected frequency for each digit in any position in a set of random numbers. This means that the chances of any number appearing in a given database are mathematically predictable. Since the expected frequency for each number in the set is known, every number that appears in the database in excess of the expected frequency requires further investigation. For instance, payment amounts authorised by a manager may be consistently just below the maximum allowed for that manager.

■ Payroll

If the auditor suspects fraud in the payroll area, he may do a number of substantive tests to detect a 'ghost employee', an employee who still 'works for the company' even though his employment has been terminated, or excessive overtime charges. Three types of analytical tests can be performed to help detect these kinds of irregularities: duplicate and validity tests, exception testing and recalculations.

Duplicate and validity tests are used to detect a ghost or a terminated employee. A CAATs program can help the auditor check for duplicate social security numbers, names, or, if direct deposit is used, bank account numbers. To find ghost employees, an auditor can also identify employees who take no sick or annual leave, or those who do not have insurance or other deductions taken out of their pay. Additionally, a CAATs program can verify that each employee's salary or wage is within the ranges for his job description and that tax withholding amounts are reasonable.

8.8 Computer Assisted Audit Techniques (CAATs) and Generalised Audit Software (GAS)

The use of computer assisted audit techniques (CAATs) may enable more extensive testing of electronic transactions and account files.[18] CAATs can be used to select sample transactions from key electronic files, to sort transactions with specific characteristics, or to test an entire population instead of a sample. CAATs generally include regression and statistical analysis as well as the more widely used file interrogation techniques using generalised audit software (GAS) such as data manipulation, calculation, data selection, data analysis, identification of exceptions and unusual transactions.

■ Regression Analysis

Complicated analytical procedures may use regression analysis. Regression analysis is the use of statistical models to quantify the auditor's expectation in financial (euro, dollar) terms, with measurable risk and precision levels. For example, an expectation for sales may be developed based on management's sales forecast, commission expense, and changes in advertising expenditures. Regression analysis provides a very high level of precision because an explicit expectation is formed in which the relevant data can be incorporated in a model to predict current year sales.

Regression analysis potentially can take into account all of the relevant operating data (sales volume by product), changes in operations (changes in advertising levels, changes in product lines or product mix), and changes in economic conditions. Regression analysis provides the benefits of statistical precision. The statistical model provides not only a 'best' expectation given the data at hand, but also provides quantitative measures of the 'fit' of the model.

■ Generalised Audit Software (GAS)

Generalised audit software (GAS) packages contain numerous computer-assisted audit techniques for both doing analytical procedures and statistical sampling bundled into one piece of software. There are widely used GAS packages such as ACL[19] and IDEA, and the Big Four audit firms have their own software such as Deloitte and Touche's STAR and MINI MAX. GAS packages provide the auditors with the ability to access, manipulate, manage, analyse, and report data in a variety of formats. This software allows the auditor to move from analytical procedures to statistical sampling for analytical procedures fairly easily.

File Interrogation Procedures Using GAS

Using GAS in an audit requires converting client data into a common format and then analysing the data. This is generally referred to as file interrogation. File interrogation is a CAAT that allows the auditor to perform automated audit routines on client computer data. It is a method of using a computer to capture accounting data and reports and test the information contained therein. Because the nature of audit evidence changes, audit techniques that take advantage of technology are often more appropriate than traditional auditing techniques. In sophisticated environments, file interrogation techniques can often create efficiency and improve the quality of audit work.

Extracting information that meets specific criteria, selecting information, and testing the accuracy of calculations can be done with file interrogation. CAATs used in GAS allows auditors to analyse and test every item on a report to determine whether it meets predefined criteria, identify significant differences, create an independent report of exceptions, select an audit sample, and export the results into audit software.

■ Audit Tasks

In general terms, file interrogation can accomplish the following six types of audit task:

1 convert client data into common format;
2 analyse data;
3 compare different sets of data;
4 confirm the accuracy of calculations and make computations;
5 sample statistically;
6 test for gaps or duplicates in a sequence.

We will discuss the first three audit tasks in this section. (For a discussion of the last three items (confirm accuracy of the calculations, statistical sampling and tests for gaps) see Appendix A to Chapter 8 'Audit Sampling and Other Selective Testing Procedures'.)

Convert Client Data into a Common Format

The auditor can use GAS (e.g. ACL)) to convert client data into a common format (e.g. files ending in the extension*.fil) that can be manipulated by the software. Audit work is more efficient since data does not have to be manually entered and the conversion is usually performed with 100 per cent accuracy. The data can then be used by the GAS or exported as several formats such as plain text, comma delimited, XML, Microsoft Word, Excel or Access.

Analyse Data

GAS can handle large volumes of data quickly. Often, file interrogation can be used to analyse an entire population in less time than it would take to test a sample of items manually. The auditor can identify all records in a data file that meet specified criteria or reformat and aggregate data in a variety of ways.

Audit tests that can be performed with GAS include the following:

■ Identify all inventory items relating to products no longer sold.
■ Select all inventory items with no recorded location.
■ Summarise inventory items by location to facilitate physical observation.
■ Review account receivable balances for amounts over credit limits or older than a specified period.
■ Summarise accounts receivable by age for comparison to the client's schedules.
■ Review inventory quantities and unit costs for negative or unusually large amounts.
■ Isolate all inventory items that have not moved since a specified date.

■ Review assets for negative net book values.

■ Summarise inventory by age to assess the reasonableness of obsolescence provisions.

Compare Different Sets of Data

If records on separate files contain comparable data, GAS can be used to compare the different sets of data. For example, the auditor could compare the following:

■ changes in accounts receivable balances between two dates **with** the details of sales and cash receipts on transaction files;

■ payroll details **with** personnel records;

■ current inventory files **with** prior period files to identify potentially obsolete or slow-moving items;

■ portfolio positions recorded in the accounting records of an investment company **with** the records maintained by the custodian.

■ Structured Approach for GAS-Based Analytical Procedures

To use analytical procedures in testing an account balance with GAS, the auditor is likely to follow the basic four-phase audit review model already discussed in Section 8.3. The four phases using GAS are shown in Illustration 8.5. When using GAS to conduct the

---

ILLUSTRATION 8.5

The Four-Phase Analytical Review Process Using GAS

Phase one in performing analytical procedures – expectations

■ Determine appropriate base data and an appropriate level of disaggregation.

■ Use regression analysis techniques to develop from the base data a plausible relationship (a regression model) between the amounts to be tested (the test variable such as accounts receivable balance) and one or more independent sets of data (predicting variables such as revenue, volume of shipments, collection history, selling square footage, number of customers, etc.) that are expected to relate to the test variable.

■ Based on this relationship, use GAS software to calculate the expectations (regression estimates) for the test variable based on the current-period values of the predicting variables.

Phase two in performing analytical procedures – identification

■ Use GAS's statistical techniques to assist in identifying significant differences for investigation (i.e. differences exceeding the materiality thresholds) based on the regression model, audit judgements as to monetary precision (MP), required audit assurance (R factor), and the direction of the test.

Phase three in performing analytical procedures – investigation

■ Investigate and corroborate explanations for significant differences between the expectations and the recorded amounts.

Phase four in performing analytical procedures – evaluation

■ Evaluate findings and determine the level of assurance, if any, to be drawn from the analytical procedures.

four-phase audit review process, the auditor must first format the data so that it might be read with the software.

Examples

To illustrate, assume that the test variable is *sales* and the predicting variable is *cost of sales*. In most cases, it is plausible that a relationship exists between these two components of the income statement. The GAS uses sales and cost of sales data from prior periods to determine the precise nature of the relationship and to develop a regression model. Then, based on audited current-period amounts for cost of sales, GAS will project the current-period expectations for sales. GAS will then compare the expectations for sales with the actual recorded amounts and calculate the differences. GAS identifies for investigation any statistically significant differences between the current-period projected amounts and the actual recorded amounts for sales.

A regression model might be constructed for a chain of retail outlets based on prior-year performance, in which annual sales per outlet are related to floor area and number of sales personnel (relationships that are expected to be reasonably constant over time). That model might then be used to develop sales expectations based on the corresponding current-year floor area and sales personnel data. The application would identify those outlets where sales results require further investigation, and may assist in selecting locations to visit.

8.9 Analytical Procedures Using Data Mining Techniques

Data mining is a set of computer-assisted techniques that use sophisticated statistical analysis, including artificial intelligence techniques, to examine large volumes of data with the objective of indicating hidden or unexpected information or patterns. In database terms, data mining is referred to as knowledge discovery in databases (KDD). Data mining can be used in all types of databases or other information repositories. Data to be mined can be numerical data, textual data or even graphics and audio.

Used most extensively in **customer relationship management** (CRM) and fraud detection, data mining is for both verification and discovery objectives. Data mining is used in a top-down approach to verify auditors' expectations or explain events or conditions observed. For example, merchandise order and delivery dates are examined to see if the delivery date falls after the order date. Discovery is a bottom-up approach that uses automated exploration of hitherto unknown patterns. For example, the auditor uses a **neural network** to sift through financial and non-financial revenue and accounts receivable data to discover unusual patterns.

■ GAS and Data Mining

GAS's capability to assist in the overall audit process while requiring little technical skill is a major reason for its success. However, GAS has been criticised because it makes some tasks easier but it cannot complete any data analysis by itself. Data mining, on the other hand, analyses data automatically but is more difficult to employ.

Data mining tools remain promising in a variety of application areas. With the development of appropriate data mining tools for the auditing profession, it may be expected to replace some professional expertise required in certain auditing processes. For now, although data mining procedures are useful in almost all steps of the audit process, its most practical and useful applications are in analytical procedures.

Data mining may use many methods and techniques and algorithms to analyse client data. Data mining methods include data description, dependency analysis, classification and prediction, cluster analysis, outlier analysis and evolution analysis The most frequently used algorithms are decision trees, apriori algorithms, and neural networks.

The purpose of **dependency analysis** is to search for the most significant relationship across large number of variables or attributes. **Classification** is the process of finding models, also known as classifiers, or functions that map records into one of several discrete prescribed classes.

The objective of **data description** is to provide an overall description of data, either in itself or in each class or concept. There are two main approaches in obtaining data description – data characterisation and data discrimination. Data characterisation is summarising general characteristics of data and data discrimination, also called data comparison, by comparing characters of data between contrasting groups or classes.

The objective of **evolution analysis** is to determine the most significant changes in data sets over time. In other words, it is other types of algorithm methods (i.e. data description, dependency analysis, classification or clustering) plus time-related and sequence-related characteristics.

The objective of **cluster analysis** is to separate data with similar characteristics from the dissimilar ones. The difference between clustering and classification is that while clustering does not require pre-identified class labels, classification does. Outliers are data items that are distinctly dissimilar to others and can be viewed as noises or errors. However, such noises can be useful in some cases, such as fraud detection, where unusual items or exceptions are major concerns.

An example of the use of the clustering method is when the auditor clusters accounting transactions in such categories as assets, liabilities, revenue, expenses, etc. This might reveal those small transactions that occur repeatedly in a certain period of the month or the same transactions recorded in different account numbers. The auditor might find that sales in some months or divisions are excessively higher or lower than the normal. Expenses that are highly variable during the year might be found. Clustering might show the repeated purchase of the same fixed asset. Loans that are transacted between related companies and subsidiaries may be uncovered.

■ Algorithms – Decision Tree, Apriori, Neural Network

Data mining most frequently uses three algorithms.

- A **decision tree** is a predictive model that classifies data with a hierarchical structure. It consists of nodes, which contain classification questions, and branches that are the result of the questions. (For example the question, 'Does this item increase at the same rate as revenue?' may be answered yes – which leads to one branch 'growth similar to revenue' or may be answered no – which leads to another branch.)
- The **apriori algorithm** attempts to discover frequent item sets using rules to find associations between the presence or absence of items (Boolean association rules). The group of item sets that most frequently come together is identified.

■ A **neural network** is a computer model based on the architecture of the brain. It first detects a pattern from data sets then predicts the best classifiers of that pattern, and finally learns from the mistakes.

8.10   Follow-Up in Case of Unexpected Deviations

When analytical procedures identify significant fluctuations or relationships that are inconsistent with other relevant information or that deviate from predicted amounts, the auditor should investigate and obtain adequate explanations and appropriate corroborative evidence.[20] A comparison of actual results with expected should include a consideration of why there is a difference.

There are primarily two reasons for a significant fluctuation or inconsistency. One is that there is a genuine business reason that was not obvious during planning procedures. The second reason is that there is a misstatement. Work must be done to determine which reason.

■ Investigation

The investigation of unusual fluctuations and relationships ordinarily begins with inquiries of management, followed by corroboration of management responses and determination if additional audit procedures are needed. Management's responses may be corroborated by comparing them with the auditor's knowledge of the business and other evidence obtained during the course of the audit.

If a reasonable explanation cannot be obtained, the auditor aggregates misstatements that the entity has not corrected. The auditor would then consider whether, in relation to individual amounts, subtotals, or totals in the financial statements, they materially misstate the financial statements taken as a whole. If management cannot provide a satisfactory explanation and there is a possibility of material misstatement, other audit procedures should be determined.

Upon finding unexpected deviations that exceed the threshold, there may be a need to do some root cause analysis. In that root cause analyses, a reassessment of the effectiveness of controls may be necessary. If the auditor detects deviations from controls upon which he intends to rely, he must make specific inquiries to understand these matters and their potential consequences. Furthermore, he must determine whether:[21]

■ the tests of controls show an appropriate basis for reliance on the controls;
■ additional tests of controls are necessary; or
■ the potential risks of misstatement need to be addressed using substantive procedures.

8.11   Summary

Analytical procedures are evaluations of financial information through analysis of plausible relationships among both financial and non-financial data. Analytical procedures also encompass such investigation as is necessary of identified fluctuations or relationships that are inconsistent with other relevant information or that differ from expected values by a significant amount. That is, analytical procedures entail the use of comparisons and relationships to determine whether account balances or other data appear reasonable. A basic premise of using analytical procedures is that there exist plausible relationships among data and these relationships can reasonably be expected to continue.

General analytical procedures include trend analysis, ratio analysis, statistical and data mining analysis, and reasonableness tests. Trend analysis is the analysis of changes in an account balance over time. Ratio analysis is the comparison of relationships between financial statement accounts, the comparison of an account with non-financial data, or the comparison of relationships between firms in an industry. Reasonableness testing is the analysis of account balances or changes in account balances within an accounting period in terms of their 'reasonableness' in light of expected relationships between accounts. Data mining is a set of computer-assisted techniques that use sophisticated statistical analysis, including artificial intelligence techniques, to examine large volumes of data with the objective of indicating hidden or unexpected information or patterns. For these tests auditors generally use computer-aided audit software (CAATs).

The process of planning, executing and drawing conclusions from analytical procedures is called **analytical review**. The four-phase process consists of the following:

1 phase one is to formulate expectations (expectations);
2 phase two is the comparison of the expected value to the recorded amount (identification);
3 phase three requires investigation of possible explanations for a difference between expected and recorded values (investigation);
4 phase four involves evaluation of the impact on the audit and the financial statements of the differences between expectation and recorded amounts (evaluation).

Expectations are developed by identifying plausible relationships that are reasonably expected to exist based on the auditor's understanding of the client and of his industry. These relationships may be determined by comparisons with the following sources:

■ comparable information for prior periods;
■ anticipated results (such as budgets and forecasts, or auditor expectations);
■ elements of financial information within the period;
■ similar industry information;
■ non-financial information.

Determining which type of analytical procedure is appropriate is a matter of professional judgment. A review of audit practice indicates that simple judgmental approaches (such as comparison and ratio analysis) are used more frequently than complex statistical approaches (such as time series modelling or regression analysis. These tests are generally carried out using computer software (i.e. CAATs).

At the planning stage of an audit, there are certain customary ratios that are always calculated to determine accounts that may represent significant risks to the entity of liquidity, solvency, profitability, and activity. Illustration 8.3 (earlier) gives a list of these ratios.

Analytical procedures are used: (a) to assist the auditor in planning the nature, timing and extent of audit procedures; (b) as substantive procedures; and (c) as an overall review of the financial statements in the final stage of the audit. The auditor is required to apply analytical procedures at the overall review stages of the audit. In the substantive testing stage of the audit, analytical procedures are used to obtain evidence to identify misstatements in account balances and thus to reduce the risk of misstatements. In the overall review stage, the objective of analytical procedures is to assess the conclusions reached and evaluate the overall financial statement presentation.

Substantive procedures in the audit are designed to reduce detection risk relating to specific financial statement assertions. Substantive tests include tests of details and analytical procedures. Auditors use analytical procedures to identify situations that require increased use of other procedures (i.e. tests of control, substantive audit procedures), but seldom to reduce audit effort. There are a number of advantages of performing substantive analytical procedures instead of tests of details. The key factors affecting business may be expected to reflect the underlying financial data. Substantive analytical procedures often enable auditors to focus on a few key factors that affect the account balance.

The use of computer-assisted audit techniques (CAATs) may enable more extensive testing of electronic transactions and account files. Computer-assisted audit techniques can be used to select sample transactions from key electronic files, to sort transactions with specific characteristics, or to test an entire population instead of a sample. CAATs generally include regression and statistical analysis as well as the more widely used file interrogation techniques using generalised audit software (GAS) such as data manipulation, calculation, data selection, data analysis, identification of exceptions, and unusual transactions.

Data mining is a set of computer-assisted techniques that use sophisticated statistical analysis, including artificial intelligence techniques, to examine large volumes of data with the objective of indicating hidden or unexpected information or patterns. Data mining is used for both verification and discovery objectives. It is used in a top-down approach to verify auditors' expectations or explain events or conditions observed. Discovery is a bottom-up approach that uses automated exploration of hitherto unknown patterns.

If the auditor detects deviations from controls upon which he intends to rely, he must make specific inquiries to understand these matters and their potential consequences. Furthermore, he must determine whether the tests of controls show an appropriate basis for reliance on the controls; additional tests of controls are necessary; or the potential risks of misstatement need to be addressed using substantive procedures. When analytical procedures identify significant fluctuations or relationships that are inconsistent with other relevant information or that deviate from predicted amounts, the auditor should investigate and obtain adequate explanations and appropriate corroborative evidence. A comparison of actual results with expected should include a consideration of why there is a difference. The investigation of unusual fluctuations and relationships ordinarily begins with inquiries of management followed by corroboration of management's responses and other audit procedures based on the results of these inquiries.

8.12 Questions, Exercises and Cases

QUESTIONS

8.2 Introduction

8-1 Define analytical procedures and give the basic premise of using them.

8-2 When should the auditor use analytical procedures? What ISA standard states when they should be used?

8.3 The Analytical Review Process

8-3 Describe the four-step theoretical approach and the four-phase process for analytical review.

8.4 Formulating Expectations

8-4 On what sources does an auditor base his expectations? Give examples of how the auditor may use each source.

8-5 Give an example of the nature of an account. Give an example of other characteristics of the data.

8.5 General Analytical Procedures

8-6 What are the five types of analytical procedures? Briefly discuss each.

8-7 In assessing going concern, list three financial indicators, three operating indicators and three other indicators.

8.6 Analytical Procedures During Different Phases in the Audit Process

8-8 Why are analytical procedures used in the planning stages? Why are they used again near the end of the audit?

8-9 Why is it useful to do analytical procedures during the completion of an audit?

8.7 Analytical Procedures as Substantive Tests

8-10 Give the advantages and disadvantages of analytical procedures used as substantive tests.

8-11 What techniques are used to corroborate an explanation for an analytical procedure finding?

8.8 Computer Assisted Audit Techniques (CAATs) and Generalised Audit Software (GAS)

8-12 What is GAS and how does an auditor use it?

8-13 What are the six audit tasks accomplished by file interrogation? Describe two in detail.

8.9 Analytical Procedures Using Data Mining Techniques

8-14 Define data mining. How is it used for verification and discovery in the audit process?

8-15 Describe two data mining methods.

8.10 Follow-Up in Case of Unexpected Deviations

8-16 What should an auditor do if he finds significant fluctuations when performing analytical procedures?

8-17 What should an auditor do if analytical procedures show significant fluctuations?

PROBLEMS AND EXERCISES

8.3 The Analytical Review Process

8-18 Four-Phase Analytical Review Process. Based on Concept and a Company 8.2 'Peregrine Systems – 37 December', discuss what you would imagine each phase of the four-phase analytical review process would involve.

8.4 Formulating Expectations

8-19 Expectation Sources. Based on the comparison of a recent year's results from Wal-Mart, Costco, Target and the retail industry, what would your expectations be about Target's revenue growth, gross margin, operating margins and number of employees this year?

	WMT	COST	TGT	Industry
Market Cap	248.07B	17.55B	36.03B	932.18M
Employees	1,400,000	61,800	306,000	10.30K
Rev. Growth	12.20%	9.80%	10.10%	4.50%
Revenue	255.08B	43.87B	46.65B	2.04B
Gross Margin	22.20%	12.45%	31.70%	27.80%
EBITDA	18.50B	1.58B	4.62B	115.53M
Operating Margins	5.35%	2.68%	5.86%	2.16%
Net Income	8.67B	735.45M	1.70B	31.56M
Earnings Per Share	1.972	1.557	1.853	0.82
Price/Earnings Ratio	29.07	24.61	21.33	24.25

Abbreviations:
WMT = Wal-Mart Corp.
COST = Costco Wholesale Corp
TGT= Target Corp
Industry = Supermarkets, Drugstores and Mass Merchandisers

8.5 General Analytical Procedures

8-20 Analytical Procedures. At the beginning of the annual audit of Porster, BV, wholesale distributor of Valkenburg, the Netherlands, Lynna Heijn, Registeraccountant, was given a copy of Porster's financial statements as prepared by the company's accountant. On reviewing these statements, Heijn noted the following abnormal conditions:

1 The accounts receivable outstanding at the year-end represent an unusually high number of average days' credit sales.
2 The inventories on hand at the year-end represent an unusually high proportion of the current assets.
3 The working capital ratio of the company is almost twice that of the previous year.
4 The percentage of gross profit on net sales is considerably in excess of that of previous years.
5 The rate of turnover of inventory is unusually low in comparison with previous years.

Required:
Taking all the above conditions together, what irregularities might Heijn suspect regarding sales and inventories?
[*Uniform Evaluation Report* (Toronto: CPA Canada)]

8-21 Ratio and Trend Analysis. When an auditor discovers a significant change in a ratio when compared with the prior year's ratio, the auditor considers the possible reasons for the change.

Required:

Give the possible reasons for the following significant changes in ratios:

A. The rate of inventory turnover (ratio of cost of sales to average industry) has decreased from the prior year's rate.

B. The number of days' sales in receivables (ratio of average of daily accounts receivable to sales) has increased over the prior year.

8.6 Analytical Procedures During Different Phases in the Audit Process

8–22 Analytical Procedures. Analytical procedures are typically done during the planning phase.

Required:

A. Define analytical procedures.

B. Other than during planning, when does an auditor do analytical procedures?

C. Name five ratios that an auditor could use to do analytical review and briefly describe each.

8.7 Analytical Procedures as Substantive Tests

8–23 Analytical Procedures. Analytical procedures are extremely useful in the initial audit planning stage.

Required:

A. Explain why analytical procedures are considered substantive tests.

B. Explain how analytical procedures are useful in the initial audit planning stage.

C. Should analytical procedures be applied at any other stages of the audit process? Explain.

D. List several types of comparisons an auditor might make in performing analytical procedures.

8.8 Computer Assisted Audit Techniques (CAATs) and Generalised Audit Software (GAS)

8–24 Using ACL or IDEA software, perform the following procedures:

Required:

A. Open the Accounts Receivable file then (1) Determine the number (count) of customers. (2) Find the customers who owe more than $5,000. (3) Perform Benford analysis.

B. Open the Inventory file then (1) Count the number of inventory items. (2) Determine the most expensive and least expensive item. (3) Find which products have a sales price less than the unit price.

8.9 Analytical Procedures Using Data Mining Techniques

8–25 Start Microsoft Access and open the Northwind Traders Sample Database (File → New → Available templates → Sample templates → Northwind).

Required:

A. Sort the Product table by unit price, reorder point, units in stock.

B. Do a visual inspection and sort the other tables. Are there any commonalities?

C. Discuss the associations that you can see in this data. What is the nature of the possible errors?

8.10 Follow-Up of Unexpected Deviations

8–26 Extent of Reliance on Analytical Procedures. The extent of reliance that the auditor places on the results of analytical procedures depends on the materiality of the items involved, other audit procedures performed by the auditor, the accuracy with which expected results can be predicted, and the assessments of inherent and control risks.

Required:

A. Give two examples of circumstances in which the auditor can rely on analytical procedures and two circumstances when reliance on analytical procedures would not be advisable.

B. Explain the relationship between company controls and reliance on analytical procedures.

CASE

8-27 Using the references in endnotes to this chapter as a beginning place and accessing journal databases such as ABI Inform, discuss the theoretical view that the review process consists of four diagnostic processes: (1) mental representation, (2) hypothesis generation, (3) information search, and (4) hypothesis evaluation.

8.13   Notes

1 IAASB, 2012, International Standards on Auditing 520 (ISA 520) 'Analytical Procedures', para. 4, *Handbook of International Quality Control, Auditing, Review, Other Assurance, and Related Services Pronouncements*, 2012 edn, Volume 1, International Federation of Accountants, New York.

2 Ibid. ISA 520, para. 6.

3 See Blocher, E. and Cooper, J., 1988, 'A Study of Auditors' Analytical Review Performance', *Auditing: A Journal of Practice and Theory*, Spring, pp. 1–28; and Koonce, L., 1993, 'A Cognitive Characterization of Audit Analytical Review', *Auditing: A Journal of Practice and Theory*, 12 (Supplement), pp. 57–76.

4 Asare, S. and Wright, A., 1997, 'Hypothesis Revision Strategies in Conducting Analytical Procedures', *Accounting, Organizations and Society*, 22, November, pp. 737–55.

5 AICPA, 2012, *AICPA Audit Guide to Analytical Procedures*, American Institute of Certified Public Accountants, New York.

6 ISA 520, op. cit, para. 5(b).

7 See: (1) Bell, T.B., Marrs, F.O., Solomon, I. and Thomas, H., 1997, *Auditing Organizations Through A Strategic-Systems Lens*, New York, NY: KPMG Peat Marwick LLP; (2) Loebbecke, J.K. and Steinbart, P.J., 1987, 'An Investigation of the Use of Preliminary Analytical Review to Provide Substantive Audit Evidence', *Auditing: A Journal of Practice and Theory*, Spring, pp. 74–89; (3) Wild, J.J., 1987, 'The Prediction Performance of a Structural Model of Accounting Numbers', *Journal of Accounting Research*, Vol. 25, No.1, pp. 139–60.

8 ISA 520, op. cit., para. 5a.

9 AICPA, 2010, AU Section 329, 'Substantive Analytical Procedures', para. 5, American Institute of Certified Public Accountants.

10 Biggs, S.F., Mock, T.J. and Simnett, R., 1999, 'Analytical Procedures: Promise, Problems and Implications for Practice', *Australian Accounting Review*, Vol. 9, No.1, pp. 42–52.

11 See Standard & Poors, *Net Advantage*, 2012, McGraw-Hill; IBISWorld, 2012, **http://www.ibisworld .com**, Los Angeles; RMA, 2012, *Annual Statement Studies: Financial Ratio Benchmarks*, Risk Management Association, Philadelphia.

12 IAASB, 2012, International Standards on Auditing 570 (ISA 570) 'Going Concern', para. 2, *Handbook of International Quality Control, Auditing, Review, Other Assurance, and Related Services Pronouncements*, 2012 edn, Volume 1, International Federation of Accountants, New York.

13 Ibid. ISA 570, para. A2.

14 See, for example, Booth, P. and Simnett, R., 1991, 'Auditors' Perception of Analytical Review Procedures', *Accounting Research Journal*, Spring, pp. 5–10.

15 ISA 520, op. cit., para. 6.

16 See, for example, Bedard, J., 1989, 'An Archival Investigation of Audit program Planning', *Auditing: A Journal of Practice and Theory*, Fall, pp. 57–71.

17 ISA 520, op. cit., para. 5.

18 IAASB, 2012, International Standards on Auditing 330 (ISA 330) 'The Auditor's Responses To Assessed Risks', para. A16, *Handbook of International Quality Control, Auditing, Review, Other Assurance, and Related Services Pronouncements*, 2012 edn, Volume 1, International Federation of Accountants, New York.

19 ACL software is developed by ACL Services Ltd (**http://www.acl.com**).

20 ISA 330, op. cit., para. 17.

21 Ibid.

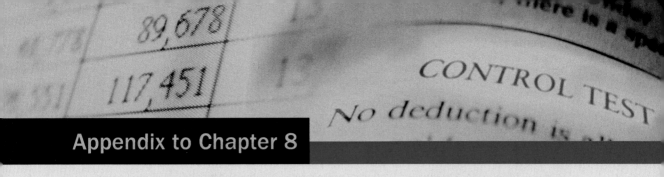

Audit Sampling and Other Selective Testing Procedures

by Lucas Hoogduin[1]

8.A.1 Preface

This appendix gives practical guidance on clarified ISA 530, 'Audit Sampling'. Unlike the previous version of the Standard, it is devoted exclusively to audit sampling. Requirements and guidance on other substantive detail testing procedures have been moved to the clarified ISA 500, 'Audit Evidence'.

The reader does not need a lot of statistical background to follow the discussions, but some mathematical skill is helpful. We have not tried to give the full mathematical derivation of formulae and results, as we believe there are some good textbooks on this matter available.

Bookkeeping scandals around the turn of the century (see the Concept and a Company cases throughout this text) have changed the audit environment considerably. Auditors feel more confident if they can base their audit conclusions on more rigid testing procedures. Nowadays, some form of audit sampling is used on almost every audit.

The clarified audit Standards are organised into two parts, Requirements, and Application and Other Explanatory Material. The Requirements paragraphs are consecutively number 1–15, and we will refer to them as 530.1, 530.2, etc. The Application and Other Explanatory Material paragraphs are consecutively numbered A1–A23, and will be referred to as 530.A1, 530.A2, etc. There are four appendices, all relating to sample size determination and sample selection.

The Standard is organised by different topics that will be discussed in this appendix:

Topic	Paragraph
Introduction	530.1–530.3
Objective	530.4
Definitions	530.5, 530.A1–530.A3
Sample design, size and selection of items for testing	530.6–530.8, 530.A4–530.A13, Appendix 1–4
Performing audit procedures	530.9–530.11, 530.A14–530.A16
Nature and cause of deviations and misstatements	530.12–530.13, 530.A17
Projecting misstatements	530.14, 530.A18–530.A20
Evaluating results of audit sampling	530.15, 530.A21–530.A23

8.A.2 Objective

The exposure draft of the standard proposed the following objective:

the objective of the auditor when using audit sampling is to design and select the audit sample, perform audit procedures on the sample items, and evaluate the results from the sample in a manner that will provide an appropriate basis for the auditor to draw conclusions about the population from which the sample is drawn.

The majority of respondents to the exposure draft were of the view that the objective to be achieved by the auditor is appropriate. Several respondents, however, were concerned that this proposed objective focused more on the process of audit sampling than on the outcome that should be accomplished. A few respondents suggested that it would be helpful if the objective were to be drafted to more closely relate to the overall objective of the auditor, that is, to obtain sufficient appropriate audit evidence.

The IAASB did not agree that the objective of the auditor in respect of audit sampling is to obtain 'sufficient appropriate audit evidence' within the broader meaning of this phrase. Rather, the objective is that, within the narrow context of audit sampling, the sample provide the auditor with a reasonable basis on which to draw conclusions about the population from which the sample was selected. The IAASB determined that this principle should be retained in the objective. Nevertheless, the IAASB accepted that the proposed objective appeared unduly procedural in nature. Accordingly, the IAASB agreed to amend the objective to the one stated above.

8.A.3 Definitions

The Standard provides definitions on a number of different concepts. We provide some background information, and cross-reference to the paragraphs where these terms come into play.

In the definition of audit sampling (530.5 (a)) a few considerations come to mind. First, the audit procedures are applied on a subset of items from the population. From a mathematical point of view that distinction is not necessary (the calculation of a point estimate becomes trivial and there is no sampling error, sampling risk, or precision associated to the estimate, because the estimate is exact). From an auditor's point of view, it is this that distinguishes a sample from, say, an analytical procedure or a substantive test carried out on the entire population using a computer-assisted audit technique (CAAT).

Secondly, it is mentioned that all sampling units have a chance of selection. If the auditor wants to draw a conclusion about the entire population, no parts of that population should be excluded from having a chance of selection. The Standard doesn't detail how the chance of selection is determined. This enables inclusion of simple random sampling techniques, where all sampling units have the same selection probability, stratified sampling, where sampling units within the same stratum have the same selection probability, and monetary-unit sampling, where selection probabilities are proportional to the book values of the sampling units. It also includes non-statistical sampling, where selection probabilities are not defined, as long as auditors attempt to not bias their selection.

■ Population

This definition may be confusing as it defines two objects that have a completely different meaning. This will become clear later in our discussion of requirement 530.9.

The set of data from which the sample is selected is commonly referred to as sampling frame. For example, when sampling accounts receivable balances for a confirmation procedure, the auditor may sample from a list of all open accounts receivable invoices or balances (these are two different examples of sampling frames that can be used). In both of these cases, the population is the accounts receivable balance in the financial statements. It is therefore important to understand which of the two is referred to when the Standards use the term 'population'.

It is even more important to understand that there may be differences between the sampling frame and the population. Not all elements from the population may be included in the frame (for example, a listing of inventories may not include items that are present in the warehouse but are not recorded), or the frame may contain sampling units that are not relevant for the test on the population (for example, the listing of accounts receivable may include intercompany receivables which the auditor may want to test with a procedure different from that used on external debtors).

■ Sampling risk (530.5(c))

The definition of sampling risk can best be explained with an easy example. Let's assume the auditor tests the operating effectiveness of a control, and has decided that a sample of 25 would be sufficient to do so. He will rely on the control if no deviations are found in the sample, and he will not rely on the control if the sample reveals any errors.

With a sample of 25 items, the auditor can be 90 per cent confident that he will find at least one deviation if the true deviation rate in the population is 8.8 per cent (his tolerable deviation rate). In other words, he runs a 10 per cent (100 per cent – 90 per cent) sampling risk of drawing an incorrect conclusion if the population contains an 8.8 per cent deviation rate. The risk is lower if the true deviation risk is greater than 8.8 per cent.

The 10 per cent risk is the risk of concluding that the controls are more effective than they actually are: the auditor finds no deviations with a chance of 10 per cent, and therefore concludes that controls are operating effectively, more effective than they actually are.

If the true deviation rate is less than 8.8 per cent, the probability of finding deviations is less than 90 per cent. For example, if the true deviation rate is only 2 per cent, the probability of finding deviations is close to 40 per cent. The sample risk now is 40 per cent, corresponding to the probability of finding deviations when the actual deviation rate is acceptably low. The auditor concludes that he cannot rely on the control when he could have.

These two examples explain the difference between the two types of erroneous conclusion as referred to in 530.5(c).

■ Anomalies (530.5(e))

This concept is subject to a lot of debate. On the one hand it may not seem justified to project anomalous misstatements or deviations to a population because the anomaly is 'demonstrably' not representative of the (entire) population. On the other hand it could be argued that an anomalous misstatement or deviation may not be representative of the population from which it was selected, but it could be representative of other anomalies that exist in the population but weren't picked up in the sample.

When ISA 530 was adapted in the United States, the concept of anomalous misstatements and deviations was stricken from the US Standards and there is no such thing as an anomaly.

■ Sampling unit (530.5(f))

In the definition of the standard, the sampling units are the individual items constituting a population

To be more exact, we would prefer to refer to the sampling units in a sampling frame and to elements in the population.

Given the definition of audit sampling, it is strange that monetary units are examples of sampling units. Since weighted selection is included in the definition of audit sampling, it is not necessary to define the monetary unit as a sampling unit. We simple define the individual balances, invoices, etc. as the sampling units and select them with any of the allowed selection techniques.

In practice, it is impossible to treat the monetary unit as the sampling unit. The auditor cannot select individual monetary units (only the 'physical' units that contain the monetary unit), and if the tested item is partially incorrect, it is difficult to tell whether the selected monetary unit was correct, partially incorrect or incorrect. As a result, an adjustment is typically made to the mathematical calculations that reflect the partial nature of the misstatements if found.

■ Statistical sampling (530.5(g))

Typically a non-statistical sample is a sample of units from a population that have not randomly been selected, but haphazardly. Because a statistical conclusion requires random selection, these samples cannot be statistical. In theory it is possible to randomly select elements from a population, and then not use probability theory to evaluate the results, but I cannot imagine why an auditor would go through the hassle of obtaining a random sample and then not statistically evaluating the results.

■ Stratification (530.5(h))

Stratification will come into play when designing the sample (530.A8), in the discussion of sample size calculation (530.7), responding to the nature and cause of deviations and misstatements (530.A17) and anomalies (530.13).

Appendix 1 to the Standard added the following with regard to stratification:

1 Audit efficiency may be improved if the auditor stratifies a population by dividing it into discrete subpopulations which have an identifying characteristic. The objective of stratification is to reduce the variability of items within each stratum and therefore allow sample size to be reduced without increasing sampling risk.

2 When performing tests of details, the population is often stratified by monetary value. This allows greater audit effort to be directed to the larger value items, as these items may contain the greatest potential misstatement in terms of overstatement. Similarly, a population may be stratified according to a particular characteristic that indicates a higher risk of misstatement, for example, when testing the allowance for doubtful accounts in the valuation of accounts receivable, balances may be stratified by age.

3 The results of audit procedures applied to a sample of items within a stratum can only be projected to the items that make up that stratum. To draw a conclusion on the entire

population, the auditor will need to consider the risk of material misstatement in relation to whatever other strata make up the entire population. For example, 20 per cent of the items in a population may make up 90 per cent of the value of an account balance. The auditor may decide to examine a sample of these items. The auditor evaluates the results of this sample and reaches a conclusion on the 90 per cent of value separately from the remaining 10 per cent (on which a further sample or other means of gathering audit evidence will be used, or which may be considered immaterial).

4 If a class of transactions or account balance has been divided into strata, the misstatement is projected for each stratum separately. Projected misstatements for each stratum are then combined when considering the possible effect of misstatements on the total class of transactions or account balance.

■ Tolerable misstatement and deviation (530.5 (i), 530.A3 and 530.5 (i))

The concept of tolerable misstatement or tolerable deviation is mainly devised as a means to establish the minimum work to be performed on a certain balance or class of transactions. It is derived from **performance materiality**,[2] acknowledging that misstatements in different accounts may (but not necessarily will) aggregate to an amount that exceeds performance materiality.

The adjective 'tolerable' may be misleading: the auditor tries his utmost to detect a misstatement or deviation rate of this size if it exists, only allowing a small permissible risk to not detect it. It would be equally appropriate to call it 'intolerable', as the tolerable deviation rate and the tolerable misstatement represent the quantity of error in the population that the auditor would like to find signs of if it existed.

8.A.4 Sample Design, Size and Selection

Now that the main terms have been defined, we can get them to work. The Standard starts with a requirement on the design of the sample.

■ Sample design (530.6)

Sample design is very important. Sample design includes consideration of the purpose of the audit procedure, as well as the characteristics of the population (in the meaning of the sampling frame) from which the sample will be drawn. Sample design also covers the sampling method and determination of the sample size. Most of the choices made in the design phase cannot be reversed after the audit evidence has been obtained. We will explain these concepts with the aid of an inventory count example.

Assume that you are the auditor of a large company that operates a central warehouse supplying more than 100 retail outlets in a certain region. At the end of the year the client performs a full count of the inventories. When attending the count, you perform procedures to address completeness, existence, accuracy and valuation of inventories.

You want to perform test counts on a selection of inventory items. How do the purpose of the audit procedure and the characteristics of the population come into play?

You have obtained a listing of all inventory items, including a description of the item, the number of items on hand, and the location at which the item is stored. This list may be a good basis for your test for existence, accuracy and valuation. But remember the distinction we made when discussing the definition of the population: the purpose of the test is to test the existence, accuracy and valuation of the total amount of the inventory as per the financial statements, and we will eventually select items from a representation of this population in the form of the sampling frame that is a listing of all inventory items. This approach is the 'list-to-floor' type. Audit teams sometimes also do 'floor-to-list' tests (i.e. completeness of inventory). Ideally, the list is a true representation of the population, with no items omitted and no items incorrectly listed. A quick test would be to reconcile the list to the general ledger, but this will prove difficult for two reasons: the list may not contain prices, and therefore the total value of the inventory may not be calculated. Furthermore, the list you obtained was likely printed at the beginning of the day when the client started counting, and doesn't reflect any differences that the client identified. The reconciliation between the sampling frame and the population can only be performed at a later point in time.

An example of the characteristics of the population is as follows. Let's assume that you selected a certain type of widgets for testing, but these widgets could be stored in a number of different locations. Will you select all occurrences of the selected widget, and test its existence in all locations, or will you select a widget at a specific location? This is a question with regard to the sampling unit, and to answer it you need to know the characteristics of the population.

Let's now focus on the completeness assertion. Although in general the completeness assertion cannot be tested with a sample, an exception can be made when a reciprocal population can be defined. In this case the collection of all inventory locations could serve for this purpose. If every physical location within the warehouse has a unique identification number, like a bin number, you could draw the sample from the sampling frame that contains all these location numbers. This may not be the most efficient test for completeness, and it certainly doesn't address the risk that inventory items are located outside the warehouse. Other tests for completeness may be more effective and should also be considered, like tag control (checking that every counted item has been tagged).

In our example, the characteristic of the items selected (530.A4) would be their quantities (for the test on existence and accuracy) and their appearance or age (for the test on valuation).

When 530.A5 goes on to discuss the completeness of the population, it is more insightful to replace population with sampling frame, the representation of the population that the auditor samples from. Paragraph 530.A6 continues the understanding of what constitutes a deviation or misstatement.

In the case of the inventory count, let's assume that the client is good at recording the correct quantity of items, but occasionally makes mistakes when recording the location number. This may lead to two different problems: an item selected from the inventory listing cannot be found, and therefore is possibly mistakenly treated as a misstatement, or a location selected appears to contain items that cannot be found on the inventory listing, thereby indicating a potential completeness issue. If an inventory item is misplaced, both problems occur at the same time, and even though they have no net effect, if only one of the two issues is identified in the sample, an audit misstatement is identified without there being one.

To avoid this problem, you may print out a listing of all empty locations and check that they, indeed, are empty. If empty locations are found that are not listed, they are reported. Likewise, if a location that is supposed to be empty actually holds goods, the number of items and **SKU (stock keeping unit) number**[3] are written down. This procedure, if carried out correctly, identifies all misplaced items. As such, this kind of difference doesn't constitute a misstatement, and the difference found does not have to be projected.

Expected rate of deviation and expected misstatement are (530.A7) are other examples of the characteristics of the population that may have an impact on sample design. If the population contains a large number of small misstatements, a technique like **classical variables sampling**[4] may be appropriate, whereas if the risk is that the population contains a small number of large misstatements, monetary unit sampling may be more appropriate. For a test of controls, if the auditor believes that the population contains some rate of error, attempting to rely on the control may not be efficient. Finally, to reduce the risk of incorrect rejection (see the discussion on the definition of sampling risk), a higher expected rate of deviation or higher expected misstatement will lead to larger sample sizes.

If the expected rate of deviation or expected misstatement is greater than tolerable, it doesn't make sense to test the population. In this case the sample results will most likely indicate that the population contains too many deviations or misstatements. The Standard suggests that a 100 per cent examination or use of a large sample size may be appropriate, but this is only true if the population can be adjusted based on the misstatements found.

Stratification (530.A8) is a technique usually connected to classical variables sampling. It is rarely encountered with monetary unit sampling.

■ Sample Size

The acceptable level of sampling risk depends on the assessments of inherent and control risk, as well as the amount of evidence obtained from other substantive procedures related to the same purpose. There is no clear-cut formula that determines the level of acceptable sampling risk based on the risk assessments. It is generally accepted that audit evidence obtained from other procedures may increase the acceptable level of sampling risk, but by how much is a matter of professional judgement.

There is one aspect that is overseen in these paragraphs. Sampling risk also depends on the number and size of the deviations or misstatements found. These are quantities that are not known when planning the sample, and we have already discussed the concept of expected misstatement to cater for a small rate of deviation or amount of misstatement, as long as it is not too close to the levels that are 'tolerable'.

From a statistical point of view, there is no necessity to formulate any requirements with regard to the sample size. As long as samples are evaluated using 'probability theory to evaluate sample results, including measurement of sampling risk' (see the definition of statistical sampling in 530.5(g)), a sample of any size can be drawn. It would just follow that if a sample was too small, sampling risk would be too large, and vice versa.

However, the Standards do not require that samples are evaluated this way. The Standards do not make a distinction between statistical and non-statistical samples. Since sampling risk cannot be measured for non-statistical samples, the only way to determine sample size and evaluate samples is to first determine the required sample size given an expected rate of deviation or amount of misstatement, then auditing the sample, and finally comparing the sample deviation rate or projected misstatement with the expected rate or amount.

Sample size calculation varies between sampling methods. It is least complicated for an attribute sample with no expected deviation rate, and most complicated for a stratified classical variables sample. The level of complication of other sampling methods (monetary unit sampling, double sampling, attribute sampling with expected misstatement) is somewhere in between these two extremes.

Given the differences there are some commonalities. The factors in Appendices 2 and 3 apply regardless of the sampling method used.

For tests of controls, the Standard recognises that the extent to which the auditor wants to rely on the control has an effect on the required sample size: the more reliance wanted, the higher the sample size.

The desired level of assurance also has an effect. The higher this level, the lower the sampling risk (level of assurance and sampling risk are each other's complement). In practice, we do not see different levels of assurance for samples for effectiveness of controls. Different levels do exist for substantive samples, where the level of assurance is dependent on the assessment of the risk of material misstatement and on the use of other substantive procedures directed at the same assertion.

The tolerable rate of deviation and the tolerable misstatement also have a direct effect on the sample size: the higher the tolerable rate of deviation or tolerable misstatement, the lower the sample size. As discussed before, the expected levels have an opposite effect: as the expected rate of deviation or the expected misstatement increase, so increases the sample size.

Stratification may decrease the required sample size if it reduces variance. It typically is done for classical variables samples and to some extent for non-statistical samples (that use elements of classical variables sampling in the projection of results), but rarely in monetary unit samples, where the variability in recorded values is addressed by a weighted selection technique.

Finally, the number of monetary units in a population has barely any effect on the sample size. Only if the total number of items is small there is a discernible difference, but as the number of population elements increases, the sample size tapers off to a constant. For substantive samples, the total number of elements in the population may have no or little effect on the sample size, the total monetary size does have an effect: for example, in monetary unit sampling, if the population value is doubled, the required sample size is doubled, all other parameters being held constant.

We can look at the effect of each of these factors for the least complicated sampling methods, attribute sampling. Particularly in its barest form, discovery sampling, where the expected deviation rate is zero, the calculations can be performed manually or with Microsoft Excel^{TM}.

In discovery sampling, we conclude on a population if the sample yields no deviations, and the sample may be inconclusive if it reveals deviations. Since the auditor wants to control the risk of inadvertent reliance, the sample size is set such that the probability of finding no deviations from a population that contains too many deviations (more than what is tolerable) is acceptable.

Let's assume the population contains 10,000 instances of a control, and that the tolerable deviation rate is 10 per cent. In other words, if the population contains more than 1,000 deviations, then the auditor would like to run not more than a certain acceptable risk of finding no deviations in the sample.

Start with a sample size of 1. If the population contains an unacceptable deviation rate (10.01 per cent or more), then the probability of finding no deviation is 89.99 per cent. This is the risk of incorrect acceptance for a sample of size one.

In most cases, a risk of this level is too high. To reduce the risk, the auditor can increase the sample size. If we increase the sample size to two, the chance of finding two instances without deviation is now:

$$\frac{8,999}{10,000} \times \frac{8,998}{9,999} = 80.98\%$$

ILLUSTRATION 8.A.1

IDEA Audit Software Screen to Determine Sample Size

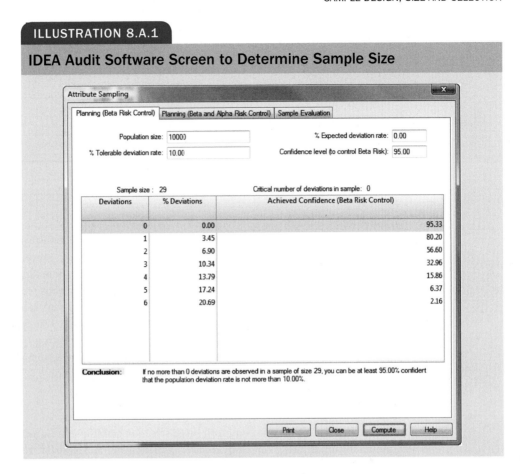

Continue this process until the sampling risk is below the acceptable level. For example, if the acceptable level is 5 per cent, the required sample size is 28.

Commercial audit sampling software, like Caseware IDEA™, has specific routines to calculate sample sizes. Illustration 8.A.1 shows a screen shot from the Attribute Sampling routine in IDEA.

To see the effect of changes in any of the parameters, we apply the same logic with different inputs. If we change the tolerable deviation rate from 10 per cent to 5 per cent, the required sample size increases to 59. Reducing the confidence level to 90 per cent (which is synonymous with increasing the acceptable sampling risk to 10 per cent), reduces the sample size to 22. Increasing the expected deviation rate from 0 per cent to 2 percent increases the sample size to 46. And finally, reducing the population size to 5,000 has no effect at all on the sample size. If we were to further reduce it to 1,000, the sample size is reduced to 28. Table 8.A.1 summarises these results.

■ Selection of Items for Testing (530.8 and 530.A12)

The requirement in 530.8 is clear: if the auditor wants to extend a conclusion from his test of a sample over the entire population, no parts from that population should be excluded from the selection process.

Table 8.A.1

Population size	Tolerable deviation rate	Acceptable sampling risk	Expected deviation rate	Sample size
10,000	10%	5%	0%	29
10,000	5%	5%	0%	59
10,000	10%	10%	0%	22
10,000	10%	5%	2%	46
5,000	10%	5%	0%	29
1,000	10%	5%	0%	28

The additional guidance in 530.A12 is clear for statistical samples. If the sample is drawn randomly (see 530.5(g)), then the sampling units have known selection probabilities. These probabilities are uniform (within a stratum) when it comes to random sampling, and proportional to the size (book value) of the sampling units when applying monetary unit sampling.

In contrast, it is challenging to understand what the Standard means when judgement is used to select sample items for non-statistical sampling. It is true that it is important that the auditor selects a representative sample, but there is no way to ascertain that a sample is representative of the population from which it was drawn (without testing 100 per cent of the population). Even when the auditor consciously avoids bias in the selection, academic studies have shown that there is a concern for unconscious bias in the selection.

■ Selection techniques (530.A13 and Appendix 4)

Systematic selection is the most commonly used selection technique. It is easily applied manually, automatically filtering out individually significant items. However, reducing the total number of possible samples introduces variation in the sampling risk. It is therefore recommended (not by the Standard, but by us) that the population is put into random order before the selection procedure is applied.

The following example explains this. Let's take the data from the bottom row of Table 8.A.1. There we found that a sample of 28 sampling units would be sufficient to reduce the acceptable sampling risk to below 5 per cent. In other words, if the true population deviation rate is 10 per cent, at least 95 per cent of all possible samples would yield a reject conclusion (at least one deviation would be found in the sample), and not more than 5 per cent of the samples would yield an accept conclusion.

We can now look at this problem from another perspective: we have a population of all possible samples, of which 95 per cent are 'good' and 5 per cent are 'bad'. When we apply systematic selection, we limit ourselves to only a subset of all possible samples. With a sample size of 28, the sampling interval is $1,000 \div 28 = 35$, so there are only 35 different samples, one for every random start. How many of these 35 samples are 'good' and how many are 'bad'? That depends on the particular order of the 1,001 deviations in the population. If the first 35 items in the population are deviations, then each of the 35 possible samples will yield at least one deviation and all 35 samples are 'good'. Sampling risk is reduced to zero. But if all control deviations occur in the first half of the sampling interval, half of our samples will be 'good' and the other half will be 'bad'. In that case sampling risk has increased to 50 per cent!

The Standards warn against a pattern of error in the population, and we agree. But we also warn against the random distribution of the deviations. If we take 35 random samples out of a very large (the number of possible samples has 54 digits) population of all possible samples, then there is a 16.6 per cent chance that no samples are 'bad' (for a real sampling risk of 0 per cent), a 30.6 per cent chance that one sample is 'bad' (the real sampling risk then is $1 \div 35$ or 2.9 per cent), etc. Table 8.A.2 summarises these results.

Table 8.A.2

Number of bad samples	Probability (A)	Real sampling risk (B)	(A) × (B)	Cumulative
0	16.6%	0.0%	0.0%	0.0%
1	30.6%	2.9%	0.9%	0.9%
2	27.4%	5.7%	1.6%	2.4%
3	15.8%	8.6%	1.4%	3.8%
4	6.7%	11.4%	0.8%	4.6%
5	2.2%	14.3%	0.3%	4.9%
6	0.6%	17.1%	0.1%	5.0%
7	0.1%	20.0%	0.0%	5.0%

We see in this example that on average sampling risk is 5 per cent. This is the expected value of sampling risk given the probability of including a certain number of 'bad' samples, but, practically, sampling risk can range between 0 per cent and 14.3 per cent, and in some cases could be even more. It is for this reason that we recommend that the population is shuffled into a random order prior to the systematic selection process. Alternatively, statistical software can be employed to draw items randomly using a more robust selection mechanism.

8.A.5 Performing Audit Procedures (530.9)

The requirement in 530.9 may seem obvious, but what should the auditor do if the audit procedure is not applicable to a selected sampling unit, or if the auditor is unable to apply the designed procedures? The next two paragraphs deal with these situations.

Paragraphs 530.10 and 530.A14 deal with a situation when a sampling frame is used that doesn't match the population about which the auditor wants to draw a conclusion. In the example, the sampling frame contains sampling units that are not relevant for the test. In such cases the sampling unit should be discarded and replaced with another sampling unit.

530.11 If the auditor is unable to apply the designed audit procedures, or suitable alternative procedures, to a selected item, the auditor shall treat that item as a deviation from the prescribed control, in the case of tests of controls, or a misstatement, in the case of tests of details.

530.A15 An example of when the auditor is unable to apply the designed audit procedures to a selected item is when documentation relating to that item has been lost.

530.A16 An example of a suitable alternative procedure might be the examination of subsequent cash receipts together with evidence of their source and the items they are intended to settle when no reply has been received in response to a positive confirmation request.

The situations described by 530.11 and 530.A15 deal with cases when the selected sampling unit is part of the population about which the auditor wants to draw a conclusion. If it is not possible to obtain sufficient appropriate audit evidence for this sampling unit, it is not allowed (contrary to the situation in 530.10) to discard the sampling unit and replace it with another sampling unit. The auditor should evaluate the sample as if the selected item were a deviation or a misstatement. This will provide the auditor with a worst case scenario. Of course it doesn't imply that the item is a deviation or a misstatement. It means that there are parts of the financial statements for which the auditor may not be able to obtain sufficient appropriate audit evidence. Treating the sampling unit as a deviation or misstatement implies that the auditor may not have obtained sufficient audit evidence.

8.A.6 Nature and Cause of Deviations (530.12 and 530.A17)

The next few paragraphs deal with the nature and cause of the deviations or misstatements identified. This is an important section from an auditing point of view. When following the requirements and guidance in these paragraphs, the auditor extends the knowledge gained in the sample from the simple occurrence to the cause, thus broadening the basis of his judgement to arrive at the correct conclusion. A mere mathematical treatment of the audit evidence is not sufficient.

Stratification may be applied ex-post, that is, after the initial sample has revealed that errors may be concentrated in one or more sub-populations. It is, however, not sufficient to just stratify, as this will barely change the projected misstatement, nor the allowance for sampling risk. The Standard suggests that audit procedures be extended in the high-error strata. Only then will the overall estimate be more precise.

It may also make sense to consider extending audit procedures in the 'clean' part of the population, for example if the initial sample underrepresented that part, but also to provide further supporting evidence for the stratification applied.

Paragraph 530.13 discusses an extreme example of post-stratification: the auditor believes that the misstatement or deviation could only have occurred in the sampled item. The Standards now require the auditor to confirm this belief by obtaining a high degree of certainty that similar misstatements or deviations did not occur in the remainder of the population.

8.A.7 Projecting Misstatements (530.14 and 530.A18)

In monetary unit sampling, for every single selected sampling unit an audit value is established, and compared to the book value. The difference between the book value and the audit value is calculated, and then expressed relative to the book value (the 'tainting'). If the book value equals the audit value, the item is correct and the tainting is 0 per cent. If the audit value is zero, the sampling unit is entirely incorrect, and its tainting is 100 per cent.

The projected misstatement is calculated by adding all taintings and multiplying the result with the sampling interval, which is the value of the population divided by the sample size. Audit software is usually used to make these calculations. They also calculate the allowance for sampling risk, a measure that represents the uncertainty about the estimate. The sum of projected misstatement and allowance for sampling risk is the upper precision limit, a worst-case assessment of the possible misstatement in the population.

If the upper precision limit is lower than the tolerable misstatement, the auditor can conclude that the population does not contain a misstatement the size of tolerable misstatement. If both projected misstatement and upper precision limit are greater than the tolerable misstatement, the auditor has gathered convincing evidence that the population contains a material misstatement. If the projected misstatement is less than the tolerable misstatement, and the upper precision limit is greater than the tolerable misstatement, the sample is inconclusive. In that case the auditor has to gather additional evidence to support a conclusion. Please refer to ISA 450 'Evaluation of Misstatements Identified during the Audit' (and Chapter 10 'Audit Evidence').

In classical variables sampling, different calculations are used, based on the assumption that the sample average is normally distributed. This usually translates to the requirement of having observed 20 or more misstatements, or alternatively uses a very large sample size. The requirement of observing 20 or more differences protects the auditor against the risk of underestimating the allowance for sampling risk.

Non-statistical samples can only be evaluated as a classical variables sample, and has haphazard selection as an additional disadvantage. This implies that a reasonable estimate of the allowance for sampling risk cannot be made if fewer than 20 misstatements were observed.

The projection of misstatements in classical variables sampling (and therefore also non-statistical sampling) can be explained with the following example. A population consists of 11,449 elements with a total book value of $522,800. The population is split into two sub-populations, one containing 2,613 elements with a higher than average value, the other containing the remaining 8,836 elements.

The auditor sampled 171 sampling units from the upper stratum and 86 from the lower stratum. The total misstatement in the top stratum adds to $429.24, in the bottom stratum to $33.13. Illustration 8.A.2 demonstrates the projection of the misstatements found using the ratio estimation method (Panel A) and difference method (Panel B) of projection.

ILLUSTRATION 8.A.2

Error Projection

Panel A Ratio Estimation Method

Stratum	Error found (A)	Book value of sampled items (B)	Error ratio (C) = (A)/(B)	Total book value in stratum (D)	Projected error (C) × (D)
Lower	33.13	1,650.20	2.0076%	159,222.33	3,196.60
Upper	429.24	24,261.28	1.7692%	363,577.67	6,432.56
Total				522,800.00	9,629.16

Panel B Difference Method

Stratum	Error found (A)	Sample size (B)	Average error (C) = (A)/(B)	Total number of items in stratum (D)	Projected error (C) × (D)
Lower	33.13	86	0.38523	8,836	3,403.91
Upper	429.24	171	2.51018	2,613	6,559.09
Total				11,449	9,963.00

8.A.8   Evaluating Results of Audit Sampling (530.15 and 530.A21-23)

The requirements and guidance provided with regard to the evaluation of results is applicable to both non-statistical and statistical sampling. Even though the auditor may use the calculated allowance for sampling risk when using statistical sampling, the Standard doesn't provide additional requirements to do so.

In non-statistical sampling, it is not possible to calculate the allowance for sampling risk. Assuming that the sample size is determined correctly using a certain expected misstatement, it could be implied that if the projected misstatement is less than or equal to the expected misstatement the sample has achieved its objective and the population can be concluded on.

In addition to the quantitative aspects of the misstatements found, ISA 450.A16 cites a list of factors that might cause the auditor to evaluate a misstatement as material:

Questions, Exercises and Cases

Questions

8A-1 Name the factors that an auditor typically takes into consideration when determining the necessary sample size.

8A-2 What is the difference between the significance level of a test and the power of a test?

8A-3 Is Type II error also part of the audit risk?

8A-4 When projecting errors for a non-statistical sampling method, the auditor can choose between extrapolating over the number of items in the population and extrapolating over the book value in the population. Typically, these methods will generate different results. Under which circumstances will the results be the same?

8A-5 Why is it difficult to determine the sample size for the estimate of the population error with a given confidence and pre-determined precision.

8A-6 To determine the completeness of accounts payable at year-end, the auditor decides to define the sampling population as the payments after year-end. Why does this test have limited value?

8A-7 What are the requirements for a representative sampling technique to qualify as a 'statistical' sample?

8A-8 Appendix 2 of ISA 530 lists a number of factors that influence sample size. Are these factors only relevant for statistical samples?

8A-9 Some people claim that an audit risk of 5 per cent implies that 5 per cent of financial statements with unqualified opinions contain material errors. What is your view on this?

Exercises

8A-10 Sampling for attributes is often used to allow an auditor to reach a conclusion concerning a rate of occurrence in a population. A common use in auditing is to test the rate of deviation from a prescribed internal control procedure to determine whether the planned assessed level of control risk is appropriate.

Required:
A. When an auditor samples for attributes, identify the factors that should influence the auditor's judgement concerning the determination of:
   1 acceptable level of risk of assessing control risk too low;
   2 tolerable deviation rate; and
   3 expected population deviation rate.
B. State the effect on sample size of an increase in each of the following factors, assuming all other factors are held constant:
   1 acceptable level of risk of assessing control risk too low;
   2 tolerable deviation rate; and
   3 expected population deviation rate.
C. Evaluate the sample results of a test for attributes if authorisations are found to be missing on seven check requests out of a sample of 100 tested. The population consists of 2,500 check requests, the tolerable deviation rate is 8 per cent, and the acceptable level of risk of assessing control risk too low is considered to be low.
D. How may the use of statistical sampling assist the auditor in evaluating the sample results described in C above?

[Adapted and reprinted with permission from AICPA. Copyright © 2000 & 1985 by the American Institute of Certified Public Accountants.]

8A–11 Rong & Wright, CA, of Hong Kong has decided to rely on an audit client's affecting receivables. Rong & Wright plans to use sampling to obtain substantive evidence concerning the reasonableness of the client's accounts receivable balances. Rong & Wright has identified the first few steps in an outline of the sampling plan as follows.

1 Determine the audit objectives of the test.
2 Define the population.
3 Define the sampling unit.
4 Consider the completeness of the population.
5 Identify individually significant items.

Required:

Identify the remaining steps which Rong & Wright should include in the outline of the sampling plan.

[Adapted and reprinted with permission from AICPA. Copyright © 2000 & 1985 by the American Institute of Certified Public Accountants.]

8.A.10   Notes

1. Lucas Hoogduin works at the Global Services Centre of KPMG LLP in Montvale, NJ. This appendix represents the views of the author(s) only, and does not necessarily represent the views or professional advice of KPMG LLP.

2. Performance materiality – the amount or amounts set by the auditor at less than materiality for the financial statements as a whole to reduce to an appropriately low level the probability that the aggregate of uncorrected and undetected misstatements exceeds materiality for the financial statements as a whole. If applicable, performance materiality also refers to the amount or amounts set by the auditor at less than the materiality level or levels for particular classes of transactions, account balances or disclosures.

3. In the field of inventory management, a stock-keeping unit or SKU is a term used (generally) by businesses as part of the process of keeping track of what they have available to sell. SKU can also refer to a unique identifier or code that refers to the items or products they have available for sale. Each SKU is attached to an item, variant, product line, bundle, service, fee, or attachment. SKUs are often used to refer to different versions of the same product.

4. Variables sampling – sampling designed to predict the value of a given variable for a population. The variables under audit are typically the total population or the arithmetic mean. An example is the CPA's estimation of the cost of a group of inventory components.

Chapter 9

AUDITOR'S RESPONSE TO ASSESSED RISK (ISA 330, ISA 500)

9.1 Learning Objectives

After studying this chapter, you should be able to:

1 List audit procedures responsive to assessed risk.

2 Know the definition of evidence in an audit and legal sense.

3 Differentiate between nature, extent and timing of audit procedures.

4 Understand the difference between legal evidence and audit evidence.

5 Identify the common management assertions for classes of transactions, account balances and disclosure.

6 Define the management standard assertions: completeness, occurrence, accuracy, rights and obligations, valuation, existence, cut-off, classification, understanding, presentation and disclosure, and measurement.

7 Discuss the systematic process of gathering evidence.

8 Recognise tests of controls for design and effectiveness.

9 Charaterise a substantive procedure.

10 Explain what is meant by the nature, timing and extent of substantive procedures.

11 List and define the two types of substantive procedure.

12 Realise the process of search for unrecorded liabilities.

13 Describe the components of and the meaning of 'sufficient appropriate audit evidence'.

14 Determine which evidence is relevant and which evidence is reliable.

Evidence-gathering procedures in auditing are directed by the assessment of risk of material misstatement. ISA 330 states,[1] 'The objective of the auditor is to obtain sufficient appropriate audit evidence regarding the assessed risks of material misstatement, through designing and implementing appropriate responses to those risks.'

■ Audit Procedures Responsive to the Assessed Risks of Material Misstatement at the Assertion Level

To meet this objective of obtaining sufficient appropriate audit evidence, the auditor must design and perform audit procedures whose nature, timing and extent are based on, and are responsive to, the assessed risks. The nature of an audit procedure refers to its purpose (that is, test of controls or substantive procedure) and its type (that is, inspection, observation, inquiry, confirmation, recalculation, re-performance or analytical procedure). The nature of the audit procedures is of most importance in responding to the assessed risks. Timing of an audit procedure refers to when it is performed, or the period or date to which the audit evidence applies.[2] Extent of an audit procedure refers to the quantity to be performed, for example a sample size or the number of observations of a control activity.

Designing and performing further audit procedures whose nature, timing and extent are based on and are responsive to the assessed risks of material misstatement at the assertion level provides a clear linkage between the auditor's further audit procedures and the risk assessment.

The auditor's assessment of the identified risks at the assertion level provides a basis for considering the appropriate audit approach for designing and performing further audit procedures. For example, the auditor may determine that only by performing tests of controls she can achieve an effective response to the assessed risk of misstatement for a particular assertion.[3] Or the auditor may find that performing only substantive procedures is appropriate for particular assertions and, therefore, she excludes the effect of controls from the relevant risk assessment. This may be because the auditor's risk assessment procedures have not identified any effective controls relevant to the assertion, or because testing controls would be inefficient and therefore the auditor does not intend to rely on the operating effectiveness of controls in determining the nature, timing and extent of substantive procedures. Of course, the auditor may try a combined approach using both tests of controls and substantive procedures. Irrespective of the approach selected, however, the auditor designs and performs substantive procedures for each material class of transactions, account balance and disclosure.

Overall responses to address the assessed risks of material misstatement at the financial statement level may include:

- Emphasising to the engagement team the need to maintain professional scepticism.
- Assigning more experienced staff or those with special skills or using experts.
- Providing more supervision.
- Incorporating additional elements of unpredictability in the selection of further audit procedures to be performed.
- Making general changes to the nature, timing or extent of audit procedures, for example: performing substantive procedures at the period end instead of at an interim date; or modifying the nature of audit procedures to obtain more persuasive audit evidence.

■ Reasons for Risk Assessment

When she designs these audit procedures to be performed, the auditor should consider the reasons for the assessment including: the likelihood of material misstatement due to inherent risk and whether the risk assessment takes account of relevant controls (that is, the control risk), thereby obtaining audit evidence to determine whether the controls are operating effectively. Such considerations have a significant bearing on the auditor's general approach; for example, an emphasis on substantive procedures (substantive approach), or an approach that uses tests of controls as well as substantive procedures (combined approach). By using an approach of gathering evidence by testing controls, the auditor is lowering the control risk. This allows the auditor to accept a higher detection risk, which allows the auditor to reduce the evidence needed from substantive procedures. This also applies the other way around. The auditor can accept a high control risk by not testing controls. This needs to be compensated by reducing the detection risk. In order to have a low detection risk, the auditor needs to gather relatively more evidence from performing substantive procedures.

The assessment of the risks of material misstatement at the financial statement level, and thereby the auditor's overall responses, is affected by the auditor's understanding of the control environment. An effective control environment may allow the auditor to have more confidence in internal control and the reliability of audit evidence generated internally within the entity and thus, for example, allow the auditor to conduct some audit procedures at an interim date rather than at the period end. Deficiencies in the control environment, however, have the opposite effect; for example, the auditor may respond to an ineffective control environment by:

- Conducting more audit procedures as of the period end rather than at an interim date.
- Obtaining more extensive audit evidence from substantive procedures.
- Increasing the number of locations to be included in the audit scope.

The higher the auditor's assessment of risk, the more persuasive audit evidence she needs. When obtaining more persuasive audit evidence because of a higher assessment of risk, the auditor may increase the quantity of the evidence, or obtain evidence that is more relevant or reliable, for example by placing more emphasis on obtaining third-party evidence or by obtaining corroborating evidence from a number of independent sources.

The auditor must consider all relevant audit evidence, regardless of whether it appears to corroborate or to contradict the assertions in the financial statements (completeness of expense, existence of revenue, etc.). If the auditor is unable to obtain sufficient appropriate audit evidence, the auditor must express a qualified opinion or disclaim an opinion on the financial statements.

Documentation in Workpapers of Responses to Assessed Risk

The auditor must include in the audit documentation the overall responses to address the assessed risks of material misstatement and the nature, timing and extent of the further audit procedures performed. The auditor should also document the linkage of those procedures with the assessed risks at the assertion level; and the results of the audit procedures, including the conclusions where these are not otherwise clear.

9.3 The Basis of Evidence

Evidence is anything that can make a person believe that a fact, proposition or assertion is true or false. Audit evidence is information used by the auditor in arriving at the conclusions on which the auditor's opinion is based.[4] Audit evidence includes both information contained in the accounting records underlying the financial statements and other information. Auditors are not expected to address all information that may exist. Audit evidence, which is cumulative in nature, includes audit evidence obtained from audit procedures performed during the course of the audit and may include audit evidence obtained from other sources such as previous audits and a firm's quality control procedures for client acceptance and continuance. Audit evidence is different from the legal evidence required by **forensic accounting**.[5]

Evidence for proof of audit assertions is different from evidence in a legal sense. Audit evidence needs only to prove reasonable assurance, whereas in a legal environment there is a more rigorous standard of proof and documentation (see Illustration 9.1).

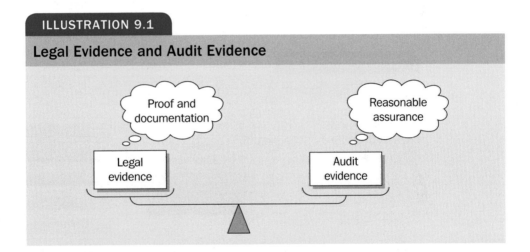

ILLUSTRATION 9.1

Legal Evidence and Audit Evidence

■ Electronic Evidence

Some of the entity's accounting data and other information may be available only in electronic form. For example, entities may use electronic data interchange (EDI) or image processing systems. In EDI, the entity and its customers or suppliers use communication links to transact business electronically. Purchase, shipping, billing, cash receipt and cash disbursement transactions are often consummated entirely by the exchange of electronic messages between the parties. In image processing systems, documents are scanned and converted into electronic images to facilitate storage and reference, and the source documents may not be retained after conversion. Certain electronic information may exist at a certain point in time, but may not be retrievable after a specified period of time if files are changed and if back-up files do not exist. The electronic nature of the accounting documentation usually requires that the auditor use computer-assisted audit techniques (CAATs).

9.4 Financial Statement Assertions

Management is responsible for the fair presentation of financial statements so that they reflect the nature and operations of the company based on the applicable financial reporting framework (IAS, GAAP, etc.). Management prepares the financial statements based upon the accounting records and other information, such as minutes of meetings; confirmations from third parties; analysts' reports; comparable data about competitors (benchmarking); and controls manuals. The auditor is likely to use the accounting records and that other information as audit evidence. In representing that the financial statements are in accordance with the applicable financial reporting framework, management implicitly or explicitly makes assertions regarding the recognition, measurement, presentation and disclosure of the various elements of financial statements and related disclosures.

Management makes assertions that can be grouped into three groups: (1) assertions about classes of transactions and events for the period under audit; (2) assertions about account balances at the period end; and (3) assertions about presentation and disclosure. Illustration 9.2 makes a graphic presentation of the areas and assertions. Assertions are representations by management, explicit or otherwise, that are embodied in the financial statements, as used by the auditor to consider the different types of potential

ILLUSTRATION 9.2

Financial Statement Assertions Grouped by Substantive Test Areas

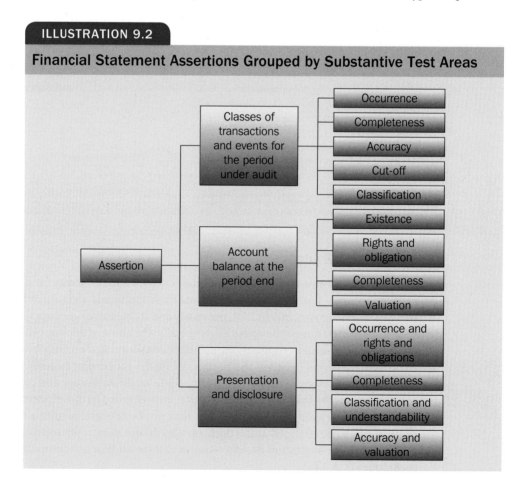

misstatements that may occur.[6] The standard assertions are occurrence, completeness, accuracy, cut-off, classification, existence, rights and obligations, valuation and allocation, and understandability. The auditor assesses risks of potential misstatements based on these assertions and designs audit procedures to discover sufficient appropriate evidence.

Standard Assertions

Auditors have identified several assertions that management makes, directly or indirectly, relating to the financial statements. The standard assertions are occurrence, completeness, accuracy, cut-off, classification, existence, rights and obligations, valuation and allocation, and understandability. In each of the three groups, the assertions are defined differently and sometimes combined; Illustration 9.3 gives the definitions of the management assertions by group.[7]

Audit evidence comprises both information that supports and corroborates management's assertions, and any information that contradicts such assertions.

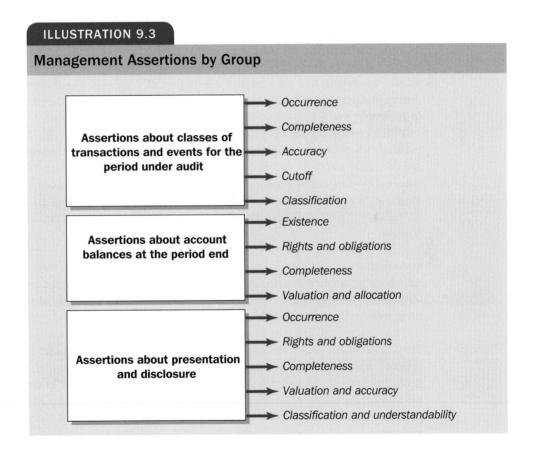

ILLUSTRATION 9.3

Management Assertions by Group

Assertions about classes of transactions and events for the period under audit
- Occurrence
- Completeness
- Accuracy
- Cutoff
- Classification

Assertions about account balances at the period end
- Existence
- Rights and obligations
- Completeness
- Valuation and allocation

Assertions about presentation and disclosure
- Occurrence
- Rights and obligations
- Completeness
- Valuation and accuracy
- Classification and understandability

9.5 Test of Controls

Test of controls are audit procedures designed to evaluate the operating effectiveness of controls in preventing, or detecting and correcting, material misstatements at the assertion level.[8] Designing tests of controls to obtain relevant audit evidence includes identifying conditions (characteristics or attributes) that indicate performance of a control, and deviation conditions which indicate departures from adequate performance. The presence or absence of those conditions can then be tested by the auditor. The auditor must design and perform tests of controls to obtain sufficient appropriate audit evidence as to the operating effectiveness of relevant controls if she assumes that the controls are operating effectively or substantive procedures alone would be inadequate to get sufficient evidence.

The auditor will perform other audit procedures in combination with inquiry to obtain audit evidence about the operating effectiveness of the controls, including details about how the controls were applied at relevant times during the period under audit; the consistency with which they were applied, and by whom or by what means they were applied. The auditor must also determine whether the controls to be tested depend upon other controls (indirect controls), and, if so, whether it is necessary to obtain audit evidence supporting the effective operation of those indirect controls.

The auditor tests controls for the particular time, or throughout the period, for which the auditor intends to rely on those controls. Audit evidence pertaining only to a point in time may be sufficient for the auditor's purpose, for example, when testing controls over the entity's physical inventory counting at the period end. If, on the other hand, the auditor intends to rely on a control over a period, tests of the control at relevant times during that period are appropriate. Such tests may include tests of the entity's monitoring of controls.

When evaluating the operating effectiveness of relevant controls, the auditor must evaluate whether misstatements that have been detected by substantive procedures indicate that controls are not operating effectively. The absence of misstatements detected by substantive procedures, however, does not mean that controls related to the assertion being tested are effective. A material misstatement detected by the auditor's procedures is a strong indicator of the existence of a significant deficiency in internal control.

If deviations from controls upon which the auditor intends to rely are detected, the auditor must make specific inquiries and determine whether the tests of controls that have been performed provide an appropriate basis for reliance on the controls. He must also determine if additional tests of controls are necessary or potential risks of misstatement need to be addressed using substantive procedures.

The concept of effectiveness of the operation of controls recognises that some deviations in the way controls are applied may occur. Deviations from prescribed controls may be caused by such factors as changes in key personnel, significant seasonal fluctuations in volume of transactions and human error. The detected rate of deviation, in particular in comparison with the expected rate, may indicate that the control cannot be relied on to reduce risk at the assertion level to that assessed by the auditor.

■ Designing and Performing Tests of Controls

Tests of controls are performed only on those controls that the auditor has determined are suitably designed to prevent, or detect and correct, a material misstatement in an assertion. If substantially different controls were used at different times during the period under audit, each is considered separately. In designing and performing tests of controls, the auditor shall obtain more persuasive audit evidence the greater the reliance the auditor places on the effectiveness of a control.

Testing the operating effectiveness of controls is different from obtaining an understanding of and evaluating the design and implementation of controls. However, the same types of audit procedures are used. The auditor may test the operating effectiveness of controls at the same time as evaluating their design and implementation. Although some risk assessment procedures may not have been specifically designed as tests of controls, they may nevertheless provide audit evidence about the operating effectiveness of the controls and, consequently, serve as tests of controls. For example, the auditor's risk assessment procedures may have included inquiring about management's use of budgets, observing management's comparison of monthly budgeted and actual expenses, and inspecting reports about the variances between budgeted and actual amounts. These audit procedures provide knowledge about budgeting policies and whether they have been implemented, but may also provide audit evidence about the effectiveness of the operation of budgeting policies in preventing or detecting material misstatements in the classification of expenses.

In some cases, the auditor may find it impossible to design effective substantive procedures that by themselves provide sufficient appropriate audit evidence. This may occur when an entity conducts its business using IT and no documentation of transactions is produced or maintained, other than through the IT system. In such cases, the auditor is required to perform tests of relevant controls.

■ Nature and Extent of Tests of Controls

The nature of the particular control influences the type of procedure required to obtain audit evidence about whether the control was operating effectively. For example, if operating effectiveness is evidenced by documentation, the auditor may decide to inspect the documents. For other controls, however, documentation may not be available or relevant. For example, documentation of operation may not exist for some factors such as assignment of authority and responsibility, or for some types of control activities, such as control activities performed by a computer. In such circumstances, audit evidence about operating effectiveness may be obtained through inquiry in combination with other audit procedures such as observation or the use of computer assisted audit techniques[9] (CAATs).

Inquiry alone is not sufficient to test the operating effectiveness of controls so other audit procedures are performed in combination with inquiry, for instance inquiry combined with inspection or re-performance may provide more assurance.

When more persuasive audit evidence is needed regarding the effectiveness of a control, the auditor increases the extent of testing of the control. As well as the degree of reliance on controls, matters the auditor may consider in determining the extent of tests of controls include the frequency of the performance of the control during the period, the expected rate of deviation from a control, the relevance and reliability of the audit evidence, and the extent to which audit evidence is obtained from tests of other controls.

Because of the inherent consistency of IT processing, it may not be necessary to increase the extent of testing of an automated control. An automated control can be expected to function consistently unless the program (including the tables, files or other permanent data used by the program) is changed. Once the auditor determines that an automated control is functioning as intended (which could be done at the time the control is initially implemented or at some other date), the auditor may consider performing tests to determine that the control continues to function effectively. Such tests might include determining that changes to the program are not made without being subject to the appropriate program change controls and the authorised version of the program is used for processing transactions.

■ Using Previous Audit Evidence

In certain circumstances, audit evidence obtained from previous audits may provide audit evidence where the auditor may perform audit procedures to establish its continuing relevance. For example, in a previous audit, the auditor may have determined that an automated control was functioning as intended. The auditor may obtain audit evidence to determine whether changes to the automated control have been made that affect its continued effective functioning through, for example, inquiries of management and the inspection of logs to indicate what controls have been changed.

Changes may affect the relevance of the audit evidence obtained in previous audits such that there may no longer be a basis for continued reliance. For example, changes in a system that enable an entity to receive a new report from the system probably do not affect the relevance of audit evidence from a previous audit; however, a change that causes data to be accumulated or calculated differently does affect it.

The auditor depends on professional judgement in deciding on whether to rely on audit evidence obtained in previous audits for controls that have not changed since they were last tested and are not controls that mitigate a significant risk. However, ISA 330[10] requires controls to be retested at least once in every third year. Factors that may decrease the period for retesting a control, or result in not relying on audit evidence obtained in previous audits at all, include the following:

- A deficient control environment.
- Deficient monitoring of controls.
- A significant manual element to the relevant controls.
- Personnel changes that significantly affect the application of the control.
- Changing circumstances that indicate the need for changes in the control.
- Deficient general IT controls.

9.6 Substantive Procedures

The main work of an auditor is to find evidence using test procedures. A substantive procedure is an audit procedure designed to detect material misstatements at the assertion level. Substantive procedures comprise: (1) tests of details (of classes of transactions, account balances and disclosures); and (2) substantive analytical procedures.

Audit evidence is the information used by the auditor in arriving at the conclusions on which the audit opinion is based. Audit evidence consists of source documents and accounting records underlying the financial statements and corroborating information from other sources and can be gathered by tests of controls as well as substantive procedures.

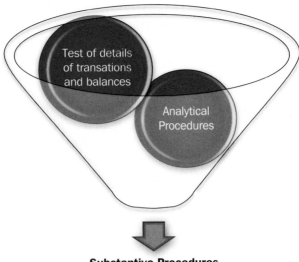

Substantive Procedures

This chapter provides guidance on the basis of evidence (**standards of proof** and documentation and financial statement assertions), what constitutes sufficient appropriate audit evidence (the quantity and quality of audit evidence) and the **substantive audit procedures** that auditors use for obtaining that audit evidence.[11]

Substantive procedures are tests performed to obtain audit evidence to detect material misstatements or significant misstatements that may in aggregate be material in the financial statements. Substantive procedures are responses to the auditor's assessment of the risk of material misstatement. The higher the assessed risk, the more likely the extent of the substantive procedures will increase and the timing of procedures will be performed close to the period.

Irrespective of the assessed risks of material misstatement, the auditor should design and perform substantive procedures for all relevant assertions related to each material class of transactions, account balance and disclosure.[12] Furthermore, if the auditor has determined that an assessed risk of material misstatement at the assertion level is a significant risk, the auditor should perform substantive procedures that are specifically responsive to that risk. For example, if there is a significant risk that management is inflating revenue to meet earnings expectations the auditor may design external confirmations (discussed in the next section) not only to confirm outstanding amounts, but also to confirm the details of the sales agreements, and then follow up those confirmations with inquiries regarding any changes in sales agreements and delivery terms.

■ Nature of Substantive Procedures

The nature of substantive procedures includes tests of details (of transactions and of balances) and substantive analytical procedures. The auditor's substantive procedures include agreeing the financial statements to the accounting records, examining material adjustments made during the course of preparing the financial statements, and other procedures relating to the financial reporting closing process. Substantive analytical procedures (discussed in Chapter 8 'Analytical Procedures') are generally more applicable to large volumes of transactions that tend to be predictable over time. Tests of details are ordinarily more appropriate to obtain audit evidence regarding certain financial statement assertions, including existence and valuation.

Tests of Balances

Tests of balances are substantive tests that provide either reasonable assurance of the validity of a general ledger balance or identify a misstatement in the account. When testing balances the auditor is concerned with overstatement or understatement of the line item in the financial statement. These tests are used to examine the actual details making up high turnover accounts such as cash, accounts receivable, accounts payable, etc. Tests of balances are important because the auditor's ultimate objective is to express an opinion on financial statements that are made up of account balances. In audits of small businesses, auditors may rely exclusively on tests of balances.

Illustration – Test of Accounts Receivable Balance

A test of balance may be illustrated as follows. If accounts receivable total €1,500,000 at the end of the year, tests of details may be made of the individual components of the total account. Assume that the accounts receivable control account balance of €1,500,000 is the total of 300 individual customer accounts. As a test of balances, an auditor might decide to confirm a sample of these 300 accounts. Based on an analysis of internal controls, the auditor may decide that the proper sample size should be 100 accounts that should be tested by confirmation. Thus the auditor tests the detail supporting the account to determine if the line item 'Accounts Receivable' is overstated – i.e. the existence of the accounts has been confirmed. As an additional test, the auditor may examine cash receipts received after year-end, testing for understatement, which provides evidence as to both the existence and measurement of the accounts.

Concept and a Company 9.1

Kmart Executives Manipulate the Contract Process

Concept	Side agreements that materially impact a company may be concealed.
Story	Kmart Corporation is a US discount retailer and a general merchandise retailer. The company operates in the general merchandise retailing industry through 1,829 Kmart discount stores with locations in all 50 states, Puerto Rico, the United States Virgin Islands and Guam. On 22 January 2002, Kmart and 37 of its US subsidiaries filed voluntary petitions for reorganisation under Chapter 11 of the federal bankruptcy laws.
	Just prior to the bankruptcy, two executives lied to Kmart accounting personnel and concealed a side letter relating to the $42 million payment from one of Kmart's vendors in order to improperly recognise the entire amount in the quarter ended 1 August 2001. Those deceptions caused Kmart to understate losses by the material amount of $0.06 per share, or 32 per cent (Merrick, 2003).

The Securities and Exchange Commission (SEC, 2003) filed civil charges against the two men responsible for this misstatement – Joseph A. Hofmeister and Enio A. Montini Jr. Montini and Hofmeister negotiated a five-year contract for which American Greetings paid Kmart an 'allowance' of $42,350,000 on 20 June 2001. The contract was for, among other things, exclusive rights to sell their product – greetings cards – in Kmart stores. American Greetings was to take over the 847 stores that were formerly supplied by Hallmark, the major competitor of American Greetings, at a rate of $50,000 per store. Under the terms of its 1997 contract with Hallmark, Kmart was obligated to repay a portion of certain prepaid allowances and other costs, and accordingly Kmart paid Hallmark $27,298,210 on or about 4 June 2001.

Accounting Makes a Difference in Bonus

Kmart classified these vendor allowances as a reduction in cost of goods sold in its statement of operations. One of the primary measures of performance for Montini and Hofmeister was contribution to gross margin. Because vendor allowances were generally accounted for as a reduction of cost of goods sold, this could help the two make their gross margin numbers and their bonuses. Montini also received an additional $750,000 forgivable cash loan after the deal was closed.

Secret Negotiations

Montini and Hofmeister conducted their negotiations with American Greetings in secret, excluding from the process key finance and accounting personnel. Since the accounting people had been frozen out of the negotiations, they depended on the two men to give them the details. Montini assured the Finance Divisional VP that there were 'no strings attached' to the $42 million. In fact, American Greetings had insisted that any and all up front monies be covered by a payback provision. American Greetings worried that, given Kmart's shaky financial condition, the retailer might not survive the contract term (SEC, 2003).

Montini had made two agreement letters with American Greetings. One agreement letter appeared to exclude the $42,350,000 from any repayment obligation. A second letter (the side letter) obligated Kmart to pay American Greetings 'liquidated damages' for early termination of the agreement. Montini and Hofmeister provided a copy of the signed 'No Strings Attached' letter, but not the 'Liquidated Damages' letter, to the Finance DVP and Internal Audit.

GAAP, as well as the company's own accounting policies and practices, required that the $42 million be recognised over the term of the agreement. Instead, Kmart improperly recognised the entire $42 million allowance during the quarter ended 1 August 2001; $27 million as an 'offset' to the payment to Hallmark and $15 million in 'incremental' merchandise allowances.

Discussion Questions	■ What procedures can Kmart's independent auditor use to uncover the side agreement? ■ What circumstances should have alerted Kmart's management and internal auditors to possible problems?
References	Merrick, A., 2003, 'Leading the News: US Indicts 2 Ex-Executives of Kmart Corp', *Wall Street Journal*, 27 February. SEC, 2003, Litigation Release No. 18000, 'SEC Charges Two Former Kmart Executives with $42 Million Accounting Fraud', US Securities and Exchange Commission, 26 February.

Test of Accounts Receivable = Test of Revenue

From this example we can see an interesting aspect of a test of balances, which is that the test makes use of the inherent properties of double-entry accounting systems. Accounting transactions involve a double entry. From the auditor's perspective, this means that a test of one side of the transaction simultaneously tests the other side of the transaction.

Direction of Testing

Testing for overstatement or understatement is called the direction of testing. By coordinating the direction of testing each account balance is simultaneously tested for both overstatement and understatement. For instance, if all liability, equity and revenue balances are tested for understatement and all asset and expense accounts are tested for overstatement, then all account balances in the balance sheet and the income statement will be tested, either directly or indirectly, for both overstatement and understatement.

Interim Testing Using Substantive Procedures

There are several considerations in determining the timing of substantive procedures. In some instances, primarily as a practical matter, substantive procedures may be performed at an interim date. Only using interim testing procedures will increase the risk that misstatements existing at the period end will not be detected. That risk increases the longer the time between interim and period end. If substantive procedures are performed at an interim date, the auditor must cover the remaining period by either performing substantive procedures combined with tests of controls for the intervening period or further substantive procedures only, as long as that will provide a reasonable basis for extending the audit conclusions from the interim date to the period end.[13]

Performing audit procedures at an interim date may assist the auditor in identifying and resolving issues at an early stage of the audit. Ordinarily, the auditor compares and reconciles information concerning the account balances at the period end with the comparable information at the interim date to identify amounts that appear unusual, investigates any such amounts, and performs substantive analytical procedures or tests of details to test the intervening period.

Extent of Substantive Procedures

The greater the risk of material misstatement, the greater the **extent** of substantive procedures. In planning tests of details of transactions or balances, the extent of testing is ordinarily thought of in terms of the sample size,[14] which is affected by the risk of material misstatement. The use of CAATs may enable more extensive testing of electronic transactions and files. For example, in performing audit procedures, such techniques may be used to test an entire population instead of a sample. Because the risk of material misstatement takes account of internal control, the extent of substantive procedures may be reduced if tests of control show that controls are adequate.

Test of Details: Search for Unrecorded Liabilities

A substantive test usually performed on accounts payable is a search for unrecorded liabilities. This test may be part of the closing procedures or done in concert with the confirmation of accounts payable. This test provides evidence as to completeness and some evidence as to valuation.

To search for unrecorded liabilities, the auditor reviews disbursements made by the client for a period after the balance sheet date, sometimes to the date of the completion of field work. Even though a client may not record accounts payable at year-end, vendors will probably pressure the client to pay the accounts payable within a reasonable period of time. Due to this pressure, most unrecorded accounts payable are paid within a reasonable time after the balance sheet date. By reviewing cash disbursements subsequent to the balance sheet date, the auditor has a good idea of the potential population of unrecorded accounts payable.

Procedures to find unrecorded liabilities start with a review of the cash disbursements journal for the period after the balance sheet date. The auditor then vouches a sample of invoices to determine to which period the payment relates. For example, vouching a January electricity payment to an unaccounted December bill will indicate that the payment relates to the period of December, prior to year-end. This would result in an unrecorded liability for which the auditor may propose an adjusting entry, if it is material.

9.7 Sufficient Appropriate Audit Evidence

According to ISA 500,[15] the objective of the auditor is to design and perform audit procedures in such a way as to enable the auditor to obtain sufficient appropriate audit evidence to be able to draw reasonable conclusions on which to base the auditor's opinion. As explained in ISA 200,[16] reasonable assurance is obtained when the auditor has obtained sufficient appropriate audit evidence to reduce audit risk (that is, the risk that the auditor expresses an inappropriate opinion when the financial statements are materially misstated) to an acceptably low level.

The sufficiency and appropriateness of audit evidence are interrelated. **Sufficiency** is the measure of the quantity of audit evidence. The quantity of audit evidence needed is affected by the auditor's assessment of the risks of misstatement (the higher the assessed risks, the more audit evidence is likely to be required) and also by the quality of such audit evidence (the higher the quality, the less may be required). Obtaining more audit evidence, however, may not compensate for its poor quality. **Appropriateness** is the measure of the quality of audit evidence; that is, its relevance and its reliability in providing support for the conclusions on which the auditor's opinion is based. The reliability of evidence is influenced by its source and by its nature, and is dependent on the individual circumstances under which it is obtained.

Audit evidence is necessary to support the auditor's opinion and report. It is cumulative in nature and is primarily obtained from audit procedures performed during the course of the audit. It may also include information obtained from other sources such as previous audits. In addition to other sources inside and outside the entity, the entity's accounting records are an important source of audit evidence. Audit evidence comprises both information that supports and corroborates management's assertions, and any information that contradicts such assertions. In addition, in some cases the absence of information (for example, management's refusal to provide a requested representation) is used by the auditor, and therefore also constitutes audit evidence.

Most of the auditor's work in forming the auditor's opinion consists of obtaining and evaluating audit evidence. Audit procedures to obtain audit evidence can include inspection, observation, confirmation, recalculation, re-performance and analytical procedures, often in some combination, in addition to inquiry. Although inquiry may provide important audit evidence, and may even produce evidence of a misstatement, inquiry alone ordinarily does not provide sufficient audit evidence of the absence of a material misstatement at the assertion level, nor of the operating effectiveness of controls.

ISA 330 requires the auditor to conclude whether sufficient appropriate audit evidence has been obtained.[17] Whether sufficient appropriate audit evidence has been obtained to reduce audit risk to an acceptably low level, and thereby enable the auditor to draw reasonable conclusions on which to base the auditor's opinion, is a matter of professional judgement. The auditor's judgement as to what constitutes sufficient appropriate audit evidence is influenced by such factors as:[18]

- the significance of the potential misstatement in the assertion and the likelihood of its having a material effect, individually or aggregated with other potential misstatements, on the financial statements: the more material the item, the greater the required sufficiency and appropriateness of evidence;
- the effectiveness of management's responses and controls to address the risks: strong controls reduce evidence requirements;
- the experience gained during previous audits with respect to similar potential misstatements: prior experience with the client will indicate how much evidence was taken before and if that was enough or appropriate;
- results of audit procedures performed, including whether such audit procedures identified specific instances of fraud or error;
- source and reliability of the available information;
- persuasiveness of the audit evidence;
- understanding of the entity and its environment, including its internal control.

Illustration 9.4 summarises the considerations for determining whether audit evidence is 'sufficient appropriate evidence'.

When designing and performing audit procedures, the auditor must consider the relevance and reliability of the information to be used as audit evidence. **Reliability** is the quality of information when it is free from material error and bias and can be depended upon by users to represent faithfully that which it either purports to represent or could reasonably be expected to represent. **Relevance of evidence** is the appropriateness (pertinence) of the evidence to the audit objective being tested. The quantity (relevance and reliability) of audit evidence needed is affected by the risk of misstatement (the greater the risk, the more audit evidence is required) and also by the quality of the audit evidence (the higher the quality of evidence, the less is required).[19] See Illustration 9.5.

■ Relevance

Relevance deals with the logical connection with, or bearing upon, the purpose of the audit procedure and the assertion under consideration. The relevance of information to be used as audit evidence may be affected by the direction of testing (overstatement or understatement of the account). For example, if the purpose of an audit procedure is to test for *overstatement* of accounts payable, testing the recorded accounts payable

ILLUSTRATION 9.4

Sufficient Appropriate Audit Evidence

Consideration	Effect on sufficient and appropriate evidence
Materiality of the item being examined.	The more material the item the greater the amount of evidence required.
Effectiveness of management's responses to risk.	More effective management responses to risk and controls decreases quality and quantity of evidence required.
Prior audit experience with the client.	Prior audit experience with the client will indicate how much evidence was taken before and if that was enough.
Auditor's assessment of inherent and control risks.	The higher the inherent or control risk, the greater the amount of evidence required.
Reliability of the available information.	The less reliable the source of information, the greater the amount of evidence required.
Whether fraud or error is suspected.	If fraud is suspected, the amount of evidence required increases.

ILLUSTRATION 9.5

The Quality of Audit Evidence

Relevance of evidence is the appropriateness (pertinence) of the evidence to the audit objective being tested.

Reliability is the quality of information when it is free from material error and bias and can be depended upon by users to represent faithfully that which it either purports to represent or could be reasonably expected to represent.

may be a relevant audit procedure. On the other hand, when testing for *understatement* of accounts payable, testing the recorded accounts payable would not be relevant, but testing such information as subsequent disbursements, unpaid invoices, suppliers' statements and unmatched receiving reports may be relevant.

A given set of audit procedures may provide audit evidence that is relevant to certain assertions, but not others. For example, inspection of documents related to the collection of receivables after the period end may provide audit evidence regarding existence and valuation of sales and the related receivable, but not necessarily cut-off (when the sales occurred). Similarly, obtaining audit evidence regarding a particular assertion, for example the existence of inventory, is not a substitute for obtaining audit evidence regarding another assertion, for example the valuation of that inventory.

Tests of controls are designed to evaluate the operating effectiveness of controls in preventing, or detecting and correcting, material misstatements at the assertion level. Designing tests of controls to obtain relevant audit evidence includes identifying conditions (characteristics or attributes) that indicate performance of a control, and deviation conditions which indicate departures from adequate performance. The presence or absence of those conditions can then be tested by the auditor.

Substantive procedures are designed to detect material misstatements at the assertion level. They comprise tests of details and substantive analytical procedures. Designing substantive procedures includes identifying conditions relevant to the purpose of the test that constitute a misstatement in the relevant assertion.

■ Reliability

When using information produced by the entity, the auditor must evaluate whether the information is sufficiently reliable for the auditor's purposes, including obtaining audit evidence about the accuracy and completeness of the information; and evaluating whether the information is sufficiently precise and detailed for the auditor's purposes.

The reliability of information to be used as audit evidence, and therefore of the audit evidence itself, is influenced by its source and its nature, and the circumstances under which it is obtained, including the controls over its preparation and maintenance where relevant. Therefore, generalisations about the reliability of various kinds of audit evidence are subject to important exceptions. Even when information to be used as audit evidence is obtained from sources external to the entity, circumstances may exist that could affect its reliability. For example, information obtained from an independent external source may not be reliable if the source is not knowledgeable, or a management's expert may lack objectivity.

While recognising that exceptions may exist, the following generalisations about the reliability of audit evidence may be useful[20] (see Illustration 9.6):

- The reliability of audit evidence is increased when it is obtained from independent sources outside the entity.
- The reliability of audit evidence that is generated internally is increased when the related controls, including those over its preparation and maintenance, imposed by the entity are effective.

ILLUSTRATION 9.6

Reliability of Evidence

	Least reliable	*Most reliable*
Source relative to entity	Internal (from inside entity)	External (from outside entity)
Source – person: employee or auditor	Employee of company	External auditor
Source – person: employee or third party	Employee of company	Third party
Source: independence of provider	Associated with company	Not associated with company
Source: qualification of provider	Little knowledge of subject	Expert in subject
Source: operation of internal controls	Not in operation	Effective operations

- Audit evidence obtained directly by the auditor (for example, observation of the application of a control) is more reliable than audit evidence obtained indirectly or by inference (for example, inquiry about the application of a control).
- Audit evidence in documentary form, whether paper, electronic or other medium, is more reliable than evidence obtained orally (for example, a contemporaneously written record of a meeting is more reliable than a subsequent oral representation of the matters discussed).
- Audit evidence provided by original documents is more reliable than audit evidence provided by photocopies or facsimiles, or documents that have been filmed, digitised or otherwise transformed into electronic form, the reliability of which may depend on the controls over their preparation and maintenance.

An audit performed in accordance with ISAs rarely involves the authentication of documents, nor is the auditor trained as or expected to be an expert in such authentication.[21] Ordinarily the auditor may accept records and documents as genuine. However, there may be circumstances where the auditor has reason to believe that a document used as evidence may not be authentic, or may have been modified without that modification having been disclosed to the auditor. In such a case, the auditor must investigate further.[22] Possible procedures to investigate further may include confirming directly with the third party and using the work of an expert to assess the document's authenticity.

While audit evidence is primarily obtained from audit procedures performed during the course of the audit, it may also include information obtained from other sources such as, for example, management's expert, the entity itself, previous audits, or a firm's quality control procedures for client acceptance and continuance. If information to be used as audit evidence has been prepared using the work of a management's expert, the auditor must evaluate the competence, capabilities and objectivity of that expert; obtain an understanding of the work of that expert; and evaluate the appropriateness of that expert's work as audit evidence.

Audit evidence to determine that the accounting records are internally consistent and agree to the financial statements is obtained by performing audit procedures to test the accounting records, for example through analysis and review, re-performing procedures followed in the financial reporting process, and reconciling related types and applications of the same information. Corroborating information, such as evidence existing within the accounting records, minutes of meetings or evidence obtained from a source independent of the entity may increase the assurance the auditor obtains from audit evidence that is generated internally. Information from sources independent of the entity that the auditor may use as audit evidence may include confirmations from third parties, analysts' reports, and comparable data about competitors (benchmarking data).

Audit evidence to draw reasonable conclusions on which to base the auditor's opinion is obtained by performing risk assessment procedures, tests of controls and substantive procedures, including tests of details and substantive analytical procedures.

■ Persuasive Evidence

Persuasive evidence has the power or ability to persuade based on logic or reason, often depending on the use of inductive or deductive reasoning. Evidence may be persuasive based on the character, credibility or reliability of the source. Unlike legal evidence, audit evidence does not have to be conclusive to be useful. Ordinarily, the auditor finds it necessary to rely on audit evidence that is persuasive rather than conclusive and will often seek audit evidence from different sources or of a different nature to support the same assertion on which the evidence is based. Not all the information available is examined. Conclusions can be reached about controls, transactions or the account balance by using a sample of the available information that is analysed by statistical sampling or judgement.

Audit evidence is more persuasive when there is consistency between items from different sources or of a different nature. Evidence is usually more persuasive for balance sheet accounts when it is obtained close to the balance sheet date. For income statements, evidence is more persuasive if it is a sample from the entire period. A random sample from the entire period is more persuasive than a sample from the first six months.

■ Cost/Benefit

The auditor also needs to think about the relationship between the cost of obtaining audit evidence and the usefulness of the information obtained. However, the matter of difficulty and expense involved is not in itself a valid basis for omitting a necessary procedure. If an auditor is unable to obtain sufficient appropriate audit evidence, he should express a qualified opinion or a disclaimer of opinion.

If the auditor has not obtained sufficient appropriate audit evidence as to a material financial statement assertion, he should attempt to obtain further audit evidence. If the auditor is unable to obtain sufficient appropriate audit evidence, he should express a qualified opinion or a disclaimer of opinion.

Concept and a Company 9.2

Mattel, Inc. Originators of 'Bill and Hold' Toy with Accounting

Concept	Sufficient appropriate audit evidence. Mattel employs several accounting tricks that went unnoticed or were not investigated in the audit.
Story	Mattel, Inc. of El Segundo, California, designs, manufactures and markets various toy products worldwide. Mattel brands include: Barbie dolls and accessories, Hot Wheels, Matchbox, Nickelodeon, Harry Potter, Yu-Gi-Oh!, He-Man and Masters of the Universe, Fisher-Price, Sesame Street, Winnie the Pooh, Blue's Clues, Barney, and View-Master, as well as games and puzzles.

Almost from its founding in 1945, Mattel was very successful, but the company began experiencing serious problems in the early 1970s. Mattel tried several accounting schemes to keep their growth high including a 'bill and hold' programme, understatement of inventory reserves, improper amortisation of tooling costs, non-payment of royalties, and booking insurance recovery in the wrong period (Knapp, 2001).

Here we will address the sales and accounts receivable 'bill and hold' issues.

Mattel Invents the Term

In order to inflate the company's reported earnings, top executives established the 'bill and hold' programme. This was the first instance of the term 'bill and hold' for the practice of billing customers for future sales, recording the sales immediately, and holding on to the inventory – bill and hold. The SEC gave several reasons why the subject sales should not have been recorded in 1971 (SEC, 1981):

- The merchandise was not shipped.
- The merchandise was not physically segregated from Mattel's inventory.
- The customer could cancel the order without penalty.
- Mattel retained the risks of ownership.
- In many instances, the invoices were prepared without knowledge of the customer.

Covering Their Tracks

To support the bill and hold sales, Mattel prepared bogus sales orders, sales invoices and bills of lading. The bills of lading were signed by the same employees as both themselves and a common carrier and were stamped 'bill and hold' on the face. When the goods were actually sold much later, Mattel's inventory records were full of errors. To resolve the problem, Mattel reversed the sales booked, but this created negative sales for the next period. To fix that problem, Mattel booked a fictitious $11 million sale in their general ledger, but not their accounts receivable subsidiary ledger, creating an unreconciled difference. They reversed another $7 million of the remaining bill and hold sales in fiscal 1972 (SEC, 1981).

The Audit of Sales

Mattel's auditors, Arthur Andersen, sent accounts receivable confirmations. The confirmations were returned with discrepancies in what the customers claimed and what Mattel booked. To resolve the discrepancies, the auditors obtained copies of bills of lading to determine whether goods had actually been shipped. Even though the bills of lading were stamped 'bill and hold', the auditors never asked Mattel to explain the phrase. Furthermore,

---

Mattel, Inc. Originators of 'Bill and Hold' Toy with Accounting (continued)

the bills of lading lacked required routeing or delivery instructions. The employee signatures as themselves and common carriers did not get noticed (SEC, 1981).

When the auditors looked at fiscal 1972 they found the $7 million reversing entry that caused that month's general ledger sales to be $7 million less than the sales figure in the corresponding sales invoice register. The staff auditor accepted the explanation of a Mattel employee that the offset to sales was due to 'invoicing errors' uncovered by Mattel employees when comparing computer-prepared invoices to bills of lading. The Andersen senior reviewing the workpapers wrote to the staff person, 'Need a better explanation. This looks like a big problem,' but the problem was investigated no further (Knapp, 2001).

Had Arthur Anderson utilised analytical procedures to evaluate the overall reasonableness of Mattel's monthly sales, they should have discovered that monthly sales varied dramatically from 1970 to 1972. This was a result of errors introduced by the bill and hold scheme and the subsequent reversals.

Discussion Questions

- What alternative audit procedures could the Andersen auditors perform when (or if) they found the inconsistencies in confirmations and bills of lading?
- Why do you think the staff auditor accepted the explanation of the $7 million discrepancy by the Mattel employee?
- Why was it not followed up?

References

Knapp, M., 2001, 'Mattel, Inc', *Contemporary Auditing Real Issues and Cases*, South Western College Publishing, Cincinnati, Ohio, pp. 3–14.

SEC, 1981, Accounting Series Release No. 292, 'SEC Charges Mattel, Inc. with Financial Fraud', US Securities and Exchange Commission, 22 June.

9.8 Summary

Evidence-gathering procedures in auditing are directed by the assessment of risk of material misstatement. ISA 330 states, 'The objective of the auditor is to obtain sufficient appropriate audit evidence regarding the assessed risks of material misstatement, through designing and implementing appropriate responses to those risks.'

To meet this objective of obtaining sufficient appropriate audit evidence, the auditor must design and perform audit procedures whose nature, timing and extent are based on, and are responsive to, the assessed risks. The nature of an audit procedure refers to its purpose (that is, test of controls or substantive procedure) and its type (that is, inspection, observation, inquiry, confirmation, recalculation, re-performance, or analytical procedure). The nature of the audit procedures is of most importance in responding to the assessed risks. Timing of an audit procedure refers to when it is performed, or the period or date to which the audit evidence applies. Extent of an audit procedure refers to the quantity to be performed, for example, a sample size or the number of observations of a control activity.

Evidence is anything that can make a person believe that a fact, proposition or assertion is true or false. Audit evidence is information used by the auditor in arriving at the conclusions on which the auditor's opinion is based. Audit evidence includes both information contained in the accounting records underlying the financial statements and other information. Auditors are not expected to address all information that may exist. Audit evidence, which is cumulative in nature, includes audit evidence obtained from audit procedures performed during the course of the audit and may include audit evidence obtained from other sources such as previous audits and a firm's quality control procedures for client acceptance and continuance. Evidence for proof of audit assertions is different from evidence in a legal sense. Audit evidence needs only to prove reasonable assurance, whereas in a legal environment there is a more rigorous standard of proof and documentation.

Management is responsible for the fair presentation of financial statements so that they reflect the nature and operations of the company based on the applicable financial reporting framework (IAS, GAAP, etc.). Management prepares the financial statements based upon the accounting records and other information, such as minutes of meetings; confirmations from third parties; analysts' reports; comparable data about competitors (benchmarking); and controls manuals. The auditor is likely to use the accounting records and that other information as audit evidence. In representing that the financial statements are in accordance with the applicable financial reporting framework, management implicitly or explicitly makes assertions regarding the recognition, measurement, presentation and disclosure of the various elements of financial statements and related disclosures. Management makes assertions that can be grouped into three groups: (1) assertions about classes of transactions and events for the period under audit; (2) assertions about account balances at the period end; and (3) assertions about presentation and disclosure. The standard assertions are occurrence, completeness, accuracy, cut-off, classification, existence, rights and obligations, valuation and allocation, and understandability.

Test of controls are audit procedures designed to evaluate the operating effectiveness of controls in preventing, or detecting and correcting, material misstatements at the assertion level. Designing tests of controls to obtain relevant audit evidence includes identifying conditions (characteristics or attributes) that indicate performance of a control, and deviation conditions which indicate departures from adequate performance. The presence or absence of those conditions can then be tested by the auditor.

The main work of an auditor is to find evidence using test procedures. A substantive procedure is an audit procedure designed to detect material misstatements at the assertion level. Substantive procedures comprise: (1) tests of details (of classes of transactions, account balances, and disclosures); and (2) substantive analytical procedures. Audit evidence is the information used by the auditor in arriving at the conclusions on which the audit opinion is based. Audit evidence consists of source documents and accounting records underlying the financial statements and corroborating information from other sources and can be gathered by tests of controls as well as substantive procedures. Substantive procedures are tests performed to obtain audit evidence to detect material misstatements or significant misstatements that may in aggregate be material in the financial statements. Substantive procedures are responses to the auditor's assessment of the risk of material misstatement. The higher the assessed risk, the more likely the extent of the substantive procedures will increase and the timing of procedures will be performed close to the period.

A substantive test usually performed on accounts payable is a search for unrecorded liabilities. This test may be part of the closing procedures or done in concert with the confirmation of accounts payable. This test provides evidence as to completeness and some evidence as to valuation. To search for unrecorded liabilities, the auditor reviews disbursements made by the client for a period after the balance sheet date, sometimes to the date of the completion of field work.

According to ISA 500, the objective of the auditor is to design and perform audit procedures in such a way as to enable the auditor to obtain sufficient appropriate audit evidence to be able to draw reasonable conclusions on which to base the auditor's opinion. As explained in ISA 200, reasonable assurance is obtained when the auditor has obtained sufficient appropriate audit evidence to reduce audit risk (that is, the risk that the auditor expresses an inappropriate opinion when the financial statements are materially misstated) to an acceptably low level. Sufficiency is the measure of the quantity of audit evidence. The quantity of audit evidence needed is affected by the auditor's assessment of the risks of misstatement (the higher the assessed risks, the more audit evidence is likely to be required) and also by the quality of such audit evidence (the higher the quality, the less may be required). Appropriateness is the measure of the quality of audit evidence; that is, its relevance and its reliability in providing support for the conclusions on which the auditor's opinion is based.

When designing and performing audit procedures, the auditor must consider the relevance and reliability of the information to be used as audit evidence. Reliability is the quality of information when it is free from material error and bias and can be depended upon by users to represent faithfully that which it either purports to represent or could reasonably be expected to represent. Relevance of evidence is the appropriateness (pertinence) of the evidence to the audit objective being tested. The quantity (relevance and reliability) of audit evidence needed is affected by the risk of misstatement (the greater the risk, the more audit evidence is required) and also by the quality of the audit evidence (the higher the quality of evidence, the less is required).

Questions, Exercises and Cases

QUESTIONS

9.2 Introduction

9-1 To meet this objective of obtaining sufficient appropriate audit evidence, what must the auditor do?

9-2 What might overall responses to address the assessed risks of material misstatement at the financial statement level include?

9-3 In what ways may an auditor respond to an ineffective control environment when planning evidence-gathering procedures?

9.3 The Basis of Evidence

9-4 Define evidence. How is Audit evidence unique?

9.4 Financial Statement Assertions

9-5 Define management assertions and discuss how they may be grouped? See Illustration 9.2.

9.5 Test of Controls

9-6 Define 'test of controls'. What are 'indirect controls'?

9-7 If the auditor hopes to rely on prior audit evidence, evidence is needed in the current audit about what areas?

9.6 Substantive Procedures

9-8 What are substantive procedures? Describe the different types of substantive procedures.

9-9 What is the difference between test of transactions and test of balances?

9-10 Discuss what is meant by direction of testing.

9-11 A substantive test usually performed on accounts payable is a search for unrecorded liabilities. Discuss this test.

9.7 Sufficient Appropriate Audit Evidence

9-12 What factors influence the auditor's judgement as to what constitutes sufficient appropriate audit evidence?

9-13 Differentiate between the most reliable evidence and the least reliable evidence.

9-14 Why does an auditor prefer persuasive evidence as opposed to conclusive evidence?

PROBLEMS AND EXERCISES

9.2 Introduction

9-15 Brack and Kabrac Corporation (BKC) of the United Arab Emirates sells financial services to clients who put up a minimum investment of €1,000,000. Abdel-Masoud, Ahrens and Spence, an auditing firm, are retained to audit BKC's financial statements. Considering the exotic financial instruments BKC deal in and the large amounts of money involved, the audit firm assesses the risk of material misstatement as high. Using the list of overall responses to address the assessed risks of material misstatement at the financial statement level from the Introduction to this chapter, discuss how the audit firm should respond. Give specific examples.

9.3 The Basis of Evidence

9-16 List and define at least ten kinds of electronic evidence that an auditor may review.

9.4 Financial Statement Assertions

9-17 Management Assertions and Audit Objectives. The following are management assertions (1 through 9) and audit objectives applied to the audit of accounts payable ((a) through (h)).

Management Assertions
1   Existence
2   Rights and obligations
3   Occurrence
4   Completeness
5   Valuation
6   Accuracy
7   Cut-off
8   Understandability
9   Classification

Specific Audit Objectives
(a) Existing accounts payable are included in the accounts payable balance on the balance sheet date.
(b) Accounts payable are properly classified.
(c) Acquisition transactions in the acquisition and payment cycle are recorded in the proper period.
(d) Accounts payable representing the accounts payable balance on the balance sheet date agree with related subsidiary ledger amounts, and the total is correctly added and agrees with the general ledger.
(e) Accounts in the acquisition and payment cycle are properly disclosed according to IASs.
(f) Accounts payable representing the accounts payable balance on the balance sheet date are valued at the correct amount.
(g) Accounts payable exist.
(h) Any allowances for accounts payable discounts are taken.

Required:
A. Explain the differences between management assertions, general audit objectives and specific audit objectives, and their relationships to each other.
B. For each specific audit objective, identify the appropriate management assertion.

9.5 Test of Controls

9-18 Tests of Controls. Auditors generally begin tests of controls by interviewing appropriate personnel who either perform or monitor control procedures. During these interviews, the auditors may also examine certain documents and reports used by persons in performing or monitoring control procedures as well as observe personnel performing their duties.

Basic Shoes, a shoe manufacturing company in Changchun, China, sells 95 per cent of its product to companies outside China. The company receives orders for shoes by fax and 20 per cent advance payment of the order price. The sales department makes up a sales order and passes it to the manufacturing manager who verifies the order with the cashier's office which receives the advance money. If the cashier okays the order, the manufacturing manager then writes a manufacturing order to produce the goods and orders the necessary raw materials for the warehouse.

The shipping officer receives a copy of the sales order and matches it to the goods manufactured and then ships, forwarding the shipping documents to accounting.

Accounting bills the customer after first matching shipping documents to the original sales order. The cashier's office receives the payment from the customer.

Required:

A. List ten questions that you might ask Basic Shoe's personnel about the sales process.
B. Discuss which person you would ask each of the questions and why you would ask them.
C. What documents would you inspect for each question? Why?
D. Which part of the sales process would you observe? Why?
E. What control procedures do you believe they might add to ensure that customers do not order goods that they cannot pay for?

9–19 Tests of Controls. Explain what types of control tests an auditor should do in each of the following circumstances and why:

1. The auditor tests controls that contribute to the reliability of accounting systems and concludes they are effective.
2. There are control failures, but in identifying and testing alternative controls the auditor finds them to be effective and therefore concludes that the accounting systems are reliable.
3. The auditor concludes that there are no effective alternative controls that address the transactions and potential errors to which failed controls relate.
4. The control failures and the absence of effective alternative controls cause the auditor to identify a specific risk.

9.6 Substantive Procedures

9–20 Substantive Tests – Analytical Procedures, Balances and Transactions. Substantive tests include (1) tests of the details of transactions, (2) tests of the details of balances, and (3) analytical procedures. Listed below are several specific audit procedures. Identify the type of substantive test – 1, 2, or 3.

A. Compare recorded travel expense with the budget.
B. Vouch entries in the cheque register to paid cheques.
C. Re-compute accrued interest payable.
D. Calculate inventory turnover ratios by product and compare with prior periods.
E. Reconcile the year-end bank account.
F. Discuss uncollectible accounts with the credit manager.
G. Count office supplies on hand at year-end.
H. Vouch entries in the sales journal to sales invoices.
I. Comparison of recorded amount of major disbursements with appropriate invoices.
J. Comparison of recorded amount of major disbursements with budgeted amounts.
K. Comparison of returned confirmation forms with individual accounts.

[Adapted from Carmichael et al., 1996, *Auditing Concepts and Methods*, McGraw-Hill, New York.]

9–21 Tests of Balances. Your client is the Nicholas van Myra Central, a shopping centre with 30 store tenants. All leases with the store tenants provide for a fixed rent plus a percentage of sales, net of sales taxes, in excess of a fixed dollar amount computed on an annual basis. Each lease also provides that the landlord may engage a Registeraccountant or Accountant-Administratieconsulent to audit all records of the tenant for assurance that sales are being properly reported to the landlord.

You have been requested by your client to audit the records of the JaiLai Chinese Ind. Restaurant to determine that the sales, totalling €725,000 for the year ended

31 December 20X4, have been properly reported to the landlord. The restaurant and the shopping centre entered into a five-year lease on 1 January 20X4. The JaiLai offers only table service. No liquor is served. During meal times there are four or five waitresses in attendance, who prepare handwritten pre-numbered bills for the customers. Payment is made at a cash register, staffed by the proprietor, as the customer leaves. All sales are for cash.

The proprietor also is the bookkeeper. Complete files are kept of bills and cash register tapes. A daily sales book and general ledger are also maintained.

Required:
List the auditing procedures that you would employ to test the annual sales of the JaiLai Chinese Ind. Restaurant. (Disregard vending machine sales and counter sales of chewing gum and sweets, and concentrate on the overall checks that would be appropriate.)

9.7 Sufficient Appropriate Audit Evidence

9–22 Sufficient Appropriate Audit Evidence. The auditor finds it necessary to rely on audit evidence that is persuasive rather than conclusive and will often seek audit evidence from different sources or of a different nature to support the same assertion. The reliability of audit evidence is not only important in determining sufficiency (quantity) of the information, but also the appropriateness (quality) of the information. Reliability of audit evidence is influenced by its source and its nature.

Required:
A. Define these terms: reliability of evidence, persuasiveness of evidence, and relevance of evidence.
B. Arrange the following people as sources of information from most reliable to least reliable and explain your reasoning:
    1 new company employee,
    2 company employee with five years' experience,
    3 company lawyer,
    4 internal auditor,
    5 external auditor,
    6 auditor's lawyer,
    7 banker,
    8 top management,
    9 board of directors,
    10 company supplier,
    11 company customer.

9–23 Reliability and Cost of Evidence-Gathering Techniques. The financial statements of Utgard Company of Drammen, Norway, a new client, indicate that large amounts of notes payable to banks were paid off during the period under audit. The auditor, Kristinge Korsvold, Statautoriseret Revisor, also notices that one customer's account is much larger than the rest, and therefore decides to examine the evidence supporting this account.

Required:
Evaluate the reliability of each of the following types of evidence supporting these transactions for:

Notes Payable:
A. Debit entries in the Notes Payable account.
B. Entries in the cheque register.

C. Paid cheques.

D. Notes payable bearing bank perforation stamp PAID and the date of payment.

E. Statement by client's treasurer that notes had been paid at maturity.

F. Letter received by auditors directly from bank stating that no indebtedness on part of client existed as of the balance sheet date.

Customer Account:

G. Computer printout from accounts receivable subsidiary ledger.

H. Copies of sales invoices in amount of the receivable.

I. Purchase order received from customer.

J. Shipping document describing the articles sold.

K. Letter received by client from customer acknowledging the correctness of the receivable in the amount shown on client's accounting records.

L. Letter received by auditors directly from customer acknowledging the correctness of the amount shown as receivable on client's accounting records.

CASES

9-24 Audit Objectives and Financial Statement Accounts. Look at the financial statements of a major public company. Pick three accounts and discuss the financial statement assertions that might be associated with those accounts. For example, the financial statement assertions might be associated with 'Accrued Product Liability' are valuation, existence, completeness, and presentation and disclosure. Valuation relates to product liability because a judgement (estimate) must be made regarding the expected cost of defective products.

9-25 Substantive Tests: Balances and Transactions. As part of systematic process of gathering and evaluating evidence regarding assertions about economic actions and events, tests of balances and tests of transactions are essential in obtaining audit evidence to detect material misstatements in the financial statements. In the following case, assume that you are an auditor. Before you conduct the actual tests you are expected to understand the concepts and procedures of tests of balances and transactions.

Required:

A. There are two types of substantive procedures. Identify each.

B. Describe the difference between tests of balances and tests of transactions. Give an example for each test and illustrate them.

C. For tests of balances, what are the major account balances in the balance sheet that need to be examined? Why are these tests important?

D. For tests of transactions, what are the major accounts that an auditor needs in order to verify transaction amounts and trace transactions to accounts in the financial statements? Why are these tests important?

E. How do inherent properties of double-entry accounting systems relate to the tests of balances? Give examples of double entries that show the simultaneous affect of one transaction has on another.

F. For certain account balances such as assets, auditors prefer to test asset accounts for overstatement. Explain why. Are there any similar preferences for understatement for other accounts? If any, explain why.

G. As an auditor, you are aware of the control risks when design tests of transactions. Explain how these risks might affect the way you design and carry out the procedures.

[Written by Maria Wise, Claudia De Santiago, Perla Barajas and Cam Long.]

9-26 **Tests of Balances.** Swartz Platten, BV, sells chemicals in large, costly returnable containers. Its procedures in accounting for the containers are as follows:

1 When containers are purchased, their cost is charged to 'Inventory – containers on
hand'.

2 Containers are billed to customers at cost; full credit is allowed for all containers
returned in usable condition. The containers remain the property of Swartz Platten
at all times.

3 The cost of containers billed to customers is debited to 'Accounts receivable –
containers' and credited to 'Liability for containers billed'. At the same time, the cost
of the containers billed is transferred to 'Inventory – containers out' from 'Inventory –
containers on hand'. Subsidiary ledgers are maintained for 'Accounts receivable –
containers' and 'Inventory – containers out'.

4 When containers are returned in usable condition, the entries in 3 are reversed.

5 A physical inventory of containers on hand is taken at the fiscal year-end.

6 As a partial control over containers in the hands of customers, sales representatives
are asked to estimate periodically the number of containers held by each customer.
These estimates are checked for reasonableness against the amount shown for the
customer in the 'Inventory – containers out' subsidiary ledger.

7 Physical shortages, unusable returned containers, and other inventory adjustments
are charged or credited to 'Containers expense – net'. The corresponding adjustments to 'Liability for containers billed' are also charged or credited to 'Containers
expense – net'.

8 Containers kept by customers for more than one year are deemed unusable. Roger
van Deelgaard had been the auditor of Swartz Platten for many years. He issued
an unqualified opinion on the financial statements for the previous fiscal year. Two
months before the current year-end, Swartz Platten's accountant requested that
van Deelgaard investigate a strange situation which had developed: the balance in
the 'Liability for containers billed' had been steadily increasing, to the point where
it exceeded the combined balances in 'Inventory – containers out' and 'Inventory –
containers on hand'.

Required:

A. What might have caused the situation described by the company's accountant?

B. List the procedures van Deelgaard should employ to determine the nature and
extent of the misstatement.

[*Uniform Evaluation Report* (Toronto: CPA Canada)]

9.10 Notes

1 International Auditing and Assurance Standards Board (IAASB), 2012, International Standard on Auditing 330 (ISA 330) 'The Auditor's Responses to Assessed Risks', para. 3, *Handbook of International Quality Control, Auditing Review, Other Assurance, and Related Services Pronouncements*, 2012 edn, Volume 1, International Federation of Accountants, New York.

2 Two different explanations are provided for timing of an audit procedure. Alternative timing of the audit procedure is when the auditor performs the procedure, for example, interim from October to December (by a year-end of 31 December) and substantive procedures after year-end. The auditor further determines the period to which the audit evidence applies, e.g. for a test of control the whole financial year, and for inventory count as close to the year-end as possible, e.g. 31 December.

3 ISA 330.21 requires the auditor to perform substantive procedures for every significant risk.

4 International Auditing and Assurance Standards Board (IAASB), 2012, International Standard on Auditing 500 (ISA 500) 'Audit Evidence', para. 5, *Handbook of International Quality Control, Auditing Review, Other Assurance, and Related Services Pronouncements*, 2012 edn, Volume 1, International Federation of Accountants, New York.

5 Forensic accounting is the application of accounting methods and financial techniques to collect civil and criminal legal evidence.

6 International Auditing and Assurance Standards Board (IAASB), 2012, International Standard on Auditing 315 (ISA 315) 'Identifying and Assessing the Risks of Material Misstatement through Understanding the Entity and Its Environment', para. A111, *Handbook of International Quality Control, Auditing Review, Other Assurance, and Related Services Pronouncements*, 2012 edn, Volume 1, International Federation of Accountants, New York.

7 Ibid. ISA 315, para. A111.

8 Ibid. ISA 500, para. A20.

9 Computer assisted audit techniques – applications of auditing procedures using the computer as an audit tool.

10 International Auditing and Assurance Standards Board (IAASB), 2012, International Standard on Auditing 330 (ISA 330) 'The Auditor's Responses to Assessed Risks', para. 14(b), *Handbook of International Quality Control, Auditing Review, Other Assurance, and Related Services Pronouncements*, 2012 edn, Volume 1, International Federation of Accountants, New York.

11 International Auditing and Assurance Standards Board (IAASB), 2012, International Standard on Auditing 500 (ISA 500) 'Audit Evidence', *Handbook of International Quality Control, Auditing Review, Other Assurance, and Related Services Pronouncements*, 2012 edn, Volume 1, International Federation of Accountants, New York.

12 See Auditing Standards Board (US), 2012, Statement on Auditing Standards: Clarification and Recodification AU-C 330 'Performing Audit Procedures in Response to Assessed Risks', para. 330.18, American Institute of Certified Public Accountants, 1 June: **http://www.aicpa.org/Research/Standards/AuditAttest/DownloadableDocuments/AU-C-00330.pdf**.

13 ISA 330, op. cit., para. 22.

14 Audit sampling is the application of audit procedures to less than 100% of items within a population of audit relevance such that all sampling units have a chance of selection in order to provide the auditor with a reasonable basis on which to draw conclusions about the entire population.

15 International Auditing and Assurance Standards Board (IAASB), 2012, International Standard on Auditing 500 (ISA 500) 'Audit Evidence', para. 5, *Handbook of International Quality Control, Auditing Review, Other Assurance, and Related Services Pronouncements*, 2012 edn, Volume 1, International Federation of Accountants, New York.

16 International Auditing and Assurance Standards Board (IAASB), 2012, International Standard on Auditing 200 (ISA 200) 'Overall Objectives of the Independent Auditor and the Conduct of an Audit in Accordance with International Standards on Auditing', para. 5, *Handbook of International Quality Control, Auditing Review, Other Assurance, and Related Services Pronouncements*, 2012 edn, Volume 1, International Federation of Accountants, New York.

17 ISA 330, para. 26.

18 ISA 330, para. A62.

19 International Auditing and Assurance Standards Board (IAASB), 2012, International Standard on Auditing 500 (ISA 500) 'Audit Evidence', para. A4, *Handbook of International Quality Control, Auditing Review, Other Assurance, and Related Services Pronouncements*, 2012 edn, Volume 1, International Federation of Accountants, New York.

20 Ibid. ISA 500, para. A31.

21 International Auditing and Assurance Standards Board (IAASB), 2012, International Standard on Auditing 200 (ISA 200) 'Overall Objectives of the Independent Auditor and the Conduct of an Audit in Accordance with International Standards on Auditing', para. A47, *Handbook of International Quality Control, Auditing Review, Other Assurance, and Related Services Pronouncements*, 2012 edn, Volume 1, International Federation of Accountants, New York.

22 International Auditing and Assurance Standards Board (IAASB), 2012, International Standard on Auditing 240 (ISA 240) 'The Auditor's Responsibilities Relating to Fraud in an Audit of Financial Statements', para. 13, *Handbook of International Quality Control, Auditing Review, Other Assurance, and Related Services Pronouncements*, 2012 edn, Volume 1, International Federation of Accountants, New York.

Chapter 10

AUDIT EVIDENCE

10.1 Learning Objectives

After studying this chapter, you should be able to:

1 Define auditing evidence.

2 Discuss what constitutes accounting records.

3 Characterise risk assessment procedures regarding evidence.

4 Understand the seven evidence-gathering techniques: inquiry, observation, inspection, re-performance, recalculation, confirmation, and analytical procedures.

5 Discuss evidence-gathering procedures for physical inventory counting, confirmation of accounts receivable, and search for unrecorded liabilities.

6 Explain the confirmation process.

7 Illustrate the main uses of audit sampling.

8 Typify the key issues in auditing management estimations.

9 Portray how an auditor approaches correction of uncorrected misstatements.

10 Depict related parties and related party transactions.

11 Obtain evidence that management acknowledges its responsibility for the fair presentation of the financial statements in a management representation letter.

10.2   Introduction

Auditing is a systematic process of objectively obtaining and evaluating evidence regarding **assertions** about economic actions and events. 'The auditor shall design and perform audit procedures that are appropriate in the circumstances for the purpose of obtaining sufficient appropriate audit evidence.'[1] **Evidence** is anything that can make a person believe that a fact, proposition or assertion is true or false. **Audit evidence** is all of the information used by the auditor in arriving at the conclusions on which the audit opinion is based. Audit evidence includes the accounting records and other information underlying the financial statements.

Audit evidence is different from the legal evidence required by **forensic accounting**.[2] In a civil lawsuit, evidence must be strong enough to incline a person to believe one side or the other. In a criminal case, evidence must establish proof of a crime beyond a **reasonable doubt**. Audit evidence provides only **reasonable assurance**.

■ Accounting Records

Accounting records, the primary basis of audit evidence, generally include the records of initial entries and supporting records. Initial entries include point of sales transactions, **electronic data interchange (EDI), electronic fund transfers (EFT)**,[3] contracts, invoices, shipping notices, purchase orders, sales orders, the general and subsidiary ledgers, journal entries, and other adjustments to the financial statements. Examples of supporting records are computer files, databases, worksheets, spreadsheets, computer and manual logs, computations, reconciliations and disclosures.

Most accounting records are initiated, recorded, processed and reported in electronic form such as a database. For the larger companies, accounting records are part of **enterprise resource planning** (ERP) which is a system that integrates all aspects of an organisation's activities (such as database maintenance, financial reporting, operations and compliance) into one accounting information system.

10.3   Audit Procedures for Obtaining Audit Evidence

The auditor performs risk assessment procedures in order to provide a basis for the assessment of risks (discussed in Chapter 6). However, risk assessment procedures by themselves do not provide sufficient appropriate audit evidence on which to base the audit opinion. Risk assessment procedures must be supplemented by further audit procedures in the form of tests of controls and substantive procedures.

We discussed tests of controls in Chapter 9. Even if the auditor tests controls, there are inherent limitations to internal control including the risk of management override, the possibility of human error, and the effect of systems changes. Therefore, substantive procedures for material classes of transactions, account balances, and disclosures are always required to obtain sufficient appropriate audit evidence.

■ Evidence Gathering Techniques

An auditor obtains audit evidence by one or more of the following evidence-gathering techniques:

- ■ inquiry;
- ■ observation;
- ■ inspection (of tangible assets, records or documents);
- ■ recalculation;
- ■ re-performance;
- ■ confirmation;
- ■ analytical procedures.

See Illustration 10.1 for a list, definition and examples of evidence-gathering techniques.

ILLUSTRATION 10.1

Audit Procedures (Evidence-Gathering Techniques)

Technique	Definition	Examples
Inquiry	Consists of seeking information of knowledgeable persons inside or outside the entity.	Obtaining written or oral information from the client in response to specific questions during the audit.
Observation	Consists of looking at a process or procedure being performed by others.	Observation by the auditor of the counting of inventories by entity's personnel, site visit at the client's facilities.
Inspection	Consists of examining records, documents or tangible assets.	Reviewing sales orders, sales invoices, shipping documents, bank statements, customer return documents, customer complaint letters, etc.
Recalculation	Consists of checking the arithmetical accuracy of source documents and accounting records or performing independent calculations.	Extending sales invoices and inventory, adding journals and subsidiary records, checking the calculation of depreciation expense and prepaid expense.
Re-performance	Consists of independent execution of procedures or controls that were originally performed as part of the entity's internal control.	Use CAATs to check controls recorded in the database. Re-perform ageing of accounts receivable.
Confirmation	Consists of response to an inquiry to corroborate information contained in the accounting records.	Used to confirm the existence of accounts receivable and accounts payable, verify bank balances with banks, cash surrender value of life insurance, notes payable with lenders or bondholders.
Analytical procedures	Consist of the analysis of significant ratios and trends including the resulting investigation of fluctuations and relationships that are inconsistent with other relevant information or that deviate from predictable amounts.	Calculating trends in sales over the past few years, comparing net profit as a percentage of sales in current year with the percentage of the preceding year, comparing client current ratio to the industry current ratio, and comparing budgets to actual results.

■ Inquiry

The most frequently used technique for evidence gathering is inquiry. Inquiry consists of seeking information of knowledgeable persons inside or outside the entity. Inquiry of the client is the obtaining of written or oral information from the client in response to specific questions during the audit. Inquiries may range from formal written inquiries, addressed to third parties, to informal oral inquiries, addressed to persons inside the entity.

Responses to inquiries may provide the auditor with information not previously possessed or with corroborative audit evidence. Alternatively, responses might provide information that differs significantly from other information that the auditor has obtained, for example, information regarding the possibility of management override of controls. In some cases, responses to inquiries provide a basis for the auditor to modify or perform additional audit procedures.

Corroboration

In a typical audit, the largest amount of audit evidence is obtained from client inquiry, but it cannot be regarded as conclusive because it is not from an independent source and might be biased in the client's favour. Therefore, the auditor must gather evidence to corroborate inquiry evidence by doing other alternative procedures. For example, the auditor generally makes inquiries about internal control, accounting entries, and procedures. Later, for corroboration, the auditor may observe the control procedures (observation) or review related documentation (inspection).

Corroborative evidence for inquiry evidence is very important. In a famous US court case, *Escott et al.* v *BarChris Const. Corp.* (1968),[4] the court ruled against the auditor because he did not follow up on management answers to inquiries. The court opinion said in part:

> Most important of all, he (the auditor) was too easily satisfied with glib answers (by management) to his inquiries. This is not to say that he should have made a complete audit. But there were enough danger signals in the materials which he did examine to require some further investigation on his part ... It is not always sufficient merely to ask questions.

■ Observation

Observation consists of looking at a process or procedure being performed by others, for example, the observation by the auditor of the counting of inventories by the entity's personnel or observation of internal control procedures that leave no audit trail. Observation provides audit evidence about the performance of a process or procedure, but is limited to the point in time at which the observation takes place and by the fact that the act of being observed may affect how the process or procedure is performed.

Observation is mostly visual, but also involves all the other senses. Hearing, touch and smell may also be used in gathering evidence. For example, it is typical for the auditor to do a site visit at the client's facilities. On site visits the auditor can get an idea of the implementation of internal controls, notice what equipment is utilised and what equipment may be collecting dust – or rusting. An auditor with a good knowledge of the industry can tell what equipment and methods are obsolete by observing.

Sufficient evidence is rarely obtained through observation alone. Observation techniques should be followed up by other types of evidence gathering procedures. For example, observation evidence such as a quick visual inspection of a printing press may be corroborated by either a thorough and detailed inspection of the printing press by an auditor's expert mechanic or specialist, or inspection of documents and records relating to the equipment, both of which are evidence gathered by inspection techniques.

Observation of Physical Inventory Procedures

A good example of an observation audit procedure is count of physical inventory. ISA 501 discusses the inspection evidence gathering technique for physical inventory counting. It states: 'If inventory is material to the financial statements, the auditor should obtain sufficient appropriate audit evidence regarding its existence and condition of the inventory by attendance at physical inventory counting.'[5]

The attendance by the auditor will enable him to evaluate management's instructions and procedures for recording and controlling the results of the entity's physical inventory counting; observe the performance of management's count procedures; inspect the inventory; perform test counts; and perform audit procedures over the entity's final inventory records to determine whether they accurately reflect actual inventory count results.

Alternative Inventory Procedures

If unable to attend the physical inventory count on the date planned due to unforeseen circumstances, the auditor should take or observe some physical counts on an alternative date and, when necessary, perform tests of controls of intervening transactions. Where attendance is impractical, due to factors such as the nature and location of the inventory where inventory is held in a location that may pose threats to the safety of the auditor, the auditor should perform alternative audit procedures to obtain sufficient appropriate audit evidence regarding the existence and condition of inventory. For example, documentation of the subsequent sale of specific inventory items acquired or purchased prior to the physical inventory count may provide sufficient evidence. If it is not possible to do so, the auditor must modify the opinion in the auditor's report in accordance with ISA 705.[6]

Planning Attendance at Inventory Count

In planning attendance at the physical inventory count or the alternative procedures, the auditor would consider:

- The risks of material misstatement related to inventory.
- The nature of the internal control related to inventory.
- Whether adequate procedures are expected to be established and proper instructions issued for physical inventory counting.
- The timing of physical inventory counting.
- Whether the entity maintains a perpetual inventory system.
- The locations at which inventory is held, including the materiality of the inventory and the risks of material misstatement at different locations, in deciding at which locations attendance is appropriate.

The auditor would review management's instructions regarding:[7]

- the application of control procedures (e.g. collection of used stock sheets, accounting for unissued stock sheets and count and re-count procedures);
- accurate identification of the stage of completion of work in progress, of slow-moving, obsolete, or damaged items and items on consignment;[8]

- the procedures used to estimate physical quantities, where applicable, such as may be needed in estimating the physical quantity of a coal pile.
- control over the movement of inventory between areas and the shipping and receipt of inventory before and after the cut-off date.

Inventory Procedures in Addition to Observation

Inventory counts involve other procedures in addition to observing the inventory take. The auditor will perform test counts. When performing counts, he would test both the completeness and the accuracy of the count records by tracing items selected from those records to the physical inventory and items selected from the physical inventory to the count records. The auditor would also review cut-off procedures including details of the movement of inventory just prior to, during, and after the count so that the accounting for such movements can be checked at a later date. The auditor would test the final inventory listing to assess whether it accurately reflects actual inventory counts. When there is a perpetual inventory system and it is used to determine the period end balance, the auditor would assess the reasons for any significant differences between the physical count and the perpetual inventory records.

Inventory Not on Company Premises

When inventory under the custody and control of a third party, or consignee, is material to the financial statements, the auditor would obtain direct confirmation from the third party as to the quantities and condition of inventory held on behalf of the entity or perform inspection or other audit procedures appropriate in the circumstances. Depending on how material the inventory is for the entity's operations, the auditor may also consider:

- the integrity and independence of the third party;
- observing, or arranging for another auditor to observe, the physical inventory count;
- obtaining another auditor's report on the adequacy of the third party's accounting and internal control systems for ensuring that inventory is correctly counted and adequately safeguarded;
- inspecting documentation regarding inventory held by third parties, for example, warehouse receipts, or obtaining confirmation from other parties when such inventory has been pledged as collateral.

■ Inspection (of Tangible Assets, Records or Documents)

Inspection consists of examining records, documents or tangible assets. Inspection is the auditor's examination of the client's documents and records to substantiate the information that is or should be included in the financial statements. Examples of evidence gathering by inspection techniques is the review by an auditor of sales orders, sales invoices, shipping documents, bank statements, customer return documents, customer complaint letters, etc. Other examples are the conduct of a thorough mechanical inspection of cash registers and point-of-sales devices and review of electronic records via Computer Assisted Audit Techniques (CAATs).

Inspection of tangible assets consists of physical examination of the assets. Inspection of tangible assets may provide reliable audit evidence with respect to their existence, but not necessarily as to the entity's rights and obligations or the valuation of the assets. Inspection of individual inventory items ordinarily accompanies the observation of inventory counting.

Inspection of Documents

Inspection of records and documents provides audit evidence of varying degrees of reliability depending on their nature, source and the effectiveness of internal controls over their processing:

- The nature of documents includes quantity of information contained, the difficulty of access to them, and who has custody.
- The source of the documents may be from inside or outside the firm.
- The source outside the firm may or may not be independent of the client.
- The source may be competent or incompetent.
- The controls over the recording process may be effective or ineffective.

Some documents represent direct audit evidence of the existence of an asset, for example a document constituting a financial instrument such as a stock or bond. Very importantly, inspecting an executed contract may provide audit evidence relevant to the entity's application of accounting principles, such as revenue recognition.

External and Internal Documents

A document's source may be internal or external to the organisation. An internal document is one that has been prepared and used within the client's organisation and is retained without ever going to an outside party. An external document is one that has been in the hands of someone outside the client's organisation who is a party to the transaction being documented. External documents may originate outside the entity and end up in their hands such as insurance policies, vendor's invoices (bills), bank statements and cancelled notes payable. Other external documents originate inside the entity, go to a third party and are then returned to the entity. Cancelled cheques are an example of client to third party and then to client documents.

In the old days external documents were considered fairly reliable evidence, but not so much today. Think of all the modern (e.g. copying) techniques of falsifying external documents. Moreover a lot of external documents are nowadays provided in a digital form, even contracts, invoices etc. In that case reliability of documents can only be secured by using digital security techniques (e.g. digital signatures). The question is if an auditor nowadays is always in able to establish if an external document is an 'original' document. Sufficient internal controls are necessary and that an auditor for a lot of external documents only can rely on them if they have been subject to adequate internal controls.

Internal documents processed under good internal controls are more reliable than those processed under weak controls. Some external documents such as title papers to property, insurance policies and contracts are reliable evidence because they may be easily verified.

Vouching and Tracing

The use of documentation to support recorded transactions or amounts is called 'vouching'. The review of how source documents lead to account balances is called 'tracing'. Vouching is an audit process whereby the auditor selects sample items from an account and goes backwards through the accounting system to find the source documentation that supports the item selected (e.g. a sales invoice). For example, to vouch the existence of recorded acquisition transactions, the audit procedure would be to trace from the acquisitions journal to supporting vendor's invoices, cancelled cheques or receiving reports. On the other hand, tracing tracks transactions in the opposite direction, form source documents to account total balance. Tracing is an audit procedure whereby the auditor selects sample items from basic source documents and proceeds forward through the accounting system to find the final recording of the transaction (e.g. in the ledger).

◼ Recalculation and Re-performance

Recalculation consists of checking the arithmetical accuracy of source documents and accounting records or of performing independent calculations. Some common recalculation audit procedures are extending sales invoices and inventory, adding journals and subsidiary records, calculating excise tax expense, and checking the calculation of depreciation expense and prepaid expense. Audit procedures to check the mechanical accuracy of recording include reviews to determine if the same information is entered correctly in point-of-sales records, receiving reports, journals, subsidiary ledgers and summarised in the general ledger. Computation evidence is relatively reliable because the auditor performs it. Recalculation may be performed through the use of CAATs (e.g. ACL), for instance to check the accuracy of totals in a file.

Re-performance is the auditor's independent execution of procedures or controls that were originally performed as part of the entity's internal control, either manually or through the use of CAATs, for example, re-performing the ageing of accounts receivable.

◼ Reliability and Cost of Audit Procedures

The most reliable evidence-gathering techniques (audit procedures) should be used whenever they are cost effective. The quality of internal controls has a significant effect on reliability. Furthermore, a specific substantive audit procedure is rarely sufficient by itself to provide competent evidence to satisfy the audit objective. However, assuming good internal controls and the ability to choose a specific method, a list of the most reliable to the least reliable evidence-gathering techniques are in general:

- recalculation,
- inspection,
- re-performance,
- observation,
- confirmation,
- analytical procedures,
- inquiry.

The most expensive evidence-gathering techniques are confirmation and inspection. Confirmation is costly because of the time and outlay required in preparation, mailing, receipt and follow-up. Inspection procedures that require the presence of both the client and auditors, such as an inventory count, are also expensive. Confirmation of documents is moderately expensive if clients are organised and have documents easily available. The three least expensive evidence-gathering procedures are observation, analytical procedures and inquiries. Observation is normally done concurrently with other audit procedures.

The evidence-gathering procedures in order of cost from most costly to least costly are in general:

- confirmation (most costly),
- inspection,

- recalculation,
- re-performance,
- observation,
- analytical procedures,
- inquiry (least costly).

10.4 External Confirmation

In general, audit evidence from external sources (e.g. external confirmation of cash account received from a bank) is more reliable than evidence generated internally. Evidence obtained directly by the auditor is more reliable than that obtained from the client entity and more reliable than evidence obtained indirectly or by inference (e.g. inquiry about the application of a control). Written documents are the second most reliable audit evidence. External confirmation combines direct participation by the auditor and written documentation from an external source.

■ Confirmation

Confirmation consists of the response to an inquiry of a third party to corroborate information contained in the accounting records. For example, the auditor ordinarily seeks direct confirmation of receivables by communication with debtors. Confirmation is the act of obtaining audit evidence from a third party in support of a fact or condition. Illustration 10.2 gives a summary of the characteristics of confirmation as an evidence-gathering technique.

ILLUSTRATION 10.2

Confirmation

Confirmation is the auditor's receipt of a written or oral response from an independent third party verifying the accuracy of information requested.

Advantage: Highly persuasive evidence.

Disadvantage: Costly and time-consuming and an inconvenience to those asked to supply them.

Four key characteristics of confirmations
1 Information requested is by the client auditor.
2 Request and response is in writing, sent to the auditor.
3 Response comes from an independent third party.
4 Positive confirmation involves a receipt of information.

Two types of positive confirmations
1 Positive confirmation with the request for information to be supplied by the recipient.
2 Positive confirmation with the information to be confirmed included on the form.

Confirmation procedures are typically used to confirm the existence of accounts receivable, investments and accounts payable, but they may be used to confirm existence, quantity and condition of inventory held by third parties (e.g. public warehouse consignee) on behalf of the entity. They may be used to verify bank balances with banks; cash surrender value of life insurance or insurance coverage with insurers; notes payable with lenders or bondholders; shares outstanding with stock transfer agents; liabilities with creditors; and contracts terms with customers, suppliers and creditors.

Because confirmations from independent third parties are usually in writing, and are requested directly by the auditor, they are highly persuasive evidence. The main disadvantage of confirmations is that they are costly, time-consuming and an inconvenience to those asked to supply them.

Confirmation of Management Assertions

Audit evidence is collected to verify management assertions. External confirmation of an account receivable provides strong evidence regarding the existence of the account as at a certain date. Confirmation also provides evidence regarding the operation of cut-off procedures. Similarly, in the case of goods held on consignment, external confirmation is likely to provide strong evidence to support the existence and the rights and obligations assertions. When auditing the completeness assertion for accounts payable, the auditor needs to obtain evidence that there is no material unrecorded liability. Therefore, sending confirmation requests to an entity's principal suppliers asking them to provide copies of their statements of account directly to the auditor, even if the records show no amount currently owing to them, will usually be effective in detecting unrecorded liabilities.

Concept and a Company 10.1

Parmalat – Milk Spills After Sour Confirmation

Concept	Importance of confirmations. Responsibility of primary auditor.
Story	Parmalat Finanziaria SpA is a Parma, Italy-based company, whose main operating subsidiary, Parmalat SpA sells dairy products around the world, employs 36,000 people, and has world-wide operations in 30 countries, including the USA. It was Italy's biggest food maker and Italy's eighth largest industrial group with market capitalisation of €1.8 billion. On 24 December 2003, Parmalat SpA filed for bankruptcy protection with a court in Parma, Italy, and on 27 December 2003, the court declared Parmalat SpA insolvent (SEC, 2003).
	The problems at Parmalat first became apparent in mid-December 2003 when Parmalat failed to meet a €150 million ($184 million) payment to bondholders. This seemed odd because the company showed €4.2 billion in cash on their 30 September balance sheet. Parmalat had raised $8 billion in bonds between 1993 and 2003. Why did they need to keep raising money with their mountain of cash? Their standard reply was that the company was on an acquisition spree and needed cash – and the liquid funds were earning good returns (Edmonson and Cohen, 2004). Now the reckoning had come.
	The following week in December, Parmalat executives admitted to their auditor Deloitte that they could not liquidate the €515 million Parmalat claimed it held in Epicurum,

a Cayman Islands fund. When Enrico Bondi, an adviser, suggested liquidating the €3.95 billion held by a Cayman Islands subsidiary called Bonlat, the rabbit popped out of the hat. Italian prosecutors say that they discovered that managers simply invented assets to offset as much as €13 billion in liabilities and falsified accounts over a 15-year period (Edmonson and Cohen, 2004).

Bonlat

Parmalat purportedly held the €3.95 billion worth of cash and marketable securities in an account at Bank of America in New York City in the name of Bonlat Financing Corporation ('Bonlat'), a wholly-owned subsidiary incorporated in the Cayman Islands. Bonlat's auditors certified its 2002 financial statements based upon a confirmation that Bonlat held these assets at Bank of America (SEC, 2003).

Confirmation Letter

Grant Thornton, auditor for the Bonlat subsidiary, sent a letter to confirm the balance in the Bonlat account to Bank of America in December 2002. On 6 March 2003, three months later, the auditors received a letter on Bank of America stationary and signed by a senior officer confirming the existence of the account with a balance of €3.95 billion. The letter was mailed, not faxed, to Grant Thornton's offices in Milan (Rigby and Michaels, 2003).

Bank of America Says Letter is a Forgery

On 19 December 2003 the letter certifying that Bank of America held €3.95 billion for Parmalat's offshore unit Bonlat was declared false by the bank in a statement to the US SEC and in a press release. The bank account and the assets did not exist and the purported confirmation had been forged. Agnes Belgrave, the signatory of the letter who worked in Bank of America's Manhattan offices, denied any involvement in Parmalat's affairs (Betts and Barber, 2004). Although documents concerning the Cayman Island subsidiary had been destroyed, Italian prosecutors found documents and a scanning machine used to forge the bank documents on Bank of America letterhead at DPA, a shell company near Parma.

Parmalat CEO Calisto Tanzi flew out of Italy the day Bank of America announced that the letter showing €3.95 billion was false. He went to Switzerland then Portugal, then an undisclosed country in Central or South America, and finally back to Milan where he was detained by police (Barber, 2003).

The Auditors

In 1999, Parmalat was forced to change its auditor under Italian law, and it replaced Grant Thornton with the Italian unit of Deloitte Touche Tohmatsu. However, Grant Thornton's Italian arm continued to audit at least 20 of Parmalat's units, including Bonlat. Deloitte became increasingly reliant on Grant Thornton for scrutiny of Parmalat's accounts. During its work on the 1999 accounts, other auditors had examined subsidiaries representing 22 per cent of Parmalat's consolidated assets. On the 2002 accounts, Deloitte said other auditors examined subsidiaries representing 49 per cent of consolidated assets (Parker et al., 2004).

A suit filed by US shareholders contends that both Deloitte and Grant Thornton issued materially false reports on Parmalat's 1998–2002 year-end financial statements. Deloitte,

▶

Parmalat – Milk Spills After Sour Confirmation (continued)

which took over as Parmalat's primary auditor, deliberately failed to verify reports from Grant Thornton on assets held by a Parmalat subsidiary. The suit also asserts that on at least eight occasions, Grant Thornton failed to send third-party confirmation request letters in connection with its audits of Parmalat's subsidiaries. Further, it asserts, the firm failed to conduct independent audits on the 17 Parmalat subsidiaries that it was engaged to audit from 1999 to 2003, but rather participated in the falsification of audit confirmation documents (*International Herald Tribune*, 2004).

Italian authorities arrested Lorenzo Penca, chairman of Grant Thornton SpA and Maurizio Bianchi, a partner in the firm's Milan office, on charges that their actions contributed to Parmalat's bankruptcy. They claimed that two men suggested ways that Parmalat executives could 'falsify the balance sheet' of a subsidiary and then 'falsely certified' the financial statements (Galloni *et al.*, 2004). Prosecutors in Italy have said Penca and Bianchi were behind the plan to create Bonlat and they failed to disclose details of two other offshore Parmalat vehicles in the Netherlands Antilles, according to court documents (US District Court, Southern New York, 2003).

In an academic paper presented at the 2nd International Conference on Corporate Governance on 29 June 2004 Andrea Melis, a researcher from the University of Cagliari, concluded that 'it is not clear whether Grant Thornton sent a second confirmation request given the time lag between the confirmation request and the response. However, they acknowledged that the request to Bank of America was done via the Parmalat chief finance director rather than getting in contact with Bank of America directly. Therefore, it seems reasonable to argue that they could have discovered the fraud if they had acted according to general auditing standards and exhibited the proper degree of professional 'scepticism' in executing their audit procedures.'

Discussion Questions	■ What audit procedures should auditors use in confirming a very material cash balance? ■ If a primary auditor is significantly dependent on the work of another auditor, what reviews and substantive tests should they conduct?

References	Barber, T., 2003, 'Tanzi Takes a Mystery Tour Amidst the Parmalat Mayhem', *Financial Times*, 30 December, p. 12. Betts, P. and Barber, T., 2004, 'Parmalat Probe Uncovers Fresh Evidence', *Financial Times*, 2 January, p. 1. Edmonson, G. and Cohn, L., 2004, 'How Parmalat Went Sour', *Business Week*, 12 January, pp. 46–48. Galloni, A., Bryan-Low, C. and Ascarelli, S., 2004, 'Top Executives are Arrested at Parmalat Auditor', *Wall Street Journal*, 2 January, A3. *International Herald Tribune*, 2004, 'Investors File Lawsuit in Parmalat Inquiry: Officials, Auditors and Lawyers Named', 7 January. Parker, A., Tessell, T. and Betts, P., 2004, 'Auditors Come Under Growing Scrutiny', *Financial Times*, 3 January, p. 9. Melis, A., 2004, 'Corporate Governance Failures: To What Extent is Parmalat a Particularly Italian Case?' presented at the 2nd International Conference on Corporate Governance on 29 June 2004. Rigby, E. and Michaels, A., 2003, 'Parmalat's Auditor 'A Victim of Fraud', *Financial Times*, 27 December, p. 8. SEC, 2003, Litigation Release No. 18527, Accounting and Auditing Enforcement Release No. 1936, 'SEC Charges Parmalat with Financial Fraud', US Securities and Exchange Commission, 30 December. US District Court for the Southern District of New York, 2003, 03CU10266 (CPKC) *Securities and Exchange Commission* v *Parmalat Finanziaria, SpA*, 29 December.

Confirmation in Response to a Significant Risk

An auditor may use a confirmation in response to a significant risk. For example, if the auditor determines that management is under pressure to meet earnings expectations, there may be a related risk that management is inflating sales by entering into sales agreements that include terms that preclude revenue recognition or by invoicing sales before delivery. In these circumstances, the auditor may design external confirmations not only to confirm outstanding amounts, but also to confirm the details of the sales agreements, including date, any rights of return and delivery terms.

Confirmation of Accounts Receivable

The confirmation of accounts receivable is typical of the confirmation process. First the auditor either decides to take a random sample of customer accounts or, alternatively, looks through accounts receivable subsidiary ledgers and picks out some customers based on his professional judgement (e.g. customers with very large balances or very small balances, customers that are slow in paying, and/or customers that buy erratically). The auditor then gives this list to the client to prepare a confirmation letter requesting that customers reply directly to the auditor. Then the auditor, not the client, mails these letters. The auditor should check randomly to see if the letters are addressed to the same customers the auditor chose and for the amounts shown on the books.

Positive and Negative Confirmations

ISA 505 identifies two forms of confirmations: positive and negative confirmation.[9] The request for **positive confirmation** asks the recipient (debtor, creditor or other third party) to confirm agreement or by asking the recipient to provide written information. A positive confirmation request is a request that the confirming party respond directly to the auditor indicating whether the confirming party agrees or disagrees with the information in the request, or providing the requested information. A response to a positive confirmation request is expected to provide reliable audit evidence. The auditor may reduce the risk that a respondent replies to the request without verifying the information by using positive confirmation requests that do not state the amount (or other information) on the confirmation request, but asks the respondent to fill in the amount. However, using this type of 'blank' confirmation request may result in lower response rates because additional effort is required of the respondents. The positive form is preferred when inherent or control risk is assessed as high because with the negative form no reply may be due to causes other than agreement with the recorded balance.

It is highly likely that there will be no response to at least a few positive confirmation letters. In that case, an alternative audit procedure is called for, especially if the confirmation is for a significant reason, for instance, confirmation of an investment account that is material (like the case of Parmalat). An alternative procedure for confirmation of cash is to prepare a reconciliation of the account based on prior investment bank statements and subsequent cash deposits and withdrawals. An alternative procedure for accounts receivables is inspection of after balance sheet date payments received from customers and then tracing them to balances at the end of the year so as to establish existence of the balances.

A **negative confirmation** request asks the respondent to reply only in the event of disagreement with the information provided in the request. However, if there is no response to a negative confirmation request, the auditor cannot be sure that intended third parties have received the confirmation requests and verified that the information contained therein is correct. For this reason, negative confirmation requests ordinarily provides less reliable evidence than the use of positive confirmation requests, and the auditor may consider performing other substantive procedures to supplement the use of negative confirmations.

The auditor must not use negative confirmation requests as the sole substantive audit procedure to address an assessed risk of material misstatement at the assertion level unless all of the following are present:[10]

- the assessed level of inherent and control risk is low;
- a large number of small, homogeneous account balances are involved;
- a substantial number of errors is not expected (exception rate is low);
- the auditor has no reason to believe that respondents will disregard these requests.

No Response to Confirmation Letter

In case the auditor does not receive a reply to a positive confirmation request, he ordinarily sends out a second confirmation letter. If the addressee still does not reply to positive confirmation, the auditor should perform alternative audit procedures to obtain relevant and reliable audit evidence. The alternative audit procedures should be such as to provide the evidence about the financial statement assertions that the confirmation request was intended to provide. If the auditor does not obtain such confirmation, the auditor shall determine the implications for the audit and the auditor's opinion.

If Audit Client Does Not Allow Confirmations

When the auditor seeks to confirm certain balances or other information, and management requests him not to do so, the auditor should consider whether there are valid grounds for management's requests and if there is evidence to support the validity of the request. If the auditor agrees to management's request not to seek external confirmation regarding a particular matter, the auditor should apply alternative procedures to obtain sufficient appropriate evidence regarding that matter.

If the auditor concludes that management's refusal to allow the auditor to send a confirmation request is unreasonable, or the auditor is unable to obtain relevant and reliable audit evidence from alternative audit procedures, the auditor shall communicate with those charged with governance. The auditor also shall determine the implications for the audit and the auditor's opinion.[11]

10.5   Sampling

The objective of the auditor, when using audit sampling, is to provide a reasonable basis for drawing conclusions about the population (e.g., invoices, shipping documents and other original source material) from which the sample is selected.[12]

Audit sampling (sampling) is the application of audit procedures to less than 100 per cent of items within a population of audit relevance such that all sampling units have a chance of selection in order to provide the auditor with a reasonable basis on which to draw conclusions about the entire population. This enables the auditor to obtain and evaluate audit evidence about some characteristic of the items selected in order to form a conclusion about the population from which the sample is drawn. Audit sampling can use either a statistical or a non-statistical approach.

It is difficult, if not impossible, to audit every source document from sales order to customer payment, purchase order to vendor payment. Sampling is necessary; however, it does not come without risk. **Sampling risk** is the risk that the auditor's conclusion based on a sample may be different from the conclusion if the entire population were subjected to the same audit procedure. Sampling risk can lead to two types of erroneous conclusions:

1 In the case of a test of controls, that controls are more effective than they actually are, or in the case of a test of details, that a material misstatement does not exist when in fact it does. The auditor is primarily concerned with this type of erroneous conclusion because it affects audit effectiveness and is more likely to lead to an inappropriate audit opinion.
2 In the case of a test of controls, that controls are less effective than they actually are, or in the case of a test of details, that a material misstatement exists when in fact it does not. This type of erroneous conclusion affects audit efficiency as it would usually lead to additional work to establish that initial conclusions were incorrect.

A detailed discussion of audit sampling appears in Chapter 8 Appendix 'Audit Sampling and Other Selective Testing Procedures' of this book.

■ Sampling Requirements

To do proper sampling, the auditor must follow certain requirements in sample design, size and selection of items for testing; performing audit procedures; the nature and cause of deviations and misstatements; projecting misstatements; and evaluating results of the sampling.

The sample design requires that the auditor consider the purpose of the audit procedure and the characteristics of the population from which the sample will be drawn. The auditor must determine a sample size sufficient to reduce sampling risk to an acceptably low level. Items for the sample should be selected in such a way that each sampling unit in the population has a chance of selection.

Of course, the auditor must perform audit procedures, appropriate to the purpose, on each item selected. If it is the case that the audit procedure is not applicable to the selected item, the auditor has to perform the procedure on a replacement item. If the auditor is unable to apply the designed audit procedures, or suitable alternative procedures, to a selected item, the auditor shall treat that item as a deviation from the prescribed control, in the case of tests of controls, or a misstatement, in the case of tests of details.

When any deviations or misstatements are found, the auditor investigates the nature and cause and evaluates their possible effect on the audit. In the extremely rare circumstances when the auditor considers a misstatement or deviation discovered in a sample to be an **anomaly**,[13] the auditor must obtain a high degree of certainty that such misstatement or deviation is not representative of the population. This degree of certainty is obtained by performing additional audit procedures to get sufficient appropriate audit evidence that the misstatement or deviation does not affect the remainder of the population.

Once misstatements are found in the sample in tests of details, they should be applied to the population as a whole by projecting that the population is the same as the sample. For example, if there are two errors per hundred in the sample (2 per cent of the sample is misstated), the auditor would project that there is a 2 per cent misstatement in the whole population from which the sample comes.

The auditor must evaluate the results of the sample; and whether the use of audit sampling has provided a reasonable basis for conclusions about the population that has been tested. See Chapter 8 Appendix 'Audit Sampling and Other Selective Testing Procedures' for more details on the techniques of sampling and Chapter 8 for information on sampling by computer assisted audit techniques (CAATs).

10.6   Audit of Estimates

Some financial statement items cannot be measured precisely, but can only be estimated. These items are accounting estimates. An **accounting estimate** is an approximation of a monetary amount in the absence of a precise means of measurement. This term is used for an amount measured at fair value where there is estimation uncertainty, as well as for other amounts that require estimation. Estimate audit standards are ISA 540 'Auditing Accounting Estimates, Including Fair Value Accounting Estimates, and Related Disclosures.'[14]

The nature and reliability of information available to management to support the making of an accounting estimate varies widely, which thereby affects the degree of estimation uncertainty associated with accounting estimates. The degree of estimation uncertainty affects the risks of material misstatement of accounting estimates, including their susceptibility to unintentional or intentional management bias. The measurement objective of accounting estimates can vary. The measurement objective for some accounting estimates is to forecast the outcome of transactions, events or conditions requiring the accounting estimate. The measurement objective is different for other accounting estimates, including many **fair value accounting**[15] estimates, and is expressed in terms of the value of a current transaction or financial statement item. This type of measurement is based on conditions prevalent at the measurement date, such as estimated market price for a particular type of asset or liability.

When considering the audit of estimates, the objective of the auditor is to obtain sufficient appropriate audit evidence about whether accounting estimates, including fair value accounting estimates, in the financial statements are reasonable and related disclosures in the financial statements are adequate.[16]

■ Risk Assessment Procedures and Related Activities

In order to provide a basis for the identification and assessment of the risks of material misstatement for accounting estimates, the auditor must obtain an understanding of how management identifies accounting estimates that are needed and how these estimates are made.[17] To determine how management identifies those transactions, events and conditions that may give rise to the need for accounting estimates, the auditor must make inquiries of management about changes in circumstances that may give rise to new, or the need to revise existing, accounting estimates. The auditor also must determine how management makes the accounting estimates, and an understanding of the data on which they are based, including:

- the method and model used in making the accounting estimate;
- relevant controls;
- whether management has used an expert;
- the assumptions underlying the accounting estimates;
- whether there has been, or ought to have been, a change from the prior period in the methods for making the accounting estimates, and if so, why; and
- whether and, if so, how management has assessed the effect of estimation uncertainty.

The auditor must review the outcome of accounting estimates included in the prior period financial statements, or their subsequent re-estimation for the current period. However, the review is not intended to call into question the judgements made in the prior periods that were based on information available at that time.

In identifying and assessing the risks of material misstatement, the auditor must evaluate the degree of estimation uncertainty associated with an accounting estimate. Do any of those accounting estimates having high estimation uncertainty give rise to significant risks?

■ Responses to the Assessed Risks of Material Misstatement

Based on the assessed risks of material misstatement, the auditor must determine whether management has appropriately applied the requirements of the applicable financial reporting framework and whether the methods for making the accounting estimates are appropriate and have been applied consistently. He must also determine whether changes from the prior period in accounting estimates or in the estimation method are appropriate in the circumstances.

In responding to the assessed risks of material misstatement, the auditor shall test how management made the accounting estimate and the data on which it is based. Further, he must make his own point estimate to compare to management's estimates. Testing management's estimate requires evaluating whether the method of measurement used is appropriate and the assumptions used by management are reasonable based on the applicable financial framework. Also tested is the operating effectiveness of the controls over how management made the accounting estimate.

The auditor develops a point estimate or a range to evaluate management's point estimate. If the auditor uses assumptions or methods that differ from management's, the auditor must establish that his point estimate takes into account relevant variables and evaluate any significant differences from management's point estimate.

For accounting estimates that give rise to significant risks, in addition to other substantive procedures the auditor must evaluate how management has considered alternative assumptions or otherwise addressed estimation uncertainty. The auditor must identify whether there are indicators of possible management bias.

Accounting estimates require certain disclosures based on the applicable financial accounting standards and framework. The auditor must obtain sufficient appropriate audit evidence about whether the estimates are disclosed in accordance with the financial reporting framework.

■ Written Representations and Documentation

The auditor must obtain written representations from management and, where appropriate, those charged with governance, saying that they believe significant assumptions used in making their accounting estimates are reasonable.

The auditor must include in the audit documentation[18] the basis for the auditor's conclusions about the reasonableness of accounting estimates and their disclosure that give rise to significant risks; and indicators of possible management bias, if any.

10.7 Evaluation of Misstatements Identified During the Audit (ISA 450)

It is the auditor's responsibility when forming an opinion on the financial statements to conclude whether reasonable assurance has been obtained about whether the financial statements as a whole are free from material misstatement.[19] The auditor's conclusion takes into account his evaluation of uncorrected **misstatements**.[20] Therefore, the objective of the auditor is to evaluate the effect of identified misstatements on the audit; and the effect of **uncorrected misstatements**[21] on the financial statements.[22]

■ Consideration of Identified Misstatements as the Audit Progresses

The auditor must accumulate misstatements identified during the audit, other than those that are clearly trivial. Findings during the audit may require the auditor to consider whether the overall audit strategy and audit plan need to be revised. For instance, the audit plan may have to be revised if the nature of identified misstatements and their circumstances indicate that other misstatements may exist that, when aggregated with misstatements accumulated during the audit, could be material.

■ Communication and Correction of Misstatements

All misstatements accumulated during the audit must be communicated to the appropriate level of management on a timely basis.[23]

Generally if misstatements are found, the auditor asks management to correct them. If management corrects the misstatements that were detected, the auditor must still perform additional audit procedures to determine whether misstatements remain. If management refuses to correct some or all of the misstatements communicated by the auditor, the auditor should take into account management's reasons for not making the corrections.

The auditor must determine whether uncorrected misstatements are material, individually or in aggregate. In making this determination, the auditor should consider the size and nature of the misstatements and the particular circumstances of their occurrence; and the effect of uncorrected misstatements related to prior periods on the relevant classes of transactions, account balances or disclosures, and the financial statements as a whole.

In addition to management, the auditor is required to communicate with those charged with governance (usually the board of directors) any uncorrected misstatements and the effect that they have on the opinion in the auditor's report. The auditor's communication will identify material uncorrected misstatements individually and request that uncorrected misstatements be corrected. The auditor also communicates the effect of uncorrected misstatements related to prior periods.

The auditor must request a written representation from management and, where appropriate, those charged with governance whether they believe the effects of uncorrected misstatements are immaterial, individually and in aggregate, to the financial statements as a whole. A summary of such items shall be included in or attached to the written representation.

In their work paper documentation the auditor must include:[24]

- the amount below which misstatements would be regarded as clearly trivial;
- all misstatements accumulated during the audit and whether they have been corrected; and
- The auditor's conclusion as to whether uncorrected misstatements are material, individually or in aggregate, and the basis for that conclusion.

10.8 Related Parties

Parties are considered to be related if one party has the ability to control the other party or exercise significant influence over the other party in making financial and operation decisions. A **related party transaction** is a transfer of resources or obligations between related parties, regardless of whether a price is charged.

In the normal course of business there may be many related party transactions. In most circumstances, they may carry no higher risk of material misstatement of the financial statements than similar transactions with unrelated parties. However, the nature of related party relationships and transactions may, in some circumstances, contribute to higher risks of material misstatements than transactions with unrelated parties. Some examples of these risk-increasing circumstances are:

- Related parties may operate through an extensive and complex range of relationships and structures, with a corresponding increase in the complexity of related party transactions.
- Information systems may be ineffective at identifying or summarising transactions and outstanding balances between an entity and its related parties.
- Related party transactions may not be conducted under normal market terms and conditions; for example, some related party transactions may be conducted with no exchange of consideration.

Two aspects of related party transactions of which an auditor must be aware is adequate disclosure of related party transactions and the possibility that the existence of related parties increases the risk of management fraud. International Financial Reporting Standards (IAS 24)[25] and other financial reporting frameworks require disclosure of the nature and volume of transactions with related parties. There are many legitimate reasons for significant transactions with related parties but the risk for an auditor is that management will conceal transactions between related parties causing the disclosures to be misstated, i.e. the related party disclosures are not complete.

Even if the applicable financial reporting framework establishes minimal or no related party requirements, the auditor nevertheless needs to obtain an understanding of the entity's related party relationships and transactions. This understanding should be sufficient to form a conclusion as to whether the financial statements achieve fair presentation (for fair presentation frameworks) or are not misleading (for compliance frameworks). In addition, an understanding of the entity's related party relationships and transactions is relevant to the auditor's evaluation of whether one or more fraud risk factors are present because fraud may be more easily committed through related parties.

Owing to the inherent limitations of an audit, there is an unavoidable risk that some material misstatements of the financial statements may not be detected. In the context of related parties, the potential effects of limitations on the auditor's ability to detect material misstatements are greater because, for example, management may be unaware of the existence of all related party relationships and transactions or related party relationships may present a greater opportunity for collusion, concealment or manipulation by management.

Procedures to Discover Related Party Transactions

Because of the possibility of related party transactions, the auditor should perform audit procedures designed to obtain sufficient appropriate audit evidence regarding the identification and disclosure by management of related parties and the effect of related party transactions. However, an audit cannot be expected to detect all related party transactions. Audit procedures must identify circumstances that increase the risk of misstatement or that indicate material misstatement regarding related parties has occurred. If these circumstances exist, the auditor should perform modified, extended or additional procedures. Illustration 10.3 shows examples of circumstances and may indicate the existence of previously unidentified related parties.

ILLUSTRATION 10.3

Circumstances That May Indicate Unidentified Related Parties

During the course of the audit, the auditor needs to be alert for transactions that appear unusual in the circumstances and may indicate the existence of previously unidentified related parties. Examples include:

- Transactions which have abnormal terms of trade, such as unusual prices, interest rates, guarantees and repayment terms.
- Transactions which lack an apparent logical business reason for their occurrence.
- Transactions in which substance differs from form.
- Transactions processed in an unusual manner.
- High-volume or significant transactions with certain customers or suppliers as compared with others.
- Unrecorded transactions such as the receipt or provision of management services at no charge.

Concept and a Company 10.2

Adelphia Communications

Concept	Related parties and unrecorded liabilities.
Story	Adelphia Communications, the sixth largest cable television provider in the USA, was the subject of a Securities and Exchange Commission (SEC) and federal grand jury investigation into its finances as its accounting practices were questioned. The company was founded and managed by John Rigas and his family.

Adelphia had fraudulently excluded from the Company's annual and quarterly consolidated financial statements portions of its bank debt, totalling approximately $2.3 billion in undisclosed, off-balance-sheet bank debt as of 31 December 2001, by systematically recording those liabilities on the books of unconsolidated affiliates, which were controlled by the Rigas family (Rigas Entities). They included in those financial statements a footnote disclosure implicitly misrepresenting that such portions had been included on Adelphia's balance sheet (SEC, 2002). Adelphia and its executives created sham transactions backed by fictitious documents to give the false appearance that Adelphia had actually repaid debts, when, in truth, it had simply shifted them to unconsolidated Rigas-controlled entities.

Since at least 1998, Adelphia used fraudulent misrepresentations and omissions of material fact to conceal rampant self-dealing by the Rigases, the family which founded and ran Adelphia, including use of Adelphia funds to: pay for vacation properties and New York City apartments; develop a golf course mostly owned by the Rigases; and purchase over $772 million of Adelphia shares of common stock and over $563 million of Adelphia notes for the Rigases' own benefit (SEC, 2002).

In addition to Adelphia's own business operations, it also managed and maintained virtually every aspect of the Rigas Entities that owned and operated cable television systems, including maintaining their books and records on a general ledger system shared with Adelphia and its subsidiaries. Rigas Entities did not reimburse or otherwise compensate Adelphia for these services.

Adelphia and the Rigas Entities, including those that are in businesses unrelated to cable systems, participated jointly in a cash management system operated by Adelphia (the 'Adelphia CMS'). Adelphia, its subsidiaries, and Rigas Entities all deposited some or all of their cash generated or otherwise obtained from their operations, borrowings and other sources in the Adelphia CMS, withdrew cash from the Adelphia CMS to be used for their expenses, capital expenditures, repayments of debt and other uses, and engaged in transfers of funds with other participants in the Adelphia CMS. This resulted in the commingling of funds among the Adelphia CMS participants, including Adelphia subsidiaries and Rigas Entities, and created numerous related party payables and receivables among Adelphia, its subsidiaries and Rigas Entities (SEC, 2002).

To conceal that the Rigases were engaged in rampant self-dealing at Adelphia's expense, Adelphia misrepresented or concealed a number of significant transactions by which the Rigases used Adelphia resources with no reimbursement or other compensation to Adelphia. The defendants engaged in these practices to afford Adelphia continued access to commercial credit and the capital markets.

In November 2002, Adelphia Corporation filed suit against its former auditor, Deloitte & Touche, claiming the firm was partly responsible for the alleged fraud that cost company

▶

383

Adelphia Communications (continued)

shareholders billions of dollars. 'If Deloitte had acted consistently with its professional responsibilities as Adelphia's outside auditor, these losses could have been preventable,' according to the complaint. The complaint alleges that some of the Rigas family's (which controlled Adelphia) acts of self-dealing were apparent to Deloitte on the books and records which Deloitte reviewed and that Deloitte knew or should have known of such acts! During its 2000 audit, for which an unqualified audit opinion was given, Deloitte asked the Rigases to disclose the full amount of the loans, which totalled $1.45 billion at the time but later amounted to more than $3 billion. The Rigases refused, and Deloitte never disclosed this issue or any disagreement to the audit committee. Adelphia's cash management system had a pool of corporate funds that the Rigases used as their personal bank account. The complaint alleges that Deloitte knew about the system and didn't report it to the audit committee (Frank, 2002).

Discussion Questions
- What audit procedures could the auditor undertake to detect the Adelphia related party transactions?
- What kind of control environment encourages related party transactions?
- At what point would the auditor report related party dealings to the board of directors?

References   Frank, R., 2002, 'The Economy: Adelphia Sues Deloitte & Touche, Accusing Former Auditor of Fraud', *Wall Street Journal* (Eastern edn), New York, NY, 7 November, p. A2.

SEC, 2002, Litigation Release No. 17837, Accounting Auditing Enforcement Release No. 1664, 'Securities And Exchange Commission v Adelphia Communications Corporation, John J. Rigas, Timothy J. Rigas, Michael J. Rigas, James P. Rigas, James R. Brown, and Michael C. Mulcahey', US Securities and Exchange Commission, 14 November.

■ Understanding the Entity's Related Party Relationships and Transactions

The engagement team discussion required by ISA 315[26] and ISA 240[27] includes specific consideration of the susceptibility of the financial statements to material misstatement due to fraud or error that could result from the entity's related party relationships and transactions.

To acquire and understanding, the auditor will inquire of management regarding:

- The identity of the entity's related parties, including changes from the prior period.
- The nature of the relationships between the entity and these related parties.
- Whether the entity entered into any transactions with these related parties during the period and, if so, the type and purpose of the transactions.
- The controls, if any, that management has established to:
  - identify, account for and disclose related party relationships and transactions in accordance with the applicable financial reporting framework;
  - authorise and approve significant transactions and arrangements with related parties; and
  - authorise and approve significant transactions and arrangements outside the normal course of business.

■ Maintaining Alertness for Related Party Information When Reviewing Records or Documents

The auditor should review information provided by the directors and management identifying related party transactions while being alert for other material related party transactions. He should review management information identifying the names of all known related parties. The auditor may perform the following procedures to determine completeness of this information:

■ review prior year working papers for names of known related parties;
■ review the entity's procedures for identification of related parties;
■ inquire as to the affiliation of directors and officers with other entities;
■ review shareholder records to determine the names of principal shareholders or, if appropriate, obtain a listing of principal shareholders from the share register;
■ review minutes of the meetings of shareholders and the board of directors and other relevant statutory records such as the register of directors' interests;
■ inquire of other auditors currently involved in the audit, or predecessor auditors, as to their knowledge of additional related parties;
■ review the entity's income tax returns and other information supplied to the regulatory agencies.

During the audit, the auditor should remain alert for arrangements that management has not disclosed that may indicate the existence of related party relationships or transactions. In particular, the auditor must inspect bank and legal confirmations and minutes of shareholders or governance bodies for indications of the existence of related party transactions

If the auditor identifies significant transactions outside the entity's normal course of business the auditor should ask management about the nature of these transactions and if related parties are involved.

■ Risks of Material Misstatement Associated with Related Party Relationships and Transactions

In meeting the audit requirement to identify and assess the risks of material misstatement, the auditor must identify and assess the risks associated with related party relationships and transactions and determine whether any of those risks are significant risks. In making this determination, the auditor must treat identified significant related party transactions outside the entity's normal course of business as giving rise to significant risks. The auditor may identify fraud risk factors (including circumstances relating to the existence of a related party with dominant influence) when performing procedures in connection with related parties.

As part of the ISA 330 requirement that the auditor respond to assessed risks,[28] he designs and performs further audit procedures to obtain sufficient appropriate audit evidence about the assessed risks of material misstatement associated with related party relationships and transactions. If the auditor identifies arrangements or information that suggests the existence of related party relationships, the auditor must promptly communicate the relevant information to the other members of the engagement team. If there is an applicable financial reporting framework (such as IFRS) which establishes related party requirements the auditor requests that management identify all transactions with

> ### ILLUSTRATION 10.4
>
> ## Procedures to Identify Related Parties' Transactions
>
> During the course of the audit, the auditor carries out procedures that may identify the existence of transactions with related parties. Examples include:
>
> - Performing detailed tests of transactions and balances.
> - Reviewing minutes of meetings of shareholders and directors.
> - Reviewing accounting records for large or unusual transactions or balances, paying particular attention to transactions recognised at or near the end of the reporting period.
> - Reviewing confirmations of loans receivable and payable and confirmations from banks. Such a review may indicate guarantor relationship and other related party transactions.
> - Reviewing investment transactions, for example purchase or sale of an equity interest in a joint venture to another entity.

the newly identified related parties and say why the entity's controls failed to identify related party relationships and transactions. The auditor should reconsider the risk that other unidentified related parties may exist. If the non-disclosure by management appears intentional, this may be indicative of fraud.

The auditor may identify significant related party transactions outside the entity's normal course of business. In that case the auditor should inspect the underlying contracts or agreements and evaluate whether the business rationale (or lack of rationale) for the transactions suggests that they may have been entered into to engage in fraudulent financial reporting or to conceal misappropriation (theft) of assets. When considering the contracts, the auditor should also determine if the terms of the transactions are consistent with management's explanations and that the transactions have been appropriately authorised, approved and disclosed.

If management has made an assertion in the financial statements to the effect that a related party transaction was conducted on terms equivalent to those prevailing in an arm's length transaction,[29] the auditor shall obtain sufficient appropriate audit evidence about the assertion.

The auditor should also carry out procedures which may identify related party transactions such as those shown in Illustration 10.4.

■ Auditor Opinion, Written Representations and Documentation

In forming an opinion on the financial statements in accordance with ISA 700,[30] the auditor must evaluate whether the identified related party relationships and transactions have been appropriately accounted for and disclosed. Further, he should consider whether the effects of the related party relationships and transactions prevent the financial statements from achieving fair presentation or make them misleading.

Where the applicable financial reporting framework (such as IFRS) establishes related party requirements, the auditor must obtain written representations from management and those charged with governance that they have disclosed to the auditor the identity of the entity's related parties and all the related party relationships and transactions of which they are aware; and that these relationships have been appropriately accounted for and disclosed.

The auditor shall communicate with those charged with governance significant matters arising during the audit in connection with the entity's related parties (unless all of those charged with governance are involved in managing the entity). The auditor shall include in the audit documentation the names of the identified related parties and the nature of the related party relationships.[31]

10.9 Written Representations (Letter of Representation)

The initial audit procedure in the closing cycle is usually to evaluate *governance* evidence, the evidence pertaining to the company and management. This means, among other things, obtaining written representation from management (sometimes called management representations letter). Written representation is a written statement by management provided to the auditor to confirm certain matters or to support other audit evidence. Written representations in this context do not include financial statements, the assertions therein, or supporting books and records. International Standard on Auditing 580 'Written Representations' states:[32] 'the auditor shall request management to provide a written representation that it has fulfilled its responsibility for the preparation of the financial statements in accordance with the applicable financial reporting framework, including, where relevant, their fair presentation, as set out in the terms of the audit engagement.'

■ Written Representations from Management

During the course of an audit, management makes many representations to the auditor, either unsolicited or in response to specific inquiries. Written representations are necessary information that the auditor requires in connection with the audit of the entity's financial statements. Written representations are audit evidence. When these representations relate to matters that are material to the financial statements, the auditor must seek corroborative audit evidence, evaluate whether the representations made by management appear reasonable and consistent with other audit evidence, and consider whether the individuals making the representations are competent to do so.

In instances when other sufficient appropriate audit evidence cannot reasonably be expected to exist, the auditor should obtain written representations from management on matters material to the financial statements. The auditor may document in his working papers evidence of management's representations by summarising oral discussions with management or by obtaining written representations from management. The possibility of misunderstandings between the auditor and management is reduced when oral representations are confirmed in writing by management.

Form and Content of Representations Letter

The management representation letter should be addressed to the auditor.[33] It should contain the information requested by the auditor, be appropriately dated as near as practicable to, but not after, the date of the auditor's report on the financial statements, and signed. The members of management who have primary responsibility for the entity and its financial aspects, usually the senior executive officer and the chief financial officer, should sign the letter.

Matters that are ordinarily included in a management representation letter are:

■ management's acknowledgement that it has fulfilled its responsibility for the preparation of the financial statements in accordance with the applicable financial reporting framework, including, where relevant, their fair presentation, as set out in the terms of the audit engagement;
■ management has provided the auditor with all relevant information and access as agreed in the terms of the audit engagement;
■ all transactions have been recorded and are reflected in the financial statements;
■ the selection and application of accounting policies are appropriate;
■ matters such as the following, have been recognised, measured, presented or disclosed in accordance with the applicable financial accounting framework:
  – plans or intentions that may affect the carrying value or classification of assets and liabilities;
  – liabilities, both actual and contingent;
  – title to, or control over, assets, the liens or encumbrances on assets, and assets pledged as collateral; and
  – aspects of laws, regulations and contractual agreements that may affect the financial statements, including non-compliance.

A sample of a management representation letter to the auditor is shown in Illustration 10.5.

ILLUSTRATION 10.5

Management Representation Letter[34]

The following illustrative letter includes written representations that are required by ISA 580 and other ISAs in effect for audits of financial statements. It is assumed in this illustration that the applicable financial reporting framework is International Financial Reporting Standards; the requirement of ISA 570 to obtain a written representation is not relevant; and that there are no exceptions to the requested written representations. If there were exceptions, the representations would need to be modified to reflect the exceptions. Representations by management will vary from one entity to another and from one period to the next.

(Entity's Letterhead)

To Auditor…
… (date)

Subject: Representation in connection with the financial statements 201X

Dear (addressee),

This representation letter is provided in connection with your audit of the financial statements 20XX of Company XYZ for the purpose of expressing an opinion as to whether the financial statements give a true and fair view of the financial position of XYZ as at December 31, 20XX and of the result for the year then ended in accordance with Part 9 of Book 2 of the Dutch Civil Code. We have made appropriate inquiries of management and officers of the entity with the relevant knowledge and experience, as we considered necessary and relevant for the purpose of appropriately informing ourselves. Accordingly, we confirm, to the best of our knowledge and belief, the following representations:

Illustration 10.5 (continued)

Financial Statements

1 We acknowledge our responsibility for the preparation and fair presentation of the financial statements and for the preparation of the management board report, both in accordance with Part 9 of Book 2 of the Dutch Civil Code. We have fulfilled our responsibilities, as set out in the terms of the audit engagement dated [insert date], for the preparation of the financial statements including its fair presentation.

2 All transactions have been recorded in the accounting records and are reflected in the financial statements)

3 Significant assumptions used by us in making accounting estimates, including those measured at fair value and...(name of elements with accounting estimates), are reasonable.

4 All events subsequent to the date of the financial statements and for which Part 9 of Book 2 of the Dutch Civil Code requires adjustment or disclosure have been adjusted or disclosed.

5 The effects of uncorrected misstatements are immaterial, both individually and in the aggregate, to the financial statements as a whole. A list of the uncorrected misstatements is attached to the representation letter.

6 [The auditor shall obtain a specific written representation regarding any restatement made to correct a material misstatement in prior period financial statements that affect the comparative information.] The restatement of the comparative information of 20XX-1 as a result of the adjustment of a material misstatement in the prior period financial statements has been appropriately recorded and disclosed in accordance with the requirements of Part 9 of Book 2 of the Dutch Civil Code.

7 [The auditor shall also obtain a specific written representation if events or conditions have been identified that may cast significant doubt on the entity's ability to continue as a going concern.]The financial statement discloses all information of which we are aware that is deemed relevant for our assessment with respect to the entity's ability to continue as a going concern. This includes all relevant key events and circumstances, mitigating factors and our plans for future action. We intend to execute these plans and consider these to be feasible. We confirm that the attached schedule contains our plans for future action relevant to the entity's ability as a going concern, which is the base for our assessment that the entity will be able to continue as a going concern [overview of plans].

Information Provided

8 We have provided you with:
 – Access to all information of which we are aware that is relevant to the preparation of the financial statements such as records, supporting documentation and other matters including all minutes of the General Meetings, Supervisory Board/Audit Committee (or similar body) and the Board of Directors, namely those held on [Data], respectively, and when applicable, summaries of actions of meetings held after period end for which minutes have not yet been prepared, namely those held on [Date].
 – Additional information that you have requested from us for the purpose of the audit; and
 – Unrestricted access to persons within the entity from whom you determined it necessary to obtain audit evidence as part of the audit of the financial statements.

Fraud and compliance with law and regulation

9 The term fraud refers to an intentional act by one or more individuals among management, those charged with governance, employees, or third parties, involving the use of deception to obtain an unjust or illegal advantage. Fraud also includes misstatements resulting from misappropriation of assets, including pledging of assets without proper authorization. Fraudulent financial reporting involves intentional misstatements or omissions of amounts or disclosures in the financial statements to deceive financial statement users.

10 We acknowledge responsibility for the design and implementation of internal control to prevent and detect fraud.

11 We have disclosed to you the results of our assessment of the risk that the financial statements may be materially misstated as a result of fraud.

12 We have disclosed to you all information in relation to suspected fraud, allegation of fraud or fraud affecting the entity involving:

Illustration 10.5 (continued)

– Management;
– Employees who have significant roles in internal control; or
– Others where the fraud could have a material effect on the financial statements.

13 We have disclosed to you all information in relation to any suspected fraud, allegations of fraud, or fraud, affecting the entity's financial statements communicated by employees, former employees, analysts, regulators or others.

14 We have disclosed to you all known instances of non-compliance or suspected noncompliance with laws and regulations whose effects should be considered when preparing financial statements.

Related parties.

15 We have disclosed to you the identity of the entity's related parties and all the related party relationships and transactions of which we are aware.

16 Related party relationships and transactions have been appropriately accounted for and disclosed in accordance with the requirements of Part 9 of Book 2 of the Dutch Civil Code.

Claims and litigations

17 We have disclosed to you all known actual or possible litigation and claims whose effects should be considered when preparing the financial statements and have appropriately accounted for and/or disclosed these in the financial statements in accordance with Part 9 of Book 2 of the Dutch Civil Code. [Other representations which considers the auditor necessary.]

Additional representation [if deemed relevant]

18 Presentation and disclosure of fair value measurements are in accordance with Part 9 of Book 2 of the Dutch Civil Code. The amounts disclosed represent our best estimate of fair value of assets and liabilities required to be disclosed by these standards. The measurement methods and significant assumptions used in determining fair value have been applied in a consistent way, are reasonable and such assumptions appropriately reflect our intent and ability to carry out specific courses of action on behalf of the entity where relevant to the fair value measurements or disclosures.

19 We have no plans or intentions that may materially alter the carrying value or classification of assets and liabilities reflected in the financial statements.

20 We believe that the carrying amounts of all fixed assets will be recoverable.

21 Information regarding financial risks exposure and our financial risk management objectives and policies has been adequately disclosed in the financial statements.

22 The entity has economic title to all assets. There are no rights of distrait or mortgage rights on the entity's assets, except for those that are disclosed in [Note X] to the financial statements.

23 We have properly recorded or disclosed in the financial statements the capital stock repurchase options and agreements, and capital stock reserved for options, warrants, conversions and other requirements.

24 We have requested the legal advisors who perform services for us to provide you with all required information and have requested them to disclose to you any matters you may request in this respect.

Yours Sincerely,
Company XYZ
[Senior Executive Officer]
[Senior Financial Officer]
Optional cc: Audit Committee

Enclosure: Schedule of uncorrected financial statement misstatements

Concept and a Company 10.3

Universal Health Services and KPMG – 'I am neither a certified public accountant nor a securities lawyer'

Concept	Management representation letter and responsibility for financial statements.

Story	Universal Health Services, Inc. (UHS) is a hospital company operating acute care and behavioural health hospitals, ambulatory surgery and radiation centres in the USA, Puerto Rico and France. UHS owns 25 acute care and 39 behavioural health hospitals in these three countries.

In February 2003, UHS's CFO Kirk Gorman, a company veteran of 16 years, was asked to resign at the urging of its auditor, KPMG LLP. KPMG were doing their first audit for the company, having just replaced the predecessor auditor Arthur Andersen. According to UHS, there was a dispute related to Gorman's theoretical views about the split of duties and responsibilities between the CFO and the auditor (Gallaro, 2003).

Gorman wrote a letter to the Philadelphia office of KPMG explaining that, while he was willing to sign the management representation letter (attesting that the financial statements he submitted for audit were, to the best of his knowledge, accurate), he was relying on KPMG to ensure that the accounting treatment was in accordance with GAAP (Leone, 2003). He asked if KPMG would be willing to sign a similar statement vouching for the accuracy of its work (*Corporate Finance*, 2003). Furthermore, the letter released by UHS stated that 'I do review and analyse the financial statements and disclosures in our 10-Q and 10-K filings, but I can't personally verify that all of our accounts are in accordance with GAAP.' Because he was 'neither a certified public accountant nor a securities lawyer' that lead him to 'rely upon KPMG to ensure that our financial statements ... are in compliance with [generally accepted accounting principles] and securities regulations' (UHS, 2002).

In a letter dated 10 February (UHS, 2003), Gorman sought to clarify his position. He wrote that he had not intended to leave the impression that he doubted the veracity of the company's financial statements or that he wanted to shift responsibility for the statements' accuracy to KPMG (Gallaro, 2003).

Nevertheless, KPMG went to the UHS board and argued that it couldn't approve the company's financial statements as long as Gorman remained CFO. Due to 'philosophical differences', the company asked Gorman to resign.

Discussion Questions	■ Who is responsible for the financial statements and why is that the case? ■ Should an auditor sign a statement vouching for the accuracy of his work? Why?

References	Corporate Finance, 2003, 'Auditors Turn up the Heat on CFOs', *Corporate Finance*, London, March, p.1. Gallaro, V., 2003, 'Executive Reservations', *Modern Healthcare*, Chicago, 24 February, Vol. 33, Issue 8, p.12. Leone, M., 2003, 'New Certification and Internal Control Requirements are Heaping New Hazards on Finance Chiefs. Here's How Some are Coping', CFO.com, Boston, 9 May, p. 1. UHS, 2002, 'Letter to KPMG from Gorman', www.uhs.com, dated 12 December.

If management refuses to provide representations that the auditor considers necessary, this will be considered a **limitation on scope**. It is also a limitation on scope if management has provided an oral representation but refuses to confirm it in writing. This scope limitation would mean that the auditor should express a qualified opinion or a disclaimer of opinion.

If management does not provide one or more of the requested written representations, the auditor must first discuss the matter with management. Next, the auditor will re-evaluate the integrity of management and evaluate the effect that this may have on the reliability of representations (oral or written) and audit evidence in general. Finally, the auditor should take appropriate actions, including determining the possible effect on the opinion in the auditor's report.

10.10 Summary

Auditing is a systematic process of objectively obtaining and evaluating evidence regarding assertions about economic actions and events. The auditor shall design and perform audit procedures that are appropriate in the circumstances for the purpose of obtaining sufficient appropriate audit evidence. Evidence is anything that can make a person believe that a fact, proposition or assertion is true or false. Audit evidence is different from the legal evidence required by forensic accounting. In a civil lawsuit, evidence must be strong enough to incline a person to believe one side or the other. In a criminal case, evidence must establish proof of a crime beyond a reasonable doubt. Audit evidence provides only reasonable assurance.

Accounting records, the primary basis of audit evidence, generally include the records of initial entries and supporting records. Initial entries include point of sales transactions, electronic data interchange (EDI), electronic fund transfers (EFT), contracts, invoices, shipping notices, purchase orders, sales orders, the general and subsidiary ledgers, journal entries, and other adjustments to the financial statements. Supporting records examples are computer files, databases, worksheets, spreadsheets, computer and manual logs, computations, reconciliations, and disclosures.

The auditor performs risk assessment procedures in order to provide a basis for the assessment of risks. Risk assessment procedures by themselves do not provide sufficient appropriate audit evidence on which to base the audit opinion, however. Risk assessment procedures must be supplemented by further audit procedures in the form of tests of controls and substantive procedures.

An auditor obtains audit evidence by one or more of the following evidence-gathering techniques: inquiry, observation, inspection (of tangible assets, records or documents), re-performance, recalculation, confirmation and analytical procedures. Inquiry consists of seeking information from knowledgeable persons inside or outside the entity. Observation consists of looking at a process or procedure being performed by others. Inspection consists of examining records, documents or tangible assets. Re-performance is the auditor's independent execution of procedures or controls that were originally performed as part of the entity's internal control. Recalculation consists of checking the arithmetical accuracy of source documents and accounting records or of performing independent calculations. Confirmation consists of the response to an inquiry to corroborate information contained in the accounting records. There are two forms of confirmations: positive and negative.

In general, audit evidence from external sources (e.g. external confirmation of cash account received from a bank) is more reliable than evidence generated internally. Evidence obtained directly by the auditor is more reliable than that obtained from the client entity and more reliable than evidence obtained indirectly or by inference (e.g. inquiry about the application of a control). Written documents are the second most reliable audit evidence. External confirmation combines direct participation by the auditor and written documentation from an external source. Confirmation consists of the response to an inquiry of a third party to corroborate information contained in the accounting records. Confirmation is the auditor's receipt of a written or oral response from an independent third party verifying the accuracy of information requested. It is the act of obtaining audit evidence from a third party in support of a fact or condition. Because confirmations from independent third parties are usually in writing, and are requested directly by the auditor, they are highly persuasive evidence.

The objective of the auditor, when using audit sampling, is to provide a reasonable basis for drawing conclusions about the population (e.g., invoices, shipping documents, and other original source material) from which the sample is selected. Audit sampling (sampling) is the application of audit procedures to less than 100 per cent of items within a population of audit relevance such that all sampling units have a chance of selection in order to provide the auditor with a reasonable basis on which to draw conclusions about the entire population. This enables the auditor to obtain and evaluate audit evidence about some characteristic of the items selected in order to form or assist in forming a conclusion concerning the population from which the sample is drawn. Audit sampling can use either a statistical or a non-statistical approach. Sampling risk is the risk that the auditor's conclusion based on a sample may be different from the conclusion if the entire population were subjected to the same audit procedure.

Some financial statement items cannot be measured precisely, but can only be estimated. These items are accounting estimates. An accounting estimate is an approximation of a monetary amount in the absence of a precise means of measurement. This term is used for an amount measured at fair value where there is estimation uncertainty, as well as for other amounts that require estimation. The nature and reliability of information available to management to support the making of an accounting estimate varies widely, affecting the risks of material misstatement of accounting estimates, including their susceptibility to unintentional or intentional management bias.

It is the auditor's responsibility when forming an opinion on the financial statements to conclude whether reasonable assurance has been obtained about whether the financial statements as a whole are free from material misstatement. The auditor's conclusion takes into account his evaluation of uncorrected misstatements. Therefore, the objective of the auditor is to evaluate the effect of identified misstatements on the audit; and the effect of uncorrected misstatements on the financial statements.

Parties are considered to be related if one party has the ability to control the other party or exercise significant influence over the other party in making financial and operation decisions. A related party transaction is a transfer of resources or obligations between related parties, regardless of whether a price is charged. The nature of related party relationships and transactions may, in some circumstances, contribute to higher risks of material misstatements than transactions with unrelated parties.

The initial audit procedure in the closing cycle is usually to evaluate *governance evidence*, the evidence pertaining to the company and management. This means, among other things, obtaining written representation from management (sometimes called management representations letter). Written representation is a written statement by management provided to the auditor to confirm certain matters or to support other audit evidence. Written representations in this context do not include financial statements, the assertions therein, or supporting books and records. International Standard on Auditing 580 'Written Representations' states:[35] 'the auditor shall request management to provide a written representation that it has fulfilled its responsibility for the preparation of the financial statements in accordance with the applicable financial reporting framework, including, where relevant, their fair presentation, as set out in the terms of the audit engagement.'

10.11 Questions, Exercises and Cases

QUESTIONS

10.2 Introduction

10-1 Define and discuss the differences between general evidence, audit evidence and legal evidence.

10-2 Name transaction and supporting records that would be considered accounting records.

10.3 Audit Procedures for Obtaining Audit Evidence

10-3 Why should an auditor corroborate evidence for inquiry? Name a famous court case and discuss.

10-4 What alternative procedures can an auditor do when he is unable to attend a physical inventory?

10-5 Discuss the reliability of external documents as evidence.

10-6 Define and give an example of recalculation and re-performance.

10-7 List the six evidence-gathering techniques in order of reliability. List the six evidence-gathering techniques in order of cost from highest to lowest.

10.4 External Confirmation

10-8 What are four key characteristics of confirmation?

10-9 Discuss the differences between positive and negative confirmation.

10-10 If a confirmation is not returned to the auditor what alternative procedures can he perform?

10.5 Sampling

10-11 Define the objective of sampling and audit sampling.

10-12 What should an auditor do when she finds deviations or misstatements when sampling?

10.6 Audit of Estimates

10-13 What issues arise in auditing accounting estimates?

10-14 The auditor must determine how management makes the accounting estimates, and an understanding of the data on which they are based. What must the auditor determine?

10.7 Evaluation of Misstatements Identified During the Audit (ISA 450)

10-15 Explain the statement, 'All misstatements accumulated during the audit must be communicated to the appropriate level of management on a timely basis.'

10.8 Related Parties

10-16 Discuss circumstances involving related parties that contribute to higher risks of material misstatements than transactions with unrelated parties.

10-17 Because of the possibility of related party transactions, the auditor should perform audit procedures designed to obtain sufficient appropriate audit evidence regarding the identification and disclosure by management of related parties and the effect of related party transactions. Name the procedures an auditor may perform regarding related party information provided by management.

10.9 Written Representations (Letter of Representation)

10-18 What should an auditor do if management refuses to provide a letter of representation (written representation of management)?

PROBLEMS AND EXERCISES

10.2 Introduction

10-19 Define Forensic Accounting. Assume that you are working at a forensic accounting firm whose speciality was Family Law Support (divorce and custody) forensics. What kind of evidence would you look for? See the website of real forensic accounting firm White, Zuckerman, Warsavsky, Luna and Hunt (**http://www.wzwlh.com/**) for ideas.

10.3 Audit Procedures for Obtaining Audit Evidence

10-20 Evidence-Gathering Techniques. An auditor obtains audit evidence by one or more of the following evidence-gathering techniques: inquiry, observation, inspection, re-performance, recalculation, confirmation and analytical procedures.

Required:

For each of the evidence-gathering technique give an example of a substantive test procedure.

10-21 Inquiry, Analytical Procedures and Observation. In the examination of financial statements, auditors must judge the validity of the audit evidence they obtain. For the following questions, assume that the auditors have considered internal control and found it satisfactory.

Required:

A. In the course of examination, the auditors ask many questions of client officers and employees.
    1 Describe the factors that the auditors should consider in evaluating oral evidence provided by client officers and employees.
    2 Discuss the validity and limitations of oral evidence.
B. Analytical procedures include the computation of various balance sheet and operating ratios for comparison to prior years and industry averages. Discuss the validity and limitations of ratio analysis as evidential matter.
C. In connection with an examination of the financial statements of a manufacturing company, the auditors are observing the physical inventory of finished goods, which consists of expensive, highly complex electronic equipment. Discuss the validity and limitations of the audit evidence provided by this procedure.

10-22 Inspection. Discuss what you would accept as satisfactory documentary evidence in support of entries in the following:
A. Sales journal.
B. Sales returns register.
C. Voucher or invoice register.
D. Payroll register.
E. Cheque register.

10-23 Attendance at Physical Inventory Counting. A processor of frozen foods carries an inventory of finished products consisting of 50 different types of items valued at approximately $2,000,000. About $750,000 of this value represents stock produced by the company and billed to customers prior to the audit date. This stock is being held for the customers at a monthly rental charge until they request shipment and is not separate from the company's inventory.

The company maintains separate perpetual ledgers at the plant office for both stock owned and stock being held for customers. The cost department also maintains a perpetual record of stock owned. The above perpetual records reflect quantities only.

The company does not take a complete physical inventory at any time during the year, since the temperature in the cold storage facilities is too low to allow one to spend more than 15 minutes inside at a time. It is not considered practical to move items outside or to defreeze the cold storage facilities for the purpose of taking a physical inventory. Because of these circumstances, it is impractical to test count quantities to the extent of completely counting specific items. The company considers as its inventory valuation at year-end the aggregate of the quantities reflected by the perpetual record of stock owned, maintained at the plant office, priced at the lower of cost or market.

Required:
A. What are the two principal problems facing the auditor in the audit of the inventory? Discuss briefly.
B. Outline the audit steps that you would take to enable you to render an unqualified opinion with respect to the inventory. (You may omit consideration of tests of unit prices and clerical accuracy.)

10.4 External Confirmation

10–24 Accounts Receivable Confirmations – Positive and Negative. In work on accounts receivable, use of confirmations is of great importance.

Required:
A. What is an audit confirmation?
B. What characteristics should an audit confirmation possess if an auditor is to consider it as sufficient appropriate audit evidence?
C. Distinguish between a positive and a negative accounts receivable confirmation.
D. In confirming a client's accounts receivable, what characteristics should be present in the accounts if the auditor is to use negative confirmations?

10.5 Sampling

10–25 The public accounting firm of Kalinowski, Czajor and Fijalkowska is auditing Whim of Warsaw, a video gaming company. The wish to get a sample of accounts receivable accounts for confirmation. Describe the procedure they would follow when selecting and performing the sampling.

10.6 Audit of Estimates

10–26 The public accounting firm of Rodrigue, Chen and Veenstra, Charted Accountants, is auditing the Windsor, Canada, company Gold Mountain which sells gold and precious metals on their website GoldMountain.com. Gold Mountain's holdings include derivative gold contracts, gold certificates and physical deposits of gold bullion. All their holding must be valued to the market equivalent. What responses to the assessed risk of material misstatement caused by the estimates must Rodrigue, Chen and Veenstra undertake?

10.7 Evaluation of Misstatements Identified During the Audit (ISA 450)

10–27 Novosibirsk Energy, a private oil transport company covering the south of Russia, is being audited by the public accounting firm of Berezinets, Frolova and Kuter (BFK). During their sampling of oil shipments BFK found a material misstatement. What procedures should BFK undertake to determine total misstatement and communicate to management and those charged with governance?

10.8 Related Parties

10–28 Related Parties. D'orsay Dore, SA is being audited by Stolowy & Oxibar, Expert Comptables. During the course of the audit Stolowy & Oxibar discover D'orsay Dore sold inventory to Parisienne de Fedora for 90-day terms, three times the typical payment period required, and the payments went directly to the president of D'orsay Dore, not to the accounting department which was the usual practice. Industriel Cuir supplies over 40 per cent of the raw materials D'orsay purchases whereas no other supplier provides more than 5 per cent of raw materials. D'orsay management says that they do so much business with Industriel Cuir because they provide D'orsay management assistance at no charge.

D'orsay's business is greatest in the last month before the fiscal year end when they book 30 per cent of their sales, some years in the last week before closing. D'orsay Dore has provided Stolowy & Oxibar with a management representation letter that states that there are no related party transactions.

Required:

A. Should Stolowy & Oxibar take D'orsay Dore's word when they say there are no related parties? Why?

B. List the circumstances at D'orsay Dore that may indicate the existence of unidentified related parties.

C. What audit procedures should Stolowy & Oxibar perform to investigate the possibility of related parties?

10.9 Written Representations (Letter of Representation)

10-29 Representation Letter. Robert Dingle, president of Alcmena Manufacturing, Ltd, of Perth, Australia, and the company's external auditor Powell, Ram and Roberts, Chartered Accountant (CA), reviewed matters that were supposed to be included in a written representation letter. Upon receipt of the following client representation letter, Powell, Ram and Roberts contacted Dingle to state that it was incomplete. The letter Powell, Ram and Roberts received is given below.

To Powell, Ram and Roberts, CA

In connection with your audit of the balance sheet of Alcmena Manufacturing as of 31 December 20X2, and the related statements of income, retained earnings, and cash flows for the year then ended, for the purpose of expressing an opinion as to whether the financial statements present fairly, in all material respects, the financial position, results of operations, and cash flows of Alcmena Manufacturing in conformity with generally accepted accounting principles, we confirm, to the best of our knowledge and belief, the following representations made to you during your audit. There were no:

- Plans or intentions that may materially affect the carrying value or classification of assets and liabilities.
- Communications from regulatory agencies concerning noncompliance with, or deficiencies in, financial reporting practices.
- Agreements to repurchase assets previously sold.
- Violations or possible violations of laws or regulations whose effects should be considered for disclosure in the financial statements or as a basis for recording a loss contingency.
- Unasserted claims or assessments that our lawyer has advised are probable of assertion and must be disclosed in accordance with International Accounting Standards No.10.
- Capital stock repurchase options or agreements or capital stock reserved for options, warrants, conversions, or other requirements.
- Compensating balance or other arrangements involving restrictions on cash balances.

R. Dingle, President
Alcmena Manufacturing Ltd.
14 March 20X3

Required:

Identify the other matters that Dingle's representation letter should specifically confirm.

CASE

10–30 Accounting Estimates. Future Focus Investments of Odense, Denmark, is being audited by the public accounting firm of Loft, Blasev and Graversen. Future Focus's primary investments are in virtual currencies such as Bitcoin. Future Focus makes a great deal of estimates in how their investments are valued. In 2013 Bitcoin's value on the Tokyo-based Mt. Gox exchange varied from DKK (Danish Krone) 287 in March to DKK 1,320 in April. Discuss the procedures Loft, Blasev and Graversen would undertake to audit the company's estimates of the Danish Krone value of the investments. Possible research sites are news stories, **https://mtgox.com/**, and United States Financial Crimes Enforcement Network guidelines on Bitcoin, **http://fincen.gov/statutes_regs/guidance/html/FIN-2013-G001.html**.

10.12 Notes

1 IAASB, 2012, International Standards on Auditing 500 (ISA 500) 'Audit Evidence', para. 6, *Handbook of International Quality Control, Auditing, Review, Other Assurance, and Related Services Pronouncements*, 2012 edn, Volume 1, International Federation of Accountants, New York.

2 Forensic accounting is the application of accounting methods and financial techniques to collect civil and criminal legal evidence.

3 Electronic data interchange (EDI) is the electronic transmission of documents between organisations in a machine-readable form. EDI allows output of one system to be electronically transmitted and input into another system. Electronic funds transfer (EFT) is a transfer of funds between two or more organisations or individuals using computer and network technology.

4 *Escott et al.* v *BarChris Const. Corp.*, 1968, United States District Court for the Southern District of New York, 283 F, Supp. 643: **http://www.casebriefs.com/blog/law/corporations/corporations-keyed-to-klein/the-duties-of-officers-directors-and-other-insiders/escott-v-barchris-const-corp/**.

5 IAASB, 2012, International Standards on Auditing 501 (ISA 501) 'Audit Evidence – Specific Considerations for Selected Items', para. 4, *Handbook of International Quality Control, Auditing, Review, Other Assurance, and Related Services Pronouncements*, 2012 edn, Volume 1, International Federation of Accountants, New York.

6 IAASB, 2012, International Standards on Auditing 705 (ISA 705) 'Modifications to the Opinion in the Independent Auditor's Report', *Handbook of International Quality Control, Auditing, Review, Other Assurance, and Related Services Pronouncements*, 2012 edn, Volume 1, International Federation of Accountants, New York.

7 Ibid. ISA 501, para. A4.

8 Consignment is a specialised way of marketing certain types of goods. The consignor delivers goods to the consignee, who acts as the consignor's agent in selling the merchandise to a third party. The consignee accepts the goods without any liability except to reasonably protect them from damage. The consignee receives a commission when the merchandise is sold. Goods on consignment are included in the consignor's inventory and excluded from the consignee's inventory since the consignor has legal title.

9 IAASB, 2012, International Standards on Auditing 505 (ISA 505) 'External Confirmations', paras 13 and 15, *Handbook of International Quality Control, Auditing, Review, Other Assurance, and Related Services Pronouncements*, 2012 edn, Volume 1, International Federation of Accountants, New York.

10 Ibid. ISA 505, para. 15.

11 Ibid. ISA 505, para. 8.

12 IAASB, 2012, International Standards on Auditing 530 (ISA 530) 'Audit Sampling', para. 4, *Handbook of International Quality Control, Auditing, Review, Other Assurance, and Related Services Pronouncements*, 2012 edn, Volume 1, International Federation of Accountants, New York.

13 Anomaly – a misstatement or deviation that is demonstrably not representative of misstatements or deviations in a population.

14 IAASB, 2012, International Standards on Auditing 540 (ISA 540) 'Auditing Accounting Estimates, Including Fair Value Accounting Estimates, and Related Disclosures', *Handbook of International Quality Control, Auditing, Review, Other Assurance, and Related Services Pronouncements*, 2012 edn, Volume 1, International Federation of Accountants, New York.

15 Fair value accounting is a financial reporting approach in which companies are required or permitted to measure and report on an ongoing basis certain assets and liabilities (generally financial instruments) at estimates of the prices they would receive if they were to sell the assets or would pay if they were to be relieved of the liabilities. Under fair value accounting, companies report losses when the fair values of their asset decrease or liabilities increase. Those losses reduce companies' reported equity and may also reduce companies' reported net income: Ryan, Stephan, 2008, *Fair Value Accounting: Understanding The Issues Raised By The Credit Crunch*, Council of Institutional Investors.

16 ISA 540, op. cit., para. 6.

17 ISA 540, op. cit., para. 8.

18 IAASB, 2012, International Standards on Auditing 230 (ISA 230) 'Audit Documentation', paras 9–11 and A6, *Handbook of International Quality Control, Auditing, Review, Other Assurance, and Related Services Pronouncements*, 2012 edn, Volume 1, International Federation of Accountants, New York.

19 IAASB, 2012, International Standards on Auditing 700 (ISA 700) ' Forming an Opinion and Reporting on Financial Statements', paras 10–11 and A6, *Handbook of International Quality Control, Auditing, Review, Other Assurance, and Related Services Pronouncements*, 2012 edn, Volume 1, International Federation of Accountants, New York.

20 Misstatement is a difference between the amount, classification, presentation or disclosure of a reported financial statement item and the amount, classification, presentation or disclosure that is required for the item to be in accordance with the applicable financial reporting framework. Misstatements can arise from error or fraud. When the auditor expresses an opinion on whether the financial statements are presented fairly, in all material respects, or give a true and fair view, misstatements also include those adjustments of amounts, classifications, presentation or disclosures that, in the auditor's judgement, are necessary for the financial statements to be presented fairly, in all material respects, or to give a true and fair view.

21 Uncorrected misstatements – misstatements that the auditor has accumulated during the audit and that have not been corrected.

22 IAASB, 2012, International Standards on Auditing 450 (ISA 450) 'Evaluation of Misstatements Identified during the Audit', para. 3, *Handbook of International Quality Control, Auditing, Review, Other Assurance, and Related Services Pronouncements*, 2012 edn, Volume 1, International Federation of Accountants, New York.

23 IAASB, 2012, International Standards on Auditing 260 (ISA 260) 'Communication with Those Charged with Governance', para. 7, *Handbook of International Quality Control, Auditing, Review, Other Assurance, and Related Services Pronouncements*, 2012 edn, Volume 1, International Federation of Accountants, New York.

24 Ibid. ISA 230, paras 8–11 and A6.

25 International Accounting Standards Board, 2009, International Accounting Standard 24 (IAS 24) 'Related Party Disclosures', London.

26 IAASB, 2012, International Standards on Auditing 315 (ISA 315) 'Identifying and Assessing the Risks of Material Misstatement through Understanding the Entity and Its Environment', para. 10, *Handbook of International Quality Control, Auditing, Review, Other Assurance, and Related Services Pronouncements*, 2012 edn, Volume 1, International Federation of Accountants, New York.

27 IAASB, 2012, International Standards on Auditing 240 (ISA 240) 'The Auditor's Responsibilities Relating to Fraud in an Audit of Financial Statements', para. 15, *Handbook of International Quality Control, Auditing, Review, Other Assurance, and Related Services Pronouncements*, 2012 edn, Volume 1, International Federation of Accountants, New York.

28 IAASB, 2012, International Standards on Auditing 330 (ISA 330) 'The Auditor's Responses to Assessed Risks', paras 5–6, *Handbook of International Quality Control, Auditing, Review, Other Assurance, and Related Services Pronouncements*, 2012 edn, Volume 1, International Federation of Accountants, New York.

29 An arm's length transaction is a transaction in which the buyers and sellers of a product act independently and have no relationship to each other. The concept of an arm's length transaction is to ensure that both parties in the deal are acting in their own self-interest and are not subject to any pressure or duress from the other party.

30 IAASB, 2012, International Standards on Auditing 700 (ISA 700) ' Forming an Opinion and Reporting on Financial Statements', paras 10–15, *Handbook of International Quality Control, Auditing, Review, Other Assurance, and Related Services Pronouncements*, 2012 edn, Volume 1, International Federation of Accountants, New York.

31 Ibid. ISA 230, paras 8–11 and A6.

32 IAASB, 2012, International Standards on Auditing 580 (ISA 580) 'Written Representations', para. 10, *Handbook of International Quality Control, Auditing, Review, Other Assurance, and Related Services Pronouncements*, 2012 edn, Volume 1, International Federation of Accountants, New York.

33 Ibid. ISA 580, Appendix 2.

34 Example Management representation letter for the audit of financial statements prepared in accordance with part 9 of Book 2 of the Dutch civil Code (Standard S80).

35 Ibid. ISA 580, para.10.

Audit Documentation and Working Papers

Introduction

The standard on documentation, ISA 230,[1] provides foundation principles of documentation. It states that audit documentation that meets the specific documentation requirements of ISAs provides evidence of the auditor's basis for a conclusion about the achievement of the overall objectives of the auditor and evidence that the audit was planned and performed in accordance with ISAs and applicable legal and regulatory requirements.

Audit documentation serves a number of additional purposes, including assisting the engagement team to plan and perform the audit and assisting members of the engagement team responsible for supervision to direct and supervise the audit work, and to discharge their review responsibilities in accordance with audit quality control standard ISA 220.[2] Audit documentation also enables the engagement team to be accountable for its work, provides a record of matters of continuing significance to future audits, enables the conduct of quality control reviews and inspections in accordance with ISQC#1[3] or national requirements that are at least as demanding, and enable the conduct of external inspections in accordance with applicable legal, regulatory or other requirements.

Audit documentation is the record of audit procedures performed, relevant audit evidence obtained, and conclusions the auditor reached (terms such as 'working papers' or 'work papers' are also sometimes used). Audit documentation is the principal record of the basis for the auditor's conclusions and provides the principal support for the representations in the auditor's report. Audit documentation also facilitates the planning, performance and supervision of the engagement and provides the basis for the review of the quality of the work by providing the reviewer with written documentation of the evidence supporting the auditor's significant conclusions. Audit documentation includes records on the planning and performance of the work, the procedures performed, evidence obtained and conclusions reached by the auditor.

The Audit Documentation standard from the US Public Company Accounting Oversight Board (PCAOB)[4] is also considered in this appendix.

■ Working Papers

Audit documentation also may be referred to as **working papers** (or **work papers**). Working papers are a record of the auditor's planning; the nature, timing and extent of the auditing procedures performed; results of those procedures; and the conclusions drawn from the evidence obtained. Working papers may be in the form of data stored on paper, film, electronic media or other media. The terms working papers, work papers and documentation are often used interchangeably in auditing.

Working papers:

- Are a direct aid in the planning, performance and supervision of the audit. If an auditor is to plan the audit adequately, the necessary reference information must be available in the working papers. The papers include a variety of planning information such as descriptive information about the internal control, background information about the client, a time budget for individual audit areas, the audit programme, and the results of the preceding year's audit.

- Record the audit evidence resulting from the audit work performed to provide support for the auditor's opinion including the representation that the audit was conducted in accordance with ISAs. Working papers are an important physical aid in recording the results of audit tests. For example, when a sample is taken, the items drawn must be recorded and computations must be made. Working papers are also necessary for coordination of the work leading to an opinion. Supervisors who perform few, if any, actual audit tests make final decisions concerning the opinion given on the financial statements. The supervisors use the working papers as a basis for evaluating the evidence gathered.

- Assist in review of the audit work. The working papers are used not only by supervisory personnel to evaluate whether sufficient competent evidence was accumulated, but also for other auditing and consulting work. Working papers are used by the consulting arm of accounting firms as a basis for income tax preparation, required government regulatory filings and other reports. They are a source of information for communications between auditors and boards of directors concerning internal control weaknesses. They are often used to train personnel.

- Provide proof of the adequacy of the audit. After the opinion has been given, working papers are the main physical proof that an adequate audit was conducted. The auditor works with original documents and accounting records that must be left with the client when the audit has been completed, so the working papers act as an index to those documents. If the auditor is called upon to prove the adequacy of the audit in a court of law or to regulatory agencies, the working papers are his basis of proof.

■ Significant Matters (Findings or Issues)

ISA 230 states: 'The auditor shall document discussions of significant matters with management, those charged with governance, and others, including the nature of the significant matters discussed and when and with whom the discussions took place.'[5] The guidance does not explain what a 'significant matter' would be.

However, for a definition of significant matters, we may look to PCAOB's documentation standard that states: 'The auditor must document significant findings or issues, actions taken to address them (including additional evidence obtained), and the basis for the conclusions reached in connection with each engagement. Significant findings or issues are substantive matters that are important to the procedures performed, evidence obtained, or conclusions reached.'[6] See Illustration 10.A.1 for a list of significant findings or issues.[7]

The auditor must identify all significant findings or issues in an engagement **completion memorandum**. This memorandum should be as specific as necessary in the circumstances

ILLUSTRATION 10.A.1

Significant Findings and Issues

Significant findings or issues are substantive matters that are important to the procedures performed, evidence obtained or conclusions reached and include, but are not limited to, the following:

a. Significant matters involving the selection, application and consistency of accounting principles, including related disclosures.

b. Results of auditing procedures that indicate a need for significant modification of planned auditing procedures, the existence of material misstatements (including omissions in the financial statements), the existence of significant deficiencies, or material weaknesses in internal control over financial reporting.

c. Accumulated misstatements and evaluation of uncorrected misstatements, including the quantitative and qualitative factors the auditor considered to be relevant to the evaluation.

d. Disagreements among members of the engagement team or with others consulted on the engagement about final conclusions reached on significant accounting or auditing matters, including the basis for the final resolution of those disagreements. If an engagement team member disagrees with the final conclusions reached, he or she should document that disagreement.

e. Circumstances that cause significant difficulty in applying auditing procedures.

f. Significant changes in the auditor's risk assessments, including risks that were not identified previously, and the modifications to audit procedures or additional audit procedures performed in response to those changes.

g. Risks of material misstatement that are determined to be significant risks and the results of the auditing procedures performed in response to those risks.

h. Any matters that could result in modification of the auditor's report.

for a reviewer to gain a thorough understanding of the significant findings or issues. This memorandum should include cross-references, as appropriate, to other supporting audit documentation.

10.A.2 Form and Content of the Working Papers

The content of the working papers should be 'sufficiently complete and detailed to provide an overall understanding of the audit'. The working papers should contain information on planning the audit work; the **nature, timing** and **extent** of the audit procedures performed; the results of the audit procedures; and the conclusions drawn leading to an opinion.

PCAOB is more specific: 'Audit documentation must contain sufficient information to enable an experienced auditor, having no previous connection with the engagement: (1) to understand the nature, timing, extent, and results of the procedures performed, evidence obtained, and conclusions reached, and (2) to determine who performed the work and the date such work was completed as well as the person who reviewed the work and the date of such review.'

The working papers should convey the auditor's reasoning on all matters, which require the exercise of judgement and the auditor's conclusions. Where the auditor encounters difficult questions of principle or judgement, working papers record the relevant facts that were known by the auditor at the time the conclusions were reached.

■ Extent of Contents

The extent of what is included in working papers is a matter of professional judgement. It is neither necessary nor practical to document every matter the auditor considers. In assessing the extent of working papers to be prepared and retained, the auditor should think about what would be necessary to provide another auditor, who has no previous experience, with an understanding of the audit work performed. The working papers should convey the basis of the principal decisions taken.

All auditing firms around the world have their own work paper formats, and these formats are modified from time to time. There is no one, standard, format. Format is influenced by audit requirements for direction, supervision and review of work performed by assistants as well as differences in audit firm methodology and technology.

Working papers are designed and organised to meet the circumstances and the auditor's needs for each individual audit. The use of standardised working papers (e.g. checklists, specimen letters, standard organisation of working papers) may improve the efficiency with which such working papers are prepared and reviewed. They facilitate the delegation of work while providing a means to control its quality.

Concept and a Company 10.1

E&Y Partner Falsifies NextCard, Inc. Work Papers

Concept	Work papers.

Story	In September 2003, former Ernst & Young partner Thomas C. Trauger was arrested for obstructing an examination into NextCard, Inc. by federal-bank regulators by altering and deleting working papers from its year 2000 audit of the company (Bryan-Low and Weil, 2003).
	On 31 October 2001, NextCard announced in a press release that the Office of the Comptroller of the Currency had asked the company to make certain changes regarding NextBank's accounting practices, including changes regarding the classification of losses on credit cards. NextBank, the bank subsidiary, was also asked to change the treatment of some allowances and securitisations of loans. In the summer of 2001, the Office of the Comptroller of the Currency asked Ernst & Young for a portion of its audit working papers regarding E&Y's audit of NextCard (Bryan-Low and Weil, 2003).
	Trauger became concerned that E&Y's audit work would be examined. Along with the help of two senior managers, Trauger is alleged to have ordered the altering of audit documents and destroying documents that were inconsistent with the changes he was directing. These alterations consisted of both addition and deletions to the work papers. Specifically, the audit partner altered the summary review memorandum as well as memoranda regarding the audit of NextCard's allowance for loan and lease losses securitisations of receivables (SEC, 2003).
	It is alleged that Trauger had ordered his senior managers change the date on their laptop computers to make it seem like the work on the documents had been done during the time

the original audit had actually occurred. The alterations and deletions made it appear as though E&Y had thoroughly considered all of the appropriate issues and available facts relating to NextCard's allowance for loan losses and NextCard's securitisation of receivables (SEC, 2003). A SEC official said Trauger, who had approved an earlier 'clean audit' of NextCard, was trying to downplay or eliminate evidence of problems that would have been red flags (Iwata, 2003).

Discussion Questions	■ How are work papers important to proving that the audit was done correctly? ■ What would an auditor accomplish by altering or destroying the work papers?
References	Bryan-Low, C. and Weil, J., 2003, 'Former Partner at Ernst is Arrested', *Wall Street Journal*, 26 September. Iwata, E., 2003, 'Accountant Arrested Under Sarbanes–Oxley; Harsher Penalties Possible for Former E&Y Senior Partner,' *USA Today*, 26 September. SEC, 2003, Litigation Release 48543, 'Commission Issues Orders Alleging That Auditors Violated Rules of Practice By Altering and Deleting Audit Working Papers', US Securities and Exchange Commission, 25 September.

10.A.3   Document Retention

ISA 230 states: 'The auditor should adopt appropriate procedures for maintaining the confidentiality and safe custody of the working papers and for retaining them for a period sufficient to meet the needs of the practice and in accordance with legal and professional requirements of record retention.' The standard provides no further guidance on documentation retention.

By contrast, the proposed International Standard on Quality Control, ISQC 1, addresses the issue of document retention in the context of the firm's system of quality control. The high-level guidance in ISQC 1 states: 'The firm retains this documentation for a period of time sufficient to permit those performing monitoring procedures to evaluate the firm's compliance with its system of quality control, or for a longer period if required by law or regulation.'

■ PCAOB and SOX Document Retention

The US SEC introduced detailed regulation (Rule 210.2-06) on document retention as mandated by the Sarbanes–Oxley Act (SOX). The regulation specifies detailed requirements regarding the types of document (e.g. working papers, memos, correspondence, etc. that contain conclusions, opinions, analyses, etc.) that should be retained and the specific period of time they should be retained, regardless of whether such documents support, or are inconsistent with, the final audit conclusions.

Under SOX Section 103, each registered public accounting firm is required to prepare and maintain audit working papers and other information related to any audit report for a period of not less than seven years. PCAOB's Documentation standard states: 'Audit documentation must be retained for seven years from the date of completion of the engagement, as indicated by the date of the auditor's report, unless a longer period of time is required by law.'

Under SOX Section 105, the PCAOB may also:

- require the testimony of the firm or of any person associated with a registered public accounting firm;
- require the production of audit work papers and any other document or information in the possession of a registered public accounting firm or any associated, and may inspect the books and records of such firm or associated person to verify the accuracy of any documents or information supplied;
- request the testimony of, and production of any document in the possession of, any other person, including any client of a registered public accounting firm.

■ Adding to or Altering Documentation

Circumstances may require subsequent additions to the audit documentation, for example if evidence is obtained after completion of the engagement, or if work performed before engagement was finished is documented after completion. When additions are made, according to PCAOB, the documentation added must indicate the date the information was added, by whom it was added, and the reason for adding it.

Audit documentation must not be deleted or discarded. SOX describes criminal penalties for altering documents: 'Whoever knowingly alters, destroys, mutilates, conceals, covers up, falsifies, or makes a false entry in any record, document, or tangible object with the intent to impede, obstruct, or influence the investigation or proper administration … shall be fined under this title, imprisoned not more than 20 years, or both.'

■ Who Owns Working Papers?

ISA 230 states that working papers are generally considered to be the property of the auditor. Although portions of or extracts from the working papers may be made available to the entity audited at the discretion of the auditor, they are not a substitute for the entity's accounting records. In international practice generally the only time anyone, including the client, has a legal right to examine the papers is when they are subpoenaed by a court as legal evidence.

During the audit a considerable amount of information of a confidential nature is gathered, including officer salaries, product cost and product plans. This information can be damaging to the client and useful to competitors if it gets out of the hands of the auditors. Therefore, auditors must take care to protect the working papers at all times.

10.A.4   Permanent and Current Files

There are two main divisions of audit working papers:

1 the permanent (or continuing) audit file;
2 the current audit file.

The **permanent file** is audit working papers containing all the data that are of continuing interest from year to year. The **current work paper file** contains all papers accumulated during the current year's audit.

■ Permanent File

The permanent file is intended to contain data of historical or continuing nature pertinent to the current audit. This file provides a convenient source of information about the audit that is of continuing interest. The permanent file of working papers ordinarily includes:

■ information concerning the legal and organisational structure of the entity such as copies or excerpts of company documents such as **corporate charter** or articles of association, **corporate bylaws**, plans, job manuals, and the corporate organisational chart;

■ extracts or copies of important legal documents, agreements and minutes such as contracts, loan agreements, pension plans, agreements with **parent company** and **subsidiaries**, minutes of board of directors or executive committees, and profit-sharing documents;

■ prior year analysis of fixed assets, long-term debt, terms of stock and bond issues, intangibles, allowances, and results of analytical procedures;

■ information concerning the industry, economic environment and legislative environment within which the entity operates.

Illustration 10.A.2 is a sample listing of the contents of a permanent file. The illustration includes items not mentioned above.

■ Current File

Working papers for the current file include all documentation applicable to the year under audit. They ordinarily include client summary information such as a description of the client, client industry, client internal controls and the auditor's materials. Auditor's materials in the working papers include:

■ evidence of the planning process including the **audit planning memorandum** (hereafter referred to as the audit plan) and the **audit programme**; and any changes thereto;

■ evidence of the auditor's understanding of the accounting and internal control systems, for instance **internal control questionnaires**, **internal control flow charts**, **organisation charts**, and a listing of controls and control weakness;

■ evidence of inherent and control risk assessments and any revisions;

■ evidence of the auditor's consideration of the work of internal auditing or another auditor and conclusions reached;

■ analyses of significant ratios and trends;

■ a record of the nature, timing and extent of audit procedures performed and the results of such procedures;

■ important current legal documents such as contracts and other agreements, leases, and minutes of high-level meetings;

■ evidence that the work performed by assistants was supervised and reviewed;

ILLUSTRATION 10.A.2

Sample Work Papers – Permanent File Contents

Permanent File		Engagement Code:	Client:
Index	# Pages	Description	
I		**General Client and Engagement Information**	
	1	Engagement letter	
	2	Client information form	
II		**Statutory and Legal Information**	
	1	Articles of association	
	2	Special legal, statutory or contractual definitions	
	3	Registrations, members register	
	4	Minutes of continuing relevance from management, directors and stockholder meetings	
	5	Insurance summary	
	6	Borrowing agreements, lease agreements	
	7	Title deeds	
	8	Details of any other important agreements	
III		**Accounting System and Internal Control**	
	1	Documentation of accounting system and internal control	
	2	Chart of accounts	
	3	Authorisation limits, initials and signature list	
	4	Accounting procedures instructions	
IV		**Audit**	
	1	Correspondence of continuing relevance	
	2	Notes and minutes of continuing relevance	
	3	Documentation: computer applications	
	4	Registration: hardware and software	
V		**Financial Statement Information**	
	1	Financial statement analysis/previous year's summary	
	2	Details: intangible fixed assets	
	3	Details: property, ships, aeroplanes	
	4	Details: other tangible fixed assets	
	5	Details: group companies and other participations	
VI		**Personnel, employment conditions**	
	1	Previous year's summary, social reports	
	2	Overview of personnel	
	3	Collective bargaining agreements, standard employment contracts, salary scales	
	4	Employment conditions board of directors	
	5	Pension/early retirement rules and regulations	
	6	Sick pay rules and regulations	
	7	Expense allowance rules and regulations	
	8	Other employment conditions	
VII		**Taxation**	

- an indication as to who performed the audit procedures and when they were performed;
- details of procedures applied regarding components whose financial statements are audited by another auditor;
- copies of communications with other auditors, experts and other third parties such as **confirmation letters**;
- copies of letters or notes concerning audit matters communicated to or discussed with the entity, including the terms of the engagement and material weaknesses in internal control;
- letters of representation received from the entity such as the *engagement letter*, and **management representation letter**;
- conclusions reached by the auditor concerning significant aspects of the audit, including how exceptions and unusual matters, if any, disclosed by the auditor's procedures were resolved or treated;
- copies of the financial statements and auditor's report;
- analyses of accounting transactions and balances such as transaction tracing, **trial balances, lead schedules**, and if necessary, recommend journal entries to correct the accounts (i.e. **adjusting** and reclassification **entries**) which are made when an auditor discovers material misstatements in the accounting records;
- various supporting schedules (discussed below).

Illustration 10.A.3 is an example of a list of the contents of a current file.

■ Lead Schedules

As early as possible after the balance sheet date, the auditor obtains a trial balance, a listing of the general ledger accounts and their year-end balances. Each line item in the trial balance is supported by a lead schedule, containing the detailed accounts from the general ledger making up the line item. Each detailed account on the lead schedule is, in turn, supported by audit work performed and the conclusions drawn. The largest portion of working papers includes the detailed schedules prepared by the client or the auditors in support of specific amounts on the financial statements.

The major types of supporting schedules are account analysis, list schedules, reconciliation of amounts, tests of reasonableness, procedures description, informational and outside documentation. An **account analysis schedule**, normally used for fixed assets, liabilities and equity accounts, shows the activity in a general ledger account during the entire period under audit, tying together the beginning and ending balances. The **list schedule** shows the detail of those items that make up an end-of-period balance in a general ledger account. A **reconciliation** relates a specific amount in the accounting records to another source of information, for example a reconciliation of accounts payable balances with vendor's statements. The **test of reasonableness schedule** contains information that enables the auditor to evaluate whether the client's balance appears to include a misstatement considering the circumstances. A **summary of procedures description schedule** summarises the result of audit procedures performed. Information schedules contain non-audit information such as tax information, regulatory information and time budgets. Outside documentation includes confirmation replies, copies of client agreements, etc. Illustration 10.A.4 shows an account analysis schedule that might be used in the audit.

ILLUSTRATION 10.A.3

Sample Work Papers – Current File

Current File		Engagement Code: Client:
Index	# Pages	Description
I		**Reports**
	1	Financial statements
	2	Auditor's report/auditor's opinion
	3	Consolidation package
	4	Interoffice memorandum to group auditor
II		**Unconsolidated Financial Statements**
	1	Trial balance
	2	Reconciliation financial statements/consolidation package/trial balance
	3	Adjusting and reclassifying entries
III		**Consolidated Financial Statements**
	1	Consolidation schedules
	2	Interoffice memoranda and reports from other offices
IV		**Engagement Planning**
	1	Strategy document
	2	Planning memorandum and audit plan
	3	Instruction to/from other offices
	4	Audit programme
	5	Audit progress reports
	6	Budget
	7	Detailed audit planning and work allocation
V		**Engagement Completion**
	1	Completion memorandum
	2	Accounting disclosure checklist
	3	Subsequent events review
	4	Notes for partner/manager
VI		**Engagement Administration**
	1	Time sheets
	2	Hours and fee-analysis
VII		**Control Overview Document**
VIII		**Representations**
	1	Letter of representation
	2	Major points discussed with management
	3	Lawyer's letter
IX		**Planning Analysis**
	1	Budget
	2	Interim financial statements
X		**Correspondence in Respect of Current Year's Audit**
XI		**Obsolete Work Papers from Permanent File**

ILLUSTRATION 10.A.4

Sample Work Papers – Account Analysis Schedule

Financial Statement Specification File		Engagement Code: Client:
Index	*# Pages*	*Description*
A		Intangible fixed assets
B		Tangible fixed assets
C		Financial fixed assets
D		Inventory (Stocks)
E		Receivables
F		Securities
G		Cash
H		Share capital and reserves
I		Provisions
J		Long-term debt
K		Current liabilities
L		Lease commitments
M		Other commitments and contingent liabilities
N		Revenue
O		Expenses (by category)
P		Expenses (by function)
Q		Financial income and expenses
R		Taxation
S		Extraordinary items
T		Discontinued operations

10.A.5 Preparation of Working Schedule

The key concept in proper preparation of working papers is to structure the information so that it is easy to interpret and gives the extent of the work in a concise form. Although the design of working papers depends on the objectives involved, they would normally be properly identified, include the conclusions that were reached, would be indexed, and clearly indicate the audit work performed.

Every individual working paper should be properly identified with the client's name, the period covered, a description of contents of the working paper, the date of preparation and index code, and, most importantly, the initials of the person who prepared it. The conclusions reached about that segment of the audit should be stated plainly.

■ Tick Marks and Indexing

The preparation of working papers has strong traditional elements that indicate the audit work performed, cross-references and suggested adjustments. These elements are tick marks, indexing and adjusting journal entries.

Tick Marks

Tick marks are symbols used by the auditor to indicate the nature and extent of procedures applied in specific circumstances. Tick marks are notations directly on the working paper schedules. Tick marks are generally done by hand with a pen or pencil alongside a specific item. With the increased use of computers for auditing, tick marks may be input in a spreadsheet program.

Tick marks must be clearly explained at the bottom of the working paper in a legend. For example, the auditor indicates that he has examined supporting vouchers for items listed on a working paper by placing a tick mark or check mark (a symbol such as ✓) beside each item on which the procedures have been carried out. The legend at the bottom of the page will say something like '✓ = voucher and supporting documents examined.' (See interest and long-term debt working papers in Illustration 10.A.5.) The illustration is from a computer spreadsheet, with check marks (✓) added by hand later when the monthly balances were checked later against the trial balance.

Indexing

Working papers are indexed and cross-referenced to aid in the organising and filing. Indexing work papers requires coding the individual sheets of paper so that necessary information may be found easily. The auditor prepares cross-references creating a trail through the working papers. A variety of indexing systems are in use. These systems include sequential numbering, combinations of letters and numbers, and digit-position index numbers. The working papers in Illustrations 10.A.2 and 10.A.3 use sequential numbering. Illustration 10.A.4 uses letters. Illustration 10.A.6 gives an example of the digit-position indexing system.

10.A.6   Adjusting Entry

An adjusting journal entry is the correcting entry required at the end of the reporting period due to a mistake made in the accounting records; also called correcting entry. The auditor does not make entries in the client's records. The auditor makes the entries on the work papers and reviews their recording by the client. The following adjusting journal entry is an example.

Repair is incorrectly debited to buildings by the following journal entry:

```
1/23/X1
Debit Buildings $2,000
    Credit Cash                    $2,000
```

To record expenditures for painting supervisor's office.

The adjusting journal entry necessary to correct this error is:

```
12/31/XI
Debit Buildings maintenance expense $2,000
    Credit Buildings                $2,000
```

To correct expenditures for painting supervisor's office incorrectly debited to fixed assets.

ILLUSTRATION 10.A.5

Sample Work Papers – Interest and Long-term Debt Work Paper

Interest and Long-term Debt Work Paper			
Client: Hu's Paradise Travel			
Topic: Overall test of interest expense			
Date: 31 December 20X5			
Index: Reasonableness schedule – 13			
Page: 1 of 1			
Prepared by: R. Mollie Hayes			
Review by _____			
Balance per General Ledger			€92,457
Short-term Loans			
Mo.	**GL Bal. Mo. End**	**Agree Trial Balance**	
Jan.	€218,316	✓	
Feb.	€214,983	✓	
Mar.	€210,459	✓	
Apr.	€315,000	✓	
May	€298,300	✓	
June	€200,000	✓	
July	€198,453	✓	
Aug.	€218,453	✓	
Sep.	€189,675	✓	
Oct.	€180,000	✓	
Nov.	€167,456	✓	
Dec.	€154,678	✓	
Total 12 Mo	€2,565,773	✓	
Ave. Bal (AB)	€213,814	✓	
AB@ 11.5%*			€24,589
Long-term Loans			
Beginning Balance	€896,897		
Ending Balance	€888,888		
Ave. Bal. (AB)	€892,893		
AB@ 7.5%**			€66,967
€			
Estimated Total Interest			€91,556
Difference from GL Balance			€900
Notes: * Based on examination of notes throughout year – 10.75% to 12.5%			
** Agrees with permanent file LT debt schedule			
✓Agree Trial Balance			

ILLUSTRATION 10.A.6

Example of Digit-Position Indexing

1000 Draft of audit report
*
*
*
*
2000 Cash
2001 Count of petty cash
2002 Bank reconciliation
2100 Accounts receivable
*
*
*
*

3000 Fixed assets
*
*
3300 Review patents and copyrights
*
*
*
4000 Accounts payable
4002 Confirmation of accounts payable
*
*

10.A.7 Summary

The auditor should document matters that are important in providing both evidence to support the audit opinion and evidence that the audit was carried out in accordance with ISAs.

Audit documentation is the principal record of the basis for the auditor's conclusions and provides the principal support for the representations in the auditor's report. Audit documentation also facilitates the planning, performance, and supervision of the engagement, and provides the basis for the review of the quality of the work by providing the reviewer with written documentation of the evidence supporting the auditor's significant conclusions. Audit documentation includes records on the planning and performance of the work, the procedures performed, evidence obtained, and conclusions reached by the auditor.

Audit documentation also may be referred to as working papers or work papers. Working papers are a record of the auditor's planning; the nature, timing and extent of the auditing procedures performed; results of those procedures; and the conclusions drawn from the evidence obtained. Working papers may be in the form of data stored on paper, film, electronic media or other media. The terms working papers, work papers and documentation are often used interchangeably in auditing.

The auditor should document matters that are important in providing evidence to support the audit opinion and evidence that the audit was carried out in accordance with International Standards on Auditing. Working papers:

- are a direct aid in the planning, performance and supervision of the audit;
- record the audit evidence resulting from the audit work performed to provide support for the auditor's opinion including the representation that the audit was conducted in accordance with ISAs;
- assist in review of the audit work;
- provide proof of the adequacy of the audit.

The auditor must document significant findings or issues, actions taken to address them (including additional evidence obtained), and the basis for the conclusions reached in an engagement completion memorandum.

The content of the working papers should be sufficiently complete and detailed to provide an overall understanding of the audit. The working papers should contain information on planning the audit work; the nature, timing and extent of the audit procedures performed; the results of the audit procedures; and the conclusions drawn leading to an opinion.

ISA 230 states: 'The auditor should adopt appropriate procedures for maintaining the confidentiality and safe custody of the working papers and for retaining them for a period sufficient to meet the needs of the practice and in accordance with legal and professional requirements of record retention.' The US SEC regulation on document retention as mandated by the Sarbanes–Oxley Act (SOX) specifies detailed requirements regarding the types of document, requires working papers be kept for not less than seven years, and describes criminal penalties for altering documents. ISA 230 states that working papers are generally considered to be the property of the auditor.

There are two main divisions of audit work papers:

1 the permanent (or continuing) audit file;
2 the current audit file.

The permanent file is audit working papers containing all the data that are of continuing interest from year to year. The current working paper file contains all papers accumulated during the current year's audit. The permanent file is intended to contain data of historical or continuing nature pertinent to the current audit. This file provides a convenient source of information about the audit that is of continuing interest.

The permanent file working papers ordinarily include:

- information concerning the legal and organisational structure of the entity;
- extracts or copies of important legal documents, agreements and minutes;
- prior year analysis of fixed assets, long-term debt, terms of stock and bond issues, intangibles, allowances, and results of analytical procedures;
- information concerning the industry, economic environment and legislative environment within which the entity operates.

Working papers for the current file include all documentation applicable to the year under audit. They ordinarily include client summary information such as a description of the client, client industry, client internal controls and the auditor's materials.

The key concept in proper preparation of working papers is to structure the information so that it is easy to interpret and gives the extent of the work in a concise form. Working papers include the conclusions that were reached; they should be indexed and clearly indicate the audit work performed. The preparation of working papers has strong traditional elements that indicate the audit work performed, cross-references and suggested adjustments. These elements are tick marks, indexing and adjusting journal entries.

10.A.8   Notes

1   International Auditing and Assurance Standards Board (IAASB), 2012, International Standard on Auditing 230 (ISA 230) 'Audit Documentation', *Handbook of International Quality Control, Auditing Review, Other Assurance, and Related Services Pronouncements*, 2012 edn, Volume 1, International Federation of Accountants, New York.

2   International Auditing and Assurance Standards Board (IAASB), 2012, International Standard on Auditing 220 (ISA 220) 'Quality Control for an Audit of Financial Statements', paras 15–17, *Handbook of International Quality Control, Auditing Review, Other Assurance, and Related Services Pronouncements*, 2012 edn, Volume 1, International Federation of Accountants, New York.

3   International Auditing and Assurance Standards Board (IAASB), 2012, International Standards on Quality Control #1 (ISQC #1) 'Quality Control for Firms that Perform Audits and Reviews of Financial Statements, and Other Assurance and Related Services Engagements', paras 32–33, 35–38 and 48, *Handbook of International Quality Control, Auditing Review, Other Assurance, and Related Services Pronouncements*, 2012 edn, Volume 1, International Federation of Accountants, New York.

4   Public Company Accounting Oversight Board (PCAOB), 2004, Auditing Standard No. 3 'Audit Documentation', Final Rule: PCAOB Release No. 2004-006: **http://pcaobus.org/Standards/Auditing/Pages/Auditing_Standard_3.aspx**.

5   ISA 230, op.cit., para 10.

6   PCAOB Audit Standard 3, op.cit., para 12.

7   Ibid.

Chapter 11

COMPLETING THE AUDIT

11.1 Learning Objectives

After studying this chapter, you should be able to:

1 Reiterate the procedures for the audit completion stage.

2 State the elements of a system of quality control of an audit firm.

3 Give the implications of the Sarbanes–Oxley Act for quality control and audit review.

4 Understand why letters from client legal counsel are necessary and what they contain.

5 Conduct a review for contingent liabilities and commitments.

6 Conduct a review after the balance sheet date for subsequent events and understand what events cause financial statement adjustments.

7 Know the auditor's responsibilities when facts are discovered after the issuance of the audit report.

8 Explain the procedures involved in the review of financial statements including disclosures and other information presented with the audited financial statements.

9 Design and perform the wrap-up procedures.

10 Determine procedures to evaluate going concern issues.

11 Discuss the design and use of matters for the attention of partners.

11.2 Introduction

The audit is not over until the audit report is signed. And even then it may not be over if facts are discovered after the balance sheet date and before the next report. After the fieldwork is almost complete, a series of procedures are generally carried out to 'complete the audit'. The intent of these procedures is to review the audit work, get certain assurances from the client, uncover any potential problems, check compliance with regulations, and check the consistency of the material that is to be presented to the users of financial statements.

In this text so far we have followed the standard audit process model (Illustration 11.1) through its phases – for client acceptance (Phase I), planning (Phase II), and elements of testing and evidence (Phase III). In this chapter, we will discuss the last phase, Phase IV, evaluation and reporting.

The procedures for completing this audit phase are: evaluate governance evidence; carry out procedures to identify **subsequent events**; review financial statements and other report material; do wrap-up procedures, prepare **Matters for Attention of Partners**; report to the board of directors and prepare audit report (which will be discussed in Chapter 12 'Audit Reports and Communication'). These procedures and the objective of the evaluation and reporting phase are shown in Illustration 11.2.

The initial audit procedure in the closing cycle is usually to evaluate **governance**[1] evidence, the evidence pertaining to the company and management. This means obtaining a **legal letter** and a **management representations letter**. The management representations letter is discussed in Chapter 10 'Audit Evidence'. Next in the governance evaluation is to look at **contingent liabilities** and **related parties**. Related parties is also discussed in Chapter 10.

Discovery of subsequent facts and events may be essential to a correct opinion. The auditor must consider events up to the date of the auditor's report and between the balance sheet date and the issuance of the statements. Discovery of facts after the financial statements' issuance are not generally as crucial.

Of course, the auditors must review financial statements and financial statement disclosures, but they must also review other information contained in the annual report. Other information that needs looking into is the board of directors' report, corporate governance disclosures (where applicable) and all other information in the annual report to shareholders.

The last work of the closing cycle is wrap-up procedures, matters for supervisors, report to the **audit committee**, and the audit report itself. Wrap-up procedures include:

- analytical procedures,
- review working papers,
- evaluation of going concern,
- client approval of adjusting entries.

Reporting and evaluation of matters for supervisory attention includes reports to managers and partners.

Prior to the final audit report the auditors will usually discuss their findings with the audit committee especially irregularities, illegal acts and **reportable conditions**. The final step in the closing cycle is the audit report (discussed in Chapter 12 'Audit Reports and Communication').

ILLUSTRATION 11.1

Standard Audit Process Model – Phase Flow Diagram

Phase I
Client Acceptance
Objective: Determine both acceptance of a client and acceptance by a client. Decide on acquiring a new client or continuation of relationship with an existing one and the type and amount of staff required.

Procedures:
(1) Evaluate the client's background and reasons for the audit.
(2) Communicate with predecesser auditor.
(3) Determine need for other professionals.
(4) Prepare client proposal.
(5) Obtain an engagement letter.
(6) Select staff to perform the audit.

Phase II
Planning the Audit
Objective: Determine the amount and type of evidence and review required to give the auditor assurance that there is no material missatement of the financial statements.

Procedures:
(1) Obtain industry, company, legal, related party and financial background information.
(2) Perform procedures to obtain an understanding of internal control.
(3) Based on the evidence, assess risk and set materiality.
(4) Prepare the planning memorandum and audit programme audit plan).

Phase III
Testing and Evidence
Objective: Test for evidence supporting internal controls and the fairness of the financial statements.

Procedures:
(1) Tests of controls.
(2) Substantive tests of transactions.
(3) Analytical procedures.
(4) Tests of details of balances.
(5) Search for unrecorded liabilities.

Phase IV
Evaluation and Judgement
Objective: Complete the audit procedures and issue an opinion.

Procedures:
(1) Evaluate governance evidence.
(2) Perform procedures to identify subsequent events.
(3) Review financial statement and other report material.
(4) Perform wrap-up procedures.
(5) Prepare matters for attention partners.
(6) Report to the board of directors.
(7) Prepare audit report.

> ## ILLUSTRATION 11.2
>
> ## Audit Process Model – Phase IV Evaluation and Reporting
>
> **Objective:** Complete the audit procedures and issue an opinion.
>
> **Procedures**
>
> 1 Evaluate governance evidence.
>
> 2 Perform procedures to identify subsequent events.
>
> 3 Review financial statements and other report material.
>
> 4 Perform wrap-up procedures.
>
> 5 Prepare Matters for Attention of Partners.
>
> 6 Report to the board of directors.
>
> 7 Prepare audit report.

11.3 Quality Control (ISQC #1, ISA 220, SOX)

According to International Standard on Quality Control #1 (ISQC #1),[2] the audit firm should establish a system of quality control designed to provide it with reasonable assurance that the firm and its personnel comply with professional standards and regulatory and legal requirements, and that reports issued by the firm or engagement partners are appropriate in the circumstances. Quality control standards are discussed in detail in Chapter 4 'An Auditor's Services'.

■ Elements of a System of Quality Control

The elements of quality control policies adopted by an audit firm normally incorporate policies related to general firm activities and personnel. General firm activities for which quality control policies and procedures are required include leadership responsibilities for quality within the firm, acceptance and retention of clients, engagement performance, and monitoring. Quality controls applied to human resources include ethical requirements. The quality control policies and procedures should be documented and communicated to the firm's personnel.

■ ISA 220 Quality Control for Audit Engagements

ISA 220 establishes standards and provides guidance on specific quality control procedures only for audit engagements. ISA 220[3] includes specific requirements for an engagement quality control reviewer to perform an objective evaluation of compliance with applicable professional standards. The responsibilities of the engagement partner under ISA 220 are shown in Illustration 11.3.

■ The Sarbanes–Oxley Act Quality Control and Audit Review

The Sarbanes–Oxley Act (SOX) addresses overall review procedures required of the auditor such as quality control, second partner review and partner rotation. It also

ILLUSTRATION 11.3

Responsibilities of the Engagement Partner

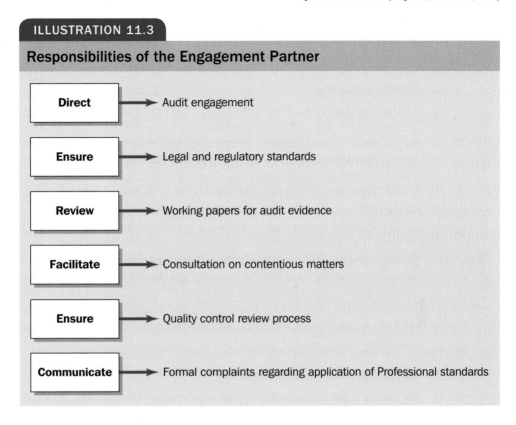

Direct	→ Audit engagement
Ensure	→ Legal and regulatory standards
Review	→ Working papers for audit evidence
Facilitate	→ Consultation on contentious matters
Ensure	→ Quality control review process
Communicate	→ Formal complaints regarding application of Professional standards

discusses the client's audit committee responsibilities and inspection by the Public Company Accounting Oversight Board (PCAOB).[4]

SOX applies not only to US audit firms, but also to audit firms throughout the world.[5] Any foreign public accounting firm that prepares or furnishes an audit report on a company publicly traded in the US is subject to SOX, in the same manner and to the same extent as a public accounting firm that is organised and operates under the laws of the USA or any state. The PCAOB may determine that a foreign public accounting firm, even though it does not issue audit reports, plays such a substantial role in the preparation and furnishing of such reports that it should be treated as a public accounting firm subject to SOX.

Quality Control Policies

The Sarbanes–Oxley Act[6] (SOX) requires that every registered public accounting firm auditing publicly traded companies include in their quality control policies standards relating to:

- monitoring of professional ethics and independence from issuers on behalf of which the firm issues audit reports;
- consultation within such a firm on accounting and auditing questions;
- supervision of audit work;
- hiring, professional development and advancement of personnel;
- the acceptance and continuation of audit engagements;

- internal inspection;
- such other requirements as the Public Company Accounting Oversight Board (PCAOB) may prescribe.

PCAOB Inspections

In order to ensure quality control, the PCAOB conducts a continuing programme[7] of inspections[8] to assess the degree of compliance of the audit firm's performance of audits and issuance of audit reports with the rules of the PCAOB and professional standards. The PCAOB evaluates the sufficiency of the quality control system of the firm, and the manner of the documentation and communication of that system by the firm; and performs such testing as appropriate of the audit, supervisory and quality control procedures of the firm.

The PCAOB is required to inspect a registered public accounting firm under SOX, section 104. The PCAOB will inspect and review selected audit and review engagements of the firm (which may include audit engagements that are the subject of ongoing litigation or other controversy between the firm and one or more third parties). A written report of the findings of the PCAOB is transmitted to the appropriate regulatory authorities. The report is made available in appropriate detail to the public, (except that the quality control portions of the report may not be made public under certain considerations).[9]

Ex-Employee Conflicts of Interest

In determining the acceptance and continuation of audit engagements the audit firm must consider ex-employee conflicts of interest and audit partner rotation. An accounting firm cannot perform any audit service for a firm if a chief executive officer, controller, chief financial officer, chief accounting officer, or equivalent position, was employed by that accounting firm and participated in any capacity in the audit of that issuer during the one-year period preceding the date of the initiation of the audit.[10]

Partnership Review and Rotation

Audits should be reviewed by partners in the accounting firm not connected with the audit and should rotate their audit partners every five years. Under SOX, section 103, auditors should provide a concurring or second partner review by a qualified person associated with the public accounting firm, other than the person in charge of the audit, or by an independent reviewer. SOX, section 303 makes it unlawful for a registered public accounting firm to provide audit services to an company if the lead audit partner having primary responsibility for the audit, or the audit partner responsible for reviewing the audit, has performed audit services for that company in each of the five previous fiscal years of that enterprise. Section 103 also states the quality control standards that were discussed above.

Audit Committee Review of Auditors

Under SOX, section 301,[11] public company audit committees are directly responsible for the appointment, compensation, and oversight of the work of any registered public accounting firm employed by their company (including resolution of disagreements between management and the auditor regarding financial reporting). Each such registered public accounting firm reports directly to the audit committee. Auditors may also have to discuss accounting complaints with the audit committee. Each audit committee must have established procedures for the receipt, retention and treatment of complaints regarding accounting, internal accounting controls or auditing matters.

11.4 Evaluate Governance Evidence

There is important governance evidence that may be acquired any time during the audit, but definitely has to be done before the final judgement and evaluation phase (Phase IV of the audit process model). The important governance information to be gathered from the client includes: a legal letter, a management representations letter, information about contingent liabilities and commitments, and identification of related parties (discussed in Chapter 10). The auditor must review legal documents, contracts, board of directors meeting notes and management communication to determine if contingent liabilities exist. A search for unrecorded liabilities is also routine.

■ Obtain Evidence and Letters Concerning Litigation, Claims and Assessments

To discover litigation, claims and assessments that affect the client, the auditor relies on both his own field procedures and a letter from the client's legal counsel. The field procedures to discover claims against the client are:

- read the corporate meetings' minutes and notes of other appropriate meetings;
- read contracts, leases, correspondence and other similar documents;
- review guarantees of indebtedness disclosed on bank confirmations;
- inspect other documents for possible client-made guarantees;
- determine if there are any side letters.

The auditor will ask management about the policies and procedures adopted for identifying, evaluating and accounting for contingencies; and obtain a description and evaluation of all pending contingencies (before or at balance sheet date). The auditor will obtain written assurance from the client that all unasserted claims[12] that require disclosure are disclosed.

Legal Letter

The primary procedure that auditors rely on for discovering litigation, claims and assessments that affect the client is a letter from the client's legal counsel called a legal letter or inquiry of client's attorneys. Auditors analyse client legal expense for the present year and sometimes the prior years. The auditor requires that the client send a standard request letter to every legal adviser. The letter goes to both outside counsel (independent law firms) and inside general counsel (lawyers that are employees of the client). The standard letter from the client's attorney is prepared on the client's letterhead and signed by one of the client company's management. The desired date of the letter from the attorney is close to the date of the auditor's report.

A sample request for such a legal letter (or inquiry of client's attorneys letter) from the client is shown in Illustration 11.4.

ILLUSTRATION 11.4

Legal Letter

Shoun Company
888 24th Street
Lubbock, Texas 79410-1894
26 January, 20X8

Duey Cheattham & Howe
69 Swindle Road
Bamboozle, Texas 78602–3847

Gentlemen:

Our auditors, Kusuda & Gasan, are now engaged in an audit of our financial statements as of 31 December 20X7 and for the year then ended. In connection with the audit, management has furnished Kusuda & Gasan with information concerning certain contingencies involving matters with respect to which you have been engaged and to which you have devoted substantive attention on behalf of the Company. These contingencies individually represent a maximum potential loss exposure in excess of $230,000.

Pending or Threatened Litigation, Claims and Assessments

We have furnished our auditors with the following information in relation to the only pending or threatened litigation, claim or assessment your firm is handling on our behalf and to which you have devoted substantive attention in the form of legal consultation or representation:

1 Description of the nature of the case – antitrust complaint filed against the company by the US Department of Justice for discriminatory pricing policies.
2 Process of case to date – case is in the discovery phase.
3 Response to the case – management intends to contest the case vigorously.
4 Evaluation of the likelihood of an unfavourable outcome and an estimate, if one can be made, of the amount or range of potential loss – management believes that the probability of an unfavourable outcome is remote. No estimate of loss can be made.

Please furnish to Kusuda & Gasan such explanation, if any, that you consider necessary to supplement the foregoing information, including an explanation of those matters as to which your views may differ from those stated and an identification of the omission of any pending or threatened litigation, claim or assessment, or a statement that the list of such matters is complete.

Unasserted Claims and Assessments

We understand that whenever, in the course of performing legal services for us with respect to a matter recognised to involve an unasserted possible claim or assessment that may call for financial statement disclosure, if you have formed a professional conclusion that we must disclose or consider disclosure concerning such possible claim or assessment, as a matter of professional responsibility to us, you will so advise us and will consult with us concerning the question of such disclosure and the applicable requirements of International Financial Reporting Standard IAS 37. Please specifically confirm to Kusuda & Gasan that our understanding is correct.

We will be representing to Kusuda & Gasan that there are no unasserted possible claims or assessments that you have advised are probable of assertion and must be disclosed in accordance with International Financial Reporting Standard IAS 37 in the financial statements currently under audit.

Other Matters

Your response should include matters that existed at 31 December 20X7 and for the period from that date to the date of your response. Please make your response effective as of 8 February 20X7, and specifically identify the nature of and reasons for any limitation on your response.

Also, please furnish Kusuda & Gasan with the amount of any unpaid fees due you as of 31 December 20X7 for services rendered through that date. Please mail your reply directly to Kusuda & Gasan, 3012 24th Street, Lubbock, Texas 79410-1894. A stamped, addressed envelope is enclosed for your convenience. Also, please furnish us a copy of your reply.

Sincerely,
Ken McPhail, President

For all litigation, claims and assessments, the inquiry of client's attorney's letter should request evidence relating to:

- existence of conditions or circumstances indicating a possible loss from litigation, claims or assessments;
- the period in which the underlying cause occurred;
- likelihood of an unfavourable outcome;
- amount of potential loss, including court costs.

Letter from Client's Legal Counsel

The letter from client's legal counsel informs the auditor of pending legislation and other information involving legal counsel that is relevant to the financial statements. It should include the following:

1 Identification of the client and the date of the audit.
2 A list, prepared by management, of material pending or threatened litigation claims or assessments for which the lawyer has been engaged. The management may also request that its lawyer prepare this list.
3 A list, prepared by management, of unasserted claims and assessments which management considers probable of assertion, and that, if asserted,[13] would have a reasonable possibility of an unfavourable outcome. There should also be a request that the lawyer indicate any disagreements with the evaluation.
4 A request that the lawyer furnish information or comment about the nature and progress to date of each listed claim or assessment. If possible, the attorney would provide an evaluation of the likelihood and amount of potential losses.
5 A request for the identification of any unlisted pending or threatened legal actions, or a statement that the client's list is complete.
6 A statement by the client informing the lawyer of his responsibility to inform management whenever, in the lawyer's judgement, there is a legal matter requiring disclosure in the financial statements.
7 A request that the lawyers identify and describe the nature of any reasons for any limitations on the response.

■ Obtain Management Representation Letter

During the course of an audit, management makes many representations to the auditor, either unsolicited or in response to specific inquiries. When these representations relate to matters that are material to the financial statements, the auditor must seek corroborative audit evidence, evaluate whether the representations made by management appear reasonable and consistent with other audit evidence, and consider whether the individuals making the representations are competent to do so. International Standard on Auditing 580 states: 'The auditor should obtain evidence that management acknowledges its responsibility for the fair representation of the financial statements in accordance with the relevant financial reporting framework, and has approved the financial statements.'

The auditor can obtain this evidence from relevant minutes of meetings of board of directors, a signed copy of the financial statements, or by obtaining a written representation from management.

Written Representations from Management

In instances when other sufficient appropriate audit evidence cannot reasonably be expected to exist, the auditor should obtain written representations from management on matters material to the financial statements. The auditor may document in his working papers evidence of management's representations by summarising oral discussions with management or by obtaining written representations from management. The possibility of misunderstandings between the auditor and management is reduced when oral representations are confirmed in writing by management. Written representations of management are discussed in Chapter 10.

■ Review for Contingent Liabilities and Commitments

Contingent liability is a potential future obligation to an outside party for an unknown amount resulting from the outcome of a past event, for example an adverse tax court decision, lawsuit, and notes receivable discounted. Footnote disclosure is ordinarily required if there are probable losses. Three conditions are required for a contingent liability to exist:

1 There is a potential future payment to an outside party or potential future assets impairment.
2 There is an uncertainty about the amount of payment or asset impairment.
3 The outcome will be resolved by some future event.

Procedures to Test for Contingencies

Audit procedures that test for contingencies are not just done in the last days of the audit, but from the beginning. Income tax disputes, investigations by government or industry authorities, and the amount of unused bank lines of credit are generally known from the start of the audit. Procedures such as reviews of contracts, correspondence, credit agreements and inquiries of management should point out possible contingencies.

One audit procedure for finding contingencies is the legal letter already discussed where the auditor analyses legal expenses and statements from legal counsel and obtains a letter from each major lawyer as to the status of pending litigation. Three other common procedures are to: review working papers; examine letters of credit to confirm used and unused balances; and evaluation of known contingent liabilities.

Contingencies that are of concern to the auditor, among others, are: pending litigation for patent infringement, product liability or other actions; guarantees of obligations of others; product warranties; income tax disputes; and notes receivable discounted.

Commitments

Similar to contingent liabilities are commitments. Commitments are agreements that the entity will hold to a fixed set of conditions, such as the purchase or sale of merchandise at a stated price, at a future date, regardless of what happens to profits or to the economy as a whole. Examples are commitments to purchase raw materials, lease premises, royalty agreements, licensing agreements and agreements to sell merchandise or services at a fixed price. There may be commitments to employees in the form of profit sharing, stock options, health benefits and pension plans.

All material commitments are ordinarily either described together in a separate footnote or combined in a footnote related to contingencies.

11.5 Review for Discovery of Subsequent Events

Review for subsequent events is the auditing procedures performed by auditors to identify and evaluate subsequent events. **Subsequent events are events occurring between the date of the financial statements**[14] and the **date of the auditor's report**,[15] and facts that become known to the auditor after the date of the auditor's report. Under International Standard on Auditing (ISA) 560[16] the auditor should consider the effect of subsequent events on the financial statements and on the auditor's report.

Concept and a Company 11.1

Arabian American Development Company – The Undisclosed Event

Concept	Subsequent events and disclosure.

Story Arabian, a Delaware corporation based in Dallas, Texas, is in the business of refining petrochemical products and developing mining operations in Saudi Arabia and the USA. Arabian maintains an office in Jeddah, Saudi Arabia, to manage its Saudi Arabian operations. Hatem El-Khalidi, age 78, a US citizen and resident of Jeddah, Saudi Arabia, helped found Arabian in 1967, and serves as the Chief Executive Officer, the President and a director of Arabian. Arabian and El-Khalidi, violated SEC rules which required Arabian to include in annual and quarterly reports any material information that might be necessary to make those reports not misleading. They failed to disclose a material lease that had a high probability of expiring, affecting severely the company's total assets.

In 1993, Arabian obtained a 30-year lease from the Saudi Arabian government to mine zinc, lead and gold in the Al Masane area of Saudi Arabia. The Al Masane lease is Arabian's largest asset, accounting for approximately $36 million (65 per cent) of Arabian's $56 million in total assets. The lease agreement requires Arabian to build the mine, and begin mining operations, pursuant to a work schedule, and if Arabian fails to comply with the work schedule, the Saudi government may have the right to terminate the lease (SEC, 2003).

In the late 1990s the economic crisis in Southeast Asia caused a sharp drop in mineral prices, making it uneconomical for Arabian to comply with the work schedule required by the lease. In May 2000, the Ministry for Petroleum and Mineral Resources of Saudi Arabia, an agency of the Saudi Arabian government, notified Arabian, via correspondence sent to El-Khalidi in Saudi Arabia, that Arabian must implement the Al Masane Project, as required by the lease agreement. If Arabian failed to do so, the Ministry would begin procedures to terminate the lease (SEC, 2003).

Ignoring this correspondence, in April 2002, El-Khalidi signed a management representation letter with Grant Thornton, Arabian's outside auditor, representing, among other things: (1) that Arabian has complied with all aspects of contractual agreements that would have a material effect on the company's financial statements in the event of non-compliance; (2) that no events have occurred which would impair the company's ability to recover its investment in the Al Masane Project and other interests in Saudi Arabia; and (3) there is no impairment of the company's investment in the Al Masane Project (SEC, 2003).

In late November 2002, El-Khalidi disclosed to Arabian's Treasurer that the Saudi government was threatening to terminate the Al Masane lease. The Treasurer promptly informed Arabian's other officers and directors and, on 23 December 2002, Arabian filed a

Form 8-K with the SEC that publicly disclosed for the first time that the Saudi government was threatening to terminate Arabian's lease. The Treasurer also informed Grant Thornton, which subsequently withdrew its audit reports for Arabian's 2000 and 2001 financial statements and resigned as Arabian's outside auditor (SEC, 2003).

Discussion Questions	■ Why should the problems with the mining lease be disclosed, even though it had no current impact on Arabian? ■ After Grant Thornton learnt of the lease problem, what were their options in relation to their prior audit opinions? ■ Why do you think Grant Thornton resigned as auditor?
References	All material from SEC, 2003, Litigation Release No. 48638, Accounting and Auditing Enforcement Release No. 1898, 'In the Matter of Arabian American Development Company and Hatem El-Khalidi', US Security and Exchange Commission, 16 October.

■ Types of Events After the Balance Sheet Date

International Financial Reporting Standard IAS 10[17] deals with the treatment of financial statement of events, favourable and unfavourable, occurring after period end. It identifies two types of events:

1 those that provide evidence of conditions that existed at the end of the reporting period (adjusting events after the reporting period); and
2 those that are indicative of conditions that arose after the reporting period (non-adjusting events after the reporting period).

The first type requires adjustment to the financial statements and the second type, if material, requires disclosure.

Events Relating to Conditions that Existed at Period End

Events relating to assets and liabilities conditions that existed at period end may require adjustment of the financial statements. For example, adjustments may be made for a loss on a trade receivable account that is confirmed by the bankruptcy of a customer that occurs after the balance sheet date. Other examples of these events that require adjustment of financial statements are:

■ settlement of litigation at an amount different from the amount recorded on the books;
■ disposal of equipment not being used in operations at a price below current book value;
■ sale of investments at a price below recorded cost.

Events Not Affecting Conditions at Period End

Events that fall into the second category, i.e. those that do not affect the condition of assets or liabilities at the balance sheet date, but are of such importance that non-disclosure would affect the ability of the users of the financial statements to make proper evaluations and decisions, should be disclosed. Examples of these types of events are:

■ a decline in the market value of securities held for temporary investment or resale;
■ issuance of bonds or equity securities;

■ a decline in the market value of inventory as a consequence of government action barring further sale of a product;

■ an uninsured loss of inventories as a result of fire.

Events up to the Date of the Auditor's Report

The auditor should perform procedures designed to obtain sufficient appropriate audit evidence that all events up to the date of the auditor's report that may require adjustment of, or disclosure in, the financial statements have been identified.[18] Some of these procedures are described in Illustration 11.5. When the auditor becomes aware of events which materially affect the financial statements, the auditor should consider whether such events are properly accounted for and adequately disclosed in the financial statements.

ILLUSTRATION 11.5

Procedures to Identify Events That May Require Adjustment of, or Disclosure in, the Financial Statements

Audit procedures

The nature of procedures performed in a subsequent events review depends on many variables, such as the nature of transactions and events and the availability of data and reports. However the following procedures are typical of a subsequent events review:

■ Enquiring into management's procedures/systems for the identification of subsequent events;

■ Inspection of minutes of board meetings;

■ Reviewing accounting records including budgets, forecasts and quarterly information;

■ Enquiring of directors if they are aware of any subsequent events that require reflection in the year-end account;

■ Obtaining, from management, a letter of representation that all subsequent events have been considered in the preparation of the financial statements;

■ Inspection of invoices and correspondence with legal advisors;

■ Gathering relevant public available information (general, industry and company);

■ Enquiring status with regards to reported provisions and contingencies; and

■ Regular audit procedures in order to verify year-end balances:

    ■ checking after date receipts from receivables;

    ■ inspecting the cash book for payments/receipts that were not accrued for at the year-end; and

    ■ checking suppliers' invoices received in the new period.

■ Facts Which Become Known to the Auditor After the Date of the Auditor's Report but Before the Date the Financial Statements Are Issued

The auditor has no obligation to perform any audit procedures or make any inquiry regarding the financial statements after the date of the auditor's report. However, if, after the date of the auditor's report but before the date the financial statements are issued, a fact becomes known to the auditor that, had it been known to the auditor at the date of the auditor's report, may have caused the auditor to amend the auditor's report, the auditor should discuss the matter with management and those charged with governance; determine if the financial statements need amendment; and inquire how management intends to address the matter in the financial statements.

When management amends the financial statements, the auditor would carry out the procedures necessary in the circumstances and would provide management with a new report on the amended financial statements dated not earlier than the date the amended financial statements are signed or approved. The procedures outlined in Illustration 11.5 would be extended to the date of the new auditor's report.

When management does not amend the financial statements in circumstances where the auditor believes they need to be amended and the auditor's report has not been released, the auditor should express either a **qualified**[19] or an **adverse**[20] opinion. If the auditor's report has been released to the entity's governance body, the auditor would notify those persons not to issue financial statements and the auditor's report. If the financial statements are subsequently issued to the regulators or public, the auditor needs to take action to prevent reliance on that auditor's report.

■ Discovery of Facts After the Financial Statements Have Been Issued

After the financial statements have been issued the auditor has no obligation to make any inquiry regarding such financial statements. If, however, after the statements have been issued, the auditor becomes aware of a fact which existed at the date of the auditor's report and which, if known then, may have caused the auditor to amend the auditor's report, the auditor should discuss it with management and consider revision of the financial statements.

The new or amended auditor's report should include an **emphasis of a matter paragraph**[21] or Other Matter paragraph referring to a note to the financial statements that more extensively discusses the reason for the revision of the previously issued financial statements and to the earlier report issued by the auditor.

11.6 Review Financial Statements and Other Report Material

The final review of the financial statements involves procedures to determine if disclosures of financial statements and other required disclosures (for corporate governance, management reports, etc.) are adequate. The auditor is responsible for all information that appears with the audited financial statements, so therefore the auditor must also see if there are any inconsistencies between this other information and the financial statements.

■ Financial Statement Disclosures

An important consideration in completing the audit is determination of whether the disclosures in the financial statements are adequate. Adequate disclosure includes consideration of all the financial statements, including related footnotes.

Under the Sarbanes–Oxley Act (SOX) auditors have the responsibility of considering certain financial statement disclosures connected with the financial statements.[22] In section 404,[23] SOX requires that each annual report of a publicly traded company contain an internal control report. The report should state the responsibility of management for establishing and maintaining an adequate internal control structure, and contain an assessment of the effectiveness of the internal control structure and the financial statement accounting procedures of company. Each public accounting firm that prepares or issues the audit report for these companies according to PCAOB Audit Standard 5[24] must attest to, and report on, the assessment made by the management. Companies must disclose all material correcting adjustments and off-balance sheet transactions. Pro-forma information included in any report must not contain an untrue statement of material fact, reconciled with the financial condition of the company.

Adequate Disclosure Ongoing

Review for adequate disclosure is an ongoing activity of the audit. For example, as part of the audit of accounts receivable, the auditor must be aware of the need to separate notes receivable and amounts due from affiliates and trade accounts due from customers because all of these may require different disclosure. Furthermore, there must be a segregation of current and non-current receivables and a disclosure of the factoring or discounting of notes receivable. An important part of verifying all account balances is determining whether financial accounting standards were applied on a basis consistent with that of the preceding year.

Financial Statement Disclosure Checklist

Many audit firms use a financial statement disclosure checklist. An independent partner or director designs these questionnaires to remind the auditor of common disclosure problems encountered on audits and also to facilitate the final review of the entire audit. Illustration 11.6 shows a partial financial statement disclosure checklist. Of course, in any given audit some aspects of the engagement require much greater expertise in accounting than can be obtained from such a checklist.

■ Corporate Governance Disclosures

Recently, there has been worldwide concern by shareholders that corporations should be governed in their best interests. This has led to a requirement on the London Stock Exchange for companies to report that they have followed a Code of Best Practice that was suggested by the Cadbury Committee.[25] The London Stock Exchange requires all listed companies registered in the UK, as a continuing obligation of listing, to state whether they are complying with the Code and to give reasons for any areas of non-compliance. The areas of greatest concern to auditors are the requirements that the directors report on internal control and going concern.

The London Stock Exchange Code of Best Practice states that[26] the directors should report on the effectiveness of the company's system of internal control and that the business is a going concern, with supporting assumptions or qualifications as necessary.

433

> **ILLUSTRATION 11.6**
>
> ## Financial Statement Disclosure Checklist: Inventory
>
> 1 Are the following disclosures included in the financial statements or notes?
>
>   (a) The accounting policies adopted in measuring inventories, including the cost formula used.
>
>   (b) The total carrying amount of inventories and the carrying amount in classifications.
>
>   (c) The carrying amount of inventories carried at net realisable value.
>
>   (d) The amount of any reversal of any write-down that is recognised as income in the period.
>
>   (e) The circumstances or events that led to the reversal or write-down of inventories.
>
>   (f) The carrying amount of inventories pledged as security for liabilities.
>
> 2 Do the financial statements disclose either:
>
>   (a) the cost of inventories recognised as an expense during the period; or
>
>   (b) the operating costs, applicable to revenues, recognised as an expense during the period, classified by their nature?

SOX Governance Disclosures

Under the Sarbanes–Oxley Act (SOX) auditors have responsibility regarding certain governance disclosures connected with the financial statements.[27] The company must also disclose whether or not – and if not, the reason why – it has adopted a **code of ethics**[28] for senior financial officers, applicable to its principal financial officer and comptroller or principal accounting officer, or persons performing similar functions.[29] SOX section 407[30] requires company disclosure of whether or not – and if not, the reasons why – their audit committee is comprised of at least one member who is a financial expert.

In other countries similar developments took place. For example in France, the Netherlands, South Africa and Canada reports about corporate governance were published and broadly discussed. The expected roles of auditors vary between countries and, in most cases; they are less highly profiled than in the UK.

Governance issues are discussed in Chapter 15 'Corporate Governance and the Role of the Auditor'.

■ Other Information in Annual Reports

ISA 720 states that the auditor should read the other information (in documents containing audited financial statements) to identify material inconsistencies with the audited financial statements.[31] 'Other information', on which the auditor may have no obligation to report but which he must check for material inconsistencies, includes documents such as an annual report,[32] a report by management or the board of directors on operations, financial summary or highlights, employment data, planned capital expenditures, financial ratios, names of officers and directors, selected quarterly data, and documents used in securities offerings. Recently, the IAASB has issued an exposure draft that revises ISA 720.[33] The exposure draft extends the scope of the standard to include documents accompanying audited financial statements and the auditor's report on those documents. The draft also extends the auditor's responsibilities (i.e. the work effort) to include not only reading the other information for consistency with the audited financial statements but also reading and considering the other information for consistency with the auditor's understanding of the entity and the environment. Furthermore, the exposure draft seeks to bring transparency of the auditor's work through new suggested auditor reporting responsibilities with respect to other information.

Material Inconsistency

A material inconsistency exists when other information contradicts information contained in the audited financial statements. A material inconsistency may raise doubts about the audit conclusions drawn from audit evidence obtained and, possibly, about the basis for the auditor's opinion on the financial statements.

If the auditor identifies a material inconsistency on reading the other information, he should determine whether the audited financial statements or the other information needs to be amended. If an amendment is necessary in the other information and the entity refuses to make the amendment, the auditor should consider including in the auditor's report an **emphasis of matter paragraph** describing the material inconsistency or taking other action. If an amendment is necessary for the audited financial statements and the entity refuses to allow it, the auditor should express a qualified or adverse opinion.

Material Misstatement of Fact

If the auditor becomes aware that the other information appears to include a material misstatement of fact he should discuss the matter with the company's management. A material misstatement of fact in other information exists when such information, not related to matters appearing in the audited financial statements, is incorrectly stated or presented. If the auditor still considers there is an apparent misstatement of fact, he should request that management consult with a qualified third party, such as the entity's legal counsel, and should consider the advice received. If management still refuses to correct the misstatement, the auditor should take appropriate action that might include notifying the board of directors.

11.7 Wrap-up Procedures

Wrap-up procedures are those procedures done at the end of an audit that generally cannot be performed before the other audit work is complete. Wrap-up procedures include: supervisory review, final analytical procedures (discussed in Chapter 8 'Analytical Procedures'), working paper review, evaluating audit findings for material misstatements, client approval of adjusting entries, review of laws and regulation, and evaluation of the company as a going concern.

Illustration 11.7 summarises the wrap-up procedures normally undertaken.

■ Supervisory Review

Wrap-up procedures start with the in-charge (senior) accountant reviewing the work of the staff accountant. In turn, the manager and partner in charge of the audit review the work submitted by the in-charge accountant. Often, for larger audits, an additional review of the engagement is performed by a manager or partner not working on the engagement to provide an objective assessment of compliance with firm standards (and SOX where applicable). For auditing firms with multiple offices, it is common practice for

ILLUSTRATION 11.7

Typical Wrap-up Procedures

Supervisory review

- in charge reviews work of staff accountant
- manager reviews work of in charge
- partner reviews manager's work

Do analytical procedures

- review of trends and important ratios
- review of unexpected audit findings

Review working papers

- reviewed by an independent member of the audit firm
- reviewed for results of audit tests
- reviewed for sufficiency of evidence
- make a completing-the-engagement checklist
- make an unadjusted error worksheet

Evaluate audit findings for material misstatement

- sign off completion of steps in audit programme
- identify monetary misstatements in financial statements
- propose adjustments to financial statements

Client approval of adjusting entries

- proposed the manager approves adjusting entries
- obtain client approval for all proposed adjusting and reclassification journal entries

Review laws and regulations

- review recent changes in statutes and regulations
- test compliance with regulations

Evaluate entity's continuance as a going concern

- review normal indications of risk
- do analytical procedures
- determine if going concern problems can be mitigated by other factors

review teams to visit the various offices periodically and review selected engagements. A checklist of review procedures is given in Illustration 11.8.

Before signing off on the audit work, the in-charge or senior accountant must make sure that all phases of the work have been concluded in accordance with the audit planning memorandum, that applicable audit procedures have been satisfactorily completed, the audit objectives have been satisfied, that all is done in line with ISAs and that the working papers reflect conclusions supporting the audit opinion. Some audit firms (as we will see in Chapter 13 'Overview of a Group Audit') draft an overall memorandum at the conclusion of the engagement commenting on the fairness of the presentation.

Resolution of Review Questions

Resolution of review questions raised by the manager and partner will usually require more extensive documentation and explanation in the working papers. This phase of the

ILLUSTRATION 11.8

Review Checklist

Client _____ Closing Date _____	Yes	No	Comments
I General Questions			
1 Have you reviewed work paper files?			
2 Are you satisfied that: (a) The judgements and conclusions reached are supported by documented evidence? (b) The work paper files contain no unresolved statements that are prejudicial to the interests of the firm? (c) Appropriate changes in the next examination, if any, have been summarised?			
3 Do the work papers include adequate documentation as to: (a) Changes in accounting policies? (b) Conformity with generally accepted accounting principles or another comprehensive basis of accounting, if appropriate? (c) Appropriate changes in the next examination, if any, have been summarised?			
4 Have you reviewed the audit conclusion on all material items in the financial statements?			
5 Based on your review and your knowledge of the client, do the financial statements fairly present the company's financial position, results of its operations and cash flow?			
6 Is the work performed consistent with the arrangements made with the client?			
7 Does the work performed comply with the firm's quality control policies in all material respects?			
8 Has the computer-assisted audit techniques-related documentation been reviewed by a qualified computer specialist?			
9 Have required job evaluation forms been completed?			
II Financial Statements			
1 Is the name of the company exact?			
2 Are the dates of the balance sheet and period covered by statements of income, stockholders' equity and cash flow exact?			
3 Are all material facts that are necessary to make the financial statements not misleading adequately disclosed?			
4 Have all material and/or extraordinary subsequent events been evaluated and properly treated and/or disclosed?			
5 Is there adequate footnote disclosure? Do the footnotes clearly communicate the facts?			
6 Do the financial statements maintain a uniform manner of format, capitalisation, headings and appearance in general within itself?			

▶

Illustration 11.8 (continued)

Client _____ Closing Date _____	Yes	No	Comments
7 Are you satisfied that other information contained agrees with the financial statements and auditor's report?			
III The Audit Report			
1 Is the audit report addressed to the proper party?			
2 Is the audit report properly worded?			
3 Is an explanatory paragraph included in our opinion when the financial statements are inconsistent?			
4 Is the date of our report proper?			
5 Is any date in the footnotes that requires special mention, with respect to the date of our report, appropriately reflected in the date of our report (e.g. dual dating)?			
6 Is the option on the supplementary financial information proper and supported by auditor examination?			
7 Are disclosures in the opinion, financial statements and notes to financial statements adequate?			
IV Client Relations			
1 Have we performed the engagement in accordance with the arrangement (including any request by the client for extra services)?			
2 Are you satisfied that the audit did not disclose any suspicions of irregularities or illegal acts?			
3 Are you satisfied that the client is a going concern?			
4 Have arrangements been made: (a) For the client's review and approval of the proposed adjustments? (b) For the client to review a draft of the report? (c) To communicate reportable conditions and material weaknesses in the internal control structure?			
5 Have suggestions been summarised for a management letter?			
6 Are we satisfied that no unusual client problem was noted during the audit?			
V Report Production			
1 Are instructions as to processing specific, including the type of report, client number, numbers of copies required, due date, delivery instruction (when and how)?			
2 Does the report style and appearance conform appropriately with the standards we have established for all reports?			
3 Is the language of the report simple and concise?			

ILLUSTRATION 11.9

Independent Review Checklist

Client _____ Closing Date_____	Yes	No	Comments
1 In-charge engagement performance and administration review performed and the appropriate questionnaires completed and signed?			
2 Have all exceptions noted on the questionnaires discussed above been resolved?			
3 Have we obtained an appropriate engagement letter, legal representation letter and client representation letter?			
4 Have you reviewed the vertical review for completeness and unusual problems?			
5 Were an audit programme, time budget and time summary prepared, approved and properly utilised?			
6 Were all problem areas adequately reviewed and conclusions properly documented?			
7 Have you concurred with alternative procedures employed to satisfy us when such procedures deviate from our firm's basic audit policies?			
8 Are the financial statements free from material errors of omission?			
9 Are the engagement files, to the extent reviewed, free from any evidence of material non-compliance with auditing standards or firm policies?			
10 Is our audit report appropriate?			
11 Does our audit report comply with generally accepted auditing standards?			
12 Do the report style and appearance conform appropriately with the standards we have established for all reports?			
13 Is the language of the report simple and concise?			
14 Have identified reportable conditions in the internal control structure been appropriately communicated?			
15 Have all conditions, that you are aware of, that require re-evaluation of our relationship with the client been appropriately considered?			
16 Have you reviewed the reference points raised in working paper review and noted the disposition thereof?			
17 Are you satisfied that there are no unresolved statements in the working paper files? If there are any, they must be properly and adequately explained.			
18 Have you removed all queries from working papers?			

By (Audit Partner): _____
Date: _____

review will usually involve a completion of a firm checklist to determine that all reporting standards have been complied with. Illustration 11.8 is a review checklist. Illustration 11.9 is a review checklist for use by those reviewers independent of the audit.

■ Working Paper Review

The 'in-charge' or 'senior' auditor will obtain the agreement of the manager that the fieldwork is complete before leaving the client's premises. This will usually involve the manager spending the last day or two of the fieldwork at the client's offices reviewing the working papers to determine that the audit programmes are complete and that sufficient evidence has been obtained to support the opinion.

Working papers (or work papers) are a record of the auditor's planning; nature, timing and extent of the auditing procedures performed; results of such procedures; and the conclusions drawn from the evidence obtained. Working papers may be in the form of data stored on paper, film, electronic or other media. A detailed discussion of audit documentation and working papers appears in Chapter 10 Appendix.

Aid in Supervision and Primary Support for Audit Opinion

Working papers serve two main functions: to aid in the conduct and supervision of the audit and as primary support for the auditor's opinion, especially the representation that the audit was conducted in accordance with ISAs.

Working papers are a physical aid in recording the results of audit tests. For example, when a sample is taken, the items sampled must be recorded and computations must be made. Since supervisors who usually perform none of the audit tests make final decisions concerning the audit opinion, the working papers serve as a basis for evaluating the evidence given. After the opinion has been given, working papers are the only physical proof that the auditor has that an adequate audit was conducted because original documents and accounting records remain with the client.

The working papers are reviewed for sufficiency of evidence. Evidence recorded in the working papers should be both relevant and valid. Relevance is largely a matter of the relationship between the evidential matter and the **financial statement assertion** involved. For example, if the assertion concerns existence of an asset, the reviewer should find that the auditor selected items included in the account balance and physically examined and confirmed those items.

Independent Review

Someone who did not take part in the audit reviews the working papers. This is called an independent review. At the completion of the audit, work papers may be reviewed by an independent member of the audit firm who has not participated in the audit for four basic reasons:

1 to evaluate the performance of inexperienced personnel;
2 to make sure that the audit meets the audit firm's standard of performance;
3 to counteract the bias that frequently enters the auditor's judgement;
4 to comply with audit regulation such as the Sarbanes–Oxley Act.

■ Evaluating Audit Findings for Material Misstatements

When the audit tests for each item in the financial statements are completed, the staff auditor doing the work will sign off completion of steps in the audit programme, identify monetary misstatements in the financial statements, and propose adjustment to the financial statements. **Monetary misstatements** are misstatements that cause a distortion of the financial statements. Monetary misstatements may result from mistakes in processing transactions (such as mistakes in quantities, prices or computations), mistakes in the selection of accounting principles, and mistakes in facts or judgements about accounting estimates.

Misstatement Worksheet

To assist the auditor in evaluating the effect of misstatements accumulated during the audit and in communicating misstatements to management and those charged with governance, ISA 320[34] suggests that it may be useful to distinguish between factual misstatements, judgmental misstatements and projected misstatements:

- **Factual misstatements** are misstatements about which there is no doubt.
- **Judgemental misstatements** are differences arising from the judgements of management concerning accounting estimates that the auditor considers unreasonable, or the selection or application of accounting policies that the auditor considers inappropriate.
- **Projected misstatements** are the auditor's best estimate of misstatements in populations, involving the projection of misstatements identified in audit samples to the entire populations from which the samples were drawn. Guidance on the determination of projected misstatements and evaluation of the results is set out in ISA 530.[35]

The most practical way to consider whether the financial statements are materially misstated at the conclusion of the audit is to use a worksheet that determines the combined effect of uncorrected misstatements, individually or in aggregate, on important totals or subtotals in the financial statements. In the combined effect worksheet procedure, a worksheet summarising the results of sampling on each account balance is combined with a worksheet giving the results of audit tests that did not use sampling. (See Chapter 10 'Audit Evidence' and Chapter 8 Appendix 'Audit Sampling and Other Selective Testing Procedures'.)

■ Review Laws and Regulation

All countries have laws that apply to businesses operating there. The auditor should know the laws that apply to their client, review the criteria required to comply with that statute, and test for the client company's compliance. The governing authorities may review publicly traded companies because they meet certain high-risk criteria. Therefore it is wise for the auditor to understand the criteria that will set the client apart for review and determine if any problems may occur. For example, the US Securities and Exchange Commission (SEC) reviews a publicly traded company if the following factors are evident:[36]

- companies that have issued material restatements of financial results;
- companies that experience significant volatility in their stock price as compared to other companies;
- companies with the largest market capitalisation;
- emerging companies with disparities in price to earnings ratios;
- companies whose operations significantly affect any material sector of the economy;
- any other factors that the SEC may consider relevant.

11.8 Going Concern Issues

Assessment of the going concern assumption is particularly important to the auditor. ISA 570[37] specifies that when performing audit procedures the auditor should consider the appropriateness of the going concern assumption underlying the preparation of the financial statements.

The going concern assumption is a fundamental principle in the preparation of financial statements. Under the going concern assumption, a company is viewed as continuing in business for the foreseeable future with neither the intention nor the necessity of liquidation, ceasing trading, or seeking protection from creditors pursuant to laws or regulations. As a result, assets and liabilities are recorded on the basis that the company will be able to realise its assets and discharge its liabilities in the normal course of business.

Most financial legislation, regulation, and accounting standards, including International Financial Reporting Standards, specifically require management to assess the entity's ability to continue as a going concern. IAS 1, 'Presentation of Financial Statements', states that when preparing financial statements, management shall make an assessment of an entity's ability to continue as a going concern. An entity shall prepare financial statements on a going concern basis unless management either intends to liquidate the entity or to cease trading, or has no realistic alternative but to do so. When management is aware, in making its assessment, of material uncertainties related to events or conditions that may cast significant doubt upon the entity's ability to continue as a going concern, the entity shall disclose those uncertainties.[38]

Illustration 11.10 gives examples of events and conditions, which individually or collectively, may cast significant doubt about the going concern assumption.[39] The significance of the indications in Illustration 11.10 can often be mitigated by other factors. For example, the effect of an entity being unable to make its normal debt repayments may be counterbalanced by management's plans to maintain adequate cash flows by alternative means, such as disposal of assets.

The auditor's responsibility is to consider the appropriateness of management's use of the going concern assumption in the preparation of the financial statements, and consider whether there are material uncertainties about the entity's ability to continue as a going concern that need to be disclosed in the financial statements.

■ Doubt of Entity's Ability to Continue as a Going Concern

If the auditor discovers events or conditions that create doubt about the audit client's ability to continue as a going concern, the auditor must perform procedures to back up the doubts with sufficient appropriate audit evidence supporting the notion that material uncertainty exists. These procedures must include the following:

- Inquire of management as to their assessment of the entity's ability to continue as a going concern.
- Evaluate management's proposed future actions to mitigate going concern issues.
- Analyse management's cash flow forecast in terms of of management's plans for future action by evaluating the reliability of the underlying data of the forecast

ILLUSTRATION 11.10

Indications That the Going Concern Assumption Might be Questioned

This listing is not all-inclusive, nor does the existence of one or more of the items always signify that a material uncertainty exists.

Financial Indications

- Net liability or net current liability position.
- Fixed-term borrowings approaching maturity without realistic prospects of renewal or repayment, or excessive reliance on short-term borrowing to finance long-term assets.
- Indications of withdrawal of financial support by creditors.
- Negative operating cash flows indicated by historical or prospective financial statements.
- Adverse key financial ratios.
- Substantial operating losses or significant deterioration in the value of assets used to generate cash flows.
- Arrears or discontinuance of dividends.
- Inability to pay creditors on due dates.
- Inability to comply with the terms of loan agreements.
- Change from credit to cash-on-delivery transactions with suppliers.
- Inability to obtain financing for essential new product development or other essential investments.

Operating Indications

- Management intentions to liquidate the entity or to cease operations.
- Loss of key management without replacement.
- Loss of major market, key customer(s), franchise, licence or principal supplier(s).
- Labour difficulties.
- Shortages of important supplies.
- Emergence of a highly successful competitor.

Other indications

- Non-compliance with capital or other statutory requirements.
- Pending legal or regulatory proceedings against the entity that may, if successful, result in claims that the entity is unlikely to be able to satisfy.
- Changes in law or regulatory or government policy expected to adversely affect the entity.
- Uninsured or underinsured catastrophes when they occur.

and determine if there is adequate support for the assumptions underlying the forecast.

- Consider whether any significant additional facts have occurred since the date of the going concern assessment.
- Request written representations from management with regards to plans for future action and the reasonableness of these plans.

■ Procedures to Gather Audit Evidence

Procedures to gather sufficient appropriate audit evidence may include:

- analysing and discussing cash flow, profit and other relevant forecasts with management;
- analysing and discussing the entity's latest available interim financial statements;
- reviewing the terms of debentures and loan agreements and determining whether any have been breached;
- reading minutes of the meetings of shareholders, the board of directors and important committees for reference to financing difficulties;
- asking the company's lawyer about the existence of litigation and claims and the reasonableness of management's assessments of their outcome and the estimate of their financial implications;
- confirming the existence, legality and enforceability of arrangements to provide or maintain financial support with related and third parties and assessing the financial ability of such parties to provide additional funds;
- considering the entity's plans to deal with unfilled customer orders;
- reviewing events after period end to identify those that either mitigate or otherwise affect the entity's ability to continue as a going concern.

If, based on the audit evidence obtained, the auditor determines a material uncertainty exists related to events or conditions that, alone or in aggregate, may cast significant doubt on the entity's ability to continue as a going concern, disclosure and a possible modification of the audit opinion might occur. This will be discussed in Chapter 12 'Audit Reports and Communications'.

11.9 Matters for Attention of Partners (MAPs)

Matters for Attention of Partners (MAPs)[40] is a report by audit managers to the partner or director detailing the audit decisions reached and the reasons for those decisions.

There is not one standard type of MAP report because the way in which an auditing firm identifies and disposes of issues affecting the audit opinion will vary. In general the MAP (or an equivalent report referred to by a different name) documents significant matters on which an initial decision has been made by the audit manager or an audit partner and details of the eventual resolution of matters that the audit partner decided should be taken up with the client, including the reasoning involved in their resolution. Examples of decisions made and reported in MAP is whether an item is sufficiently material to require adjustment of or disclosure in the accounts. Typically the audit manager prepares the MAP and each item is read and commented on by the partner or director.

The areas discussed in the MAP relate to difficult questions of principle where there is a possibility that the auditor's judgement may subsequently be questioned, particularly by a third party. It is therefore important that the working papers record all those relevant facts available at the time the decision was made. This will allow determination at some future time of the reasonableness of the conclusion reached based on the facts.

■ Contents of MAP

The items included in the MAP are a cover page signed by audit manager and partners stating the basic conclusions of the audit; general matters; management comments; comments on results; discussions of accounts that required special consideration; compliance with statutory laws; comments on accounting systems; comments on management letters; and discussion of any matters that were outstanding at that date. It should be standard that the audit is performed in accordance with ISA.

Results of the audit and discussion of specific accounts may include explanation of findings about inadequate ratios, unusual trends, or decreases in sales or profits. For example, a matter discussed might be: 'Decreases in gross margin are attributable to lower pricing necessitated by increased competition from Zego's Design Rite and General Software's Room Zoom and increased cost of producing CD ROMs.' Major concerns about the accounts are mentioned. An example would be: 'There have been large increases in research and development costs because of the company's policy of developing a major interactive design software product, code-named Walkabout.'

The Matters for Attention should mention that the accounts have been prepared in accordance with the legal statutes (e.g. the Company Act in the UK). Matters for Attention might mention that all ISAs and IFRS have been complied with. Any upgrade or additions to accounting systems (computerised accounting systems especially) would be mentioned for comment. Any matters involving management letters would be mentioned. Finally, any matters outstanding would be presented for comments.

11.10 Reports to the Board of Directors

The board of directors (or, more generally, the audit committee of the board of directors) has significant influence over accounting and financial policies of the entity. The audit committee also has the responsibility for hiring an independent auditor. The auditor must communicate important findings to the board.

■ Matters Discussed With the Board of Directors (Audit Committee)

Auditors may attend board of directors' meetings to discuss accounting and auditing matters. Some matters that might be discussed are the accounting system, internal controls, and impacts of changes in accounting standards, and disclosure. Discussion with the board is essential for matters that cannot be successfully resolved with the executive officers.

Auditors are required by the Security and Exchange Commission[41] to report to the audit committee of the publicly traded company:

■ all critical accounting policies and practices to be used;
■ all alternative treatments of financial information within generally accepted accounting principles that have been discussed with management officials of the issuer, ramifications of the use of such alternative disclosures and treatments, and the treatment preferred by the registered public accounting firm;
■ other material written communications between the registered public accounting firm and the management of the issuer, such as any management letter or schedule of unadjusted differences.

■ Long-Form Audit Report

In some countries, such as Germany, the board of directors gets a special report that is longer and much more detailed than the audit opinion. It is called the long-form report to the board. It may include a number of items, as there is no standard form. Typical areas of discussion in the report are information that the client has omitted from its notes and the errors the auditor has found in performing his work. Chapter 12, 'Audit Reports and Communications', will discuss the long-form audit report in more detail and also communications with the directors and audit committee.

Illustration 11.11 summarises the documents to be obtained or reviewed by the auditor, and to be generated by the auditor and audit team, during the course of the audit.

ILLUSTRATION 11.11

Summary of Audit Process Documents

(a)   Documents to be obtained or reviewed by the auditor during the course of the audit:

Predecessor auditor's working papers	Minutes of board of directors and shareholders
Industry reports, trends, and information	Management representations letter
Engagement letter	Legal letter – letter of inquiry from client counsel
Financial statements	Side letters, if any
Notes to financial statements	Related parties lists and relationship to firm
	Work of other auditors and experts, if any

(b)   Documents to be generated by the auditor and audit team during the course of the Audit:

Client proposal	Completing-the-engagement checklist (optional)
Planning memorandum	Report to audit committee
Audit programme plan	Report to board of directors
Working papers	Unadjusted error worksheet
Confirmation letters to lenders and creditors	Adjustments to financial statements
Matters for Attention of Partners (MAPs)	Audit report

11.11   Summary

This chapter describes the fourth and last phase of the audit. The procedures for completing this audit phase are:

- evaluate governance evidence;
- carry out procedures to identify subsequent events;
- review financial statements and other report material;
- carry out wrap-up procedures;
- prepare Matters for Attention of Partners;
- report to the board of directors and prepare audit report.

Presently two IAASB standards apply to audit quality: International Standards on Quality Control (ISQC) and ISA 220, 'Quality Control for Audit Work'. IAASB issues International Standards on Quality Control (ISQCs) as the standards to be applied for all services falling under the Standards of the IAASB (i.e. ISAs, International Standards on Assurance Engagements (ISAEs), and International Standards on Related Services (ISRSs)).

The elements of quality control policies adopted by an audit firm normally incorporate policies related to general firm activities and personnel. General firm activities for which quality control policies and procedures are required include leadership responsibilities for quality within the firm, acceptance and retention of clients, engagement performance, and monitoring. Quality controls applied to human resources include ethical requirements. The quality control policies and procedures should be documented and communicated to the firm's personnel.

The Sarbanes–Oxley Act, which applies to both US audit firms and audit firms throughout the world, addresses overall review procedures required of the auditor such as second partner review, partner rotation, and quality control. It also discusses the client's audit committee responsibilities and inspection by the Public Company Accounting Oversight Board.

There is important governance evidence that may be acquired any time during the audit, but definitely has to be acquired before the final reporting and evaluation phase (Phase IV of the audit process model). The important governance information to be gathered from the client includes: a legal letter, a management representations letter, information about contingent liabilities and commitments, and identification of related parties.

International Financial Reporting Standard IAS 10 deals with the treatment of financial statement of events, favourable and unfavourable, occurring after period end. It identifies two types of events: (1) those that provide evidence of conditions that existed at the end of the reporting period (adjusting events after the reporting period); and (2) those that are indicative of conditions that arose after the reporting period (non-adjusting events after the reporting period). The first type requires adjustment to the financial statements and the second type, if material, requires disclosure.

The final review of the financial statements involves procedures to determine if disclosures of financial statements and other required disclosures (for corporate governance, management reports, etc.) are adequate. The auditor is responsible for all information that appears with the audited financial statements, so therefore the auditor must also see if there are any inconsistencies between this other information and the financial statements.

Wrap-up procedures are those procedures done at the end of an audit that generally cannot be performed before the other audit work is complete. Wrap-up procedures include: supervisory review, final analytical procedures, working paper review, evaluating audit findings for material misstatements, client approval of adjusting entries, review of laws and regulation, and evaluation of the company as a going concern.

Assessment of the going concern assumption is particularly important to the auditor. ISA 570 specifies that when performing audit procedures the auditor should consider the appropriateness of the going concern assumption underlying the preparation of the financial statements. The auditor's responsibility is to consider the appropriateness of management's use of the going concern assumption in the preparation of the financial statements, and consider whether there are material uncertainties about the entity's ability to continue as a going concern that need to be disclosed in the financial statements.

Matters for Attention of Partners (MAPs) is a report by audit managers to the partner or director detailing the audit decisions reached and the reasons for those decisions. The areas discussed in the MAP relate to difficult questions of principle where there is a possibility that the auditor's judgement may subsequently be questioned, particularly by a third party. Typically the audit manager prepares the MAP and each item is read and commented on by the partner or director.

The board of directors (or, more generally, the audit committee of the board of directors) has significant influence over accounting and financial policies of the entity. The board also has the responsibility for hiring an independent auditor. The auditor must communicate important findings to the board.

11.12 Questions, Exercises and Cases

QUESTIONS

11.2 Introduction

11-1 What are the general procedures for completing the audit as shown in the standard audit process model?

11.3 Quality Control (ISQC #1, ISSA 220, SOX)

11-2 Describe the elements of quality control policies adopted by an audit firm.

11-3 The Sarbanes–Oxley Act (SOX) requires that every registered public accounting firm auditing publicly traded companies include quality control policies standards relating to what areas?

11.4 Evaluate Governance Evidence

11-4 What should be included in the letter from client's legal counsel?

11-5 What kind of evidence does ISA 580 suggest that the auditor get from management? Where might an auditor find evidence to fulfil this requirement?

11-6 What is a contingent liability? What three conditions must be met for a contingent liability to exist?

11.5 Review for Discovery of Subsequent Events

11-7 What is a review for discovery of subsequent events? What should an auditor do if he becomes aware of facts that existed at the date of the auditor's report after the financial statements have been issued?

11-8 If the auditor becomes aware of a fact that may materially affect the financial statements after the date of the auditor's report but before the financial statements have been issued, what should an auditor do and how may this affect the financial statements? What if a material fact is discovered after the financial statements have been issued?

11.6 Review of Financial Statements and Other Report Material

11-9 When reviewing for adequate disclosure, what does an auditor look for? Give some examples.

11-10 When does a material inconsistency exist in information other than the financial statements? What other information must an auditor review for material inconsistencies? What should an auditor do if a material inconsistency is found?

11.7 Wrap-up Procedures

11-11 What are wrap-up procedures? Give some examples.

11-12 What must the audit supervisor do before he can consider the audit work complete?

11-13 What are monetary misstatements? What mistakes can cause a monetary misstatement?

11.8 Going Concern Issues

11-14 What are some indications that the continuance of the company as a going concern may be questionable?

11-15 What procedures should an auditor perform when events or conditions have been identified which may cast significant doubt on the entity's ability to continue as a going concern?

11.9 Matters for the Attention of Partners (MAPs)

11–16 What is meant by MAP? What items are discussed in MAP and why are they important?

11.10 Reports to the Board of Directors

11–17 What are auditors required to discuss with the board of directors? The audit committee?

PROBLEMS AND EXERCISES

11.3 Quality Control (ISQC #1, ISA 220, SOX)

11–18 Quality Review. Charalambos Viachoutsicos is assigned the responsibility of setting up a quality review programme at his St Petersburg, Russia, audit firm, Levenchuk.

Required:
A. What should the verification procedures include? Who should perform the procedures?
B. What type of documentation is required?
C. What should be covered in the report on the quality review programme?
D. What organisational authority is required for the personnel who carry out the quality audit?
E. What qualifications should the personnel have?

11.4 Evaluation of Governance Evidence

11–19 Inquiry of Client's Attorney. Morgan LeFay, AS, of Horsens, Denmark, auditor Jan Ogier, Statsautoriseret Revisor, determines that LeFay has paid legal fees to four different law firms during the year under audit. Ogier requests standard attorney letters as of the balance sheet date from each of the four law firms.

Jan Ogier receives the following responses:

1 One attorney furnished the following opinion: 'It is our opinion that, based on a complete investigation of the facts known to us, no liability will be established against LeFay in the suits referred to in your letter of inquiry.'

2 Attorney number two states that there may be a potentially material lawsuit against the client but refuses to comment further to protect the legal rights of the client.

3 By the last day of field work, Ogier has not received any letter from the third attorney.

4 The letter from the fourth attorney writes that their firm deals exclusively in registering song copyrights and cannot comment on LeFay lawsuits or any other legal affairs.

Required:
A. Discuss the adequacy of the attorney's response in each of the four cases. What procedures should Ogier take in response to each letter?
B. What impact will each of these letters have on Ogier's audit report? Explain.
C. Should you refer to the attorney's opinion in your audit report or disclosures?

11–20 Management Representation Letter. Robert Dingle, president of Alcmena Manufacturing, Ltd., of Perth, Australia, and the company external auditor Deny H. Lawrence, Chartered Accountant (CA), reviewed matters that were supposed to be included in a written representation letter. Upon receipt of the following client representation letter, Lawrence contacted Dingle to state that it was incomplete. The letter Lawrence received is given below.

> To D.H. Lawrence, CA
> In connection with your audit of the balance sheet of Alcmena Manufacturing as of 31 December 20X2, and the related statements of income, retained earnings, and cash flows for the year then ended, for the purpose of expressing an opinion as to whether the financial

statements present fairly, in all material respects, the financial position, results of operations, and cash flows of Alcmena Manufacturing in conformity with generally accepted accounting principles, we confirm, to the best of our knowledge and belief, the following representations made to you during your audit. There were no:

■ Plans or intentions that may materially affect the carrying value or classification of assets and liabilities.
■ Communications from regulatory agencies concerning noncompliance with, or deficiencies in, financial reporting practices.
■ Agreements to repurchase assets previously sold.
■ Violations or possible violations of laws or regulations whose effects should be considered for disclosure in the financial statements or as a basis for recording a loss contingency.
■ Unasserted claims or assessments that our lawyer has advised are probable of assertion and must be disclosed in accordance with International Accounting Standards No.10.
■ Capital stock repurchase options or agreements or capital stock reserved for options, warrants, conversions, or other requirements.
■ Compensating balance or other arrangements involving restrictions on cash balances.

R. Dingle, President
Alcmena Manufacturing Ltd.
14 March 20X3

Required:
Identify the other matters that Dingle's representation letter should specifically confirm.

11.5 Review for Discovery of Subsequent Events

11–21 Subsequent Facts and Events. The following unrelated events occurred after the balance sheet date but before the audit report was prepared:
1 The granting of a retrospective pay increase to selected employees.
2 Receipt of a letter from the tax authorities stating that additional income tax is due for a prior year.
3 Filing of an antitrust suit by the federal government.
4 Declaration of a stock dividend.
5 Sale of a fixed asset at a substantial profit.

Required:
A. Define 'review for discovery of subsequent events' and 'subsequent events'.
B. Identify what procedure to identify events the auditor might have used to bring each of these items to the auditor's attention. (Hint: See Illustration 11.8.)
C. Discuss the auditor's responsibility to recognise each of these in connection with the audit report.
[Adapted and reprinted with permission of AICPA. Copyright © 2000 & 1985 by American Institute of Certified Public Accountants.]

11–22 Subsequent Facts and Events. In connection with their audit of the financial statements of Swan Mfg. Corporation of Ayutthay, Thailand, for the year ended 31 December 20X4, Virameteekul, Kanchana & Banharn, Chartered Accountants (CA) review of subsequent events disclosed the following items:
1 3 January 20X5: The government approved a plan for the construction of an express highway. The plan will result in the expropriation of a portion of the land owned by Swan Mfg. Corporation. Construction will begin in late 20X5. No estimate of the condemnation award is available.
2 4 January 20X5: The funds for Baht 1,000,000 loan to the corporation made by the company president, Somsak Na Lan, on 15 July 20X4, were obtained by him from a loan on his personal life insurance policy. The loan was recorded in the account 'loan from officers'. Mr Somsak's source of the funds was not disclosed in the company records.

451

The corporation pays the premiums on the life insurance policy, and Mrs Somsak, wife of the president, is the beneficiary.

3   7 January 20X5: The mineral content of a shipment of ore, en route on 31 December 20X4, was determined to be 72 per cent. The shipment was recorded at year-end at an estimated content of 50 per cent by a debit to raw material inventory and a credit to accounts payable in the amount of Baht 824,000. The final liability to the vendor is based on the actual mineral content of the shipment.

4   31 January 20X5: As a result of reduced sales, production was curtailed in mid-January and some workers were laid off. On 5 February 20X5, all the remaining workers went on strike. To date the strike is unsettled.

Required:

Assume that the items described above came to your attention prior to completion of your audit work on 15 February 20X5. For each item:

A. Give the audit procedures, if any, that would have brought the item to your attention. Indicate other sources of information that may have revealed the item.

B. Discuss the disclosure that you would recommend for the item, listing all details that you would suggest should be disclosed. Indicate those items or details, if any, that should not be disclosed. Give your reasons for recommending or not recommending disclosure of the items or details.

11.6 Review of Financial Statements and Other Report Material

11–23 Board of Directors Disclosures. The board of directors of Celestial City Corporation of Taejon, Korea, is issuing a corporate governance report. In this audit year Celestial City lost 1,280,000,000 South Korean Won (won) due to a weakness in their internal controls in the treasury department which represents 11 per cent of their current assets. The controller's assistant, Dongsung Young, a Certified Public Accountant (CPA), is asked to write the first draft of the internal control portion of the report.

Required:

Pretend that you are Mr Dongsung and write a draft of the internal controls portion of Celestial City Corporation's corporate governance report. Since Celestial City is publicly traded on the American Stock Exchange and a Depository Receipt use the SEC requirements for the report. See 'Final Rule: Management's Report on Internal Control Over Financial Reporting and Certification of Disclosure in Exchange Act Periodic Reports': http://www.sec.gov/rules/final/33-8238.htm.

11.7 Wrap-up Procedures

11–24 Independent Review Checklist. Compare the general checklist used by an audit firm to assure that the review of the audit work is thorough and complete (Illustration 11.8) with the checklist used by a person independent of the audit (Illustration 11.9).

Required:

A. Which questionnaire is the longest?

B. What questions does each questionnaire ask about the in-charge accountant? About the client?

C. What questions does each checklist ask about the audit report?

D. What is the primary difference between the review questionnaire and the independent review questionnaire? What are the similarities between the two?

11–25 Working Paper Review. Berins & Trichet, Reviseurs d'Entreprises, of Brussels, Belgium has a policy of having their audit papers reviewed by both the partner in charge and an independent reviewer.

Required:

A. Define 'working paper'.

B. Describe the difference between a regular working paper review and an independent review.

C. What items does the regular reviewer examine? The independent reviewer?

11.8 Going Concern Issues

11-26 Going Concern. When an auditor finds the ability of a company to continue as a going concern is questionable, the auditor will use certain audit procedures to obtain further evidence. Jocques Entremont, Expert Comptable, the external auditor for Japonaiseries SA, a company which retails Japanese art and woodcuts in Boulogne, France, suspects that there is a going concern problem.

Required:

A. List the procedures the auditor would perform.

B. Write the auditor's opinion if disclosure of the problem is considered adequate.

C. Write the auditor's opinion if adequate disclosure is not made.

11.9 Matters for the Attention of Partners (MAPs)

11-27 Matters for Attention of Partners. Mneme Monos, a Greek manufacturer of computer chip memories, is being audited by you and you are to make a report to the partner in charge, Abderus Calliope, Soma Orkoton Logiston (SOL). The chief executive officer, Zephyrus Briareus, is determined to make Mneme Monos the number one memory maker and has set up contracts with several distributors around the world, largely on his own initiative.

An analysis of financial statements shows that sales have increased 50 per cent, but profits have dropped 13 per cent. Cost of goods sold as a percentage of sales has increased although there have been only minor increases in inventory due to increase in the cost of silicon. Accounts receivable have increased 60 per cent over last year. Expenses are up as a result of research and development expenditures.

Required:

Write a brief Matters for Attention of Partners memo about Mneme Monos to your managing partner, Abderus Calliope, including a cover page.

CASES

11-28 SEC Regulation, Tax and Working Papers. Marshall and Wyatt, CPA, have been for several years the independent auditors of Interstate LDC Land Development Corporation of New Orleans, Louisiana. During these years, Interstate LDC prepared and filed its own annual income tax returns.

During 20X3, Interstate LDC requested Marshall and Wyatt to audit all the necessary financial statements of the corporation to be submitted to the US Securities and Exchange Commission (SEC) in connection with a multi-state public offering of one million shares of Interstate Land Development Corporation common stock. This public offering came under the provisions of the US Securities Act of 1933. The audit was performed carefully and the financial statements were fairly presented for the respective periods. These financial statements were included in the registration statement filed with the SEC.

While the registration statement was being processed by the SEC, but before the effective date, the US taxing authority, the Internal Revenue Service (IRS), obtained a federal court subpoena directing Marshall and Wyatt to turn over all of its working papers relating to Interstate LDC for the years 20X0–X2. Marshall and Wyatt initially refused to comply for two reasons. First, Marshall and Wyatt did not prepare Interstate LDC's tax returns. Second, Marshall and Wyatt claimed that the working papers were confidential matters subject to the privileged communications rule. Subsequently, however, Marshall and Wyatt did relinquish the subpoenaed working papers. Upon receiving the subpoena, Wyatt called Dan Dunkirk, the chairman of Interstate LDC's board of directors, and asked him about IRS investigation. Dunkirk responded, 'I'm sure the IRS people are on a "fishing expedition" and that they will not find any material deficiencies.'

A few days later Chairman Dunkirk received a written memorandum from the IRS stating that Interstate LDC had underpaid its taxes during the period under review. The memorandum revealed that Interstate LDC was being assessed $800,000, including penalties and interest for the three years. Dunkirk forwarded a copy of this memorandum to Marshall and Wyatt.

This $800,000 assessment was material relative to the financial statements as of 31 December 20X3. The amount for each year individually, exclusive of penalty and interest, was not material relative to each respective year.

Required:

A. In general terms, discuss the extent to which a US CPA firm's potential liability to third parties is increased in an SEC registration audit.

B. Discuss the implications of the IRS investigation, if any, relative to Marshall and Wyatt's audit of Interstate LDC's 20X3 financial statements. Discuss any additional investigative procedures that the auditors should undertake or any audit judgments that should be made as result of this investigation.

C. Can Marshall and Wyatt validly refuse to surrender the subpoenaed working papers to the IRS? Explain.

11.13 Notes

1 Governance – the term 'governance' describes the role of persons entrusted with the supervision, control and direction of an entity. Those charged with governance ordinarily are accountable for ensuring that the entity achieves its objectives, financial reporting, and reporting to interested parties. Those charged with governance include management only when it performs such functions.

2 International Auditing and Assurance Standards Board (IAASB), 2012, International Standard on Quality Control#1 (ISQC#1) 'Quality Control for Firms That Perform Audits and Reviews of Historical Financial Information, and Other Assurance and Related Services Engagements', para. 11, *Handbook of International Quality Control, Auditing, Review, Other Assurance, and Related Services Pronouncements*, 2012 edn, Volume 1, International Federation of Accountants, New York.

3 International Auditing and Assurance Standards Board (IAASB), 2012, International Standard on Auditing 220 (ISA 220) 'Quality Control for an Audit of Financial Statements', paras 9–12, *Handbook of International Quality Control, Auditing, Review, Other Assurance, and Related Services Pronouncements*, 2012 edn, Volume 1, International Federation of Accountants, New York.

4 The Public Company Accounting Oversight Board (PCAOB) was established under SOX section 101. It was established to oversee the audit of public companies that are subject to the securities laws of the USA in order to protect the interests of investors and the public in the preparation of informative, accurate and independent audit reports.

5 107th US Congress, 2002, Sarbanes–Oxley Act of 2002, Public Law 107–204, section 106, 'Foreign Public Accounting Firms', Senate and House of Representatives of the United States of America in Congress assembled, Washington, DC, 30 July.

6 107th US Congress, 2002, Sarbanes–Oxley Act of 2002, Public Law 107–204, section 103-a-2-B, Senate and House of Representatives of the United States of America in Congress assembled, Washington, DC, 30 July.

7 Inspections are made annually with respect to each registered public accounting firm that regularly provides audit reports for more than 100 issuers (companies reporting to the US SEC); and not less frequently than once every three years with respect to each registered public accounting firm that regularly provides audit reports for 100 or fewer issuers.

8 PCAOB, 2003, PCAOB Release No. 2003-019, 'Inspection of Registered Public Accounting Firms', Public Company Accounting Oversight Board, 7 October. Required by 107th US Congress, 2002, Sarbanes–Oxley Act of 2002, Public Law 107–204, section 104, 'Inspections of Registered Public Accounting Firms', Senate and House of Representatives of the United States of America in Congress assembled, Washington, DC, 30 July.

9 No portions of the inspection report regarding quality control systems criticisms is made public if those criticisms or defects are being addressed by the public accounting firm inspected.

10 107th US Congress, 2002, Sarbanes–Oxley Act of 2002, Public Law 107–204, section 206, 'Conflicts of Interest', Senate and House of Representatives of the United States of America in Congress assembled, Washington, DC, 30 July.

11 107th US Congress, 2002, Sarbanes–Oxley Act of 2002, Public Law 107–204, Title III – Corporate Responsibility, section 301, 'Public Company Audit Committees', Senate and House of Representatives of the United States of America in Congress assembled, Washington, DC, 30 July.

12 Unasserted claim – a potential legal claim against a client where the condition for a claim exists but no claim has been filed.

13 Asserted claims are existing lawsuits.

14 Date of the financial statements – the date of the end of the latest period covered by the financial statements.

15 Date of the auditor's report – the date the auditor dates the report on the financial statements in accordance with ISA 700.

16 International Auditing and Assurance Standards Board (IAASB), 2012, International Standard on Auditing 560 (ISA 560) 'Subsequent Events', *Handbook of International Quality Control, Auditing,*

Review, Other Assurance, and Related Services Pronouncements, 2012 edn, Volume 1, International Federation of Accountants, New York.

17 International Accounting Standards Board (IASB), 2013, International Financial Reporting Standards IAS 10 'Events After the Balance Sheet Date', IASB, London and ISA 560 'Subsequent Events', op. cit.

18 International Auditing and Assurance Standards Board (IAASB), 2012, International Standard on Auditing 560 (ISA 560) 'Subsequent Events', *Handbook of International Quality Control, Auditing, Review, Other Assurance, and Related Services Pronouncements*, 2012 edn, Volume 1, International Federation of Accountants, New York.

19 Qualified opinion – a qualified opinion is expressed when the auditor concludes that an unqualified opinion cannot be expressed but that the effect of any disagreement with management, or limitation on scope, is not so material and pervasive as to require an adverse opinion or a disclaimer of opinion.

20 Adverse opinion – an adverse opinion is expressed when the effect of a disagreement is so material and pervasive to the financial statements that the auditor concludes that a qualification of the report is not adequate to disclose the misleading or incomplete nature of the financial statements.

21 Emphasis of matter paragraph – the explanatory paragraph placed after the opinion paragraph in an unqualified auditor's opinion which emphasises a matter related to the entity or its financial statements.

22 107th US Congress, 2002, Sarbanes–Oxley Act of 2002, Public Law 107–204, section 501, 'Disclosure in Periodic Reports', Senate and House of Representatives of the United States of America in Congress assembled, Washington, DC, 30 July.

23 Ibid. Section 404.

24 Public Company Accounting Oversight Board (PCAOB), 2007, Auditing Standard No. 5 'An Audit of Internal Control over Financial Reporting That is Integrated with an Audit of Financial Statements', **PCAOB: http://pcaobus.org/Standards/Auditing/Pages/Auditing_Standard_5.aspx**.

25 Committee on the Financial Aspects of Corporate Governance, 1992, Report of the Committee on the Financial Aspects of Corporate Governance (the Cadbury Report), Gee and Co. Ltd, London, December.

26 Financial Reporting Council, 2003, the Combined Code, Financial Reporting Council, July.

27 107th US Congress, 2002, Sarbanes–Oxley Act of 2002, Public Law 107–204, section 501, 'Disclosure in Periodic Reports', Senate and House of Representatives of the United States of America in Congress assembled, Washington, DC, 30 July.

28 In SOX section 406, the term 'code of ethics' means such standards as are reasonably necessary to promote:
  1 honest and ethical conduct, including the ethical handling of actual or apparent conflicts of interest between personal and professional relationships;
  2 full, fair, accurate, timely, and understandable disclosure in the periodic reports required to be filed by the issuer;
  3 compliance with applicable governmental rules and regulations.

29 107th US Congress, 2002, Sarbanes–Oxley Act of 2002, Public Law 107–204, section 406, 'Code of Ethics for Senior Financial Officers', Senate and House of Representatives of the United States of America in Congress assembled, Washington, DC, 30 July.

30 Ibid. Section 407.

31 International Auditing and Assurance Standards Board (IAASB), 2012, International Standard on Auditing 720 (ISA 720) 'The Auditor's Responsibilities Relating to Other Information in Documents Containing Audited Financial Statements', para. 1, *Handbook of International Quality Control, Auditing, Review, Other Assurance, and Related Services Pronouncements*, 2012 edn, Volume 1, International Federation of Accountants, New York.

32 Annual report – an entity ordinarily issues on an annual basis a document which includes its financial statements together with the audit report thereon. This document is frequently referred to as the 'annual report'.

33 International Auditing and Assurance Standards Board, 2013, International Standard on Auditing (ISA) 720 (Revised) exposure draft, 'The Auditor's Responsibilities Relating to Other Information in Documents Containing or Accompanying Audited Financial Statements and the Auditor's Report Thereon', International Federation of Accountants, New York.

34 International Auditing and Assurance Standards Board (IAASB), 2012, International Standard on Auditing 450 (ISA 450) 'Evaluation of Misstatements Identified During the Audit', para. A3, *Handbook of International Quality Control, Auditing, Review, Other Assurance, and Related Services Pronouncements*, 2012 edn, Volume 1, International Federation of Accountants, New York.

35 International Auditing and Assurance Standards Board (IAASB), 2012, International Standard on Auditing 530 (ISA 530) 'Audit Sampling', paras 14–15, *Handbook of International Quality Control, Auditing, Review, Other Assurance, and Related Services Pronouncements*, 2012 edn, Volume 1, International Federation of Accountants, New York.

36 107th US Congress, 2002, Sarbanes–Oxley Act of 2002, Public Law 107–204, section 408, 'Enhanced Review of Periodic Disclosures by Issuers', Senate and House of Representatives of the United States of America in Congress assembled, Washington, DC, 30 July.

37 International Auditing and Assurance Standards Board (IAASB), 2012, International Standard on Auditing 570 (ISA 570) 'Going Concern', para. 2, *Handbook of International Quality Control, Auditing, Review, Other Assurance, and Related Services Pronouncements*, 2012 edn, Volume 1, International Federation of Accountants, New York.

38 International Accounting Standards Board (IASB), 2012, 'Technical Summary IAS 1 Presentation of Financial Statements': **http://www.ifrs.org/Documents/IAS1.pdf**.

39 International Auditing and Assurance Standards Board (IAASB), 2012, International Standard on Auditing 570 (ISA 570) 'Going Concern', para. A2, *Handbook of International Quality Control, Auditing, Review, Other Assurance, and Related Services Pronouncements*, 2012 edn, Volume 1, International Federation of Accountants, New York.

40 The term 'Matters for the Attention of Partners' was once in widespread use, although there has been a trend away from its use. There is concern about use of the term because it implies that the partner is not part of the audit engagement team. The reality is that the partner is primarily responsible for the conduct of the audit. However, as there is not now a term to replace it in widespread use, we will use the term in this chapter.

41 107th US Congress, 2002, Sarbanes–Oxley Act of 2002, Public Law 107–204, section 204, 'Auditor Reports to Audit Committees', Senate and House of Representatives of the United States of America in Congress assembled, Washington, DC, 30 July.

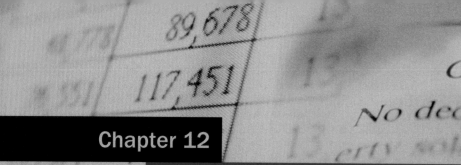

Chapter 12

AUDIT REPORTS AND COMMUNICATIONS

12.1 Learning Objectives

After studying this chapter, you should be able to:

1 Grasp who has responsibility for the financial statements and why.

2 Understand the basic elements of the auditor's report: contents and form.

3 Explain the contents and importance of the unmodified (unqualified) audit opinion.

4 List the considerations of an auditor in giving an unmodified (unqualified) opinion.

5 Distinguish between the different types of opinions given in audit reports on financial statements.

6 Describe the circumstances under which the auditor will modify an opinion.

7 Understand how some uncertainties lead to qualification of opinions in the audit report on financial statements.

8 Provide circumstances in which the unmodified opinion requires an emphasis of a matter paragraph.

9 State the two circumstances that require an auditor's report containing an opinion other than an unmodified (unqualified) one.

10 Discuss the audit matters of governance interest arising from the audit of financial statements that the auditor must communicate to those charged with governance of an entity.

11 Give details contained in the long-form audit report.

12 List the general content of a management letter.

13 Reason why an auditor may attend a meeting of the stockholders of a corporation.

An audit report is very brief, occupying no more than a few lines. Because of its brevity those not knowledgeable in auditing may view it as constituting little more than a necessary legal formality, lacking in substance. This is a paradox because the audit report, although comprising only a few words, requires great care and is the consummation of a rigorous and lengthy audit process.

As an illustration of a long process being reduced to a few words, a study in the USA[1] found that in one given year a global audit firm's five largest clients required average audit work of 128,000 hours per client. This resulted in external reports of only 175 words or less. Currently the audit opinions are longer, but still fewer than 300 words. One might conclude that to get so many hours into so few words, accountants must be poets. More likely, this brevity is out of concern for the users of financial statements. The authors of that same study suggest that the anxious investor does not want to muddle through a lengthy catalogue of work done and detailed findings (imagine how long that would be after 128,000 hours of work) when the final message is 'It is OK'.

However, in addition to this brief external audit report, the auditor is expected to address accounting and auditing issues more extensively in a long-form audit report (see Section 12.9). Also, currently the International Auditing and Assurance Standards Board (IAASB), the US Public Company Accounting Oversight Board (PCAOB) and others are contemplating a more lengthy and detailed report for the near future.

■ Management Responsibility for Audit Report

Up until 2002, corporate officers of publicly traded companies in the USA were not held liable for misstated financial statements unless fraud could be proven. (In other words, the officers knew it was misstated and that was their intent.) All that changed with the Sarbanes–Oxley Act of 2002 (SOX) which now requires[2] that the principal executive officer or officers and the principal financial officer or officers certify in each annual or quarterly report filed or submitted to the US Securities and Exchange Commission (SEC) the following:

- the signing officer has reviewed the report;
- the report does not contain any untrue statement of a material fact or omit to state a material fact;
- the financial statements, and other financial information, fairly present in all material respects the financial condition of the company;
- the signing officers:
  - are responsible for establishing and maintaining internal controls;
  - have evaluated the effectiveness of the company's internal controls;
  - have presented in the report their conclusions about the effectiveness of their internal controls based on their evaluation;
- the signing officers have disclosed to the company's auditors and the audit committee of the board of directors:
  - all significant deficiencies in the design or operation of internal controls which could adversely affect the company's ability to record, process, summarise, and report financial data, and have identified for the company's auditors any material weaknesses in internal controls;

- any fraud, whether or not material, that involves management or other employees who have a significant role in the company's internal controls;
■ the signing officers have indicated in the report whether or not there were significant changes in internal controls or in other factors that could significantly affect internal controls subsequent to the date of their evaluation, including any corrective actions with regard to significant deficiencies and material weaknesses.

This applies also to officers of corporations headquartered outside the USA whose company's stock is traded on US stock exchanges.. This may prove in future to be a sticky point and already there is much international debate. In several European countries it is required by law that all members of the board of directors (or, in a two-tier system, the executive board and the supervisory board) sign the financial statements, thereby demonstrating that their responsibility for these statements is a joint one rather than only that of the CEO and CFO. However, this does not detract from the principle that the responsibility for the financial statements and the internal controls rests with those charged with governance, which is the key issue in SOX.

The Sarbanes–Oxley Act of 2002 is discussed in greater detail in Chapter 2 'The Audit Market' and Chapter 14 'Other Assurance and Non-Assurance Engagements'.

Illustration 12.1 is the certification of Schlumberger Limited's Chairman and Chief Executive Officer Andrew Gould that was submitted in the 10-K report to the SEC for 2003.

12.3 Basic Elements of the Auditor's Report

ISA 700, 'Forming an Opinion and Reporting on Financial Statements', states: 'The auditor shall evaluate whether the financial statements are prepared, in all material respects, in accordance with the requirements of the applicable financial reporting framework. This evaluation shall include consideration of the qualitative aspects of the entity's accounting practices, including indicators of possible bias in management's judgment.'[3] The auditor's report should contain a clear written expression of opinion on the financial statements taken as a whole.

In the first and second edition of this book, the auditor's report (auditor's opinion) had a different format. That format applied generally around the world. However, we now have a new format as set out by ISA 700 and this format is different from that used in many countries. The format will stabilize to the ISA standard in the near future, but today the audit standards organisations of the world are wrestling with providing a format that will give the user of the auditor's report more information about the audit process. In the United States, for instance, the PCAOB has issued a concept release to solicit public comment on the potential direction of a proposed standard-setting project on the content and form of reports on audited financial statements.[4]

■ Contents of the Auditor's Report

The auditor's report should be written and include the following basic elements[5] that are discussed in more detail in the balance of this section (see Illustration 12.2):[6]

■ A title, e.g. 'Independent Auditor's Report'.
■ An addressee, as required by the circumstances of the engagement, e.g. 'Shareholders of ABC company'.

ILLUSTRATION 12.1

Certification of Schlumberger Financial Statements by Corporate Officers

Certification of Chief Executive Officer

I, Andrew Gould, certify that:

1. I have reviewed this annual report on Form 10-K of Schlumberger Limited.

2. Based on my knowledge, this report does not contain any untrue statement of a material fact or omit to state a material fact necessary to make the statements made, in light of the circumstances under which such statements were made, not misleading with respect to the period covered by this report.

3. Based on my knowledge, the financial statements, and other financial information included in this report, fairly present in all material respects the financial condition, results of operations and cash flows of the registrant as of, and for, the periods presented in this report.

4. The registrant's other certifying officer and I are responsible for establishing and maintaining disclosure controls and procedures (as defined in Exchange Act Rules 13a–15(e) and 15d–15(e)) for the registrant and have:

(a) Designed such disclosure controls and procedures, or caused such disclosure controls and procedures to be designed under our supervision, to ensure that material information relating to the registrant, including its consolidated subsidiaries, is made known to us by others within those entities, particularly during the period in which this report is being prepared.

(b) Evaluated the effectiveness of the registrant's disclosure controls and procedures and presented in this report our conclusions about the effectiveness of the disclosure controls and procedures, as of the end of the period covered by this report based on such evaluation.

(c) Disclosed in this report any change in the registrant's internal control over financial reporting that occurred during the registrant's most recent fiscal quarter (the registrant's fourth fiscal quarter in the case of an annual report) that has materially affected, or is reasonably likely to materially affect, the registrant's internal control over financial reporting.

5. The registrant's other certifying officer and I have disclosed, based on our most recent evaluation of internal control over financial reporting, to the registrant's auditors and the audit committee of the registrant's board of directors (or persons fulfilling the equivalent functions):

(a) all significant deficiencies and material weaknesses in the design or operation of internal control over financial reporting which are reasonably likely to adversely affect the registrant's ability to record, process, summarise and report financial information; and

(b) any fraud, whether or not material, that involves management or other employees who have a significant role in the registrant's internal control over financial reporting.

Date: 3 March 2004   /s/ Andrew Gould

_____

Andrew Gould
Chairman and Chief Executive Officer

Source: US Securities and Exchange Commission, http://www.sec.gov.

```
ILLUSTRATION 12.2
```

An Auditor's Report on Financial Statements Prepared in Accordance with a Fair Presentation Framework Designed to Meet the Common Financial Information Needs of a Wide Range of Users

---

INDEPENDENT AUDITOR'S REPORT

To: Appropriate addressee

Report on the financial statements

We have audited the accompanying financial statements 20XX of Company XYZ, Amsterdam, which comprise the consolidated and company statement of financial position as at 20XX, the consolidated and company statements of comprehensive income, changes in equity and cash flows for the year then ended and notes, comprising a summary of the significant accounting policies and other explanatory information.

Management's responsibility

Management is responsible for the preparation and fair presentation of these financial statements in accordance with International Financial Reporting Standards as adopted by the European Union and with Part 9 of Book 2 of the Dutch Civil Code, and for the preparation of the management board report in accordance with Part 9 of Book 2 of the Dutch Civil Code. Furthermore management is responsible for such internal control as it determines is necessary to enable the preparation of the financial statements that are free from material misstatement, whether due to fraud or error.

Auditor's responsibility

Our responsibility is to express an opinion on these financial statements based on our audit. We conducted our audit in accordance with Dutch law, including the Dutch Standards on Auditing. This requires that we comply with ethical requirements and plan and perform the audit to obtain reasonable assurance about whether the financial statements are free from material misstatement.

An audit involves performing procedures to obtain audit evidence about the amounts and disclosures in the financial statements. The procedures selected depend on the auditor's judgment, including the assessment of the risks of material misstatement of the financial statements, whether due to fraud or error.

In making those risk assessments, the auditor considers internal control relevant to the entity's preparation and fair presentation of the financial statements in order to design audit procedures that are appropriate in the circumstances, but not for the purpose of expressing an opinion on the effectiveness of the entity's

internal control. An audit also includes evaluating the appropriateness of accounting policies used and the reasonableness of accounting estimates made by management, as well as evaluating the overall presentation of the financial statements. We believe that the audit evidence we have obtained is sufficient and appropriate to provide a basis for our audit opinion.

Opinion with respect to the financial statements

In our opinion, the financial statements give a true and fair view of the financial position of XYZ as at December 31, 20XX and of its result and its cash flows for the year then ended in accordance with International Financial Reporting Standards as adopted by the European Union and with Part 9 of Book 2 of the Dutch Civil Code.

Report on other legal and regulatory requirements5

Pursuant to the legal requirement under Section 2:393 sub 5 at e and f of the Dutch Civil Code, we have no deficiencies to report as a result of our examination whether the management board report, to the extent we can assess, has been prepared in accordance with Part 9 of Book 2 of this Code, and whether the information as required under Section 2:392 sub 1 at b-h has been annexed.

Illustration 12.2 (continued)

Further we report that the management board report, to the extent we can assess, is consistent with the financial statements as required by Section 2:391 sub4 of the Dutch Civil Code.

Place, date
(Name and Audit firm)
(Name external auditor and his signature)

- An introductory paragraph that identifies the financial statements audited.
- A description of the responsibility of management for the preparation of the financial statements.
- A description of the auditor's responsibility to express an opinion on the financial statements and the scope of the audit, which includes:
  - A reference to International Standards on Auditing and the law or regulation; and
  - A description of an audit in accordance with those standards.
- An opinion paragraph containing an expression of opinion on the financial statements and a reference to the applicable financial reporting framework used to prepare the financial statements (including identifying the jurisdiction of origin of the financial reporting framework that is not International Financial Reporting Standards or International Public Sector Accounting Standards).
- The auditor's signature.
- The date of the auditor's report.
- The auditor's address.

Title

The auditor's report should have an appropriate title that helps the reader to identify it and easily distinguish it from other reports, such as that of management. The most frequently used title is 'Independent Auditor' or 'Auditor's Report' in the title to distinguish the auditor's report from reports that might be issued by others.

Addressee

The report should be addressed as required by the circumstances of the engagement and the local regulations. The report is usually addressed either to the shareholders or supervisory board or the board of directors of the entity whose financial statements have been audited. In some countries, such as the Netherlands, auditor's reports are not addressed at all because the reports are meant to be used by (the anonymous) public at large.

Opening or Introductory Paragraph

The report should identify the entity whose financial statements that have been audited. This should include the name of the entity and the date and period covered by the financial statements. The report should state that the financial statements have been audited, identifying the title of each statement that comprises the financial statements. The report should also refer to the summary of significant accounting policies and other explanatory information.

Management's Responsibility for the Financial Statements

The Management's Responsibility section of the auditor's report describes the responsibilities of those in the organisation that are responsible for the preparation of the financial statements. The auditor's report need not refer specifically to 'management', but shall use the term appropriate to the legal framework in that particular country. In some jurisdictions, the appropriate reference may be to those charged with governance. The auditor's report shall include a section with the heading 'Management's [or other appropriate term] Responsibility for the Financial Statements'.

The auditor's report must describe management's responsibility for the preparation of the financial statements. The description shall include an explanation that management is responsible for the preparation of the financial statements in accordance with the applicable financial reporting framework, and for internal control to enable the preparation of financial statements that are free from material misstatement, whether due to fraud or error. Where the financial statements are prepared in accordance with a fair presentation framework, the explanation of management's responsibility for the financial statements in the auditor's report shall refer to 'the preparation and fair presentation of these financial statements' or 'the preparation of financial statements that give a true and fair view', as appropriate in the circumstances.

Auditor's Responsibility

The auditor's report will include a section with the heading 'Auditor's Responsibility'. The auditor's report shall state that the responsibility of the auditor is to express an opinion on the financial statements based on the audit. The auditor's report shall also state that the audit was conducted in accordance with International Standards on Auditing. The audit report explains that ISA standards require that the auditor comply with ethical requirements and that the auditor plan and perform the audit to obtain reasonable assurance about whether the financial statements are free from material misstatement.

Historically discussed in the second paragraph, or 'scope paragraph', the present auditor's report format under 'auditor's responsibility' (the third, fourth and fifth paragraph) describes the scope of an audit by stating that:

- An audit involves performing procedures to obtain audit evidence about the amounts and disclosures in the financial statements.
- The procedures selected depend on the auditor's judgement, including the assessment of the risks of material misstatement of the financial statements, whether due to fraud or error. In making those risk assessments, the auditor considers internal control relevant to the entity's preparation of the financial statements in order to design audit procedures that are appropriate in the circumstances, but not for the purpose of expressing an opinion on the effectiveness of the entity's internal control. (In circumstances when the auditor also has a responsibility to express an opinion on the effectiveness of internal control in conjunction with the audit of the financial statements, the auditor shall omit the phrase that the auditor's consideration of internal control is not for the purpose of expressing an opinion on the effectiveness of internal control.)

■ An audit also includes evaluating the appropriateness of the accounting policies used and the reasonableness of accounting estimates[5] made by management, as well as the overall presentation of the financial statements.

Where the financial statements are prepared in accordance with a fair presentation framework, the description of the audit in the auditor's report must refer to 'the entity's preparation and fair presentation of the financial statements' or 'the entity's preparation of financial statements that give a true and fair view', as appropriate in the circumstances. The auditor's report shall state whether the auditor believes that the audit evidence the auditor has obtained is sufficient and appropriate to provide a basis for the auditor's opinion.

Opinion Paragraph

The auditor's report will include a section with the heading 'Opinion'.

When expressing an unmodified (unqualified) opinion on financial statements prepared in accordance with a fair presentation framework, the auditor's opinion shall use one of the following phrases, which are regarded as being equivalent:

■ The financial statements present fairly, in all material respects … in accordance with [the applicable financial reporting framework]. Or
■ The financial statements give a true and fair view of … in accordance with [the applicable financial reporting framework].

When expressing an unmodified opinion on financial statements prepared in accordance with a compliance framework, the auditor's opinion shall be that the financial statements are prepared, in all material respects, in accordance with [the applicable financial reporting framework]. If the reference to the applicable financial reporting framework in the auditor's opinion is not to International Financial Reporting Standards issued by the International Accounting Standards Board or International Public Sector Accounting Standards issued by the International Public Sector Accounting Standards Board, the auditor's opinion shall identify the jurisdiction of origin of the framework.

The opinion paragraph of the auditor's report should clearly indicate the financial reporting framework used to prepare the financial statements (including identifying the country of origin of the financial reporting framework when the framework used is not International Financial Reporting Standards) and state the auditor's opinion as to whether the financial statements give a true and fair view (or are presented fairly, in all material respects) in accordance with that financial reporting framework and, where appropriate, whether the financial statements comply with statutory requirements.[7]

International Standard on Auditing (ISA) 200,[8] states that the purpose of an audit is to enhance the degree of confidence of intended users in the financial statements. This is achieved by the expression of an opinion by the auditor on whether the financial statements are prepared, in all material respects, in accordance with an applicable financial reporting framework. he financial reporting framework is determined by International Financial Reporting Standards (IFRSs), rules issued by professional bodies, and the development of general practice within the country, with the appropriate consideration of fairness and with due regard to local legislation.

To advise the reader of the context in which fairness is expressed, the auditor's opinion would indicate the framework upon which the financial statements are based by using words such as '… in accordance with International Accounting Standards (or [title of financial reporting framework with reference to the country of origin]) …'.

Report on Other Legal and Regulatory Requirements

If the auditor addresses other reporting responsibilities in the auditor's report on the financial statements that are in addition to the auditor's responsibility under the ISAs to report on the financial statements, these other reporting responsibilities shall be addressed in a separate section in the auditor's report that shall be subtitled 'Report on Other Legal and Regulatory Requirements', or otherwise as appropriate to the content of the section.

Signature of the Auditor and Date of the Report

The auditor's report must be signed.

The report must be dated. The auditor shall date the report no earlier than the date on which the auditor has obtained sufficient appropriate audit evidence on which to base the auditor's opinion on the financial statements including evidence that: (a) all the statements that comprise the financial statements, including the related notes, have been prepared; and (b) those with recognised authority have asserted that they have taken responsibility for those financial statements. This informs the reader that the auditor has considered the effect on the financial statements and on the report of events or transactions about which the auditor became aware and that occurred up to that date. Since the auditor's responsibility is to report on the financial statements as prepared and presented by management, the auditor should not date the report earlier than the date on which the financial statements are signed or approved by management.[9]

Auditor's Address

The report should name a specific location, which is usually the city in which the auditor maintains an office that serves the client audited. PCAOB's Auditing Standard No.1 [10] also requires that an auditor include the city and state (or city and country, in the case of non-local auditors) from which the auditor's report has been issued. Note: in some countries it is not required that the audit report give the specific address for the auditor.

Signature

The report should be signed in the name of the audit firm, or the personal name of the auditor, or both, as appropriate. The auditor's report is ordinarily signed in the name of the firm because the firm assumes responsibility for the audit. Note: in several countries (e.g. the USA, the UK, the Netherlands) it is currently not required that the personal name of the auditor be signed. Inclusion of the name in a reference is sufficient.

■ Other Formats of the Auditor's Report

An auditor may be required to conduct an audit in accordance with the auditing standards of a specific jurisdiction (the 'national auditing standards'), but may additionally have complied with the ISAs in the conduct of the audit. If this is the case, the auditor's report may refer to International Standards on Auditing in addition to the national auditing standards. However, the auditor shall make reference to ISAs and the national standards only if there is no conflict between the requirements of the two sets of standards that would lead the auditor to form a different opinion, or not to include an Emphasis of Matter paragraph that, in the particular circumstances, is required by ISAs. Furthermore, the auditor's report must still include each of the elements required by the ISA format when he uses the layout or wording specified by the national auditing standards. When the auditor's report refers to both the national auditing standards and International Standards on Auditing, the auditor's report must identify the jurisdiction of origin of the national auditing standards. If the company audited is traded on a US stock exchange, PCAOB's Auditing Standard No. 1[11] requires that in a report the auditor must instead refer to 'the standards of the Public Company Accounting Oversight Board', which is currently reported in the second, or scope, paragraph.

■ Form of an Auditor's Report

The most common type of audit report is the standard unmodified (historically called an 'unqualified') audit report. It is used for more than 90 per cent of all audit reports.[12] Other audit reports are referred to as 'other than unmodified reports'. Other than unmodified reports include those reports that express: an adverse opinion, disclaimer of opinion, and modified opinion (see Section 12.4).

The form of an auditor's report will generally be the form of the unmodified report which traditionally consisted of just three paragraphs (introduction, scope, and opinion), but now it may consist of several paragraphs so long as the basic elements are covered (Introduction, Management's Responsibility, Auditor's Responsibility (including audit scope), and Auditor's Opinion). For unmodified financial statement opinions the PCAOB currently requires the traditional, three-paragraph report. Reports can also include a paragraph after the opinion paragraph called 'an Emphasis of a Matter paragraph' (see ISA 706).[13] In some countries a paragraph referring a qualification as a result of inadequate accounting procedures or disclosure may be inserted just before the opinion paragraph.

Illustration 12.3 shows the standard wording for an unmodified audit report.

The final paragraph in the standard unmodified report states the auditor's conclusion based on the results of the audit examination. This paragraph is so important that the entire audit report is frequently referred to as 'the auditor's opinion'. The opinion paragraph is stated as an opinion rather than as statement of absolute fact or a guarantee. The intent is to indicate that the conclusions are based on professional judgement.

PCAOB auditing standards in the USA currently require the use of a four-paragraph opinion. First is the introduction, the scope paragraph is the second paragraph, the opinion paragraph is third and then there is a paragraph explaining that the auditor has also audited internal controls. Illustration 12.3 is an unmodified report from the US company Wal-Mart Stores.

■ Modified Opinion

An auditor's report is considered to be modified in the two different situations:

1 Matters that do not affect the Auditor's Opinion (which would mean adding an **Emphasis of Matter paragraph**).[14]
2 Matters that do affect the Auditor's Opinion (instances that call for either a (a) **qualified opinion**, (b) **disclaimer of opinion**, or (c) **adverse opinion**).

As the user's understanding will be better if the form and content of each type is uniform, ISA 705, 'Modifications to the Opinion in the Independent Auditor's Report', includes suggested wording to express a qualified, adverse or disclaimer of opinion.

ILLUSTRATION 12.3

Sample US Unmodified Report for Wal-Mart Stores, Inc

Report of Independent Registered Public Accounting Firm

The Board of Directors and Shareholders of Wal-Mart Stores, Inc

We have audited the accompanying consolidated balance sheets of Wal-Mart Stores, Inc. as of 31 January 2012 and 2011, and the related consolidated statements of income, comprehensive income, shareholders' equity, and cash flows for each of the three years in the period ended 31 January 2012. These financial statements are the responsibility of the Company's management. Our responsibility is to express an opinion on these financial statements based on our audits.

We conducted our audits in accordance with the Standards of the Public Company Accounting Oversight Board (United States). Those Standards require that we plan and perform the audit to obtain reasonable assurance about whether the financial statements are free of material misstatement. An audit includes examining, on a test basis, evidence supporting the amounts and disclosures in the financial statements. An audit also includes assessing the accounting principles used and significant estimates made by management, as well as evaluating the overall financial statement presentation. We believe that our audits provide a reasonable basis for our opinion.

In our opinion, the financial statements referred to above present fairly, in all material respects, the consolidated financial position of Wal-Mart Stores, Inc. at 31 January 2012 and 2011, and the consolidated results of its operations and its cash flows for each of the three years in the period ended 31 January 2012, in conformity with US Generally Accepted Accounting Principles.

We also have audited, in accordance with the Standards of the Public Company Accounting Oversight Board (United States), Wal-Mart Stores, Inc.'s internal control over financial reporting as of 31 January 2012, based on criteria established in Internal Control – Integrated Framework issued by the Committee of Sponsoring Organizations of the Treadway Commission and our report dated 27 March 2012 expressed an unqualified opinion thereon.

Ernst & Young
Rogers, Arkansas
27 March 2012

12.4 Types of Report Expressing Audit Opinions

The opinion expressed in the auditor's report may be one of four types: unmodified, qualified, adverse or disclaimer of opinion.

■ Standard Unmodified Opinion Auditor's Report

The auditor's unmodified report should be expressed when the auditor concludes that the financial statements are prepared, in all material respects, in accordance with the identified financial reporting framework.[15] An auditor's report containing an unmodified opinion also indicates implicitly that any changes in accounting principles or in the method of their application, and their effects, have been properly determined and disclosed in the financial statements. Illustration 12.2, earlier, shows sample wording for an auditor's unmodified report.

Requirements to Give Unmodified Opinion

In order to form that opinion, the auditor shall conclude as to whether he has obtained reasonable assurance about whether the financial statements as a whole are free from material misstatement, whether due to fraud or error. That conclusion shall take into account whether sufficient appropriate audit evidence has been obtained, if uncorrected misstatements are material, individually or in aggregate; and certain evaluations as to correspondence of financial statements to the requirements of the applicable financial reporting framework. Evaluation of the compliance to the reporting framework includes consideration of the qualitative aspects of the entity's accounting practices, including indicators of possible bias in management's judgements. In particular, the auditor must evaluate:

- whether the financial statements adequately disclose the significant accounting policies selected and they are consistent and appropriate;
- accounting estimates made by management are reasonable;
- information presented in the financial statements is relevant, reliable, comparable and understandable;
- disclosures to enable the intended users to understand the effect of material transactions and events on the information conveyed in the financial statements; and
- terminology used in the financial statements, including the title of each financial statement, is appropriate.

When the financial statements are prepared in accordance with a fair presentation framework, the evaluation above will also include whether the financial statements achieve fair presentation. The auditor's evaluation as to whether the financial statements achieve fair presentation includes consideration of the overall presentation, structure and content of the financial statements; and whether the financial statements and related notes represent the underlying transactions and events achieve fair presentation.

If the auditor concludes, based on the audit evidence, that the financial statements as a whole are not free from material misstatement, or he is unable to obtain sufficient appropriate audit evidence, he must modify the opinion in the auditor's report by expressing a qualified, adverse or disclaimer of opinion.

■ Auditor's Report Containing a Modified Opinion

The auditor will express a qualified opinion when:[16]

- having obtained sufficient appropriate audit evidence, the auditor concludes that misstatements, individually or in the aggregate, are material, but not pervasive, to the financial statements; or
- the auditor is unable to obtain sufficient appropriate audit evidence on which to base the opinion, but the auditor concludes that the possible effects on the financial statements of undetected misstatements, if any, could be material but not pervasive.

The key concepts to consider are materiality and pervasiveness. Information is **material** if its omission or misstatement could influence the economic decisions of users taken on the basis of the financial statements. Materiality depends on the size of the item or error judged in the particular circumstances of its omission or misstatement. Thus, materiality provides a threshold or cut-off point rather than being a primary qualitative characteristic which information must have if it is to be useful. **Pervasive** is a term used to describe the effects on the financial statements of misstatements or the possible effects on the financial statements of misstatements that are undetected due to an inability to obtain sufficient appropriate audit evidence. Pervasive effects on the financial statements are those that, in the auditor's judgement:

- are not confined to specific elements, accounts or items of the financial statements;
- if so confined, represent or could represent a substantial proportion of the financial statements; or
- in relation to disclosures, are fundamental to users' understanding of the financial statements.[17]

An example of the wording of a qualified report is given in Illustration 12.4.[18] This illustration is a qualified opinion report based on inability to obtain sufficient appropriate audit evidence. It should be noted that in some countries the auditor would not be allowed to accept an engagement when there is a known limitation of scope.

ILLUSTRATION 12.4

Qualified Independent Auditor's Report Due to the Inability to Obtain Sufficient and Appropriate Audit Evidence

Independent Auditor's Report

To: Appropriate addressee

Report on the financial statements[1]
We have audited the accompanying financial statements 20XX of Company XYZ Amsterdam, which comprise the consolidated and company balance sheet as at December 31, 20XX, the consolidated and company profit and loss account for the year then ended and the notes, comprising a summary of the accounting policies and other explanatory information.

Management's responsibility
Management is responsible for the preparation and fair presentation of these financial statements and for the preparation of the management board report, both in accordance with Part 9 of Book 2 of the Dutch Civil Code. Furthermore management is responsible for such internal control as it determines is necessary to enable the preparation of the financial statements that are free from material misstatement, whether due to fraud or error.

Auditor's responsibility
Our responsibility is to express an opinion on these financial statements based on our audit. We conducted our audit in accordance with Dutch law, including the Dutch Standards on Auditing. This requires that we comply with ethical requirements and plan and perform the audit to obtain reasonable assurance about whether the financial statements are free from material misstatement.

Illustration 12.4 (continued)

An audit involves performing procedures to obtain audit evidence about the amounts and disclosures in the financial statements. The procedures selected depend on the auditor's judgment, including the assessment of the risks of material misstatement of the financial statements, whether due to fraud or error. In making those risk assessments, the auditor considers internal control relevant to the entity's preparation and fair presentation of the financial statements in order to design audit procedures that are appropriate in the circumstances, but not for the purpose of expressing an opinion on the effectiveness of the entity's internal control. An audit also includes evaluating the appropriateness of accounting policies used and the reasonableness of accounting estimates made by management, as well as evaluating the overall presentation of the financial statements.

We believe that the audit evidence we have obtained is sufficient and appropriate to provide a basis for our qualified audit opinion.

Basis for qualified opinion
XYZ s investment in Company ABC, a foreign associate acquired during the year and accounted for by the equity method, is carried at ... on the balance sheet as at ..., XXXX, and XYZ s share of ABC s net income of ... is included in XYZ BVs income for the year then ended. We were unable to obtain sufficient appropriate audit evidence about the carrying amount of XYZ s investment in ABC as at ..., XXXX, and XYZ s share of ABC s net income for the year because we were denied access to the financial information, management and the auditors of ABC. Consequently, we were unable to determine whether any adjustments to these amounts were necessary.

Qualified opinion 4 with respect to the financial statements
In our opinion, except for the possible effects of the matter described in the Basis for qualified opinion paragraph, the financial statements give a true and fair view of the financial position of XYZ as at December 31, 20XX and of its result for the year then ended in accordance with Part 9 of Book 2 of the Dutch Civil Code.

Report on other legal and regulatory requirements
Pursuant to the legal requirement under Section 2:393 sub 5 at e and f of the Dutch Civil Code, we have no deficiencies to report as a result of our examination whether the management board report, to the extent we can assess, has been prepared in accordance with Part 9 of Book 2 of this Code, and whether the information as required under Section 2:392 sub 1 at b-h has been annexed. Further we report that the management board report, to the extent we can assess, is consistent with the financial statements as required by Section 2:391 sub 4 of the Dutch Civil Code.

Place, date
... (Name and Audit firm)
... (Name external auditor and his signature)

■ Auditor's Report Containing an Adverse Opinion

The auditor shall express an adverse opinion when the auditor, having obtained sufficient appropriate audit evidence, concludes that misstatements, individually or in the aggregate, are both material and pervasive to the financial statements.

An adverse opinion is issued when the effect of a disagreement is so material and pervasive to the financial statements that the auditor concludes that a qualification of his report is not adequate to disclose the misleading or incomplete nature of the financial statements.

471

An example of the wording of an auditor's report containing an adverse opinion for materially misstated financial statements due to the non-consolidation of a subsidiary is given in Illustration 12.5.[19]

Notice that the adverse opinion report has a paragraph, before the adverse opinion paragraph, which is the paragraph discussing the disagreement. For example, in Illustration 12.5, the auditor has a disagreement with management as to the consolidation of a subsidiary.

It is obvious from reading the opinion paragraph that an adverse opinion report is likely to have a very negative effect on the readers of the report and the related financial statements; therefore, such reports are issued only after all attempts to persuade the client to adjust the financial statements have failed. The only other option available to the auditor in this situation is withdrawal from the engagement.

■ Auditor's Report Containing a Disclaimer of Opinion

The auditor will disclaim an opinion when he is unable to obtain sufficient appropriate audit evidence on which to base the opinion, and he concludes that the possible effects on the financial statements of undetected misstatements could be both material and pervasive. The auditor would also disclaim an opinion when, in extremely rare circumstances involving multiple uncertainties, the auditor concludes that, notwithstanding having obtained sufficient appropriate audit evidence regarding each of the individual uncertainties, it is not possible to form an opinion on the financial statements due to the potential interaction of the uncertainties and their possible cumulative effect on the financial statements.

An auditor's report containing a disclaimer of opinion should be expressed when the possible effect of a limitation on scope is so material and pervasive that the auditor has

---

ILLUSTRATION 12.5

Adverse Independent Auditor's Report Due to a Fundamental Departure from Generally Accepted Accounting Principles

Independent Auditor's Report

[To: Appropriate Addressee]

Report on the financial statements
We have audited the accompanying financial statements 20XX of Company XYZ , Amsterdam, which comprise the consolidated and company statement of financial position as at December 31, 20XX, the consolidated and company statements of comprehensive income, changes in equity and cash flows for the year then ended and notes, comprising a summary of the significant accounting policies and other explanatory information.

Management's responsibility
Management is responsible for the preparation and fair presentation of these financial statements in accordance with International Financial Reporting Standards as adopted by the European Union and with Part 9 of Book 2 of the Dutch Civil Code, and for the preparation of the management board report in accordance with Part 9 of Book 2 of the Dutch Civil Code . Furthermore management is responsible for such internal control as it determines is necessary to enable the preparation of the financial statements that are free from material misstatement, whether due to fraud or error.

Auditor's responsibility
Our responsibility is to express an opinion on these financial statements based on our audit. We conducted our audit in accordance with Dutch law, including the Dutch Standards on Auditing. This requires that we comply with

Illustration 12.5 (continued)

ethical requirements and plan and perform the audit to obtain reasonable assurance about whether the financial statements are free from material misstatement. An audit involves performing procedures to obtain audit evidence about the amounts and disclosures in the financial statements. The procedures selected depend on the auditor's judgment, including the assessment of the risks of material misstatement of the financial statements, whether due to fraud or error. In making those risk assessments, the auditor considers internal control relevant to the entity's preparation and fair presentation of the financial statements in order to design audit procedures that are appropriate in the circumstances, but not for the purpose of expressing an opinion on the effectiveness of the entity's internal control. An audit also includes evaluating the appropriateness of accounting policies used and the reasonableness of accounting estimates made by management, as well as evaluating the overall presentation of the financial statements.

We believe that the audit evidence we have obtained is sufficient and appropriate to provide a basis for our adverse audit opinion.

Basis for adverse opinion
A provision for unconditional pension liabilities is not recorded in the balance sheet as required by Part 9 Book 2 of the Dutch Civil Code. At the balance sheet date the required provision amounts to approximately ... As a consequence, the company's equity and net result, tax effects taken into account, are overstated by ... and ..., respectively.

Adverse opinion with respect to the financial statements
In our opinion, because of the significance of the matter described in the Basis for adverse opinion paragraph, the financial statements do not give a true and fair view of the financial position of XYZ as at December 31, 20XX, and of its result and its cash flows for 20XX in accordance with International Financial Reporting Standards as adopted by the European Union and with Part 9 of Book 2 of the Dutch Civil Code.

Report on other legal and regulatory requirements6
Pursuant to the legal requirement under Section 2:393 sub 5 at e and f of the Dutch Civil Code, we have no deficiencies to report as a result of our examination whether the management board report, to the extent we can assess, has been prepared in accordance with Part 9 of Book 2 of this Code, and whether the information as required under Section 2:392 sub 1 at b-h has been annexed. Further we report that the management board report, to the extent we can assess, is consistent with the financial statements as required by Section 2:391 sub 4 of the Dutch Civil Code.

Place, date
... (Name and Audit firm)
... (Name external auditor and his signature)

not been able to obtain sufficient appropriate audit evidence and therefore is unable to express an opinion on the financial statements.

An example of the wording of a disclaimer of opinion report for limitation of scope (due to the auditor's inability to obtain sufficient appropriate audit evidence about a single element of the financial statements) is given in Illustration 12.6.[20]

When an auditor issues a disclaimer of opinion, more often than not there is a finding regarding the internal controls (controls or either ineffective or are missing/not in place, or a combination). Therefore it is helpful to understand ISA 265 'Communicating Deficiencies in Internal Control to Those Charged with Governance and Management'.[21]

Whenever the auditor issues a report that is other than unmodified, he should include a clear description of all the substantive reasons that should be included in the report and a qualification of the possible effect(s) on the financial statements. This information should be set out in a separate paragraph, preceding the opinion or disclaimer of opinion and may include a reference to a more extensive discussion, if any, in a note to the financial statements.

ILLUSTRATION 12.6

Independent Auditor's Report with a Disclaimer of Opinion Due to the Auditor's Inability to Obtain Sufficient Appropriate Audit Evidence About Multiple Elements in the Financial Statements

INDEPENDENT AUDITOR'S REPORT

To: Appropriate addressee

Report on the financial statements
We were engaged to audit the accompanying financial statements 20XX of Company XYZ, Amsterdam, which comprise the balance sheet as at December 31, 20XX, the profit and loss account for the year then ended and the notes, comprising a summary of the accounting policies and other explanatory information.

Management's responsibility
Management is responsible for the preparation and fair presentation of these financial statements and for the preparation of the management board report, both in accordance with Part 9 of Book 2 of the Dutch Civil Code . Furthermore management is responsible for such internal control as it determines is necessary to enable the preparation of the financial statements that are free from material misstatement, whether due to fraud or error.

Auditor's responsibility
Our responsibility is to express an opinion on the financial statements based on conducting the audit in accordance with Dutch law, including the Dutch Standards on Auditing. Because of the matter described in the Basis for disclaimer of opinion paragraph, however, we were not able to obtain sufficient appropriate audit evidence to provide a basis for an audit opinion.

Basis for disclaimer of opinion
We were not appointed as auditors of the company until after ..., 20XX and thus did not observe the counting of physical inventories at the beginning and end of the year. We were unable to satisfy ourselves by alternative means concerning the inventory quantities held at ..., 20XX-1 and 20XX which are stated in the balance sheet at ... and ..., respectively.
In addition, the introduction of a new computerized accounts receivable system in September 20XX resulted in numerous errors in accounts receivable. As of the date of our audit report, management was still in the process of rectifying the system deficiencies and correcting the errors. We were unable to confirm or verify by alternative means accounts receivable included in the balance sheet at a total amount of ... as at ..., 20XX. As a result of these matters, we were unable to determine whether any adjustments might have been found necessary in respect of recorded or unrecorded inventories and accounts receivable, and the elements making up the profit and loss account.

Disclaimer of opinion with respect to the financial statements
Because of the significance of the matter described in the Basis for disclaimer of opinion paragraph, we have not been able to obtain sufficient appropriate audit evidence to provide a basis for an audit opinion. Accordingly, we do not express an opinion on the financial statements.

Report on other legal and regulatory requirements
Pursuant to the legal requirement under Section 2:393 sub 5 at e and f of the Dutch Civil Code, we have no deficiencies to report as a result of our examination whether the management board report, to the extent we can assess, has been prepared in accordance with Part 9 of Book 2 of this Code, and whether the information as required under Section 2:392 sub 1 at b-h has been annexed. Further we report that the management board report, to the extent we can assess, is consistent with the financial statements as required by Section 2:391 sub 4 of the Dutch Civil Code.

Place, date
... (Name and Audit firm)
... (Name external auditor and his signature)

■ Consequence of an Inability to Obtain Sufficient Appropriate Audit Evidence Due to a Management-Imposed Limitation after the Auditor Has Accepted the Engagement

If, after accepting the engagement, the auditor becomes aware that management has imposed a limitation on the scope of the audit that the auditor considers likely to result in the need to express a qualified opinion or to disclaim an opinion on the financial statements, the auditor must request that management remove the limitation. If management refuses to remove the limitation, the auditor must communicate the matter to those charged with governance and determine whether it is possible to perform alternative procedures to obtain sufficient appropriate audit evidence.

If the auditor is unable to obtain sufficient appropriate audit evidence, the auditor shall determine if the possible effects on the financial statements of undetected misstatements. If the effects could be material but not pervasive, the auditor shall qualify the opinion. If the auditor concludes that the possible effects on the financial statements of undetected misstatements could be both material and pervasive he must withdraw from the audit. If withdrawal from the audit before issuing the auditor's report is not practicable or possible, the auditor should disclaim an opinion on the financial statements. Before withdrawing, the auditor will communicate to those charged with governance any matters regarding misstatements identified.

When the auditor considers it necessary to express an adverse opinion or disclaim an opinion on the financial statements as a whole, the auditor's report shall not also include an unmodified opinion with respect to the same financial reporting framework on a single financial statement or one or more specific elements, accounts or items of a financial statement. To include such an unmodified opinion in the same report in these circumstances would contradict the auditor's adverse opinion or disclaimer of opinion on the financial statements as a whole.

■ Form and Content of the Auditor's Report When the Opinion Is Modified

When the auditor modifies the opinion on the financial statements, the auditor will include a paragraph in the auditor's report that provides a description of the basis for the modification. This paragraph is placed immediately before the opinion paragraph in the auditor's report under the heading 'Basis for Qualified Opinion', 'Basis for Adverse Opinion' or 'Basis for Disclaimer of Opinion', as appropriate. The auditor includes in the basis for modification paragraph a description and quantification of the financial effects of the misstatement. If it is not practical to quantify the financial effects, the auditor shall state that in the basis for modification paragraph. If the modification results from an inability to obtain sufficient appropriate audit evidence, the auditor shall include in the basis for modification paragraph the reasons for that inability.

If there is a material misstatement of the financial statements that relates to narrative disclosures, an explanation of how the disclosures are misstated should be included in the basis for modification paragraph. If a material misstatement relates to the non-disclosure of information required to be disclosed, the auditor shall discuss the non-disclosure with those charged with governance; describe in the basis for modification paragraph the nature of the omitted information; and include the omitted disclosures.

■ Opinion Paragraph When the Opinion Is a Modified One

When the auditor modifies the audit opinion, the auditor uses the heading 'Qualified Opinion', 'Adverse Opinion' or 'Disclaimer of Opinion', as appropriate, for the opinion paragraph. When the auditor expresses a qualified opinion, the auditor states in the opinion paragraph that, in the auditor's opinion, *except for* the effects of the matter(s) described in the Basis for Qualified Opinion paragraph, the financial statements present fairly, in all material respects (or give a true and fair view) in accordance with the applicable financial reporting framework when reporting in accordance with a fair presentation framework *or* in accordance with the applicable financial reporting framework when reporting in accordance with a compliance framework. When the modification arises from an inability to obtain sufficient appropriate audit evidence, the auditor shall use the corresponding phrase 'except for the possible effects of the matter(s) …' for the modified opinion.

When the auditor expresses an **adverse opinion**, the auditor will state in the opinion paragraph that, in the auditor's opinion, because of the significance of the matter(s) described in the Basis for Adverse Opinion paragraph the financial statements do not present fairly (or give a true and fair view) in accordance with the applicable financial reporting framework when reporting in accordance with a fair presentation framework; or in accordance with the applicable financial reporting framework when reporting in accordance with a compliance framework.

When the auditor *disclaims* an opinion due to an inability to obtain sufficient appropriate audit evidence, the auditor states in the opinion paragraph that because of the significance of the matter(s) described in the Basis for Disclaimer of Opinion paragraph, the auditor has not been able to obtain sufficient appropriate audit evidence to provide a basis for an audit opinion; and, accordingly, the auditor does not express an opinion on the financial statements.

■ Description of Auditor's Responsibility for Qualified, Adverse or Disclaimer

When the auditor expresses a qualified or adverse opinion, the auditor must amend the description of the auditor's responsibility to state that the auditor believes that the audit evidence he has obtained is sufficient and appropriate to provide a basis for the auditor's modified audit opinion.

When the auditor disclaims an opinion due to an inability to obtain sufficient appropriate audit evidence, the auditor must amend the **introductory** paragraph of the auditor's report to state that the auditor was engaged to audit the financial statements. The auditor shall also amend the description of the auditor's responsibility and the description of the scope of the audit to state only the following:[22]

> Our responsibility is to express an opinion on the financial statements based on conducting the audit in accordance with International Standards on Auditing. Because of the matter(s) described in the Basis for Disclaimer of Opinion paragraph, however, we were not able to obtain sufficient appropriate audit evidence to provide a basis for an audit opinion.

12.5 Emphasis of a Matter Paragraph

The auditor, having formed an opinion on the financial statements, sometimes must draw the financial statement users' attention to a matter, although appropriately presented or disclosed in the financial statements, that is of such importance that it is fundamental to users' understanding of the financial statements; or any other matter that is relevant to users' understanding of the audit, the auditor's responsibilities, or the auditor's report. This part of the opinion is called an emphasis of a matter paragraph or other matter paragraph. An **Emphasis of Matter paragraph** is a paragraph included in the auditor's report that refers to a matter appropriately presented or disclosed in the financial statements that, in the auditor's judgement, is of such importance that it is fundamental to users' understanding of the financial statements. The **Other Matter paragraph** is a paragraph included in the auditor's report that refers to a matter other than those presented or disclosed in the financial statements that, in the auditor's judgement, is relevant to users' understanding of the audit, the auditor's responsibilities or the auditor's report.

When the auditor includes an Emphasis of Matter paragraph in the auditor's report, the auditor shall include it immediately after the Opinion paragraph in the auditor's report and use the heading 'Emphasis of Matter'. Furthermore, the auditor will include in the paragraph a clear reference to the matter being emphasised and to where relevant disclosures that fully describe the matter can be found in the financial statements and indicate that the auditor's opinion is not modified in respect of the matter emphasised.

If the auditor considers it necessary to communicate a matter other than those that are presented or disclosed in the financial statements that is relevant to users' understanding of the audit, the auditor shall do so in a paragraph in the auditor's report, with the heading 'Other Matter'. This paragraph is placed immediately after the Opinion paragraph and any Emphasis of Matter paragraph.

In certain circumstances, an auditor's report may be modified by adding an emphasis of matter paragraph to highlight a matter affecting the financial statements. The addition of an emphasis of matter paragraph does not affect the auditor's opinion. The paragraph should follow the opinion paragraph and state that the auditor's opinion is not modified by this.[23]

Ordinarily, an auditor might write an emphasis of a matter paragraph:

- if there is a significant uncertainty which may affect the financial statements, the resolution of which is dependent upon future events. Examples of uncertainties that might be emphasised include: the existence of related party transactions, important accounting matters occurring subsequent to the balance sheet date, matters affecting the comparability of financial statements with those of previous years (e.g. change in accounting methods), and litigation, long-term contracts, recoverability of asset values, losses on discontinued operations;
- to highlight a material matter regarding a going concern problem (Illustration 12.8 shows an emphasis of matter paragraph relating to going concern; also see Chapter 11 'Completing the Audit' and ISA 570 'Going Concern');
- other matters.

An illustration of an emphasis of matter paragraph for a significant uncertainty in an auditor's report follows:[24]

> Emphasis of Matter
> We draw attention to Note X to the financial statements which describes the uncertainty related to the outcome of the lawsuit filed against the company by XYZ Company. Our opinion is not qualified in respect of this matter.

Or:

> Without qualifying our opinion we draw attention to Note X to the financial statements. The Company is the defendant in a lawsuit alleging infringement of certain patent rights and claiming royalties and punitive damages. The Company has filed a counter action, and preliminary hearings and discovery proceedings on both actions are in progress. The ultimate outcome of the matter cannot presently be determined, and no provision for any liability that may result has been made in the financial statements.

■ Uncertainties in the Emphasis of a Matter Paragraph

Examples of uncertainties that might be emphasised include the existence of related-party transactions, important accounting matters occurring subsequent to the balance sheet date (discussed in Chapter 11 'Completing the Audit'), and matters affecting the comparability of financial statements with those of previous years (e.g. change in accounting methods). Illustration 12.7[25] gives a complete qualified audit opinion when there is uncertainty. Illustration 12.8[26] provides sample wording for uncertainty paragraphs for a going concern uncertainty.

ILLUSTRATION 12.7

Sample Wording – Auditor's Qualified Report with Emphasis of Matter Paragraph

Independent Auditor's Report

[Appropriate Addressee]

Report on the Financial Statements
We have audited the accompanying financial statements of ABC Company, which comprise the statement of financial position as at 31 December 20X1, and the statement of comprehensive income, statement of changes in equity and statement of cash flows for the year then ended, and a summary of significant accounting policies and other explanatory information.

Management's Responsibility for the Financial Statements
Management is responsible for the preparation and fair presentation of these financial statements in accordance with International Financial Reporting Standards, and for such internal control as management determines is necessary to enable the preparation of financial statements that are free from material misstatement, whether due to fraud or error.

Auditor's Responsibility
Our responsibility is to express an opinion on these financial statements based on our audit. We conducted our audit in accordance with International Standards on Auditing. Those standards require that we comply

Illustration 12.7 (continued)

with ethical requirements and plan and perform the audit to obtain reasonable assurance about whether the financial statements are free from material misstatement.

An audit involves performing procedures to obtain audit evidence about the amounts and disclosures in the financial statements. The procedures selected depend on the auditor's judgement, including the assessment of the risks of material misstatement of the financial statements, whether due to fraud or error. In making those risk assessments, the auditor considers internal control relevant to the entity's preparation and fair presentation of the financial statements in order to design audit procedures that are appropriate in the circumstances, but not for the purpose of expressing an opinion on the effectiveness of the entity's internal control. An audit also includes evaluating the appropriateness of accounting policies used and the reasonableness of accounting estimates made by management, as well as evaluating the overall presentation of the financial statements.

We believe that the audit evidence that we have obtained is sufficient and appropriate to provide a basis for our qualified audit opinion.

Basis for Qualified Opinion
The company's short-term marketable securities are carried in the statement of financial position at xxx. Management has not marked these securities to market but has instead stated them at cost, which constitutes a departure from International Financial Reporting Standards. The company's records indicate that had management marked the marketable securities to market, the company would have recognised an unrealised loss of xxx in the statement of comprehensive income for the year. The carrying amount of the securities in the statement of financial position would have been reduced by the same amount at 31 December 20X1, and income tax, net income and shareholders' equity would have been reduced by xxx, xxx and xxx respectively.

Qualified Opinion
In our opinion, except for the effects of the matter described in the Basis for Qualified Opinion paragraph, the financial statements present fairly, in all material respects (or give a true and fair view of), the financial position of ABC Company as at 31 December 20X1, and (of) its financial performance and its cash flows for the year then ended in accordance with International Financial Reporting Standards.

Emphasis of Matter
We draw attention to Note X to the financial statements which describes the uncertainty related to the outcome of the lawsuit filed against the company by XYZ Company. Our opinion is not qualified in respect of this matter.

Report on Other Legal and Regulatory Requirements
[Form and content of this section of the auditor's report will vary depending on the nature of the auditor's other reporting responsibilities.]

[Auditor's signature]
[Date of the auditor's report]
[Auditor's address]

ILLUSTRATION 12.8

Unqualified Independent Auditor's Report with a Compulsory Emphasis of Matter Due to Significant Uncertainty with Respect to the Appropriateness of the Going Concern Principle

INDEPENDENT AUDITOR'S REPORT

To: Appropriate addressee

Report on the financial statements

We have audited the accompanying financial statements 20XX of Company XYZ, Amsterdam, which comprise the consolidated and company statement of financial consolidated and company statement of financial position as at December 31, 20XX, the consolidated and company statements of comprehensive income, changes in equity and cash flows for the year then ended and notes, comprising a summary of the significant accounting policies and other explanatory information.

Management's responsibility

Management is responsible for the preparation and fair presentation of these financial statements in accordance with International Financial Reporting Standards as adopted by the European Union and with Part 9 of Book 2 of the Dutch Civil Code, and for the preparation of the management board report in accordance with Part 9 of Book 2 of the Dutch Civil Code . Furthermore management is responsible for such internal control as it determines is necessary to enable the preparation of the financial statements that are free from material misstatement, whether due to fraud or error.

Auditor's responsibility

Our responsibility is to express an opinion on these financial statements based on our audit. We conducted our audit in accordance with Dutch law, including the Dutch Standards on Auditing. This requires that we comply with ethical requirements and plan and perform the audit to obtain reasonable assurance about whether the financial statements are free from material misstatement. An audit involves performing procedures to obtain audit evidence about the amounts and disclosures in the financial statements. The procedures selected depend on the auditor's judgment, including the assessment of the risks of material misstatement of the financial statements, whether due to fraud or error.

In making those risk assessments, the auditor considers internal control relevant to the entity's preparation and fair presentation of the financial statements in order to design audit procedures that are appropriate in the circumstances, but not for the purpose of expressing an opinion on the effectiveness of the entity's internal control. An audit also includes evaluating the appropriateness of accounting policies used and the reasonableness of accounting estimates made by management, as well as evaluating the overall presentation of the financial statements.

We believe that the audit evidence we have obtained is sufficient and appropriate to provide a basis for our audit opinion

Opinion with respect to the financial statements

In our opinion, the financial statements give a true and fair view of the financial position of XYZ as at December 31, 20XX and of its result and its cash flows for the year then ended in accordance with International Financial Reporting Standards as adopted by the European Union and with Part 9 of Book 2 of the Dutch Civil Code.

Emphasis of uncertainty with respect to the going concern assumption

We draw attention to note X to the financial statements which indicates that the company incurred a net loss of ... during the year ended ..., 20XX and, as of that date, the company's current liabilities exceeded its total assets by ... These conditions, along with other matters as set forth in note X, indicate the existence of a material uncertainty which may cast significant doubt about the company's ability to continue as a going concern. Our opinion is not qualified in respect of this matter.

Illustration 12.8 (continued)

Report on other legal and regulatory requirements
Pursuant to the legal requirement under Section 2:393 sub 5 at e and f of the Dutch Civil Code, we have no deficiencies to report as a result of our examination whether the management board report, to the extent we can assess, has been prepared in accordance with Part 9 of Book 2 of this Code, and whether the information as required under Section 2:392 sub 1 at b-h has been annexed. Further we report that the management board report, to the extent we can assess, is consistent with the financial statements as required by Section 2:391 sub 4 of the Dutch Civil Code.

Place, date
... (Name and Audit firm)
... (Name external auditor and his signature)

Other uncertainties, depending on their materiality and a country's laws, may lead to a modification of the unmodified report or a modified report or disclaimer. Examples include: the outcome of major litigation and the outcome of long-term contracts, estimates of recoverability of asset values, and losses on discontinued operations. If an entity refuses to make a necessary amendment to information accompanying the financial statements, and when there are additional statutory reporting responsibilities, the report may also be modified.

If the uncertainty is significant and material and not adequately disclosed in the notes, the auditor may wish to issue a modified opinion or a disclaimer of opinion.

Illustrations 12.9 and 12.10 show unqualified reports of two large international companies, Wal-Mart and Apple, each requiring an emphasis of matter paragraph.

■ Going Concern Emphasis of Matter

The going concern assumption is one of the fundamental assumptions underlying preparation of financial statements. An enterprise is normally viewed as a going concern, that is, as continuing in operation for the foreseeable future. ISA 570[27] establishes standards and provides guidance on the auditor's responsibilities regarding the appropriateness of the going concern assumption as a basis for preparing financial statements. When a question arises regarding the appropriateness of the going concern assumption, the auditor should gather sufficient appropriate audit evidence to attempt to resolve, to the auditor's satisfaction, the question regarding the entity's ability to continue in operation for the foreseeable future.

If adequate disclosure is made in the financial statements, the auditor must express an unmodified opinion and include an Emphasis of Matter paragraph in the auditor's report to highlight the existence of a material uncertainty relating to the event or condition that may cast significant doubt on the entity's ability to continue as a going concern and draw attention to the note in the financial statements that discloses the event or condition.

ILLUSTRATION 12.9

Wal-Mart 2011 Unmodified Audit Report

Report of Independent Registered Public Accounting Firm

The Board of Directors and Shareholders of Wal-Mart Stores, Inc
We have audited the accompanying consolidated balance sheets of Wal-Mart Stores, Inc. as of 31 January 2011 and 2010, and the related consolidated statements of income, shareholders' equity, and cash flows for each of the three years in the period ended 31 January 2011. These financial statements are the responsibility of the company's management. Our responsibility is to express an opinion on these financial statements based on our audits.

We conducted our audits in accordance with the Standards of the Public Company Accounting Oversight Board (United States). Those Standards require that we plan and perform the audit to obtain reasonable assurance about whether the financial statements are free of material misstatement. An audit includes examining, on a test basis, evidence supporting the amounts and disclosures in the financial statements. An audit also includes assessing the accounting principles used and significant estimates made by management, as well as evaluating the overall financial statement presentation. We believe that our audits provide a reasonable basis for our opinion.

In our opinion, the financial statements referred to above present fairly, in all material respects, the consolidated financial position of Wal-Mart Stores, Inc. at 31 January 2011 and 2010, and the consolidated results of its operations and its cash flows for each of the three years in the period ended 31 January 2011, in conformity with US Generally Accepted Accounting Principles.

As discussed in Note 2 to the consolidated financial statements, effective 1 May 2010, the company has elected to change its method of accounting for inventory under the retail inventory method.

We also have audited, in accordance with the Standards of the Public Company Accounting Oversight Board (United States), Wal-Mart Stores, Inc.'s internal control over financial reporting as of 31 January 2011, based on criteria established in Internal Control – Integrated Framework issued by the Committee of Sponsoring Organizations of the Treadway Commission and our report dated 30 March 2011 expressed an unqualified opinion thereon.

/S/ Ernst & Young LLP
Rogers, Arkansas
30 March 2011

Illustration 11.13 (see Chapter 11 'Completing the Audit') shows some of the indications that the company may have going concern problems. These indications may be mitigated by other factors; for instance, delinquency in loan repayment may be countered by management plans to reschedule loans, sale of assets, etc.

■ Going Concern Disclosure

After the auditor has carried out the additional procedures deemed necessary, obtained all required information and considered the effect of management's plans, he should determine whether the questions raised regarding going concern have been satisfactorily resolved. If the going concern questions are not resolved, the auditor must adequately

ILLUSTRATION 12.10

Apple Inc 2008 Audit Report

Report of Independent Registered Public Accounting Firm

The Board of Directors and Shareholders of Apple Inc

We have audited the accompanying consolidated balance sheets of Apple Inc. and subsidiaries (the Company) as of 27 September 2008 and 29 September 2007, and the related consolidated statements of operations, shareholders' equity and cash flows for each of the years in the three-year period ended 27 September 2008. These consolidated financial statements are the responsibility of the company's management. Our responsibility is to express an opinion on these consolidated financial statements based on our audits.

We conducted our audits in accordance with the Standards of the Public Company Accounting Oversight Board (United States). Those Standards require that we plan and perform the audit to obtain reasonable assurance about whether the financial statements are free of material misstatement. An audit includes examining, on a test basis, evidence supporting the amounts and disclosures in the financial statements. An audit also includes assessing the accounting principles used and significant estimates made by management, as well as evaluating the overall financial statement presentation. We believe that our audits provide a reasonable basis for our opinion.

In our opinion, the consolidated financial statements referred to above present fairly, in all material respects, the financial position of Apple Inc. and subsidiaries as of 27 September 2008 and 29 September 2007, and the results of their operations and their cash flows for each of the years in the three-year period ended 27 September 2008, in conformity with US Generally Accepted Accounting Principles.

As discussed in Note 1 to the consolidated financial statements, effective 30 September 2007, the company adopted Financial Accounting Standards Board Interpretation No. 48, Accounting for Uncertainty in Income Taxes – an interpretation of FASB Statement No. 109.

We also have audited, in accordance with the Standards of the Public Company Accounting Oversight Board (United States), Apple Inc.'s internal control over financial reporting as of 27 September 2008, based on criteria established in Internal Control – Integrated Framework issued by the Committee of Sponsoring Organizations of the Treadway Commission (COSO), and our report dated 4 November 2008 expressed an unqualified opinion on the effectiveness of the company's internal control over financial reporting.

KPMG LLP
Mountain View, California
4 November 2008

disclose in his report the principal conditions that raise doubt about the entity's ability to continue in operation in the foreseeable future. The disclosure should:

- describe the principal conditions that raise doubt;
- state that there are doubts about going concern; therefore, the entity may be unable to realise its assets and discharge its liabilities in the normal course of business;
- state that the financial statements do not include any adjustments relating to the recoverability and classification of recorded asset amounts or to amounts and classification of liabilities that may be necessary should the entity be unable to continue as a going concern.

Illustration 12.8, earlier, illustrates sample wording for a going concern if the problem is adequately disclosed.

12.6 Circumstances That May Result in Other Than an Unmodified Opinion

Based on ISA 700,[28] there are at least two circumstances where the auditor may not be able to express an unmodified opinion:

1 a limitation in scope (inability to obtain sufficient appropriate audit evidence);
2 the auditor's judgement about the pervasiveness of the effects or possible effects of the matter on the financial statements.

The circumstances described in 1 – scope limitation such as auditor is unable to obtain sufficient appropriate audit evidence – could lead to a qualified opinion or a disclaimer of opinion. The circumstances described in 2 – auditor's judgement about the pervasiveness of the effects or possible effects of the matter on the financial statements – could lead to a modified opinion or an adverse opinion.

In addition to scope limitation and disagreement with management, audit reports are often modified if there are material uncertainties such as financial statements not in conformity with accounting standards and lack of independence.

If the auditor concludes that, based on the audit evidence obtained, the financial statements as a whole are not free from material misstatement; or he is unable to obtain sufficient appropriate audit evidence to conclude that the financial statements as a whole are free from material misstatement, the auditor shall modify the opinion in the auditor's report in accordance with ISA 705.

■ Limitation on Scope

Scope limitations arise when the auditors are unable for any reason to obtain the information and explanations considered necessary for the audit. Scope may be limited by the inability to carry out a procedure the auditors consider necessary and the absence of proper accounting records.

The client, for example, may sometimes impose a limitation on the scope of the auditor's work when the terms of the engagement specify that the auditor will not carry out an audit procedure that the auditor believes is necessary. Scope limitations may also be caused by circumstances beyond the control of either the client or the auditor. When restrictions are due to conditions beyond the client's control, a modified opinion is more likely.

A scope limitation may be imposed by circumstances, for example, when the timing of the auditor's appointment makes it difficult to observe the counting of physical inventories. It may also arise when the accounting records are inadequate or when the auditor is unable to carry out a necessary audit procedure. In these circumstances, the auditor should attempt to carry out reasonable alternative procedures to obtain sufficient audit evidence to support an unmodified opinion.

Describe the Limitation

When there has been a limitation on the scope of the auditor's work (an inability to obtain sufficient appropriate audit evidence) that prevents him from issuing an auditor's report containing an unmodified opinion, the report should describe the limitation. When the modification arises from an inability to obtain sufficient appropriate audit evidence, the auditor shall use the corresponding phrase 'except for the possible effects of the matter(s) …' for the modified opinion. The wording of the opinion should indicate that it is modified as to the possible adjustments to the financial statements that might have been necessary had the limitation not existed.[29] In cases where the limitation is so significant that the auditor is unable to express an opinion, an auditor's report containing a disclaimer of opinion is called for. Illustration 12.8, earlier in this chapter, gives an auditor's report containing a qualified opinion due to the auditor's inability to obtain sufficient appropriate audit evidence.

Do Not Accept Engagement

ISA 210[30] states that when the limitation in terms of a proposed engagement is such that the auditor believes that he would need to issue an auditor's report containing a disclaimer of opinion, he would ordinarily not accept the audit engagement unless required to do so by statute or law. A statutory auditor should not accept an audit engagement when the limitation infringes on his statutory duties.

■ Disagreement with Management

The auditor may disagree with management regarding:

- the acceptability of the accounting policies selected;
- the method of policy application, including the adequacy of valuations and disclosures in the financial statements; or
- the compliance of the financial statements with relevant regulations and statutory requirements.

If any of these disagreements are material, the auditor should express a qualified opinion. If the effect of the disagreement is so material and pervasive to the financial statements that the auditor concludes that a qualification would not be adequate to disclose the misleading or incomplete nature of the financial statements, an adverse opinion should be expressed.

The table below illustrates how the auditor's judgement about the nature of the matter giving rise to the modification, and the pervasiveness of its effects or possible effects on the financial statements, affects the type of opinion to be expressed.[31]

Nature of matter giving rise to the modification	Auditor's judgement about the pervasiveness of the effects or possible effects on the financial statements	
	Material but not pervasive	Material and pervasive
Financial statements are materially misstated	Qualified opinion	Adverse opinion
Inability to obtain sufficient appropriate audit evidence	Qualified opinion	Disclaimer of opinion

12.7 Uncertainties Leading to Qualification of Opinions

The international standards of IAASB specify qualification of opinions based on limitation of scope and disagreement with management as conditions that lead to an auditor's report containing a modified or adverse opinion. However, certain uncertainties may lead to an auditor's report containing a qualification of opinion in many countries. These uncertainties include: material uncertainties, lack of consistency, independence of auditor, reports in reference to an expert and fraud.

■ Materiality and Lack of Consistency

Materiality is an essential consideration in determining the appropriate type of report for a given set of circumstances. During the performance of an audit, materiality means the amount set by the auditor below which the undetected misstatement would be unlikely to affect the user's perception of the financial statements as a whole. Auditors may also view an item as material if inclusion or exclusion of the item on the financial statements is sufficiently important to influence a decision made by a reasonable user of financial statements. If the amounts of a misstatement in the financial statements are so significant that the financial statements are materially affected as a whole, it is necessary to issue either a qualified or an adverse opinion, depending on the nature of the misstatement.

Lack of consistency in the application of accounting principles in the current period in relation to the preceding period may require a modification to an unmodified opinion based on standards in many countries. For instance, US GAAP requires that changes in accounting principles or their application be adequately disclosed and that the audit report be modified by adding an explanatory paragraph that describes the nature of the change. If the auditor does not concur with the appropriateness of the accounting principle change, in most countries, a modified opinion is called for.

We discuss the modifications required by going concern problems, fraud, and noncompliance with laws elsewhere in this chapter. Going concern problems are discussed in Section 12.5, earlier. Fraud and non-compliance issues as discussed with those charged with governance are set out in Section 12.8.

■ Independence of Auditor

IFAC's Guideline on Ethics for Professional Accountants (see Chapter 3 'Ethics for Professional Accountants') stresses the great importance of auditor independence both in fact and appearance. However, the ISA auditing standards do not require a modified opinion or a disclaimer of opinion if the auditor is not independent, although this is the case in several countries. Some countries, such as the Netherlands, do not allow the auditor to accept the engagement in case he is not independent.

■ Reference to Expert

When expressing an unmodified opinion the auditor generally should not refer to the work of an expert in his report because such a reference might be misunderstood to be a qualification of the auditor's opinion or a division of responsibility. If the auditor, as a result of the other auditor's or expert's work, issues an opinion other than unmodified, he may in some circumstances describe the work of the expert.

12.8 Communications with those Charged with Governance

The auditors are required to communicate their audit findings to the management and board of directors of a corporation. This is not only given in the ISA standards, but also required by law in some countries.[32] Audit matters of governance interest to be communicated by the auditor to the board or audit committee ordinarily include: material weaknesses in internal control, non-compliance with laws and regulations, fraud involving management, questions regarding management integrity, and other matters.

Concept and a Company 12.1

Tyco International Ltd – Management's Piggy Bank

Concept	Financial statement disclosure, corporate governance and loans.
Story	Tyco is a US company that manufactures a wide variety of products, from electronic components to healthcare products. It operates in over 100 countries around the world and employs more than 240,000 people. In 2002, three former top executives of Tyco (former CEOs Dennis Kozlowski, Mark Swartz and the chief legal officer Mark Belnick) were sued by the SEC. Kozlowski and Swartz granted themselves hundreds of millions of dollars in secret low-interest and interest-free loans from Tyco that they used for personal expenses. They later caused Tyco to forgive tens of millions of dollars they owed the company, without disclosure to investors as required by the federal securities laws (SEC, 2002). Kozlowski and Swartz engaged in numerous highly profitable related party transactions with Tyco and awarded themselves lavish perquisites – without disclosing either the transactions or perquisites to Tyco shareholders (US District Court, 2002). 'Messrs. Kozlowski and Swartz … treated Tyco as their private bank, taking out hundreds of millions of dollars of loans in compensation without ever telling investors,' said Stephen M. Cutler, the SEC's Director of Enforcement (SEC, 2002).

But Not What He Told Them

At the same time that Kozlowski and Swartz engaged in their massive covert fraudulent use of corporate funds, Kozlowski regularly assured investors that at Tyco 'nothing was hidden behind the scenes', that Tyco's disclosures were 'exceptional' and that Tyco's management 'prided itself on having sharp focus with creating shareholder value'. Similarly, Swartz regularly assured investors that 'Tyco's disclosure practice remains second to none' (US District Court, 2002).

KELP and Relocation Loans

Most of Kozlowski's and Swartz's improper Tyco loans were taken through abuse of Tyco's Key Employee Corporate Loan Program (the 'KELP'). A disclosure description of the plan, as filed with the SEC, explicitly described its narrow purpose (US District Court 2002):

Tyco International Ltd – Management's Piggy Bank (continued)

[U]nder the Program, loan proceeds may be used for the payment of federal income taxes due upon the vesting of Company common stock from time to time under the 1983 Restricted Stock Ownership Plans for Key Employees, and to refinance other existing outstanding loans for such purpose.

Kozlowski and Swartz bestowed upon themselves hundreds of millions of dollars in KELP loans which they used for purposes not legitimately authorised by the KELP. From 1997 to 2002, Kozlowski took an aggregate of approximately $270 million charged as KELP loans – even though he only used $29 million of that to cover taxes from the vesting of his Tyco stock. The rest was used for impermissible and unauthorised purposes. For example, with his KELP loans, Kozlowski amassed millions of dollars in fine art, yachts and estate jewellery, as well as an apartment on Park Avenue and a palatial estate in Nantucket. He also used the KELP to fund his personal investments and business ventures (US District Court, 2002).

Kozlowski and Swartz also abused Tyco's relocation loan programme to enrich themselves. When Tyco moved its corporate offices from New Hampshire to New York City, an interest-free loan programme was established. It was designed to assist Tyco employees who were required to relocate from New Hampshire to New York. Kozlowski used approximately $21 million of 'relocation' loans for various other purposes, including the purchase of prestigious properties in New Hampshire, Nantucket and Connecticut. Kozlowski even used approximately $7 million of Tyco's funds to purchase a Park Avenue apartment for his wife from whom he had been separated for many years and whom he subsequently divorced (US District Court, 2002).

Kozlowski and Swartz did not stop there. Instead, they oversaw and authorised transactions by which tens of millions of dollars of their KELP loans and relocation loans were forgiven and written off Tyco's books. They also directed the acceleration of the vesting of Tyco common stock for their benefit (US District Court, 2002).

They Deserve Bonuses

In December 2000, Kozlowski and Swartz engineered another programme whereby Tyco paid them bonuses comprised of cash, Tyco common stock, and/or forgiveness of relocation loans. From that programme, Kozlowski received 148,000 shares of Tyco common stock, a cash bonus of $700,000, and $16 million in relocation loan forgiveness. Swartz received 74,000 shares of Tyco common stock, a cash bonus of $350,000, and $8 million in relocation loan forgiveness. None of these payments were disclosed as part of Kozlowski's and Swartz's executive compensation in Tyco's annual reports (US District Court, 2002).

The Auditor

In 2003, the SEC sued Richard P. Scalzo, CPA, the PricewaterhouseCoopers LLP (PwC) audit engagement partner for Tyco from 1997 through 2001 (SEC, 2003a).

The SEC alleged that Scalzo received 'multiple and repeated facts' regarding the lack of integrity of Tyco's senior management, but he did not take appropriate audit steps in the face of this information. The SEC maintained that those facts were sufficient to obligate Scalzo to re-evaluate the risk assessment of the Tyco audits and to perform additional audit procedures, including further audit testing of certain items (most notably, certain executive benefits, executive compensation, and related party transactions). He did not perform these procedures (SEC, 2003a).

Red Flags and Post Period Adjustments

In the 30 September 1997 audit, factual red flags appeared in the audit working papers. The working papers contained 26 pages of reports prepared by the company, listing the activity in the various KELP accounts of Tyco employees. Three of those 26 pages listed the KELP account activity for L. Dennis Kozlowski. Most of the line items for the Kozlowski account also include a brief description, and 18 carry descriptions that are immediately recognisable as not being for the payment of taxes on the vesting of restricted stock. For example, one item reads 'WINE CELLAR', another reads 'NEW ENG WINE', another 'BMW REG/TAX', another 'ANGIE KOZLOWS', and 13 read either 'WALDORF', 'WALDORF RENT', 'WALDORF EXPEN', 'WALDORF RENT A' or WALDORF RENT S' (SEC, 2003b).

In the 30 September 1998 audit, the audit team noticed a series of transactions in which three Tyco executives exercised Tyco stock options, by borrowing from the KELP, and then sold the shares back to the company the next business day through an offshore Tyco subsidiary. Tyco then wrote a cheque to the executives, representing a net settlement of the transactions. After consulting with PwC national partners, the PwC audit team came to the conclusion that Tyco should include a compensation charge of approximately $40 million (SEC, 2003b).

Faced with the reality of having to book an unanticipated $40 million compensation charge, Tyco suddenly arrived at $40 million in additional, contemporaneous, post-period adjustments which had the effect of negating the impact of the $40 million charge. The $40 million in credits raise significant issues – $7.8 million resulted from Tyco reversing a previous 'fourth quarter charge for restricted stock expense for certain executives no longer required'. The rationale advanced for that reversal was that the executives had decided to forego the corresponding bonuses in the fourth quarter.

The company's treatment for certain executive bonuses provided evidence of problems. For example, Tyco made an initial public offering (IPO) of its previously wholly-owned subsidiary, TyCom Ltd. Because of the IPO's success, Kozlowski decided to grant $96 million in bonuses to Tyco officers and employees. Tyco accounted for the bonuses as: (1) a TyCom offering expense, (2) a credit for previous over-accruals of general and administrative expense, and (3) a contra-accrual for federal income taxes. None of it was booked as compensation expense.

Discussion Questions

- What tests should an auditor perform to find evidence concerning misstatement of executive compensation expense?
- Are public statements by the CEO to investors considered a disclosure that requires the attention of the auditor?
- If the Sarbanes–Oxley Act, Section 402 Enhanced Conflict Provisions was in effect in 2001, would that have made a difference to the disclosure requirements?

References

SEC, 2002, Press Release 2002-135, 'SEC Sues Former Tyco CEO Kozlowski, Two Others for Fraud', Securities and Exchange Commission, 12 September.

SEC, 2003a, Press Release 2003-95, 'Former Tyco Auditor Permanently Barred from Practicing before the Commission,' Securities and Exchange Commission, 13 August.

SEC, 2003b, Securities Exchange Act of 1934 Release No. 48328. Accounting And Auditing Enforcement Release No. 1839, 'In the Matter of Richard P. Scalzo, CPA', Securities and Exchange Commission, 13 August.

United States District Court Southern District of New York, 2002, 'Securities and Exchange Commission v. L. Dennis Kozlowski, Mark H. Swartz, and Mark A. Belnick', Securities and Exchange Commission, 12 September.

■ Communications with the Audit Committee

ISA 260 states that effective two-way communication is important in assisting the auditor and those charged with governance in understanding matters related to the audit in context, and in developing a constructive working relationship. Communication is important for the auditor in obtaining from those charged with governance information relevant to the audit. (For example, those charged with governance may assist the auditor in understanding the entity and its environment, in identifying appropriate sources of audit evidence, and in providing information about specific transactions or events.)[33]

'Governance' is the term used to describe the role of persons entrusted with the supervision, control and direction of an entity. Those persons are the ones responsible for financial reporting and for ensuring that the company achieves its objectives. Those charged with corporate governance are usually the board of directors or supervisory board or the audit committee.

The audit committee is a body formed by a company's board of directors to allow the board to focus on issues affecting external reporting and, in some cases, internal control. In general, the board of directors is composed of **outside directors**. The audit committee selects and appraises the performance of the auditing firm. It develops a professional relationship with the external auditing firm to ensure that accounting and control matters are properly discussed. Besides evaluating external audit reports, the committee may evaluate internal audit reports, review management representations, and get involved with public disclosure of corporate activities. International Standards on Auditing 250, 260 and 300 all apply to communications between the external auditor and the audit committee.

■ Comunications of Deficiencies in Internal Control

ISA 265[34] discusses the auditor's communications to management and those charged with governance when the auditor has identified internal control deficiencies in an audit of financial statements. A **deficiency in internal control** exists when: (1) a control is designed, implemented or operated in such a way that it is unable to prevent, or detect and correct, misstatements in the financial statements on a timely basis; or (2) a control necessary to prevent, or detect and correct, misstatements in the financial statements on a timely basis is missing. A **significant deficiency in internal control** is a deficiency or combination of deficiencies in internal control that, in the auditor's professional judgement, is of sufficient importance to merit the attention of those charged with governance. The auditor is required to obtain an understanding of internal control relevant to the audit when identifying and assessing the risks of material misstatement.

The auditor must communicate to management at an appropriate level of responsibility on a timely basis and in writing, significant deficiencies in internal control that were those in charge of governance and any other deficiencies in internal control identified during the audit that have not been communicated to management by other parties and that, in the auditor's professional judgement, are of sufficient importance to merit management's attention.

The auditor is required to include in the written communication of significant deficiencies in internal control:

- A description of the deficiencies and an explanation of their potential effects.
- Sufficient information to enable those charged with governance and management to understand the context of the communication. In particular, the auditor shall explain that:
  - the purpose of the audit was for the auditor to express an opinion on the financial statements;
  - the audit included consideration of internal control relevant to the preparation of the financial statements in order to design audit procedures that are appropriate in the circumstances, but not for the purpose of expressing an opinion on the effectiveness of internal control; and
  - the matters being reported are limited to those deficiencies that the auditor has identified during the audit and that the auditor has concluded are of sufficient importance to merit being reported to those charged with governance.

■ Governance Structures

The structures of governance vary from country to country reflecting cultural and legal backgrounds. For example, in some countries, the supervision function, and the management function are legally separated into different bodies, such as a supervisory (wholly or mainly non-executive) board and a management (executive) board. In other countries, like the USA, both functions are the legal responsibility of a single, unitary board.

The requirements of national professional accountancy bodies, legislation, or regulation may impose obligations on the auditor to make communications on governance related matters. These additional communications requirements are not covered by International Standards on Auditing; however, they may affect the content, form and timing of communications with those charged with governance.

■ Audit Matters of Governance Interest

'Audit matters of governance interest' are those that arise from the audit of financial statements and are important for people in charge of governance. Audit matters of governance interest to be communicated by the auditor to the board or audit committee ordinarily include:

- material weaknesses in internal control;
- non-compliance with laws and regulations;
- fraud involving management;
- questions regarding management integrity;
- the general approach and overall scope of the audit;
- the selection of, or changes in, significant accounting policies and practices that have a material effect on the financial statements;
- the potential effect on the financial statements of any significant risks and exposures, such as pending litigation, that requires disclosure in the financial statements;
- significant audit adjustments to the accounting records;
- material uncertainties related to the entity's ability to continue as a going concern;
- disagreements with management about matters that could be significant to the entity's financial statements or the auditor's report (these communications include consideration of whether the matter has, or has not, been resolved and the significance of the matter);
- expected modifications to the auditor's report.

■ Reportable Conditions

Major internal control problems (material weakness or **reportable conditions**) should be reported to management, and where necessary, the board of directors. In deciding whether a matter is a reportable condition, the auditor considers factors such as the size of the company and its ownership characteristics, the organisational structure, and the complexity and diversity of company activities. For example, an internal control structure deficiency that is a reportable condition for a large sophisticated financial institution may not be a reportable condition for a small manufacturing concern.

The reportable conditions are generally communicated in a separate letter, the so-called **management letter**. The management letter (discussed later in this chapter in Section 12.10) also includes suggestions for improvement of internal controls focused on financial, compliance and operational processes.

■ Fraud and Non-Compliance with Laws

As required by ISA 240, the auditor should communicate to management any material weaknesses in internal control related to the prevention or detection of fraud and error, which have come to the auditor's attention as a result of the performance of the audit. The auditor should also be satisfied that those charged with governance have been informed of any material weaknesses in internal control related to the prevention and detection of fraud that either have been brought to the auditor's attention by management or have been identified by the auditor during the audit.

Based on the risk assessment the auditor should design audit procedures to obtain reasonable assurance that misstatements arising from fraud and error that are material to the financial statements taken as a whole are detected. When the auditor encounters circumstances that may indicate that there is a material misstatement in the financial statements resulting from fraud or error, the auditor should perform procedures to determine whether the financial statements are materially misstated.

Auditor Withdrawal

If the auditor concludes that it is not possible to continue performing the audit as a result of a misstatement resulting from fraud or suspected fraud, withdrawal from the engagement must then be seriously considered. If the auditor withdraws, he should:

- discuss with those charged with governance the auditor's withdrawal from the engagement and the reasons for the withdrawal;
- consider whether there is a professional or legal requirement to report to regulatory authorities, the auditor's withdrawal from the engagement and the reasons for the withdrawal.

Reporting Fraud or Error to a Third Party

The auditor's duty of confidentiality would ordinarily preclude reporting fraud or error to a third party. However, in certain circumstances, statute or law overrides this duty. For instance, in the USA, the auditor is required to report fraud or error by financial institutions to the supervisory authorities. In the Netherlands, if the directors do not take sufficiently corrective measures and the fraud is considered material, the auditors have to withdraw from the engagement. If such engagement is a statutory audit, the auditor must report the withdrawal to the Ministry of Justice. In France, auditors must report illegal acts and fraud to the government. UK auditors are obligated to pursue matters of a suspicious nature and have a reporting duty similar to that in the USA. German auditors have to report fraud to the boards of directors in their auditor's report; this is also indicated in the tax return of the company and, therefore indirectly, it is also a report to the authorities. In Mexico, auditors are liable for negligence if the auditor should have known of internal control failures, or if he was aware, and did not report them. Auditors may not be liable if they told management of shortcomings in internal control in the area in which a crime has been committed, did not tell because the area in which the crime was committed had no close relationship to financial statements, the crime occurred in collusion with others, or the criminal had 'extraordinary ability'.

Matters Communicated to those Charged with Governance

The matters communicated by the auditor to those charged with governance is a matter of professional judgement but ordinarily would include:

- questions regarding management competence and integrity;
- fraud involving management;
- other fraud that results in a material misstatement of the financial statements;
- material misstatements resulting from error;
- misstatements that indicate material weaknesses in internal control, including the design or operation of the entity's financial reporting process;
- misstatements that may cause future financial statements to be materially misstated.

The auditor should communicate with the audit committee, the board of directors and senior management, each as appropriate in the circumstances, regarding noncompliance with applicable laws and regulations that comes to the auditor's attention. If the auditor suspects that members of senior management, including members of the board of directors, are involved in non-compliance, the auditor should report the matter to the next higher level of authority at the entity, if it exists, such as an audit committee or a supervisory board.

12.9 Long-Form Audit Report

In many countries it is customary for the auditor to prepare a long-form report to the entity's board of directors in addition to the publicly published short-form report discussed in this chapter. The topics covered in the report may vary as there are no standards, but a typical long-form report will include:

- an overview of the audit engagement;
- an analysis of the financial statements;
- a discussion of risk management and internal control;
- various optional topics subject to the circumstances;
- auditor independence and quality control;
- fees.

In the overview, the long-form report will discuss nature, scope, organisation, level of materiality, new audit work and work with other auditors and experts.

■ Discussion of Financial Issues

Highlights of the financial statements are discussed. Accounting issues need to be clarified. Several issues may require judgement in accounting such as provisions, accruals and contingent liabilities. Changes in client, national, and international accounting policies are explained in terms of their impact on the financial statements. Acquisitions and divestments and their effect on the accounts should be covered. The financial position of the company for possible financing or refinancing and the related debt covenant ratios and defaults are gone into.

Other financial statement topics such as disagreement or discussion with management and future client developments are reviewed. Management and auditors may disagree on certain financial statement issues, so the long-form report must address these. Future client development affecting the annual report may include a discussion of future uncertainties and subsequent events.

■ Risk Discussion

Risk management and internal controls are ever more important to the board of directors. A discussion of risk in the long-form report may include:

■ major operational and financial risks;
■ effectiveness of the client's risk management;
■ quality of internal reporting and management accounting;
■ frauds and irregularities;
■ ethics compliance and special areas such as treasury, new business and quality control.

Internal control topics unveiled might include: strengths and weaknesses of internal controls, recommendations for improving controls, information technology and internal audit department.

Risk management is an important topic for board members. Of course, the client is interested in major operational and financial risks, so they are reviewed at least in so far as they are related to the audit. The effectiveness of the client's risk management and quality of internal reporting and management accounting are meaningful to the board. Of crucial importance is the discussion of any frauds and irregularities suspected by the auditor or uncovered in the audit. Industry ethics affect the moral and legal position of the client so a discussion of compliance with ethics standards is very important. Popular areas for quality management are treasury effectiveness, new business development and quality control.

■ Other Topics Discussed

There may be topics not typically addressed that the auditor may feel warrant discussion because of the circumstances of the company, the economy, or the audit. These topics may include tax, pension, treasury function and audit-related requirements.

Audit-related areas that might be discussed include special advisory projects on the financial statements, risk control, insurance coverage, and pension arrangements. Other areas related to the audit that may be reviewed are tax compliance work and constancy projects such as cost benchmarking, information technology and logistics.

Furthermore, it becomes best practice or is already required by law in some countries, that the auditor describes how his independence has been warranted, and what quality control procedures he has applied to deliver a high-quality audit report. Also, an overview of audit fees compared to budget, and of other fees, might be presented.

12.10 Management Letter

The management letter identifies issues not required to be disclosed in the Annual Financial Report but represent the auditors concerns and suggestions noted during the audit. The management letter is the auditor's letter addressed to the client. It contains the public accountant's conclusions regarding the company's accounting policies and procedures, internal controls and operating policies. An evaluation is made of the present system, pointing out problems. Recommendations for improvement are cited. Also included is a discussion of any problem which may require immediate action to correct. The management letter is sort of a 'feel good' letter that is designed to point out the problems but also offer solutions and provide any special approach that might benefit the enterprise.

There is no format or requirements for management letters given in the standards of the International Auditing and Assurance Standards Board or most other national standards. The audit firm may develop a format and typical contents for their own organisation over time. Some may choose to incorporate just the communications required under ISA 240 'The Auditor's Responsibilities Relating to Fraud in an Audit of Financial Statements', ISA 250 'Consideration of Laws and Regulations in an Audit of Financial Statements', ISA 260 'Communication with Those Charged with Governance' and ISA 265 'Communicating Deficiencies in Internal Control to Those Charged with Governance and Management'. Other firms have adopted alternative language that they prefer. In certain cases, due to an audit client's specific circumstance, additional or modified wording may be used. When communicating material that is not required by standards and statute, the auditor must be sure that there is no conflict with the general purpose of communication set forth by IAASB standards.

Illustration 13.12 gives a sample format of a management letter. A sample letter for a government management letter may be different.[35]

12.11 Summary

An audit report is very brief, occupying no more than a few lines. This is a paradox because the audit report, although comprising only a few words, requires great care and is the consummation of a rigorous and lengthy audit process.

In many countries management of the enterprise must take responsibility for the audit report. For example, the US Sarbanes–Oxley Act of 2002 requires that the principal executive officer or officers and the principal financial officer or officers of any firm, foreign or domestic, that is publicly traded, certify certain conditions in each annual or quarterly report filed or submitted to the US Securities and Exchange Commission (SEC). In Europe and other parts of the world, similar developments are observed. They may differ in practice due to national or regional legal and cultural differences, but in principle they have much in common.

The auditor's unmodified report, under ISA 700, should include the following basic elements: title, addressee, opening or introductory paragraph, a description of the responsibility of management for the preparation of the financial statements, a description of the auditor's responsibility to express an opinion on the financial statements and the scope of the audit; opinion paragraph containing an expression of opinion on the financial statements,, a report on other reporting responsibilities, the date of the report, the auditor's address and auditor's signature.

The most common type of audit report is the standard unmodified (historically called an 'unqualified') audit report. It is used for more than 90 per cent of all audit reports. Other audit reports are referred to as 'other than unmodified reports'. Other than unmodified reports include those reports that express: an adverse opinion, disclaimer of opinion and modified opinion. The form of an auditor's report will generally be the form of the unmodified report which traditionally consisted of just three paragraphs (introduction, scope and opinion), but now it may consist of several paragraphs so long as the basic elements are covered (Introduction, Management's Responsibility, Auditor's Responsibility (including audit scope), and Auditor's Opinion). Reports can also include a paragraph after the opinion paragraph called 'an emphasis of a mater paragraph' (see ISA 706). In some countries a paragraph referring a qualification as a result of inadequate accounting procedures or disclosure may be inserted just before the opinion paragraph.

The auditor's unmodified report should be expressed when the auditor concludes that the financial statements are prepared, in all material respects, in accordance with the identified financial reporting framework. In order to form that opinion, the auditor shall conclude as to whether he has obtained reasonable assurance about whether the financial statements as a whole are free from material misstatement, whether due to fraud or error. The auditor must evaluate:

- whether the financial statements adequately disclose the significant accounting policies selected and they are consistent and appropriate;
- accounting estimates made by management are reasonable;
- information presented in the financial statements is relevant, reliable, comparable and understandable;
- disclosures to enable the intended users to understand the effect of material transactions and events on the information conveyed in the financial statements; and
- terminology used in the financial statements, including the title of each financial statement, is appropriate.

The auditor must modify the opinion in the auditor's report (give an adverse, qualified or disclaimer) when the auditor concludes that, based on the audit evidence obtained, the financial statements as a whole are not free from material misstatement or the auditor is unable to obtain sufficient appropriate audit evidence to conclude that the financial statements as a whole are free from material misstatement. The auditor expresses a qualified opinion when having obtained sufficient appropriate audit evidence, the auditor concludes that misstatements, individually or in the aggregate, are material, but not pervasive, to the financial statements; or the auditor is unable to obtain sufficient appropriate audit evidence on which to base the opinion, but the auditor concludes that the possible effects on the financial statements of undetected misstatements, if any, could be material but not pervasive. The auditor expresses an adverse opinion when the auditor, having obtained sufficient appropriate audit evidence, concludes that misstatements, individually or in the aggregate, are both material and pervasive to the financial statements. The auditor will disclaim an opinion when he is unable to obtain sufficient appropriate audit evidence on which to base the opinion, and he concludes that the possible effects on the financial statements of undetected misstatements could be both material and pervasive.

The auditor, having formed an opinion on the financial statements, sometimes must draw the financial statement users' attention to a matter, although appropriately presented or disclosed in the financial statements, that is of such importance that it is fundamental to users' understanding of the financial statements; or any other matter that is relevant to users' understanding of the audit, the auditor's responsibilities, or the auditor's report. This part of the opinion is called an emphasis of a matter paragraph or other matter paragraph. The addition of an emphasis of matter paragraph does not affect the auditor's opinion. The paragraph should follow the opinion paragraph and state that the auditor's opinion is not modified by this. Ordinarily, an auditor might write an emphasis of matter paragraph if there is a significant uncertainty that may affect the financial statements, the resolution of which is dependent upon future events and to highlight a material matter regarding a going concern problem.

Based on ISA 700, there are two circumstances that require an auditor's report containing an opinion other than an unmodified one: a limitation in scope and the auditor's judgement about the pervasiveness of the effects or possible effects of the matter on the financial statements. Scope limitation could lead to a modified opinion or a disclaimer of opinion. The pervasive of the effects could lead to a modified opinion or an adverse opinion. In addition, some countries require modified reports based on uncertainties arising from financial statements not in conformity with accounting standards and lack of independence.

The auditors are required to communicate their audit findings to the management or board of directors of a corporation. This is not only given in the ISA standards, but also required by law in some countries. The auditor should communicate audit matters of governance interest arising from the audit of financial statements with those charged with governance of an entity. 'Governance' is the term used to describe the role of persons entrusted with the supervision, control and direction of an entity. Those persons are the ones responsible for financial reporting and for ensuring that the company achieves its objectives. Those charged with corporate governance are usually the board of directors or supervisory board or the audit committee.

In many countries it is customary for the auditor to prepare a long-form report to the entity's board of directors in addition to the publicly published short-form report discussed in this chapter. The topics covered in the report may vary as there are no standards, but a typical long-form report will include: an overview of the audit engagement, an analysis of the financial statements, a discussion of risk management and internal control, various optional topics subject to the circumstances, and fees.

The management letter identifies issues not required to be disclosed in the Annual Financial Report but represent the auditors concerns and suggestions noted during the audit. The management letter is the auditor's letter addressed to the client. It contains the public accountant's conclusions regarding the company's accounting policies and procedures, internal controls and operating policies. An evaluation is made of the present system, pointing out problem areas. Recommendations for improvement are cited. Also included is a discussion of any problem which may require immediate action to correct.

12.12   Questions, Exercises and Cases

QUESTIONS

12.2 Introduction

12-1   How long should an audit report be? Can all important information be conveyed in the standard length?

12-2   What must the principal executive officer or officers and the principal financial officer or officers certify in each annual or quarterly report filed or submitted to the US Securities and Exchange Commission (SEC) according to the Sarbanes–Oxley Act of 2002 (SOX)?

12.3 Basic Elements of the Auditor's Report

12-3   What elements make up an audit report? Briefly discuss each.

12-4   What are the phrases used to express the auditor's opinion that the financial statements have been prepared according to local legislation, rules issued by professional bodies, etc.?

12-5   What are the forms of an auditor's report?

12.4 Types of Reports Expressing Audit Opinions

12-6   There are the four different opinions an auditor can issue. Briefly discuss each and the requirements to give that opinion.

12-7   When does an auditor express a qualified opinion? Discuss the terms 'material' and 'pervasive'.

12-8   When is an adverse opinion given? How is the wording of an adverse opinion different from that of an unqualified (unmodified) opinion?

12-9   When is a disclaimer opinion issued? How is the wording of a disclaimer opinion different from that of an unqualified (unmodified) opinion?

12.5 Emphasis of a Matter Paragraph

12-10 Define emphasis of a matter paragraph and 'other matter paragraph'. In what circumstances would an auditor write an emphasis of a matter paragraph?

12-11 If the going concern questions are not resolved, the auditor must adequately disclose in his report the principal conditions that raise doubt about the entity's ability to continue in operation in the foreseeable future. What are the characteristics of this disclosure?

12.6 Circumstances That May Result in Other Than an Unqualified Opinion

12-12 Explain the circumstances where the auditor may not be able to express an unmodified opinion.

12-13 Define limitations of scope. Under what circumstances do scope limitations arise? Give some examples of scope limitations. What should an auditor do if a limitation on scope is imposed by circumstances beyond the client's control?

12.7 Uncertainties Leading to Qualification of Opinions

12-14 Discuss why uncertainties may lead to an auditor's report containing a qualification of opinion in many countries.

12-15 When can an auditor make reference to an expert work in his audit report? When may he not make reference to an expert? Why? What is the international standard involved in this issue?

12.8 Communications with those Charged with Governance

12-16 Define governance, audit committee and outside directors.

12-17 What audit matters of governance interest would ordinarily be communicated by the auditor to the board of directors or audit committee?

12-18 When reporting fraud how would an auditor proceed if he were in France, the UK, Germany or Mexico?

12.9 Long-Form Audit Report

12-19 What topics are included in a typical 'long-form' audit report? Briefly discuss each.

12.10 Management Letter

12-20 What is the purpose of the management letter and what does it usually contain?

PROBLEMS AND EXERCISES

12.3 Basic Elements of the Auditor's Report

12-21 Basic Elements of Audit Report. When fieldwork was finished on 31 December 20X0, the following standard unqualified auditor's report was given by Eldridge and Lloyd, Chartered Accountants (CAs), of Surrey, England:

> Auditor's Report
> We have audited the accompanying financial statements.
> In our opinion, the financial statements correctly show the account balances and comply with the Companies Acts 1948 to 1981.
> Eldridge and Lloyd, CAs

Required:

A. List the basic elements that should appear in an unmodified (unqualified) auditor's report.

B. List and explain the deficiencies and omissions in the Eldridge and Lloyd auditor's report.

12-22 Form of the Audit Report. The most common type of audit report is the standard unqualified report.

Required:

Review Illustration 12.2, the standard wording of the IAS audit report, and Illustration 12.3, the unmodified (unqualified) report of Wal-Mart Stores.

A. List the differences, paragraph-by-paragraph, between the two reports.

B. List the similarities, paragraph-by-paragraph, between the two reports.

12.4 Types of Reports Expressing Audit Opinions

12-23 Unmodified (Unqualified) Audit Report. Upon completion of all fieldwork on 23 September 20X1, the following audit report was rendered by Alexander Dlouhy, Auditor, to the directors of Rabochaya Raum Company of Docesky, the Czech Republic.

> To the Directors of the Rabochaya Raum Company:
> We have examined the balance sheet and the related statement of income and retained earnings of the Rabochaya Raum Company as of 31 July 20X1. In accordance with your instructions, a complete audit was conducted.
> In many respects, this was an unusual year for the Rabochaya Raum Company. The weakening of the economy in the early part of the year and the strike of plant employees in the summer of 20X1 led to a decline in sales and net income. After making several tests of sales records, nothing came to our attention that would indicate that sales have not been properly recorded.

In our opinion, with the explanation given above, and with the exception of some minor errors that are considered immaterial, the aforementioned financial statements present fairly the financial position of the Rabochaya Raum Company at 31 July 20X1, and the results of its operations for the year then ended, in conformity with pronouncements of International Accounting Standards Committee applied consistently throughout the period.

Alexander Dlouhy, Auditor
23 September 20X1

Required:

List and explain the deficiencies and omissions in the auditor's report. Organise your answer sheet by section (introduction, management's responsibility, auditor's responsibility and opinion) of the auditor's report.

12–24 Adverse Audit Opinion. Bheda Bhasya, Ltd, a company from Ahmadabad, India, without consulting its Chartered Accountant (CA), has changed its accounting so that it is not in accordance with International Accounting Principles (IASs). During the regular audit engagement the CA discovers that the statements based on the accounts are so grossly misleading that they might be considered fraudulent.

Required:

A. Discuss the specific action to be taken by the CA.
B. What type of opinion would the CA issue? Why?
C. In this situation what obligation does the CA have to a new auditor if he is replaced? Discuss briefly.

12–25 Modification of Unqualified Opinion. Jorge Leyva, Licenciado en Contaduría Público, has completed the examination of the financial statements of Medina Construcción of Caracas, Venezuela, for the year ended 31 July 20X4. Leyva also examined and reported on the Medina financial statements for the prior year. Leyva's report is as follows:

Auditor's report to Board of Directors of Medina Construcción.

We have audited the accompanying balance sheet of Medina Construcción as of 31 December 20X3, and the related statements of income and retained earnings for the year then ended. These financial statements are the responsibility of the Company's management. Our responsibility is to express an opinion on these financial statements based on our audit.

We conducted our audit in accordance with International Standards on Auditing and approved Auditing Standards of the Federación de Collegios de Contadores Publicos. Those standards require that we plan and perform the audit to obtain reasonable assurance about whether the financial statements are free of material misstatement. An audit includes examining, on a test basis, evidence supporting the amounts and disclosures in the financial statements. An audit also includes assessing the accounting principles used and significant estimates made by management, as well as evaluating the overall financial statement presentation. We believe that our audit provides a reasonable basis for our opinion.

In our opinion, the financial statements referred to above present fairly, in all material respects, the financial position of Medina Construcción as of 31 December 20X3, and the results of its operations for the year then ended in conformity with International Accounting Standards and comply with Venezuela's national law, applied on a basis consistent with that of the preceding year.

Jorge Leyva, LCP
13 November 20X4
International Centre
456 Alhambra
Calabozo, Venezuela

Other information:

1 Medina is presenting comparative financial statements
2 During 20X3, Medina changed its method of accounting for long-term construction contracts and properly reflected the effect of the change in the current year's financial statements and restated the prior year's financial statements. Leyva is satisfied with Medina's justification for making the change. The change is discussed in footnote number 8 to the report.
3 Leyva was unable to perform normal accounts receivable confirmation procedures, but alternate procedures were used to satisfy Leyva as to the validity of the receivables.
4 Medina Construcción is the defendant in a litigation, the outcome of which is highly uncertain. If the case is settled in favour of the plaintiff, Medina will be required to pay a substantial amount of cash, which might require the sale of certain fixed assets. The litigation and the possible effects have been properly disclosed in footnote number 11 to the report.
5 Medina issued debenture bonds payable on 31 January 20X6, in Venezuela Bolivars (VB), for the amount of VB 1,000,000,000. The funds obtained from the issuance were used to finance the expansion of plant facilities. The debenture agreement restricts the payment of future cash dividends to earnings after 31 December 20X6. Medina declined to disclose this essential data in the footnotes to the financial statements.

Required:

Consider all facts given and rewrite the auditor's report in acceptable and complete format incorporating any necessary departures from the standard unqualified report.

Explain any items included in 'Other Information' that need not be part of the auditor's report.

12.5 Emphasis of a Matter Paragraph

12–26 Ordinarily, an auditor might write an emphasis of a matter paragraph (1) if there is a significant uncertainty which may affect the financial statements, the resolution of which is dependent upon future events; (2) to highlight a material matter regarding a going concern problem, and (3) other matters. Write an emphasis of a matter paragraph for each of three circumstances.

12–27 Going Concern. In the audit of Cerberus, SA, of Bydgoszcz, Poland, Merek Olzewski, Certified Public Accountant (CPA), found indications that Cerberus may have going concern problems.

Required:

A. List three financial, two operating and two other indications that Olzewski might have found that show Cerberus may have going concern problems.
B. Because the going concern assumption is in question, what additional audit procedures would Olzewski undertake?

12.6 Circumstances That May Result in Other Than an Unqualified Opinion

12–28 Limitation on Scope. Lorts Corporation of Maastricht, the Netherlands (whose fiscal year will end 31 December 20X3), informs you on 18 December 20X3 that it has a serious shortage of working capital because of heavy operating losses incurred since 1 October 20X3. Application has been made to a bank for a loan, and the bank's loan officer has requested financial statements.

The management of Lorts Corporation requests a meeting with you. You try to imagine the following independent sets of circumstances.

1 Lorts asks that you save time by auditing the financial statements prepared by Lorts' chief accountant as of 30 September 20X3. The scope of your audit would not be limited by Lorts in any way.

2 Lorts asks that you conduct an audit as of 15 December 20X3. The scope of your audit would not be limited by Lorts in any way.

3 Lorts asks that you conduct an audit as of 31 December 20X3 and render a report by 16 January. To save time and reduce the cost of the audit, it is requested that your examination not include confirmation of accounts receivable or observation of the taking of inventory.

4 Lorts asks that you prepare financial statements as of 15 December 20X3 from the books and records of the company without audit. The statements are to be submitted on plain paper without your name being associated in any way with them. The reason for your preparing the statements is your familiarity with proper form for financial statements.

Required:

Indicate the type of opinion you would render under each of the above set of circumstances. Give reasons for your decision.

12-29 **Disagreement with Management.** Emiko Iamiva, Certified Public Accountant (CPA), audited the Satsuma Company's earthquake insurance policies. All routine audit procedures with regard to the earthquake insurance register have been completed (i.e. vouching, footing, examination of cancelled cheques, computation of insurance expense and repayment, tracing of expense charges to appropriate expense accounts, etc.).

After the insurance review, Iamiva came to the conclusion that the insurance coverage against loss by earthquake is inadequate and that, if loss occurs, the company may have insufficient assets to liquidate its debts. After a discussion with Iamiva, management refuses to increase the amount of insurance coverage.

Required:

A. What mention will Iamiva make of this condition and contingency in his standard report? Why?

B. What effect will this condition and contingency have upon the audit opinion? Give reasons for your position.

12.7 Uncertainties Leading to Qualification of Opinions

12-30 **Uncertainty Concerning Future Events.** Vilma Castro, Contador Público Autorizado, has completed fieldwork for her examination of the Wigwam Winche company of Panama City, Panama, for the year ended 31 December 20X1, and now is in the process of determining whether to modify her report. Presented below are two independent, unrelated situations which have arisen.

Situation 1

In September, 20X1, a lawsuit was filed against Wigwam to have the court order it to install pollution-control equipment in one of its older plants. Wigwam's legal counsel has informed Castro that it is not possible to forecast the outcome of this litigation. However, Wigwam's management has informed Castro that the cost of the pollution-control equipment is not economically feasible and that the plant will be closed if the case is lost. In addition, Castro has been told by management that the plant and its production equipment would have only minimal resale values and that the production that would be lost could not be recovered at other plants.

Situation 2

During 20X1, Wigwam purchased a franchise amounting to 20 per cent of its assets for the exclusive right to produce and sell a newly patented product in the north-eastern USA. There has been no production in marketable quantities of the product anywhere to date. Neither the franchiser nor any franchisee had conducted any market research with respect to the product.

In deciding the type of report or modification, if any, Castor will take into account such considerations as follows:

1   Uncertainty of outcome.
2   Likelihood of error.
3   Expertise of the auditor.
4   Pervasive impact on the financial statements.
5   Inherent importance of the item.

Required:

Discuss Castro's type of report decision for each situation in terms of the above and other appropriate considerations. Assume each situation is adequately disclosed in the notes to the financial statements. Each situation should be considered independently. In discussing each situation, ignore the other.

12.8 Communications with those Charged with Governance

12-31 Nordtek, A/S, a manufacturer of fine skiing equipment based in Skien, Norway, has retained the firm of Berzins, Dybtsyna and Kaarboe (BDK) as their auditors. BDK have found significant deficiencies in internal control which they are required to report to Nortek's audit committee.

During the audit BDK discovered that Nordtek does not have manuals of policies and procedures for monitoring and reporting on internal controls. The board has no code of business ethics. New employees undergo minimal background checks and knowledge testing. The company has no employee training programme.

Eight of the ten members of the board of directors are not independent of the company and none of the audit committee members are independent (non-executive) directors. There are no board committees for executive remuneration, government relations and investment review.

Management does not have a budgeting process. They have no internal audit department. Employees never switch tasks. The internal controls have never been tested for effectiveness. Nordtek's inventory storerooms were unlocked and there were no checks on those who entered or left the premises.

Required:

Write a written communication to the Audit Committee explaining the deficiencies based on the requirements for such a report described in ISA 265.

12.9 Long-Form Audit Report

12-32 Pick a publically traded company from the SEC website www.sec.gov, search for the 10K, review risk factors, Controls and Procedures, Changes in and Disagreements with Accountants on Accounting and Financial Disclosure, Management's Discussion and Analysis of Financial Condition and Results of Operations, the financial statements, auditor's fees, and disclosure notes. Imagine that you are the auditor for the most recent 10K. Write up a long-form audit report for that publically traded company.

CASE

12–33 Material Misstatements or Omissions in Audit Reports. Auditors are required to report internal control weaknesses to management. The auditors, however, have no responsibility to report internal control weaknesses in the audit report and failing to do so does not constitute a material misstatement or omission.

Required:

A. Using the library, Lexis-Nexis or internet, find the case of *James G. Monroe and Penelope E. Monroe* v *Gary C. Hughes: Thomas R. Hudson and Deloitte & Touche* (1994 US App. LEXIS 18003). Summarise the case.

B. List the reasons why the auditing firm was not found guilty of issuing an audit report with a material misstatement or omission.

12.13 Notes

1 In Woolf, Emile, 1997, *Auditing Today*, 6th edn, Prentice Hall, Hertfordshire, UK.

2 PCAOB, 2007, Auditing Standard No. 5, 'An Audit of Internal Control over Financial Reporting that is Integrated with an Audit of Financial Statements', para. 85, Public Company Accounting Oversight Board, June, 2007.

3 International Auditing and Assurance Standards Board (IAASB), 2012, International Standard on Auditing 700 (ISA 700) 'Forming an Opinion and Reporting on Financial Statements', para. 12, *Handbook of International Quality Control, Auditing Review, Other Assurance, and Related Services Pronouncements*, 2012 edn, Volume 1, International Federation of Accountants, New York.

4 Public Company Accounting Oversight Board of the US (PCAOB), 2011, 'Concept Release on Possible Revisions to PCAOB Standards Related to Reports on Audited Financial Statements', PCAOB Release No. 2011-003, PCAOB, USA.

5 ISA 700, op. cit., para. 43.

6 Example report for a company and consolidated financial statements, both prepared in accordance with Dutch Law and IFRS as adopted in the EU, combined in one set.

7 ISA 700, op. cit., paras. 36–38.

8 International Auditing and Assurance Standards Board (IAASB), 2012, International Standard on Auditing 200 (ISA 200) 'Overall Objectives of the Independent Auditor and the Conduct of an Audit in Accordance with International Standards on Auditing', para. 3, *Handbook of International Quality Control, Auditing Review, Other Assurance, and Related Services Pronouncements*, 2012 edn, Volume 1, International Federation of Accountants, New York.

9 Ibid. ISA 700, paras. 41.

10 PCAOB, 2004, 'Auditing Standard No. 1 – References in Auditors' Reports to the Standards of the Public Company Accounting Oversight Board', para. 3, Public Company Accounting Oversight Board, September 2004.

11 Ibid.

12 Arens, A.A., Elder, R.J. and Beasley, M.S., 2003, *Essentials of Auditing and Assurance Services: An Integrated Approach*, Pearson Education/Prentice Hall, Upper Saddle River, New Jersey.

13 International Auditing and Assurance Standards Board (IAASB), 2012, International Standard on Auditing 706 (ISA 706) 'Emphasis of Matter Paragraphs and Other Matter Paragraphs in the Independent Auditor's Report', *Handbook of International Quality Control, Auditing Review, Other Assurance, and Related Services Pronouncements*, 2012 edn, Volume 1, International Federation of Accountants, New York.

14 Emphasis of matter paragraph(s) – an auditor's report may be modified by adding an emphasis of matter paragraph(s) to highlight a matter affecting the financial statements which is included in a note to the financial statements that more extensively discusses the matter. The addition of such an emphasis of matter paragraph(s) does not affect the auditor's opinion. The auditor may also modify the auditor's report by using an emphasis of matter paragraph(s) to report matters other than those affecting the financial statements.

15 International Auditing and Assurance Standards Board (IAASB), 2012, International Standard on Auditing 700 (ISA 700) 'Forming an Opinion and Reporting on Financial Statements', para. 16, *Handbook of International Quality Control, Auditing Review, Other Assurance, and Related Services Pronouncements*, 2012 edn, Volume 1, International Federation of Accountants, New York.

16 International Auditing and Assurance Standards Board (IAASB), 2012, International Standard on Auditing 705 (ISA 705) 'Modifications to the Opinion in the Independent Auditor's Report', para. 7, *Handbook of International Quality Control, Auditing Review, Other Assurance, and Related Services Pronouncements*, 2012 edn, Volume 1, International Federation of Accountants, New York.

17 Ibid. ISA 705, paras. 5.

18 Model report for a company and consolidated financial statements, both prepared in accordance with IFRS as adopted in the EU, combined in one set.

19 Model report for a company and consolidated financial statements, both prepared in accordance with IFRS as adopted in the EU, combined in one set.

20 Model report for financial statements, prepared in accordance with Part 9 of Book 2 of the Dutch Civil Code (no consolidated financial statement, prepared).

21 International Auditing and Assurance Standards Board (IAASB), 2012, International Standard on Auditing 265 (ISA 265) 'Communicating Deficiencies in Internal Control to Those Charged with Governance and Management', *Handbook of International Quality Control, Auditing Review, Other Assurance, and Related Services Pronouncements*, 2012 edn, Volume 1, International Federation of Accountants, New York.

22 Ibid. ISA 705, para.27.

23 International Auditing and Assurance Standards Board (IAASB), 2012, International Standard on Auditing 706 (ISA 706) 'Emphasis of Matter Paragraphs and Other Matter Paragraphs in the Independent Auditor's Report', para. 7, *Handbook of International Quality Control, Auditing Review, Other Assurance, and Related Services Pronouncements*, 2012 edn, Volume 1, International Federation of Accountants, New York.

24 Ibid. ISA 706, Sample Reports in Appendix.

25 Ibid. ISA 706, Appendix 3.

26 Model report for a company and consolidated financial statements, both prepared in accordance with IFRS as adopted in the EU, combined in one set

27 Ibid. ISA 570, para. 6.

28 International Auditing and Assurance Standards Board (IAASB), 2012, International Standard on Auditing 700 (ISA 700) 'Forming an Opinion and Reporting on Financial Statements', para. 17, *Handbook of International Quality Control, Auditing Review, Other Assurance, and Related Services Pronouncements*, 2012 edn, Volume 1, International Federation of Accountants, New York.

29 International Auditing and Assurance Standards Board (IAASB), 2012, International Standard on Auditing 705 (ISA 705) 'Modifications to the Opinion in the Independent Auditor's Report', para. 20, *Handbook of International Quality Control, Auditing Review, Other Assurance, and Related Services Pronouncements*, 2012 edn, Volume 1, International Federation of Accountants, New York.

30 International Auditing and Assurance Standards Board (IAASB), 2012, International Standard on Auditing 210 (ISA 210) 'Agreeing the Terms of Audit Engagements', para. 7, *Handbook of International Quality Control, Auditing Review, Other Assurance, and Related Services Pronouncements*, 2012 edn, Volume 1, International Federation of Accountants, New York.

31 Ibid. ISA 705, para. A1.

32 For instance, in the USA, the Sarbanes–Oxley Act requires auditors to report directly to the audit committee of the board of directors.

33 International Auditing and Assurance Standards Board (IAASB), 2012, International Standard on Auditing 260 (ISA 260) 'Communication with Those Charged with Governance', para. 4, *Handbook of International Quality Control, Auditing Review, Other Assurance, and Related Services Pronouncements*, 2012 edn, Volume 1, International Federation of Accountants, New York.

34 Ibid. ISA 265, 'Communicating Deficiencies in Internal Control to Those Charged with Governance and Management'.

35 A sample management letter from US Office of inspector General is at **http://www.treasury.gov/about/organizational-structure/ig/Documents/oig09020.pdf**.

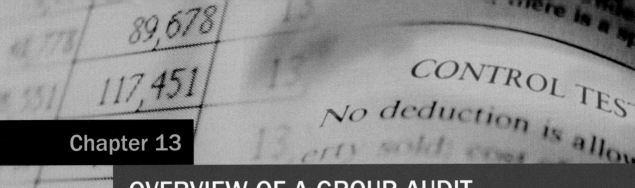

Chapter 13

OVERVIEW OF A GROUP AUDIT

After studying this chapter, you should be able to:

1 Grasp the scope and contents of ISA 600.

2 Know the meaning of component, component auditor and group engagement partner.

3 Trace the requirements and considerations for acceptance of a group audit client.

4 Recognise how audit strategy is determined for a group audit.

5 Identify what components of a group company might be.

6 Recognise the required communications between group auditor, component auditor and those charged with governance.

7 Fathom what is involved in consolidation.

8 Comprehend the reporting and documentation requirements of a group auditor.

9 Grasp what is required to understand the component auditor.

10 Have a handle on materiality considerations in a group audit.

11 Comprehend the work performed by a component auditor.

12 Understand the use of group audit instructions on international audits.

13 Discern the differences between the various documents used in planning an audit.

14 Describe the contents of group audit instructions.

15 Understand what is included in audit scope and coverage.

16 Discuss the meaning of critical and significant audit areas.

17 Discuss the issues involved in the audit planning memorandum.

18 Evaluate critical and significant audit areas in the audit planning process.

19 Distinguish between an audit planning memorandum and an audit programme.

20 Describe the components of the audit programme.

21 Identify components of the completion memorandum.

22 Distinguish between how critical and significant audit areas are described in the completion memorandum and in the audit planning memorandum.

13.2   Introduction

This chapter takes you through the documents and procedures of an international audit, based on group audit instructions. The contents of this chapter are based on the working experience of the authors. ISA 600[1] deals with special considerations that apply to group audits, in particular those that involve component auditors. A **component auditor** is the auditor who, at the request of the group engagement team, performs work on the financial information related to a component. A **component** is an entity or business activity which financial information is included in the group financial statements. Although component auditors may perform work on the financial information of the components and are responsible for their work, the **group engagement partner**[2] is responsible for the direction, supervision and performance of the audit engagement and the auditor's report. The group engagement partner should be satisfied that those performing the group audit engagement, including component auditors, collectively have the appropriate competence and capabilities. The review of the overall group audit strategy and audit plan is an important part of fulfilling the group engagement partner's responsibility for the direction of the group audit engagement.

13.3   Acceptance and Continuance

The group engagement partner must determine whether sufficient appropriate audit evidence can reasonably be expected to be obtained about the consolidation process and the financial information of the components. To do this, the group engagement team shall obtain an understanding of the group, its components and their environments to identify components that are likely to be significant. The group engagement partner must evaluate the component auditors who perform work on the financial information of the components to determine whether the group engagement team should also be involved in the work of those component auditors in order to obtain sufficient audit evidence.

In the case of a new engagement the understanding of the group to be audited may be obtained from group management and from the previous auditor, component management or component auditors. Important matters to be considered are:[3]

- The structure of the group (consolidated company).
- Significant components (of the consolidated company).
- The use of service organisations.
- A description of group-wide controls.
- The complexity of the consolidation process.
- Component auditors not being part of the network of the group auditor.
- Having unrestricted access to relevant persons and information.
- Ability to perform work on the financial information of the components.

When dealing with a continuing engagement the focus will be on changes of the above matters.

If the group engagement partner concludes that it will not be possible for the group engagement team to obtain sufficient appropriate audit evidence due to restrictions imposed by group management and the possible effect will result in a disclaimer of opinion report on the group financial statements, the group engagement partner shall either not accept the engagement, or in the case of a continuing engagement, withdraw from the engagement. Where law or regulation prohibits an auditor from declining an engagement or where withdrawal from an engagement is not otherwise possible, a disclaimer of opinion report should be issued.

13.4 Overall Audit Strategy and Audit Plan

■ Understanding the Group Being Audited, Its Components and Their Environments

The auditor is required to identify and assess the risk of material misstatements through obtaining an understanding of the entity and its environment. The group engagement team must enhance its understanding of the group auditee, its components and their environments, including group-wide controls obtained during the acceptance or continuance stage. The team must also obtain an understanding of the consolidation process, including the instructions issued by group management to components.

Matters to be considered are:

- Industry, regulatory and other external factors.
- The applicable financial reporting framework.
- The nature of the entity.
- Objectives and strategies and related business risks.
- Measurement and review of the entity's performance.

- Instructions issued by group management to components: accounting manual, reporting package and a timetable.
- Identification and assessment of risks of fraud: the key members of the engagement team (may include component auditors) are required to discuss the susceptibility of an entity to material misstatement of the financial statements due to fraud or error, specifically emphasising the risks due to fraud.

The previous matters to be considered possess a more generic character. Matters specific to a group, including the consolidation process, are:

- Group-wide controls: regular meetings between group management and component management, monitoring of components' operations and their financial results, group management's risk assessment process, intra- group transactions, process for financial information received from components, control activities within the IT environment, internal audit, code of conduct and arrangements for assigning authority and responsibility to component management.
- Consolidation process: matters relating to the applicable reporting framework, matters relating to the consolidation process and matters relating to consolidation adjustments.

The group engagement team shall obtain an understanding that is sufficient to confirm or revise its initial identification of significant components and to assess the risks of material misstatement of the group financial statements. Examples of conditions or events that may indicate risks of material misstatement of the group financial statements are:

- A complex group structure.
- Poor corporate governance.
- Ineffective group-wide controls.
- Components operating in foreign jurisdictions with, for example, unusual governance intervention.
- Business activities that involve high risk.
- Specific consolidation items.
- Unusual related party relationships and transactions.
- Reconciliation issues.
- Complex transactions;
- Components' accounting policies differ from group policies.
- Components with different financial year-ends.
- Unauthorised or incomplete consolidation adjustments.
- Aggressive tax planning.
- Frequent changes of auditors.

Specific attention is required to identify the risks of material misstatement of the financial statements due to fraud. Group management's assessment of the risks and their process for identifying and responding to the risks is important. There may be components for which the risk of fraud is more likely. Moreover the monitoring of those charged with governance of management's processes for identifying and responding to the risks of fraud and the controls to mitigate the risks are important.

   The key members of the engagement team are required to discuss the susceptibility of an entity to material misstatement of the financial statements due to fraud or error, specifically emphasising the risks due to fraud. These discussions may include the component auditors. The discussions provide an opportunity to share knowledge of the components and the business risks of the group and the components. They key members will exchange ideas how group management and component management could perpetrate and conceal fraudulent reporting, including earning management or revenue recognition practices that do not follow the accounting framework. They will consider external and internal pressures affecting the group that may create an incentive, opportunity or indicate a culture for fraud. The key members will consider the risk that management may override controls. Furthermore they will consider how differences in accounting policies are identified and adjusted, discuss identified fraud and share information that may indicate non-compliance with laws or regulations.

Identifying Components

A component could be a head office, parent, division, location, business unit, branch, subsidiary, activity, shared service centre, joint venture, associated company, or other entity whose financial information is included in the group financial statements. Determining what is a component will require professional judgement and is guided by: the structure of the group, the flow of the financial information and the audit approach.

The group engagement team shall obtain an understanding of the group, its components and their environment that is sufficient to identify significant components. The group engagement team may apply a percentage to a chosen benchmark as an aid to identify significant components. Identifying a benchmark and determining a percentage involves professional judgement. For example, components exceeding 15 per cent of the chosen benchmark may be considered significant. The group engagement team may also identify a component as likely to include significant risks of material misstatement of the group financial statements due to its specific nature or circumstances: risks that require special audit consideration. In other words, a component can be significant based on size (quantitative consideration) or based on risks (qualitative consideration).

Understanding the Component Auditor

If the group engagement team plans to request a component auditor to perform work on the financial information of a component, the group engagement team must obtain an understanding of the following:[4]

- Whether the component auditor understands and will comply with the ethical requirements that are relevant to the group audit and, in particular, is independent. If a component auditor does not meet the independence requirements or the group engagement team has serious concerns about the component auditor's ethical requirements, the group engagement team shall obtain sufficient appropriate evidence without the component's auditor involvement.
- The component auditor's professional competence. This may include whether the auditor possesses an understanding of auditing standards and other standards applicable to the group audit, special skills (for example, industry knowledge), and an understanding of the applicable financial reporting framework.
- Whether the group engagement team will be able to be involved in the work of the component auditor to the extent necessary to obtain sufficient appropriate evidence.
- Whether the component auditor operates in a regulatory environment that actively oversees auditors.

In addition the group engagement team considers factors such as:

- The significance of the component, its materiality and the identified significant risks.
- The level of work to be requested of the component auditor.
- The complexity of the component.
- Whether the component auditor is part of the network of the group auditor. Consideration of this point is easily underestimated in actual practice. There are differences in the level of cooperation within networks. Big Four firms tend to have a high level of cooperation and standardisation of policies and procedures. Smaller firms tend to have network relations with less integration and coordination.

■ Materiality

In the context of a group audit materiality levels are established for both the group financial statements as a whole and for the financial information of the components. The group engagement team shall determine the following:[5]

- Materiality for the group financial statements as a whole when establishing the overall group audit strategy.
- The materiality level (amount) to be applied when there are particular transactions, balances or disclosures for which misstatements of any larger amounts could be expected to influence the economic decisions of users.[6]
- The performance materiality: to reduce to an appropriate level the probability that the aggregate of uncorrected and undetected misstatements in the financial information exceeds overall materiality.
- The threshold above which misstatements cannot be regarded as clearly trivial to the group financial statements.
- Component materiality for those components where component auditors will perform an audit for the group audit. To reduce to an appropriate low level the probability that the aggregate of uncorrected and undetected misstatements in the group financial statements exceeds materiality, component materiality shall be lower than materiality for the group financial statements as a whole.

For those components where component auditors perform audit or review work for the group audit, the group engagement team determines the overall materiality, the performance materiality and the amount applicable to group reporting. The group auditor communicates the levels to the component auditors, or confirms approval of the levels to the component auditors.

Professional judgement is to be applied in establishing the overall materiality for a component. Component materiality need not to be an arithmetical portion of the materiality for the group financial statements as a whole and consequently the aggregate of component materiality for the different components may exceed the materiality for the group financial statements as a whole. Factors that may influence component materiality are: the number of components where audit procedures will be performed, the existence of a sound control environment, the expected number of misstatements, the complexity of accounting judgements and the existence of inter-company transactions. Component performance materiality needs to be established at an amount lower than component overall materiality. In practice a haircut between 25 per cent to 50 per cent is to be applied.[7]

Misstatements identified in the financial information of the component that are above the threshold (clearly trivial) are communicated to the group engagement team. Usually in group audits the amount is the same for each component. In practice a percentage between 5 and 10 is to be applied.

If a component is subject to audit by statue, regulation or other reason and the group engagement team decides to use that audit to provide audit evidence for the group audit, the group engagement team shall determine whether the overall and performance materiality at the component level meet the requirements of ISA 600.

■ Determining the Type of Work with Respect to Components

The group or component auditor performs one of the following types of work:

- An audit of the financial information of the component using component materiality.
- An audit of one or more account balances, classes of transactions or disclosures.
- Specified procedures relating to likely significant risks of material misstatement of the group financial statements.
- A review of the financial information of a non-significant component using component materiality.

Illustration 13.1 gives an overview of the type of work to be performed for the components.

ILLUSTRATION 13.1

Type of Work to Be Performed for Components

Significant components	Audit of financial statements (component materiality)
Components likely to include significant risks	■ Audit of the financial information ■ Audit of one or more account balances, classes of transactions or disclosures relating to the significant risks ■ Specified audit procedures relating to the significant risks
Not significant components	■ Analytical procedures ■ If insufficient audit evidence is available, the group engagement team selects non-significant components and performs or requests the component auditor to perform one or more of the following procedures: audit of the financial information, audit of one or more account balances, classes of transactions or disclosures, a review of specific procedures

The objective of an audit of a group is to obtain sufficient evidence on the consolidated financial statements as a whole. The work on the significant components is a key part of the work that has to be done. Where there are components that are not significant individually, but account for an important proportion of the group, it is necessary to obtain sufficient evidence about some of those 'not significant components' in order to have sufficient evidence on the group as a whole. The group engagement team's decision as to how many and which 'not significant components' to select and the type of work to be performed is affected by:

- The extent of audit evidence expected to be obtained on the significant components.
- Whether the component has been newly formed or acquired.
- Whether significant changes have taken place in the component.
- Whether internal audit has performed work at the component.
- Whether components apply common systems and processes.
- The operating effectiveness of group-wide controls.
- Abnormal fluctuations identified by analytical procedures.
- Individual financial significance of, or the risk posed by, the component in comparison with other components within this category.
- Whether the component is subject to audit required by statue, regulation or for another reason.

An important consideration is when executing a group audit is the 'scope of the audit' expected of the component auditors. The **scope of an audit** refers to the audit procedures deemed necessary in the circumstances to achieve the objective of the audit. The scope may be 'full scope', 'specific scope', 'limited scope' or 'no scope'. Full scope involves performing a full audit of the component's financial statements. This scoping is required when a component by itself is significant due to its individual financial importance to the group. If a component is likely to include significant risks of material misstatement of the group financial statements due to its specific nature or circumstances, either a full scope or a specific scope is the right response. A specific scope involves doing audit procedures in those areas where significant risks were identified. Those areas can be one or more account balances, classes of transactions or disclosures relating to the likely significant risks. A limited scope involves a review of the component entity's financial statements.

Limited scope is an option when a component is not significant based on size or specific risks identified, but the group engagement team believes less audit procedures are not enough. Other audit responses to components that are not significant are also possible, depending on the circumstance, including upgrading to full scope or specific scope. If a component is not significant, the group engagement team should at least perform analytical procedures at group level. The results of the analytical procedures corroborate the group engagement team's conclusions that there are no significant risks of material misstatement of the financial information of components that are not significant components. This minimum level of scoping is called 'no scope', as it does not contain specific audit procedures at the level of the component.

Illustration 13.2 illustrates setting of different scopes for the component audit.

It is possible that the group engagement team uses another auditor for performing audit procedures on group components (component auditors). The group engagement team shall determine the nature, timing and extent of its involvement in the work of the component auditors. If a component auditor performs an audit of the financial information of a significant component, the group engagement team shall be involved in the component auditor's risk assessment to identify significant risks

ILLUSTRATION 13.2

Audits of Group Financial Statements (The Work of Component Auditors)

Audits of group financial statements
The work of component auditors

Is the component of the individual of financial significance to the group? **YES** → **Audit of the component's financial information** *(further work to be determined and performed) (ISA 600.29)*

NO ↓

Is the component likely to include significant risk of misstatement of the group financial statements due to its specific nature or circumstances? **YES** → **Audit of the component's financial information** *(further work to be determined and performed) (ISA 600.29),* **or audit of one or more account balances, classes of transactions or disclosures relating to the likely significant risks; or specified audit procedures relating to the likely significant risks**

NO ↓

→ **Analytical procedures performed at group level for components that are not significant components**

Is the planned scope such that sufficient appropriate audit evidence on which to base the group audit opinion can be obtained?

NO ↓   **YES** ↓

For further selected components: Audit of the component's financial information (further work to be determined and performed (ISA 600.29), or audit of one or more accounts balances, classes of transactions or disclosures; or review of the component's financial information; or specified procedures

Communication with component auditors

of material misstatement of the group financial statements. The involvement shall include at a minimum:[8]

- Discussing with the component auditor or component management those of the component's business activities that are significant to the group.
- Discussing with the component auditor the susceptibility of the component to material misstatement of the financial information due to fraud or error.
- Reviewing the component auditor's documentation of identified significant risks of material misstatement of the group financial statements.

If significant risks of material misstatement of the group financial statements have been identified in a component on which a component auditor performs the work, the group engagement team shall evaluate the appropriateness of the further audit procedures to be performed to respond to the identified significant risks. Based on its understanding of the component auditor, the group engagement team shall determine whether it is necessary to be involved in the further audit procedures.

13.5 Communication

This section deals with the communication of the group auditor and component auditor and communications with group management and those charged with governance. First the communication with the component auditor will be considered, then communication with those charged with governance of the group auditee

■ Group Auditor and Component Auditor Communication

The group engagement team sets out the work to be performed, the use to be made of that work and the form and content of the communication with the group engagement team. The communication shall include the information shown in Illustration 13.3.

In conformity with the ISA 600 standard the component auditor shall communicate matters relevant to the group engagement team's conclusion with regard to the group audit. Such communication shall include the information given in Illustration 13.4.[9]

ILLUSTRATION 13.3

Information Required in Group Auditor Communication to the Component Auditor

- Confirmation that the component auditor will cooperate with the group engagement team
- Work to be performed by the component auditor
- Ethical requirements that are relevant to the group, in particular the independence requirements
- Component materiality and the threshold above which misstatements cannot be regarded as clearly trivial to the group financial statements
- Identified significant risks of material misstatements of the group financial statements due to fraud or error that are relevant to the work of the component auditor

Illustration 13.3 (continued)

- List of related parties
- Timetable
- Dates of planned visits
- List of key contacts
- Work to be performed on intra-group transactions
- Guidance on other statutory reporting responsibilities (for example on the effectiveness of internal control)
- Specific instructions for subsequent events
- Findings of the group engagement team's tests of control activities of a processing system that is common for all or some components and tests of controls to be performed by the component auditor
- Findings of internal audit
- Request for timely communication of audit evidence that contradicts the audit evidence on which the group engagement team originally based the risk assessment at group level
- Request for a written representation on component management's compliance with the applicable financial reporting framework
- Matters to be documented
- Request for reporting: significant accounting, financial reporting and auditing matters, going concern issues, litigation or claim events, significant deficiencies in internal control and information that indicates the existence of fraud
- Request for notification of any significant or unusual events
- Request that the component auditor shall communicate, when the work on the financial information of the component is completed, matters relevant to the group engagements team's conclusion with regard to the group audit

ILLUSTRATION 13.4

The Component Auditor Must Communicate to the Group Auditor

- Component auditor's compliance with ethical requirements, including independence and professional competence
- Component auditor's compliance with group engagement's requirements
- Identification of the financial information of the component
- Information on non-compliance with laws and regulations that could give rise to a material misstatement at group level
- List of uncorrected misstatements (unless below the threshold for clearly trivial)
- Indicators of possible management bias
- Description of any identified deficiencies in internal control
- Other significant matters that the component auditor communicated or expects to communicate with those charged with governance, including fraud or suspected fraud
- Any other matters that may be relevant to the group audit, or that the component auditor wishes to draw to the attention of the group engagement team
- Component auditor's overall findings, conclusions or opinion

Based on the received information the group auditor shall evaluate the component auditor's communication and adequacy of their work. The group engagement team shall discuss significant matters arising from that evaluation with the component auditor, component management or group management. They determine whether it is necessary to review other relevant parts of component auditor's documentation. If the group engagement team concludes that the work of the component auditor is insufficient, they shall determine what additional procedures are to be performed and whether they are to be performed by the component auditor or by the group engagement team. The group engagement team shall evaluate whether sufficient appropriate evidence has been obtained from the audit procedures performed on the consolidation process and the work performed by the group engagement team and the component auditors on which to base the group audit opinion. The group engagement partner shall evaluate the effect on the group audit opinion of any uncorrected misstatements and any instances where there has been an inability to obtain sufficient appropriate audit evidence.

■ Group Auditor Communication with Management and Those Charged with Governance

Another important element in a group audit is the communication with group management and those charged with governance. The group engagement team shall determine which deficiencies in internal control shall be communicated with group management. Fraud issues must be communicated on a timely basis to the appropriate level of group management. If a component auditor is required to express an audit opinion on the financial statements of a component, the group engagement team shall request group management to inform component management of any matter of which the group engagement team becomes aware that may be significant to the financial statements of the component, but of which component management may be unaware.

The following matters shall be communicated by the group engagement team to those charged with governance of the group:[10]

- An overview of the type of work to be performed on the financial information of the components.
- An overview of the nature of the group engagement team's planned involvement in the work performed by the component auditors on the financial information of significant components.
- Instances where the group engagement team's evaluation of the work of a component auditor gave rise to a concern about the quality of that auditor's work.
- Any limitations on the group audit.
- Fraud or suspected fraud involving group management, employees who have significant roles in group-wide controls or others where the fraud resulted in a material misstatement of the group financial statements.

13.6 Consolidation

The group auditor is required to obtain an understanding of the consolidation process, including the instructions issued by group management to components.[11] 'The consolidation process' includes: the recognition, measurement, presentation and disclosure of the financial information of the components in the group financial statements by way of consolidation, proportionate consolidation, or the equity or cost methods of accounting. The consolidation process also means the aggregation in combined financial statements of the financial information of components that have no parent but are under common control.

The group engagement team obtains an understanding of group-wide controls and the consolidation process, including the instructions issued by group management to components. If group-wide controls are operating effectively, or if substantive procedures alone cannot provide sufficient appropriate audit evidence, the group engagement team or the component auditor tests the operating effectiveness of the group-wide controls. The group engagement team shall evaluate the appropriateness, completeness and accuracy of consolidation adjustments and reclassifications. When consolidation adjustments relate to a component, the group engagement team needs to consider communicating adjustments to component auditors as appropriate.

If the financial information of a component has not been prepared in accordance with the same accounting policies applied to the group financial statements, the group engagement team shall evaluate whether the financial information of the component has been appropriately adjusted to the accounting policies of the group entity. The group engagement team shall determine whether the financial information identified in the component auditor's communication is the same financial information that is incorporated in the group financial statements. When the group financial statements include financial statements of a component with a financial reporting period-end that differs from that of the group, the group engagement team shall evaluate whether appropriate adjustments have been made.

13.7 Subsequent Events

Subsequent events are events occurring between the date of the financial statements and the date of the auditor's report, and facts that become known to the auditor after the date of the auditor's report. In performing subsequent event procedures the component auditor needs to gain an understanding of the controls and procedures component management and group management have in place that affect the component. Normally the group engagement team will ask the component auditor to perform the relevant procedures. The aforementioned procedures are only required when performing an audit of the financial information of a component. For all other types of work there is a requirement for the component auditor to inform the group engagement team if they become aware of any events.

13.8 Reporting

The group engagement partner must evaluate the effect on the group audit opinion of any uncorrected misstatements and inability to obtain sufficient appropriate audit evidence. This evaluation allows her to determine whether the group financial statements as a whole are materially misstated.

When the group audit opinion is modified because the group engagement team was unable to obtain sufficient appropriate audit evidence in relation to the financial information of one or more components, the auditor's report on the group financial statements describes the reasons for that without referring to the component auditor (unless such a reference is necessary for an adequate explanation of the circumstances).

Where access to information is restricted by circumstances the group engagement team may still be able to obtain sufficient appropriate audit evidence; however, this becomes less likely as the significance of the component increases. If the component is not a significant component and the group engagement team has a complete set of financial statements of the component, including the auditor's report and has access to information kept by group management in relation to that component, the group engagement team may conclude that this information constitutes sufficient appropriate audit evidence. Although the group engagement team may in this situation be able to obtain sufficient appropriate audit evidence, the reason for the restriction may affect the group audit opinion. For example, it may affect the reliability of group management's responses and representations to the group engagement team. If the component is a significant component, the group engagement team will not be able to comply with the requirements of ISA 600. Further guidance is available in ISA 705.[12]

13.9 Documentation

In addition to documentation required by ISA 230[13] and other ISAs the group engagement team shall include in the audit documentation the following matters:[14]

- An analysis of components, indicating those that are significant and the type of work performed on the financial information of the components.
- The nature, timing and extent of the group engagement team's involvement in the work performed by the component auditors on significant components, including, where applicable, the group engagement team's review of relevant parts of the component auditor's audit documentation and conclusions thereon.
- Written communications between the group engagement team and the component auditors about the group engagement team's requirements.

Disposition of matters raised by the component auditor(s), materiality levels used for group purposes and the evaluation of the adequacy of the component auditor's work are part of the documentation.

13.10 Extended Example of a Group Audit

The remainder of this chapter will describe a typical group audit based on several actual cases.

The US office of BIG, a major audit firm, wants you to audit some European subsidiaries of its client, United States of America Technology, Inc. (USATec), which is listed at the New York Stock Exchange. The company that will be your primary audit client is Maastricht Technology (MaasTec), a subsidiary of USATec.

The documents in the package are the **group audit instructions**. These documents are to familiarise you with what is expected by the BIG office, which is in charge of the USATec audit.[15] Based on these you and the partner in charge of the audit will put together an audit planning memorandum and an audit programme (audit plan). A last document, a completion memorandum, will be required to summarise your audit findings.

The instructions from the US office are important to your understanding of the background of the client and the applicable accounting and auditing standards to be used in the audit. They point out some of the key audit objectives for this client. In this particular case, there have been several acquisitions by both USATec and MaasTec, which will require increased substantive tests. There has also been a spin-off of a subsidiary independent distributor.

Your audit team will prepare an audit planning memorandum, the audit programme and the completion memorandum. The audit planning memorandum incorporates most of the important ideas of the audit. It is put together by your senior audit staff person and approved by you, the manager, and by the partner. It is also discussed with the client when in draft form. Discussion with the client rarely produces major changes. The audit programme serves as a set of procedures to be performed by assistants involved in the audit and as a means to control proper execution of the work. It is prepared based on BIG's auditing software. The report on your auditing findings, the completion memorandum, describes critical and significant audit areas, accounting issues, and any matters that need to be highlighted.

◼ Reviewing the Group Audit Instructions

It is Monday morning and you have come to work at the Netherlands office of BIG loaded down with work that you took home for the weekend and did not finish. There is a package on your desk, delivered over the weekend, from BIG's US office. It is better to get straight to work on these projects, so you put everything else away, and pick up your yellow marker pen.

You first read the contents pages of the documents which are given in Illustration 13.5, then you read the documents and highlight certain important items with your yellow marker.

ILLUSTRATION 13.5

Contents of Group Audit Instructions

Sections

A. General

B. Specific procedures

C. Company

D. Audit scope, fees and coverage

E. Critical and significant audit concerns

F. Management letters

G. New accounting standards

H. Independence

■ Sections A (General) and B (Specific Procedures) of the Group Audit Instructions

The first two sections of the group audit instructions contain general information and specific procedures. The general information is about subsidiaries and audit standards required. Specific procedures include discussion on:

- reporting package and deadline;
- separate report information;
- currency exchange considerations;
- supplemental statements;
- details about the completion memorandum;
- potential material weakness in internal control;
- written representation[16] of management (management letter) comments;
- material differences;
- specific details of the client audited.

Specific procedures listed in section B are numbered. You read the first procedure required which is to document planning policies in accordance with professional accounting literature and the audit service manual. You highlight the next section – the deadline for the reporting package – with your yellow marker. Other procedures such as identifying related parties, illegal or questionable acts (document who, where, results) and fraud are mentioned. You highlight legal and questionable acts because you know that this aspect is becoming more and more important to BIG and to national governments, especially under ISA 240[17] and 250[18] and the local laws.

The reporting package and deadline deals with audited financial statements, local currency and the national accounting principles applicable to USATec. The required supplemental schedules, completion memo, tax working papers and management letter comments (those that USATec management will see or those for BIG eyes only) are mentioned. You are asked to describe any unresolved issues or audit requirements not completed.

Financial Reporting Requirements

There is a fairly detailed discussion about compliance with the national accounting principles applicable to USATec. In the case of MaasTec's, the business you are auditing, there is a separate financial report for statutory purposes required by local laws. Differences between financial statements in local currency and in accordance with the national accounting principles applicable to USATec, and issued financial statements, should be detailed as a footnote. You highlight the last item because you know there are some differences.

Completion Memorandum

You highlight the next item about the completion memorandum because you know that it is the most important document sent back to BIG's group engagement partner. The completion memorandum should include a statement that the audit is in accordance with BIG's audit manual, working papers are prepared and reviewed, and that your working papers support your audit opinion. BIG also want to see a statement that you used a disclosure checklist and documentation of partner or senior inquiries of illegal or questionable acts with senior management, and discussion of any matters disclosed in the inquiries.

■ Section C of the Group Audit Instructions – United States of America Technology (USATec) – the Company

Section C opens with information about the main client United States of America Technology (USATec), the 'Company'. Details are given about the company including when it was organised, where, products, markets, service, sales force, type of customers and the industry's marketing strategy. You highlight the information about sales force, types of products, and industry's marketing strategy because you know this could be important in assessing inherent risk.

Organisation Structure of USATec

The next piece of information is on the organisation of USATec which lists all subsidiaries by location, principal activities, with any subsidiaries sold, acquired, spun off or shutdown noted. You highlight the subsidiaries sold, acquired, etc. Where there is a change in ownership, there might be some accounting problems. The subsidiaries, which are important to your audit, are shown in Illustration 13.6.

You highlight 'the industry', 'rapid technological advances' and 'competitors' because of possible inherent risk. Internal factors that are of importance are: product changes and customer reaction to those changes, acquisitions over the last ten years, and MaasTec's overall strategy. You highlight 'product changes' because this will increase control risk in that old control may not work for new products.

ILLUSTRATION 13.6

Subsidiaries Important to the Audit

Company	*Structure*	
Parent Company – Home Office Technology (USATec)	**USATec Subsidiary –** Local Office Technology **(MaasTec)**	**Local Subsidiary–** Brother Office Technology (Brother)*
	Sister Information Systems (SIS)	Zap
	Brother Research Organisation (BRO)	Design Info Planning and Programming Resources (DIPPER)
	Cousin Office Technology (Cousin)	Finance Investment National Enterprises (FINE)
	Uncle Office Technology (Uncle)	SIS subsidiary Newco

*Note: Brother owns Sister Information Systems (SIS), which owns Newco.

Questions about MaasTec (USATec subsidiary)

General questions the auditor should ask are about MaasTec's legal situation, industry and products. Legal questions include:

■ Is there an in-house legal department?
■ Is there an in-charge manager?
■ Who is MaasTec's general counsel?

Regarding related parties, you must provide a list of: (a) directors, (b) non-director officers, (c) subsidiaries and (d) others. Also required is an analysis of the competition related to characteristics of the industry, evidence of rapid technological advances, and a list of competitors.

■ Section D of the Group Audit Instructions – Audit Scope, Fees and Coverage

Section D includes subsections on BIG home office participation, audit fees, audit coverage, timing of certain audit procedures, computer assisted auditing techniques, the audit timetable and quarterly reviews.

The section begins with a list of names and telephone numbers of key personnel responsible for the United States of America Technology (USATec) audit: the partner, manager and in-charge senior manager. There is also a list of key personnel names and telephone numbers, partner and manager at BIG's US office. The agreed audit scope and related amount of the audit fees are given.

Schedule of Planned Scope and Coverage

An audit coverage schedule of planned scope and coverage is detailed. They give you a schedule of the percentage of estimated total consolidated amounts at 31 December 20XX for each company and the scope of the audit; for example, USATec's revenues represent 52 per cent of the total consolidated revenues. A partial schedule looks like Illustration 13.7.

ILLUSTRATION 13.7

USATec and Subsidiaries

Revenue, total assets and accounts rec. as a percentage of Consolidated Values

	Revenues		Total Assets		Accounts Rec.		Scope of Audit
	Total	Audit	Total	Audit	Total	Audit	
USATec	52	52	50	50	62	62	Full scope
MaasTec	13	13	8	8	14	14	Full scope
Uncle	12	lr	8	lr	9	lr	Limited review
Others	5	dr	2	dr	–	na	Desk review

na = not audited   dr = desk review   lr = limited review

Timing of Audit Procedures

The timing of certain audit procedures is considered next. The general audit plan gives you a list of the audit area and a description of audit procedures, which you can perform prior to year-end. The schedule is as follows:

Audit area	Discussion of audit procedures
Accounts receivable	Confirm balances as of 30 November and roll forward to year-end
Research and development costs	Test of transactions for third quarter and roll forward to year-end
Investments	Test of balances as of 30 November and roll forward to year-end
Property plant and equipment	Test of balances as of 30 November and roll forward to year-end

Deadlines

The audit timetable calls for all working papers, reports and supporting schedules to be received by 30 January 20XX at BIG group audit office in the USA. The audit-planning memorandum will be due 12 December. You highlight that date because that is the most pressing one.

■ Section E of the Group Audit Instructions – Critical and Significant Audit Concerns

Section E is described as 'Critical and Significant Audit Concerns'. This is an important section that shows which items you will need to concentrate on during the audit. The specific areas of concern are revenue, research and development costs, third-party regulation, acquisitions, restructure accruals, management letters, benchmarking and new accounting standards that need to be applied.

MaasTec Management's Revenue Recognition Policies

You must review if management's revenue recognition procedures are being followed. Management's procedure for revenue recognition is to record revenue only when four conditions are met. These four conditions are:

1 a signed purchase order is received;
2 creditworthiness of the customer is reviewed and the sale is documented;
3 the product has been shipped;
4 the product shipped is only the currently authorised product, not test products or samples.

Research and Development Costs

The final concerns for the audit are review of research and development costs, third-party royalties, acquisitions and restructuring accruals. MaasTec pays royalties to third parties on some of their software, which will require review.

■ Sections F (Management Letters) and G (New Accounting Standards) of the Group Audit Instructions

Management letters are important to BIG. The Management Letter is the auditor's written communications to management to point out weaknesses in the internal control, other reportable conditions, and possibilities for operational improvements. The instructions convey the suggestions for the management letter to be reviewed with MaasTec managers. You also make sure that your comments are supported in the working papers and typed for inclusion in the consolidated management letter.

The final part of the group audit instructions discusses benchmarking[19] and the new accounting standards that apply this year. MaasTec is to be compared to benchmarks developed on several other companies and results are to be discussed with managers. New GAAP standards in the US include standards on financial instruments used as investments or hedging and certain internal controls.

■ Section H (Independence) of the Group Audit Instructions

It is requested that you and your audit team have a sufficient understanding of, and have complied with, the applicable independence requirements.[20]

You will write emails to your audit team members in order to determine and document their compliance with these rules.

13.11 The Audit Planning Memorandum – Strategy Part

After reading the group audit instructions, the first order of business is to meet with the audit staff and discuss strategy for the audit. Based on the results of the meeting, your senior staff auditor will write up an audit planning memorandum that will be reviewed by senior team members. So, early on Friday morning, everyone meets at the office and discusses the BIG overseas materials and the audit plan.

Things get pretty well structured and the meeting is over by 11 o'clock, which is just as well because the partner has another meeting that day. You discuss some fine points with your audit senior that will have the memorandum for your review by Wednesday.

Wednesday afternoon your senior gives you the draft memorandum. He has split the audit-planning memorandum into a Strategy Part and a Plan Part.

An outline of the contents of the Strategy Part is shown in Illustration 13.8.

■ Section II and III of the Audit Planning Memorandum – Follow-up and Insights

Follow-up Section

Since MaasTec is a continuing client, the audit should be started by following up on last year. The Follow-up from Last Year section discusses some questions:

- Has MaasTec fixed the problems it had last year?
- How has the situation been improved?
- If they have improved, what tests will be done to ensure this conclusion?

ILLUSTRATION 13.8

Contents of Audit Planning Memorandum – Strategy Part

I. Introduction

II. Follow-up from last year

III. Insights
   A. Critical success factors and key performance indicators
   B. Objectives and strategies
   C. Business activities and influence on controls
   D. Market position – position and competitors
   E. Important customer/suppliers
   F. New developments
   G. Changed business structure
   H. Financing and financial reporting environment
   I. Information system changes

IV. Initial risk analysis

V. Internal controls and control procedures

VI. Identification of critical audit objectives

VII. Client service aspects item – action
   A. New structure of internal control due to new systems
   B. Functional currency charged to USATec
   C. Proposed CIS review

VIII. Important contacts
   A. At MaasTec
   B. MaasTec professional advisers

IX. Service Audit Team

Insights Section

The insights section gives some of the audit staff's insights into the company. One of MaasTec's business activities, service contracts, has changed. Therefore, a change in controls is needed. Market position, new developments and problems involving revenue auditing are considered. Important customers and suppliers should be reviewed, especially big customers and new contracts. Confirmations of accounts receivable may prove difficult for MaasTec because business custom in this country discourages sending confirmations to customers. The team will find another way to audit the revenue cycle.

Some of the changes at MaasTec may require more extensive audit procedures and investigation. MaasTec has made some change in its business structure by taking over Newco and Design Information Planning & Programming Resources (DIPPER). This could cause control and accounting problems. MaasTec has had information system changes, which may cause misstatement and control problems.

Concept and a Company 13.1

Ahold – Rapid Global Expansion and the Group Audit

Concept	Difficulties of a group audit.
Story	In 2003, Koninklijke Ahold N.V. (Royal Ahold), a 115-year-old Netherlands company, had 9,000 stores in 27 countries that served 40 million customers a week, and owned or had interest in about 9,000 supermarkets as well as discount and speciality stores in some 25 countries in Asia, Europe and the Americas. In February 2003, Ahold revealed improperly booked profit of approximately $1.12 billion (Sams, 2003).

Ahold's auditor, Deloitte & Touche (DT), discovered the company's accounting irregularities as part of its 2002 year-end audit. As a result of the discovery, Ahold had to restate its audited financial statements for 2001 which had been given an unqualified audit opinion (Weil, 2003). Speaking at the company's annual meeting, Henry de Ruiter, in his last official engagement as Ahold chairman, said that Ahold's supervisory and executive boards felt responsible for the 'horrendous' events. He added that Ahold would not replace DT, saying there was no evidence the auditor knew of the fraud prior to its discovery (Bickerton and Watkins, 2003).

Irregularities involving improper booking of vendor allowances were discovered in US subsidiaries US Foodservice and Tops Markets. The company's Disco subsidiary engaged transactions that were illegal and improperly accounted for. Unauthorised side letters (supplements to contracts) created errors of consolidation regarding joint ventures in Sweden/Norway, Brazil, Guatemala and Argentina (Mirabella, 2003).

Ahold's executive and supervisory boards ordered an investigation by a forensic team from PricewaterhouseCoopers (PwC). For the period 1 April 2000 (the effective date of Ahold's acquisition of US Foodservice) to 28 December 2002, (the end of Ahold's 2002 fiscal year), PwC has identified total overstatements of pre-tax earnings of approximately $880 million. Of this amount, approximately $110 million relates to fiscal year 2000, approximately $260 million relates to fiscal year 2001, and approximately $510 million relates to fiscal year 2002. In addition, PwC identified approximately $90 million of adjustments required to be made to the opening balances for US Foodservice at the date of its acquisition. This consists of a reclassification of such amount from current assets to goodwill primarily as a result of required write-offs of vendor receivables (NACS, 2003).

The forensic accounting work at Albert Heijn, Stop & Shop, Santa Isabel in Chile, Ahold's operations in Poland and the Czech Republic, and the ICA Ahold Scandinavian joint venture found no evidence of financial fraud (NACS, 2003).

The main problem in the US was improper booking of vendor allowances. The allowances are a broad industry term that covers everything from vendor payments for prime shelf space in a store, to rebates awarded to retailers who hit sales targets for suppliers' products. These payments were allegedly booked too high and were, in some cases, booked without the manufacturers' permission. Subsidiaries were also faulted for booking vendor allowances as revenue, when, in most cases, they should be booked as a reduction in the cost of sales. Ahold says that Tops was principally to blame for $29 million in overstated income. Another of its US subsidiaries, US Foodservice, overstated its pre-tax income by $880 million over three years (Glenn, 2003).

Cees van der Hoeven, Ahold's Chief Executive, took the retailer on a worldwide buying spree, from Chile to Thailand, running up net debts of around €13 billion. Ahold began its buying spree in 1976 when it acquired a Spanish supermarket and the Bi-Lo chain in the American South. In 1996, it bought Stop & Shop for $2.9 billion and added dozens of chains in Latin America, Europe and Asia. It tried to buy Pathmark Stores in 1999, but that deal was blocked by the US Federal Trade Commission. Ahold subsequently turned to food service for growth, acquiring US Foodservice for $3.6 billion in 2000 (Knowledge@Wharton, 2004). Also, in 2000, Ahold acquired PYAO Monarch for $2.57 billion and paid $75 million for Peapod.

Ahold's broad strategy was to buy regional supermarket retailers and gain economies of scale and savings through consolidation of back-office and buying operations. Other chains sought to do the same thing, modelling themselves on the successful expansion of chain drugstores. However, grocery stores are more complicated than drugstores and depend to a greater extent on regional suppliers and marketing (Knowledge@Wharton, 2004).

Discussion Questions	■ Discuss ways that a buying spree like that of Mr Van der Hoeven can create problems for the group auditor. ■ What pressures may be applied to the management of newly acquired divisions that would encourage misstatement of income? ■ What special audit procedures should be applied to an audit of an acquisitive company?
References	Bickerton, I. and Watkins, M., 2003, 'Ahold Says Up to 10 people to Blame for Fraud', *Financial Times*, London, 27 November, p.15. Glynn, M., 2003, 'Vendor Rebates to Retailers Are Under the Microscope', *Buffalo News*, Buffalo, NY, 1 June, p. B.9. Knowledge@Wharton, 2004, 'Royal Ahold's Royal Hold Up', http://knowledge.wharton.upenn.edu/, 12 March. Mirabella, L., 2003, 'Dutch Grocery Chain Raided', *Cincinnati Post*, Cincinnati, Ohio, 8 July, p. C.9.0. NACS 2003, 'Ahold Releases Results of US Foodservice Forensic Accounting Investigation', *Daily News*, National Association of Convince Stores, 9 May. Sams, R., 2003, 'Ahold Accounting Probes Reveal More Irregularities', *Washington Business Journal*, 1 July. Weil, J., 2003, 'Deloitte's Work for Ahold Raises Questions on Auditing', *Wall Street Journal* (Eastern edition), New York, NY, 25 February, p. A.10.

■ Section IV of the Audit Planning Memorandum – Initial Risk Analysis

Initial risk analysis must be conducted to determine main risks. You and the team made a schedule of risk arranged by process (sales, accounts receivable and salary) and information source as follows (example):

Process	Information Source	Inherent Risk	Control Risk	Critical Audit Objective
Intangibles	Groot Warnsborn	High	High	Valuation
Sales of software	John Smith	High	High	Completeness
Accounts receivable	Patricia Hayward	High	Average	Valuation
Salary	Robert de Niro	Low	Low	None

■ Section V of the Audit Planning Memorandum – Internal Controls and Control Procedures

The team members noted that at MaasTec no one feels responsible for controls. That is not a good sign. A review of CIS showed that MaasTec is highly dependent on user dependent controls of the CIS. After the planned installation of new software this year, controls must be tested again, including boundary testing. **Boundary testing** is audit testing of documentation at the lowest level of the information stream; for example, testing the first document (i.e. purchase order) that initiates an exchange.

■ Section VI of the Audit Planning Memorandum – Identification of Critical Audit Objectives

The strategy part identifies critical audit objectives. One of the critical audit objectives relates to the purchase of certain subsidiaries creating substantial goodwill. You feel that MaasTec should speed up the recovery of the goodwill intangible fixed assets due to these recurring (substantial) operating losses. The audit team suggested to MaasTec at the beginning of the year that they write off this goodwill immediately. No reaction from MaasTec management has been received.

■ Section VII to IX of the Audit Planning Memorandum – Client Service, Important Contacts and Audit Team

Because auditing is a service and offered in a competitive business environment, a major concern of BIG is client service aspects of the audit. The team feels that changing the functional currency to US dollars, which is USATec's functional currency, may result in tax problems and proposes an information system review because of the new finance system that has just been installed at MaasTec. There is a note to contact BIG's tax office and BIG's CIS department.

List of Important MaasTec Contacts

The team put together a list of MaasTec's professional advisors and important contacts among MaasTec employees. The list of important contacts at MaasTec is categorised by name, quality (good/bad) of contact, frequency of contact and by whom the contact should be made (partner, manager or senior).

Audit Team

The final item in the strategy part of the audit planning memorandum is a schedule of the audit team. The schedule includes the audit team's names and experience at the client. Also listed will be other professionals at BIG who may be called for assistance (e.g. tax personnel, CIS consultants and others).

Everyone on the team reviews the strategy part of the planning memorandum. It is now your job to combine their comments with the following discussion of the draft plan part of the audit planning memorandum. You call MaasTec to set up interviews and a walk-through with some of the team for two days next week to develop a better under-standing of MaasTec and some of the areas that may require investigation.

13.12 The Audit Planning Memorandum – Plan Part

The strategy part of the audit planning memorandum sets the broad direction for the audit. The plan part of the audit planning memorandum summarises technical matters, client service matters and logistical matters. Technical matters include further planning of our approach of critical audit objectives and internal control. It expands on the strategy part and provides, among other things, an overview of the client company, the industry environment, significant audit concerns, and areas of interest to the audit team. In other words, an audit has to be planned in greater detail using the strategy as a basis. An outline of this plan part appears in Illustration 13.9.

ILLUSTRATION 13.9

Contents of Audit Planning Memorandum – Plan Part

I. Introduction
   A. Client background
   B. Group structure
   C. Analytical review to assist in audit planning

II. Audit approach
   A. Scope
   B. Audit materiality (gauge)
   C. Assessment of inherent risk and preliminary assessments of control risk

III. Critical audit objectives
   A. Intangibles
   B. Sales of software
   C. Accounts receivable

IV. Significant audit areas and accounting issues
   A. Accounts receivable
   B. Accounts payable
   C. Inter-company receivables and payables
   D. Revenue recognition
   E. Unearned revenue
   F. Taxation
   G. Forward exchange contracts
   H. Related party
   I. Assets
   J. Statutory financial statements

V. Fees

VI. Timetable
   A. Format financial statement and items requested
   B. Draft of management letter

VII. Client contacts

VIII. MaasTec firm service team

We will not discuss audit approach and critical audit objectives in greater detail, but we will sketch some considerations in audit planning to be made based upon risk analysis. We call these considerations 'significant audit areas' and 'accounting issues'. These considerations (and, of course, the critical audit objectives) should be dealt with in the audit programme (audit plan) that will be discussed below. Please note that the audit programme primarily focuses on substantive year-end procedures to provide guidance for the audit work in a practical way. Of course, tests of control should be performed. However, these have been described in more detail in Chapter 7 'Internal Control and Control Risk'.

Concept and a Company 13.2

ZZZZ Best – How to Fool the Auditors

Concept	**I had to fool accountants and auditors into believing those numbers were real before I could perpetrate the fraud,' Barry Minkow (ACFE, 2002).**
Story	ZZZZ Best began operations in the fall of 1982 as a door-to-door carpet cleaning business operating out of the Reseda, California, the garage of 16-year-old Barry Minkow. In the three-year period from 1984 to 1987, net income grew from less than $200,000 to more than $5 million on a revenue of $50. In the spring of 1987, ZZZZ Best had a market value of $200 million. By the end of 1987 the company was in bankruptcy and the assets were auctioned off for only $64,000 (Knapp, 2004). The company for almost its entire history was a fraud.

ZZZZ Best had a legitimate carpet-cleaning business that accounted for 20 per cent of reported revenue and a phoney building restoration business which was 80 per cent of revenue. To create loans for the company, ZZZZ Best management made fraudulent invoices, set up cheque accounts for front companies, created fraudulent vendors, wrote cheques for phoney expenses, and kept the money circulating by cheque kiting at several banks (Knapp, 2004).

False Documents

Thousands of company cheques in the company written by hand, in large numbers, and often payable to cash were made out to different people or firms but paid into the same account. The same money – obtained from ZZZZ Best investors and lenders – kept going around and around from ZZZZ Best to phoney vendors and customers and back to ZZZZ Best. The purpose of all these movement was to make ZZZZ Best look like a legitimate business (Akst and Berton, 1988).

'Accounts receivable are a wonderful thing,' Barry Minkow said, 'They are a tool used by a fraudster like me to ask to borrow money and to show earnings' (ACFE, 2002). He would create an invoice from a phoney customer, write a cheque to ZZZZ Best from the front company's cheque account, and deposit it to the company account. 'One way you cannot dispute a receivable is if it has been paid … I was a paperwork manufacturing machine,' he said (ACFE, 2002).

Convincing the Auditors

To avoid the auditors finding anything, Minkow employed a number of tricks besides false documentation. He steered the auditors to examine the legitimate carpet cleaning business instead of the non-existent building restoration business. 'The restoration business was 80 per cent of the revenue, but I made sure that the auditors did 80 per cent of due diligence in the carpet cleaning business,' he said. He also intimidated the auditors, ingratiated himself to the auditors, and in one instance created a completely false audit environment.

Auditing is a very competitive business. 'Competition is what you leverage,' Minkow said. 'I can't remember how many times [I said] "Larry, I just know Coopers and Lybrand would love this account." Does he want to go back to his clients and managers and say that he lost the ZZZZ Best account because he wanted to be petty? No, he does not want to lose the ZZZZ Best account, and I leveraged that to the hilt, too' (ACFE, 2002).

Minkow's charm and entrepreneurial spirit caused the media to tout him as an example of what America's youth could obtain if they applied themselves. As a guest on the *The Oprah Winfrey Show* on US network television in April 1987 he encouraged his peers to adopt his personal motto, 'The sky is the limit' (Knapp, 2004). He ingratiated himself by having dinner with the auditors and their wives. He felt that if the wives like him and the auditor wanted to be hard on Minkow, the wives would say, 'but he is such a nice kid.' Minkow said, 'The final touch was "Well, the kid is on Wall Street. If there was something wrong, someone would have found out by now"' (ACFE, 2002).

Classic Tricks

Minkow's tricks to mislead the accountants doing audit procedures are classic. They included phoney confirmations, financial statements manipulated to reflect industry standards, false documentation and, in one instance, creation of an entire false audit environment.

Minkow paid an insurance claims adjuster from a legitimate company to confirm over the telephone to banks and any other interested third parties that ZZZZ Best was the recipient of insurance restoration contracts. ZZZZ Best's first external auditor, George Greenspan, maintained that he performed analytical procedures comparing the company to the industry, confirmed the existence of contracts, and obtained and reviewed copies of key documents. Greenspan, however, did not inspect any restoration sites (US Congress, 1988).

Ernst & Whinney (E&W) took over as ZZZZ Best's auditor in 1986. E&W repeatedly insisted on visiting several of the largest of the contract sites, so that finally Minkow agreed to a visit. E&W wanted to visit a large site in Sacramento, California, for which ZZZZ Best claimed to have a multi-million dollar contract.

Minkow sent two associates to Sacramento to find a large building under construction or renovation that would be a plausible site for a restoration contract. Posing as leasing agents, they convinced the supervisor of the construction site to provide keys to the building one weekend on the pretext that a possible future tenant wanted to tour the building. Before E&W visited the site, placards were placed on the walls indicating that ZZZZ Best was the contractor for building renovation. The building's security officer was paid to greet the visitors and demonstrate that he was aware in advance of the auditor's visit (US Congress, 1988).

Another site visit by E&W required that ZZZZ Best lease a partially completed building and hire subcontractors to do a large amount of work on the site. In total ZZZZ Best spent several million dollars just to deceive its auditors (US Congress, 1988).

ZZZZ Best required that E&W sign a confidentiality agreement before the visits were made on the pretext that the insurance company required it. The agreement required that E&W not disclose the location of the building and not 'make any follow-up telephone calls to any contractors, insurance companies, building owner or other individuals' (Knapp, 2004).

Minkow and 10 other ZZZZ Best insiders were indicted by a Los Angeles federal grand jury in January 1988 on 54 counts of racketeering, securities fraud, money laundering, embezzlement, mail fraud, tax evasion and bank fraud. On 27 March 1989 he was sentenced to 25 years in prison. He was also placed on five years' probation and ordered to pay $26 million in restitution.

After being released from jail, Minkow became a preacher and a fraud investigator, and spoke at schools about ethics. This all came to an end in 2011, when he admitted to helping deliberately drive down the stock price of homebuilder Lennar and was ordered back to prison.

Discussion Questions	■ What procedures should an auditor carry out to determine the validity of a significant source of company revenue? ■ What actions of Minkow and the company's audit history would have caused an auditor to become suspicious? ■ How does signing a confidentiality agreement affect auditor substantive procedures?
References	ACFE, 2002, 'Cooking the Books' video, Introduction to Higher Education, Association of Certified Fraud Auditors, Austin, Texas, 12 February. Akst, D. and Berton, L., 1988, 'Accountants Who Specialise in Detecting Fraud Find Themselves in Great Demand', *The Wall Street Journal*, 26 February. Knapp, M, 2004, 'ZZZZ Best Company, Inc', *Contemporary Auditing Real Issues and Cases*, South-Western College Publishing, pp. 41–56. US Congress, House, Subcommittee on Oversight and Investigation of the Committee on Energy and Commerce, 1988, 100th Congress, *Hearing 100-115*, 'Failure of ZZZZ Best Co', US Government Printing Office, Washington, DC, 27 January to 1 February. http://en.wikipedia.org/wiki/Barry_Minkow#Conviction_and_prison.

■ Revenue Recognition Procedures Key

The group audit instructions from BIG Overseas stated that revenue recognition would be a key area. You plan to review revenue recognition policy by first testing cut-off procedures; then make a review of shipping documents as an alternative procedure to confirmation of accounts receivable, and boundary testing on the revenue cycle.

The almost continuous revision of financial instruments standards from IAS 30 and IAS 39 to IFRS 7 and IFRS 9 about financial instruments and disclosures reinforces your feeling about being careful when financial instruments are a significant portion of the current assets. MaasTec uses forward exchange contracts.

■ Fees, Timetable and Client Contacts

Fees and the timetable for the audit are important parts of the audit plan for obvious reasons. You calculate the budgeted hours and related fees for partner, manager, staff, and out-of-pocket expenses. The timetable for audit was given to you in the instructions as follows:

(1) planning memo, time and fee estimate are due 12 December 20XX; (2) format financial statement and items requested by group audit instructions are due on 23 January 20XX and (3) a draft of management letter is due on 30 January 20XX.

You and the partner review and approve the plan and take it to the client for discussion. MaasTec management and audit committee review the plan and meet with you. They recommend only a few changes in the plan based on timing. Now you are ready to finalise the audit planning memorandum and conduct the audit.

13.13 Audit Programme (Audit Plan)

Using BIG's audit software, BIGdealer, you write the audit programme. You use standardised audit procedures suggested by the software that are needed to substantially test the account balances and transactions outlined in the audit planning memorandum. Major steps that can be included are given (as example) in Illustration 13.10.

ILLUSTRATION 13.10

Audit Programme

Investments

Balances:	
Investments	25,000,000
Income or (losses)	200,000
Gain or (loss) on sales	300,000

OBJECTIVES:

I. All dividend, interest and other income is recorded; gains and losses on sales and other dispositions are recognised; premiums and discounts and related amortisation are recorded. (Completeness and accuracy.)

II. Investments exist and are owned by the entity. (Existence and ownership.)

III. Valuation methods (e.g. equity, market, lower of cost or market) applied are in conformity with applicable accounting principles consistently applied, and write-down, or provision for write-down, is recorded, when appropriate. (Valuation, presentation and disclosures.)

	Obj.	Done By	Refer.
1 Verify accuracy of relevant supporting schedules and agree to trial balance and subsidiary records. (a) Obtain and check mathematical accuracy of a detailed schedule of securities, including transactions for the year, classified as to (1) short-term investments, (2) long-term investments, (3) affiliated companies, and (4) other; agree beginning balances to the prior year's workpapers; and reconcile ending balances to the trial balance, general ledger, and subsidiary records, if any. Identify separately marketable equity securities.	I, II		
2 Confirm investments held by third parties.	II		
3 For major acquisitions or dispositions of investments, agree to authorisation in the minutes of the Board of Directors.	II		
4 Vouch purchases of investments to supporting documentation.	I, II		
5 Vouch sales of investments to supporting documentation and recompute gain or loss on disposal. Trace collections to cash receipts.	I, II		
6 Examine latest financial statements of investees.	II, II, III		
7 Review disclosures (e.g. basis, assets pledged, related parties, equity method details interests, gross unrealised gain/losses). (a) Perform detail procedures as considered necessary.	I		
8 Determine the application of correct rates of exchange for amounts denominated in foreign currency	III		

▶

Illustration 13.10 (continued)

	Obj.	Done By	Refer.
9 Conclude (a) With respect to the set of assertions and related audit objective(s), the audit procedures applied were in accordance with firm and professional requirements; subject to any differences documented in the workpapers, the recorded amounts are materially correct and the accounting principles are proper and consistently applied; the information in the workpapers is sufficient to draw a conclusion as to proper disclosure.	II, II, III		

Expenses and Payables

Balances: Prepaid Expenses Trade Accounts Payables and Accruals	10,000,000 10,000,000

OBJECTIVES:
I. All unpaid amounts due to suppliers or others for goods and services received prior to year-end are included or otherwise accrued. (Completeness, existence, accuracy, and ownership.)
II. All cash disbursements are valid and properly recorded (i.e. they are for goods and services received by the entity; classification as asset expense, liability, and other accounts is appropriate). (Existence and accuracy.)
III. Accounting principles are appropriate and applied consistently (e.g. interest adjustments, if required, are recognised). (Valuation, presentation and disclosures.)

	Obj.	Done By	Refer.
1 Compare amounts for trade payables, accruals, purchases, period expenses, and payments to prior periods and budgets.	I, II		
2 Verify the mathematical accuracy of relevant supporting schedules and agree to trial balance and subsidiary records.	I, II		
3 Review liabilities recorded after the end of the period and review subsequent cash payments. (a) Determine propriety of year-end accounts for both accounts payable and accrued liabilities by searching for unrecorded liabilities. Such review should encompass the period subsequent to the balance sheet date and include a review of unpaid vendor invoices, cash disbursements, unmatched receiving reports, significant liabilities recorded after year-end, and other relevant items. (b) Verify computation of period accruals. (c) Determine the extent to which it is necessary to examine documents supporting period-end accruals and check underlying mathematical calculations. Perform any necessary tests of details. (d) Verify cut-off for: purchases, payments, supplier returns, and shipments direct to customer from suppliers. (e) For the period before and after the balance sheet date, check vendor invoices to and from receiving records to determine that a proper cut-off was made. (f) For the period before and after the balance sheet date. Check debit memos for purchase returns to and from shipping records to determine that a proper cut-off was made. (g) Request or confirm suppliers' statements. (h) Check suppliers' statements to recorded balances and investigate differences. (i) Send second requests where requested statements are not received or apply alternative auditing procedures (e.g. review subsequent payments, agree to receiving reports, purchase orders, correspondence files).	I		

Illustration 13.10 (continued)

	Obj.	Done By	Refer.
4 Vouch purchases of inventory from perpetual records.	I		
5 Vouch claims for credit from suppliers (e.g. receivables from suppliers) to supporting documents.	I		
6 Vouch purchases and other disbursements from voucher register to supporting documents including relevant data.	II		
7 Vouch purchases of inventory to and from perpetual records.	II		
8 Trace purchases from receiving reports to suppliers' invoices and voucher register including relevant data (e.g. party, price, description, quantity and date).	II		
9 Determine the application of correct rates of exchange for amounts expressed in foreign currency.	III		
10 Review classification and description of accounts (e.g. debit balance, current/non-current trade, related parties).	III		
11 Review accounting principles for appropriateness and consistency.	III		
12 Conclude (a) With respect to the set of assertions and related audit objective(s), the audit procedures applied were in accordance with firm and professional requirements; subject to any differences documented in the working papers, the recorded amounts are materially correct and the accounting principles are proper and consistently applied; the information in the working papers is sufficient to draw a conclusion as to proper disclosure.	II, II, III		

Revenue/Accounts Receivable

Balances: Revenue Accounts Receivable	35,000,000 35,000,000

OBJECTIVES:

I. All revenue from the sale of goods and performance of service are recorded accurately. (Completeness and accuracy.)

II. Recorded revenues are in conformity with proper revenue recognition methods consistently applied and adequately disclosed. (Valuation, presentation and disclosure.)

III. Cut-off is proper. (Completeness and existence.)

IV. Trade accounts receivable represent uncollected sales or other charges to bona fide customers and are owned by the entity. (Existence and ownership.)

V. All cash collections are accurately recorded. (Completeness and accuracy.)

VI. Non-cash credit to receivables (e.g. returns, allowances) are valid and accurate. (Existence and accuracy.)

VII. Valuation of trade receivables is appropriate (i.e. provision is made for uncollectable amounts). (Valuation, presentation and disclosure.)

	Obj.	Done By	Refer.
1 Vouch sales from shipping records to sales authorisation, sales invoices, and sales register, including relevant data (e.g. party, price, description, quantity, and dates).	I		
2 Test sales invoice price of items to authorised lists.	I, VII		
3 Test processing to general and subsidiary ledgers.	I		
4 Determine sequential numbering of sales invoices.	I		
5 Analyse the VAT-payable to total sales (Netherlands).	I		

Illustration 13.10 (continued)

	Obj.	Done By	Refer.
6 Evaluate propriety and consistency of accounting principles. Consider: (a) Revenue recognition (current and deferred); Bill and hold transactions; Discontinued operations; Non-monetary exchanges; Warranties; Sales of receivables with or without recourse; Commissions; Special discounts and rebates; Consignment sales; Trade notes receivable; Troubled debt restructuring of customers; and Scrap sales.	II		
7 Verify cut-off for sales, cash receipts, returns, etc.	II, III		
8 Verify the mathematical accuracy of relevant supporting schedules and agree to trial balance and subsidiary records.	IV		
9 Confirm recorded receivables (amount, date, terms, interest rate, etc.). (a) Check replies to confirmations and investigate exceptions. (b) Send second requests where replies to positive requests are not received. (Exceptions to sending second requests for non-responding positive confirmations should be rare and the reasons for not sending them should be fully documented.) (c) Investigate undelivered requests returned by post office. If possible obtain better addresses and mail again. (d) Where replies are not received to positive requests for confirmation apply alternative audit procedures (e.g. check subsequent remittance advices, shipping documents, billing records, customer orders and correspondence files). (e) Summarise results of confirmation requests and all iterative procedures.	IV, V, VII		
10 Vouch recorded receivables to subsequent cash receipts.	IV, V VII		
11 Vouch sales from sales register to shipping records (including relevant data).	IV		
12 Vouch write-offs of uncollectable receivables to supporting documentation.	VI, VII		
13 Vouch ageing details to supporting documents, discuss collectability of receivables with responsible officials, and review correspondence.	V, VI, VII		
14 Determine the extent to which it is necessary to perform the following tests of details: (a) Select credit memos, examine supporting documents and trace posting to the sales register. (b) Review credit memos issued after the balance sheet date and ascertain whether significant amounts relate to sales for the period under review. (c) Vouch returns to supporting documentation.	VI		
15 Verify the accuracy of client schedules supporting their analysis of the allowance for doubtful accounts. (a) Obtain an aged listing of trade receivables as of the balance sheet date. Reconcile the balance with the general ledger and trial balance, and compare a selected number of individual accounts of the listing with the detailed subsidiary trade receivable records. Verify the mathematical accuracy of any schedules.	V, VII		
16 Determine the application of correct rates of exchange for amounts expressed in foreign currency.	V		
17 Review disclosures (e.g. assets pledged, related parties, segments, significant customer data, economic dependency). (a) Perform additional procedures considered necessary.	V		
18 Conclude: (a) With respect to the set of assertions and related audit objective(s), the audit procedures applied were in accordance with BIG's and professional requirements; subject to any differences documented in the workpapers, the recorded amounts are materially correct and the accounting principles are proper and consistently applied; the information in the working papers is sufficient to draw a conclusion as to proper disclosure.	I, II, III, IV, V, VI		

Illustration 13.10 (continued)

Inventory/Cost of Sales

Balances: Inventories Cost of Sales	2,000,000 15,000,000			

OBJECTIVES:				

I. Inventory is accurately compiled and priced in conformity with acceptable methods (e.g. FIFO, LIFO) consistently applied. (Accuracy.)

II. Cut-off is proper. (Completeness and existence.)

III. Valuation of inventories is appropriate (e.g. write-down, or provision for write-down, is recorded when amounts otherwise exceed net realised values). (Valuation, presentation and disclosure.)

	Obj.	Done By	Refer.
1 Verify accuracy of supporting schedules and agree to trial balance and subsidiary records.	I		
2 Test priced inventory listing. Obtain the client's final extended inventory listing and perform the following procedures:	I		

(a) Check the mathematical accuracy of the listing.
(b) Agree test counts with recorded quantities.
(c) Compare items on final inventory listing to physical inventory tags, sheets, or lists and vice versa.
(d) Determine that unused, voided, and no-quantity tags are accounted for property.
(e) Reconcile totals with general ledger control totals.
(f) Ascertain that corrections and adjustments to the final listing are proper.
(g) Scan the inventory listing and investigate unusual quantities or amounts.
   (**Note:** The procedures enumerated below provide only general guidance for the examination of the three principal components of inventory costs and will require further modification. The cost methods and cost accumulation systems used to value inventories will vary from entity to entity. Also, depending upon the nature of the business, the components of inventory will vary. In some entities, material cost will represent a significant portion of the inventory's cost, while in others, labour costs represent the major component of cost. The audit procedures designed to test inventory costs should recognise the components of costs that are most significant and the appropriateness of the cost accumulation system.)
(h) **Purchased Items (Materials)**
   Compare the unit cost of selected purchased items to vendor invoices. Consider the treatment of freight, duty, discounts, and so forth in arriving at unit cost. This test should encompass purchased items included in raw materials, work-in-process, and finished goods.
(i) **Labour Costs**
   ■ Test direct and indirect labour costs included in inventory by tracing such costs to payroll registers, time cards, labour distribution reports, and so forth (This step should be coordinated with the work in the Payroll and Related Costs audit area.)
   ■ Compare direct and indirect labour application rates and individual direct and indirect labour accounts between periods and within periods and investigate reasons for unusual fluctuations.

Illustration 13.10 (continued)

	Obj.	Done By	Refer.
(j) Overhead Costs Determine the composition and allocation of factory overhead included in inventory. Evaluate the reasonableness of (a) the basis used to distribute overhead to departments, products, and so forth, and (b) expenses included in overhead. Investigate period-to-period fluctuations in overhead application rates and in individual overhead accounts. Review analysis of standard cost variance accounts to determine reasonableness of allocation to period costs and inventories. ■ If the physical inventory was not taken as of the balance sheet date, perform substantive analysis and other substantive procedures, as appropriate, during the roll-forward period.			
3 Vouch purchases of inventory to and from perpetual records.	I		
4 Vouch sales from perpetual inventory records.	I		
5 Ascertain that cut-off is proper. ■ Consider: – Sales/shipments to trade customers; – Purchases/receiving; – Intercompany activity; – Stage of production; – Customer returns; – Returns to suppliers; – Shipments direct to customers from suppliers. (Note: Care should be taken not to duplicate procedures performed in connection with the Accounts Payable and Trade Receivables cycles.) ■ Trace and test receiving reports noted during inventory observation to accounts payable or cash disbursements of the appropriate period. ■ For a period after inventory observation date, trace purchase invoices to and from receiving reports to test for inclusion in the proper period. Coordinate this procedure with similar procedures in the accounts payable area. ■ If inventory was in transit during the physical inventory, ascertain whether the cost of the items was accounted for properly. ■ Review open purchase orders and open receiving reports for possible unrecorded items. ■ Trace latest shipping reports noted during inventory observation to postings in the sales register of the appropriate period. Coordinate this work with work on the revenue cycle. ■ Ascertain that proper cut-off was obtained between classes of inventories (e.g. transfers of purchased items between raw materials and work-in-process and between work-in-process and finished goods).	II		
6 Determine the application of correct rates of exchange for amounts expressed in foreign currency.	III		
7 Review accounting principles for appropriateness and consistency. ■ For each major inventory classification, determine the basis of pricing (lower of cost or market, market, etc.), the method of determining cost (FIFO, LIFO, average, etc.), and the method of determining market (replacement, net realisable value, etc.). Verify that the basis of pricing and determination of cost of sales are in accordance with GAAP and consistent with the prior year.	III		
8 Review disclosures (e.g. valuation, liens, unusual market write-downs) and perform additional procedures as necessary.	III		
9 Conclude: ■ With respect to the set of assertions and related audit objective(s), the audit procedures applied were in accordance with firm and professional requirements; subject to any differences documented in the workpapers, the recorded amounts are materially correct and the accounting principles are proper and consistently applied; the information in the working papers is sufficient to draw a conclusion as to proper disclosure.	I, II, III		

Illustration 13.10 (continued)

Asset Balances/Expense

Balances: Asset Balances	125,000,000

OBJECTIVES:
I. Amounts prepaid, deferred, or capitalised are expected to provide future benefits for matching with expected future income; amounts and related amortisation are calculated correctly; write-down or loss provision recorded, if appropriate. (Existence, Accuracy, Valuation, Ownership, Presentation and Disclosure.)

	Obj.	Done By	Refer.
1 Verify the mathematical accuracy of relevant supporting schedules and agree to trial balance and subsidiary records.	I		
2 Agree beginning balances in schedules to prior period's workpapers.	I		
3 Vouch significant additions during the period.	I		
4 Ascertain that the amortisation period is appropriate.	I		
5 Test calculations of amortisation and unamortised balances.	I		
6 Test write-offs during the period.	I		
7 Review disclosures (e.g. valuation, liens, unusual write downs, amortisation period) and perform additional procedures as necessary.	I		

Expense and Capitalised Balances

Balances: Expense Capitalised Balances	2,000,000 6,000,000

OBJECTIVES:
I. All capitalised leases are recorded at the appropriate amounts and operating base, rentals are appropriately charged to expense. (Completeness and accuracy).

	Obj.	Done By	Refer.
1 Compare operating lease rent expense to prior periods and budgets.	I		
2 Consider performing substantive analysis procedures (as an alliterative or supplement to tests of details) for: ■ Operating lease expense; ■ Interest expense on obligation under capital leases; ■ Related rent and interest balance sheet accruals; and ■ Amortisation expense.	I		
3 Verify classification and accounting treatment of leases accounted for as operating leases based on review and/or confirmation of lease terms.	I		
4 Recompute expense, accruals, and prepayments related to operating leases.	I		
5 Conclude: ■ With respect to the set of assertions and related audit objective(s), the audit procedures applied were in accordance with firm and professional requirements; subject to any differences documented in the workpapers, the recorded amounts are materially correct and the accounting principles are proper and consistently applied; the information in the working papers is sufficient to draw a conclusion as to proper disclosure.	I		

The audit programme starts out with the basic data about value of assets and revenue, the basis on which the testing will be made and the gauge or monetary precision or materiality, the amount of maximum misstatements allowed. This data for the MaasTec audit is shown on the first part of the audit programme, Illustration 13.10.

The rest of the audit programme consists of objectives and procedures of each critical area tested. For example, the first area tested is investments. There is one audit objective and several audit procedures given for testing investments.

The remainder of this section will refer to the audit programme (see Illustration 13.10). We will pick a few of the procedures and their related audit objectives to discuss in detail and explain how these procedures are carried out from your viewpoint as the audit manager.

■ Investments

For investments audit procedures there are three objectives:

I   All dividend, interest and other income is recorded; gains and losses on sales and other dispositions are recognised; premiums and discounts and related amortisation are recorded. (The financial statement assertions of management are completeness and accuracy.)

II Investments exist and are owned by the entity. (The financial statement assertions of management are existence and ownership.)

III Valuation methods applied are in conformity with applicable accounting principles consistently applied, and write-down or provision for write-down is recorded when appropriate. (The financial statement assertions of management are valuation, presentation and disclosure.)

Procedure Number 3: Agree to Authorisation in the Minutes of the Board of Directors

Looking at Illustration 13.9, you are responsible for procedure number 3, which is based on objective II: For major acquisitions or dispositions of investments, agree to authorisation in the minutes of the board of directors.

MaasTec this year bought controlling interest in Newco, Design Information Planning and Programming Resources (DIPPER), Financial Investment National Enterprises (FINE) and 15 per cent of Zap. You check the minutes of the board of directors to see if the board of directors authorised the purchases.

Procedure Number 4: Vouch Purchases of Investments to Supporting Documentation (Based on Objectives I and II)

You need to verify the existence of the investments and the ownership. If the investment is a minority ownership (like the stock ownership of 15 per cent of Zap), you need to check for the stock certificates. There are three ways this can be done. If they are bearer stock certificates in a third-party custodian vault you need to request a confirmation of custody by the custodian. If the certificates are in a MaasTec's safe, you would just do a count and inspection of the stock certificates. It is also possible to request an up-to-date shareholder register from the company in which MaasTec has invested.

A custodian, the stockbroker Smidt Barne, holds the stock certificates evidencing ownership of Zap. You send a confirmation request to Smidt Barne. You also send a request to Zap for a recent stockholder register.

Review Purchase Contracts, Due Diligence

If a company has a major, or controlling, interest (like the ownership in Newco, Design Information Planning and Programming Resources (DIPPER), and Financial Investment National Enterprises (FINE)) you need to review the purchase contracts, review the deeds of transfer, and check the bank statement to see if there was a cash outflow at the time of the purchase. If a **due diligence report** was carried out when MaasTec was acquiring the company, you should see that, along with any other documentation that was done for the acquisition.

You ask management for purchase agreements for Newco, DIPPER and FINE. Your audit team reviews the purchase agreements for DIPPER and FINE to see that they were purchased and the time the purchase took place. Your team finds the amounts are appropriate. The team then traces the purchase amounts to the bank statement to verify the amount and payment. There is a due diligence report for the purchase of FINE, so you review that.

Oohh – Oh

You find that one purchase agreement shows Sister Information Systems (SIS), not MaasTec, has entered into a share purchase agreement to purchase all shares of Newco for US\$3,000,000 in six semi-annual payments. You find from your discussion with management that Newco is owned by SIS, which is owned by Brother, which is owned by MaasTec. There is no documentation supporting ownership of Brother by MaasTec. You make a note on your working papers and send out a confirmation request to Newco to verify that their shares are owned by SIS.

Review Accounting of Three Companies

Zap is carried on MaasTec's books at cost. You think that accounting treatment is appropriate because the ownership of Zap by MaasTec is only 15 per cent, but you feel you can give no opinion on Zap unless you have their financial statements. You ask for financial statements, preferably audited.

You review the notes of the three controlled companies to see if there are any differences in accounting. This is important, because these companies will be consolidated and any differences in the financial statements must be adjusted on the consolidated statements.

Different auditors not from your own firm prepare two of the financial statements of the three controlled companies. Doiever, RA, is the auditor of Financial Investment National Enterprises (FINE) and Lickanapromise, RA, audited Design Information Planning and Programming Resources (DIPPER). You know the firms' backgrounds and make a note of it in your working papers. You also send a questionnaire about the audit and a request for working papers to Doiever, RA, and to Lickanapromise, RA. It is important to determine these auditors' reputations and that they took due care in the audit.

■ Expenses and Payables

Expenses and payables auditing have three audit objectives. For procedure number 3 which we will discuss, the audit objective is: All unpaid amounts due to suppliers or others for goods and services received prior to year-end are included or otherwise accrued. (Financial statement assertions are: completeness, existence, accuracy and ownership.) See Illustration 13.10.

Procedure Number 3: Review Liabilities Recorded After the End of the Period and Review Subsequent Cash Payments

You request that the client provide you with a list of all invoices for payment received after the balance sheet date. You pick invoices from the list on a random basis and see if they pertain to the period before or after the balance sheet date. If the invoice shows the payables are incurred before the balance sheet date, your team traces the invoices through the journals and ledgers to the balance sheet to see if they show up as accrued liabilities or accounts payable for that period.

You take the bank statements after the balance sheet date, pick out items randomly, and vouch them back to the corresponding payment invoice to see if they show up as accrued liabilities or accounts payable.

Procedure Number 5: Vouch Claims for Credit from Suppliers (e.g. Receivable from Suppliers) to Supporting Documents

First, your team reviews any contracts MaasTec has with their main suppliers. If MaasTec has any credit with the suppliers, you would check purchase administration to see what items were returned or what extra payments were made to create the credit. You determine whether MaasTec's policy regarding credits has been followed. Finally, you vouch the credits back to the original documents.

■ Revenue and Accounts Receivables (Confirmations)

Auditing sales and receivables has seven audit objectives. Here are three of them, numbers IV, V and VII:

IV   Trade accounts receivable represent uncollected sales or other charges to bona fide customers and are owned by the entity. (Financial statement assertions are: existence and ownership.)

V   All cash collections are accurately recorded. (Financial statement assertions are: completeness and accuracy.)

VII Valuation of trade receivables is appropriate (i.e. provision is made for uncollectable amounts). (Financial statement assertions are: valuation, presentation and disclosure.)

Concept and a Company 13.3

ComROAD – From Whence Those Sales?

Concept	Revenue recognition audit.
Story	The Neuer Markt of the Frankfurt Stock exchange, Europe's version of Nasdaq-style capital raising and equity trading, closed its doors in late 2002. Deutsche Borse set up the Frankfurt-based Neuer in 1997 to latch onto the technology boom and provide a source of financing for German tech start-ups. In the first three years it brought nearly 350 companies public, peaking at above 8,500 in March 2000, a near tenfold increase. In the next two years, plagued by scandal and hurt by the global economic and technology downturn, the Neuer's main index plummeted more than 95 per cent, wiping out more than $200 billion in market value (Rombel, 2002).

The most notorious scandal to hit the Neuer involved ComROAD Aktiengesellschaft, a German navigation-technology company that went public in 1999. It was delisted from the exchange in 2002 following the revelation that 97 per cent of its claimed $94 million in revenue in 2001 was non-existent. Bodo Schnabel, the chief executive of ComROAD, was tried for insider trading and financial manipulation (Ewing and Byrnes, 2002).

ComROAD licensed technology it had developed to companies in the telecommunications, security and automotive markets (GTTS Partners). The GTTS Partner would pay a start-up fee of from €200,000 to €500,000 for ComROAD to deliver and install telematic service centres. The GTTS Partner then bought the car computer, StreetGuard software, StreetMachine software, and StreetPC, and marketed them through telecommunications, security, and automotive markets distribution channels. GTTS Partners generated monthly income from the use of their services and ComROAD would receive 10 per cent of their gross profit. In early 2001, a reported 32 telematic service centres were installed (ComROAD, 2001).

ComROAD invented revenues from a non-existent client in Hong Kong, VT Electronics, which contributed between 63 per cent and 97 per cent of ComROAD's revenue between 1998 and 2000 (Smith, 2002). It was a German journalist who discovered the fraud at ComROAD. She found it odd that almost all ComROAD's sales came from a company in Hong Kong. While on vacation, she went to Hong Kong at her own expense and tried to locate the company. She could find no record it existed (Ewing, 2003).

KPMG, ComROAD's external auditor, resigned in February 2002 after withdrawing its opinion on the accounts for 1998, 1999 and 2000. During those audit periods KPMG also assisted the company with its cash-flow statements. KPMG said it had helped compile the cash-flow statement, but that the cash-flow statements had not been audited and were based on second-hand information from the company (Smith, 2002).

Discussion Questions	■ What are the typical audit procedures to test for existence of revenue? ■ What additional procedures would an auditor perform if a majority of sales came from a single customer? ■ What aspect of ComROAD's business model made revenue recognition fraud relatively easy? ■ Did the existence of the Neuer reduce scrutiny of revenue?

References	ComROAD, 2001, 'Shareholder Information' press release, ComROAD, 13 August. Ewing, J. and Byrnes, N., 2002, 'Continental Drift at KPMG: Already Beset at Home, the Firm is Reeling From Scandal and Stumbles in Germany', *Business Week*, New York, p. 27. Ewing, J., 2003, 'Business Investigations and Cooking the Books', presented at Investigative Journalism Summer School, London, 18–20 July, May, Issue 3784, p. 70. Rombel, A., 2002, 'Germany: Germany's Symbol of Dot-com Excess Heads for the Scrap Heap', *Global Finance*, New York, November, Vol. 16, Issue 11, p.10. Smith, P., 2002, 'KPMG Dragged into German Fraud', Accountancy Age.com, 25 April.

Procedure Number 9: Confirm Recorded Receivables

Audit procedure number 9, confirm recorded receivable (amount, date, terms, interest rate, etc.), has several sub-procedures. Objectives IV and V apply.

(9a) Check Replies to Confirmations and Investigate Exceptions

First you look through the accounts receivable sub-ledgers and pick out some customers based on your professional judgement, referred to as a **scope sample**. You consider customers with very large balances or very small balances, customers that are slow in paying, and customers that buy erratically, i.e. a lot one week and nothing for several weeks.

Positive Confirmation

You give this list to MaasTec to prepare a confirmation letter. It is a brief letter that says something to the effect, 'We show that you owe us €XX as of 31 December 20XX. Will you please confirm directly to our auditors that this figure is accurate?' Because you expect a reply, this is a **positive confirmation**. Then you, not the client, mail these letters, checking randomly to see if they are the customers you chose and for the amounts shown on the books.

Differences in Amounts

Some of the confirmation letters come back from customers stating that there are differences between the amount MaasTec's books show they owe and the amount their books show they owe at 31 December 20XX. The customer may say, for instance, that they paid off the account balance on 28 December. Your team checks the bank statements before and after 31 December to see when MaasTec's customer's cheque was received. For most of these letters you find that the money was not received until after 31 December so MaasTec's customer still owed the amounts on the balance sheet date and the balances are correct. In one case you find a minor, immaterial, error in recording that you nevertheless note in your working papers for later follow-up.

(9b) Send Second Requests Where Replies to Positive Requests are Not Received

Since the type of confirmation you are using as evidence is a positive confirmation, for those letters sent where you did not receive replies, you send out a second confirmation letter.

(9c) Investigate Undelivered Requests Returned by Post Office

Requests that are returned by the post office for incorrect addresses are investigated by asking the salesperson assigned to the customer the customer's correct address. Typically the salesperson has the current address if the customer has moved. For this audit there were only two returned letters and the salesperson quickly gave you the new, correct address.

However, if the problem continues, you would go to the last shipping invoice to see where the last order was sent. If you still cannot find a correct address, you may try telephoning the customer or resending to the same address. You may also apply alternative procedures.

(9d) Where Replies are Not Received to Positive Requests for Confirmation, Apply Alternative Audit Procedures

For those customers who did not reply to the two confirmation letters or as a result of lack of time, you may decide to perform alternative procedures. One procedure is to trace the accounts receivable to cash receipts to answer the question, 'Has the money come in yet?' If money has not come in based on cash receipts, you look at the shipping records to see if the merchandise was shipped. You can also check the warehouse's order list to see if they prepared the order for pick-up. Check that the transport agent signed for the item when it was picked up. Other procedures are checking customer correspondence files, customer orders and subsequent remittance advices.

Because of the lack of time, your team performs cash receipts and shipping traces on one third of the customers that had not replied by your deadline. Your team also checks customer orders. All are accurate. You also review customer correspondence files, which show no problems.

(9e) Summarise Results of Confirmation Requests and Alternative Procedures

Proper documentation always requires making extensive notes on accounts receivable audit activities.

Procedure Number 10, Based on Audit Objectives IV, V and VII: Vouch Recorded Receivables to Subsequent Cash Receipts.

You take a random sample of the accounts receivable sub-ledger customers who were not included in the scope sample that received confirmation letters and trace their payments to the cash receipts journal and the bank statement.

Procedure Number 11, Based on Audit Objective IV: Vouch Sales from Sales Register to Shipping Records

Your team takes a random sample of items from the sales register and vouches them to the shipping records. This determines if the items listed as sales were shipped. Your team finds that all amounts tested from the sales register equal amounts stated on the shipping document.

■ Inventory and Cost of Sales

Inventory audit has three audit objectives. We will discuss a procedure that concerns Objective I: Inventory is accurately compiled and priced in conformity with consistently applied acceptable methods. (The financial statement assertion related to this is accuracy.)

Procedure Number 2

Look at Illustration 13.10 for audit procedure number 2, which has several sub-procedures: Test priced inventory listing. Obtain the client's final extended inventory listing and perform the following procedures:

(2a) Check the Mathematical Accuracy of the Listing

You attend the physical count of the inventory. You read the count instructions. At the count you make sure:

- all inventory locations get a 'tag' (a description of the item and the quantity and perhaps the item number);
- there are two people counting – one counting the items and the other verifying the count;
- every count team has people from separate departments on the team (e.g. no two people on the same team are from accounting, no two persons on a team are from the warehouse, etc.);
- there is a pre-numbered count list and that you get back all the copies of the list;
- every location has a count sheet and you have all sheets returned;
- you take a random sample of items and make sure they have been counted correctly.

(2b) Agree Test Counts with Recorded Quantities

You agree test counts with recorded quantities by taking a random sample of inventory items from the sub-ledgers and comparing the number of items recorded with the number of items counted. You then take a random sample of the inventory items counted and compare the number of items counted with the number of items recorded in the ledger.

To verify the price you take a sample of items from the inventory price list and compare that with shipping invoices. Determine if the pricing is FIFO, LIFO, etc. and verify the correct valuation formula was used.

(2c) Compare Items on Final Inventory Listing to Physical Inventory Tags, Sheets, or Lists and Vice Versa

You review the final inventory list and take a random sample of items and trace them to the inventory tags, sheets, etc.

(2d) Determine That Unused, Voided and No-quantity Tags are Accounted for Properly

If there are any unused, voided, and no-quantity tags, you must investigate. You find that there are a few of these tags, but it all checks out.

(2e) Reconcile Totals with General Ledger Control Totals

Counted inventory totals rarely agree with the totals in the inventory control account. The process of reconciliation is determining where the differences come from and making sure that the control account balance is adjusted to the counted amounts. You make adjusting entries in your working papers and suggest that MaasTec's accounting department make these adjustments.

There is a difference between the counted inventory and the control totals. Tests of purchases and deliveries show that more raw material inventory was purchased and delivered than was counted. You are reasonably certain that the count is correct. The physical controls over inventory are fairly good; most of the valuable materials that were under lock and key in the storage room are still there. Other inventory sits on the shop floor, providing access to practically everyone. You suspect that the reduction in inventory was due to theft or wastage in the production process. You make a note for the management letter.

(2f) Ascertain That Corrections and Adjustments to the Final Listing are Proper

You need to find if obsolete inventory is written off, the lower of cost or market valuations are correct, work in process is accounted for correctly, and if there are any errors in overhead allocation to inventory.

Obsolete Inventory

To review if inventory is obsolete you talk to management and see if they have any products or product lines they plan to cancel in the future. You also take a look at the sales budget to see what products sales are based on. Based on this knowledge you choose three products that your professional judgement tells you may become obsolete: one product management is thinking of cancelling and two products because sales projections include them in 'misc. sales' and they are not detailed. You look at inventory turnover on a historical basis and determine that the product management intends to cancel is a very slow-moving product and should have increased allowances for obsolescence.

Cost Allocation for Inventory

You then take a look at the procedures for allocating labour and overhead to work-in-progress. First you review the written allocation procedures and then talk to the accountants who carry this allocation out. You must determine if the assumptions of inventory turnover are correct. That means finding if there are any cost, efficiency or utilisation differences in actual inventory and standard costing. One machine has a maximum output of 100,000 units. The standard cost assumption is that the output hours less downtime would be 80,000 units. Machine costs are allocated to inventory based on this assumption. You discover the machine produces only 40,000 units. That utilisation loss should be accounted for. You make a note on your working papers.

Based on the written allocation procedures and what management says they do, allocations seem reasonable. Furthermore, management updates standard costing every season and have recently experienced very few differences between actual and standard costs. Standard costing is periodically compared to, and revised, based on actual experience. The utilisation of certain machines is less than expected, but these utilisation differences have been accounted for. You recalculate month-end inventory allocations for two months to determine consistence of application of management's standard costing formula.

(2g) Scan the Inventory Listing and Investigate Unusual Quantities or Amounts

You review the inventory listing to see if there are any quantities that are in larger or smaller amounts than on previous inventory takes. There are two inventory items that did not appear on the last inventory take, one item that has increased 25 per cent from last year and another item that has dropped 60 per cent. The item that has dropped 60 per cent is the item that the company plans to cancel and an allowance account has already been set up to write it off in the future. Management says the item that increased 25 per cent is their hottest item this year and sales projections predict it will grow an additional 30 per cent next year. The items that appeared this year for the first time are new items.

Procedure Number 3: Vouch Purchases of Inventory To and From Perpetual Records

It is important to test if cut-off was properly made. Did the count instructions have procedures for separating inventory into those items that were shipped and those that were stored? Did the procedures allow for goods that were going from one department to another? You review the count instructions to see if these separating procedures were requested. You supervise the count so that the inventory that needed to be separated was separated.

The warehouse department gives you their shipping and receiving log. You pick all items just before and after the balance sheet date and a random sample of other items. You see if any of these items are still in inventory based on the inventory count.

■ Asset Balances/Expense

Asset auditing has only one audit objective: amounts prepaid, deferred or capitalised are expected to provide future benefits for matching with expected future income; amounts and related amortisation are calculated correctly; write-down or loss provision is recorded. The financial statement assertions are: existence, accuracy, valuation, ownership, presentation and disclosure.

Procedure Number 6: Test Write-offs During the Period

Audit procedure number 6: Test write-offs during the period. Write-offs are a valuation issue about the recoverability of long-lived assets. Many questions could be asked.

- Does the board of directors authorise assumptions by which the write-offs are calculated?
- Have these assumptions changed because of change in financial accounting standards?
- Are the projections management used to determine recoverability of assets reasonable and are they upgraded on a regular basis?
- Are the valuation methods used in the projections the same as those used in the financial statements?
- Is the allocation of overheads properly and consistently done?
- Is the recovery of goodwill amortised over a reasonable period of time?

■ A Look at Accounting Standards and Assumptions

You talk to management and read corporate minutes to see if the write-off assumptions are authorised. You find reference to update assumptions in an attachment to corporate minutes for the July meeting. The national accounting standards that apply to USATec require that research and development be charged to expenses in the year that it is paid. The national standards for accounting for MaasTec allow you to capitalise and amortise certain research and development costs, but the GAAP standards used by USATec, which require charging to expenses all research and development, must be applied to MaasTec, requiring that adjustments be made in the financial statements. You calculate these adjustments in your working papers and recommend MaasTec book them.

You review the projections to see if they use the same assumptions on amortisation as the financial statements and to see if the allocations are realistic. The same assumptions on amortisation are used in both projections and financial statements. You see that raw materials are projected as increasing in cost by only 10 per cent next year. You take a look at the financial statements and see that historically raw materials cost has been increasing at close to 15 per cent per year and this last year it increased by over 20 per cent. You look at the basic profit drivers, sales income and service income and determine that projections are unrealistic.

MaasTec management projects that goodwill paid for two subsidiaries three years ago should be amortised over another ten years. You note that the subsidiaries have lost money every year. You determine that the goodwill related to the purchase of these subsidiaries should be written off more quickly and you make a note in your working papers.

■ The End in Sight

You are sitting at your desk just staring out of the window. You look from the view of the motorway from your window back to the pile of work on your desk and then to the large picture on your office wall. Today is 15 January. The audit is almost over. You sent copies of the audit plan and strategy memorandum to BIG's US branch just last week. Now you have to perform the last procedures and prepare the last documents – the completion memorandum and the management letter.

The sun is setting over the motorway. You have work to do before it rises again.

13.14 Completion Memorandum

Illustration 13.11 shows the outline of the Completion Memorandum.

■ General

The first item in the completion memorandum is the statement that the engagement manager and partner have reviewed the audit papers related to critical areas. This is an essential procedure, because a review by the manager and the partner can uncover weak or incomplete areas of the audit which the audit staff might have overlooked or are not experienced enough to recognise as a problem.

The other important elements to discuss immediately are audit schedules, going concern considerations and your overall opinion on the work. You state in the completion memo that

ILLUSTRATION 13.11

Contents of Completion Memorandum

I. General
   A. Manager and partner review
   B. Schedules of MaasTec and FS
   C. Going concern
   D. Opinion

II. Critical audit areas
   A. Inventories
   B. Accounts receivable
   C. Revenue recognition
   D. Intercompany accounts
   E. Accounts payable

III. Accounting issues
   A. Accounting for Newco
   B. Accounting for Design by MaasTec
   C. Accounting for Finance Subsidiary (FS) by MaasTec
   D. Accounting for ZAP
   E. Foreign exchange
   F. Pension plan
   G. Post-retirement benefits
   H. Group structure

IV. Special audit problems

V. Other matters
   A. Illegal and questionable acts
   B. Management letter
   C. Summary of unadjusted audit differences
   D. Status of statutory financial statements

VI. Outstanding matters

VI. Attached schedules

schedules of MaasTec and FINE are audited in accordance with BIG's manual. MaasTec is a going concern, provided adjustments are made regarding recoverability of assets. Your audit opinion will be based upon the follow-up of subject matters like reorganisation cost, taxation and inventory and follow-up of the outstanding matters. You are aware of the fact that your audit opinion is of much importance for the group auditor in order for him to sign off on the consolidated financial statements. The group auditor is responsible for expressing an audit opinion on whether the group financial statements give a true and fair view (or are presented fairly, in all material respects) in accordance with the applicable financial reporting framework.

■ Critical Audit Areas

The areas you consider critical are discussed in the completion memorandum. Critical means with risk and significant areas.

Inventory and accounts receivable are reviewed. A full inventory take was done and the audit team was assured on test basis that the inventory was correctly counted. The team agreed the count sheets to the inventory sub-ledger and reconciled to the general ledger. The team used confirmation letters to test receivables. For outstanding invoices for non-respondents, they used alternative methods.

The collectability of the inter-company accounts was not tested for the audit for consolidation purposes. There were no confirmations by related parties. It is your opinion that further assurance from BIG's US branch is needed.

Accounts payable were tested with a confirmation process for main local suppliers. Other accounts payable procedures performed were cut-off test work, search for unrecorded liabilities on invoices and payments at year-end, test work on accrued expenses and analytical review on expenses. In your opinion accounts payable are understated by €300,000.

■ Accounting Issues

Accounting issues are broadly defined as accounting for Newco, for DIPPER by MaasTec, for Financial Investment National Enterprises (FINE) by MaasTec, and for ZAP. Other topics described in the completion memorandum are foreign exchange, pension plan and post-retirement benefits.

Sister Information Systems (SIS) entered into a share purchase and assignment agreement with Newco to purchase all existing shares of Newco. The purchase price of Newco was €6,000,000 payable in two semi-annual payments. Deferred payment for the purchase is €550,000. For MaasTec accruals, neither the deferred purchase price nor related payables are recorded. Deferred payments are capitalised as an investment rather than loan or receivable from SIS.

MaasTec's pension plan is a defined contribution plan. The enclosed statements disclose employees covered as a basis for contributions and the amount of cost recognised. The team reviewed the pension schedule.

■ Special Audit Problems: Financial Investment National Enterprises (FINE)

In this report, a special section is added on Financial Investment National Enterprises (FINE) because of audit problems with cash and cash equivalents, prepaid expenses and taxation.

Under a pledge agreement with the Oneandonly bank, USATec shall pledge to Oneandonly bank €3,530,000 in cash and securities. Forward Rate Notes (FRNs) of

€1,700,000 with maturity dates over three months are classified as short-term investments. Disclosure is according to the GAAP applicable to USATec.

■ Other Matters

Other matters are a round-up of miscellaneous matters including illegal and questionable acts, management letter, summary of **unadjusted audit differences** and the status of statutory financial statements.

Possible occurrence of illegal and questionable acts and fraud was evaluated by making inquiries of management about occurrence of illegal and questionable acts and status of any investigations by regulatory agencies. Management is in a position to be aware of these activities and no illegal or questionable acts occurred and no investigations are underway.

Enclosed is a draft of the management letter (see outline in Illustration 13.12). The audit team noted no material weaknesses. Unadjusted audit differences are stated in

---

ILLUSTRATION 13.12

Outline of Management Letter to MaasTec

I. Introduction

A Management Letter could have the following format:
- Finding
- Comment (e.g. short description of finding)
- Recommendation
- Management response
- Action (including timetable)

II. Material weaknesses in the design or operation of internal control

Typically BIG reports material weaknesses in writing, but an auditor may also report orally if they prepare minutes of the meetings. Material weaknesses are defined in laws and regulations as well as professional standards; therefore, their condition may have regulatory implications.

For MaasTec: No material weaknesses in internal control were found; therefore, this part of the report reviews the auditor's reliance on internal controls.

III. Other reportable conditions relating to internal control

Deficiencies in internal control, although not sufficiently important to be classified as material weaknesses, may be important. Management is informed of these deficiencies. For MaasTec: No copy of a notarised deed of transfer was found for the transaction between HO, Cousin and MaasTec. There were no confirmations by related parties. These details are discussed. Tests of purchases and deliveries show that more raw material inventory was purchased and delivered than was counted. We are reasonably certain that the count is correct. We suspect that the reduction in inventory was due to theft or wastage in the production process. The standard cost assumption for one machine is that the output hours less downtime would be 80,000 units. Machine costs are allocated to inventory based on this assumption. The auditor discovers the machine produces only 40,000 units. That utilisation loss should be expensed.

IV. Efficiency of internal control

Additional control activities can be recommended and the auditor may suggest that present control procedures are too complex. Improvements may be recommended through simplification and elimination of outdated policies and introduction of more cost effective procedures. For MaasTec: Internal control procedures are not too complex. They are reasonable.

▶

Illustration 13.12 (continued)

V. Prior year's suggestions

The auditor may inquire about actions taken on suggestions made in BIG's previous reports to management. Matters of continuing significance may be reported. For MaasTec had been audited in the prior year by BIG. The suggestions made at that time were carried out by MaasTec during the past year.

VI. Accounting and auditing matters

The auditor may comment on the accounting treatment adopted for some of the items in the financial statements, on foreseeable accounting changes and the implications.

For MaasTec: In the auditor's opinion accounts payable are understated by €300,000. New reorganisation announced after balance sheet date (a subsequent event). Based on discussion with management new reorganisation was a post balance sheet event and as a consequence no opinion is given on provision. Taxation expense is €6,357,000. A provision for these taxes is not recorded in MaasTec balance sheet because it applies to Sister company. We have no opinion on reasonableness of this change. There was no documentation on three payments to Newco of €117,000.

MaasTec management projects that goodwill paid for two subsidiaries three years ago should be amortised over another ten years. We note that the subsidiaries have lost money every year. We determine that the goodwill related to the purchase of these subsidiaries should be written off more quickly and you make a note in your working papers.

VII. Other matters arising during the audit

The auditor may comment on changes in significant accounting policies, accounting estimates, audit adjustments, and disagreements with management.

For MaasTec: MaasTec considers USATec's national currency to be its functional currency in terms of values and size. Gains and losses on hedged contracts for foreign currencies are charged to current year income. The discount on contracts is amortised over the life of the contract. Gain from long-term intercompany loans translation was charged directly to stockholders equity because they have a long-term financing nature. Loans due are from Bro, Sis and Cousin. Bro, Sis and Cousin are subsidiaries of MaasTec. There is no agreement with employees to pay post retirement benefits; therefore, MaasTec need not record a provision for post retirement benefits.

Different auditors than your own firm prepare two of the financial statements of the three controlled companies. Doiever, RA, is the auditor of Finance Subsidiary and Lickanapromise audited Design. BIG sent a questionnaire about the audit and a request for working papers to Doiever, RA, and to Lickanapromise.

MaasTec uses forward exchange contracts. To audit them the auditor reviews to see if accounting treatment is in line with the IAS 32 on financial instruments IAS and the national accounting standards of USATec. The investments meet the conditions to be considered hedges. Several international accounting standards apply to related parties; however, the Group Audit Instructions require that related parties be reported in accordance with USATec national accounting standards.

VIII. Other services consistent with role as an auditor

Work that goes beyond the audit plan, such as tax or management consulting work. For MaasTec: MaasTec has permanent tax differences to be carried forward in accordance with a contract between MaasTec and the national tax authorities. This requires disclosure and may lead to valuation problems. Our team consulted BIG's tax department and MaasTec's tax advisers who review the agreement and found no problems. Our team proposed a CIS review by BIG's CIS department because of the new finance system that has just been installed at MaasTec. It will be necessary to bring in CIS experts.

ILLUSTRATION 13.13

Summary of Unadjusted Audit Differences Found in the Audit

The following is a summary of unadjusted audit differences:

A. Cost assumption for machine 143 is that the output hours less downtime would be 80,000 units. Machine costs are allocated to inventory based on this assumption. The machine produces only 40,000 units. That utilisation loss should be expensed.

21 Dec 20XX	Utilisation Loss	120,000	
	Inventory		120,000

To record allocation of 40,000 excessive units to inventory.

B. In the auditor's opinion accounts payable are understated by €300,000.

21 Dec 20XX	Accounts Payable	300,000	
	Inventory		300,000

To reduce accounts payable by overstated amount.

C. Taxation expense, which has not been accrued, is €6,357,000. A provision for these taxes is not recorded in MaasTec balance sheet because it applies to Sister company.

21 Dec 20XX	Taxation Expense – MaasTec	5,000,000	
	Taxation Expense – Sister	1,357,000	
	Taxes Payable – MaasTec		5,000,000
	Taxes Payable – Sister		1,357,000

To record tax expense for 20XX.

D. There was no documentation on three payments to Newco of €117,000 each.

21 Dec 20XX	Interest Expense	351,000	
	Interest Payable		351,000

To record payments to Newco

Illustration 13.13. All differences were approved by the partner and discussed with management.

A copy of the financial statements is enclosed. The issue of statement is awaiting classification of ownership of Newco and group structure.

■ Outstanding Matters

There may be some matters that are still pending because of time limitations or other complications during an audit. The Completion Memorandum lists the following items necessary before the audit can be considered closed.

1 Receipt of forecast to ensure the appropriateness of book value of intangible assets.
2 Receipt of confirmations that accounts receivables are collectable.
3 Receipt of certain bank confirmations.
4 Receipt of documents supporting ownership of subsidiaries.
5 Receipt of financial statement of ZAP.

6 Receipt of management representation letter.

7 Receipt of lawyers' letters.

8 Receipt of confirmation by USATec firm that USATec has pledged $12,000,000 under agreement with Oneandonly bank.

■ Attached Schedules

Attached to the memorandum are the following schedules:

1 Summary of audit difference (see Illustration 13.13).

2 Elimination entries.

3 USATec balance sheet, income statement, other income (expense) schedule.

4 Financial statements in local currency (Euro) and USATec currency (USD).

5 Working papers.

6 Tax papers.

The completion memorandum is concluded with the signature of the auditor, the date and place of the signature.

The last sentence of the completion memorandum is finished. You put it in the out-basket for review by the partner. You look at the pile of papers on your desk, then at the view from the window. You see only a few sets of headlights going down the motorway this time of night. You drain the last drops of your cold coffee and put on your coat. It will be nice to get home.

13.15 Summary

ISA 600 deals with special considerations that apply to group audits, in particular those that involve component auditors. A component auditor is the auditor who, at the request of the group engagement team, performs work on the financial information related to a component. A component is an entity or business activity which financial information should be included in the group financial statements. Although component auditors may perform work on the financial information of the components and are responsible for their work, the group engagement partner is responsible for the direction, supervision and performance of the audit engagement and the auditor's report. The group engagement partner should be satisfied that those performing the group audit engagement, including component auditors, collectively have the appropriate competence and capabilities. The review of the overall group audit strategy and audit plan is an important part of fulfilling the group engagement partner's responsibility for the direction of the group audit engagement.

The group engagement partner must determine whether sufficient appropriate audit evidence can reasonably be expected to be obtained about the consolidation process and the financial information of the components. To do this, the group engagement team shall obtain an understanding of the group, its components and their environments to identify components that are likely to be significant. The group engagement partner must evaluate the component auditors who perform work on the financial information of the components to determine whether the group engagement team should also be involved in the work of those component auditors in order to obtain sufficient audit evidence.

The auditor is required to identify and assess the risk of material misstatements through obtaining an understanding of the entity and its environment. The group engagement team must enhance its understanding of the group auditee, its components and their environments, including group-wide controls obtained during the acceptance or continuance stage. The team must also obtain an understanding of the consolidation process, including the instructions issued by group management to components.

A component could be a head office, parent, division, location, business unit, branch, subsidiary, activity, shared service centre, joint venture, associated company, or other entity whose financial information is included in the group financial statements. Determining what is a component will require professional judgement and is guided by: the structure of the group, the flow of the financial information and the audit approach.

If the group engagement team plans to request a component auditor to perform work on the financial information of a component, the group engagement team must obtain an understanding of the following: whether the component auditor understands and will comply with ethical requirements and in particular, is independent; the component auditor's professional competence; whether the group engagement team will be able to be involved in the work of the component auditor; and whether the component auditor operates in a regulatory environment that actively oversees auditors.

The group engagement team shall determine the following: materiality for the group financial statements as a whole; materiality level of transactions, account balances or disclosures in the group financial statements for which misstatements of lesser amounts than materiality could be expected; the performance materiality; and component materiality for those components where component auditors will perform an audit for the group audit.

The work on the significant components is a key part of the work that has to be done. Where there are components that are not significant individually, but account for an important proportion of the group, it is necessary to obtain sufficient evidence about some of those 'not significant components' in order to have sufficient evidence on the group as a whole. The group engagement team's decision as to how many and which 'not significant components' to select and the type of work to be performed is affected by several factors.

The communication of the group auditor and component auditor and communications with group management and those charged with governance are very important. The group engagement team sets out the work to be performed, the use to be made of that work and the form and content of the communication with the group engagement team. In conformity with the ISA 600 standard the component auditor shall communicate certain matters relevant to the group engagement team's conclusion with regard to the group audit. The group engagement team shall determine which deficiencies in internal control shall be communicated with group management.

The group auditor is required to obtain an understanding of the consolidation process, including the instructions issued by group management to components. 'The consolidation process' includes: the recognition, measurement, presentation and disclosure of the financial information of the components in the group financial statements by way of consolidation, proportionate consolidation, or the equity or cost methods of accounting.

The group engagement team obtains an understanding of group-wide controls and the consolidation process, including the instructions issued by group management to components. If group-wide controls are operating effectively, or if substantive procedures alone cannot provide sufficient appropriate audit evidence, the group engagement team or the component auditor tests the operating effectiveness of the group-wide controls.

The group engagement partner shall evaluate the effect on the group audit opinion of any uncorrected misstatements and any instances where there has been an inability to obtain sufficient appropriate audit evidence. When the group audit opinion is modified because the group engagement team was unable to obtain sufficient appropriate audit evidence in relation to the financial information of one or more components, the auditor's report on the group financial statements describes the reasons for that without referring to the component auditor, unless such a reference is necessary for an adequate explanation of the circumstances.

The documents typically required in an audit of a subsidiary are a general audit plan with specific instructions and a general audit programme guide from the primary auditor. Based on these documents and additional inquiry, the auditor will put together an audit planning memorandum, an audit programme and a completion memorandum.

The parent company's auditors issue group audit instructions to participating offices. They may start with two opening sections – one with general information and one with specific procedures.

The strategy part of the audit planning memorandum may incorporate most of the important ideas of the audit. The whole audit team puts it together. The plan part of the audit planning memorandum will follow the concepts addressed in the strategy part and is a general outline of the auditors' approach to the audit.

The audit programme (audit plan) serves as a set of instructions to assistants involved in the audit and as a means to control proper execution of the work. It is commonly prepared based on the auditing firm's audit programme software.

The report on your auditing findings, the completion memorandum, describes critical and significant audit areas, accounting issues, and any matters that need to be highlighted. The completion memorandum, including the audit opinion, is the final document in the audit.

13.16 Questions, Exercises and Cases

QUESTIONS

13.2 Introduction

13-1 Define and discuss the terms 'component auditor', 'component' and 'group engagement partner'.

13.3 Acceptance and Continuance

13-2 What matters should and auditor consider concerning a new group audit client which can be obtained from group management.

13.4 Overall Audit Strategy and Audit Plan

13-3 What matters must be considered when understanding the group entity and its environment?

13-4 If the group engagement team plans to request a component auditor to perform work on the financial information of a component, what must the group engagement team understand about the component auditor?

13-5 What is meant by 'scope of an audit'? What are the considerations when determining the scope of the component audit.

13.5 Communication

13-6 What information must the group auditor communicate to the component auditor? What information must the component auditor communicate to the group auditor.

13.6 Consolidation

13-7 What should the group and component audit team understand about consolidation?

13.9 Documentation

13-8 In addition to documentation required by ISA 230 and other ISAs, the group engagement team must include what other matters in the audit documentation?

13.10 Extended Example of a Group Audit

13-9 Name the sections of the 'Group Audit Instructions' and describe each.

13-10 What kind of differences are there between the accounting for the main company (USATec) and your local client (MaasTec)?

13-11 What information are you required to provide about your client, MaasTec, regarding their legal situation, related parties and industry?

13-12 What concerns are 'Critical and Significant Audit Concerns' for the MaasTec audit? Why are they significant?

13.11 The Audit Planning Memorandum – Strategy Part

13-13 What is the purpose of the strategy memorandum? What are the elements contained in this memorandum?

13.12 The Audit Planning Memorandum – Plan Part

13-14 What is the plan part of the audit planning memorandum? What are the contents of the plan part?

13.13 Audit Programme (Audit Plan)

13-15 What are the objectives for MaasTec's investments audit procedures? Discuss the procedures used to test one of these objectives.

13-16 What may an auditor do if positive confirmations were not replied to on the second mailing?

13-17 When you as an auditor attend a physical count of inventory what things should you look for?

13-18 List the procedures for testing priced inventory listings.

13-19 What are the objectives when auditing an asset?

13.14 Completion Memorandum

13-20 What are the different areas in a completion memorandum? Briefly discuss each area.

13-21 What schedules do you attach to a completion memorandum?

PROBLEMS AND EXERCISES

13.3 Acceptance and Continuance

13-22 Newtight is a Japanese manufacturer of high technology adhesives traded on the Tokyo Nikkei stock exchange. The Kobe audit firm of Noda, Haider, and Itabashi, CPAs, is doing a group audit on the company.

Newtight has 14 subsidiaries located in 10 different countries. They own 100 per cent of four subsidiaries, 50 per cent of 5 and 10 per cent of the last five. The most important subsidiaries are Newtight USA in Compton, California, owned 100 per cent and Euro-Newtight of Brussels owned 10 per cent with the rest owned by the government of Belgium. They use service organisations for payroll and collection of receivables. The company has only three internal auditors for all their operations. Management believes they know everything that happens in the organisation and all important decisions are made by the CEO. There are no group-wide controls. Management believes that each component division will handle internals their own way. The accounts of the full company are consolidated one month after the end of the fiscal year by their accounting department. Currency exchange rates are determined by using the best rate for the prior year. One of the 50 per cent owned subsidiaries is located in Nigeria and another one is in Syria.

Management has warned the audit firm of Noda, Haider and Itabashi, CPAs, that they will have very limited access to top executives and the chief executive of each of the divisions to protect company industrial secrets.

Required:
Write a memo describing an understanding of Newtight based on important matters to be considered.

13.4 Overall Audit Strategy and Audit Plan

13-23 Describe a company that would have a high risk of material misstatement of the group financial statements. Make sure it reflects a complex group structure; poor corporate governance; ineffective group-wide controls; has components operating in foreign jurisdictions with for unusual governance intervention; and conducts business activities that involve high risk. The company should have unusual related party relationships and transactions, reconciliation issues and complex transactions. The group company and the component companies have important differences: the components' accounting policies differ from group policies and components with different financial year-ends. The board of directors encouraged aggressive tax planning and made frequent changes of auditors.

13-24 The Taipei, Taiwan, audit firm of Hung, Pan and Wu is being considered as a component auditor to audit the manufacturing component of Forever Teen clothing company, a Munich, Germany, based firm. Forever Teen's auditors are Claassen, Sohn, Schanz and Kupper, Wirtschaftsprufers (CSSK). What questions would CSSK ask of Hung, Pan and Wu to determine if they are qualified to be component auditors?

13-25 The Tel Aviv, Israel, firm of Levi, Bar-Hava, Kama and Segal, CPAs, are the auditors for ZoomZa Optical Devices, a manufacturer of high technology scopes and viewing devices. They have a manufacturing plant in Guangzhou, China, which will be audited by Rui, Li and Chen, CPAs. The group auditors Levi, Bar-Hava, Kama and Segal, CPAs consider the component manufacturing plant in Guangzhou as 'not significant' and wants to select and the type of work to be performed by Rui, Li and Chen. What considerations would affect the decisions of Levi, Bar-Hava, Kama and Segal, CPAs?

13.5 Communication

13-26 Sweetheart Junkyard, a Sao Paulo based worldwide online dating site for individuals who feel they have been unlucky in love, has hired Chiquento Da Silva, Aquino, Franco de Lima and Coda (CAFC) as their group auditor. CAFC proposes a financial statement audit of the Sweetheart Junkyard and the main subsidiaries SJ Euro and SJ USA. Three other subsidiaries – SJ China, SJ Asia and SJ South America – will get a review. CAFC will work with a different component auditor for each of the locations. The subsidiary SJ Asia audit by Wu and Wang, CPAs, was not up to the quality standards of CAFC because they offered no safeguards against self-interest and self-review threats. The group auditors, CAFC, will not do an internal control audit and will limit their management letter comments. There is a suspected employee fraud involving accounts payable at the SJ Euro location.

Required:
Write a communication to the board of directors explaining the audit of Sweetheart Junkyard.

13.6– 13.8 Consolidation, Subsequent Events, and Reporting

13-27 Siffre Industries of Port Elizabeth, South Africa, has several subsidiaries which are consolidated into the Siffre Industries financial statements. Empire Manufacturing is a manufacturing subsidiary that is one of the components that is being consolidated into Siffre's financial statement. Empire Manufacturing's largest customer, Turley Distributing, has gone bankrupt one month after the balance sheet date. Siffre is being audited by Van der Merwe, Coetzee and Schmulian (VCS).

Required:
A. Discuss the consolidation process.
B. Discuss how the work on subsequent events should be handled.
C. If Siffre refuses to revise their financial statements and disclosures because of the subsequent event, how will this affect the opinion of audit firm Van der Merwe, Coetzee and Schmulian?

13.10 Extended Example of a Group Audit

13-28 Parallell Medical Devices is a distributer of medical devises to large hospitals in South America based in Santiago Chile. Their auditor is Pena and Batistella, Contador Publicos. The audit based on International Financial Reporting Standards (IFRS) and International Standards on Auditing (ISA) is to be a financial statement audit due 30 March. A separate report is required for government medical regulators. All subsidiaries should have financial statements converted to the Chilean Peso (CLP). The completed package of audit material should be returned to Pena and Batistella, CPs, on 15 March. A completion memorandum in the standard form for Pena and Batistella is required. The completion memorandum should include key accounting issues, disagreements with management and outstanding matters. The audit could include a risk analysis of potential material weakness in internal control and our standard internal control questionnaires. A written representation of management (management letter) should be included in the returned material. A full description of any material differences between financial statements and audit tests is required. Provide any specific details of the client audited.

Required:

Using Illustration 13.5 and the material in this chapter write the 'General' and 'Specific Procedures' sections of the Group Audit Instructions.

13.11 The Audit Planning Memorandum – Strategy Part

13–29 Audit Planning Memorandum – Strategy Part. The following are three situations in which you are required to develop an audit strategy and prepare a partial strategy memorandum:

■ You are on the first year audit of Jaani, a medium-sized company of Parnu, Estonia, that is considering selling its business because of severe under-financing. A review of the acquisitions and payments indicates that controls over cash disbursements are excellent, but controls over acquisitions are not effective. The Jaani lacks shipping and receiving reports. They have no policy as to when to record acquisitions. When you review the general ledger, you observe that there are many large adjusting entries to correct accounts payable.

■ You are doing the audit of Lacplesis Bank, a small loan company in Latvia. It has extensive receivables from customers. Collections are an ongoing problem because many of the customers have severe financial problems resulting from adjustments to a capitalist economy. Because of these adverse economic conditions, loans receivable have significantly increased and collections are less than historical levels. Controls over granting loans, collections, and loans outstanding are considered effective. There is extensive follow-up weekly of all outstanding loans. In previous years, Lacplesis has had relatively few adjusting entries.

■ Cazadas Cooperative Vineyards with headquarters in Debreczen, Hungary, has inventory at approximately 40 locations in a two country region. The inventory can only be observed by travelling to the field locations by automobile. The internal controls over acquisitions, cash disbursements, and inventory perpetual records are considered effective. This is the sixth year that you have done the audit, and audit results in past years have always been excellent. The client is in excellent financial condition and is privately held.

Required:

For each of the three situations above:

A. Write a risk analysis of the main risks for the Strategy Memorandum.
B. Identify difficult questions you would address in the Strategy Memorandum.
C. List the techniques for gathering evidence (inquiry of client personnel, observation, examination of documents, re-performance, confirmation, analytical procedures and physical examination) you would use in the audit.

13.12 The Audit Planning Memorandum – Plan Part

13–30 Audit Planning Memorandum – Plan Part. Wigila Swaiaty, a for-profit cooperative, was organised in 1954 in Gdansk, Poland, to produce and distribute local crafts such as natural material Christmas decorations (82 per cent of sales), woodwork, folk art, sculpture and embroidery. Their sales by region are approximately 20 per cent Poland, 45 per cent Europe, 25 per cent North America and 10 per cent the rest of the world.

They sell directly to retailers in Poland and have a sales force of ten people. Outside of Poland they sell primarily to wholesalers of Christmas decorations. Their sales strategy is to increase sales of their non-Christmas decoration products overall and to increase sales to North America.

Wigila has one subsidiary company, Wigila BV (started in 1993) in Amsterdam, which is responsible for European sales. Wigila has a board of directors and an audit committee made up of outside directors. Both Gdansk and Amsterdam offices have the latest network hardware and software and Gdansk has a website. The computers run the most up-to-date versions of word processor, communications, accounting and financial software.

Wigila Swaiaty's Gadansk office has one employee who is responsible for legal matters and they use the services of a local solicitor firm Klodka & Waldemar. The company has six directors: Tom Miller, chairman and chief executive; Edward Miller, vice chairman; Doriusz Kaxzmarek and Marek Miller are directors who also work for Wigila as vice-president operations and chief executive officer of Wigila BV respectively. Outside directors are Paul Pollorz and Gregorz Locoski.

The market for their main product line, natural material Christmas decorations, is worldwide. Wigila's main competitor in Poland is Gwiazdka who has 60 per cent of the market versus Wigila's 30 per cent. Wigila market share and main competitors in their other sales area are: 11 per cent of North America, main competitor is You'lltyde with 26 per cent; 26 per cent of Europe, main competitor is Tauschung Tadesco with 14 per cent; and the rest of the world share is less than 1 per cent.

The industry has seen a rapid growth in computer usage to manage distribution and operations, but the manufacturing tools and techniques are hundreds of years old. Products are made by hand by individual craftsmen and collected by distributors such as Wigila. Unlike most distributors, Wigila is a cooperative. It is operated for profit and owned 50 per cent by the craftsmen who provide the products. There is pressure on the management to increase sales and the compensation of all executives is tied to increases in sales.

The craftsmen-owners of Wigila receive their wages based on a per-piece basis. For artfully made 'spheres' (the size of large apples and individually decorated) they may receive 10 per cent of the wholesale price the company charges customers. For sculpture, on the other hand, they may receive up to 40 per cent of the wholesale price. The craftsmen-owners wish the company to increase sales of non-Christmas decoration products as they have a higher profit margin for the craftsmen.

The auditor is Wieslaw Borowski, Auditor. The firm determines that one partner, one audit manager, three audit supervisors and 10 audit staff will require 1,000 hours audit time at Polish Zloty (zloty) 600 for partner hours, 400 for audit manager, 250 for supervisors and 150 for audit staff. Staff telephone and email numbers are provided in the Audit Plan.

A schedule of percentage of Revenues and Total Assets for Wigila Swaiaty and the subsidiary Wigila BV and the percentage of proposed audit scope is below.

Company	Revenues		Total Assets		Accts. Rec.		Scope of Audit
	Total	Audit	Total	Audit	Total	Audit	
Wigila S.	55	55	85	100	45	70	Full scope
Wigila BV	45	45	15	0	55	30	Limited

Required:
A. As part of the General Audit Plan, describe five audit procedures that you believe Wieslaw Borowski can perform in the accounts receivable and sales audit areas.
B. Describe what you believe will be the critical and significant auditing concerns in Borowski's General Audit Plan.

13.13 Audit Programme

13-31 Audit Programme. The following are eight audit procedures taken from an audit programme:

1 Review board of directors' minutes to verify approval of equipment purchases.
2 Review sales, cash receipts and sales returns cut-offs.
3 Examine the initials on vendors' invoices that indicate internal verification of pricing, extensions (price X units), and footing by a clerk.
4 Reconcile marketable security summary schedules to general ledger.
5 Compare the balance in payroll tax expense with previous years taking into consideration any changes in payroll tax rates.
6 Count a sample of inventory and check against inventory sheets.
7 Account for a sequence of cheques in the cash disbursements journal to determine whether any have been omitted.
8 Confirm accounts payable balances in writing with a sample of vendors.

Required:

A. For each of the above audit procedures, give the audit area (accounts receivable, cash, etc.), and an example of an audit objective and a financial statement assertion.
B. For each audit procedure, list a technique for gathering evidence used (inquiry of client personnel, inspection, observation, examination of documents, re-performance, confirmation, analytical procedures and physical examination.)

13-32 Audit Programme. A normal procedure in the audit of a corporate client consists of a careful reading of the minutes of meetings of the board of directors. One of the auditors' objectives in reading the minutes is to determine whether the transactions recorded in the accounting records are in agreement with actions approved by the board of directors.

Required:

A. What is the reasoning underlying this objective of reconciling transactions in the corporate accounting records with actions approved by the board of directors? Describe fully how the auditors achieve the stated objective after they have read the minutes of directors' meetings.
B. Discuss the effect that each of the following situations would have on specific audit steps in the auditors' examination and on the auditors' opinion:
   1 The minutes book does not show approval for the sale of an important manufacturing division that was consummated during the year.
   2 Some details of a contract negotiated during the year with the labour union are different from the outline of the contract included in the minutes of the board of directors.
   3 The minutes of a meeting of directors held after the balance sheet date have not yet been written, but the corporation's secretary shows the auditors notes from which the minutes are to be prepared when the secretary has time.
C. What corporate actions should be approved by stockholders and recorded in the minutes of the stockholders' meetings?

13-33 Audit of Investments. In connection with an examination of the financial statements of Moravia of Prague (Praha), the Czech Republic, Libusa Stadic, Auditor, is considering the necessity of inspecting marketable securities on the balance sheet date, 31 May, or at some other date. The marketable securities held by Moravia include negotiable bearer bonds, which are kept in a safe in the treasurer's office, and miscellaneous stocks and bonds kept in a safe-deposit box at Bohemia Bank. Both the negotiable bearer bonds and the miscellaneous stocks and bonds are material to proper presentation of Moravia's financial position.

Required:

A. What are the factors that Stadic should consider in determining the necessity for inspecting these securities on 31 May, as opposed to other dates?

B. Assume that Stadic plans to send a member of her staff to Moravia's offices and Bohemia Bank on 31 May to make the security inspection. What instructions should she give to this staff member as to the conduct of the inspection and the evidence to be included in the audit working papers? (Note: do not discuss the valuation of securities, the revenue from securities, or the examination of information contained in the accounting records of the company.)

C. Assume that Stadic finds it impracticable to send a member of her staff to Moravia's offices and Bohemia Bank on 31 May. What alternative procedures may she employ to assure herself that the company had physical possession of its marketable securities on May 31, if the securities are inspected on (1) 28 May? (2) 5 June?

13-34 Audit of Expense and Payables for Defalcations. On 11 January at the beginning of Elijah Domacin's annual audit of the financial statements for the year ended 31 December of Zedruga Manufacturing Company of Skoplje, Serbia, the Company president confides in Domacin that an employee is living on a scale in excess of that which his salary would support.

The employee has been a buyer in the purchasing department for six years and has charge of purchasing all general materials and supplies. He is authorised to sign purchase orders for amounts up to Yugoslavian New Dinar (New Dinar) 1,000. Purchase orders in excess of New Dinar 1,000 require the countersignature of the general purchasing agent.

The president understands that the usual examination of financial statements is not designed, and cannot be relied upon, to disclose fraud or conflicts of interest, although their discovery may result. The president authorises Domacin, however, to expand his regular audit procedures and to apply additional audit procedures to determine whether there is any evidence that the buyer has been misappropriating company funds or has been engaged in activities that involve a conflict of interests.

Required:

A. List the audit procedures that Domacin would apply to Zedruga's records and documents in an attempt to:

1 Discover evidence within the purchasing department of defalcations being committed by the buyer. Give the purpose of each audit procedure.

2 Provide leads as to possible collusion between the buyer and suppliers. Give the purpose of each audit procedure.

B. Assume that Domacin's investigation disclosed that some suppliers have been charging the Zedruga Manufacturing Company in excess of their usual prices and apparently have been making 'kick-backs' to the buyer. The excess charges are material in amount. What effect, if any, would the defalcation have upon:

1 the financial statements that were prepared before the defalcation was uncovered; and

2 Domacin's auditor's report? Discuss.

13-35 Confirmation of Accounts Receivables. You have been assigned to the first audit of the accounts of the Super Blinchiki Company of St Petersburg, Russia, for the year ending 31 March 20X8. The accounts receivable were confirmed 31 December 20X7, and at that date the receivables consisted of approximately 200 accounts with balances totalling Russian Roubles (Rouble) 956,750. Seventy-five of these accounts, with balances totalling Rouble 650,725, were selected for confirmation. All but 20 of the confirmation requests have been returned; 30 were signed without comments, 14 had minor differences that have been cleared satisfactorily, while 11 confirmations had the following comments:

1 'We are sorry but we cannot answer your request for confirmation of our account as we use an accounts payable voucher system.'
2 'The balance of Roubles 1,050 was paid on 23 December 20X7.'
3 'The above balance of Roubles 7,750 was paid on 5 January 20X8.'
4 'The above balance has been paid.'
5 'We do not owe you anything at 31 December 20X7, as the goods, represented by your invoice dated 30 December 20X7, number 25,050, in the amount of Roubles 11,550, were received on 5 January 20X8, on FOB destination terms.'
6 'An advance payment of Roubles 2,500 made by us in November 20X7 should cover the two invoices totalling Roubles 1,350 shown on the statement attached.'
7 'We never received these goods.'
8 'We are contesting the propriety of this Roubles 12,525 charge. We think the charge is excessive.'
9 'Amount okay. As the goods have been shipped to us on consignment we will remit payment upon selling the goods.'
10 'The Roubles 10,000 representing a deposit under a lease, will be applied against the rent due to us during 20X9, the last year of the lease.'
11 'Your credit dated 5 December 20X7, in the amount of Roubles 440 cancels the above balance.'

Required:
What steps would you take to clear satisfactorily each of the above 11 comments?

13-36 Audit of Inventory. Late in December, the Registeraccountant (RA) firm of Radbod & van Weg accepted an audit engagement at Brandewyn Juwelen, BV, a company that deals largely in diamonds. Brandewyn Juwelen has retail jewellery stores in several Netherlands cities and a diamond wholesale store in Amsterdam. The wholesale store also sets the diamonds in rings and other quality jewellery.

The retail stores place orders for diamond jewellery with the wholesale store in Amsterdam. A buyer employed by the wholesale store purchases diamonds in the Amsterdam diamond market; the wholesale store then fills orders from the retail stores and from independent customers and maintains a substantial inventory of diamonds. The corporation values its inventory by the specific identification cost method.

Required:
Assume that at the inventory date you are satisfied that Brandewyn Juwelen has no items left by customers for repair or sale on consignment and that no inventory owned by the corporation is in the possession of outsiders.

A. Discuss the problems the auditors should anticipate in planning for the observation of the physical inventory on this engagement because of the:
   1 different locations of inventories;
   2 nature of the inventory.

B. Assume that a shipment of diamond rings was in transit by corporation messenger from the wholesale store to a retail store on the inventory date. What additional audit steps would you take to satisfy yourself as to the gems that were in transit from the wholesale store on the inventory date?

13-37 Audit of Assets. Yarilo Company of Vinnista, Ukraine, owns and operates gas wells which are accounted for in three classifications:

1 *Producing* – for wells currently producing; there are engineers' estimates of the gas reserves. Each well is depleted on the basis of the gas produced as compared to its total reserve.

2   *Suspended* – although engineers' estimates indicate that these wells have considerable reserves of gas; they will not be operated until such time as additional production is required.

3   *Abandoned* – these wells either never produced commercially useful quantities of gas or the gas reserves have been used up.

The properties on which the wells are located are leased from the Russian and Ukraine governments at a specified annual rental, and payments are made until the well is abandoned. In addition, royalty payments are made at a specified rate, based on every 1,000 cubic feet of gas extracted from each well. The wells are recorded on the books at cost (including engineers' fees, materials and equipment purchased, labour, etc.), depleted only while producing, and written off when abandoned.

Required:

What procedures should the auditor follow to substantiate that all wells owned by the company are properly recorded, classified, and valued? What supporting evidence would the auditor examine in this connection?

13.14 Completion Memorandum

13-38 Completion Memorandum. In the course of his initial examination of the financial statements of Yenitscheri Company, Omar Pishdadian, Sworn Financial Advisor (SFA), the auditor, obtained an understanding of the internal control structure relating to the purchasing, receiving, trade accounts payable, and cash disbursement cycles and has decided not to proceed with any tests of controls. Based upon analytical procedures, Pishdadian believes that the trade accounts payable balance on the balance sheet as of 31 December 20X2 may be understated.

Pishdadian requested and obtained a client-prepared trade accounts payable schedule listing the total amount owed to each vendor. Pishdadian ascertains that of the substantial amount of accounts payable outstanding at the close of the period, approximately 75 per cent is owed to six creditors. Pishdadian has requested that he be permitted to confirm the balances owing to these six creditors by communicating with the creditors, but the president of the company is unwilling to approve Pishdadian's request on the grounds that correspondence in regard to the balances – all of which contain some overdue items – might give rise to demands on the part of the creditors for immediate payment of the overdue items and thereby embarrass Yenitscheri Company.

Accounts receivable represent a significant portion of the total assets of the company. At the beginning of the audit Pishdadian mailed out positive confirmations on a test basis. Included in his tests were confirmations requested from several Turkish government departments; the confirmation request for this one department was returned, along with the following notation: 'The Pishdadian confirmation letter is returned herewith without action because the type of information requested cannot be compiled by the office with sufficient accuracy to be of any value.'

Yenitscheri Company does not conduct a complete annual physical count of purchased parts and supplies in its principal warehouse, but uses statistical sampling instead to estimate the year-end inventory. Yenitscheri Company maintains a perpetual inventory record of parts and supplies and believes that statistical sampling is highly effective in determining inventory values and is sufficiently reliable to make a physical count of each item of inventory unnecessary.

Required:

When Pishdadian, SFA, writes up the Completion Memo:

A. What should he discuss in the 'Critical audit areas' and 'Significant Audit Areas' segments of the Memorandum?

B.   You are Pishdadian's senior auditor. He is running short of time and wants you to write the 'Accounting Issues' segment. Write the segment.

CASES

13-39 Audit of Investments. For several years you have made the annual audit for Sichou Jinhuangse Company of Nanjing, China. This company is not a dealer in securities. A list of presently held securities is kept, but an investment register is not maintained. During the audit, the following worksheet was prepared:

A Columns 1–7

Description of security (name, maturity, rate, etc.)	Balance at beginning of year	Face value or number of shares	Cost or book value additions during period	Date	Face value or number of shares	Cost deductions during period

B Columns 8–14

Date	Face value or number of shares	Cost or book value	Proceeds on disposals (net)	Profit or (loss) on disposals Balance at end of year	Face value or number of shares	Cost or book value

C Columns 15–20

Market value Interest and dividends	Accrued at beginning of year	Purchased	Earned	Received	Accrued at end of year	

Required:
Draw a line down the middle of a lined sheet of paper.
A.   On the left of the line, state the specific source(s) of information to be entered in each column and, where required, how the data of previous columns are combined.
B.   On the right of the line, state the principal way(s) that such information would be tested.

13.17 Notes

1 IAASB, 2012, International Standards on Auditing 600 (ISA 600) 'Special Considerations – Audits of Group Financial Statements (Including the Work of Component Auditors)', *Handbook of International Quality Control, Auditing, Review, Other Assurance, and Related Services Pronouncements*, 2012 edn, Volume 1, International Federation of Accountants, New York.

2 Group engagement partner – the partner or other person in the firm who is responsible for the group audit engagement and its performance, and for the auditor's report on the group financial statements that is issued on behalf of the firm. Where joint auditors conduct the group audit, the joint engagement partners and their engagement teams collectively constitute the group engagement partner and the group engagement team.

3 ISA 600 op. cit., para. A11.

4 ISA 600 op. cit., para. 19.

5 ISA 600 op. cit., para. 21.

6 This and the next two bullet points are consistent with ISA 320. IAASB, 2012, International Standards on Auditing 320 (ISA 320) 'Materiality in Planning and Performing an Audit', *Handbook of International Quality Control, Auditing, Review, Other Assurance, and Related Services Pronouncements*, 2012 edn, Volume 1, International Federation of Accountants, New York.

7 In a recent PhD thesis and article, Trevor Stewart introduces a model with which materiality for components (GUAM model) can be determined: Stewart, Trevor, 2013, 'A Bayesian Audit Assurance Model with Application to the Component Materiality Problem in Group Audits', PhD thesis, Vrije Universiteit Amsterdam; and 'Group Audits, Group-Level Controls, and Component Materiality: How Much Auditing Is Enough?', 2013, *Accounting Review*, March.

8 ISA 600 op. cit., para. 30.

9 ISA 600 op. cit., para. 41.

10 ISA 600 op. cit., para. 49.

11 ISA 600 op. cit., para. 17.

12 IAASB, 2012, International Standards on Auditing 705 (ISA 705) 'Modifications to the Opinion in the Independent Auditor's Report', *Handbook of International Quality Control, Auditing, Review, Other Assurance, and Related Services Pronouncements*, 2012 edn, Volume 1, International Federation of Accountants, New York.

13 IAASB, 2012, International Standards on Auditing 230 (ISA 230) 'Audit Documentation', paras 8–11 and A6, *Handbook of International Quality Control, Auditing, Review, Other Assurance, and Related Services Pronouncements*, 2012 edn, Volume 1, International Federation of Accountants, New York.

14 Ibid. ISA 600, para. 50.

15 When an auditor, acting as group auditor, decides to use the work of a related auditor or other auditor in the audit of group financial statements, the group auditor should communicate to the related auditors and other auditors to provide them with the group auditor's requirements. This communication is ordinarily in the form of Group Audit Instructions. More information on the requirements of the group auditor can be found in ISA 600.

16 Written representation – a written statement by management provided to the auditor to confirm certain matters or to support other audit evidence. Written representations in this context do not include financial statements, the assertions therein, or supporting books and records.

17 IAASB, 2012, International Standards on Auditing 240 (ISA 240) 'The Auditor's Responsibilities Relating to Fraud in an Audit of Financial Statements', *Handbook of International Quality Control, Auditing, Review, Other Assurance, and Related Services Pronouncements*, 2012 edn, Volume 1, International Federation of Accountants, New York.

18 IAASB, 2012, International Standards on Auditing 250 (ISA 250) 'Consideration of Laws and Regulations in an Audit of Financial Statements', *Handbook of International Quality Control,*

Auditing, Review, Other Assurance, and Related Services Pronouncements, 2012 edn, Volume 1, International Federation of Accountants, New York.

19 Benchmarking – the comparison of actual performance to a standard of typical competence developed by testing or a published standard.

20 Applicable independence requirements can be the IESBA Code of Ethics for Professional Accountants, or the United States Sarbanes–Oxley Act 2002.

Chapter 14

OTHER ASSURANCE AND NON-ASSURANCE ENGAGEMENTS

14.1 Learning Objectives

After studying this chapter, you should be able to:

1 Give the distinguishing characteristics of the special area reports.

2 Understand what distinguishes a review from a compilation.

3 Describe the key users of reports on prospective financial information.

4 Explain the requirements of internal control reporting standards.

5 Give the distinguishing characteristics of sustainability reports.

6 Define agreed-upon procedures and accounting compilation engagements.

14.2 Introduction

Auditor services are work that an audit firm performs for their clients. Except for consulting services, the work that auditors do for their clients falls under the guidance of engagement standards set by the International Auditing and Assurance Standards Board (IAASB). All auditor services have as their basis the *IESBA Code of Ethics* and *International Standards on Quality Control* (ISQC).

Some engagement standards are based on the 'International Framework for Assurance Engagements' (assurance engagements), and others fall under the 'Related Services Framework' (related services engagements). Three sets of standards (ISAs, ISREs and ISAEs) share the assurance engagement framework and one standard (ISRS) is based on the related services framework. ISAs, ISAEs, ISREs and ISRSs are collectively referred to as the IAASB's Engagement Standards (see Chapter 4, Illustration 4.1).

International Standards on Auditing (ISAs) describe the main concepts applicable to financial statement audit and special area engagements.

International Standards for Review Engagements (ISREs) are to be applied in the review of historical financial information. Two standards exist for review engagements: 2400 'Engagements to Review Financial Statements' and 2410 'Review of Interim Financial Information Performed by the Independent Auditor of the Entity'.

International Standards on Assurance Engagements (ISAE) 3000 'Assurance Engagements Other than Audits or Reviews of Historical Financial Information' describes concepts applicable to assurance services whose subject matter is not related to historical financial information. The ISAE standards are divided into two parts: (1) ISAEs 3000–3399, which are topics that apply to all assurance engagements; and (2) ISAEs 3400–3699, which are subject specific standards, for example standards relating to examination of prospective financial information and sustainability reporting.

Engagements covered by International Standards on Related Services (ISRSs) are based on the 'Related Services Framework'. Standards under this framework (ISRSs) are applied currently to two related services: agreed-upon procedures (ISRS 4400) and compilations (ISRS 4410).

■ Other Engagements Performed by Auditors

Not all engagements performed by auditors are assurance engagements. Other engagements frequently performed by auditors do not meet the definition of an assurance engagement and are therefore not covered by the framework for assurance engagements. They include:

- engagements covered by International Standards for Related Services (ISRSs);
- the preparation of tax returns where no assurance is expressed;
- consulting engagements such as tax consulting, or engagements in which a practitioner is engaged to testify as an expert witness in accounting, auditing, taxation or other matters, given stipulated facts.

14.3 Special Areas Engagements

Standard audit reports are based on the financial statements 'taken as a whole'. However, sometimes the auditor may have a request for a financial statement based on historical financial information, but which is not based on the financial statements as a whole or on IFRS or the requisite national accounting standard. Auditors refer to this type of work as examination of historical financial information, the prime example being special area engagements.

Auditors may examine historical financial information for special purpose reports. An auditor may be called upon to report on components of the financial statements, such as when a bank requests an audit of the accounts receivable (a component of the balance sheet) in anticipation of financing. Sometimes there are audits that give an opinion on compliance with legal agreements required of a company. For instance, a subcontractor may ask for an audit to give comfort to a main contractor. Management or the board of directors may request a summarised financial statement. Small businesses are generally not required to comply with IFRS or a national standard. Small businesses may want to have financial statements based on the cash basis, an income tax basis, or a basis required by regulatory agencies.

■ List of Special Areas Reports

The special areas engagements reports include any of the following:

1 Reports on Financial Statements Prepared in Accordance with the Special Purpose Framework (ISA 800), such as reports based on a tax basis of accounting, the cash receipts and disbursements basis of accounting, the financial reporting provisions established by a regulator or the financial reporting provisions of a contract.[1]
2 Reports on Audits of Single Financial Statements and Specific Elements, Accounts or Items of Financial Statement (ISA 805).
3 Reports on Summarised Financial Statements (ISA 810).

Reports on Financial Statements Prepared in Accordance with the Special Purpose Framework (ISA 800)

The Special Purpose Framework is a financial reporting framework designed to meet the financial information needs of specific users and relates to a complete set of special purpose financial statements, including related notes. The financial reporting framework may be a fair presentation framework or a compliance framework.[2]

Examples of special purpose frameworks are:

■ A tax basis of accounting for a set of financial statements that accompany an entity's tax return.
■ The cash receipts and disbursements basis of accounting for cash flow.
■ Information that an entity may be requested to prepare for creditors.
■ The financial reporting provisions established by a regulator to meet the requirements of that regulator.
■ The financial reporting provisions of a contract, such as a bond indenture, a loan agreement, or a project grant.[3]

The auditor's report on special purpose financial statements must describe the purpose for which the financial statements are prepared and, if necessary, the intended users, or refer to a note in the special purpose financial statements that contains that information. If management has a choice of financial reporting frameworks in the preparation of such financial statements, the report gives an explanation of management's responsibility for the financial statements and shall also make reference to management's responsibility for determining the financial reporting framework used is acceptable in the circumstances.

The auditor's report on special purpose financial statements shall include an emphasis of matter paragraph alerting users of the auditor's report that the financial statements are prepared in accordance with a special purpose framework and that, as a result, the financial statements may not be suitable for another purpose. The auditor shall include this paragraph under an appropriate heading.[4]

The auditor's report on financial statements prepared in accordance with the Special Purpose Framework should include a statement that indicates the basis of accounting used. The opinion paragraph of the report should state whether the financial statements are prepared, in all material respects, in accordance with the identified basis of accounting. Illustration 14.1 gives a sample report for financial reports prepared on provisions of a contract.[5]

ILLUSTRATION 14.1

Form of Examples of Reports on Financial Statements Prepared in Accordance with the Special Purpose Framework

---

INDEPENDENT AUDITOR'S REPORT

To: Appropriate addressee

We have audited the accompanying financial statements of Company XYZ, which comprise the balance sheet as at 31 December 20XX, and the profit and loss account for the year then ended and the notes comprising of a summary of accounting policies and other explanatory information. The financial statements have been prepared by management of XYZ based on Dutch fiscal accounting principles as included in Dutch Tax Law.

Management's Responsibility

Management is responsible for the preparation of these financial statements in accordance with the Dutch fiscal accounting policies as included in Dutch Tax Law. Furthermore, management is responsible for such internal control as it determines is necessary to enable the preparation of financial statements that are free from material misstatement, whether due to fraud or error.

Auditor's Responsibility

Our responsibility is to express an opinion on these financial statements based on our audit. We conducted our audit in accordance with International Standards on Auditing. Those standards require that we comply with ethical requirements and plan and perform the audit to obtain reasonable assurance about whether the financial statements are free from material misstatement.

An audit involves performing procedures to obtain audit evidence about the amounts and disclosures in the financial statements. The procedures selected depend on the auditor's judgment, including the assessment of the risks of material misstatement of the financial statements, whether due to fraud or error. In making those risk assessments, the auditor considers internal control relevant to the entity's preparation of the financial statements in order to design audit procedures that are appropriate in the circumstances, but not for the purpose of expressing an opinion on the effectiveness of the entity's internal control. An audit also includes evaluating the

Illustration 14.1 (continued)

appropriateness of accounting policies used and the reasonableness of accounting estimates made by management, as well as evaluating the overall presentation of the financial statements.

We believe that the audit evidence we have obtained is sufficient and appropriate to provide a basis for our audit opinion.

Opinion

In our opinion, the financial statements of XYZ for the year ended 31 December 20XX are prepared, in all material respects, in accordance with the Dutch fiscal accounting policies as included in Dutch Tax Law.

Basis of accounting and restriction on distribution and use

Without modifying our opinion we draw attention to note X to the financial statements, which describes the special purpose of the statements including the basis of accounting. The financial statements are intended solely for .... and are prepared to assist XYZ to comply with the Tax Law). As a result, the financial statements may not be suitable for another purpose. Therefore, our auditor's report is intended solely for XYZ and the Dutch Tax Authorities and should not be distributed to or used by other parties than XYZ and the Dutch Tax Authorities.

Place, date,

... (Name Audit firm)
... (Name auditor)

Reports on Audits of Single Financial Statements and Specific Elements, Accounts or Items of a Financial Statement (ISA 805)

The auditor may be requested to express an opinion on one or more elements of financial statements (for example, accounts receivable, inventory, an employee's bonus calculation, or a provision for income taxes). This type of engagement may be done as a separate engagement or in conjunction with an audit of the entity's financial statements. However, this type of engagement does not result in a report on the financial statements taken as a whole and, accordingly, the auditor would express an opinion only as to whether that specific element audited is prepared in accordance with the accounting standards.

The auditor's report on an element of financial statements should include a statement that indicates what the basis of accounting is for the element is presented or refers to an agreement that specifies the basis.

The opinion should state whether the element is prepared, in all material respects, in accordance with the identified basis of accounting. Illustration 14.2 gives an example of a report on a specific element: a schedule of the liability for 'incurred but not reported' claims in an insurance portfolio.[6]

When an adverse opinion or disclaimer of opinion on the entire financial statements has been expressed, the auditor should report on elements of the financial statements only if those elements are not so extensive as to constitute a major portion of the financial statements. To do otherwise may overshadow the report on the entire financial statements.

ILLUSTRATION 14.2

Report on an Element of a Financial Statement – Schedule of the Liability for 'Incurred but not Reported' Claims in an Insurance Portfolio

Independent Auditor's Report

[Appropriate Addressee]

We have audited the accompanying schedule of the liability for 'incurred but not reported' claims of ABC Insurance Company as at 31 December 20X1 ('the schedule'). The schedule has been prepared by management based on [describe the financial reporting provisions established by the regulator].

Management's Responsibility for the Schedule

Management is responsible for the preparation of the schedule in accordance with [describe the financial reporting provisions established by the regulator], and for such internal control as management determines is necessary to enable the preparation of the schedule that is free from material misstatement, whether due to fraud or error.

Auditor's Responsibility

Our responsibility is to express an opinion on the schedule based on our audit. We conducted our audit in accordance with International Standards on Auditing. Those standards require that we comply with ethical requirements and plan and perform the audit to obtain reasonable assurance about whether the schedule is free from material misstatement.

An audit involves performing procedures to obtain audit evidence about the amounts and disclosures in the schedule. The procedures selected depend on the auditor's judgement, including the assessment of the risks of material misstatement of the schedule, whether due to fraud or error. In making those risk assessments, the auditor considers internal control relevant to the entity's preparation of the schedule in order to design audit procedures that are appropriate in the circumstances, but not for the purpose of expressing an opinion on the effectiveness of the entity's internal control.

An audit also includes evaluating the appropriateness of accounting policies used and the reasonableness of accounting estimates made by management, as well as evaluating the overall presentation of the schedule. We believe that the audit evidence we have obtained is sufficient and appropriate to provide a basis for our audit opinion.

Opinion

In our opinion, the financial information in the schedule of the liability for 'incurred but not reported' claims of ABC Insurance Company as at 31 December 20X1 is prepared, in all material respects, in accordance with [describe the financial reporting provisions established by the regulator].

Basis of Accounting and Restriction on Distribution

Without modifying our opinion, we draw attention to Note X to the schedule, which describes the basis of accounting. The schedule is prepared to assist ABC Insurance Company to meet the requirements of Regulator DEF. As a result, the schedule may not be suitable for another purpose. Our report is intended solely for ABC Insurance Company and Regulator DEF and should not be distributed to parties other than ABC Insurance Company or Regulator DEF.

[Date of the auditor's report]   [Auditor's signature]

[Auditor's address]

Reports on Summarised Financial Statements (ISA 810)

Some financial statement users may only be interested in the highlights of a company's financial position. Therefore, a company may only require statements summarising its annual audited financial statements. An auditor should only take an engagement to report on summarised financial statements if he has expressed an audit opinion on the financial statements from which the summary is made.

Summarised financial statements are much less detailed than annual audited financial statements. Therefore, the summarised nature of the information reported needs to be clearly indicated. The report must caution the reader that summarised financial statements should be read in conjunction with the company's most recent audited financial statements.

What sets the summarised financial statements apart from the other reports in this section is that they include the elements (c) through (e) below. The following are the basic elements in the report on summarised statements:

(a) A title clearly indicating it as the report of an independent auditor.
(b) An addressee.
(c) An introductory paragraph that:
    (i)   identifies the summary financial statements on which the auditor is reporting;
    (ii) identifies the audited financial statements;
    (iii) refers to the auditor's report on the audited financial statements, the date of that report, and the fact that an unmodified opinion is expressed on the audited financial statements;
    (iv) if the date of the auditor's report on the summary financial statements is later than the date of the auditor's report on the audited financial statements, states that the summary financial statements and the audited financial statements do not reflect the effects of events that occurred subsequent to the date of the auditor's report on the audited financial statements; and
    (v) a statement indicating that the summary financial statements do not contain all the disclosures required by the financial reporting framework applied in the preparation of the audited financial statements, and that reading the summary financial statements is not a substitute for reading the audited financial statements.
(d) A description of management's responsibility for the summary financial statements, explaining that management is responsible for the preparation of the summary financial statements in accordance with the applied criteria.
(e) A statement that the auditor is responsible for expressing an opinion on the summary financial statements based on the procedures required by this ISA.
(f) A paragraph clearly expressing an opinion.
(g) The auditor's signature.
(h) The date of the auditor's report.
(i) The auditor's address.[7]

Illustration 14.3 gives an example of an auditor's reports on summarised financial statements when an unmodified opinion has been expressed on the company's annual financial statements.[8] The auditor's report on the summary financial statements is dated later than the date of the auditor's report on the financial statements from which summary financial statements are derived.

ILLUSTRATION 14.3

Report on Summarised Financial Statements When an Unmodified Opinion Was Expressed on the Annual Audited Financial Statements

Report of the Independent Auditor on the Summary Financial Statements

[Appropriate Addressee]

The accompanying summary financial statements, which comprise the summary balance sheet as at 31 December 20X1, the summary income statement, summary statement of changes in equity and summary cash flow statement for the year then ended, and related notes, are derived from the audited financial statements of ABC Company for the year ended 31 December 20X1. We expressed an unmodified audit opinion on those financial statements in our report dated 15 February 20X2. Those financial statements, and the summary financial statements, do not reflect the effects of events that occurred subsequent to the date of our report on those financial statements.

The summary financial statements do not contain all the disclosures required by [describe financial reporting framework applied in the preparation of the audited financial statements of ABC Company]. Reading the summary financial statements, therefore, is not a substitute for reading the audited financial statements of ABC Company.

Management's Responsibility for the Summary Financial Statements

Management is responsible for the preparation of a summary of the audited financial statements in accordance with [describe established criteria].

Auditor's Responsibility

Our responsibility is to express an opinion on the summary financial statements based on our procedures, which were conducted in accordance with International Standard on Auditing (ISA) 810 Engagements to Report on Summary Financial Statements.

Opinion

In our opinion, the summary financial statements derived from the audited financial statements of ABC Company for the year ended 31 December 20X1 are consistent, in all material respects, with (or a fair summary of) those financial statements, in accordance with [describe established criteria].

[Date of the auditor's report]   [Auditor's signature]

[Auditor's address]

14.4 Review Engagements

■ Engagements to Audit Financial Statements

The objective of an audit of financial statements is to enable the auditor to express an opinion whether the financial statements are prepared, in all material respects, in accordance with an identified financial reporting framework. The expression of a conclusion by an auditor is designed to enhance the degree of confidence intended users can have about historical financial statements. Audit engagements standards include ISA200 to ISA 299. The rest of this book is about historical financial statement audit engagements, so these will not be discussed here.

■ Engagements to Review Financial Statements (ISRE 2000–2699)

A review of financial statements is similar to an audit of financial statements in the way it requires terms of an engagement, planning, consideration of work performed by others, documentation, and paying attention to subsequent events.[9] These concerns are discussed throughout this book, especially Chapter 5 on client acceptance, Chapter 6 on planning, Appendix 10 on audit documentation and working papers and Chapter 11 which considers completing the audit. Where reviews of financial statements differ most from a financial statement audit is that in a review report engagement only limited procedures are performed (primarily inquiry of management and analytical procedures).

The objective of a review of financial statements is to enable an auditor to state (based on procedures that are not as extensive as would be required in a full financial statement audit) 'nothing has come to the auditor's attention that causes the auditor to believe that the financial statements do not give a true and fair view (or are not presented fairly, in all material respects) in accordance with [an identified financial reporting framework].' This way of expressing an opinion is called negative assurance.

Limited Audit Procedures

Sufficient appropriate evidence for a financial statement review is limited to inquiry, analytical procedures, limited inspection and, in certain cases only, additional evidence gathering procedures. Inquiry consists of seeking information of knowledgeable persons inside or outside the entity. Analytical procedures (discussed in Chapter 8) consist of the analysis of significant ratios and trends including the resulting investigation of fluctuations and relationships that are inconsistent with other relevant information or deviate from predictable amounts. Inspection (discussed in Chapter 10), which consists of examining records, documents, or tangible assets, is carried out on a limited basis.

A review engagement, unlike a full financial statement audit, usually does not involve collecting evidence about the design and operation of internal control, or obtaining evidence to back up the findings from inquiries or analytical procedures (i.e. corroborating evidence). Review engagements do not employ the evidence gathering techniques used in a financial statement audit such as observation, confirmation, recalculation, re-performance or extensive inspection.

Review Report of Financial Statements

The report on a review of financial statements should contain the following basic elements, ordinarily in the following layout[10] (see Illustration 14.4 for a sample unqualified review report):[11]

(a) Title.
(b) Addressee.
(c) Opening or introductory paragraph including:
  (i) identification of the financial statements on which the review has been performed; and
  (ii) a statement of the responsibility of the entity's management and the responsibility of the auditor.
(d) Scope paragraph, describing the nature of a review, including:
  (i) a reference to this ISRE applicable to review engagements, or to relevant national standards or practices;

ILLUSTRATION 14.4

Form of Unqualified Review Report

Review Report to ...

We have reviewed the accompanying balance sheet of ABC Company at 31 December 19XX, and the income statement, statement of changes in equity and cash flow statement for the year then ended. These financial statements are the responsibility of the Company's management. Our responsibility is to issue a report on these financial statements based on our review.

We conducted our review in accordance with the International Standard on Review Engagements 2400 (or refer to relevant national standards or practices applicable to review engagements). This Standard requires that we plan and perform the review to obtain moderate assurance as to whether the financial statements are free of material misstatement. A review is limited primarily to inquiries of company personnel and analytical procedures applied to financial data and thus provides less assurance than an audit. We have not performed an audit and, accordingly, we do not express an audit opinion.

Based on our review, nothing has come to our attention that causes us to believe that the accompanying financial statements do not give a true and fair view (or are not presented fairly, in all material respects) in accordance with International Accounting Standards.

[Date]   [Practitioner]

[Address]

(ii) a statement that a review is limited primarily to inquiries and analytical procedures; and

(iii) a statement that an audit has not been performed, that the procedures undertaken provide less assurance than an audit, and that an audit opinion is not expressed.

(e) Statement of negative assurance.

(f) Date of the report.

(g) Practitioner's address.

(h) Practitioner's signature.

Review Conclusion

The review conclusion will be either an **unqualified, qualified** or **adverse opinion**. The unqualified opinion offers negative assurance, as we have discussed. If matters that impair a true and fair view in accordance with the identified financial reporting framework have come to the auditor's attention, the auditor may express a **qualification** of the negative assurance provided; or give an adverse opinion. When the effect of the matter is so material and pervasive to the financial statements that a qualification is not adequate an adverse statement states that the financial statements do not give a true and fair view (or 'are not presented fairly, in all material respects') in accordance with the identified financial reporting framework.

The auditor should date the review report as of the date the review is completed, which includes performing procedures relating to events occurring up to the date of the report. However, the auditor should not date the review report earlier than the date on which the financial statements were approved by management.

14.5 Assurance Engagements Other Than Audits or Reviews of Historical Financial Information (ISAE 3000–3699)

The International Standard on Assurance Engagements (ISAE) establishes basic principles and essential procedures for professional accountants in public practice for the performance of assurance engagements on subject matters other than historical financial information. Examples of engagements other than historical financial information can be internal control reporting, sustainability reporting and engagements regarding prospective financial information.

The standards regarding assurance engagements other than historical financial information have two main components:

1 topics that apply to all assurance engagements (ISAEs 3000–3399); and
2 subject specific standards (ISAEs 3400–3699).

■ Topics that Apply to All Assurance Engagements (ISAEs 3000–3399)

Several things must be considered when providing assurance services other than audit or review of historical financial information. Some of the considerations are similar to those of a financial statement audit including ethics, quality control, terms of engagement, planning, materiality, using the work of an expert, subsequent events, and documentation. These topics are discussed throughout this book. The primary considerations of an assurance report that differ from an audit of financial statements are the choice in level of assurance, engagement acceptance, subject matter and reporting.

Currently standard ISAE 3000 is the only standard that applies to all subject matters (ISAEs 3000–3399). This standard establishes a framework for assurance engagements other than audits or reviews of historical financial information. Additional standards will be added by the IAASB as needed.

■ Reasonable and limited Assurance Engagements

The ISAEs permit the auditor to perform two types of assurance engagements: 'reasonable assurance engagements' and 'limited assurance engagements'.

The objective of a reasonable assurance engagement is a reduction in assurance engagement risk to an acceptably low level in the circumstances of the engagement as the basis for a positive form of expression of the practitioner's conclusion.

The objective of a limited assurance engagement is a reduction in assurance engagement risk to a level that is acceptable in the circumstances of the engagement, but where that risk is greater than for a reasonable assurance engagement, as the basis for a negative form of expression of the practitioner's conclusion.[12] See also Chapter 4 for the differences between reasonable and limited assurance engagements.

■ Engagement Acceptance

As under the ISAEs assurance can be provided regarding a wide range of subject matters, an adequate engagements acceptance process is essential. At the phase of engagement acceptance the auditor should be verify that all five elements of an assurance engagements[13] can be applied to the specific engagement, before signing an engagement letter.

When the client requests the auditor to change the engagement to a non-assurance engagement or from a reasonable assurance engagement to a limited assurance engagement, the auditor should not agree to a change without reasonable justification. A change in circumstances that affects the intended users' requirements, or a misunderstanding concerning the nature of the engagement, ordinarily will justify a request for a change in the engagement. If such a change is made, the auditor does not disregard evidence that was obtained prior to the change.[14]

■ Assurance Report Regarding ISAE Engagements

The assurance report should contain the following basic elements, ordinarily in the following layout:[15]

(a) Title.
(b) Addressee.
(c) Identification and description of the subject matter information.
(d) Identification of the criteria.
(e) Where appropriate, a description of any significant, inherent limitation associated with the evaluation or measurement of the subject matter against the criteria.
(f) When the criteria used to evaluate or measure the subject matter are available only to specific intended users, or are relevant only to a specific purpose, a statement restricting the use of the assurance report to those intended users or that purpose.
(g) A statement to identify the responsible party and to describe the responsible party's and the practitioner's responsibilities.
(h) A statement that the engagement was performed in accordance with ISAEs.
(i) A summary of the work performed.
(j) The practitioner's conclusion.
(k) The assurance report date.
(l) The name of the firm or the practitioner, and a specific location.

Although currently not mentioned in ISAE 3000, the report will also contain the practitioner's signature.

■ Subject Specific Standards (ISAEs 3400–3699)

The ISAEs can cover a wide range of non-historical financial subject matters, like prospective financial information, corporate governance, internal controls and sustainability. The subject matter currently covered by IAASB's pronouncements are:

■ ISAE 3400 'The Examination of Prospective Financial Information';
■ ISAE 3402 'Assurance Reports on Controls at a Service Organisation';
■ ISAE 3410 'Assurance Engagements on Greenhouse Gas Statements';
■ ISAE 3420 'Assurance Engagements to Report on the Compilation of Pro Forma Financial Information Included in a Prospectus'.

■ Example Existing Standards Other Than IAASB Used in an Assurance Engagement

Examples of existing standards that may be considered in systems and processes, non-financial information, or behaviour assurance engagements are:

- Sarbanes–Oxley Section 404 internal control audit standard;[16]
- Global Reporting Initiative (GRI) *Sustainability Reporting Guidelines*;[17]
- SA8000 standards for social accountability towards employees.[18]

In this section we will discuss the ISAE-subject specific standards. We will also discuss the Sarbanes–Oxley internal control audit standard and the GRI *Sustainability Reporting Guidelines*, as these are the most influential non-IAASB standards currently.

The Examination of Prospective Financial Information (ISAE 3400)

'Prospective financial information' means financial information based on assumptions about events that may occur in the future. Prospective financial information can be in the form of a forecast, a projection or a combination of both. A 'forecast' is prospective financial information prepared on the basis of management's assumptions as to future events (best-estimate assumptions). A 'projection' means prospective financial information prepared on the basis of hypothetical assumptions about future events and management actions which may or may not take place, such as a possible merger of two companies. A projection is a 'what-if' scenario.

A report on an examination of prospective financial information may take several forms. It may be a prospectus to provide potential investors with information about future expectations. The report may take the form of an annual report to provide information to shareholders, regulatory bodies, and other interested parties. It might be a report to lenders of cash flow forecasts.

Prospective Financial Information Offers Moderate Level of Assurance

Reporting on prospective financial information is highly subjective. Prospective financial information relates to events and actions that have not yet occurred and may not occur. While evidence may be available to support the assumptions, the evidence is future oriented and, therefore, speculative in nature. This means that this evidence does not offer the same level of assurance as historical financial information. The auditor is, therefore, not in a position to express an opinion as to whether the results shown in the prospective financial information will be achieved.

Given the types of evidence available, it may be difficult for the auditor to obtain a level of satisfaction sufficient to provide a positive expression of opinion. The auditor can generally only provide a moderate level of assurance.

Report on Examination of Prospective Financial Information

The report by an auditor on an examination of prospective financial information differs from the reports on historical financial information in that it contains the following:[19]

- identification of the prospective financial information;
- a statement that management is responsible for the prospective financial information including the assumptions on which it is based;
- when applicable, a reference to the purpose and/or restricted distribution of the prospective financial information;
- a statement of negative assurance as to whether the assumptions provide a reasonable basis for the prospective financial information;
- an opinion as to whether the prospective financial information is properly prepared on the basis of the assumptions and is presented in accordance with the relevant financial reporting framework;

■ appropriate caveats concerning the achievability of the results indicated by the prospective financial information.

The warnings in the report on prospective financial statements should be clear. They would state that actual results are likely to be different from the prospective financial information since anticipated events frequently do not occur as expected and the variation could be material. In the case of a projection, the caveat would be that 'the prospective financial information has been prepared for [state purpose], using a set of assumptions that include hypothetical assumptions about future events and management's actions that are not necessarily expected to occur.'

Illustration 14.5 shows examples of extracts from both an unmodified report on a forecast and unmodified report on a projection.[20]

■ Internal Controls Over Financial Reporting Assurance Engagements

Currently various standards for internal control reporting exist. Most common is reporting according to SOX 404, which is required for all companies that trade on the stock exchanges in the USA including companies headquartered outside the USA. For listed companies in Japan Japanese-SOX is applicable. As of June 2011 the IAASB standard ISAE 3402 'Assurance Reports on Controls at a Service Organisation' is effective, which set standards for auditing internal controls of service organisations. As SOX is most common worldwide, we focus on SOX as an example of Internal Control Reporting. Further we discuss ISAE 3402

SOX 404 Reporting

The Sarbanes–Oxley Act of 2002 (SOX) requires certification of internal control by the Chief Executive Officer (CEO) and Chief Financial Officer (CFO) of all companies that trade on the stock exchanges in the USA including companies headquartered outside the USA. SOX also requires that the company's auditor give an opinion on management's report on internal control.

The rules on internal control reporting published by the SEC[21] require a company's annual report to include an internal control report of management that contains:[22]

■ A statement of management's responsibility for establishing and maintaining adequate internal control over financial reporting for the company.
■ A statement identifying the framework used by management to evaluate the effectiveness of the company's internal control over financial reporting.
■ Management's assessment of the effectiveness of the company's internal control over financial reporting, including a statement as to whether or not the company's internal control over financial reporting is effective.[23] The assessment must include disclosure of any 'material weaknesses'[24] in the company's internal control over financial reporting identified by management.
■ A statement that the registered public accounting firm that audited the financial statements included in the annual report has issued an attestation report on management's assessment of the registrant's internal control over financial reporting.[25]

Standards for Preparation and Issuance of Audit Reports

The US Public Company Accounting Oversight Board (PCAOB) established an internal control audit standard (Audit Standard 5)[26] required by US publicly traded companies. The PCAOB rules require that public accounting firms describe in the audit report the

ILLUSTRATION 14.5

Prospective Financial Report Examples

(A) Extract from an Unmodified Report on a Forecast

Auditor's Report to ...

We have examined the forecast in accordance with International Standards on Auditing applicable to the examination of prospective financial information. Management is responsible for the forecast including the assumptions set out in Note X on which it is based.

Based on our examination of the evidence supporting the assumptions, nothing has come to our attention that causes us to believe that these assumptions do not provide a reasonable basis for the forecast. Further, in our opinion the forecast is properly prepared on the basis of the assumptions and is presented in accordance with [name of standard].

Actual results are likely to be different from the forecast since anticipated events frequently do not occur as expected and the variation may be material.

[Date]   [Auditor]

[Address]

(B) Extract from an Unmodified Report on a Projection

Auditor's Report to ...

We have examined the projection in accordance with International Standards on Auditing applicable to the examination of prospective financial information. Management is responsible for the projection including the assumptions set out in Note X on which it is based.

This projection has been prepared for (describe purpose). As the entity is in a start-up phase the projection has been prepared using a set of assumptions that include hypothetical assumptions about future events and management's actions that are not necessarily expected to occur. Consequently, readers are cautioned that this projection may not be appropriate for purposes other than that described above.

Based on our examination of the evidence supporting the assumptions, nothing has come to our attention that causes us to believe that these assumptions do not provide a reasonable basis for the projection, assuming that (state or refer to the hypothetical assumptions). Further, in our opinion the projection is properly prepared on the basis of the assumptions and is presented in accordance with [standards].

Even if the events anticipated under the hypothetical assumptions described above occur, actual results are still likely to be different from the projection since other anticipated events frequently do not occur as expected and the variation may be material.

[Date]   [Auditor]

[Address]

scope of its testing of the company's internal control structure and procedures performed in its internal control evaluation under SOX Section 404(b). In the audit report, the registered public accounting firm also must describe, at a minimum, material weaknesses in company internal controls and any material noncompliance found.[27] See Illustration 14.6 for a sample auditor's opinion on internal control.[28]

ILLUSTRATION 14.6

Illustrative Report Expressing an Unqualified Opinion on Internal Control over Financial Reporting (Separate Report)

Report of Independent Registered Public Accounting Firm

[Introductory paragraph]

We have audited the accompanying balance sheets of W Company as of 31 December 20X8 and 20X7, and the related statements of income, stockholders' equity and comprehensive income, and cash flows for each of the years in the three-year period ended 31 December 20X8. We also have audited W Company's internal control over financial reporting as of 31 December 20X8, based on [identify control criteria, for example 'criteria established in *Internal Control – Integrated Framework issued by the Committee of Sponsoring Organizations of the Treadway Commission (COSO)*']. W Company's management is responsible for these financial statements, for maintaining effective internal control over financial reporting, and for its assessment of the effectiveness of internal control over financial reporting, included in the accompanying [title of management's report]. Our responsibility is to express an opinion on these financial statements and an opinion on the company's internal control over financial reporting based on our audits.

[Scope paragraph]

We conducted our audits in accordance with the standards of the Public Company Accounting Oversight Board (United States). Those standards require that we plan and perform the audits to obtain reasonable assurance about whether the financial statements are free of material misstatement and whether effective internal control over financial reporting was maintained in all material respects. Our audits of the financial statements included examining, on a test basis, evidence supporting the amounts and disclosures in the financial statements, assessing the accounting principles used and significant estimates made by management, and evaluating the overall financial statement presentation. Our audit of internal control over financial reporting included obtaining an understanding of internal control over financial reporting, assessing the risk that a material weakness exists, and testing and evaluating the design and operating effectiveness of internal control based on the assessed risk. Our audits also included performing such other procedures as we considered necessary in the circumstances. We believe that our audits provide a reasonable basis for our opinions.

[Definition paragraph]

A company's internal control over financial reporting is a process designed to provide reasonable assurance regarding the reliability of financial reporting and the preparation of financial statements for external purposes in accordance with generally accepted accounting principles. A company's internal control over financial reporting includes those policies and procedures that (1) pertain to the maintenance of records that, in reasonable detail, accurately and fairly reflect the transactions and dispositions of the assets of the company; (2) provide reasonable assurance that transactions are recorded as necessary to permit preparation of financial statements in accordance with generally accepted accounting principles, and that receipts and expenditures of the company are being made only in accordance with authorizations of management and directors of the company; and (3) provide reasonable assurance regarding prevention or timely detection of unauthorized acquisition, use, or disposition of the company's assets that could have a material effect on the financial statements.

[Inherent limitations paragraph]

Because of its inherent limitations, internal control over financial reporting may not prevent or detect misstatements. Also, projections of any evaluation of effectiveness to future periods are subject to the risk that controls may become inadequate because of changes in conditions, or that the degree of compliance with the policies or procedures may deteriorate.

[Opinion paragraph]

In our opinion, the financial statements referred to above present fairly, in all material respects, the financial position of W Company as of 31 December 20X8 and 20X7, and the results of its operations and its cash flows for each of the years in the three-year period ended 31 December 20X8 in conformity with accounting principles generally accepted in the United States of America. Also in our opinion, W Company maintained, in all material respects, effective internal control over financial reporting as of 31 December 20X8, based on [identify control criteria, for example 'criteria established in *Internal Control – Integrated Framework issued by the Committee of Sponsoring Organizations of the Treadway Commission (COSO).*'].

[Signature]

[City and State or Country]

[Date]

Management's Assessment of Internal Control over Financial Reporting

Management provides a written report of their assessment similar to Illustration 14.7.

ILLUSTRATION 14.7

Sample Written Report of Management

Management is responsible for establishing and maintaining adequate internal control over financial reporting for the company. Management assessed the Company's internal control over financial reporting as of 31 December 201X. Because of its inherent limitations, internal control over financial reporting is not intended to provide absolute assurance that a misstatement of our financial statements would be prevented or detected.

Based on management's assessment, management believes that, as of 31 December 200X, the Company maintained effective internal control over financial reporting including maintenance of records that in reasonable detail accurately and fairly reflect the transactions and dispositions of the assets of the Company, and policies and procedures that provide reasonable assurance that (a) transactions are recorded as necessary to permit preparation of financial statements in accordance with accounting principles generally accepted in the United States of America and (b) receipts and expenditures of the Company are being made only in accordance with authorisations of management and directors of the Company based on the criteria for effective internal control over financial reporting established in Internal Control – Integrated Framework issued by the Committee of Sponsoring Organisations (COSO) of the Treadway Commission.

[Name of the independent registered public audit firm] has audited the financial statements of the Company for the fiscal year ended 31 December 20X8 and the Company's internal control over financial reporting as of 31 December 20X8.

Illustrative Report on an Unqualified Opinion on the Effectiveness of Internal Control

Auditors must report on management's assertions. Illustration 14.6 gives a sample auditor's report on internal control. The introductory paragraph says the practitioner audited management's assessment that it maintained effective internal control over financial reporting. It also gives the responsibilities of management and auditor. The definition paragraph gives the company's internal control policies and procedures. The scope paragraph tells how the auditor followed PCAOB standards in its audit, which serves as a reasonable basis for its opinion. The inherent limitations paragraph is a disclaimer that internal controls may not detect or prevent misstatements. The opinion paragraph gives the opinion of the auditor regarding the effectiveness of internal controls over financial reporting. It also refers to the audit of the financial statements.

Assurance Reports on Controls at a Service Organisation (ISAE 3402)

Various companies (user entities) use service organisations for specific services, for example payroll services. As these user entities would like to rely on controls of services organisations, the IAASB came with a standard to audit the controls at a service organisation that is likely to be relevant to user entities' internal control as it relates to financial reporting. This standard complements ISA 402 'Audit Considerations Relating to an Entity Using a Service Organisation'.[29]

The objectives of the service auditor are to obtain reasonable assurance about whether, in all material respects, based on suitable criteria:

(i) The service organisation's description of its system fairly presents the system as designed and implemented throughout the specified period (or in the case of a type 1 report, as at a specified date).

(ii) The controls related to the control objectives stated in the service organisation's description of its system were suitably designed throughout the specified period (or in the case of a type 1 report, as at a specified date).

(iii) Where included in the scope of the engagement, the controls operated effectively to provide reasonable assurance that the control objectives stated in the service organisation's description of its system were achieved throughout the specified period.

And to report on these matters in accordance with the service auditor's findings.[30]

Some of the considerations are similar to those of a financial statement audit, which are discussed throughout this book. The primary considerations of an assurance report on controls at service organisations that differ from an audit of financial statements are the subject matter and reporting (type 1 or 2).

Type of Report

According to ISAE 3402 two types of reports are applicable related to control reporting of service organisations:

- a type 1 report, a report on the description and design of controls at a service organisation;
- a type 2 report, a report on the description, design and operating effectiveness of controls at a service organisation.

To be able to verify the effectiveness of the operating controls of the service organisation, user entities need to request a type 2 report from the service organisation.

■ Sustainability Assurance Engagements

Sustainability Reporting

The verification of sustainability reports providing assertions regarding economic, environmental and social performance has become a mature assurance service. Important drivers of this demand are:

- the legal requirement to report on environmental issues in several countries;
- required as part of an emission trading scheme;
- voluntary sustainability reporting to inform stakeholders.

Besides separate sustainability reports, integrated reporting is becoming common practice. Integrated reporting is a process that results in communication, most visibly a periodic 'integrated report', about value creation over time. An integrated report is a concise communication about how an organisation's strategy, governance, performance and prospects lead to the creation of value over the short, medium and long term. An integrated report should be prepared in accordance with the International Integrated Reporting Framework. While the communications that result from integrated reporting will be of benefit to a range of stakeholders, they are principally aimed at providers of financial capital.[31]

In the European Union, all Member States have transposed the EU Modernisation Directive (2003/51) in national laws, under which companies must provide a Business Review including non-financial, environmental and social performance indicators, to the extent necessary for an understanding of a company's performance. However, the Modernisation Directive does not contain specific disclosure requirements. Some countries have gone further such as France, where the Grenelle II Act (2012) is a step forward to integrated reporting as companies have to include in their annual management report information regarding social and environmental consequences of its activity as well as its societal commitments for sustainable development. In Denmark the 2008 Financial Statements Act requires specific CSR disclosures by large companies and in Sweden all state-owned companies have to publish a sustainability report. In the UK the government has announced new mandatory carbon reporting for all companies listed on the main London Stock Exchange starting in 2013. Around the world, many countries have requirements for environmental (financial) risks, such as the USA, Canada and Australia where the Corporations Act (2001) requires companies that prepare a Director's Report to provide details of performance in relation to environmental regulations. In other countries local stock exchanges have introduced a range of sustainability reporting requirements for listed companies, such as in China (Shanghai/Shenzen), South Africa (Johannesburg) and Brazil (Bovespa).

Most common standards for sustainability are the GRI Sustainability Reporting Guidelines. Regarding assurance standards, the IAASB developed standard ISAE 3410 'Assurance Engagements on Greenhouse Gas Statements', effective as of 30 September 2013.

The Greenhouse Gas Protocol (GHG Protocol) is the most widely used international accounting tool to understand, quantify, and manage greenhouse gas emissions. The GHG Protocol is a partnership between the World Resources Institute (WRI) and the World Business Council for Sustainable Development (WBCSD). The GHG Protocol is working with businesses, governments, and environmental groups around the world to build a new generation of credible and effective programmes for tackling climate change.[32]

Besides discussing economic, environmental and social sustainability, we will discuss the GRI guidelines and standard ISAE 3410.

■ Economic Sustainability

The economic dimension of sustainability concerns an organisation's impact on the economic circumstances of its stakeholders and on economic systems at the local, national and global levels. Economic indicators in the sustainability-reporting context focus on the manner in which an organisation affects the stakeholders with whom it has direct and indirect economic interactions.

■ Environmental Sustainability

The environmental dimension of sustainability concerns an organisation's impact on living and non-living natural systems, including ecosystems, land, air and water. The reporting organisation provides both normalised (e.g. resource use per unit of output) and absolute figures. Organisations are encouraged to relate their individual performance to the broader ecological systems within which they operate. For example, organisations could seek to report their pollution output in terms of the ability of the environment (local, regional or global) to absorb the pollutants.

■ Social Sustainability

The social dimension of sustainability concerns an organisation's impact on the social systems within which it operates. Social performance can be gauged through an analysis of the organisation's impact on stakeholders at the local, national and global levels. In some cases, social indicators influence the organisation's intangible assets, such as its human capital and reputation. GRI has selected indicators by identifying key performance aspects surrounding labour practices, human rights, and broader issues affecting consumers, community and other stakeholders in society.

The assurance report by Philips is a very good example of this type of reporting. This report is based on the third generation guidelines of the Global Reporting Initiative (G3.1) and has a GRI application level of A+. Illustration 14.8, from the Philips integrated report, gives the auditor's assurance on the report of Philips management.[33]

ILLUSTRATION 14.8

Independent Limited Assurance Report Regarding Sustainability Reporting

Independent Auditor's Report

To the Supervisory Board and Shareholders of Koninklijke Philips Electronics N.V.:

Introduction

We were engaged by the Supervisory Board of Koninklijke Philips Electronics N.V. (further 'Philips') to provide assurance on the information in the chapter Sustainability statements in the Annual Report 2012 including the information referred to in the sections Social performance and Environmental performance (further 'The Sustainability Information'). The Board of Management is responsible for the preparation and fair presentation of The Sustainability Information, including the identification of material issues. Our responsibility is to issue an assurance report based on the engagement outlined below.

Scope

Our assurance engagement was designed to provide reasonable assurance on whether The Sustainability Information is presented fairly, in all material respects, in accordance with the reporting criteria. We do not provide any assurance on the achievability of the objectives, targets and expectations of Philips.

Reporting Criteria and Assurance Standard

Philips applies the Sustainability Reporting Guidelines G3.1 of the Global Reporting Initiative supported by internally developed guidelines as described in Approach to sustainability reporting in the chapter Sustainability statements, of this Annual Report. It is important to view the performance data in the context of this explanatory information. We believe these criteria are suitable in view of the purpose of our assurance engagement.

We conducted our engagement in accordance with the International Standard for Assurance Engagement (ISAE 3000): Assurance Engagement other than Audits or Reviews of Historical Financial Information, issued by the International Auditing and Assurance Standards Board. This standard requires, among others, that the assurance team possesses the specific knowledge, skills and professional competencies needed to provide assurance on sustainability information, and that they comply with the requirements of the Code of Ethics for Professional Accountants of the International Federation of Accountants to ensure their independence.

Work Undertaken

Our procedures included assessing the appropriateness of the accounting policies used, evaluating the design and implementation, and testing the operating effectiveness of the systems and processes for collecting and processing the qualitative and quantitative information in The Sustainability Information

Illustration 14.8 (continued)

(including the implementation of these at a number of sites), and evaluating the overall presentation of sustainability information within our scope. Also we held interviews with relevant management and evaluated documentation on a sample basis to determine whether the information is supported by sufficient evidence.

We have also reviewed, to the extent of our competence, whether the information on sustainability in the rest of the Annual Report 2012 is consistent with The Sustainability Information.

Opinion

In our opinion, The Sustainability Information is fairly presented, in all material respects, in accordance with the reporting criteria.

We also report, to the extent of our competence, that the information on sustainability in the rest of the Annual Report 2012 is consistent with The Sustainability Information.

Amsterdam, The Netherlands
February 25, 2013
KPMG Accountants N.V.
J.F.C. van Everdingen RA

Independent Assurance Report

To the Supervisory Board and Shareholders of Koninklijke Philips Electronics N.V.:

Introduction

We have been engaged by the Supervisory Board of Koninklijke Philips Electronics N.V. to provide assurance on the information in the chapter Sustainability statements in the Annual Report 2011. The Board of Management is responsible for the preparation and fair presentation of the information in the chapter Sustainability statements. Our responsibility is to provide assurance on this information contained in this Annual Report.

Scope

Our engagement was designed to provide:

- limited assurance on whether the information in Sustainability statements is, in all material respects, fairly stated in accordance with the reporting criteria;
- reasonable assurance on whether the information on 2011 in Chapter 14, Sustainability statements, in the sections 14.1 to 14.6 with the exclusion of section 14.3 and the section 'Health and Safety' in section 14.4 of this Annual Report is, in all material respects, presented in accordance with the reporting criteria.

Procedures performed to obtain a limited level of assurance are aimed at determining the plausibility of data and are less extensive than those for a reasonable level of assurance.

Our procedures for limited level of assurance included reviewing systems and processes for data management, assessing the appropriateness of the accounting policies used, assessing the design and existence of data collection and reporting process at a limited number of sites and evaluating the overall presentation of sustainability information within our scope.

For the information subject to a reasonable level of assurance additional procedures were carried out. These procedures included testing of the operational effectiveness of systems and methods used to collect and process the data and information reported.

We have also reviewed, to the extent of our competence, whether the information on sustainability in the Performance highlights of this Annual Report, the Management's report as defined in the introduction paragraph of Group financial statements is consistent with the information in Sustainability statements.

Reporting Criteria

Koninklijke Philips Electronics N.V. applies the Sustainability Reporting Guidelines of the Global Reporting Initiative (G3.1) supported by internally developed guidelines, as detailed in Approach to sustainability reporting

Illustration 14.8 (continued)

in Sustainability statements. It is important to view the performance data in the context of this explanatory information. We believe that these criteria are suitable in view of the purpose of our assurance engagement.

Standards

We conducted our engagement in accordance with the International Standard for Assurance Engagements (ISAE) 3000: Assurance Engagements other than Audits or Reviews of Historical Financial Information, issued by the International Auditing and Assurance Standards Board. This Standard requires, amongst others, that the assurance team possesses the specific knowledge, skills and professional competencies needed to understand sustainability information, and that they comply with the requirements of the Code of Ethics for Professional Accountants from the International Federation of Accountants to ensure their independence.

Conclusion

Based on our work described in this report, we conclude that:

■ nothing came to our attention to indicate that the information in Sustainability statements is not, in all material respects, fairly stated in accordance with the reporting criteria;
■ the 2011 information in Chapter 14, Sustainability statements, in sections 14.1 to 14.6 with the exclusion of section 14.3 and the section 'Health and Safety' in section 14.4 of this Annual Report is, in all material respects, presented in accordance with the reporting criteria and

We also report, to the extent of our competence, that the information on sustainability in the Performance highlights, the Management's report as defined in the introduction paragraph of Group financial statements is consistent with the information in Sustainability statements.

Amsterdam, The Netherlands
February 23, 2012
KPMG ACCOUNTANTS N.V.
M.A. Soeting RA

GRI Sustainability Reporting Guidelines

Most environmental and social reporting by large corporations follows the guidelines of the Global Reporting Initiative (GRI) *Sustainability Reporting Guidelines*.[34] These Guidelines are for voluntary use by organisations for reporting on the economic, environmental and social dimensions of their activities, products and services. Reports can be used for the following purposes, among others:

■ Benchmarking and assessing sustainability performance with respect to laws, norms, codes, performance standards, and voluntary initiatives.
■ Demonstrating how the organisation influences and is influenced by expectations about sustainable development.
■ Comparing performance within an organisation and between different organisations over time.

The latest available GRI Guideline at the moment of publishing of this book is GRI Guideline 3.1. A report under GRI Guideline 3.1 comprises two parts:

Part 1 – Reporting Principles and Guidance

■ Principles to define report content:
  – materiality: the information in a report should cover topics and indicators that reflect the organisation's significant economic, environmental, and social impacts or that would substantively influence the assessments and decisions of stakeholders;

- stakeholder inclusiveness: the reporting organisation should identify its stakeholders and explain in the report how it has responded to their reasonable expectations and interests;
- sustainability context: the report should present the organisation's performance in the wider context of sustainability;
- completeness: coverage of the material topics and indicators and definition of the report boundary should be sufficient to reflect significant economic, environmental and social impacts and enable stakeholders to assess the reporting organisation's performance in the reporting period.

■ Principles to define report quality: balance, comparability, accuracy, timeliness, reliability and clarity.

■ Guidance on how to set the report boundary.

Part 2 – Standard Disclosures

■ Strategy and profile: a description of the reporting organisation's strategy and analysis, organisation's profile, report parameters, governance, commitments to external initiatives and stakeholder engagement.

■ Management approach: a description of management's goals and performance, policy, organisational responsibility, training and awareness, and monitoring and follow-up.

■ Performance indicators: measures of the impact or effect of the reporting organisation divided into economic, environmental and social performance indicators. The social category is broken down further by labour, human rights, society and product responsibility sub-categories.[35]

During 2013 GRI Guideline G4 will become available, which will provide more guidelines regarding integrated reporting. The latest GRI Guidelines are available on the GRI website: **http://www.globalreporting.org**.

Assurance Engagements on Greenhouse Gas Statements (ISAE 3410)

ISAE 3410 deals with assurance engagements to report on an entity's greenhouse gas (GHG) statement. The objectives of the practitioner are:

(a) To obtain reasonable or limited assurance, as appropriate, about whether the GHG statement is free from material misstatement, whether due to fraud or error, thereby enabling the practitioner to express a conclusion conveying that level of assurance.

(b) To report, in accordance with the practitioner's findings, about whether:
   (i) in the case of a reasonable assurance engagement, the GHG statement is prepared, in all material respects, in accordance with the applicable criteria; or
   (ii) in the case of a limited assurance engagement, anything has come to the practitioner's attention that causes the practitioner to believe, on the basis of the procedures performed and evidence obtained, that the GHG statement is not prepared, in all material respects, in accordance with the applicable criteria; and

(c) To communicate as otherwise required by this ISAE, in accordance with the practitioner's findings.[36]

Some of the considerations are similar to those of a financial statement audit, which are discussed throughout this book. The primary considerations of an assurance report that differ from an audit of financial statements are the choice in level of assurance (limited versus reasonable assurance), engagement acceptance, subject matter and reporting.

Reporting on Greenhouse Gas Statement

The report by an auditor on greenhouse gas differs from the reports on historical financial information in that it contains the following:

■ Identification of the GHG statement, including the period(s) it covers, and, if any information in that statement is not covered by the practitioner's conclusion, clear identification of the information subject to assurance as well as the excluded information, together with a statement that the practitioner has not performed any procedures with respect to the excluded information and, therefore, that no conclusion on it is expressed.

■ A statement that GHG quantification is subject to inherent uncertainty.

■ If the GHG statement includes emissions deductions that are covered by the practitioner's conclusion, identification of those emissions deductions, and a statement of the practitioner's responsibility with respect to them.

■ Identification of the applicable criteria.

■ A description of the practitioner's responsibility, including:
  – A statement that the engagement was performed in accordance with ISAE 3410, Assurance Engagements on Greenhouse Gas Statements; and
  – A summary of the practitioner's procedures. In the case of a limited assurance engagement, this shall include a statement that the procedures performed in a limited assurance engagement vary in nature from, and are less in extent than for, a reasonable assurance engagement. As a result, the level of assurance obtained in a limited assurance engagement is substantially lower than the assurance that would have been obtained had a reasonable assurance engagement been performed.

■ The practitioner's conclusion, expressed in the positive form in the case of a reasonable assurance engagement or in the negative form in the case of a limited assurance engagement, about whether the GHG statement is prepared, in all material respects, in accordance with the applicable criteria.[37]

Illustration 14.9 shows an example of a reasonable assurance report on Greenhouse Gas Statement.[38]

ILLUSTRATION 14.9

Greenhouse Gas Statement Report Example

**Independent Practitioner's Reasonable Assurance Report on ABC's
Greenhouse Gas (GHG) Statement**

[Appropriate Addressee]

Report on GHG Statement (*this heading is not needed if this is the only section*)

We have undertaken a reasonable assurance engagement of the accompanying GHG statement of ABC for the year ended 31 December 20X1, comprising the Emissions Inventory and the Explanatory Notes on pages xx–yy. [This engagement was conducted by a multidisciplinary team including assurance practitioners, engineers and environmental scientists.]

Illustration 14.9 (continued)

ABC's Responsibility for the GHG Statement

ABC is responsible for the preparation of the GHG statement in accordance with [*applicable criteria*], applied as explained in Note 1 to the GHG statement. This responsibility includes the design, implementation and maintenance of internal control relevant to the preparation of a GHG statement that is free from material misstatement, whether due to fraud or error.

[As discussed in Note 1 to the GHG statement] GHG quantification is subject to inherent uncertainty because of incomplete scientific knowledge used to determine emissions factors and the values needed to combine emissions of different gases.

Our Independence and Quality Control

We have complied with the *Code of Ethics for Professional Accountants* issued by the International Ethics Standards Board for Accountants, which includes independence and other requirements founded on fundamental principles of integrity, objectivity, professional competence and due care, confidentiality and professional behaviour. In accordance with International Standard on Quality Control 1 [*name of firm*] maintains a comprehensive system of quality control including documented policies and procedures regarding compliance with ethical requirements, professional standards and applicable legal and regulatory requirements.

Our Responsibility

Our responsibility is to express an opinion on the GHG statement based on the evidence we have obtained. We conducted our reasonable assurance engagement in accordance with International Standard on Assurance Engagements 3410, *Assurance Engagements on Greenhouse Gas Statements* ('ISAE 3410'), issued by the International Auditing and Assurance Standards Board. That standard requires that we plan and perform this engagement to obtain reasonable assurance about whether the GHG statement is free from material misstatement.

A reasonable assurance engagement in accordance with ISAE 3410 involves performing procedures to obtain evidence about the quantification of emissions and related information in the GHG statement. The nature, timing and extent of procedures selected depend on the practitioner's judgement, including the assessment of the risks of material misstatement, whether due to fraud or error, in the GHG statement. In making those risk assessments, we considered internal control relevant to ABC's preparation of the GHG statement. A reasonable assurance engagement also includes:

- assessing the suitability in the circumstances of ABC's use of [*applicable criteria*], applied as explained in Note 1 to the GHG statement, as the basis for preparing the GHG statement;
- evaluating the appropriateness of quantification methods and reporting policies used, and the reasonableness of estimates made by ABC; and
- evaluating the overall presentation of the GHG statement.

We believe that the evidence we have obtained is sufficient and appropriate to provide a basis for our opinion.

Opinion

In our opinion, the GHG statement for the year ended 31 December 20X1 is prepared, in all material respects, in accordance with the [*applicable criteria*] applied as explained in Note 1 to the GHG statement.

Report on Other Legal and Regulatory Requirements (*applicable for some engagements only*)

[Form and content of this section of the assurance report will vary depending on the nature of the practitioner's other reporting responsibilities.]

[Practitioner's signature]

[Date of the assurance report]

[Practitioner's address]

ISAE 3420 Assurance Engagements to Report on the Compilation of Pro Forma Financial Information Included in a Prospectus (ISAE 3420)

The ISAE 3420 'Assurance Engagement to Report on the Compilation of Pro Forma Financial Information Included in a Prospectus' is effective dated on or after 31 March 2013. This ISAE deals with reasonable assurance engagements undertaken by a practitioner to report on the responsible party's compilation of pro forma financial information included in a prospectus.[39]

14.6 Related Services

Besides assurance engagement, auditors can be engaged for non-assurance engagements. The IAASB covers two types of non-assurance engagements in the 'Related Services Framework': engagements to perform agreed-upon procedures regarding financial information (ISRS 4400) and compilation engagements (ISRS 4410). These are the International Standards on Related Services (ISRS) currently covered in the 'Related Services Framework' (see Chapter 4, Illustration 4.1, 'Related Services Framework').

A report issued by an auditor in connection with an engagement that does not exhibit all of the elements described in the Assurance Framework,[40] such as a compilation or engagement to perform agreed-upon procedures, should specifically state it does not offer assurance.

Furthermore, it does not purport to enhance the degree of confidence intended users can have.

A related service engagement is generally an examination of historical financial statements to develop a conclusion based on the criteria, but no audit opinion. In some instances, this kind of engagement could also be linked to information in other historical financial statements.

Engagements to Perform Agreed-Upon Procedures Regarding Financial Information (ISRS 4400)[41]

An agreed-upon procedures engagement is an engagement in which the party engaging the professional accountant or the intended user determines the procedures to be performed and the auditor provides a report of factual findings as a result of undertaking those procedures.

Agreed-upon procedures are not considered an assurance engagement. While the intended user of the report may derive some assurance from the report of factual findings, the engagement is not intended to provide, nor does the auditor express, a conclusion that provides a level of assurance. Rather, the intended user assesses the procedures and findings and draws his own conclusions[42] (see Illustration 4.1, 'Agreed-upon procedures').

Objective

The objective of an agreed-upon procedures engagement is for the auditor to carry out procedures of an audit nature to which the auditor, the company, and some third party have agreed and to report on factual findings. The report is restricted to those parties that have agreed to the procedures since others, unaware of the reasons for the procedures, may misinterpret the results.

Independence Not Required

Independence is not a requirement for agreed-upon procedures engagements; however, the terms or objectives of an engagement or national standards may require the auditor to comply with the independence requirements of IESBA Code of Ethics. Where the auditor is not independent, a statement to that effect would be made in the report of factual findings.[43]

Matters to Be Agreed

The auditor should ensure that all involved parties have a clear understanding regarding the agreed procedures and the conditions of the engagement. Matters to be agreed between auditor and management include the:[44]

■ Nature of the engagement including the fact that no assurance will be expressed on the procedures performed.
■ Identification of the financial information to which the agreed-upon procedures will be applied.
■ Nature, timing and extent of the specific procedures to be applied.
■ Anticipated form of the report of factual findings.
■ Limitations on distribution of the report of factual findings. When such limitation would be in conflict with the legal requirements, if any, the auditor would not accept the engagement.

Procedures Performed

An engagement to perform agreed-upon procedures may involve the auditor in performing certain procedures on subject matter information like financial data (e.g. accounts payable, accounts receivable, purchases from related parties, and sales and profits of a segment of an entity), a financial statement (e.g. a balance sheet) or even a complete set of financial statements.

The procedures applied in an engagement to perform agreed-upon procedures may include: inquiry and analysis, recompilation, comparison and other clerical accuracy checks, observation, inspection and obtaining confirmations (these are discussed in Chapter 9 'Auditor's Response to Assessed Risk' and Chapter 10 'Audit Evidence').

Report

The report on an agreed-upon procedures engagement needs to describe the purpose and the agreed-upon procedures of the engagement in sufficient detail to enable the reader to understand the nature and the extent of the work performed. The report of factual findings should contain,[45] among other things, a description of the auditor's factual findings including sufficient details of errors and exceptions found and a statement that the report is restricted to those parties that have agreed to the procedures to be performed.

Illustration 14.10 contains an example of a report of factual findings issued in connection with an engagement to perform agreed-upon procedures regarding financial information.[46]

Engagements to Compile Financial Information (ISRS 4410)[47]

The objective of a compilation engagement is for the accountant to use accounting expertise, as opposed to auditing expertise, to collect, classify and summarise financial information. This ordinarily entails reducing detailed data to a manageable and understandable form without a requirement to test the assertions underlying that information.

ILLUSTRATION 14.10

Example of a Report of Factual Findings in Connection with Accounts Payable

REPORT OF FACTUAL FINDINGS

To (those who engaged the auditor)

We have performed the procedures agreed with you and enumerated below with respect to the accounts receivable of Company XYZ as per ..... 20XX, set forth in the accompanying schedules (not shown in this example). Our engagement was undertaken in accordance with the International Standard on Related Services applicable to agreed-upon procedures engagements. The procedures were performed solely to assist you in evaluating the existence of the accounts receivable and are summarized as follows:

1   We obtained and checked the ..... and we compared the total to the balance in the related general ledger account.
2   We compared the attached list of major customers and the amounts outstanding at ... 20XX to the related names and amounts in the trial balance.
3   We obtained confirmations of balances outstanding as per .... 20XX.
4   We compared such confirmations to the amounts referred to in 3. For amounts which did not agree, we contacted where appropriate, the sales department, the customer and examined order, delivery and freight documentation.

We report our findings below:

(a) With respect to item 1 we found
(b) With respect to item 2 we found
(c) With respect to item 3 we found
(d) With respect to item 4 we found

(Detail the exceptions)

Because the above procedures do not constitute either an audit or a review made in accordance with International Standards on Auditing or International Standards on Review Engagements (or relevant national standards or practices), we do not express any assurance on the accounts receivable as of .... 20XX.

Had we performed additional procedures or had we performed an audit or review of the financial statements in accordance with International Standards on Auditing or International Standards on Review Engagements (or relevant national standards or practices), other matters might have come to our attention that would have been reported to you.

Our report is solely for the purpose set forth in the first paragraph of this report and for your information and is not to be used for any other purpose or to be distributed to any other parties. This report relates only to the accounts and items specified above and does not extend to any financial statements of Company XYZ, taken as a whole.

Place, date

... (Name Audit Firm)

... (Name Auditor)

The procedures employed do not enable the accountant to express any assurance on the financial information.

Independence

Unlike assurance engagements, independence is not a requirement for a compilation engagement. However, national ethical codes or laws or regulations may specify requirements or disclosure rules pertaining to independence.[48]

Understanding Terms of the Engagement

The accountant should ensure that there is a clear understanding between the client and the accountant regarding the terms of the engagement. Matters to be considered, among other things, include:[49]

- The intended use and distribution of the financial information, and any restrictions on either its use or its distribution where applicable.
- Identification of the applicable financial reporting framework.
- The objective and scope of the compilation engagement.
- The responsibilities of the practitioner, including the requirement to comply with relevant ethical requirements.
- The responsibilities of management.
- The expected form and content of the practitioner's report.

Compilation Procedures

A compilation engagement would ordinarily include the preparation of financial statements (which may or may not be a complete set of financial statements) but may also include the collection, classification and summarisation of other financial information.

The accountant should read the compiled information and consider whether it appears to be appropriate in form and free from obvious material misstatements. If this compiled information does not satisfy the accountant, he should bring it to the attention of management and request for additional or corrected information.

The accountant is **not ordinarily** required to: assess internal controls; verify any matters or explanations; or make any inquiries of management to assess the reliability and completeness of the information provided.

Reporting on a Compilation Engagement

Reports on compilation engagements should contain, among other requirements:[50]

- A statement that the practitioner has compiled the financial information based on information provided by management.
- A description of the responsibilities of management, or those charged with governance as appropriate, in relation to the compilation engagement, and in relation to the financial information.
- A description of the practitioner's responsibilities in compiling the financial information, including that the engagement was performed in accordance with this ISRS, and that the practitioner has complied with relevant ethical requirements.
- Explanations that:
  - since a compilation engagement is not an assurance engagement, the practitioner is not required to verify the accuracy or completeness of the information provided by management for the compilation; and

– accordingly, the practitioner does not express an audit opinion or a review conclusion on whether the financial information is prepared in accordance with the applicable financial reporting framework.

The financial information compiled by the accountant should contain a reference such as 'Unaudited', 'Compiled without Audit or Review' or 'Refer to Compilation Report' on each page of the financial information or on the front of the complete set of financial statements.

Illustration 14.11 contains an example of a compilation report.[51]

ILLUSTRATION 14.11

Example of a Report on an Engagement to Compile Financial Statements

COMPILATION REPORT

[To Management of Company XYZ]

We have compiled the accompanying financial statements of Company XYZ, based on information you have provided. These financial statements comprise the statement of financial position of XYZ as at December 31, 20XX, the statement of comprehensive income, statement of changes in equity and statement of cash flows for the year then ended, and a summary of significant accounting policies and other explanatory information.

We performed this compilation engagement in accordance with International Standard on Related Services 4410, Compilation Engagements. We have applied our expertise in accounting and financial reporting to assist you in the preparation and presentation of these financial statements in accordance with International Financial Reporting Standards for Small- and Medium-sized Entities. We have complied with relevant ethical requirements, including principles of integrity, objectivity, professional competence and due care. These financial statements and the accuracy and completeness of the information used to compile them are your responsibility.

Since a compilation engagement is not an assurance engagement, we are not required to verify the accuracy or completeness of the information you provided to us to compile these financial statements. Accordingly, we do not express an audit opinion or a review conclusion on whether these financial statements are prepared in accordance with IFRS for SMEs.

Place, date

... (Name Audit Firm)

... (Name Auditor)

14.7 Summary

Auditor services are work that an audit firm performs for their clients. Except for consulting services, the work that auditors do is under the guidance of engagement standards set by the International Auditing and Assurance Standards Board (IAASB).

Some engagement standards are based on 'International Framework for Assurance Engagements' (assurance engagements), and others result from the 'Related Services Framework' (related services engagements). Three sets of standards (ISAs, ISREs and ISAEs) share the assurance engagement framework and one standard set (ISRS) is based on the related services framework. ISAs, ISREs, ISAEs and ISRSs are collectively referred to as the IAASB's Engagement Standards. All auditor services standards have as their basis the IESBA Code of Ethics (see Chapter 3) and International Standards on Quality Control (ISQC).

International Standards on Auditing (ISAs) ISA 100 'Audits and Reviews of Historical Financial Information' describes the main concepts applicable to audit, review and special purpose area engagements.

International Standards for Review Engagements (ISREs) are to be applied in the review of historical financial information. Two standards exist for review engagements: 2400 'Engagements to Review Financial Statements' and 2410 'Review of Interim Financial Information Performed by the Independent Auditor of the Entity'.

International Standards on Assurance Engagements (ISAE) 3000 'Assurance Engagements on Subject Matter Other than Audits or Reviews of Historical Financial Information' describes concepts applicable to assurance services whose subject matter is not related to historical financial information. The ISAE standards are divided into two parts: (1) ISAEs 3000–3399, which are topics that apply to all assurance engagements, and (2) ISAEs 3400–3699, which are subject specific standards, for example standards relating to examination of prospective financial information and sustainability reporting.

Engagements covered by International Standards on Related Services (ISRSs) are based on the 'Related Services Framework' – a framework that is in the development stage at the IAASB. Standards under this framework (ISRSs) are applied currently to two related services: agreed-upon procedures (ISRS 4400) and compilations (ISRS 4410).

There are two types of assurance engagement: a reasonable assurance engagement and a limited assurance engagement. The objective of a reasonable assurance engagement is a reduction in assurance engagement risk to an acceptably low level based on the circumstances of the engagement as the basis for a positive form of expression of the practitioner's conclusion. The objective of a limited assurance engagement is a reduction in assurance engagement risk to a level that is acceptable in the circumstances of the engagement, but where that risk is greater than for a reasonable assurance engagement, as the basis for a negative form of expression of the practitioner's conclusion. Where reviews of financial statements differ most from audits is in the limited procedures performed (limited in inquiry of management and analytical procedures) and the review report. The objective of a review of financial statements is to enable an auditor to state whether anything has 'come to the auditor's attention that causes the auditor to believe that the financial statements are not prepared, in all material respects, in accordance with an identified financial reporting framework (negative assurance).'

Sometimes the auditor may have a request for a financial statement audit based on historical financial information, but which is not based on the financial statements as a whole or on IFRS or the requisite national standard. An auditor may be called upon to do special area reports. Sometimes there are audits that give an opinion on compliance with legal agreements required of a company. Management or the board of directors may request a summarised financial statement. Small businesses, which generally are not required to comply with IFRS or a national standard required of publicly traded companies, may feel that an audit based on the cash basis, an income tax basis, or a basis required by regulatory agencies is needed.

1 Reports on Financial Statements Prepared in Accordance with the Special purpose Framework (ISA 800), such as:
   (a) a tax basis of accounting for a set of financial statements that accompany an entity's tax return;
   (b) the cash receipts and disbursements basis of accounting for cash flow information that an entity may be requested to prepare for creditors;
   (c) the financial reporting provisions established by a regulator to meet the requirements of that regulator; or
   (d) the financial reporting provisions of a contract, such as a bond indenture, a loan agreement or a project grant.
2 Reports on Audits of Single Financial Statements and Specific Elements, Accounts or Items of a Financial Statement (ISA 805).
3 Reports on Summarised Financial Statements (ISA 810).

The International Standard on Assurance Engagements (ISAE) 3000 establishes basic principles and essential procedures for professional accountants in public practice for the performance of assurance engagements on subject matters other than historical financial information. Assurance engagements other than historical financial information have two main components: (1) topics that apply to all assurance engagements (ISAEs 3000–3399) and (2) subject specific standards (ISAEs 3400–3699). The subject matter currently covered by IAASB's pronouncements are:

- ISAE 3400 The Examination of Prospective Financial Information;
- ISAE 3402 Assurance Reports on Controls at a Service Organisation;
- ISAE 3410 Assurance Engagements on Greenhouse Gas Statements;
- ISAE 3420 Assurance Engagements to Report on the Compilation of Pro Forma Financial Information Included in a Prospectus.

Prospective financial information means financial information based on assumptions about events that may occur in the future. Prospective financial information can be in the form of a forecast, a projection, or a combination of both. A 'forecast' is prospective financial information prepared on the basis of management's best-estimate assumptions about future events. A 'projection' means prospective financial information prepared on the basis of hypothetical assumptions about future events and management actions which may or may not take place, such as a possible merger of two companies.

Standards that apply in all these subject matter areas are currently being developed. The most influential standards in this specific subject matter area are the Global Reporting Initiative and the Sarbanes–Oxley internal control reporting standards. The Sarbanes–Oxley Act of 2002 (SOX) and PCAOB Audit Standard 2 require certification of internal control by the CEO and CFO of all companies that trade on the stock exchanges in the USA including companies headquartered outside the USA. SOX also requires that the company's auditor give an opinion on management's report on internal control. Most environmental and social reporting by large corporations follows the guidelines of the Global Reporting Initiative (GRI) Sustainability Reporting Guidelines. These Guidelines are for voluntary use by organisations for reporting on the economic, environmental and social dimensions of their activities, products and services.

Besides separate sustainability reports, integrated reporting is becoming common practice. Integrated reporting is a process that results in communication, most visibly a periodic 'integrated report', about value creation over time. An integrated report is a concise communication about how an organisation's strategy, governance, performance and prospects lead to the creation of value over the short, medium and long term. An integrated report should be prepared in accordance with the International Integrated Reporting Framework.

An accounting-related service engagement is an examination of historical financial statements to develop a conclusion based on the criteria, but no audit opinion. The most common of the accounting-related services non-assurance report are agreed-upon procedures (ISRS 4400) and accounting compilation (ISRS 4410). An agreed-upon procedures engagement is an engagement in which the party engaging the professional accountant or the intended user determines the procedures to be performed and the professional accountant provides a report of factual findings as a result of undertaking those procedures. The objective of a compilation engagement is for the accountant to use accounting expertise, as opposed to auditing expertise, to collect, classify, and summarise financial information. This ordinarily entails reducing detailed data to a manageable and understandable form without a requirement to test the assertions underlying that information.

14.8 Questions, Exercises and Cases

QUESTIONS

14.2 Introduction

14-1 What are auditor services? List the major categories (except for consulting) of auditor's services.

14-2 Which assurance engagements have historical financial information as subject matter? Discuss the differences between these assurance engagements.

14.3 Special Areas Engagements

14-3 The auditor's report on special purpose financial statements shall include an emphasis of matter paragraph. Why is this necessary?

14.4 Review Engagements

14-4 What are the basic elements required being included in the assurance report according to International Standards for Review Engagements 2400?

14.5 Assurance Engagements Other than Audits or Reviews of Historical Financial Information (ISAE 3000–3699)

14-5 Describe the difference between 'reasonable assurance engagements' and 'limited assurance engagements'.

14-6 Describe what is meant by 'prospective financial information'. Give some examples of when a prospective financial information report might be used.

14-7 What must auditors cover in their internal control report under the PCAOB standards?

14-8 Various companies use service organisations for specific services, for example payroll services. As these user entities would like to rely on controls of services organisations, the IAASB came with a standard to audit the controls at a service organisation that is likely to be relevant to user entities' internal control as it relates to financial reporting. According to ISAE 3402 two types of reports are applicable related to control reporting of service organisations. Briefly describe the types of reports.

14.6 Related Services

14-9 How does the related services framework differ from the assurance framework?

14-10 In an agreed-upon procedures engagement what matters generally have to be agreed between auditor and management?

PROBLEMS AND EXERCISES

14.3 Special Areas Engagements

14-11 List the types of special area engagement and give some examples of each.

14-12 Using Illustrations 14.1 through 14.3, compare the following three reports:
1 A report on financial statements prepared in accordance with the special purpose framework: a statement of provisions of a contract.
2 A Report on an element of a financial statement: schedule of the liability for 'incurred but not reported' claims in an insurance portfolio.
3 A report on summarised financial statement.

Make a comparison on the following three paragraphs:

Required:
A. Using the introductory paragraph as the basis of comparison.
B. Using the auditor's responsibility paragraph as the basis of comparison.
C. Using the opinion paragraph as the basis of comparison.

14.4 Review Engagements

14-13 Da Xing Fan, CPA, is engaged by the management of Ky-lin, a non-public company, to review the company's financial statements for the year ended 28 February 20XX.

Required:
A. Discuss the content of the report on a review of financial statements.
B. Summarise Fan's responsibilities if she finds the financial statements contain a material departure from IFRS.

14.5 Assurance Engagements Other than Audits or Reviews of Historical Financial Information (ISAE 3000–3699)

14-14 Haruspex is a new consulting company. They specialise in analysis of the market and process of producing sellable products from industrial waste. They have asked Sophia Coronis to prepare an examination of prospective financial information report of the prospective company financial statements for the first two years. This will be presented to Apollo Bank as part of a loan request.

Required:
A. What type of report would Coronis prepare – a forecast or a projection?
B. Draft the report for Apollo Bank.

14-15 Diamond Jousts, a UK Limited Company, is traded on the American Stock Exchange as American Depository Receipts (ADRs). They hire Lancelot, Elaine and Guinevere, Chartered Accountants, to prepare an internal control report to meet Sarbanes–Oxley requirements.

Required:
A. What should the report of management contain?
B. Draft an unqualified opinion on management's assessment of the effectiveness of internal control for the CA firm. (See Illustration 14.6 for an example.)

14-16 British Airways, Philips, ING, H&M, Nike, Shell, Heineken, Volkswagen, Coca-Cola and Samsung are companies that produce annual sustainability verification statements.

Required:
A. Chose two of the companies listed above.
B. Download a copy of their sustainability verification statements from their websites.
C. Compare the two reports on the basis of GRI guidelines (3.1 or most recent ones).

14.6 Related Services

14-17 The following list describes seven situations Certified Accountants may encounter, or contentions they may have to deal with, in their association with and preparation of *unaudited* financial statements. Briefly discuss the extent of the certified accountant's responsibilities and, if appropriate, the actions they should take to minimise any misunderstandings.
A. Armando Almonza, CPA, was engaged by telephone to perform accounting work including the compilation of financial statements. The client believes that Almonza

has been engaged to audit the financial statements and will examine the records accordingly.

B.   A group of investors who own a farm that is managed by an independent agent engage An Nguyen, CPA, to compile quarterly unaudited financial statements for them.

C.   In comparing the trial balance with the general ledger, Thynie Pukprayura, CPA, finds an account labelled 'Audit Fees' in which the client has accumulated his CPA firm's quarterly billings for accounting services including the compilation of quarterly unaudited financial statements.

D.   Unaudited financial statements for a public company were accompanied by the following letter of transmittal from Franz Ravel, Expert Comptable:

> To determine appropriate account classification, Jose Torres, CP Titulado, examined a number of the client's invoices. He noted in his working papers that some invoices were missing, but did nothing further because it was felt that the invoices did not affect the unaudited financial statements he was compiling. When the client subsequently discovered that invoices were missing, he contended that the Torres should not have ignored the missing invoices when compiling the financial statements and had a responsibility to at least inform him that they were missing.

E.   Omar El Qasaria, CA, compiled a draft of unaudited financial statements from the client's records. While reviewing this draft with his client, El Qasaria learnt that the land and building were recorded at appraisal value.

F.   Tomoko Nakagawa, CPA, is engaged to compile the financial statements of a non-public company. During the engagement, Nakagawa learns of several items for which IFRS would require adjustments of the statements and note disclosure. The controller agrees to make the recommended adjustments to the statements, but says that she is not going to add the notes because the statements are unaudited.

1 IAASB, 2012, International Standards on Auditing 800 (ISA 800) 'Special Considerations – Audits of Financial Statements Prepared in Accordance with Special Purpose Frameworks', *Handbook of International Quality Control, Auditing Review, Other Assurance, and Related Services Pronouncements*, International Federation of Accountants, New York.

2 IAASB, 2012, International Standards on Auditing 800 (ISA 800) 'Special Considerations – Audits of Financial Statements Prepared in Accordance with Special Purpose Frameworks,' paras 6 and 7, *Handbook of International Quality Control, Auditing Review, Other Assurance,and Related Services Pronouncements*, International Federation of Accountants, New York.

3 IAASB, 2012, International Standards on Auditing 800 (ISA 800) 'Special Considerations – Audits of Financial Statements Prepared in Accordance with Special Purpose Frameworks', para. A-1, *Handbook of International Quality Control, Auditing Review, Other Assurance, and Related Services Pronouncements*, International Federation of Accountants, New York.

4 IAASB, 2012, International Standards on Auditing 800 (ISA 800) 'Special Considerations – Audits of Financial Statements Prepared in Accordance with Special Purpose Frameworks', para. 17, *Handbook of International Quality Control, Auditing Review, Other Assurance, and Related Services Pronouncements*, International Federation of Accountants, New York.

5 Auditor's report on a complete set of financial statements prepared in accordance with fiscal accounting principles (Compliance framework).

6 IAASB, 2012, International Standards on Auditing 805 (ISA 805) 'Special Considerations – Audits of Single Financial Statements and Specific Elements, Accounts or Items of a Financial Statement', Appendix 2, Illustration 3, *Handbook of International Quality Control, Auditing Review, Other Assurance, and Related Services Pronouncements*, International Federation of Accountants, New York.

7 IAASB, 2012, International Standards on Auditing 810 (ISA 810) 'Engagements to Report on Summary Financial Statements', para. 14, *Handbook of International Quality Control, Auditing Review, Other Assurance, and Related Services Pronouncements*, International Federation of Accountants, New York.

8 IAASB, 2012, International Standards on Auditing 810 (ISA 810) 'Engagements to Report on Summary Financial Statements', Appendix, Illustration 1, *Handbook of International Quality Control, Auditing Review, Other Assurance, and Related Services Pronouncements*, International Federation of Accountants, New York.

9 Subsequent events – events occurring between the date of the financial statements and the date of the auditor's report, and facts that become known to the auditor after the date of the auditor's report.

10 IAASB, 2012, International Standards on Review Engagements 2400 (ISRE 2400) 'Engagements to Review Financial Statements', para. 26, *Handbook of International Quality Control, Auditing Review, Other Assurance, and Related Services Pronouncements*, International Federation of Accountants, New York.

11 IAASB, 2012, International Standards on Review Engagements 2400 (ISRE 2400) 'Engagements to Review Financial Statements', Appendix 3, *Handbook of International Quality Control, Auditing Review, Other Assurance, and Related Services Pronouncements*, International Federation of Accountants, New York.

12 IAASB, 2012, International Standards on Assurance Engagements 3000 (ISAE 3000) 'Assurance Engagements other than Audit or Review of Historical Financial Information', para. 2, *Handbook of International Quality Control, Auditing Review, Other Assurance, and Related Services Pronouncements*, International Federation of Accountants, New York.

13 IAASB, 2012, International Standards on Assurance Engagements 3000 (ISAE 3000) 'International Framework for Assurance Engagements', para. 20, *Handbook of International Quality Control, Auditing Review, Other Assurance, and Related Services Pronouncements*, International Federation of Accountants, New York.

14 IAASB, 2012, International Standards on Assurance Engagements 3000 (ISAE 3000) 'Assurance Engagements other than Audit or Review of Historical Financial Information', para. 11, *Handbook*

of International Quality Control, Auditing Review, Other Assurance, and Related Services Pronouncements, International Federation of Accountants, New York.

15 IAASB, 2012, International Standards on Assurance Engagements 3000 (ISAE 3000) 'Assurance Engagements other than Audit or Review of Historical Financial Information', para. 49, *Handbook of International Quality Control, Auditing Review, Other Assurance, and Related Services Pronouncements*, International Federation of Accountants, New York.

16 US Securities and Exchange Commission (SEC), 2003, Release No. 33-8238, Section II.A(1), *Final Rule: Management's Reports on Internal Control Over Financial Reporting and Certification of Disclosure in Exchange Act Periodic Reports*, SEC, 5 June.

17 Global Reporting Initiative, 2011, *Sustainability Reporting Guidelines*, GRI Secretariat, **http://www.globalreporting.org**, Amsterdam, Netherlands.

18 The SA8000* standard is the central document of our work at Social Accountability International. It is one of the world's first auditable social certification standards for decent workplaces, across all industrial sectors. It is based on conventions of the ILO, UN and national laws (**http://www.sa-intl.org**).

19 IAASB, 2012, International Standards on Assurance Engagements 3400 (ISAE 3400) 'The Examination of Prospective Financial Information', para. 27, *Handbook of International Quality Control, Auditing Review, Other Assurance, and Related Services Pronouncements*, International Federation of Accountants, New York.

20 IAASB, 2012, International Standards on Assurance Engagements 3400 (ISAE 3400) 'The Examination of Prospective Financial Information', paras 29 and 30, *Handbook of International Auditing, Assurance, and Ethics Pronouncements*, International Federation of Accountants, New York.

21 US Securities and Exchange Commission (SEC), 2003, Release. No. 33-8238, Section II.A(1), *Final Rule: Management's Reports on Internal Control Over Financial Reporting and Certification of Disclosure in Exchange Act Periodic Reports*, SEC, 5 June.

22 US Securities and Exchange Commission (SEC), 2003, Release. No. 33-8238, Section II.B(3), *Final Rule: Management's Reports on Internal Control Over Financial Reporting and Certification of Disclosure in Exchange Act Periodic Reports*, SEC, 5 June.

23 Management must state whether or not the company's internal control over financial reporting is effective. A negative assurance statement indicating that nothing has come to management's attention to suggest that the company's internal control over financial reporting is not effective will not be acceptable.

24 For the purposes of these standards, a 'material weakness' is defined the same as in US GAAS Statement on Auditing Standards No. 115 (codified in Codification of Statements on Auditing Standards AU §325) as a reportable condition in which the design or operation of one or more of the internal control components does not reduce to a relatively low level the risk that misstatements caused by errors or fraud in amounts that would be material in relation to the financial statements being audited may occur and not be detected within a timely period by employees in the normal course of performing their assigned functions.

25 Final rules also require a company to file, as part of the company's annual report, the attestation report of the registered public accounting firm that audited the company's financial statements.

26 Public Company Accounting Oversight Board (PCAOB), 2007, PCAOB Release No. 2007-005A, Auditing Standard No.5 'An Audit of Internal Control Over Financial Reporting That is Integrated With An Audit of Financial Statements', PCAOB, Washington, DC, 12 June.

27 See Sections 103(a)(2)(A)(iii)(I), (II) and (III) of the Sarbanes–Oxley Act.

28 Public Company Accounting Oversight Board (PCAOB), 2007, PCAOB Release No. 2007-005A, Auditing Standard No.5 'An Audit of Internal Control Over Financial Reporting That is Integrated With an Audit of Financial Statements', paragraph 87, PCAOB, Washington, DC, 15 November.

29 IAASB, 2012, International Standards on Assurance Engagements 3402 (ISAE 3402) 'Assurance Reports on Controls at a Service Organization', para. 1, *Handbook of International Quality Control, Auditing Review, Other Assurance, and Related Services Pronouncements*, International Federation of Accountants, New York.

30 IAASB, 2012, International Standards on Assurance Engagements 3402 (ISAE 3402) 'Assurance Reports on Controls at a Service Organization', para. 8, *Handbook of International Quality Control,*

*Auditing Review, Other Assurance, and Related Services Pronouncements,*International Federation of Accountants, New York.

31 Based on **http://www.theiirc.org**, the website of International Integrated Reporting Council.

32 Based on **http://www.ghgprotocol.org**, the website regarding the Greenhouse Gas Protocol.

33 Extract from the Philips integrated report, 2012; **http://www.philips.com/about/sustainability/ integrated annual report/index.Page** used with permission from Philips and KPMG.

34 Global Reporting Initiative, 2011, *Sustainability Reporting Guidelines 3.1*, GRI Secretariat, **http://www.globalreporting.org**, Amsterdam, Netherlands.

35 Global Reporting Initiative, 2011, *Sustainability Reporting Guidelines 3.1*, GRI Secretariat, **http://www.globalreporting.org**, Amsterdam, Netherlands.

36 IAASB, 2012, International Standards on Assurance Engagements 3410 (ISAE 3410) 'Assurance Engagements on Greenhouse Gas Statements', para. 13, *Handbook of International Quality Control, Auditing Review, Other Assurance, and Related Services Pronouncements*, International Federation of Accountants, New York.

37 IAASB, 2012, International Standards on Assurance Engagements 3410, (ISAE 3410)' Assurance Engagements on Greenhouse Gas Statements, paragraph 76, international Federation of Accountants, New Work.

38 IAASB, 2012, International Standards on Assurance Engagements 3410 (ISAE 3410) 'Assurance Engagements on Greenhouse Gas Statements', Appendix 2, Illustration 1, *Handbook of International Quality Control, Auditing Review, Other Assurance, and Related Services Pronouncements*, International Federation of Accountants, New York.

39 IAASB, 2012, International Standards on Assurance Engagements 3420 (ISAE 3420) 'Assurance Engagements to Report on the Compilation of Pro Forma Financial Information Included in a Prospectus', para. 1, *Handbook of International Quality Control, Auditing Review, Other Assurance, and Related Services Pronouncements*, International Federation of Accountants, New York.

40 IAASB, 2012, *Handbook of International Quality Control, Auditing Review, Other Assurance, and Related Services Pronouncements,* International Framework of Assurance Engagements, para. 20: An assurance engagement performed by a practitioner must exhibit all of the following elements, (1) A three party relationship involving: a practitioner, a responsible party; and the intended users; (2) A subject matter; (3) Suitable criteria; (4) Evidence; and (5) An assurance report, International Federation of Accountants, New York.

41 Based on IAASB, 2012, *Handbook of International Quality Control, Auditing Review, Other Assurance, and Related Services Pronouncements*, International Standards on Related Services, (ISRS 4400) 'Engagements to Perform Agreed-Upon Procedures Regarding Financial Information', International Federation of Accountants, New York.

42 However, if, in the judgement of the professional accountant, the procedures agreed to be performed are appropriate to support the expression of a conclusion that provides a level of assurance on the subject matter, then that engagement becomes an assurance engagement governed by the International Standards on Assurance Engagements and the Assurance Framework.

43 Based on IAASB, 2012, *Handbook of International Quality Control, Auditing Review, Other Assurance, and Related Services Pronouncements*, International Standards on Related Services, (ISRS 4400) 'Engagements to Perform Agreed-Upon Procedures Regarding Financial Information', para. 7, International Federation of Accountants, New York.

44 Based on IAASB, 2012, *Handbook of International Quality Control, Auditing Review, Other Assurance, and Related Services Pronouncements*, International Standards on Related Services, (ISRS 4400) 'Engagements to Perform Agreed-Upon Procedures Regarding Financial Information', para. 9, International Federation of Accountants, New York.

45 Based on IAASB, 2012, *Handbook of International Quality Control, Auditing Review, Other Assurance, and Related Services Pronouncements*, International Standards on Related Services, (ISRS 4400) 'Engagements to Perform Agreed-Upon Procedures Regarding Financial Information', para. 18, International Federation of Accountants, New York.

46 Based on IAASB, 2012, *Handbook of International Quality Control, Auditing Review, Other Assurance, and Related Services Pronouncements*, International Standards on Related Services,

(ISRS 4400) 'Engagements to Perform Agreed-Upon Procedures Regarding Financial Information', Appendix 2, International Federation of Accountants, New York.

47 Based on IAASB, 2012, *Handbook of International Quality Control, Auditing Review, Other Assurance, and Related Services Pronouncements*, International Standards on Related Services, (ISRS 4410) 'Compilation Engagements', International Federation of Accountants, New York.

48 Based on IAASB, 2012, *Handbook of International Quality Control, Auditing Review, Other Assurance, and Related Services Pronouncements*, International Standards on Related Services, (ISRS 4410) 'Compilation Engagements', para. A21, International Federation of Accountants, New York.

49 Based on IAASB, 2012, *Handbook of International Quality Control, Auditing Review, Other Assurance, and Related Services Pronouncements*, International Standards on Related Services, (ISRS 4410) 'Compilation Engagements', para. 24, International Federation of Accountants, New York.

50 Based on IAASB, 2012, *Handbook of International Quality Control, Auditing Review, Other Assurance, and Related Services Pronouncements*, International Standards on Related Services, (ISRS 4410) 'Compilation Engagements', para. 40, International Federation of Accountants, New York.

51 Based on IAASB, 2012, *Handbook of International Quality Control, Auditing Review, Other Assurance, and Related Services Pronouncements*, International Standards on Related Services, (ISRS 4410) 'Compilation Engagements', Appendix 2, Illustrations 1 and 2, International Federation of Accountants, New York.

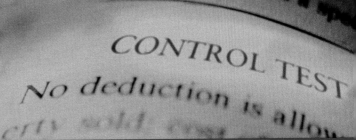

Chapter 15

CORPORATE GOVERNANCE AND THE ROLE OF THE AUDITOR

15.1 Learning Objectives

After studying this chapter, you should be able to:

1 Understand the concept of corporate governance.

2 Explain causes for corporate governance being in the spotlight.

3 Distinguish between different corporate governance structures.

4 Give examples of corporate governance codes.

5 Identify major elements of corporate governance.

6 Evaluate the role of the auditor in corporate governance.

15.2   Introduction

This chapter will discuss the concept of **corporate governance** and its different components. We also will sketch differences in corporate governance structures that exist all over the world. The distinction between a market-oriented versus network-oriented structure is central. The importance of the auditor in corporate governance will be described as well as some recent developments in corporate governance.

Topics covered in this chapter are: the nature of corporate governance, corporate governance structures, corporate governance committees and reports, law and regulation and practical issues like the relationship with audit committees. We will also discuss corporate governance and the role of the auditor.

The current attention for corporate governance originated after the Watergate affair in the USA during the 1970s, gained steam based on the financial debacles in the US saving and loans industries in the early 1980s (see Chapter 3, Concept and a Company 3.2 on Lincoln Savings & Loan) and has come under the spotlight again after Enron, Parmalat, US financial institution failures, etc. Similar financial debacles and discussions about transparency of capital markets and shareholders activated the attention for corporate governance in the early nineties in countries like the UK, Australia, South Africa and New Zealand. Because of the internationalisation and harmonisation of capital markets, the discussions also arose in continental Europe and Asia.

Illustration 15.1 shows four causes of the current corporate governance discussion:

1   bankruptcies, fraud and mismanagement;
2   the influence of public, customers and media;
3   globalisation of capital markets;
4   developments in information technology (IT).

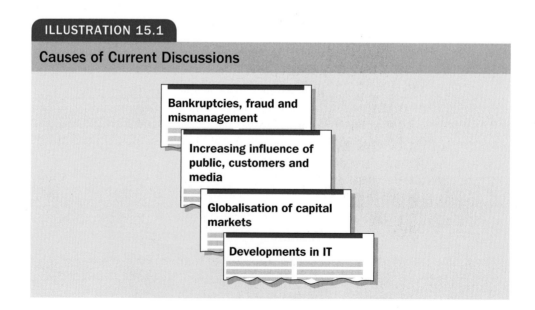

ILLUSTRATION 15.1

Causes of Current Discussions

- **Bankruptcies, fraud and mismanagement**
- **Increasing influence of public, customers and media**
- **Globalisation of capital markets**
- **Developments in IT**

■ Bankruptcies, Fraud and Mismanagement

Major reasons for corporate governance being in the spotlight are unexpected bankruptcies, fraud and mismanagement. Some examples of notorious disasters are names like Barings (UK), BCCI (UK), Daiwa (Japan), Polly Peck (US), Orange County (US), Maxwell (UK), Metallgesellschaft (Germany), Enron (US), Worldcom (US), ComROAD (Germany), Vivendi (France), Parmalat (Italy), Ahold (Netherlands), Lernhout & Hauspie (Belgium), Satyam (India) and Olympus (Japan).

■ Influence of Shareholders and Public

A second development is the increasing demand for shareholder participation, and also the increasing influence of other stakeholders like customers and the general public. Just think about the following dilemma. You are board member of a large oil and gas company and you have to decide to sink an outdated oil platform at sea or to dismantle it on land. Both options are legally acceptable. Also, assume that sinking the platform at sea is cheaper and will cause less environmental pollution than dismantling it on land. However, a well-known influential interest group gently demands that the platform be dismantled on land. What do you decide to do?

This example is a complicated dilemma, because the interest group could influence public opinion, including your customers and suppliers! The worst-case scenario is that these important stakeholders decide to stop doing business with your company. It is not very difficult to calculate the financial burden should this scenario materialise. These new type of dilemmas are central to current corporate governance discussions.[1] One of the consequences is the need for further transparency. Arguments used to decide in this kind of dilemmas should be reported. One of the current developments is the development of an Integrated Reporting Framework by the International Integrated Reporting Council (IIRC) in which the issuance of relevant information to all stakeholders is central.

■ Globalisation of Capital Markets

A third factor that places corporate governance in the spotlight is globalisation of capital markets and businesses. Events like application of International Financial Reporting Standards (IFRS) in all European Countries as of 2005 and the requirement of referring to ISA for statutory audits.[2] Another interesting development influencing the global capital markets is the extra territorial scope of the US Sarbanes–Oxley Act of 2002. As consequence of this law all companies issuing stocks in the US have to comply with this Act. This led to competition between governments and stock exchanges[3] as well as unintended side effects. Competition and globalisation recently resulted in a US Securities and Exchange Commission's attack on the Chinese affiliates of five major accounting firms, calling into question the future of China-based companies listing on the US stock exchanges at a time when accounting scandals have eroded investor appetite for these companies.[4]

Empirical studies show that institutional investors are increasingly making investment decisions on the basis of whether an enterprise meets the demands of corporate governance.[5]

■ Information Technology

Finally, it should not be a surprise that Information Technology (IT) is a major enabler of the new economy and, consequently, of corporate governance developments and discussions. IT introduces new XML[6] languages like XBRL[7] for standard business reporting.

This may lead to fundamental changes in disclosure of information for decision making. We also refer to the growing impact of social media, cloud computing and big data on business as a consequence of reporting and auditing. And then think of the political and fiscal consequences of loss of control over value added tax as transactions are being processed via the internet, the growing impact of worldwide cyber-crime and automation of major parts of business processes. These are all interesting IT-related issues that drive corporate governance developments.

15.3   The Nature of Corporate Governance

Corporate governance has been defined in many different ways by many different authors in many different countries. All aspects of corporate governance are subject to discussion in many parts of society, in both the private and the public sector.

We can liken 'governance' to a game of darts.[8] The **board of directors** sets the mission, vision, objectives and strategy of the entity. (These are like the target in the game of darts.) Governance deals with **managing** as a key responsibility of the board. (Managing includes coordination and skill required to hit the bull's eye of the target.) It is also the board's responsibility to design and monitor **controls** that reasonably assure that objectives are met (the darts player should ensure a good night's rest, make sure that windows are closed and that the audience is quiet). The third element of Governance is **supervision**. Independent supervision of management performance and remuneration is especially crucial (the umpire should supervise the darts game as crossing the line with your foot is not permitted). We all know that conflicts of interests between management and stakeholders do exist on a day-to-day basis, and can result in bankruptcies or major frauds. These potential conflicts of interests are one of the major reasons of incorporating monitoring by non-executive board members as well as introducing external (stock exchange or banking) oversight and external auditors as important gatekeepers. Governance also includes transparency[9] to all stakeholders that can be recognised (principles and rules of the darts match should be disclosed).

Source: sergign. Shutterstock

Concept and a Company 15.1

Li & Fung Third Generation Corporate Governance

Concept 'The techniques are modern, but the culture is still Confucian,' Victor Fung, Chairman (*Economist*, 2000).

Story A 2001 study of 495 companies by CLSA Emerging Markets found a strong link between good corporate governance, earnings and stock values. According to the study, the correlation between good corporate governance and share performance for the largest companies is 'a near perfect fit'. In that study, Li & Fung were rated as one of the top companies (Day, 2001). A corporate governance poll conducted by *Euromoney* magazine rated Li & Fung fourth highest globally in corporate governance and second highest in Asia (*Euromoney*, 2003).

Li & Fung, a family-owned company founded in 1906 during the Ching Dynasty, acted as a trader – basically a broker, charging a fee to put buyers and sellers together. When they decided to make a public stock offering on the Hong Kong Stock Exchange in 1973, they had already begun changing their governance. William Fung, managing director of the company put it this way, 'We typify the transition from a first-generation entrepreneurial firm to a company that is being made more professional to compete with Japan and the multinationals' (Kraar, 1994).

In 1989, to pay relatives who wanted to cash out, William Fung and his elder brother Victor, who is chairman of both the family company and Prudential Asia, arranged an LBO with bank financing. After cleaning up the privatised company and selling off fringe businesses like chartered boats, the brothers took it public again in 1992 (Kraar, 1994).

At Li & Fung, the Harvard-trained management has replaced family members in the company with professional managers, imported performance-related pay and instituted an open, western-style management regime. It accepts the need for stakeholding and transparent governance (Caulkin, 1996). Victor Fung explains, 'You can run a large empire with very few people making few decisions. Now you need a large number of small decisions' (*Economist*, 2000).

Li & Fung represent good corporate governance in several ways: leadership in outsourcing to customise customer products, leadership in employee management and fiscal controls, and encouraging best practices among its suppliers.

Distributed Manufacturing around the Customer's Needs

Li & Fung performs the high-value-added tasks such as design and quality control in Hong Kong, and outsources the lower-value-added tasks to the best possible locations around the world. For example, to produce a garment the company might buy yarn from Korea, have it woven and dyed in Taiwan, then shipped to Thailand for final assembly, using zippers from Japan. For every order, the goal is to customise the product to meet the customer's specific needs. They call this supply chain outsourcing 'distributed manufacturing' (Magretta, 1998).

Li & Fung is uniquely organised around the customer. They are divided into divisions and each division is structured around an individual customer or a group of customers with similar needs. Consider, for example, the Gymboree division where everyone is focused solely on meeting Gymboree's needs. On every desk is a computer with direct software links to Gymboree. The staff is organised into specialised teams in such areas as

▶

Li & Fung Third Generation Corporate Governance (continued)

technical support, merchandising, raw material purchasing, quality assurance and shipping (Magretta, 1998).

People Management and Fiscal Controls

For the creative parts of the business, Li & Fung gives people considerable operating freedom. Substantial financial incentives tied directly to the unit's bottom line motivate the division leaders. There's no cap on bonuses. On the other hand, when it comes to financial controls and operating procedures, Li & Fung does not want creativity or entrepreneurial behaviour. In these areas, Li & Fung centralises and manages tightly. They have a fully computerised operating system for executing and tracking orders, and everyone in the company uses the system (Magretta, 1998).

Since 1993, Li & Fung have changed from a Hong Kong-based Chinese company that was 99.5 per cent Chinese into a truly regional multinational with a workforce from at least 30 countries. Victor Fung says, 'We are proud of our cultural heritage. But we don't want it to be an impediment to growth, and we want to make people comfortable that culturally we have a very open architecture' (Magretta, 1998).

Best Practices at Suppliers

Wherever Li & Fung operates, it follows local rules and best practices. It makes sure its suppliers are doing the right thing when it comes to issues such as child labour, environmental protection and country-of-origin regulations. If it finds factories that don't comply, it will not work with them. This generally does not happen because of the company's long relationship with the suppliers (Magretta, 1998).

Li & Fung, in the course of monitoring its supplier network, constantly compares the performance of hundreds of different companies. It then shares the information with all of them, giving them a detailed understanding of their performance gaps, ideas for addressing them, and strong incentives for taking action. Benchmarking, rather than being an occasional event, is an intrinsic part of process management (Hagel, 2002).

Discussion Questions	■ How might Li & Fung's reputation for good corporate governance impact its on-going business? ■ As Li & Fung's auditor, which areas of the business would require the greatest test of controls? ■ Which are the most significant substantive tests?

References	Caulkin, S., 1996, 'Chinese walls', *Management Today*, London, September, p. 62. Day, P., 2001, 'Corporate Governance Can Be Strong Indicator of Stock Performance within Emerging Markets', *Wall Street Journal*, New York, 1 May, p. C14. *Economist*, 2000, 'The End of Tycoons', 29 April, Vol. 355, Issue 8168, p. 67. *Euromoney*, 2003, 'Good Practice Boosts Performance', September, Vol. 34, Issue 412, p. 222. Hagel III, J., 2002, 'Leveraged Growth: Expanding Sales without Sacrificing Profits', *Harvard Business Review*, October, Vol. 80, Issue 10, p. 68. Kraar, L., 1994, 'The Overseas Chinese', *Fortune*, New York, 31 October, Vol. 130, Issue 9, p. 91. Magretta, J., 1998, 'Fast, Global, and Entrepreneurial: Supply Chain Management, Hong Kong Style. An interview with Victor Fung', *Harvard Business Review*, September/October, Vol. 76, Issue 5, p.102.

■ Definitions of Corporate Governance

A generally accepted definition of corporate governance does not exist, so we will refer to several descriptions of the concept of corporate governance. Using the wording of the Toronto Stock Exchange,[10] 'Corporate Governance is the process and structure used to direct and manage the business and affairs of the corporations with the objective of enhancing shareholder value, which includes ensuring the financial viability of the business. The process and structure define the division of power and establish mechanisms for achieving accountability among shareholders, the board and management.' Corporate governance has been defined by the Cadbury Committee as 'the system by which companies are directed and controlled'.[11]

The Hampel Committee[12] made the point that this definition does not give sufficient recognition to other stakeholders groups who have legitimate interest in the organisation. The Netherlands Corporate Governance Code[13] noted that governance includes aspects like management and power, responsibility and influence and accountability and supervision, while integrity and transparency play an important part.

According to the Organisation for Economic Cooperation and Development (OECD),[14] corporate governance is affected by the relationships among participants in the governance system. The OECD specifies the distribution of rights and responsibilities among the different participants in the organisation – such as the board, managers, shareholders and other stakeholders – and lays down the rules and procedures for decision making.

Summarising, corporate governance essentially focuses on the dilemmas that result from the separation of ownership and control, and addresses, in particular, the principal–agent relationship between shareholders and directors on the one hand and the relationship between company agents and stakeholders on the other.[15] Other parties are lenders to the corporation: its trading partners (workers, customers and suppliers) as well as competitors and the general public. All of these parties have an interest in the success of corporation. All except competitors (and possibly the general public and analysts) stand to lose financially as a result of corporate failure. Each of the stakeholders has a different kind of relationship with the firm and specified rights to receive financial reports. These rights and relationships must be extensively described if we want to understand each claim and propose a reporting system that answers adequately this demand.[16]

■ Stakeholders

In general, corporate governance (CG) is the process and structure used to manage and direct the business, with the objective of enhancing shareholder value. But it has been recognised that directors of the business should also take into account the impact of their decisions on other stakeholders.

Usually, a list of stakeholders would also include the community, the general public, consumer groups, etc. However, these groups have no legal rights and no legal power to enforce any contract. The stakeholder relationships include a relationship between the community and the firm, between governments and firms, and between community and governments. Through this legal network, members of the community can influence the firm and express their opinion.

By some opinions, members of the community are not direct stakeholders of the firm but mediated stakeholders through the government. However, in some cases, members of community may believe that the legal network does not provide them with adequate or sufficiently efficient means to be heard. They choose to bypass the legal system with legitimate actions like consumer boycotts or even illegitimate and illegal actions.

■ Transparency

Transparency forms the backbone of good corporate governance. Transparency within governance is like a 'lubricant' for an engine. Transparency includes concepts like openness, reporting and disclosure.

In a business environment, transparency requires a sophisticated system of accounting. Such an accounting system should:

■ allow investors to assess the magnitude and timing of future cash flows to be generated by a business;
■ encourage efficient operations and maximisation of results;
■ provide an early warning of problems in meeting objectives of the firm;
■ lead to quick corrective action whenever things go bad.

Let us now turn to some of the causes of the current global corporate governance discussion.

Concept and a Company 15.2

Vivendi – Increasing Company Value through 'Operational Free Cash Flow'

Concept	Corporate disclosure and transparency.

Story   Vivendi Universal, SA is a media and telecommunications conglomerate with substantial holdings in the USA and Europe. Vivendi was formed in December 2000 as a result of a three-way merger of Vivendi's predecessor company with the Seagram Company Ltd ('Seagram') and French cable giant Canal Plus, SA ('Canal!'). Ordinary shares trade on the EuroNext Paris, SA (the Paris Bourse), and its American Depository Shares trade on the New York Stock Exchange and are registered with the SEC (US District Court, 2003).

Relevant subsidiaries include: Cegetel Group, based in France, a privately held telecommunications operator; Elektrim Telekomunikacja Sp.zoo (Telco), based in Poland, a holding company that owns various telecommunications assets; Maroc Telecom, based in Morocco, a telecommunications operator; Universal Music Group (UMG), based in the USA; and Houghton Mifflin Company, MP3.com, and USA Networks.

The cost of the company's listed above and other acquisitions totalled more than $60 billion in cash, stock and assumed debt. In July 2002, Vivendi reported that it experienced a liquidity crisis and began selling many of its assets. Prior to this reported liquidity crisis, it is alleged that Vivendi, Jean-Marie Messier, former CEO, and Guillaume Hannezo, former CFO, committed multiple violations of the anti-fraud, books and records, internal controls and reporting provisions of the federal securities laws (US District Court, 2003).

SEC Complaint

Vivendi, under the direction of Messier and Hannezo, reported materially false and misleading information about growth and liquidity of its earnings before income taxes, depreciation and amortisation (EBITDA) (US District Court, 2003). Specifically, the SEC's complaint includes the following allegations (SEC 2003):

- During 2001 and the first half of 2002, Vivendi issued misleading press releases authorised by Messier, Hannezo, and other senior executives. The press releases falsely portrayed Vivendi's liquidity and cash flow as 'excellent' or 'strong' and as sufficient to meet Vivendi's future liquidity requirements.
- Vivendi failed to disclose future financial commitments regarding two of its subsidiaries. Vivendi failed to disclose the commitments in SEC filings and in meetings with analysts.
- Vivendi, at the direction of its senior executives, made improper adjustments that raised Vivendi's EBITDA.
- Vivendi and the other defendants failed to disclose all of the material facts about Vivendi's investment in a fund that purchased a 2 per cent stake in Elektrim Telekomunikacja Sp. zoo (Telco), a Polish telecommunications company in which Vivendi already held a 49 per cent stake.

Reports of Liquidity

Vivendi emphasised two non-US GAAP measurements when it announced its financial results to the public. First, Vivendi typically announced in press releases and other public statements its EBITDA. Second, Vivendi reported its 'Operating Free Cash Flow' (also referred to as 'Operational Free Cash Flow'), which Vivendi defined in its earnings releases as 'EBITDA minus capital spending minus changes in working capital minus other expenses.'

On 26 June 2002, Vivendi issued a press release in response to media speculation regarding the company's liquidity. In that press release, Vivendi claimed that it had 'around 3.3 billion euro in unused credit lines to back up its commercial paper outstanding of nearly 1 billion euro. The cash situation has greatly improved since the beginning of the year.' Vivendi's access to credit, however, was much worse than this press release indicated.

In reality, Vivendi's overall cash flow was 'zero or negative', and Vivendi 'produced negative cash flow from [its] core holdings' such as its entertainment businesses 'that [was] barely offset by inaccessible cash flow from minority interests' (SEC, 2003). Vivendi did not have the ability to unilaterally access the earnings and cash flow of two of its most profitable subsidiaries, Cegetel and Maroc Telecom (US District Court, 2003).

Financial Commitments with Subsidiaries

Vivendi owned the majority of Cegetel and Maroc Télécom, but due to legal restrictions, Vivendi (as a parent company) was not permitted unilaterally to access the cash flow of subsidiaries. In fact, during the relevant time period, Maroc Télécom did not transfer cash to Vivendi, and Vivendi only accessed Cegetel's cash through a short-term current account that Vivendi had to repay by 31 July 2002. During the relevant time period, over 30 per cent of Vivendi's EBITDA and almost half of its cash flow were attributable to those two companies.

EBITDA

Concerned that Vivendi's EBITDA growth for the quarter ended 30 June 2001 might not meet or exceed market expectations, Vivendi personnel made various improper adjustments that raised Vivendi's EBITDA by almost €59 million (5 per cent of the total EBITDA of €1.12 billion).

Vivendi – Increasing Company Value through 'Operational Free Cash Flow' (continued)

Vivendi's EBITDA was increased primarily by causing Cegetel to depart from its historical methodology for determining its reserve for bad debts (accounts receivable). This improper departure caused Cegetel's bad debts reserve for the second quarter of 2001 to be €45 million less than it should have been given historical methods. As a result, Vivendi's overall EBITDA for that period was increased by the same amount.

In order to reach an EBITDA figure of €250 million, UMG prematurely recognised just over €3 million in deferred revenue that it received in connection with a contract between UMG and other parties. This payment should not have been recognised because it would need to be refunded if Vivendi failed to meet certain conditions by mid-December 2001 (US District Court, 2003).

Investment in Telco

Vivendi's did not disclose its investment in a fund that purchased a 2 per cent stake in Telco, a Polish telecommunications holding company.

In June 2001, Vivendi, which owned 49 per cent of Telco's equity, publicly announced its intention to purchase an additional 2 per cent of Telco's shares (increasing Vivendi's ownership of Telco equity from 49 per cent to 51 per cent). After this announcement, Vivendi learnt that Poland's antitrust authorities would have to approve the acquisition and that the credit rating agencies might react negatively to Vivendi's acquisition of additional Telco shares. As a result, rather than directly purchasing the 2 per cent interest in Telco, Vivendi deposited $100 million into an investment fund administered by Société Générale Bank & Trust Luxembourg. That fund subsequently purchased a 2 per cent stake in Telco in September 2001 (US District Court, 2003).

Sarbanes–Oxley-based Settlements

Vivendi and its executives were one of the first cases where fines and repayment of salaries were required under the Sarbanes–Oxley Act of 2002. The settlements include Vivendi's consent to pay a $50 million civil money penalty. The settlements also include Messier's agreement to relinquish his claims to a €21 million severance package that he negotiated just before he resigned his positions at Vivendi, and payment of disgorgement and civil penalties by Messier and Hannezo that total over $1 million (SEC, 2003).

Discussion Questions	■ What audit procedures should have been undertaken at Vivendi to assure proper disclosures were made? ■ Why is it not in the shareholders' best interest to use EBITDA reporting? ■ Discuss if management-determined measurements like 'Operational Free Cash Flow' should be allowed in reporting.
References	SEC, 2003, Litigation Release No. 18523, Accounting and Auditing Enforcement Release No. 1935, 'SEC Files Settled Civil Fraud Action Against Vivendi Universal, SA, its Former CEO, Jean-Marie Messier, and its Former CFO, Guillaume Hannezo', US Security and Exchange Commission, 24 December. US District Court, 2003, '*Securities and Exchange Commission v Vivendi Universal, S.A., Jean-Marie Messier, and Guillaume Hannezo*', United States District Court Southern District of New York, 23 December.

To understand current developments, one should understand differences in national corporate governance structures as well. These differences are caused by factors like culture, history, legal systems, and so on. In other words, corporate behaviour is influenced by history and culture of the country. Geert Hofstede, a social economist, characterised the Anglo-Saxon culture as masculine and Continental culture as feminine.[17]

To illustrate, we briefly sketch some differences between the **market** corporate governance structure and **network** corporate governance structure (see Illustration 15.2). Examples of countries with a market-oriented corporate governance structure are countries like the USA and the Commonwealth countries. Examples of network-oriented corporate governance structure countries are those in Continental Europe and some Asian countries. Market-oriented countries are more aggressive and confrontation-seeking, while 'network cultures' seek consensus instead of conflict. In general, network oriented countries apply civil law (principle of legality) while common law (case law) is one of the characteristics of market oriented countries.

Of course differences are not that black and white, but nevertheless, cultural distinction is a most powerful factor in explaining global differences in corporate governance (CG).[18] In Germany and Japan, there is a culture of long-term support from shareholders because of influence from banks, which are equity providers as well as lenders. In France and Italy, there is a tradition of companies being family-oriented and, indeed, many companies still have a major shareholder from the founding family. Such shareholders are usually represented on the board. Because shareholder interests are not the only yardstick by which corporate performance is measured, there is a greater expectation from shareholders that profits will be ploughed back into the organisation. This, coupled with a lack

---

ILLUSTRATION 15.2

Market-Oriented Versus Network-Oriented CG Structures

CG structures

Market-oriented (Anglo-Saxon)	Network-oriented (Continental)

• Confrontation
• Shareholders:
  – greater spread,
    individual private investors
• Shareholder relations
• One-tier boards
	• Consensus
	• Shareholders:
	  – banks
	  – individual investors
	• Stakeholder approach
	• Two-tier boards

of an aggressive takeover culture, helps to create a more long-term environment, without the fear of displacement engendered by the prospect of a hostile takeover.

In Anglo-Saxon countries, shares are widely distributed among individuals. In Continental countries, banks, insurance companies and other institutions mainly hold shares. As a consequence, stock exchanges play a more important role in market-oriented countries. At US high schools, share prices are a common basis for discussions among students. Because of this shareholder focus, directors often choose a short-term strategy to keep shareholders satisfied. One other characteristic of 'short termism' is a large variable component of remuneration as an incentive to maximise shareholder return. Examples of this component are incentives linked to EBITDA, share based and stock options awards.

■ Governance Boards

Another difference between the market-oriented and the network-oriented corporate governance structures is the two-tier separation between the board of management and the supervisory board in the network structure. In the market-oriented, one-tier system, the complete board (that is, both executive and non-executive directors) is formally responsible for day-to-day operating activities. However, this responsibility is delegated to the executive members, while the non-executive board members have a supervisory role. This means that non-executives supervise **and**, at the same time, are jointly responsible for day-to-day operations. In the two-tier system, supervising and management are formally separated: the monitoring of executive board members is exclusively the responsibility of the supervisory board. Therefore supervisory board members seem to be more independent than their non-executive counterparts. Despite these differences in structure role and tasks of boards are generally accepted and characterised by differentiating decision management and decision control.[19]

■ Demand for Supervision vs. Shareholder Rights

Given the previously mentioned fraud cases and bankruptcies, in Anglo-Saxon countries we observe a demand for stronger supervision and control. While in Continental countries such as France and the Netherlands, the demand for more shareholder rights is apparent, because of the globalisation of capital markets and a more active role for the supervisory board.

Given these worldwide developments, in several countries special corporate governance committees have been installed to prepare guidelines for good corporate governance.

15.5   Corporate Governance Committees and Reports

The most famous corporate governance codes are the Cadbury report in the UK (which focuses on the financial aspects of CG), the Dey Report[20] in Canada and the King Report[21] in South Africa. But there are others (shown in Illustration 15.3).

In the Netherlands, the Peters Report[22] was published in 1997. As concluded by Peters[23] in 2002, the code was not applied by most public companies in the Netherlands.

ILLUSTRATION 15.3

Corporate Governance Committees and Reports

- US – COSO Report [1992], Sarbanes–Oxley [2002], Report of the New York Stock Exchange Commission on Corporate Governance [2010]
- UK – Cadbury [1992], The Combined Code [2008], The UK Corporate Governance Code [2012]
- Canada – Dey: 'Where Were the Directors?' [1994], Corporate Governance: Guide to Good Disclosure [2006]
- Germany – [1998] 'Kontrag', Cromme Commission [2002], German Corporate Governance Code [2012]
- France – [1995, 1999] Viénot Rapport, Bouton [2002], Corporate Governance Code of Listed Corporations [2010]
- Netherlands – Peters Committee [1997], Tabaksblat [2003], Dutch Corporate Governance Code [2008]
- South Africa – [1994] 'The King Report', King Code of Governance for South Africa (King III) [1 September 2009]
- Australia – [1994] 'Bridging the Expectation Gap', Corporate Governance Principles and Recommendations [2010]
- OECD – 'Improving Competitiveness and Access to Capital in Global Markets' [1999], OECD Principles of Corporate Governance [2004]

Therefore, a new committee chaired by former Unilever Chair Morris Tabaksblat was installed. It presented a new code in December 2003. Like the French one, the Dutch capital market is increasingly influenced by Anglo-Saxon practice. As a consequence, the main CG guidelines focus on improving shareholders' rights and powerful supervision.

The interesting conclusion that can be derived from the different reports is the ongoing convergence of corporate governance structures. In other words, globalising financial and investment markets seeks the best of both worlds in corporate practices and policies, and hence 'best practice behaviour'.

■ Sarbanes–Oxley Act of 2002[24]

After the financial failures in 2001 and 2002, the US Congress passed a new law to prevent future disasters like Enron, Global Crossing, Adelphia, Tyco, and WorldCom. On 31 July 2002 US president George W. Bush signed the law championed by Senators Sarbanes and Oxley. The rush to pass the law was driven by a sense of escalating financial failures, Congressional pressure, near-term congressional elections, and calls for oversight of public company auditors by the SEC.

The Sarbanes–Oxley Act consists of 11 'Sections':

I   Public Company Accounting Oversight Board
II   Auditor Independence
III   Corporate Responsibility
IV   Enhanced Financial Disclosures
V   Analyst Conflicts of Interest

VI   Commission Resources and Authority

VII   Studies and Reports

VIII Corporate and Criminal Fraud Accountability Act of 2002

IX   White-Collar Crime Penalty Enhancements

X   Corporate Tax Returns

XI   Corporate Fraud and Accountability.

Most of the details of the law were not clearly worked out as it was written very rapidly. The SEC has since worked out further details. For example, a 93-page final rule[25] was written based on the two-paragraph Section 404 of the law. It is certain that the law will influence performance of the board of directors and auditors. The main characteristic is its legal force. Deviation from law leads to clear punishments. Company executives who fraudulently report financial statements are subject to criminal penalties if they 'knowingly' violate the law ($1 million or ten years' imprisonment) or if they are 'wilful and knowing' in their violation ($5 million or 20 years' imprisonment).

Not Just US Companies

Another characteristic of the law is its scope. All US-listed companies (domestic and foreign registrants and auditors) have to comply with the Sarbanes–Oxley Act, despite the differences in culture and laws of foreign companies. Recognising potential difficulties for foreign registrants, the SEC is not willing to provide exemptions to guarantee a level playing field.[26] The SEC ruled that exemptions to compliance with the Act will only be allowed in instances where the countries in which companies are domiciled have laws and regulations similar to that contained in the Sarbanes–Oxley Act.

■ European Union Laws

Partly in response to the Sarbanes–Oxley Act of 2002, the EU modernised company law and enhanced corporate governance in the European Union.[27] Good company law and good corporate governance practices throughout the EU will enhance the real economy. An effective approach fosters the global efficiency and competitiveness of business in the EU and help to strengthen shareholders' rights and third parties' protection.

EU Company Law

In 2002, a comparative study[28] concluded that the EU should not devote time and effort to the development of a European corporate governance code. This study identified more valuable areas for the European Commission to focus its efforts on; namely the reduction of legal and regulatory barriers to shareholder engagement in cross-border voting (participation barriers) as well as the reduction of barriers to shareholder's ability to evaluate the governance of companies (information barriers). Because of differences in European Law, a European Code would have to allow for many different options and, therefore, a common approach should be adopted with respect to a few essential rules and adequate coordination of corporate governance codes within Europe would then be ensured.[29]

In its 2003 Action Plan on modernising company law and enhancing corporate governance in the European Union the Commission considered as a priority to encourage the coordination and convergence of national codes through regular high level meetings of the European Corporate Governance Forum. The European Corporate Governance Forum was first set up at the end of 2004. Part of the work programme is an evaluation of the effectiveness of monitoring and enforcement systems that the Member States have put in place with a view to the national corporate governance codes. The Forum publishes annually a report on its activities.[30]

Furthermore, the EU Commission Communication 'Action Plan: European company law and corporate governance – a modern legal framework for more engaged shareholders and sustainable companies' of 2012 outlines the initiatives which the Commission intends to take in this area in the coming years in order to modernise and enhance the current framework.

The initiatives, which will be both legislative and non-legislative, follow three main lines:

- Enhancing transparency between companies and investors.
- Encouraging long-term shareholder engagement.

Improving the framework for cross-border operation of companies.

In addition, the Action Plan also launches a process of codification of most company law directives.

15.6 Best Practice from a Global Perspective

Here we discuss some of the best practices that are on the worldwide agenda for modernisation of governance related to the four elements of governance we mentioned: managing including board responsibility, supervision, internal control and transparency. We can only highlight some choice examples of what is currently seen as best practice from a global point of view. Among others, important sources are the OECD report *Corporate Governance, Improving Competitiveness and Access to Capital in Global Markets*,[31] the Sarbanes–Oxley Act, the UK Corporate Governance Code, and the ongoing proposals reforming corporate governance in the EU.

■ Managing Best Practice

An important element of governance is 'managing' which includes the concepts of mission, strategy, objectives, and compatibility with societal objectives.

Best practice requires that boards take leadership in defining corporate mission and strategy, as these issues are often seen as 'corporate glue' and consequently are essential for the success and vitality of the company. To illustrate its importance, we refer to the Royal Dutch Shell Group. This company started to formulate and disclose its mission and principles way back in the 1970s, because of the sharp attacks of pressure groups on the multinational's relationships with South Africa's apartheid regime. Nowadays – based upon years of experiences – Shell's board publicly discusses its mission and principles to provide cohesion, common purpose and shared values for a global and decentralised organisation. Some other companies that more recently responded to 'attacks' of pressure groups, such as non-governmental organisations, employee unions or consumer representatives, are Adidas, Novartis, Nike, BP, Wal-Mart and Apple. It can be expected that new social media like twitter and blogs will further influence 'management'.

Closely related to mission and strategy, key objectives of the company are to engage profitably, efficiently and responsibly in selected businesses. These objectives lead us to another management best practice, namely 'recognising societal interest'.

Recognising Societal Interest

As companies do not act independently from the societies in which they operate, corporate actions must be compatible with societal objectives concerning social cohesion, individual welfare and equal opportunities for all. Attending to legitimate social concerns should benefit all parties in the long run, including shareholders. At times, however, there may be a trade-off between short-term social costs and the long-term benefits to society of having a healthy, competitive private sector.

The current debate and search for sustainability is a very interesting example of societal interest. Sustainability is often indicated by the triple bottom-line reporting, about 'economic, social and environmental issues'. We quote Mark Moody Stuart[32] as Chair of Shell's Committee of Managing Directors: 'My colleagues and I are totally committed to a business strategy that generates profits while contributing to the well-being of the planet and its people. We see no alternative.'

Companies in the raw material industry, like Shell, are scared of losing reputation and consequently profit, and therefore want to control reputational risk. For that reason, best practice means that management has to focus on stakeholders' interest instead of having an exclusive focus on shareholders' interest.[33] The owner of the company should of course play an active role in corporate governance.

Concept and a Company 15.3

Hollinger International – 'Greed has been severely underestimated and denigrated, unfairly so, in my opinion' – Conrad Black, CEO (Newman, 2004)

Concept Board responsibility, executive control.

Story Conrad Black (Lord Black of Crossharbour) was CEO of publicly traded Hollinger International (HI) and other related companies for 25 years. HI is a newspaper publisher with 270-odd publications, the most important being London's *Daily Telegraph*, the *Jerusalem Post*, London's *Spectator* magazine and the *Chicago Sun-Times*. The story of HI involves several other companies controlled by Lord Black, his wife and his associate David Radler, former president of HI. These controlled companies include: holding companies Ravelston, Argus, and publicly traded Hollinger Inc. (H); Black's private management services firm, Ravelston Management Inc. (RMI); and newspaper companies Horizon and Bradford.

Hollinger International's board included some well-known individuals, such as Margaret Thatcher, Henry Kissinger, his eminence Emmett Cardinal Carter, Chaim Herzog, a former president of Israel, James Thompson, a former governor of Illinois, Lord Carrington, the former secretary general of NATO, Richard Perle, one of the architects of George W. Bush's Iraq policy, as well as half a dozen other British lords, plus the Italian industrialist Giovanni Agnelli. Not a single one of them (except Agnelli, who runs Fiat) was trained to read a balance sheet well enough to spot some of the irregularities taking place.

Unusual Governance Structure

HI corporate governance employed an unusual ownership model. HI was controlled by H through a device called 'super voting shares', which allowed H to cast 72.6 per cent of any vote while holding only 30.3 per cent of the company's combined equity. H is, in turn,

77.8 per cent owned by private companies Ravelston and Argus, which are owned primarily by Black, his wife and David Radler (McDonald, 2004). So the controlling interest in HI is held by Black via holding companies Ravelston, Argus and H.

Unusual Payments

Cash flows between the companies are even more complex. Argus depends on dividend payments from H. In turn, H depends on support payments from RMI, which depends on management fees from HI. RMI billed HI an annual average of US$28 million for its services between 1996 and 2004. The board waved through substantial fees going to Ravelston – about $24 million in 2002 – for what was vaguely defined as 'advisory, consultative, procurement and administrative services', and a comparable payment in 2003. The companies also borrowed from each other – Ravelston owed $59.2 million to Argus as at September 2003 (*Wall Street Journal*, 2004).

Whenever HI sold any assets (such as a newspaper), they paid H, Ravelston and Black, and his associates directly in 'non-compete fees' – fees paid by the newspaper acquirer to prevent the seller from going into the same market with another newspaper. Of the US$73.7 million non-compete fees paid to Black and his associates, the board of directors did not approve $32 million (*Wall Street Journal*, 2004).

Events Leading to the Fall

Events that led to Conrad Black losing control of his media empire started 10 March 2003 when H issued US$120 million in debt at 11.875 per cent, pledging most of its HI stock as collateral. A default on this loan would cause H to lose the HI controlling shares. One month later, H said it was uncertain if it could meet future financial obligations. In May, Standard & Poor's Rating Services downgraded H's credit rating to 'selective default', In October, Moody's downgraded H because of 'questionable corporate governance practices' (Newman, 2004).

In November, HI stopped making payments to Ravelston, upon which H depends for cash flow. In January 2004, worried about loan default, thereby losing the HI shares pledged as collateral, Black and Ravelston agreed to sell its controlling interest in H and its newspaper assets to Press Holdings International Ltd for $605.5 million (Newman, 2004).

Shareholder reaction began 19 May 2003 when investment firm Tweedy Browne Co. LLC, one of HI largest minority shareholders, filed its concerns about management with the US Securities and Exchange Commission. Among them were sales of HI assets to Horizon Publications Inc. (controlled by David Radler, HI's president, who also owns 14.2 per cent of Ravelston). The complaint also questioned both 'services agreements' in which HI paid US$203 million to Ravelston and affiliated firms from 1995 to 2002; and US$73.7 million in 'non-compete payments' made directly to Black, other officers, and Ravelston, instead of to the company. Within one month, HI set up a special committee to investigate Tweedy Browne allegations (Newman, 2004).

The HI shareholder battles culminated on 17 November 2003 when HI announced the resignations of Black as CEO and Radler as president. One basis for dismissal is US$32 million in unauthorised non-compete payments made to Black. In January 2004, HI removed Black as chairman of the board. HI filed a lawsuit against Hollinger Inc., Ravelston, Black and Radler to recover 'damages and disgorgement of more than US$200 million' (Newman, 2004).

Black and Radler each agreed to repay US$7.2 million in unauthorised non-compete fees. In December, Black missed his first US$850,000 scheduled payment to H. Black told HI he would not repay 'certain disputed non-compete payments' because he believed they were approved by independent directors.

Hollinger International – 'Greed has been severely underestimated and denigrated, unfairly so, in my opinion' – Conrad Black, CEO (Newman, 2004) (continued)

At H's annual meeting, Black called the controversy over corporate governance a 'sideshow'. H announced that all or part of the firm was up for sale. Four independent directors (friends of Black) who made up the H audit committee resigned after the company's board rejected their recommendations to keep Black.

In November, KPMG, H's outside auditor, received subpoenas from the SEC requesting documents. On 20 November, Conrad Black resigned as CEO of H, two days earlier than expected, so he would not be required to sign the quarterly CEO certification of statements required by the SEC (Heinzl, 2003). In December, KPMG LLP quit as auditor of Hollinger Inc. after the company refused to make management changes.

H disclosed the possibility of conflicts of interest. In 2003's annual information form, H warned shareholders: 'There may be a conflict between his [Black's] interests and interests of other shareholders.' The same document pointed out that HI routinely did business with other companies controlled by Black. Those deals 'may not be as favourable to the Company as those that could be negotiated with non-affiliated third parties,' it stated (McClearn, 2004).

Selling Out

Lord Black never disclosed his deal to sell control of H, and therefore the controlling interest in HI. HI learnt of Black's clandestine dealings along with the rest of the world on 18 January 2004 when Black and Press Holdings International Ltd announced their agreement. To stop the HI board and special committee looking for a buyer for HI from interfering with the sale to Press Holdings, Ravelston filed action in Ontario court to pre-empt any effort by Hollinger International to halt the sale.

Court Judgment

The action to stop HI from interfering with Black's sale to Press Holdings went to trial before Judge Leo Strine. Strine ruled against Conrad Black and said that Black's plan to sell control of his H newspaper empire to Press Holdings was about the legality of Black's business practices. Strine determined that Black had misled his former colleagues at HI, violated his fiduciary duties to its shareholders on numerous occasions and acted in bad faith on others. Strine even said the manner in which the board was led to 'approve' one non-compete payment to Black was possibly 'a fraud on the board'. Ultimately, he didn't trust Black: 'It became impossible for me to credit his word, after considering his trial testimony in light of the overwhelming evidence of his less-than-candid conduct towards his fellow directors,' Strine wrote. 'His explanations of key events and of his own motivations do not have the ring of truth' (McClearn, 2004).

Aftermath

Black was convicted in US District Court in Chicago on 13 July 2007 and sentenced to serve 6.5 years in federal prison and pay Hollinger $6.1 million, in addition to a fine of $125,000. Black was found guilty of diverting funds for personal benefit from money due (to) Hollinger International, and of other irregularities. After this sentencing, a series of lawsuits occurred dealing with the definition of 'Honest Services Fraud'. Black was released. However, the final resentencing on 24 June 2011 resulted in Black receiving a reduced term of 42 months and a fine of $125,000, returning him to prison on 6 September 2011 to serve the remaining 13 months of his sentence.

Discussion Questions	■ What are the main problems with the corporate governance structure describe above? ■ Given all the related party transactions, what audit procedures would you recommend?

References	Heinzl, M., 2003, 'Hollinger Faces an SEC Inquiry: Unauthorised Payments Are the Apparent Subject; Colson Gets Broader Duties', *Wall Street Journal*, New York, 20 November, p. B10. Newman, P.C., 2004, 'Epitaph for a Heavyweight', *Mcclean's*, Toronto, 2 February, Vol. 117, Issue 5, p. 44. McClearn, M., 2004, 'The Verdict', *Canadian Business*, Toronto, 1–14 March, Column 77, Issue 5, p. 22. McDonald, D., 2004, 'The Man Who Wanted More', *Vanity Fair*, April, p. 148. *Wall Street Journal*, 2004, 'Hollinger's Black Out', New York, 20 January, p. A10. http://en.wikipedia.org/wiki/Conrad_Black#Order_of_Canada.

■ Board Responsibility

The board defines the company's strategy, appoints the corporate officers responsible for managing the company and implementing this strategy, oversees management and ensures the quality of information provided to shareholders and to financial markets through the financial statements.[34]

Certification by Executives

Given fierce pressure caused by fraudulent financial reporting and bankruptcies, chief executive and financial officers of US-listed companies have to certify annual and quarterly reports filed with the SEC. Certification means that these executives reviewed the reports and based on their knowledge there are no untrue statements or omissions of material fact, and the statements fairly present the company's financial condition. Signing officers also sign for evaluating the effectiveness of disclosure controls and procedures as of a date within 90 days prior to the filing date of the report and for the fact that they presented their conclusions about effectiveness in the report. By signing they also confirm that disclosures have been made to auditors and the audit committee of all significant deficiencies in internal control or any fraud that involves employees with a significant role in internal control.

Penalties

Severe penalties are imposed for knowing that a report does not conform to requirements of the Act. The Sarbanes–Oxley Act forces responsibility on boards by forfeiture of certain bonuses and profits in case of fraudulent financial reporting. Also, board members can be barred from acting as a director in cases of non-compliance with the law. Another restrictive law to prevent board members from acting in a way that conflicts with the interest of the company is the prohibition of personal loans to executives. According to Sarbanes–Oxley, companies have to disclose whether a Code of Ethics for the CEO/CFO has been adopted, including contents, or if not, why not.

■ Supervising Best Practice

We now come to some best practices related to the 'supervising' component of governance. Global debates lead to an agreed vision that good corporate governance requires a system of independent supervision and active oversight of management. The result today is a view of governance best practice that is largely designed to prevent directors being influenced too much by management.

Independent Directors

A director is independent when he has no relationship of any kind whatsoever with the corporation, its group or the management of either that is such as to colour his judgement.[35] A reduction on management influence over boards is generally achieved by rules that ensure the independence of non-executive members of the board or, in Continental European countries, supervisory board members. An important issue is the influence of shareholders, employees and other stakeholders on the appointment of supervisory board members.

Who the Board Represents

According to Anglo-Saxon best practice, the board represents the shareholders – not other constituencies. On the other hand, according to best practice in the Netherlands, the board should represent all stakeholders. Nowadays, shareholders and work councils elect supervisory members in Germany and in the Netherlands (where members are appointed by themselves, a so-called system of co-optation, creating a sphere of 'old boys' network'). Here convergence to the Anglo-Saxon structure can be recognised, because of some hesitation of foreign investors like large pension funds (e.g. California employees' pension fund CalPERs) to invest in Dutch-listed companies. As a result, a current debate in some network-oriented structures is focusing on how to increase the influence of shareholders and employees in the nomination process.

Appraisal of Directors

With respect to re-appointment of individual board members, appraisal of individual directors is a key element of corporate governance. Boards have a special responsibility for designing and approving appropriate remuneration schemes and this has been globally accepted as best practice. A special remuneration committee should therefore be installed and report to the shareholders each year on remuneration of both directors and management.

■ Audit Committee

A separate audit committee is another expression of best practice. Regulated corporate governance via audit committees began in the USA in 1978 with audit committee requirements by stock exchanges based on recommendations of the Cohen Commission.[36] As of 1978, the major American stock exchanges have required listed firms to have audit committees comprised of independent, outside, directors who own relatively little stock in a firm and who are not members of management. Over time and over various corporate failure eras, audit committees have been assigned increasing responsibilities for monitoring management, corporate reporting, and relations with the independent auditor. The audit committee acts on the behaviour of stockholders in this regard.

The European Union Directive of 2006/43/EC, article 41.2 states that:

> ... the audit committee shall, inter alia: (a) Monitor the financial reporting process; (b) Monitor the effectiveness of the company's internal control, internal audit where applicable, and risk management systems; (c) Monitor the statutory audit of the annual and consolidated accounts; (d) Review and monitor the independence of the statutory auditor or audit firm, and in particular the provision of additional services to the audited entity.

According to this Directive, the audit committee oversees the audit process and communicates directly with the auditor without going through management. The committee would also select the auditor and propose the appointment to shareholders. In addition, if a company dismissed an auditor it would need to explain the reasons to the relevant authority in the Member State concerned.

Currently, the committees are charged with conducting meetings with the internal and external auditors, reviewing financial statements before they are issued to the public, and, in certain circumstances, taking action to control management. Audit committees are typically the primary locus for suggestions for improvement of the process and also focus of recent failures. These committees should focus on high quality financial reporting and risk management (including identification and control). Furthermore, audit committees should maintain a charter, and regularly assess the performance against this charter.

Independent Directors

Sarbanes–Oxley explicitly establishes an independence definition for audit committee members. An audit committee member should not receive fees other than for board service and should not be an 'affiliated person' of the issuer (publicly listed company) or any subsidiary.

Financial Expert

Section 407 of the Sarbanes–Oxley Act states[37] that the SEC shall issue rules to require issuers to disclose whether at least one member of its audit committee is a 'financial expert'. The final SEC rules state[38] that the audit committee financial expert's expertise should be related to the body of generally accepted accounting principles used in the issuer's primary financial statements filed with the SEC. The company must disclose the name of the audit committee financial expert and whether that person is independent.

Auditor Oversight

As they are responsible for oversight of external reporting, internal controls and auditing, the audit committee should play a role in guarding independence of the auditor. In this respect, Sarbanes–Oxley and 'best practice' teach that the audit committee is directly responsible for the appointment, compensation, and oversight of the auditor. In 2006 the International Forum of Independent Audit Regulators (IFIAR) was established based on the following activities:

1 to share knowledge of the audit market environment and practical experience of independent audit regulatory activity;
2 to promote collaboration in regulatory activity; and
3 to provide a focus for contacts with other international organisations which have an interest in audit quality.

Currently, almost 50 national independent audit oversight authorities are member of IFIAR.[39]

Auditor Reports to Audit Committee

To support the supervisory role of the audit committee, the Sarbanes–Oxley Act (as well as most of the Corporate Governance Codes) requires the auditor to report directly to the audit committee:[40]

- all critical accounting policies and practices in use by the publicly listed company;
- GAAP alternatives discussed with management and any alternative preferred by the audit firm;
- other material written communications such as management letters and unadjusted audit differences.

Whistle-Blower Communications

To be able to perform its tasks, Sarbanes–Oxley requires the audit committee to establish a protocol to address 'whistle blower' communications.[41] This duty comprises:

- receipt, retention and treatment of complaints received by the company regarding accounting, internal controls or auditing matters;
- confidential and anonymous submissions by employees.

Financial Expert on Audit Committee

A next interesting requirement in the USA's strive to have effective audit committees is the requirement to disclose in the annual report that the audit committee has at least one financial expert to be defined by the SEC.[42] The audit committee should consider 'whether a person, through education and experience as a public accountant or auditor or a principal financial officer, comptroller, or principal accounting officer of an issuer, or from a position involving the performance of similar functions, has:

- an understanding of generally accepted accounting principles and financial statements;
- experience in:
  - the preparation or auditing of financial statements of generally comparable issuers; and
  - the application of such principles in connection with the accounting for estimates, accruals, and reserves;
- experience with internal accounting controls; and
- an understanding of audit committee functions.'

To emphasise the importance of audit committees, Sarbanes–Oxley states that non-compliance with audit committee requirements can lead to de-listing of US stock exchanges.

To prevent any misunderstanding to occur, most of the current Corporate Governance Codes do include best practices requiring similar expertise or experience of at least one member of the audit committee.

Board Training

Finally, according to 'best practice' in the UK, France and the Netherlands, every new board member should follow appropriate training. Training should include general orientation for new supervisory board members, contact with the company's higher management officers and ongoing permanent education by means of external seminars and reading material. Once again, these requirements should be put onto the world-wide agenda for modernisation of governance. In other words, best practice should recognise that supervising is a professional task, requiring specific expertise, experience and skills.

■ Internal Control Best Practice

The US Treadway Commission[43] recommended in 1978 that prevention and detection of fraud should be guaranteed through strong internal controls. Treadway also recommended that guidelines be developed on internal control to allow management to report against some framework. Such internal-control guidelines were published in 1992 and are known as the COSO Report.[44]

Cadbury Committee

The Cadbury Committee in the UK was also established in response to a concern about the reliability of financial reporting. The Code of Best Practice issued by Cadbury deals with internal controls as defined by COSO. The current UK Code[45] even requires that 'The board should, at least annually, conduct a review of the effectiveness of the company's risk management and internal control systems and should report to shareholders that they have done so. The review should cover all material controls, including financial, operational and compliance controls.'

Since the publication of Cadbury's Code of Best Practice, several regulators and corporate governance committees followed in the footsteps of their UK trend-setting cousins and have also developed similar recommendations concerning internal control. Most of the national corporate governance codes that have been issued since include a similar best practice.

SOX 404

Section 404 (SOX 404) of the Sarbanes–Oxley Act[46] requires the annual report of issuers to contain management reports which shall:

1 state management responsibility for internal control structure and procedures;
2 give an assessment of effectiveness.

To be able to perform such an assessment, management should select a set of criteria that are established like the COSO criteria. Management should document internal controls; perform a gap analyses and revise/redesign controls that seem to be inadequate; examine, monitor and evaluate the internal controls; and conclude on their design and operating effectiveness. Detailed standards for the report to comply with SOX 404 were discussed in Chapter 4 'An Auditor's Services'.

Auditor Report on Management's Assertion about Internal Controls

Sarbanes–Oxley requires that the auditor report on management's assertion of the effectiveness of internal controls. The auditors' internal control attestation engagement is inseparable from the engagement to conduct an audit.

To be able to attest the auditor should:

- obtain understanding of internal control and management's evaluation;
- evaluate design effectiveness of controls;
- test and evaluate the operating effectiveness of controls;
- form an opinion.

This requirement has not been copied into many corporate governance codes. Among those countries that introduced a SOX (Act) approach are South Korea, Israel and China. China SOX, China's version of the Sarbanes–Oxley Act of 2002 was issued in 2008, with supporting guidelines issued in 2010. Supplementing Guidelines require listed companies and non-listed large and medium-sized enterprises to disclose an annual self-evaluation report on the effectiveness of their internal control as well as engage an accounting firm to issue an auditor's reports on the effectiveness of their internal control in financial reporting. Application Guidelines include 18 aspects for enterprises to focus on in establishing internal controls, along with definitions and examples (see Illustration 15.4), while Evaluation Guidelines provide an outline for enterprises to perform comprehensive assessments on the design and operation of their internal controls. These guidelines are generally in line with international materials.

ILLUSTRATION 15.4

China SOX – Aspects of Internal Control

Organisational Structure	■ Ensure that decision-making, execution and supervision are separate and from adequate checks and balances ■ Conduct an overall evaluation of the efficiency and effectiveness of the design and operation of its organisation on a regular basis
Development Strategy	■ Set up strategy committee to be in charge of the management of development strategies and formulation of a development strategy proposal, which will be implemented after adoption upon deliberation by the board of directors and approval at the shareholders' meeting
Human Resources	■ Formulate annual plans on human resource needs and evaluate its execution on a regular basis
Social Responsibilities	■ Establish stringent work safety management systems, rigorous product quality control and inspection systems ■ Diligently perform energy conservation and emission reduction responsibilities ■ Establish a scientific employee remuneration system and incentive mechanism ■ Ensure the entitlement of staff members to rest and leave days
Corporate Culture	■ Actively cultivate a corporate culture and a corporate culture assessment system which focuses on whether the directors, supervisors, managers and other senior management personnel have performed their duties in corporate cultural building and whether all employees identify with the enterprise's core values
Fund-related Activities	■ Based on its fund-raising goals and planning, draft fund-raising programs in light of the annual overall budget, specify the purposes, amount and structure of the funds to be raised and the fund -raising methods, and make sufficient estimates of the fund-raising costs and potential risks
Procurement Activities	■ Put procurement operations under centralised management, and avoid procurement from too many suppliers or decentralised procurement
Asset Management	■ Adopt advanced inventory management technologies and methods and standardize inventory management processes ■ Establish inventory management post accountability system
Sales	■ Strengthen market research and promptly adjust sales strategies according to market changes ■ Strengthen the management of bad debts of accounts receivable ■ Where the accounts receivables cannot be recovered in whole or in part, the enterprise should find out the reasons, clarify the responsibilities, and handle the issues in strict compliance with the examination and approval procedures and pursuant to China's uniform accounting standards
Research and Development	■ Establish a research achievement protection system, and strengthen the management of patents, non-patented technologies, trade secrets, as well as various kind of confidential drawings, programs and data formed during the R&D process ■ Establish a R&D activity assessment system to enhance the comprehensive assessment of project initiation and research, and research, and other process
Engineering Projects	■ Designate a special department to manage engineering projects on a centralised basis ■ Select contractors and supervision entities based on merits for its engineering projects through open bidding.

Illustration 15.4 (continued)

Guarantee	■ Designate relevant departments to be responsible for guarantee operations, conduct credit investigation and risk assessment of applicants, and issue written reports on assessment results ■ Establish a guarantee accountability system, and strictly hold accountable the departments and personnel that make major errors in guarantee decision-making, fail to go through the collective examination and approval process, or fail to manage guarantee operations as required
Business Outsourcing	■ Establish and improve the business outsourcing management systems, specifying the scope, manner, conditions, procedures and implementation of business outsourcing, make clear the duties and authority of relevant departments and positions, and reinforce the monitoring of the entire outsourcing process
Financial Reports	■ Hold financial analysis meetings on a regular basis, and make full use of he comprehensive information reflected in the financial reports to conduct a thorough analysis of the operation and management situation and the existing problems of the enterprise, and constantly improve its operation and management level
Comprehensive Budgeting	■ Establish a budgeting managements committee to perform the duties of comprehensive budgeting management ■ Prepare an annual comprehensive budget by adhering to its development strategies and annual production and operation plan, by taking into comprehensive consideration the economic policies, market conditions and other factors during the budget period
Contract Management	■ Designate a centralised contract management department; specify the procedures and requirements for contract drafting, examination and approval, performance and other aspects, conduct regular inspection and evaluation. ■ Establish a contract performance assessment system, analyse and assess the overall situation of contract performance and the specific situations of the performance of major contracts at least once at the end of each year
Internal Informal Communication	■ Formulate a rigorous internal reporting process, make full use of information technology, reinforce the integration and sharing of internal reporting information, and include internal reports into its unified information platform, so as to build a scientific internal reporting network ■ Make effective use of internal reports in risk assessment, accurately identify and systemically analyse the internal and external risks in its production and operation activities, and determine the strategies to tackle such risks, so as to achieve effective control of risks
Information Systems	■ Designate a department to manage the building of information systems on a centralised basis ■ Strengthen the management of critical information equipment such as the severs

Source: The Basic Standard Supporting Guidelines, Articles 4–18. Adapted from 'Internal Control and Audit', *China Briefing Magazine*, March 2012. Also see Ku, E., 2013, 'Internal Control and Anti-Corruption Regulations in China', 23 July, http://www.china-briefing-com.

Internal Audit Department

Referring to the COSO, internal control component 'monitoring' includes the contribution of an internal audit department. The UK Code of Best Practice recommended that 'Companies which do not have an internal audit function should from time to time review the need for one.' The Code also states that although internal audit should maintain independence from management, it can perform more than just a monitoring role. Internal audit arrangements naturally vary, but they have the potential to play a central role within the monitoring process.

Best Practice: Transparency

Finally, we discuss best practice transparency. Elements of transparency include timely disclosure of reliable, adequate and relevant information for decision making. Annual and consolidated financial statements should record the level of success that the executive board has enjoyed over the previous financial year. This helps to serve both the supervisory board and the capital market in their control and disciplining of management. Financial statements also contain information that can point to future corporate development, thus helping to create a basis for investment decisions. Investors want clear, reliable and internationally comparable information about enterprises. Available information should meet these needs.[47]

Corporate Governance Disclosure

Wall Street's pressure for profits can be great, with the potential risk that companies manage their earnings and disclosures. Stakeholders therefore call for reliable and relevant reporting of financial and non-financial information. Regulators and best practices are setting the tone.

In addition to the 'comply or explain' requirement, the UK Corporate Governance Code (2012)[48] includes specific requirements for disclosure which must be provided in order to comply (paragraph references to the Code are in parentheses):

- a statement of how the board operates, including a high level statement of which types of decisions are to be taken by the board and which are to be delegated to management (A.1.1);
- the names of the chairman, the deputy chairman (where there is one), the chief executive, the senior independent director and the chairmen and members of the board committees (A.1.2);
- the number of meetings of the board and those committees and individual attendance by directors (A.1.2);
- where a chief executive is appointed chairman, the reasons for their appointment (this only needs to be done in the annual report following the appointment) (A.3.1);
- the names of the non-executive directors whom the board determines to be independent, with reasons where necessary (B.1.1);
- a separate section describing the work of the nomination committee, including the process it has used in relation to board appointments; a description of the board's policy on diversity, including gender; any measurable objectives that it has set for implementing the policy, and progress on achieving the objectives. An explanation should be given if neither external search consultancy nor open advertising has been used in the appointment of a chairman or a non-executive director. Where an external search consultancy has been used it should be identified and a statement made as to whether it has any other connection with the company (B.2.4);
- any changes to the other significant commitments of the chairman during the year (B.3.1);

- a statement of how performance evaluation of the board, its committees and its directors has been conducted (B.6.1). Where an external facilitator has been used, they should be identified and a statement made as to whether they have any other connection to the company (B.6.2);
- an explanation from the directors of their responsibility for preparing the accounts and a statement that they consider that the annual report and accounts, taken as a whole, is fair, balanced and understandable and provides the information necessary for shareholders to assess and provide the company's performance, business model and strategy. There should also be a statement by the auditor about their reporting responsibilities (C.1.1);
- an explanation from the directors of the basis on which the company generates or preserves value over the longer term (the business model) and the strategy for delivering the objectives of the company (C.1.2);
- a statement from the directors that the business is a going concern, with supporting assumptions or qualifications as necessary (C.1.3);
- a report that the board has conducted a review of the effectiveness of the company's risk management and internal controls systems (C.2.1);
- where there is no internal audit function, the reasons for the absence of such a function (C.3.6);
- where the board does not accept the audit committee's recommendation on the appointment, reappointment or removal of an external auditor, a statement from the audit committee explaining the recommendation and the reasons why the board has taken a different position (C.3.7);
- a separate section describing the work of the audit committee in discharging its responsibilities, including: the significant issues that it considered in relation to the financial statements, and how these issues were addressed; an explanation of how it has assessed the effectiveness of the external audit process and the approach taken to the appointment or reappointment of the external auditor, including the length of tenure of the current audit firm and when a tender was last conducted; and, if the external auditor provides non-audit services, an explanation of how auditor objectivity and independence is safeguarded (C.3.8);
- a description of the work of the remuneration committee as required under the Large and Medium-Sized Companies and Groups (Accounts and Reports) Regulations 2008, including, where an executive director serves as a non-executive director elsewhere, whether or not the director will retain such earnings and, if so, what the remuneration is (D.1.2);
- where remuneration consultants are appointed they should be identified and a statement made as to whether they have any other connection with the company (D.2.1); and
- the steps the board has taken to ensure that members of the board, and in particular the non-executive directors, develop an understanding of the views of major shareholders about their company (E.1.2).
- The following information should be made available (which may be met by placing the information on a website that is maintained by or on behalf of the company):
  - the terms of reference of the nomination, audit and remuneration committees, explaining their role and the authority delegated to them by the board (B.2.1, C.3.3 and D.2.1); and
  - the terms and conditions of appointment of non-executive directors (B.3.2).

- The board should set out to shareholders in the papers accompanying a resolution to elect or re-elect directors:
  - sufficient biographical details to enable shareholders to take an informed decision on their election or re-election (B.7.1);
  - why they believe an individual should be elected to a non-executive role (B.7.2); and
  - on re-election of a non-executive director, confirmation from the chairman that, following formal performance evaluation, the individual's performance continues to be effective and to demonstrate commitment to the role (B.7.2).
- The board should set out to shareholders in the papers recommending appointment or reappointment of an external auditor. if the board does not accept the audit committee's recommendation, a statement from the audit committee explaining the recommendation and from the board setting out reasons why they have taken a different position (C.3.6).

Introduction of a New Business Reporting Model

The modernisation of current business reporting models is another best practice issue. Illustration 15.5 sketches some of the changes that closely follow changes in the corporate governance environment. The current model does serve as an effective foundation from which business reporting should start. However, 'real time' decisions are made by looking at both the lagging indicators (the historical financial statement) and leading indicators that enhance business reporting as the information is much closer to the event. The fact of the matter is that the one size fits all concepts to financial reporting are over 20 years out of date. The loss of relevance, or at least the need for more information, can easily be identified.

ILLUSTRATION 15.5

Current and Future Business Reporting Models

Current Reporting Model	Future Reporting Model
Shareholder focus	Stakeholder focus
Paper-based reporting	Web-based reporting
Standardised information	Customised information (relevant information for decision making)
Periodic reporting	Continuous (online, real-time)
Distribution of information	Dialogue (i.e. a two-way communication)
Financial information	Integrated reporting (based on relevant value drivers)

The International Integrated Reporting Council (IIRC) is a global coalition of regulators, investors, companies, standard setters, the accounting profession and non-governmental organisations (NGOs). Over 80 global businesses and 50 institutional investors are currently directly involved in the IIRC's work. This includes some of the world's most iconic brands, such as Coca-Cola, Clorox, Microsoft, Hyundai, Tata, Unilever, Marks & Spencer, SAP and National Australia Bank.[49] Together, this coalition shares the view that communication about businesses' value creation should be the next step in the evolution of corporate reporting. Integrated reporting (IR) is a process that results in communication, most visibly a periodic 'integrated report', about value creation over time. An integrated report is a concise communication about how an organisation's strategy, governance, performance and prospects lead to the creation of value over the short, medium and long term. While the communications that result from IR will be of benefit to a range of stakeholders, they are principally aimed at providers of financial capital.

Integrated reporting (IR) aims to:

- Catalyse a more cohesive and efficient approach to corporate reporting that draws together other reporting strands and communicates the full range of factors that materially affect the ability of an organisation to create value over time.
- Provide information on resource allocation by providers of financial capital that supports long-term, as well as short- and medium-term, value creation.
- Enhance accountability and stewardship with respect to the broad base of capitals (financial, manufactured, human, intellectual, natural, and social and relationship) and promote understanding of the interdependencies between them.
- Promote integrated thinking, decision-making and actions that focus on the creation of value in the long term, as well as short and medium term.

For the purpose of the IR Framework, the components of an organisation can be depicted in Illustration 15.6. These components are aligned with the content elements of an integrated report and are given in Illustration 15.7.

Organisations may seek independent, external assurance to enhance the credibility of their reports. Independent, external assurance may also provide comfort, in addition to internal mechanisms, to those charged with governance. The IR Framework provides criteria to which organisations and assurance providers assess a reporting organisation's adherence; it is not intended to provide the protocols for performing assurance engagements.

ILLUSTRATION 15.6

IR Framework

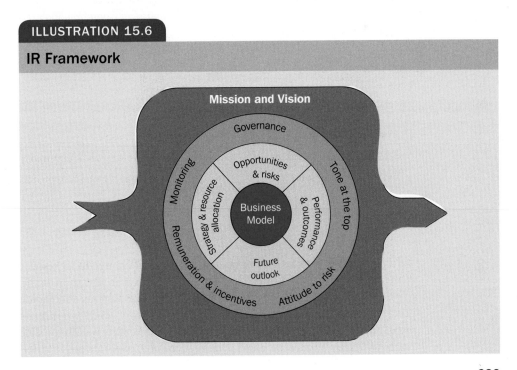

ILLUSTRATION 15.7

Content Elements of an Integrated Report

CONTENTS

1. **OVERVIEW**
2. **FUNDAMENTAL CONCEPTS**
   A. Introduction
   B. The capitals
   C. The business model
   D. Creating value

3. **GUIDING PRINCIPLES**
   A. Strategic focus and future orientation
   B. Connectivity of information
   C. Stakeholder responsiveness
   D. Materiality and conclseness
   E. Reliability
   F. Comparability and consistency

4. **CONTENT ELEMENTS**
   A. Organisational overview and operating context
   B. Governance
   C. Opportunities and risks
   D. Strategy and resource allocation plans
   E. Business model
   F. Performance and outcomes
   G. Future outlook

5. **PREPARATION AND PRESENTATION**
   A. Disciosure of material matters and the materiality determination process
   B. Frequency of reporting
   C. Time frames for short, medium and long term
   D. Reporting boundary
   E. Aggregation and disaggregation
   F. Involvement of those charged with governance
   G. Use of technology
   H. Assurance
   I. Other considerations

GLOSSARY
APPENDICES
   A. Other IIRC publicatons and resources
   B. Basis for conclusions

In conclusion, we can simply say that the pace of change in all respects is accelerating in this global, online and inter-connected world. This acceleration is affecting all aspects of our business and industries, and involves all our various stakeholders' and interest groups. It must be accepted that while corporate governance is concerned with harnessing of energy and power, the ability of a company to create wealth for stakeholders should not be stifled by bureaucracy and over-regulation. Corporate governance is not an end in itself. However, the transparency of governance practices can help to play a role in maintaining public confidence. Dialogue on these practices can lead to informed reflection on the dynamic and interdependent relationships, which constitute the corporate environment and hopefully 'best of both worlds.'

How do we proceed? We agree with the OECD's view that public policy makers and regulators should encourage the development of improved governance practices, with strong emphasis on government enabling voluntary private sector development rather than attempting to regulate it.

15.7 Corporate Governance and the Role of the Auditor

The external auditor plays a central role in good corporate governance. Despite the fact that auditors are indirect stakeholders, their core role is to provide assurance regarding:

- financial and non-financial information;
- internal control statements;
- corporate governance statements.

The auditor's role of auditing financial statements, including the identification and communication of deficiencies in internal control to those in charge of governance, is discussed throughout this book while an engagement to provide assurance on non- financial information and an audit of internal control statements have been elaborated on earlier in the text (see Chapters 14 and 4). That leaves the third important governance role – the audit or review of corporate governance statements. Providing assurance to these statements is only possible when verifiable and suitable criteria are available.

Concept and a Company 15.4

HIH Insurance Board Failure to 'See, Remedy and Report the Obvious'

Concept	Corporate culture, poor corporate governance model, the role of the auditor.
Story	HIH was one of Australia's biggest home-building market insurers selling home warranty insurance and builders' warranty insurance. Raymond Williams and Michael Payne established the business in 1968.
	Despite Australian regulation designed to detect solvency problems at an early stage, 'the corporate officers, auditors and regulators of HIH failed to see, remedy or report what should have been obvious.' Poor leadership, inept management and indifference to company problems marked the last years of HIH. Those involved in HIH management ignored or concealed the true state of the company's steadily deteriorating financial position, which led by 2001 to the largest corporate failure in Australian history (HIH Royal Commission, 2003). The problematic aspects of the corporate culture of HIH were caused by a number of factors. One was blind faith in a leadership that was ill-equipped for the task. Risks were not properly identified and managed. Unpleasant information was hidden, filtered or sanitised. Finally, there was no sceptical questioning and analysis.

HIH Insurance Board Failure to 'See, Remedy and Report the Obvious' (continued)

Underwriting Losses

The main reason for HIH's financial decline was several billion dollars in underwriting losses based on claims arising from insured events in previous years. Past claims on policies that had not been properly priced had to be met out of present income, i.e. a deficiency resulted from 'under-reserving' or 'under-provisioning'. The reserves were based on reports of independent actuaries and the assessment of those reports by the auditors. Actuaries were never called in before the board of directors to describe the report.

From as far back as 1997 their underwriting losses increased dramatically. In the year ending 31 December 1997 HIH made an underwriting loss of $33.8 million on net premium earned of $1,233.5 million. The comparative figures for the year ending 30 June 2000 are $103.5 million and $1,995.4 million respectively. Between 1997 and 1999 the underwriting loss was up 206 per cent while the net earned premium rose by only 25 per cent. The reported underwriting losses were high, but without several one-off entries they would have been much worse. On 12 September 2000 Andersen, HIH's auditor, made a presentation to the HIH audit committee. They said that in the 12 months to December 1999, one-off adjustments reduced the underwriting loss by $157 million; and at 30 June 2000 they reduced the loss by $360 million.

Reliance on intangibles

Another feature of the financial trend was the increasing reliance on intangible assets to support shareholders' equity. In addition to goodwill and management rights, HIH had on its balance sheet future income tax benefits, deferred information technology costs, and deferred acquisition costs. Goodwill alone represented 50 per cent of HIH's shareholders funds. By way of comparison, QBE and NRMA (two comparable Australian insurance companies) had a ratio of goodwill to shareholders funds of 4.9 per cent and 0.4 per cent respectively.

Acquisitions

At board level, there was little, if any, analysis of the future strategy of the company. Indeed, the company's strategy was not documented. As one director conceded, if he had been asked to commit to writing what the long-term strategy was, he would have had difficulty doing so. Examples of this lack of strategy were the acquisition of a UK branch (where losses amounted to $1.7 billion), reacquisition of US operations (causing losses of $620 million), and a joint venture with Alliance Australia Limited.

The most disastrous business transaction involved joint venture arrangements agreed between HIH and Allianz which ultimately caused HIH to experience an insurmountable cash flow crisis in early 2001 and largely dictated the timing of HIH's collapse. In addition to the transfer of HIH's most profitable retail lines to the joint venture, HIH was required to contribute $200 million received for the retail lines plus an additional $300 million in cash and assets to a trust to cover claims. All premium income (about $1 billion) was paid into the trust, and HIH was not allowed access to the funds until an actuarial assessment, about five months after the transfer.

The agreement to proceed with the Allianz proposal took a mere 75 minutes of the board of directors' meeting. The trust provisions and their potential adverse effect on cash flow were either completely overlooked or not properly appreciated.

Corporate Governance Model

The corporate governance model at HIH was deficient in a number of ways. There was a dearth of clearly defined and recorded policies or guidelines. There were no clearly defined limits on the authority of the chief executive in areas such as investments, corporate donations, gifts and staff emoluments. The board did not have a well-understood policy on matters that would be reserved to itself, but depended on the chief executive. In addition, it was heavily dependent on the advice of senior management. There were very few occasions when the board either rejected or materially changed a proposal put forward by management. The board was reluctant to disclose related-party transactions. The Chairman of the board gave board agendas to the CEO, but not to the board members, for comments.

Discussion Questions	■ What were the warning signs of financial decline that the auditors should have addressed in their procedures? ■ Describe why assessment of the corporate governance model is important to the audit. ■ What types of strategy and action could the board of directors initiate which could have changed the outcome?
References	HIH Royal Commission, Justice Owen, R., 2003, *The Failure of HIH Insurance*, Commonwealth of Australia.

As 'best practice' of the auditor's role of reviewing or auditing corporate governance statements, we refer to one of the earliest governance codes, the Cadbury report (1992). According to Cadbury, the accountant has to be engaged to review correctness of management's statement regarding compliance with the code of best practice. Following the work of the Hampel Committee on Corporate Governance in June 1998 the London Stock Exchange published a new listing rule together with related *Principles of Good Governance and Code of Best Practice* ('the Combined Code'). As before, a company's auditors are required to review such compliance statements (the second statement referred to above) before publication, but only in so far as it relates to certain Code provisions. These are as follows:

1 The directors should explain in the annual report their responsibility for preparing the annual report and accounts, and state that they consider the annual report and accounts, taken as a whole, is fair, balanced and understandable and provides the information necessary for shareholders to assess the company's performance, business model and strategy. There should be a statement by the auditor about their reporting responsibilities.

2 The board should, at least annually, conduct a review of the effectiveness of the company's risk management and internal control systems and should report to shareholders that they have done so. The review should cover all material controls, including financial, operational and compliance controls.

3 The board should establish an audit committee of at least three, or in the case of smaller companies, two, independent non-executive directors. In smaller companies the company chairman may be a member of, but not chair, the committee in addition to the independent non-executive directors, provided he or she was considered independent on appointment as chairman.

4 The board should satisfy itself that at least one member of the audit committee has recent and relevant financial experience.

5 The main role and responsibilities of the audit committee should be set out in written terms of reference and should include:

   (a) to monitor the integrity of the financial statements of the company and any formal announcements relating to the company's financial performance, reviewing significant financial reporting judgements contained in them;

   (b) to review the company's internal financial controls and, unless expressly addressed by a separate board risk committee composed of independent directors, or by the board itself,

   (c) to review the company's internal control and risk management systems;

   (d) to monitor and review the effectiveness of the company's internal audit function;

   (e) to make recommendations to the board, for it to put to the shareholders for their approval in general meeting, in relation to the appointment, reappointment and removal of the external auditor and to approve the remuneration and terms of engagement of the external auditor;

   (f) to review and monitor the external auditor's independence and objectivity and the effectiveness of the audit process, taking into consideration relevant UK professional and regulatory requirements;

   (g) to develop and implement policy on the engagement of the external auditor to supply non-audit services, taking into account relevant ethical guidance regarding the provision of non-audit services by the external audit firm; and to report to the board, identifying any matters in respect of which it considers that action or improvement is needed and making recommendations as to the steps to be taken; and

   (h) to report to the board on how it has discharged its responsibilities.

6 The terms of reference of the audit committee, including its role and the authority delegated to it by the board, should be made available.

7 Where requested by the board, the audit committee should provide advice on whether the annual report and accounts, taken as a whole, is fair, balanced and understandable and provides the information necessary for shareholders to assess the company's performance, business model and strategy.

8 The audit committee should review arrangements by which staff of the company may, in confidence, raise concerns about possible improprieties in matters of financial reporting or other matters. The audit committee's objective should be to ensure that arrangements are in place for the proportionate and independent investigation of such matters and for appropriate follow-up action.

9 The audit committee should monitor and review the effectiveness of the internal audit activities. Where there is no internal audit function, the audit committee should consider annually whether there is a need for an internal audit function and make a recommendation to the board, and the reasons for the absence of such a function should be explained in the relevant section of the annual report.

10 The audit committee should have primary responsibility for making a recommendation on the appointment, reappointment and removal of the external auditors. FTSE 350 companies should put the external audit contract out to tender at least every ten years. If the board does not accept the audit committee's recommendation, it should include in the annual report, and in any papers recommending appointment or reappointment, a statement from the audit committee explaining the recommendation and should set out reasons why the board has taken a different position.

See Illustration 15.8 which gives sample wording for the management's statement regarding compliance with the code of best practice.

If, in the opinion of the auditors the listed company has not complied with any of the requirements set out in the code, the listed company must ensure that the auditor's report includes, to the extent possible, a statement giving details of the non-compliance.

ILLUSTRATION 15.8

Sample Wording for the Management's Statement Regarding Compliance with the Code of Best Practice

Matters on which we are required to report by exception

We have nothing to report in respect of the following items that we are required to review under the Listing Rules:

- the Directors' statement, set out on page x, in relation to going concern; and
- the part of the Corporate Governance statement relating to the Company's compliance with the nine provisions of the UK Corporate Governance Code specified for our review; and
- certain elements of the Directors' report to the shareholders on Directors' remuneration.

Opinion on other matters because of voluntary compliance with the UK Companies Act 2006

- The part of the Directors' remuneration report to be audited has been properly prepared in accordance with the Companies Act 2006.
- In our opinion the information given in the Directors' report for the financial year for which the Group financial statements are prepared is consistent with the Group financial statements.

Matters on which we report by exception because of voluntary compliance with the UK Companies Act 2006

We have nothing to report in respect of the following items that we are required to report to you under the UK Companies Act 2006 if, in our opinion:

- adequate accounting records have been kept by the Group, or returns adequate for our audit have not been received from branches not visited by us; or
- the consolidated financial statements and the part of the Directors' remuneration report to be audited are not in agreement with the accounting records and returns; or
- certain disclosures of Directors' remuneration specified by law are not made; or
- we have not received all the information and explanations we require for our audit.

15.8 The Audit Profession and Corporate Governance

The audit profession not only plays a significant role in corporate governance, but is also forced to look after its own corporate governance structure! Financial reporting scandals and the collapse of Arthur Andersen prompted several regulators and professional institutes to develop new legislation and best practices. We will first look into some important new developments hitting the profession as introduced by the Sarbanes–Oxley Act. Central in the Sarbanes–Oxley Act is the establishment of the Public Company

Accounting Oversight Board (PCAOB) with the objective of closely monitoring the audit profession to restore investor confidence. One of the consequences of this is the end of self-regulation by the US audit profession.

Duties of the PCAOB are:

- Register public accounting firms that prepare audit reports for issuers. Public accounting firms must register and disclose (1) names of public clients; (2) fees received for audit services, other accounting services and non-audit services; (3) statement of quality control policies; (4) list of all accountants; (5) any penalties pending against the firm or individuals; and (6) copies of client issuer disclosures of accounting disagreements.
- Establish or adopt rules on auditing, quality control, ethics, independence, as related to preparation of audit reports. Conduct investigations and disciplinary proceedings involving registered public accounting firms. Establish auditing standards.
- Establish quality control standards. Quality control standards could include rules to require monitoring professional ethics and independence.[50] Availability of a formal consultation process, supervision of audit work, client acceptance and continuation procedures and internal inspection policies are further examples.

Audit firms in the US and individuals associated with audit firms listed in the US are required to comply with requests for testimony and production of documents concerning their clients who have issued publicly traded equity or debt. This requirement applies to all audit firms of US registrants and implies that foreign auditors can be forced to testify in US courts.

■ EU Directive on Statutory Audit

In 2006, the Commission of the European Union approved a major revision of the Eighth Company Law Directive. The main objectives of the Directive are to strengthen consistency and credibility of the external audit. The Directive set out a new structure for audit and corporate governance in the following areas:

- Qualifications to be a statutory auditor.
- Characteristics of a statutory auditor.
- Performance standards.
- Transparent information about statutory auditors.
- Independent quality assurance (QA).

Furthermore, the Directive requires that audits must be carried out in accordance with international auditing standards (ISAs) and that the group auditor bears full responsibility. The Directive also requires Public Interest Entities to set up an audit committee to strengthen the monitoring of the financial reporting process and the statutory audit, and help to prevent any possible undue influence of the executive management on the financial reporting of the audited entity. To enhance the quality of financial reporting, the statutory auditor or audit firm must communicate to the audit committee on key matters of governance arising from the audit, in particular on any material weaknesses observed in internal controls relating to the financial reporting process.

Other relevant requirements are:

- **Annual transparency report**: Statutory auditors or audit firms that carry out statutory audits of public interest entities must publish on their websites, within three months of each financial year, an annual transparency report that includes, among other information, a description of the governance structure of the audit firm, a description of its internal quality control system, and a statement by its administrative or management body on the effectiveness of its functioning (Art. 38).

- **Mandatory audit partner rotation** (note: not audit firm rotation): The key audit partner is to rotate within a maximum period of seven years after the date of appointment. The audit partner can be allowed to participate in the audit of the audited entity again after a minimum period of two years.
- **A cooling-off period of two years**: The statutory auditor or the key audit partner who carries out the statutory audit on behalf of an audit firm is not allowed to take up a key management position in the audited entity before two years have elapsed from their resignation. The full text of the Eight Directive can be found at the website of the European Union (http://www.europa.eu.int/comm) under the 'Internal Markets' caption by selecting 'Financial Reporting' followed by 'Auditing' and 'Directives and other official Documents'.

Measures Applicable to All Statutory Auditors and Audit Firms

Some of the measures from the Directive that concern all statutory auditors and audit firms follow:[51]

- Educational curriculum for auditors must include knowledge of international accounting standards (IAS) and international auditing standards (ISA).
- The ownership and the management of audit firms will be opened to statutory auditors of all Member States (not just the home country).
- Auditors and audit firms in all Member States have to be registered with the EU.
- Basic principles of professional ethics and auditor independence are defined very closely to IFAC's ethics (see Chapter 3 'Ethics for Professional Accountants').
- Member States will set rules for audit fees that ensure audit quality and prevent 'low-balling' – in other words, preventing audit firms from offering the audit service for a marginal fee and compensating this with the fee income from other non-audit services.
- Auditors must use international auditing standards for all EU statutory audits once those standards have been endorsed under an EU procedure; Member States can only impose additional requirements in certain defined circumstances.
- Member States are obliged to introduce effective investigative and disciplinary systems.
- Common rules concerning the appointment and the resignation of statutory auditors and audit firms are adopted (e.g. statutory auditors to be dismissed only if there is a significant reason why they cannot finalise the audit). A requirement for companies to document their communication with the statutory auditor or audit firm is introduced.
- Companies must disclose in the notes to their financial statements the audit fee and other fees for non-audit services delivered by the auditor.

Measures Applied to Statutory Auditors and Audit Firms of Public Interest Companies

Provisions in the Directive applying specifically to auditors of public interest companies (defined broadly as listed companies, banks or insurance companies) are the introduction of an annual transparency report, auditor rotation, audit quality review every three years, a requirement that auditors to be selected by an audit committee, and mandated report of the auditor to the audit committee on audit key matters (especially material weaknesses of the internal control system), and discussion with the audit committee of any threats to the auditor's independence and confirmation in writing to the audit committee of his independence.

The transparency report and auditor rotation are important requirements. The annual transparency report for audit firms includes information on the governance of the audit firm, its international network, its quality assurance systems and the fees collected for audit and non-audit services (to demonstrate the relative importance of audit in the firm's overall business). Member States have the option of requiring either a change of the key audit partner dealing with an audited company every five years, if the same audit firm keeps the work, or a change of audit firm every seven years.

15.9 Summary

Corporate governance has been defined in many different ways, by many different authors, in many different countries. In general, corporate governance includes the process and structure used to manage and direct the business, with the objective of enhancing shareholder value. The Organisation for Economic Cooperation and Development (OECD) Corporate Governance Principles state: 'Corporate governance involves a set of relationships between a company's management, its board, its shareholders and other stakeholders. Corporate governance also provides the structure through which the objectives of the company are set, and the means of attaining those objectives and monitoring performance are determined.'

The board of directors sets the mission, vision, objectives and strategy of the entity. Governance deals with 'managing' as a key responsibility of the board. It is also the board's responsibility to design and monitor controls that reasonably assure that objectives are met. The third element of governance is supervision. Independent supervision of management performance and remuneration is especially crucial. We all know that conflicts of interests between management and stakeholders do exist on a day-to-day basis, and can result in bankruptcies or major frauds. Governance also includes transparency to all stakeholders that can be recognised.

Corporate governance essentially focuses on the dilemma's that result from the separation of ownership and control, and addresses, in particular, the principal–agent relationship between shareholders and directors on the one hand and the relationship between company agents and stakeholders on the other. Other parties are lenders to the corporation; their trading partners (workers, customers and suppliers); as well as competitors and the general public. All of these parties have an interest in the success of the corporation. Each of the stakeholders has a different kind of relationship with the company and specified rights to receive financial reports. These rights and relationships must be extensively described if we want to understand each claim and propose a reporting system that answers adequately this demand.

There are four causes of the current corporate governance discussion:

1 bankruptcies, fraud and mismanagement;
2 the influence of public, customers and the media;
3 globalisation of capital markets;
4 developments in information technology (IT).

Major reasons for corporate governance being in the spotlight are unexpected bankruptcies, fraud and mismanagement. A second development is the increasing demand for shareholder participation, and also the increasing influence of customers' and public opinion. Globalisation supports striving for harmonisation of law and legislation. IT is major enabler of the new economy and, consequently, of corporate governance developments and discussions.

To understand current developments, one should understand differences in national corporate governance structures. These differences are caused by factors like culture, history, legal systems, and so on. There are two basic systems of corporate governance: market and network corporate governance structures. Examples of countries with a market-oriented corporate governance structure are countries like the USA and the Commonwealth countries. Examples of network-oriented corporate governance structure countries are those in continental Europe and some Asian countries. Market-oriented countries are more aggressive and confrontation seeking, while 'network cultures' seek consensus instead of conflict. Of course, differences are not that black and white, but nevertheless, cultural distinction is a most powerful factor in explaining global differences in corporate governance. The major difference between the market-oriented and the network-oriented corporate governance structures is the two-tier separation between the board of management and the supervisory board in the network structure. In the market-oriented, one-tier system, the complete board, that is both executive and non-executive directors, is formally responsible for day-to-day operating activities.

The most famous corporate governance codes are the Cadbury Report in the UK (which focuses on the financial aspects of corporate governance), the Dey Report in Canada and the King Report in South Africa. But there are others (shown in Illustration 15.3 earlier). In the Netherlands, the Peters Report was published in 1997. As concluded by Peters in 2002, the code was not applied by most public companies in the Netherlands; the Committee Tabaksblat presented a new code in December 2003.

The best practices that are on the worldwide agenda for modernisation of governance are related to managing, board responsibility, supervision, internal control and transparency. Managing includes the concepts of mission, strategy, objectives, and compatibility with societal objectives. The board defines the company's strategy, appoints the corporate officers responsible for managing the company and implementing this strategy, oversees management and ensures the quality of information provided to shareholders and to financial markets through the financial statements. Global debates lead to an agreed vision that good corporate governance requires a system of independent supervision and active oversight of management. The US Treadway Commission recommended that prevention and detection of fraud should be guaranteed through strong internal controls. Treadway also recommended that guidelines be developed on internal control to allow management to report against some framework. Such internal-control guidelines were published in 1992 in what is known as the COSO Report. The Cadbury Committee in the UK was also established in response to a concern about the reliability of financial reporting. Section 404 of the Sarbanes–Oxley Act requires the annual report of issuers to contain a management report which: (1) states management's responsibility for internal control structures and procedures; and (2) give an assessment of effectiveness. Best practice transparency includes the elements of timely disclosure of reliable, adequate and relevant information for decision making. Transparency is another best practice issue, being the modernisation of current business reporting models.

The external auditor plays a central role in good corporate governance. Despite the fact that auditors are indirect stakeholders, their core role is to provide assurance regarding:

- financial and non-financial information;
- internal control statements;
- corporate governance statements.

Central in the Sarbanes–Oxley Act is the establishment of the Public Company Accounting Oversight Board (PCAOB) with the objective of closely monitoring the audit profession to restore investor confidence. One of the consequences of this is the end of self-regulation by the US audit profession. Duties of the PCAOB are: (1) to register public accounting firms that prepare audit reports for issuers; (2) to establish or adopt rules relating to auditing, quality control, ethics, independence, as related to the preparation of audit reports; (3) to conduct investigations and disciplinary proceedings involving registered public accounting firms; (4) to establish auditing standards; and (5) to establish quality control standards.

The 8th EU Directive clarifies the duties of statutory auditors and sets out certain ethical principles to ensure their objectivity and independence; for example, where audit firms are also providing their clients with other services. It includes requirements for external quality assurance, ensure robust public oversight over the audit profession and improve cooperation between regulatory authorities in the EU. The Directive also requires compliance with international standards on auditing for all statutory audits conducted in the EU and provides a basis for balanced and effective international regulatory co-operation with third country regulators such as the US Public Company Accounting Oversight Board (PCAOB).

15.10   Questions, Exercises and Cases

QUESTIONS

15.2 Introduction

15–1   Explain why the concept of corporate governance is being discussed all over the globe at the beginning of the 21st century.

15–2   Talk about why IFRS and XBRL could contribute to good corporate governance.

15.3 The Nature of Corporate Governance

15–3   Explain the concept of Corporate Governance

15–4   Describe the difference between shareholders and stakeholders and discuss why differences play a central role in the corporate governance discussion.

15–5   Describe the positive and negative effects the corporate governance components 'Transparency' and 'Internal Control' could have in meeting the company objectives.

15.4 Corporate Governance Structures

15–6   Describe the differences between a market-oriented and a network-oriented corporate governance structure.

15–7   What are advantages and disadvantages of a one-tier board structure.

15.5 Corporate Governance Committees and Reports

15–8   Should a corporate governance code be developed by governmental bodies and enforced by law or should a code be developed by private institutions such as companies, shareholder representatives, lawyers and accountants and compliance be left to self-regulation? Describe the motivation for your answer.

15.6 Best Practice from a Global Perspective

15–9   Should auditors be appointed by management or the audit committee? Why?

15–10 According to Sarbanes–Oxley, at least one audit committee member should be a 'financial expert'. Discuss some criteria that should be met.

15–11 Should the audit committee review design and operating effectiveness of internal controls? Do you think the audit committee is part of 'internal control'?

15–12 Describe the steps of the audit of internal controls over financial reporting.

15–13 Transparency is an important element of good corporate governance. Visit www.iirc.org and study the guidance and content of the Integrated Reporting Framework. What conditions should be met for an external auditor to be able to provide assurance (refer to International Standard on Assurance Engagements 3000)?

15–14 Describe the concept of Integrated Thinking.

15.7 Corporate Governance and the Role of the Auditor

15–15 List major differences between the internal and external audit.

15–16 What is meant with the statement 'Corporate governance is not an end in itself'?

15–17 Describe the role of the external auditor in corporate governance.

15.8 The Audit Profession and Corporate Governance

15–18 Describe advantages and disadvantages of mandatory firm rotation.

15–19 Select a transparency report of one of the (EU) Big Four firms. Summarise the measures the firm implemented to guarantee good (audit firm) governance.

PROBLEMS AND EXERCISES

15.2 Introduction

15-20 Using the example of basketball, explain the nature of governance in terms of a basketball team.

15.3 The Nature of Corporate Governance

15-21 Bakka Bee is a Canadian construction firm, of which 30 per cent of the shares are listed at the Toronto Stock Exchange and 70 per cent are held by management. They are a firm with 200 employees in five countries. One of their divisions – in Peru – has encountered difficulties linked to the statutory accounts and might be involved in violating human rights. Because of recent discussions about the company in national parliament, it may have to be liquidated.

Required:
Discuss Bakka Bee in terms of three of the four causes of the current corporate governance discussion: (1) bankruptcies, fraud and mismanagement; (2) the influence of public, customers and media; (3) globalisation of capital markets.

15.4 Corporate Governance Structures

15-22 Pick one listed US-based company and one listed continental European company and compare and contrast their board of directors and other supervisory boards.

15.5 Corporate Governance Committees and Reports

15-23 According to the US Sarbanes–Oxley Act, auditors should audit the internal controls of financial reporting (SOX 404). However, from prior research it can be concluded that users of the auditor's opinion on financial statements assume an unqualified opinion implicates internal controls being adequately designed and operating. Explain why this expectation cannot be met by an audit of financial statements. Describe major differences in evaluating internal controls over financial reporting in a financial statements audit and auditing internal controls over financial reporting as a separate engagement.

15.6 Best Practice from a Global Perspective

15-24 Discuss the duties of the PCAOB.

15-25 Royal Shell publishes a Report in which they report about economic, social and environmental issues. This report (called 'The Shell Sustainability Report') can be found at **http://www.shell.com**. Review this Report and summarise potential stakeholders that could be interested in this report. For each potential stakeholder formulate a financial or non-financial performance indicator.

15.7 Corporate Governance and the Role of the Auditor

15-26 Why is self-regulation by the audit profession in the US no longer in place? Find some arguments 'pro and con' self-regulation?

15.8 The Audit Profession and Corporate Governance

15-27 Write a short essay (2 pages) describing which (new) way(s) the audit profession could contribute to an effective future corporate governance system. Give reasons.

15.11 Notes

1 This development influences business, corporate governance, corporate reporting and auditing. The members of the International Integrated Reporting Council (IIRC), a global coalition of regulators, investors, companies, standard setters, the accounting profession and NGOs, share the view that communication about businesses' value creation should be the next step in the evolution of corporate reporting (**http://www.theIIRC.org**).

2 A statutory audit is one that is required by law or statute.

3 Ribstein, L., 2002, 'Market vs. Regulatory Responses to Corporate Fraud: A Critique of the Sarbanes–Oxley Act of 2002', *Illinois Law and Economics Working Papers Series,* September 2002.

4 Chu, Kathy, Rapoport, Michael, and Dummett, Ben, 2012, 'SEC Probe Puts China Listings in Doubt', *The Wall Street Journal,* 4 December.

5 Masulis, R., Want., C. and Xie, F., 2007, 'Corporate Governance and Acquirer Returns', *The Journal of Finance,* August 2007. Also Gugler, K., Mueller, D. and Yurtoglu, B., 2004, 'Returns on Investment', *Journal of Law and Economics,* October 2004.

6 XML (eXtensible Mark-up Language) – a set of rules, guidelines or conventions for designing text formats for such data, in a way that produces files that are easy to generate and read (by a computer), that are unambiguous, and that avoid common pitfalls, such as lack of extensibility, lack of support for internationalisation/localisation, and platform dependency. XML is an extension of the World Wide Web Consortium's (W3C) Standard Generalised Mark-up Language, SGML that allows creation of custom (extensible) data tags, provides a universal data format, allows data objects to be serialised into text streams, and can be parsed by all internet browsers.

7 XBRL (Extensible Business Reporting Language) – based on XML, this is a tagging system for financial data. It provides taxonomy for US Generally Accepted Accounting Principles and International Financial Reporting Standards, and can be used on a transactional basis. An offshoot of XML, XBRL is a freely licensed, open technology standard that makes it possible to store and/or transfer data along with the complex hierarchies, data-processing rules and descriptions.

8 Darts is a game in which darts (slender, pointed missiles with tail fins) are thrown by hand at a target of concentric circles.

9 Transparency – for corporations, practices that make rules, regulations and accounting methods open and accessible to the public. Transparency includes concepts like openness, reporting and disclosure.

10 Toronto Stock Exchange Committee on Corporate Governance (Dey Committee), 1994, *Where were the Directors? Guidelines for Improved Corporate Governance in Canada*, Toronto Stock Exchange. Note that the Toronto Stock Exchange issued 'Request for Comments Corporate Governance Policy – Proposed New Disclosure Requirement and Amended Guidelines' on 26 March 2002. These new amendments did not offer a definition of corporate governance.

11 Committee on the Financial Aspects of Corporate Governance, 1992, *Report of the Committee on the Financial Aspects of Corporate Governance* (The Cadbury Report), Gee and Co. Ltd, London.

12 Hampel Committee, 1998, *Committee on Corporate Governance, Final Report,* Gee Publishing, London, January.

13 The Netherlands Corporate Governance Code, 2008, Monitoring Committee Corporate Governance.

14 Business Sector Advisory Group on Corporate Governance, 1998, *Corporate Governance, Improving Competitiveness and Access to Capital in Global Markets*, A Report to the OECD by the Business Sector Advisory Group on Corporate Governance, Ira M. Millstein (Chairman) *et al.*, OECD. Also see OECD, 2004, OECD Principles of Corporate Governance, Organisation for Economic Cooperation and Development, Paris, **http://www.oecd.org/home/**.

15 For further discussion of the agency theory, we refer to Jensen, M.C. and Meckling, W.H., 1976, 'Theory of the Firm: Managerial Behavior, Agency Costs and Ownerhsip Structure', *Journal of Financial Economics*, October.

16 Instead of primarily focusing on shareholder interests, stakeholder theory takes into account a broader perspective. We refer to Donaldson, T. and Preston, L.E., 1995, 'The Stakeholder Theory of the Corporation: Concepts, Evidence, and Implications', *Academy of Management Review,* 20(1).

17 Hofstede, Geert, 1980, 'International Differences in Work-Related Values', *Culture's Consequences*, Sage Publications, California.

18 See, for example, International Capital Markets Group, 1995, *International Corporate Governance: Who Holds the Reins?*, London.

19 Fama, E.F. and Jensen, M.C., 1983, Separation of ownership and control, *Journal of Law and Economics*, 26, 301–25.

20 Toronto Stock Exchange Committee on Corporate Governance (Dey Committee), 1994, *Where Were the Directors? Guidelines for Improved Corporate Governance in Canada*, December, Toronto Stock Exchange.

21 Institute of Directors in Southern Africa, 1994, *King I Report on Corporate Governance*.

22 Committee on Corporate Governance (Peters Committee), 1997, *Corporate Governance in the Netherlands, Forty Recommendations*, Amsterdam, June.

23 De stand van zaken, 2002, Corporate Governance in Nederland 2002, *Eenuitgaveonderauspiciën van de Nederlandse Corporate Governance Stichting*, De stand van zaken, Amsterdam, 2002.

24 107th US Congress, 2002, Sarbanes–Oxley Act of 2002, Public Law 107–204, Senate and House of Representatives of the United States of America in Congress assembled, Washington, DC, 30 July.

25 SEC, 2003, *Final Rule: Management's Reports on Internal Control Over Financial Reporting and Certification of Disclosure in Exchange Act Periodic Reports*, US Securities and Exchange Commission, 11 June.

26 See PCAOB, 2003, PCAOB Release No. 2003–024, 'Proposed Rules Relating to the Oversight of Non-US Public,' Public Company Accounting Oversight Board, 10 December.

27 Commission to the Council and the European Parliament, 2003, *Communication from the Commission to the Council and the European Parliament*, Brussels, May.

28 EU, 2002, *Comparative Study of Corporate Governance Codes Relevant to the EU and its Member States*, European Union, Brussels, March.

29 In developing its approach, the Commission has paid attention to the following needs: considering where possible (a) the use of alternatives to legislation and (b) the preference to be given to disclosure requirements (because they are less intrusive in corporate life, and they can prove to be a highly effective market-led way of rapidly achieving results).

30 European Corporate Governance Forum at: **http://ec.europa.eu/internal_market/company/ecgforum/index_en.htm#overview**.

31 Business Sector Advisory Group on Corporate Governance, 1998, *Corporate Governance, Improving Competitiveness and Access to Capital in Global Markets*, A Report to the OECD by the Business Sector Advisory Group on Corporate Governance, Ira M. Millstein (Chairman), *et al.*, OECD.

32 The Shell Report, 1999, **http://www.shell.com**.

33 Ibid. Shell Report, Triple Bottom Line.

34 Le conseil d'administration des societies côteés, 1995, *Vienot Report*, Le conseil d'administration des societies côteés, July.

35 Bouton, R., 2002, 'Pour un meilleur gouvernement des entreprises côteés', September.

36 Cohen Commission, 1978, *The Commission of Auditors' Responsibilities: Report, Conclusions and Recommendations*, American Institute of Certified Public Accountants, New York.

37 107th US Congress, 2002, Sarbanes–Oxley Act of 2002, Public Law 107–204, section407, 'Disclosure of Audit Committee Financial Expert,' Senate and House of Representatives of the United States of America in Congress assembled, Washington, DC, 30 July.

38 SEC, 2003, Release No. 33-8220, File No. S7-02-03, 'Standards Relating to Listed Company Audit Committees', US Securities And Exchange Commission, 10 April.

39 See their website: **http://www.ifiar.org**.

40 107th US Congress, 2002, SEC, 2004, 'Auditor Reports To Audit Committees', Sarbanes–Oxley Act of 2002, Public Law 107–204, Senate and House of Representatives of the United States of America in Congress assembled, Washington, DC, 30 July.

41 107th US Congress, 2002, SEC, 806, 'Protection for Employees of Publicly Traded Companies Who Provide Evidence of Fraud', Sarbanes–Oxley Act of 2002, Public Law 107–204, Senate and House of Representatives of the United States of America in Congress assembled, Washington, DC, 30 July.

42 107th US Congress, 2002, SEC, 103.4, 'Auditing, Quality Control, and Independence Standards and Rules', *Sarbanes–Oxley Act of 2002*, Public Law 107–204, Senate and House of Representatives of the United States of America in Congress assembled, Washington, DC, 30 July.

43 National Commission on Fraudulent Financial Reporting (Treadway Commission), 1987, *Report of the National Commission on Fraudulent Financial Reporting*, Washington, October.

44 Committee of Sponsoring Organizations of the Treadway Commission (COSO), 1992, *Internal Control – Integrated Framework*, American Institute of Certified Public Accountants, Jersey City, New Jersey.

45 The KPMG Review, 1999, *The Combined Code: A Practical Guide*, KPMG, United Kingdom, January.

46 107th US Congress, 2002, SEC, 404 'Management Assessment of Internal Controls', *Sarbanes–Oxley Act of 2002*, Public Law 107–204, Senate and House of Representatives of the United States of America in Congress assembled, Washington, DC, 30 July.

47 IDW, 2003, *Financial Reporting, Auditing and Corporate Governance*, IDW, Düsseldorf, April.

48 UK Corporate Governance Code (2012). Paragraphs referred to are given after each bullet point statement.

49 See website at **http://www.iirc.org**.

50 For further details about the independence requirements, refer to Chapter 3.

51 Adapted from EU, 2004, *MEMO/04/60 European Commission Proposal for a Directive on Statutory Audit: Frequently Asked Questions*, Brussels, 16 March.

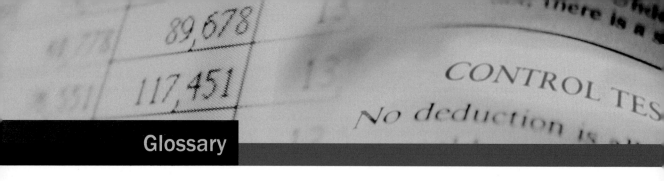

Remember: If you see a term in this glossary, then that term and its related process are discussed in the book. If you cannot find a term here, let the authors know at **rhayes@ calstatela.edu**.

Access controls – Procedures designed to restrict access to online terminal devices, programs and data. Access controls consist of 'user authentication' and 'user authorisation'. 'User authentication' typically attempts to identify a user through unique logon identifications, passwords, access cards or biometric data. 'User authorisation' consists of access rules to determine the computer resources each user may access. Specifically, such procedures are designed to prevent or detect:

- unauthorised access to online terminal devices, programs and data;
- entry of unauthorised transactions;
- unauthorised changes to data files;
- the use of computer programs by unauthorised personnel; and
- the use of computer programs that have not been authorised.

Account analysis schedule – Normally used for fixed assets, liabilities and equity accounts, shows the activity in a general ledger account during the entire period under audit, tying together the beginning and ending balances.

Accounting estimate – An approximation of the amount of an item in the absence of a precise means of measurement.

Accounting system – The series of tasks and records of an entity by which transactions are processed as a means of maintaining financial records. Such systems identify, assemble, analyse, calculate, classify, record, summarise, and report transactions and other events.

Accounts receivable turnover – The ratio of operating revenues to accounts receivable; it measures a company's ability to convert revenues into cash.

Accuracy assertion – The assertion that amounts and other data relating to recorded transactions and events have been recorded accurately.

Adjusting journal entry – The correcting entry required at the end of the reporting period due to a mistake made in the accounting records; also called 'correcting entry'.

Adverse opinion – see **Modified auditor's report** and **Opinion**.

Advertising – The communication to the public of information as to the services or skills provided by professional accountants in public practice with a view to procuring professional business.

Advocacy threat – Occurs when a member of the assurance team promotes, or seems to promote, an assurance client's position or opinion.

Affiliate – A party that, directly or indirectly, controls, is controlled by, or is under common control with an enterprise.

Agency theory – A company is viewed as the result of more or less formal contracts, in which several groups make some kind of contribution to the company, given a certain price. A reputable auditor is appointed not only in the interest of third parties, but also in the interest of management. (See Watts, R.L. and Zimmerman J.L., 1978, 'Towards a Positive Theory of the Determination of Counting Standards', *The Accounting Review* (January), pp. 112–134; and Watts, R.L. and Zimmerman J.L., 1979, 'The Demand for and Supply of Accounting Theories: The Market for Excuses', *The Accounting Review* (April), pp. 273–305.)

Agree – An audit procedure whereby the auditor takes one document or set of documents and compares it to another document or set which should contain the same information to determine if the two match (agree with each other).

Agreed-upon procedures – see **Agreed-upon procedures engagement**.

Agreed-upon procedures engagement – An engagement in which the party engaging the professional accountant or the intended user determines the procedures to be performed and the auditor provides a report of factual findings as a result of undertaking those procedures.

Analytical procedures – Evaluations of financial information through analysis of plausible relationships among both financial and non-financial data. Analytical procedures also encompass such investigation as is necessary of identified fluctuations or relationships that are inconsistent with other relevant information or that differ from expected values by a significant amount.

Analytical review – The process of planning, executing and drawing conclusions from analytical procedures.

Annual report – An entity ordinarily issues on an annual basis a document which includes its financial statements together with the audit report thereon. This document is frequently referred to as the 'annual report'.

Anomalous error – see **Audit sampling**.

Applicable financial reporting framework – The financial reporting framework adopted by management and, where appropriate, those charged with governance in the preparation of the financial statements that is acceptable in view of the nature of the entity and the objective of the financial statements, or that is required by law or regulation.

Application controls in computer information systems – The specific controls over the relevant accounting applications maintained by the computer. The purpose of application controls is to establish specific control procedures over the accounting applications in order to provide reasonable assurance that all transactions are authorised and recorded, and are processed completely, accurately and on a timely basis.

Appropriateness – Appropriateness is the measure of the quality of audit evidence and its relevance to a particular assertion and its reliability.

Arm's length transaction – A transaction in which the buyers and sellers of a product act independently and have no relationship to each other. The concept of an arm's length transaction is to ensure that both parties in the deal are acting in their own self-interest and are not subject to any pressure or duress from the other party.

ASCII (American Standard Code for Information Interchange) – A standard translation scheme used to translate computer bytes into readable characters; commonly used in microcomputers, minicomputers and non-IBM mainframes.

Asserted claims – Existing law suits.

Assertions – Assertions are representations by management, explicit or otherwise, that are embodied in the financial statements as used by the auditor to consider the different types of potential misstatements that may occur. Sometimes called 'financial statements assertions', they can be categorised as follows: *existence, rights and obligations, occurrence, completeness, valuation, accuracy cut-off, classification, understandability, measurement,* and *presentation and disclosure.*

Asset/Liability management – A planning and control process, the key concept of which is matching the mix and maturities of assets and liabilities.

Assistants – Assistants are personnel involved in an individual audit other than the audit supervisor or manager.

Assurance – see **Reasonable assurance**.

Assurance client – An entity in respect of which a firm conducts an assurance engagement.

Assurance engagement – Means an engagement in which a practitioner expresses a conclusion that is designed to enhance the degree of confidence intended users can have about the evaluation or measurement of a subject matter, which is the responsibility of a party other than the intended users or the practitioner, against criteria.

Assurance team – (1) All professionals participating in the assurance engagement; (2) All others within a firm who can directly influence the outcome of the assurance engagement, including: (a) Those who recommend the compensation of, or who provide direct supervisory, management or other oversight of the assurance engagement partner in connection with the performance of the assurance engagement; (b) Those who provide consultation regarding technical or industry specific issues, transactions or events for the assurance engagement; and (c) Those who provide quality control for the assurance engagement; and (3) For the purposes of an audit client, all those within a network firm who can directly influence the outcome of the audit engagement.

Attendance – Attendance consists of being present during all or part of a process being performed by others; for example, attending physical inventory taking will enable the auditor to inspect inventory, to observe compliance of management's procedures to count quantities and record such counts and to test-count quantities.

Attestation – A professional opinion in report form on compliance of the responsible party with some specific criteria.

Audit – The objective of an audit of financial statements is to enable the auditor to express an opinion whether the financial statements are prepared, in all material respects, in accordance with an identified financial reporting framework. The phrases used to express the auditor's opinion are 'give a true and fair view' or 'present fairly, in all material respects', which are equivalent terms. A similar objective applies to the audit of financial or other information prepared in accordance with appropriate criteria.

Audit assurance – The expression of a conclusion by an auditor that is designed to enhance the degree of confidence intended users can have about the evaluation or measurement of historical financial statements that is the responsibility of the auditee against the criteria of International Financial Reporting Standards or other national accounting standards.

Audit client – An entity in respect of which a firm conducts an audit engagement. When the audit client is a listed entity, it will always include its related entities.

Audit committee – Selected members of a company's outside directors, who take an active role in overseeing the company's accounting and financial reporting policies and practices.

Audit documentation – The record of audit procedures performed, relevant audit evidence obtained, and conclusions the auditor reached (terms such as 'working papers' or 'workpapers' are also sometimes used).

Audit engagement – An assurance engagement to provide a high level of assurance that financial statements are free of material misstatement, such as an engagement in accordance with International Standards on Auditing. This includes a statutory audit which is an audit required by national legislation or other regulation.

Audit evidence – The information obtained by the auditor in arriving at the conclusions on which the audit opinion is based. Audit evidence will comprise source documents and accounting records underlying the financial statements and corroborating information from other sources.

Audit expectation gap – A gap that results from the fact that users of audit services have expectations regarding the duties of auditors that exceed the current practice in the profession.

Audit firm – Audit firm is either a firm or entity providing audit services, including where appropriate its partners, or a sole practitioner.

Audit matters of governance interest – Matters that arise from the audit of financial statements and, in the opinion of the auditor, are both important and relevant to those charged with governance in overseeing the financial reporting and disclosure process. Audit matters of governance interest include only those matters that have come to the attention of the auditor as a result of the performance of the audit.

Audit objective – The specific expression of a financial statement assertion or assertions for which evidence needs to be obtained. For example, the objective 'Investments exist and are owned by the entity.'

Audit of financial statements – see **Financial statement audit**.

Audit opinion – see **Opinion**.

Audit plan – A work plan that reflects the design and performance of all audit procedures, consisting of a detailed approach for the nature, timing and extent of audit procedures to be performed (including the performance of risk assessment procedures) and the rationale for their selection. The audit plan begins by planning risk assessment procedures and once these procedures have been performed it is updated and changed to reflect the further audit procedures needed to respond to the results of the risk assessments. Also called **audit programme**.

Audit planning memorandum – A document prepared by the auditor which gives an overview of the client company, the industry environment, significant audit concerns, and areas of interest to the audit team. Furthermore, it details the planned audit approach and budget.

Audit programme – An audit programme sets out the nature, timing, and extent of planned audit procedures required to implement the overall audit plan. The audit programme serves as a set of instructions to assistants involved in the audit and as a means to control the proper execution of the work. Also called **audit plan**.

Audit report – An audit report in usually synonymous with an **Audit opinion**, but it may be a more comprehensive report. The comprehensive audit report contains all important administrative data related to the audit, including comments, results, and the corrective/ preventive actions that have been determined. The audit report is an official document that is signed by the lead auditor and the head of the audited area.

Audit risk – Audit risk is the risk that the auditor gives an inappropriate audit opinion when the financial statements are materially misstated. Audit risk has three components: inherent risk, control risk and detection risk.

- **Control risk** – The risk that a misstatement that could occur in an account balance or class of transactions and that could be material, individually or when aggregated with misstatements in other balances or classes, will not be prevented or detected and corrected on a timely basis by the accounting and internal control systems.
- **Detection risk** – The risk that an auditor's substantive procedures will not detect a misstatement that exists in an account balance or class of transactions that could be material, individually or when aggregated with misstatements in other balances or classes.
- **Inherent risk** – A component of audit risk. It is the susceptibility of an account balance or class of transactions to misstatement that could be material, individually or when aggregated with misstatements in other balances of classes, assuming that there were no related internal controls.

Audit sampling – Audit sampling (sampling) involves the application of audit procedures to less than 100 per cent of items within an account balance or class of transactions such that all sampling units have a chance of selection. This will enable the auditor to obtain and evaluate audit evidence about some characteristic of the items selected in order to form or assist in forming a conclusion concerning the population from which the sample is drawn. Audit sampling can use either a statistical or a non-statistical approach.

- **Anomalous error** – Anomalous error means an error that arises from an isolated event that has not recurred other than on specifically identifiable occasions and is therefore not representative of errors in the population.
- **Confidence level** – As used in sampling, the probability of being correct in assessing the level of control risk. The term is used interchangeably with *reliability*.
- **Error** – Either control deviations, when performing tests of control, or misstatements, when performing substantive procedures. Total error is either the rate of deviation or total misstatement.
- **Expected error** – The error that the auditor expects to be present in the population.
- **Homogeneity** – All items in the population have similar characteristics.
- **Monetary unit sampling** – A statistical sampling method that provides upper and lower misstatement bounds expressed in monetary amounts; also referred to as dollar unit sampling, cumulative monetary amount sampling, and sampling with probability proportional to size.
- **Non-sampling risk** – Non-sampling risk arises from factors that cause the auditor to reach an erroneous conclusion for any reason not related to the size of the sample. For example, most audit evidence is persuasive rather than conclusive, the auditor might use inappropriate procedures, or the auditor might misinterpret evidence and fail to recognise an error.

- **Population** – Population means the entire set of data from which a sample is selected and about which the auditor wishes to draw conclusions. A population may be divided into strata, or sub-populations, with each stratum being examined separately. The term population is used to include the term stratum.
- **Power of the test** – It is a measure of how effective the test employed is in discriminating between populations that contain material errors and populations that contain non-material errors.
- **Representativeness** – A sample having essentially the same characteristics as the population. Haphazard selection or a random-based selection method can be expected to produce a sample that is representative of the population.
- **Sampling risk** – Sampling risk arises from the possibility that the auditor's conclusion, based on a sample, may be different from the conclusion reached if the entire population were subjected to the same audit procedure.
- **Sampling unit** – Sampling unit means the individual items constituting a population, for example, cheques listed on deposit slips, credit entries on bank statements, sales invoices or debtors' balances, or a monetary unit.
- **Statistical sampling** – Statistical sampling means any approach to sampling that has the following characteristics:
  (a) random selection of a sample;
  (b) use of probability theory to evaluate sample results, including measurement of sampling risk.
- A sampling approach that does not have characteristics (a) and (b) is considered non-statistical sampling.
- **Stratification** – Stratification is the process of dividing a population into subpopulations, each of which is a group of sampling units which have similar characteristics (often monetary value).
- **Tolerable error** – Tolerable error means the maximum error in a population that the auditor is willing to accept.
- **Type I error** – The auditor concludes, in the case of a test of control, that control risk is lower than it actually is, or in the case of a substantive test, that a material error does not exist when in fact it does. This type of risk affects audit effectiveness and is more likely to lead to an inappropriate audit opinion.
- **Type II error** – The auditor concludes, in the case of a test of control, that control risk is higher than it actually is, or in the case of a substantive test, that a material error exists when in fact it does not. This type of risk affects audit efficiency as it would usually lead to additional work to establish that initial conclusions were incorrect.

Audit team – People who make up the group of auditors responsible for planning and executing an audit.

Audit trail – The information that is used to trace the status and contents of an individual transaction record backwards or forwards between output, processing, and source document.

Auditee – The entity which is audited.

Auditor – 'Auditor' is used to refer to the person or persons conducting the audit, usually the engagement partner or other members of the engagement team, or, as applicable, the firm. Where an ISA expressly intends that a requirement or responsibility be fulfilled by the engagement partner, the term 'engagement partner' rather than 'auditor' is used. 'Engagement partner' and 'firm' are to be read as referring to their public sector equivalents where relevant.

- **Continuing auditor** – The auditor who audited and reported on the prior period's financial statements and continues as the auditor for the current period.
- **External auditor** – Where appropriate, the terms 'external auditor' and 'external audit' are used to distinguish the external auditor from an internal auditor and to distinguish the external audit from the activities of internal auditing.
- **Existing auditor** – The auditor who is currently holding an audit or assurance services appointment with the prospective client.
- **Incoming auditor** – The incoming auditor is a current period's auditor who did not audit the prior period's financial statements.
- **Other auditor** – An independent auditor other than the group auditor or a related auditor.
- **Personnel** – Personnel includes all partners and professional staff engaged in the audit practice of the firm.
- **Predecessor auditor** – The auditor who was previously the auditor of an entity and who has been replaced by an incoming auditor.
- **Proposed professional accountant** – A professional accountant in public practice who will act as the current financial statement period's auditor who did not audit the prior period's financial statements.
- **Principal auditor** – The principal auditor is the auditor with responsibility for reporting on the financial statements of an entity when those financial statements include financial information of one or more components audited by another auditor.
- **Related auditor** – An independent auditor from the group auditor's office, other office of the group auditor's firm, a network firm or another firm operating under common quality control policies and procedures as described in International Standard on Quality Control (ISQC) 1, 'Quality Control for Audit, Assurance and Related Services Practices'.

Auditor's association – An auditor is associated with financial information when the auditor attaches a report to that information or consents to the use of the auditor's name in a professional connection.

Auditor's expert – An individual or organisation possessing expertise in a field other than accounting or auditing, whose work in that field is used by the auditor to assist the auditor in obtaining sufficient appropriate audit evidence. An auditor's expert may be either an auditor's internal expert (who is a partner or staff, including temporary staff, of the auditor's firm or a network firm), or an auditor's external expert.

Authorisation – The delegation of initiation of transactions and obligations on the company's behalf.

Bank reconciliation – A test of the agreement between a balance on the bank statement and the same balance on the company's books.

Basel Committee on Banking Supervision – A committee of banking supervisory authorities that was established by the central bank Governors of the Group of Ten countries in 1975. It consists of senior representatives of banking supervisory authorities and central banks from Belgium, Canada, France, Germany, Italy, Japan, Luxembourg, the Netherlands, Spain, Sweden, Switzerland, the UK and the USA. It usually meets at the Bank for International Settlements in Basel, where its permanent Secretariat is located.

Basis – The difference between the price of the hedged item and the price of the related hedging instrument.

Basis Risk – The risk that the basis will change while the hedging contract is open and, thus, the price correlation between the hedged item and hedging instrument will not be perfect.

Bearer securities – A document of title to stocks, bonds, shares, debentures, etc. transferable by hand, being made out to bearer (any person who has it in hand) and not a named person.

Benchmarking – The comparison of actual performance to a standard of typical competence developed by testing or a published standard.

Benford's Law – Provides the expected frequencies of the digits and digit combinations in tabulated data.

Board of directors – Individuals responsible for overseeing the affairs of an entity, including the election of its officers. The board of a corporation that issues stock is elected by stockholders.

Bookkeeping services – Services including payroll services and the preparation of financial statements or financial information which forms the basis of the financial statements on which the audit report is provided for audit clients that are listed entities.

Boundary testing – Audit testing of documentation at the lowest level of the information stream; for example, testing the first document (i.e. purchase order) that initiates an exchange.

Breach of contract – A failure of one or both parties in a contract to fulfil the requirements of the contract.

Business operations – The ongoing activities of the business.

Business risks – Risks that result from significant conditions, events, circumstances, or actions that could adversely affect the entity's ability to achieve its objectives and execute its strategies.

Bylaws – Includes rules and procedures of the corporation including fiscal year, frequency of stockholder meetings, method of voting for board of directors, and the duties and powers of the corporate officer.

Cap – A series of call options based on a notional amount. The strike price of these options defines an upper limit to interest rates.

Capital structure – The proportions of capital of an entity that are derived from each source of financing, i.e. the proportion of debt versus equity.

Checklists – A list of considerations or procedures which are followed by the auditor.

Circumstantial evidence – Evidence based on facts and circumstances from which a court may infer that a factual matter has been proved.

Classes of transactions – Groups of accounting entries in an accounting cycle of transactions such as the revenue cycle, expenditure cycle, production cycle, or personnel cycle, or any sub-categories of those cycles.

Classification – The process of finding models, also known as classifiers, or functions that map records into one of several discrete prescribed classes.

Clear and convincing evidence – A proof that is stronger than a mere preponderance of evidence, but not convincing beyond a reasonable doubt.

Client account – Any bank account, which is used solely for the banking of clients' monies.

Clients' monies – Any monies, including documents of title to money (e.g. bills of exchange, promissory notes and documents of title) which can be converted into money (e.g. bearer bonds received by a professional accountant in public practice to be held or paid out on the instruction of the person from whom or on whose behalf they are received).

Close family – A parent, non-dependent child or sibling.

Close out – The consummation or settlement of a financial transaction.

Cluster Analysis – A technique that aggregates data based on certain specified common characteristics.

Collateral – Assets pledged by a borrower to secure a loan or other credit; these are subject to seizure in the event of default.

Collusion – The act of two or more employees to steal assets or misstate records.

Combined Code (of the Committee on Corporate Governance) – Represents the Code of Best Practice of the London Stock Exchange. (See the Committee on Corporate Governance, 1998, *The Combined Code*, London Stock Exchange, London, January; or KPMG Review, 1999, *The Combined Code: A Practical Guide*, KPMG, United Kingdom, January.)

Commitments – Agreements that the entity will hold to a fixed set of conditions, such as the purchase or sale of merchandise at a stated price, at a future date, regardless of what happens to profits or to the economy as a whole.

Commodity – A physical substance, such as food, grains, and metals that is interchangeable with other product of the same type.

Company bylaws – The rules and procedures adopted by a company's stockholders, including the company's fiscal year as well as duties and powers of the officers.

Comparatives – Comparatives in financial statements, may present amounts (such as financial position, results of operations, cash flows) and appropriate disclosures of an entity for more than one period, depending on the framework. The frameworks and methods of presentation are as follows:

- Corresponding figures where amounts and other disclosures for the preceding period are included as part of the current period financial statements, and are intended to be read in relation to the amounts and other disclosures relating to the current period (referred to as 'current period figures'). These corresponding figures are not presented as complete financial statements capable of standing alone, but are an integral part of the current period financial statements intended to be read only in relationship to the current period figures.
- Comparative financial statements where amounts and other disclosures for the preceding period are included for comparison with the financial statements of the current period, but do not form part of the current period financial statements.

Competence – The knowledge and skills necessary to accomplish tasks that define the individual's job.

Compilation – see **Compilation engagement**.

Compilation engagement – In a compilation engagement, the accountant is engaged to use accounting expertise as opposed to auditing expertise to collect, classify and summarise financial information.

Complementary user entity controls – Controls that the service organisation assumes, in the design of its service, will be implemented by user entities, and which, if necessary to achieve control objectives, are identified in the description of its system.

Completeness assertion – see **Financial statement assertions**.

Completion memorandum – A report on auditing findings at the completion of the audit that ordinarily describes critical and significant audit areas, accounting issues and any matters that need to be highlighted.

Compliance auditing – Is a review of an organisation's procedures to determine whether the organisation is following a specific set of criteria (e.g. government regulation, commercial contract, lease).

Component – An entity or business activity which financial information should be included in the group financial statements.

Component auditor – The auditor who, at the request of the group engagement team, performs work on the financial information related to a component.

Components of audit risk – There are three components of audit risk: inherent risk, control risk and detection risk.

Components of financial statements – The auditor may be requested to express an opinion on one or more components of a financial statement, for example, accounts receivable, inventory, an employee's bonus calculation, or a provision for income taxes. This is described in ISA 800.

Components of internal control – There are five components of internal control: control environment, risk assessment, control procedures (activities), information and communication system, and monitoring.

Component management – Management responsible for the preparation and presentation of a component's financial information.

Comprehensive basis of accounting – A comprehensive basis of accounting comprises a set of criteria used in preparing financial statements which applies to all material items and which has substantial support.

Computation – Computation consists of checking the arithmetical accuracy of source documents and accounting records or of performing independent calculations.

Computer assisted audit techniques – Applications of auditing procedures using the computer as an audit tool are known as computer assisted audit techniques (CAATs).

Computer information systems – A computer information systems (CIS) environment exists when a computer of any type or size is involved in the processing by the entity of financial information of significance to the audit, whether that computer is operated by the entity or by a third party.

Confidentiality – To respect the confidentiality of information acquired as a result of professional and business relationships and, therefore, not disclose any such information to third parties without proper and specific authority, unless there is a legal or professional right or duty to disclose, nor use the information for the personal advantage of the professional accountant or third parties.

Confidence level – see **Audit sampling**.

Confirmation – Consists of the response to an inquiry of a third party to corroborate information contained in the accounting records – see **External confirmation**.

Confirmation letter – A letter sent to a third party to request information about, confirm, or corroborate a particular item affecting assertions made by management in the financial statements.

Consignment – A specialised way of marketing certain types of goods. The consignor delivers goods to the consignee who acts as the consignor's agent in selling the merchandise to a third party. The consignee accepts the goods without any liability except to reasonably protect them from damage. The consignee receives a commission when the merchandise is sold. Goods on consignment are included in the consignor's inventory and excluded from the consignee's inventory since the consignor has legal title.

Consulting services – Services that are designed to improve the effectiveness and efficiency of clients' operations, broadly defined as any services other than attestation and related services. Examples are executive search, legal services, financial services, strategic planning, and development of management information systems.

Contingency fee – An arrangement whereby no fee will be charged unless a specified finding or result is obtained or when the fee is otherwise contingent on the findings or results of these services.

Contingent fees – Fees calculated on a predetermined basis relating to the outcome or result of a transaction or the result of the work performed.

Contingent liability – A potential future obligation to an outside part for an unknown amount resulting from the outcome of a past event.

Continuing auditor – see **Auditor**.

Continuous reporting – The real-time disclosure of transaction data.

Contracts – Include long-term notes and payables, stock options, pension plans, contracts with vendors, government contracts, royalty agreements, union contracts and leases.

Control activities – Those policies and procedures that help ensure that management directives are carried out. Control activities are a component of internal control. Control activities are the policies and procedures that help ensure risk responses are properly executed. Control activities occur throughout the organisation, at all levels and in all functions. Control activities are part of the process by which an enterprise strives to achieve its business objectives. They usually involve two elements: a policy establishing what should be done and procedures to effect the policy.

Control environment – Includes the governance and management functions and the attitudes, awareness and actions of those charged with governance and management concerning the entity's internal control and its importance in the entity. The control environment is a component of internal control.

Control procedures – see **Control activities**.

Control risk – see **Audit risk**.

Controls – All the organisational activities aimed at having organisational members co-operate to reach the organisational goals.

Corporate bylaws – The rules and procedures adopted by a company's stockholders, including the company's fiscal year, as well as duties and powers of the officers.

Corporate charter – A legal document granted by the country, state or province in which a company is incorporated and recognises a company as a separate legal entity. Included in the charter is the name of the company, date of incorporation, capital stock authorised, and the types of business activities the company may undertake.

Corporate finance and similar activities – Promoting, dealing in, or underwriting a client's share; committing the client to the terms of the transaction; and consummating a transaction on behalf of the client.

Corporate governance – see **Governance**.

Corporate minutes – Official record of the meetings of the board of directors and stockholders. Include authorisation of compensation of officers, new contracts, acquisition of fixed assets, loans, and dividends payments.

Correcting entry – see **Adjusting journal entry**.

Correlation – The degree to which contract prices of hedging instruments reflect price movements in the cash-market position. The correlation factor represents the potential effectiveness of hedging a cash-market instrument with a contract where the deliverable financial instrument differs from the cash-market instrument. Generally, the correlation factor is determined by regression analysis or some other method of technical analysis of market behaviour.

Corroborate – To attest the truth or accuracy of an inquiry.

Counterparty – The other party to a derivative transaction.

Credit risk – The risk that a customer or counterparty will not settle an obligation for full value, either when due or at any time thereafter.

Currency risk – The risk of loss arising from future movements in the exchange rates applicable to foreign currency assets, liabilities, rights and obligations.

Custody – Physical control over assets or records.

Customer relationship management (CRM) – A software package that helps organise detailed data about customers so that the data can be used to facilitate better customer service.

Cut-off – Transactions and events have been recorded in the correct accounting period.

Cut-off procedures – Refers to recognising assets and liabilities as of a proper date and accounting for revenue, expense and other transactions in the proper period.

Data description – A technique that provides an overall description of data, either in itself or in each class or concept, typically in summarised, concise, and precise form. It summarises general characteristics of data and compares characteristics of data between contrasting groups or classes.

Data mining – A set of computer-assisted techniques that use sophisticated statistical analysis, including artificial intelligence techniques, to examine large volumes of data with the objective of indicating hidden or unexpected information or patterns.

Database – A collection of data that is shared and used by a number of different users for different purposes.

Date of the auditor's report – The date the auditor dates the report on the financial statements in accordance with ISA 700.

Date of the financial statements – The date of the end of the latest period covered by the financial statements.

Dealer (for the purposes of IAPS 1012) – The person who commits the entity to a derivative transaction.

Defalcation – Theft of an entity's assets, also referred to as misappropriation of assets.

Deficiency in internal control – This exists when:
- a control is designed, implemented or operated in such a way that it is unable to prevent, or detect and correct, misstatements in the financial statements on a timely basis; or
- a control necessary to prevent, or detect and correct, misstatements in the financial statements on a timely basis is missing.

Dependency analysis – A technique that searches data for the most significant relationship across large number of variables or attributes. One use is to describe data items or events that frequently occur together or in sequence.

Derivative – A generic term used to categorise a wide variety of financial instruments whose value 'depends on' or is 'derived from' an underlying rate or price, such as interest rates, exchange rates, equity prices, or commodity prices. Many national financial reporting frameworks and the International Accounting Standards contain definitions of derivatives. For example, International Accounting Standard (IAS) 39 'Financial Instruments: Recognition and Measurement' defines a derivative as a financial instrument:
- whose value changes in response to the change in a specified interest rate, security price, commodity price, foreign exchange rate, index of prices or rates, a credit rating or credit index, or similar variable (sometimes called the 'underlying');
- that requires no initial net investment or little initial net investment relative to other types of contracts that have a similar response to changes in market conditions; and
- that is settled at a future date.

Detection risk – see **Audit risk**.

Direct evidence – Comes from personal knowledge of the witnesses under oath as to specific facts.

Direct financial interest – A financial interest: (1) Owned directly by and under the control of an individual or entity (including those managed on a discretionary basis by others); or (2) Beneficially owned through a collective investment vehicle, estate, trust or other intermediary over which the individual or entity has control.

Directors and officers – Those charged with the governance of an entity, regardless of their title, which may vary from country to country.

Disclaimer of opinion – see **Modified auditor's report** and **Opinion**.

Disclosure – Typically required when accounts of interest (revenue, joint venture accounts) exceed certain amounts or have certain characteristics. (Revenue segments amounts are disclosed if they exceed 10 per cent of total revenue and joint venture amounts, and consolidated if the company has effective control.)

Documentary evidence – Evidence gathered from written, printed or electronic sources.

Documentation – Documentation is the material (working papers) prepared by and for, or obtained and retained by the auditor in connection with the performance of, the audit.

Due diligence – An investigation of a business prior to signing a contract. Due diligence refers to exercising maximum care in a given transaction. Due diligence is most often used in the process of buying a business. The buyer needs to understand target company's financial situations, legal obligations, customer records and subsequences which may arise of those. Due diligence is also important issue of determining a price to offer for a business.

Due diligence report – A report based on the analysis by an acquiring company's auditing firm of a company to be acquired.

Due professional care – The activities of a professional fulfilling his duties diligently and carefully. Due care for an auditor includes the completeness of the working papers, the sufficiency of the audit evidence, and the appropriateness of the audit report.

Edit check – An accuracy check performed by a computer accounting system edit program.

Electronic data interchange (EDI) – The electronic transmission of documents between organisations in a machine-readable form. EDI allows output of one system to be electronically transmitted and input into another system.

Electronic funds transfer (EFT) – A transfer of funds between two or more organisations or individuals using computer and network technology.

Embedded audit modules (EAM) – Database software routines that are placed at predetermined points to gather information about transactions or events within the system that auditors deem to be material. EAMs allow auditors to proactively monitor auditable conditions.

Embedded derivative instruments – Implicit or explicit terms in a contract or agreement that affect some or all of the cash flows or the value of other exchanges required by the contract in a manner similar to a derivative.

Emphasis of matter paragraph – The explanatory paragraph placed after the opinion paragraph in an unqualified auditor's opinion which emphasises a matter related to the entity or its financial statements.

Employed professional accountant – A professional accountant employed in industry, commerce, the public sector, or education.

Encryption (cryptography) – The process of transforming programs and information into a form that cannot be understood without access to specific decoding algorithms (cryptographic keys). For example, the confidential personal data in a payroll system may be encrypted against unauthorised disclosure or modification. Encryption can provide an effective control for protecting confidential or sensitive programs and information from unauthorised access or modification. However, effective security depends upon proper controls over access to the cryptographic keys.

End user – An entity that enters into a financial transaction, either through an organised exchange or a broker, for the purpose of hedging, asset/liability management or speculating. End users consist primarily of corporations, government entities, institutional investors and financial institutions. The derivative activities of end users are often related the production or use of a commodity by the entity.

Engagement circumstances – The terms of the engagement, the characteristics of subject matter, the criteria to be used, the needs of the intended users, relevant characteristics of the responsible party, and its environment and other matters (e.g. events, transactions, conditions and practices) that may have a significant effect on the subject matter and the engagement.

Engagement letter – An engagement letter documents and confirms the auditor's acceptance of the appointment, the objective and scope of the audit, the extent of the auditor's responsibilities to the client and the form of any reports.

Engagement partner – The partner or other person with sufficient and appropriate experience and authority in the firm who has responsibility for the engagement and its performance, for issuing the report on the subject matter on behalf of the firm, and who is permitted by law, regulation or a professional body to act in the role in the relevant jurisdiction.

Engagement proposal – A written proposal from the auditor or audit firm to the proposed or existing client proposing that an audit or assurance engagement be undertaken.

Engagement quality control review – A process designed to provide an objective evaluation, before the report is issued, of the significant judgements the engagement team made and the conclusions they reached in formulating the report.

Engagement quality control reviewer – A partner, other person in the firm, suitably qualified external person, or a team made up of such individuals, with sufficient and appropriate experience and authority to objectively evaluate, before the report is issued, the significant judgements the engagement team made and the conclusions they reached in formulating the report.

Engagement team – The individuals involved in performing an engagement, including any experts employed or engaged by the firm in connection with that engagement.

Entity – A separate or self-contained existence that provides goods or services; for example, a company, organisation or agency.

Entity's objectives – The overall plans for the company as determined by those charged with governance and management.

Enterprise resource planning (ERP) – A system that integrates all aspects of an organisation's activities (such as recording accounting transactions, database maintenance, financial reporting, operations and compliance) into one accounting information system.

Environmental matters – Environmental matters are defined as:
- initiatives to prevent, abate or remedy damage to the environment, or to deal with conservation of renewable and non-renewable resources (such initiatives may be required by environmental laws and regulations or by contract, or they may be undertaken voluntarily);
- consequences of violating environmental laws and regulations;
- consequences of environmental damage done to others or to natural resources;
- consequences of vicarious liability imposed by law (e.g. liability for damages caused by previous owners).

Environmental performance report – An environmental performance report is a report, separate from the financial statements, in which an entity provides third parties with qualitative information on the entity's commitments towards the environmental aspects of the business, its policies and targets in that field, its achievement in managing the relationship between its business processes and environmental risk, and quantitative information on its environmental performance.

Environmental risk – In certain circumstances, factors relevant to the assessment of inherent risk for the development of the overall audit plan may include the risk of material misstatement of the financial statements due to environmental matters.

Error – An error is an unintentional mistake in financial statements. See also **Audit sampling**.

Ethics – A set of moral principles, rules of conduct or values. The discipline dealing with values relating to human conduct, with respect to the rightness and wrongness of certain actions and to the goodness and badness of the motives and ends of such actions.

Evaluation assertion – Not an assertion given in the IFAC definitions (see **Financial statement assertions**). It is particular to specific firms. It means that the account balance has been evaluated for consistency.

Evidence – Anything that can make a person believe that a fact, proposition or assertion is true or false.

Evidence-gathering techniques – Those techniques employed by an auditor to obtain evidence. There are six types of evidence-gathering techniques including inquiry, observation, inspection (physical evidence and examination of documents), computation (reperformance or mechanical accuracy), confirmation, and analytical procedures.

Evolution analysis – A technique that determines the most significant changes in data sets over time. It includes other types of algorithm methods (i.e. data description, dependency analysis, classification or clustering) plus time-related and sequence-related characteristics.

Exchange-traded derivatives – Derivatives traded under uniform rules through an organised exchange.

Existence – see **Financial statement assertion**.

Existing accountant – A professional accountant in public practice currently holding an audit appointment or carrying out accounting, taxation, consulting or similar professional services for a client.

Existing auditor – The auditor who is currently holding an audit or assurance services appointment with the prospective client.

Expected error – see **Audit sampling**.

Experienced auditor – An individual (whether internal or external to the firm) who has practical audit experience, and a reasonable understanding of:
(i)   audit processes;
(ii) ISAs and applicable legal and regulatory requirements;
(iii) the business environment in which the entity operates; and
(iv) auditing and financial reporting issues relevant to the entity's industry.

Expert – A person or firm possessing special skill, knowledge and experience in a particular field other than accounting and auditing.

Extent of audit procedures – The size of the evidence sample audited.

External audit/auditor – see **Auditor**.

External confirmation – External confirmation is the process of obtaining and evaluating audit evidence through a direct communication from a third party in response to a request for information about a particular item affecting assertions made by management in the financial statements.

Factual misstatements – see **Misstatement**.

Fair value – The amount for which an asset could be exchanged, or a liability settled, between knowledgeable, willing parties in an arm's length transaction.

Familiarity threat – Occurs when, by virtue of a close relationship with an assurance client, its directors, officers or employees, an auditor becomes to sympathetic to the client's interests.

Fiduciary risk – The risk of loss arising from factors such as failure to maintain safe custody or negligence in the management of assets on behalf of other parties.

Fields – A group of bytes that make up a meaningful unit of information (e.g. account number, account balance, or account name).

File – Set of related data records.

File interrogation – A technique that performs automated routines on computer data.

File interrogation specifications – A document prepared by the engagement team that describes the file interrogation tests to be performed, documents any selection or calculation criteria, and documents control totals of one or more key fields.

File interrogation specialist – A professional in the firm who has appropriate training and experience in identifying, designing, and running file interrogation applications.

Financial instruments – Common stock, preferred stock, bonds, and other contracts or rights to assets, liabilities, or equity which convey financial interest to the holder.

Financial interest – An interest in an equity or other security, debenture, loan or other debt instrument of an entity, including rights and obligations to acquire such an interest and derivatives directly related to such interest.

Financial reporting policies – Company policies and accounting methods related to the reporting of accounting information.

Financial statement assertions – Financial statement assertions are assertions by management, explicit or otherwise, that are embodied in the financial statements and can be categorised as follows:

- **Accuracy** – Amounts and other data relating to recorded transactions and events have been recorded appropriately.
- **Classification** – Transactions and events have been recorded in the proper accounts.
- **Completeness** – All transactions, events, assets, liabilities, and equity interests that should have been recorded have been recorded.
- **Cut-off** – Transactions and events have been recorded in the correct accounting period.
- **Existence** – Assets, liabilities and equity interests exist.
- **Measurement** – A transaction or event is recorded at the proper amount and revenue or expense is allocated to the proper period.
- **Occurrence** – An assertion that a transaction or event took place which pertains to the entity during the period.

- **Presentation and disclosure** – An item is disclosed, classified, and described in accordance with the applicable financial reporting framework.
- **Rights and obligations** – An entity holds or controls the rights to assets, and liabilities are the obligations of the entity.
- **Transparency** – Financial information is appropriately classified and disclosures are understandable.
- **Valuation and allocation** – Assets, liabilities and equity interests are included in the financial statements at appropriate amounts and any resulting valuation or allocation adjustments are appropriately recorded.

Financial statement audit – An audit of financial statements guided by ISAs 100–799 and IAPSs 1000–1100.

Financial statements – The balance sheets, income statements or profit and loss accounts, statements of changes in financial position (which may be presented in a variety of ways, for example, as a statement of cash flows or a statement of fund flows), notes, and other statements and explanatory material which are identified as being part of the financial statements.

Firewall – A combination of hardware and software that protects a WAN, LAN or PC from unauthorised access through the internet and from the introduction of unauthorised or harmful software, data or other material in electronic form.

Firm – (a) A sole practitioner, partnership or corporation of professional accountants; (b) An entity that controls such parties; and (c) An entity controlled by such parties.

Floor – A series of put options based on a notional amount. The strike price of these options defines a lower limit to the interest rate.

Forecast – A forecast is prospective financial information prepared on the basis of assumptions as to future events which management expects to take place and the actions management expects to take as of the date the information is prepared (best-estimate assumptions).

Foreign exchange contracts – Contracts that provide an option for, or require a future exchange of foreign currency assets or liabilities.

Foreign exchange risk – The risk of losses arising through re-pricing of foreign currency instruments because of exchange rate fluctuations.

Forensic accounting – The application of accounting methods and financial techniques to collect civil and criminal legal evidence.

Forward contracts – A contract negotiated between two parties to purchase and sell a specified quantity of a financial instrument, foreign currency, or commodity at a price specified at the origination of the contract, with delivery and settlement at a specified future date.

Forward rate agreements – An agreement between two parties to exchange an amount determined by an interest rate differential at a given future date based on the difference between an agreed interest rate and a reference rate (LIBOR, Treasury bills, etc.) on a notional principal amount.

Fraud – Refers to an intentional act by one or more individuals among management, employees, or third parties, which results in a misrepresentation of financial statements.

Functional audit quality – The degree to which the process of carrying out the audit and communicating its results meets a consumer's expectations.

Futures contracts – Exchange-traded contracts to buy or sell a specified financial instrument, foreign currency or commodity at a specified future date or during a specified period at a specified price or yield.

General controls in computer information systems – The establishment of a framework of overall control over the computer information systems activities to provide a reasonable level of assurance that the overall objectives of internal control are achieved.

General IT controls – Policies and procedures that relate to many applications and support the effective functioning of application controls by helping to ensure the continued proper operation of information systems. General IT controls commonly include controls over data centre and network operations; system software acquisition, change and maintenance; access security; and application system acquisition, development and maintenance.

Generalised audit software (GAS) – A computer software package (e.g., ACL, Idea) that performs automated routines on electronic data files based on auditor expectations. GAS functions generally include reformatting, file manipulation, calculation, data selection, data analysis, file processing, statistics and reporting on the data. It may also include statistical sampling for detailed tests, generating confirmation letters.

Generally Accepted Auditing Standards (GAAS) – A set of auditing standards accepted by professional accountants.

Going concern assumption – Under the going concern assumption, an entity is ordinarily viewed as continuing in business for the foreseeable future with neither the intention nor the necessity of liquidation, ceasing trading, or seeking protection from creditors pursuant to laws or regulations. Accordingly, assets and liabilities are recorded on the basis that the entity will be able to realise its assets and discharge its liabilities in the normal course of business.

Governance – Describes the role of person(s) or organisation(s) with responsibility for overseeing the strategic direction of the entity and obligations related to the accountability of the entity. Those charged with governance ordinarily are accountable for ensuring that the entity achieves its objectives, financial reporting, and reporting to interested parties. Those charged with governance include management only when it performs such functions.

Government business enterprises – Government business enterprises are businesses which operate within the public sector ordinarily to meet a political or social interest objective. They are ordinarily required to operate commercially, that is, to make profits or to recoup, through user charges, a substantial proportion of their operating costs.

Group audit instructions – A communication from a group auditor to the related auditors and other auditors to provide them with the group auditor's requirements.

Group engagement partner – The partner or other person in the firm who is responsible for the group audit engagement and its performance, and for the auditor's report on the group financial statements that is issued on behalf of the firm. Where joint auditors conduct the group audit, the joint engagement partners and their engagement teams collectively constitute the group engagement partner and the group engagement team.

Group auditor – The independent auditor who signs the auditor's report on the group financial statements.

Group financial statements – Financial statements that include or should include financial information of more than one component by means of consolidation procedures or equity accounting methods. It may also mean a combination of components' financial information or an equivalent presentation.

Group management – Management responsible for the preparation and presentation of the group financial statements.

Gross negligence – see **Negligence of auditor**.

Hedge – A strategy that protects an entity against the risk of adverse price or interest rate movements on certain of its assets, liabilities or anticipated transactions. A hedge is used to avoid or reduce risks by creating a relationship by which losses on certain positions are expected to be counterbalanced, in whole or in part, by gains on separate positions in another market.

Hedge effectiveness – The degree to which offsetting changes in fair value or cash flows attributable to a hedged risk are achieved by the hedging instrument.

Hedged item – An asset, liability, firm commitment or forecasted future transaction that:
- exposes an entity to risk of changes in fair value or changes in future cash flows;
- for hedge accounting purposes, is designated as being hedged.

Hedging (for accounting purposes) – Designating one or more hedging instruments so that their change in fair value is an offset, completely or in part, to the change in fair value or cash flows of a hedged item.

Hedging instrument (for hedge accounting purposes) – A designated derivative or (in limited circumstances) another financial asset or liability whose value or cash flows are expected to offset changes in the fair value or cash flows of a designated hedged item.

Hidden reserves – Some financial reporting frameworks allow banks to manipulate their reported income by transferring amounts to non-disclosed reserves in years when they make large profits and transferring amounts from those reserves when they make losses or small profits. The reported income is the amount after such transfers. The practice served to make the entity appear more stable by reducing the volatility of its earnings, and would help to prevent a loss of confidence in the bank by reducing the occasions on which it would report low earnings.

Homogeneity – see **Audit sampling**.

HTML (Hypertext Mark-up Language) – The language used to format web pages. Web browsers like Internet Explorer transmit information using the hypertext transport protocol (HTTP).

Illegal act – An act or omission that violates any law or any rule having the force of law.

Immediate family – A spouse (or equivalent) or dependant.

Incoming auditor – see **Auditor**.

Independence – (a) Independence of mind – the state of mind that permits the provision of an opinion without being affected by influences that compromise professional judgement, allowing an individual to act with integrity, and exercise objectivity and professional scepticism; and (b) Independence in appearance – the avoidance of facts and circumstances that are so significant a reasonable and informed third party, having knowledge of all relevant information, including any safeguards applied, would reasonably conclude a firm's, or a member of the assurance team's, integrity, objectivity or professional scepticism had been compromised.

Independent director – A director is independent when he has no relationship of any kind whatsoever with the corporation, its group or the management of either that is such as to colour his judgement (See Bouton, D. (Chair), 2002, *Promoting Better Corporate Governance in Listed Companies*, report of working group, Mouvement des Entreprises de France, Paris.).

Indirect financial interest – A financial interest beneficially owned through a collective investment vehicle, estate, trust or other intermediary over which the individual or entity has no control.

Information asymmetry – A condition in which at least some relevant information is known to some but not all parties involved. Information asymmetry causes markets to become inefficient, since all the market participants do not have access to the information they need for their decision making processes.

Information technology – The computing, communications and management information systems technology. This technology includes computer hardware and software systems such as operating systems, networks, databases and operating applications (word processing, presentation, monitoring and design systems), as well as communications.

Inherent limitations in an audit – Limitations that result from such factors as the use of testing, the inherent limitations of any accounting and internal control system, and the fact that most audit evidence is persuasive rather than conclusive. Furthermore, the work performed by an auditor to form an opinion is permeated by judgement.

Inherent risk – see **Audit risk**.

Inquiry – Consists of seeking information of knowledgeable persons inside or outside the entity.

Inspection – Inspection consists of examining records, documents or tangible assets.

Inspection – In relation to completed engagements, procedures designed to provide evidence of compliance by engagement teams with the firm's quality control policies and procedures.

Inspired confidence, theory of – The demand for audit services is the direct consequence of the participation of outside stakeholders (*third parties*) in the company. These stakeholders demand accountability from the management, in return for their contribution to the company. Since information provided by management might be biased, because of a possible divergence between the interests of management and outside stakeholders, an audit of this information is required. (See Limperg, T.H., 1932, *Theory of Inspired Confidence*, University of Amsterdam, Amsterdam.)

Integrity – To be straightforward and honest in all professional and business relationships.

Intended users (for assurance services) – The class or classes of persons for whom the practitioner prepares the assurance report. It includes cases when there is only one intended user. The responsible party can be one of the intended users, but not the only one.

Interest rate risk – The risk that a movement in interest rates would have an adverse effect on the value of assets and liabilities or would affect interest cash flows.

Interest rate swap – A contract between two parties to exchange periodic interest payments on a notional amount (referred to as the notional principal) for a specified period. In the most common instance, an interest rate swap involves the exchange of streams of variable and fixed-rate interest payments.

Interim financial information or statements – Financial information (which may be less than full financial statements as defined above) issued at interim dates (usually half-yearly or quarterly) in respect of a financial period.

Internal auditing – An appraisal activity established within an entity as a service to the entity. Its functions include, amongst other things, examining, evaluating and monitoring the adequacy and effectiveness of the accounting and internal control systems.

Internal auditors – Those individuals who perform the activities of the internal audit function. Internal auditors may belong to an internal audit department or equivalent function.

Internal audit function – An appraisal activity established or provided as a service to the entity. Its functions include, among other things, examining, evaluating and monitoring the adequacy and effectiveness of internal control.

Internal control – A process, effected by an entity's board of directors, management and other personnel, designed to provide reasonable assurance regarding the achievement of objectives in the following categories: effectiveness and efficiency of operations, reliability of financial reporting, and compliance with applicable laws and regulations – Committee of Sponsoring Organisations of the Treadway Commission.

Internal control flow chart – A symbolic, diagrammatic representation of the client's documents and their sequential flow in the organisation.

Internal control questionnaire – A series of questions about the controls in each audit area as a means of indicating to the auditor aspects of the internal control structure that may be inadequate.

Internal control narrative – A written description of a client's internal control structure.

Internal control structure – The set of policies and procedures designed to provide management with reasonable assurance that the goals and objectives it believes are important will be met.

Internal control system – An internal control system consists of all the policies and procedures (internal controls) adopted by the management of an entity to assist in achieving management's objective of ensuring, as far as practicable, the orderly and efficient conduct of its business, including adherence to management policies, the safeguarding of assets, the prevention and detection of fraud and error, the accuracy and completeness of the accounting records, and the timely preparation of reliable financial information. The internal control system extends beyond these matters which relate directly to the functions of the accounting system.

International Financial Reporting Standards (IFRS) – The international standards for financial statements developed by the International Accounting Standards Board (IASB). IFRS set out recognition, measurement, presentation and disclosure requirements dealing with transactions and events that are important in general purpose financial statements.

International Standards on Assurance Engagements (ISAEs) – Standards applied in assurance engagements dealing with *subject matters* other than historical financial information. Developed by IAASB.

International Standards on Auditing (ISAs) – Standards applied, as appropriate, in the *audit* or *review* of historical financial information. Developed by IAASB.

International Standards on Quality Control (ISQCs) – The standards relating to quality of audit applied to all services falling under the standards of the IAASB.

International Standards on Related Services (ISRSs) – Standards applied to *compilation engagements*, engagements to apply *agreed-upon procedures* to information and other related services engagements as specified by the IAASB.

International Standards on Review Engagements (ISREs) – Standards applied to the *review* of historical financial information. Developed by IAASB.

Intimidation threat – Occurs when a member of the assurance team may be deterred from acting objectively and exercising professional scepticism by threats, actual or perceived, from the directors, officers, or employees of an assurance client.

IT environment – The policies and procedures that the entity implements and the IT infrastructure (hardware, operating systems, etc.) and application software that it uses to support business operations and achieve business strategies.

Joint and several liability – All parties involved are liable for losses.

Judgemental misstatements – see **Misstatement**.

Key performance indicators (KPIs) – Quantitative measurements, both financial and non-financial, of the process's ability to meet its objectives and of the process performance. They are usually analysed through trend analyses within a company, or benchmarking against a peer of the company or its industry. The KPIs that should be listed must be relevant to the critical success factors and/or the process objectives. The KPIs listed must have relevance to the organisation. Taken together they should provide a key set of measures for measuring process performance and achieving process objectives.

Knowledge of the business – The auditor's general knowledge of the economy and the industry within which the entity operates and a more particular knowledge of how the entity operates.

Lead engagement partner – In connection with an audit, the partner responsible for signing the report on the consolidated financial statements of the audit client and, where relevant, the partner responsible for signing the report in respect of any entity whose financial statements form part of the consolidated financial statements and on which a separate stand-alone report is issued. When no consolidated financial statements are prepared, the lead engagement partner would be the partner responsible for signing the report on the financial statements.

Lead schedule – A listing of the detailed accounts which make up the line item total on a general ledger trial balance.

Legal letter (or *inquiry of client's attorneys*) – A letter from the client's legal counsel informing the auditor of pending litigation or other information involving legal counsel that is relevant to financial statement disclosure.

Legal and documentary risk – The risk that contracts are documented incorrectly or are not legally enforceable in the relevant jurisdiction in which the contracts are to be enforced or where the counterparties operate. This can include the risk that assets will turn out to be worthless or liabilities will turn out to be greater than expected because of inadequate or incorrect legal advice or documentation. In addition, existing laws may fail to resolve legal issues involving a bank; a court case involving a particular bank may have wider implications for the banking business and involve costs to it and many or all other banks; and laws affecting banks or other commercial enterprises may change. Banks are particularly susceptible to legal risks when entering into new types of transactions and when the legal right of a counterparty to enter into a transaction is not established.

Legal risk – The risk that a legal or regulatory action could invalidate or otherwise preclude performance by the end user or its counterparty under the terms of the contract.

Lending Credibility Theory – Audited financial statements are used by management to enhance the stakeholders' faith in management's stewardship.

LIBOR (London Interbank Offered Rate) – An international interest rate benchmark. It is commonly used as a reprising benchmark for financial instruments such as adjustable rate mortgages, collateralised mortgage obligations, and interest rate swaps.

Limitation on scope – A limitation on the scope of the auditor's work may sometimes be imposed by the entity (e.g. when the terms of the engagement specify that the auditor will not carry out an audit procedure that the auditor believes is necessary). A scope limitation may be imposed by circumstances (e.g. when the timing of the auditor's appointment is such that the auditor is unable to observe the counting of physical inventories). It may also arise when, in the opinion of the auditor, the entity's accounting records are inadequate or when the auditor is unable to carry out an audit procedure believed desirable.

Linear contracts – Contracts that involve obligatory cash flows at a future date.

Liquidity – The capability of a financial instrument to be readily convertible into cash.

Liquidity risk – Changes in the ability to sell or dispose of the derivative. Derivatives bear the additional risk that a lack of sufficient contracts or willing counterparties may make it difficult to close out the derivative or enter into an offsetting contract.

List schedule – Shows the detail of those items that make up an end-of-period balance in a general ledger account.

Listed entity – An entity whose shares, stock or debt are quoted or listed on a recognised stock exchange, or are marketed under the regulations of a recognised stock exchange or other equivalent body.

Litigation support – The making of managerial decisions on behalf of an audit client or acting for an audit client in the resolution of a dispute or litigation when the amounts involved are material to the financial statements of the audit client.

Local area network (LAN) – A communications network that serves users within a confined geographical area. LANs were developed to facilitate the exchange and sharing of resources within an organisation, including data, software, storage, printers, and telecommunications equipment. They allow for decentralised computing. The basic components of a LAN are transmission media and software, user terminals and shared peripherals.

Management – Management comprises officers and others who also perform senior managerial functions. Management includes directors and the audit committee only in those instances when they perform such functions.

Management assertion – see **Financial statement assertions**.

Management letter – The auditor's written communications to management to point out weaknesses in the internal control, other reportable conditions, and possibilities for operational improvements.

Management report – A report that is needed for publicly traded companies in the US.

Management representations – Representations made by management to the auditor during the course of an audit, either unsolicited or in response to specific inquiries.

Management representations letter – A written communication from the client to the auditor formalising representations made by management to the auditor about matters pertinent to the audit.

Margin – (1) The amount of deposit money a securities broker requires from an investor to purchase securities on behalf of the investor on credit. (2) An amount of money or securities deposited by both buyers and sellers of futures contracts and short options to ensure performance of the terms of the contract, i.e. the delivery or taking of delivery of the commodity, or the cancellation of the position by a subsequent offsetting trade. Margin in commodities is not a payment of equity or down payment on the commodity itself, but rather a performance bond or security deposit.

Margin call – A call from a broker to a customer (called a maintenance margin call) or from a clearinghouse to a clearing member (called a variation margin call) demanding the deposit of cash or marketable securities to maintain a requirement for the purchase or short sale of securities or to cover an adverse price movement.

Market risk – The risk of losses arising because of adverse changes in the value of derivatives due to changes in equity prices, interest rates, foreign exchange rates, commodity prices or other market factors. Interest rate risk and foreign exchange risk are sub-sets of market risk.

Material inconsistency – A material inconsistency exists when other information contradicts information contained in the audited financial statements. A material inconsistency may raise doubt about the audit conclusions drawn from audit evidence previously obtained and, possibly, about the basis for the auditor's opinion on the financial statements.

Material misstatement – A significant mistake in financial information which would arise from errors and fraud if it could influence the economic decisions of users taken on the basis of the financial statements.

Material misstatement of fact – A material misstatement of fact in other information exists when such information, not related to matters appearing in the audited financial statements, is incorrectly stated or presented.

Material weaknesses – The weaknesses in internal control that could have a material effect on the financial statements.

Materiality – Information is material if its omission or misstatement could influence the economic decisions of users taken on the basis of the financial statements. Materiality depends on the size of the item or error judged in the particular circumstances of its omission or misstatement. Thus, materiality provides a threshold or cut-off point rather than being a primary qualitative characteristic which information must have if it is to be useful.

Materiality threshold – In substantive testing, the amount of audited difference between the book value of an account and the tested value that an auditor will accept before he determines that an account is misstated.

Matters for Attention of Partners (MAP) – A report by audit managers to be reviewed by a partner or director detailing the audit decisions reached by managers or partners and the reasons for those decisions.

Measurement – see **Financial statement assertions**.

Minutes of the board of directors – The written notes of a meeting of the board of directors which lists the names of the attendees, summarises the key topics discussed, and reports the results of any votes of the board.

Misappropriation – Employee theft of assets. Especially susceptible accounts are inventory and cash.

Misstatement – Incorrect information as a result of error, inappropriate application of standards or fraud.

- **Factual misstatements** – Misstatements about which there is no doubt.
- **Judgemental misstatements** – Differences arising from the judgements of management concerning accounting estimates that the auditor considers unreasonable, or the selection or application of accounting policies that the auditor considers inappropriate.
- **Projected misstatements** – The auditor's best estimate of misstatements in populations, involving the projection of misstatements identified in audit samples to the entire populations from which the samples were drawn. Guidance on the determination of projected misstatements and evaluation of the results is set out in ISA 530.

Modelling risk – The risk associated with the imperfections and subjectivity of valuation models used to determine the values of assets or liabilities.

Modified auditor's report – An auditor's report is considered to be modified if either an emphasis of matter paragraph(s) is added to the report or if the opinion is other than unqualified.

Monetary unit sampling – see **Audit sampling**.

Monitoring – For an audit firm a process comprising an ongoing consideration and evaluation of the firm's system of quality control, including a periodic inspection of a selection of completed engagements, designed to enable the firm to obtain reasonable assurance that its system of quality control is operating effectively.

National practices (auditing) – A set of auditing guidelines not having the authority of standards defined by an authoritative body at a country level and commonly applied by auditors in the conduct of an audit or related services.

National standards (auditing) – A set of auditing standards defined by law or regulations or an authoritative body at a country level, the application of which is mandatory in conducting an audit or related services and which should be complied with in the conduct of an audit or related services.

Nature of audit procedures – Primarily substantive (tests of transactions and tests of balances) tests, tests of controls, and analytical procedures.

Negative confirmation – A letter, addressed to the debtor, creditor, or third party, requesting a response only if the recipient disagrees with the amount of the stated account balance.

Negligence of auditor – An auditor in the performance of his duty may not use an appropriate level of care and therefore be legally liable.

- **Gross negligence** – Reckless behaviour with not even slight care.
- **Ordinary negligence** – The absence of reasonable care that can be expected in similar circumstances.

Network – A group of interconnected computers and terminals; a series of locations tied together by communications channels.

Network firm – An entity under common control, ownership, or management with the firm or any entity that a reasonable and informed third party having knowledge of all relevant information would reasonably conclude as being part of the firm nationally or internationally.

Neural network – A computer model based on the architecture of the brain. It first detects a pattern from data sets then predicts the best classifiers of that pattern, and finally learns from the mistakes.

Non-compliance – Used to refer to acts of omission or commission by the entity being audited, either intentional or unintentional, which are contrary to the prevailing laws or regulations.

Non-executive directors – A member of the board of directors who is not an executive of the entity supervised.

Non-linear contracts – Contracts that have option features where one party has the right, but not the obligation to demand that another party deliver the underlying item to it.

Non-sampling risk – see **Audit sampling**.

Nostros – Accounts held in the bank's name with a correspondent bank.

Notional amount – A number of currency units, shares, bushels, pounds or other units specified in a derivative instrument.

Object of an audit – see **Audit objective**.

Objectivity – To not allow bias, conflict of interest or undue influence of others to override professional or business judgements.

Observation – Observation consists of looking at a process or procedure being performed by others, for example, the observation by the auditor of the counting of inventories by the entity's personnel or the performance of internal control procedures that leave no audit trail.

Occurrence assertion – see **Financial statement assertions**.

Off-balance-sheet instrument – A derivative financial instrument that is not recorded on the balance sheet, although it may be disclosed.

Off-balance-sheet risk – The risk of loss to the entity in excess of the amount, if any, of the asset or liability that is recognised on the balance sheet.

Office – A distinct sub-group, whether organised on geographical or practice lines.

Opening balances – Opening balances are those account balances which exist at the beginning of the period. Opening balances are based upon the closing balances of the prior period and reflect the effects of transactions of prior periods and accounting policies applied in the prior period.

Operational auditing – A study of a specific unit of an organisation for the purpose of measuring its performance.

Operational risk – The risk of direct or indirect loss resulting from inadequate or failed internal processes, people and systems, or from external events.

Opinion – The auditor's report contains a clear written expression of opinion on the financial statements as a whole.

- **Adverse opinion** – An adverse opinion is expressed when the effect of a disagreement is so material and pervasive to the financial statements that the auditor concludes that a qualification of the report is not adequate to disclose the misleading or incomplete nature of the financial statements.

- **Disclaimer of opinion** – A disclaimer of opinion is expressed when the possible effect of a limitation on scope is so material and pervasive that the auditor has not been able to obtain sufficient appropriate audit evidence and accordingly is unable to express an opinion on the financial statements.

- **Qualified opinion** – A qualified opinion is expressed when the auditor concludes that an unqualified opinion cannot be expressed but that the effect of any disagreement with management, or limitation on scope, is not so material and pervasive as to require an adverse opinion or a disclaimer of opinion.

- **Unmodified (Unqualified) opinion** – An audit opinion expressed when the auditor concludes that the financial statements give a true and fair view (or are presented fairly, in all material respects) in accordance with the identified financial reporting framework. (See also **Modified auditor's report.**)

Option – A contract that gives the holder (or purchaser) the right, but not the obligation to buy (call) or sell (put) a specific or standard commodity, or financial instrument, at a specified price during a specified period (the American option) or at a specified date (the European option).

Ordinary negligence – see **Negligence of auditor.**

Other auditor – see **Auditor.**

Organisation chart – A visual diagram of an organisation's structure that depicts formal lines of reporting, communication and responsibility among managers.

Organisation for Economic Cooperation and Development (OECD) – The OECD groups 30 member countries sharing a commitment to democratic government and market economy in a unique forum to discuss, develop and, refine economic and social policies. Countries compare experiences, seek answers to common problems and work to coordinate domestic and international policies to help members and non-members deal with an increasingly globalised world. Their exchanges may lead to agreements to act in a formal way, for example by establishing legally binding agreements to crack down on bribery, or codes for free flow of capital and services. Together, they produce around two-thirds of the world's goods and services.

Outcome of the audit process – The end results after planning and performing procedures on financial statements.

Outlier analysis – Analysis of data items (outliers) that are distinctly dissimilar to others, fall outside the standard distribution of data, and ordinarily are viewed as noises or errors in the data sets.

Outside directors – Directors on an entity's board of directors who are neither officers nor employees of the entity.

Parent – The entity in respect of which group financial statements are or should be prepared.

Parent company – The owner of a subsidiary company and this could be a holding company not engaged in a trade or business.

Partner – Any individual with authority, whether through office or otherwise, to bind the firm.

PCs or personal computers (also referred to as *microcomputers*) – Economical yet powerful self-contained general purpose computers consisting typically of a monitor (visual display unit), a case containing the computer electronics, and a keyboard (and mouse). These features may be combined in portable computers (laptops). Programs and data may be stored internally on a hard disk or on removable storage media such as CDs or floppy disks. PCs may be connected to online networks, printers and other devices such as scanners and modems.

Performance materiality – The amount or amounts set by the auditor at less than materiality for the financial statements as a whole to reduce to an appropriately low level the probability that the aggregate of uncorrected and undetected misstatements exceeds materiality for the financial statements as a whole. If applicable, performance materiality also refers to the amount or amounts set by the auditor at less than the materiality level or levels for particular classes of transactions, account balances or disclosures.

Performance reviews – Independent checks on performance by a third party not directly involved in the activity.

Permanent audit file – A file of audit work papers containing all the data that is of continuing interest from year to year.

Personnel – Partners and staff (see **Auditor**).

Persuasive evidence – Evidence that has the power or ability to persuade based on logic or reason, often depending on the use of inductive or deductive reasoning. Evidence may be persuasive based on the character, credibility or reliability of the source.

Pervasive – A term used, in the context of misstatements, to describe the effects on the financial statements of misstatements or the possible effects on the financial statements of misstatements, if any, that are undetected due to an inability to obtain sufficient appropriate audit evidence. Pervasive effects on the financial statements are those that, in the auditor's judgement:
(a) are not confined to specific elements, accounts or items of the financial statements;
(b) if so confined, represent or could represent a substantial proportion of the financial statements; or
(c) in relation to disclosures, are fundamental to users' understanding of the financial statements.

Physical controls – Procedures to ensure the physical security of assets.

Planning – Planning involves developing a general strategy and a detailed approach for the expected nature, timing and extent of the audit.

Planning memorandum – A written discussion of the audit strategy and audit plan which incorporates most of the important ideas of the audit.

Policeman theory – An auditor's job was to focus on arithmetical accuracy and on prevention and detection of fraud.

Policy – Management's dictate of what should be done to effect control. A policy serves as the basis for procedures and their implementation.

Population – see **Audit sampling**.

Position – The status of the net of claims and obligations in financial instruments of an entity.

Positive confirmation – The process of obtaining and evaluating audit evidence through a direct communication from a third party in response to a request for information about a particular item affecting assertions made by management in the financial statements. The request for *positive confirmation* asks the recipient (debtor, creditor, or other third party) to confirm agreement or by asking the respondent to fill in information.

Post balance sheet events – see **Subsequent events**.

Power of the test – see **Audit sampling**.

Practice – A sole practitioner, a partnership or a corporation of professional accountants which offers professional services to the public.

Practitioner – A professional accountant in public practice.

Predecessor auditor – The auditor who was previously the auditor of an entity and who has been replaced by an incoming auditor. (See also **Auditor**.)

Pre-formatting – An online data entry control in which the computer displays a form on the screen and the user fills in the blanks on the form.

Preponderance of evidence – Upon listening to both sides, the weight of the evidence inclines a person with an impartial mind to one side rather than the other.

Presentation and disclosure assertion – see **Financial statement assertions**.

Price risk – The risk of changes in the level of prices due to changes in interest rates, foreign exchange rates, or other factors that relate to market volatility of the underlying rate, index or price.

Principal auditor – see **Auditor**.

Privity – A relationship that is established by contract between entities. There can be privity of contract without a written agreement under common law.

Probable cause – Serves as the basis for arrest and search warrants.

Procedures to obtain an understanding – Procedures used by the auditor to gather evidence about the design and placement in operation of specific control policies and procedures.

Professional accountant – That person, whether in public practice (including a sole practitioner, partnership or corporate body), industry, commerce, the public sector or education who is a member of an IFAC member body.

Professional accountant in public practice – Each partner or person occupying a position similar to that of a partner, and each employee in a practice providing professional services to a client irrespective of their functional classification (e.g. audit, tax or consulting) and professional accountants in a practice having managerial responsibilities. This term is also used to refer to a firm of professional accountants in public practice.

Professional behaviour – To comply with relevant laws and regulations and avoid any action that discredits the profession.

Professional competence and due care – To maintain professional knowledge and skill at the level required to ensure that a client or employer receives competent professional services based on current developments in practice, legislation and techniques and act diligently and in accordance with applicable technical and professional standards.

Professional judgement – The application of relevant training, knowledge and experience, within the context provided by auditing, accounting and ethical standards, in making informed decisions about the courses of action that are appropriate in the circumstances of the audit engagement.

Professional service – Any service requiring accountancy or related skills performed by a professional accountant including accounting, auditing, taxation, management consulting, and financial management services.

Professional scepticism – Having a questioning mind and performing a critical assessment of audit evidence through the audit process.

Professional standards – IAASB engagement standards and relevant ethical requirements, which ordinarily comprise Parts A and B of the IESBA Code of Ethics for Professional Accountants and national ethical requirements.

Programming controls – Procedures designed to prevent or detect improper changes to computer programs that are accessed through online terminal devices. Access may be restricted by controls such as the use of separate operational and program development libraries, and the use of specialised program library software. It is important for online changes to programs to be adequately documented, controlled and monitored.

Projected misstatements – see **Misstatement**.

Projection – A projection is prospective financial information prepared on the basis of: (a) Hypothetical assumptions about future events and management actions which are not necessarily expected to take place, such as when some entities are in a start-up phase or are considering a major change in the nature of operations; or (b) A mixture of best-estimate and hypothetical assumptions.

Proportionate liability – A defendant is not liable for the entire liability or loss incurred by plaintiffs, but only to the extent to which the loss is attributable to the defendant.

Proposed professional accountant – A professional accountant in public practice who will act as the current financial period's auditor (and who did not audit the prior period's financial statements).

Prospective financial information – Prospective financial information is financial information based on assumptions about events that may occur in the future and possible actions by an entity. Prospective financial information can be in the form of a forecast, a projection or a combination of both. (See also **Forecast** and **Projection**).

Provision – An adjustment to the carrying value of an asset to take account of factors that might reduce the asset's worth to the entity. Sometimes called an allowance.

Prudential ratios – Ratios used by regulators to determine the types and amounts of lending a bank can undertake.

Public Company Accounting Oversight Board (PCAOB) – An independent board established under the US Sarbanes–Oxley Act of 2002 to oversee the audit of public companies that are subject to the securities laws of the USA in order to protect the interests of investors and the public in the preparation of informative, accurate and independent audit reports.

Public interest companies – Broadly defined by the EU 2004 proposal for statutory audits as listed (publicly-traded) companies, banks or insurance companies.

Public sector – Refers to national governments, regional (e.g. state, provincial, territorial) governments, local (e.g. city, town) governments and related governmental entities (e.g. agencies, boards, commissions and enterprises).

Publicity – The communication to the public of facts about a professional accountant which are not designed for the deliberate promotion of that professional accountant.

Qualified opinion – see **Modified auditor's report** and **Opinion**.

Quality controls – The policies and procedures adopted by a firm to provide reasonable assurance that all audits done by the firm are being carried out in accordance with the Objective and General Principles Governing an Audit of Financial Statements, as set out in International Standard on Auditing 220 'Quality Control for Audit Work' and International Standard on Quality Control (ISQC).

Ratio analysis – The comparison of relationships between financial statement accounts, the comparison of an account with non-financial data, or the comparison of relationships between firms in an industry.

Reasonable assurance – In the context of audit engagements, and in quality control is a high, but not absolute, level of assurance. In an audit engagement, the auditor provides a high, but not absolute, level of assurance, expressed positively in the audit report as reasonable assurance, that the information subject to audit is free of material misstatement.

Reasonable doubt – The degree of certainty a person has in accomplishing or transacting the more important concerns in everyday life.

Reasonableness testing – The analysis of account balances or changes in account balances within an accounting period in terms of their 'reasonableness' in light of expected relationships between accounts.

Recalculation – Checking the arithmetical accuracy of source documents and accounting records or performing independent calculations.

Receiving accountant – A professional accountant in public practice to whom the existing accountant or client of the existing accountant has referred audit, accounting, taxation, consulting or similar appointments, or who is consulted in order to meet the needs of the client.

Reconciliation – Relates a specific amount in the accounting records to another source of information (e.g. a reconciliation of accounts payable balances with vendor's statements).

Recording – The creation of documentary evidence of a transaction and its entry into the accounting records.

Regression analysis – The use of statistical models to quantify the auditor's expectation in dollar terms, with measurable risk and precision levels.

Regulatory risk – The risk of loss arising from failure to comply with regulatory or legal requirements in the relevant jurisdiction in which the bank operates. It also includes any loss that could arise from changes in regulatory requirements.

Related auditor – An independent auditor from the group auditor's office, other office of the group auditor's firm, a network firm or another firm operating under common quality control policies and procedures as described in International Standard on Quality Control (ISQC) #1 'Quality Control for Audit, Assurance and Related Services Practices'.

Related entity – An entity that has any of the following relationships with the client: (a) An entity that has direct or indirect control over the client provided the client is material to such entity; (b) An entity with a direct financial interest in the client provided that such entity has significant influence over the client and the interest in the client is material to such entity; (c) An entity over which the client has direct or indirect control; (d) An entity in which the client, or an entity related to the client under (c) above, has a direct financial interest that gives it significant influence over such entity and the interest is material to the client and its related entity in (c); and (e) An entity which is under common control with the client (hereinafter a 'sister entity') provided the sister entity and the client are both material to the entity that controls both the client and sister entity.

Related party – Parties are considered to be related if one party has the ability to control the other party or exercise significant influence over the other party in making financial and operating decisions.

Related party transaction – A transfer of resources or obligations between related parties, regardless of whether a price is charged.

Related services – Related services comprise reviews, agreed-upon procedures and compilations.

Relational database – A database in which all data elements are logically viewed as being stored in the form of two-dimensional tables called 'relations'. Each column represents a field where the record's attributes are stored.

Relevance of evidence – The appropriateness (pertinence) of the evidence to the audit objective being tested.

Reliability – The quality of information when it is free from material error and bias and can be depended upon by users to represent faithfully that which it either purports to represent or could reasonably be expected to represent.

Re-performance – Performance of an auditor of a task done by an employee to verify the result of the transaction.

Replacement risk (sometimes called *performance risk*) – The risk of failure of a customer or counterparty to perform the terms of a contract. This failure creates the need to replace the failed transaction with another at the current market price. This may result in a loss to the bank equivalent to the difference between the contract price and the current market price.

Reportable conditions – Significant deficiencies in the design or operation of the internal control structure which could adversely affect the organisation's ability to record, process, summarise, and report financial data consistent with the assertions of management in the financial statements (AICPA SAS 60 (AU 325)).

Report on the description and design of controls at a service organisation (referred to in ISA 402 as a type 1 report) – A report that comprises:
- a description, prepared by management of the service organisation, of the service organisation's system, control objectives and related controls that have been designed and implemented as at a specified date; and
- a report by the service auditor with the objective of conveying reasonable assurance that includes the service auditor's opinion on the description of the service organisation's system, control objectives and related controls and the suitability of the design of the controls to achieve the specified control objectives.

Report on the description, design and operating effectiveness of controls at a service organisation (referred to in ISA 402 as a type 2 report) – A report that comprises:

- a description, prepared by management of the service organisation, of the service organisation's system, control objectives and related controls, their design and implementation as at a specified date or throughout a specified period and, in some cases, their operating effectiveness throughout a specified period; and
- a report by the service auditor with the objective of conveying reasonable assurance that includes:
  - the service auditor's opinion on the description of the service organisation's system, control objectives and related controls, the suitability of the design of the controls to achieve the specified control objectives, and the operating effectiveness of the controls; and
  - a description of the service auditor's tests of the controls and the results thereof.

Representativeness – see **Audit sampling**.

Reputational risk – The risk of losing business because of negative public opinion and consequential damage to the entity's reputation arising from failure to properly manage some significant risks, or from involvement in improper or illegal activities by the entity or its senior management, such as money laundering or attempts to cover up losses.

Responsible party – Someone other than the intended user or the practitioner who is responsible for the subject matter (e.g. board of directors, management).

Revenue cycle – The recurring set of business activities and information-processing operations associated with providing goods and services to customers and collecting cash in payment for those sales.

Review – see **Review of financial statements**.

Review of financial statements – The objective of a review of financial statements engagement is to enable an auditor to state whether, on the basis of procedures which do not provide all the evidence that would be required in an audit, anything has come to the auditor's attention that causes the auditor to believe that the financial statements are not prepared, in all material respects, in accordance with an identified financial reporting framework.

Rights and obligations assertions – see **Financial statement assertions**.

Risk assessment procedures – The audit procedures performed to obtain an understanding of the entity and its environment, including the entity's internal control, to identify and assess the risks of material misstatement, whether due to fraud or error, at the financial statement and assertion levels.

Risk assessment process (of the entity) – Forms the basis for how management determines the risks to be managed. If that process is appropriate to the circumstances, including the nature, size and complexity of the entity, it assists the auditor in identifying risks of material misstatement.

Risk management – Using derivatives and other financial instruments to increase or decrease risks associated with existing or anticipated transactions.

Roll forward – An audit procedure whereby a month-end closing (hand close) is audited and then transactions in the intervening months, before the fiscal year-end closing (balance sheet date) are audited and combined with the results of the hand close.

Sales cycle – see Revenue cycle.

Sampling risk – see **Audit sampling**.

Sampling unit – see **Audit sampling**.

Sarbanes–Oxley Act of 2002 – This Act was passed by US Congress and signed into law by President W. Bush on 30 July 2002. The Act is intended to establish investor confidence by improving the quality of corporate disclosure and financial reporting, strengthen the independence of accounting firms, and increase the role and responsibility of corporate officers and directors in financial statements and corporate disclosures. It required the US Securities and Exchange Commission (SEC) to create a Public Company Accounting Oversight Board (PCAOB). The most famous sections are on internal control reporting in Section 404 'Management Assessment of Internal Controls' (107th US Congress, 2002, Sarbanes–Oxley Act of 2002, Public Law 107–204, Senate and House of Representatives of the United States of America in Congress assembled, Washington, DC, 30 July).

Scope limitation – see **Limitation on scope**.

Scope of an audit – The term 'scope of an audit' refers to the audit procedures deemed necessary in the circumstances to achieve the objective of the audit.

Scope of a review – The term 'scope of a review' refers to the review procedures deemed necessary in the circumstances to achieve the objective of the review.

Scope paragraph – The paragraph in an audit opinion that describes the nature of the audit and the standards by which it was carried out. It is the second paragraph in an unqualified and qualified audit opinion.

Scope sample – A sample of data from a subsidiary ledger or account classification (customer invoices, shipping documents) based on auditor judgement that represents a variety of types of information from that classification.

Second-tier audit firm – An audit firm that is not one of the Big Four (first-tier firms), but is one level below them in terms of revenue, assets, etc.

Segment information – Information in the financial statements regarding distinguishable components or industry and geographical aspects of an entity.

Segregation of duties – A segregation of the following activities in an organisation: custody of assets, accounting (or recording), and authorisation.

Self-interest threat – Occurs when an auditor could benefit from the financial interest in, or other self-interests conflict with, an assurance client.

Self-review threat – Occurs when (a) when any product or judgement of a previous assurance engagement or non-assurance engagement needs to be re-evaluated in reaching conclusions on the assurance engagement; or (b) when a member of the assurance team was previously a director or officer of the assurance client or was an employee in a position to exert direct and significant influence over the subject matter of the assurance engagement.

Sensitivity Analysis – A general class of models designed to assess the risk of loss in market-risk-sensitive instruments based upon hypothetical changes in market rates or prices.

Sequence check – An edit check that determines if a batch of input data is in the proper numerical or alphabetical sequence.

Service auditor – An auditor who, at the request of the service organisation, provides an assurance report on the controls of a service organisation.

Service organisation – A third-party organisation (or segment of a third-party organisation) that provides services to user entities that are part of those entities' information systems relevant to financial reporting.

Service organisation's system – The policies and procedures designed, implemented and maintained by the service organisation to provide user entities with the services covered by the service auditor's report.

Subservice organisation – A service organisation used by another service organisation to perform some of the services provided to user entities that are part of those user entities' information systems relevant to financial reporting.

Settlement date – The date on which derivative transactions are to be settled by delivery or receipt of the underlying product or instrument in return for payment of cash.

Settlement risk – The risk that one side of a transaction will be settled without value being received from the customer or counterparty. This will generally result in the loss to the bank of the full principal amount.

Side agreements – see **Side letters**.

Side letters – Agreements made outside the standard company contracts. These otherwise undisclosed agreements may be signed by senior officers, but not approved by the board of directors.

Significance – Significance is related to materiality of the financial statement assertion affected.

Significant risk – A type of business risk that generally relates to judgemental matters and significant non-routine transactions requiring special audit consideration.

Small entity – A small entity is any entity in which:
  (a) there is concentration of ownership and management in a small number of individuals (often a single individual); and
  (b) one or more of the following are also found:
    (i) few sources of income;
    (ii) unsophisticated record-keeping;
    (iii) limited internal controls together with the potential for management override of controls.
Small entities will ordinarily display characteristic (a), and one or more of the characteristics included under (b).

Solicitation – An approach to a potential client for the purpose of offering professional services.

Solvency risk – The risk of loss arising from the possibility of the bank not having sufficient funds to meet its obligations, or from the bank's inability to access capital markets to raise required funds.

Special purpose auditor's report – A report issued in connection with the independent audit of financial information other than an auditor's report on financial statements, including:
  (a) Financial statements prepared in accordance with a comprehensive basis of accounting other than International Accounting Standards or national standards.

(b) Specified accounts, elements of accounts, or items in a financial statement.

(c) Compliance with contractual agreements.

(d) Summarised financial statements.

Special purpose engagement – An independent audit of financial information other than financial statements in accordance with IFRS or the national financial reporting standards, including:

■ Financial statements prepared in accordance with a comprehensive basis of accounting other than International Accounting Standards or national standards.

■ Specified accounts, elements of accounts, or items in a financial statement.

■ Compliance with contractual agreements.

■ Summarised financial statements.

Special purpose entity (SPE) – Defined as an entity (e.g. corporation, partnership, trust, joint venture) created for a specific purpose or activity. SPEs may be used to transfer assets and liabilities from an entity; accounted for as a gain for that entity. Between 1993 and 2001, Enron created over 3,000 SPEs.

Speculation – Entering into an exposed position to maximise profits; that is, assuming risk in exchange for the opportunity to profit on anticipated market movements.

Staff – Individuals, other than the engagement partner, involved in performing engagements, including any experts employed or engaged by the firm in connection with that engagement.

Stakeholders – Individuals and entities who have a stake (claim, share, involvement, interest) in a company. Stakeholders may include shareholders, employees, government, banks, etc.

Standards of proof – Concepts that describe the quality of evidence for most legal systems. There are four standards of proof: (1) beyond a reasonable doubt, (2) preponderance of evidence, (3) clear and convincing evidence, and (4) probable cause.

Statistical sampling – see **Audit sampling**.

Statutory audit – Audits established by law.

Strategies – The operational approaches by which management intends to achieve its objectives.

Stratification – see **Audit sampling**.

Stress testing – Testing a valuation model by using assumptions and initial data outside normal market circumstances and assessing whether the model's predictions are still reliable.

Subject matter – In an assurance engagement, the topic about which the assurance is conducted. Subject matter could be financial statements, statistical information, non-financial performance indicators, capacity of a facility, etc.

Subsequent events – Events occurring between the date of the financial statements and the date of the auditor's report, and facts that become known to the auditor after the date of the auditor's report.

Subsequent events – International Accounting Standard 10 identifies two types of events both favourable and unfavourable occurring after period end:

(a) Those that provide further evidence of conditions that existed at period end;

(b) Those that are indicative of conditions that arose subsequent to period end.

Subsidiary company – A firm in which a controlling interest is owned by another company, called a parent company.

Substantive procedure – An audit procedure designed to detect material misstatements at the assertion level. Substantive procedures comprise: (a) tests of details (of classes of transactions, account balances, and disclosures); and (b) substantive analytical procedures.

Substantive testing – see **Substantive procedures**.

Sufficiency – The measure of the quantity of audit evidence.

Sufficient appropriate audit evidence – *Sufficiency* is the measure of the quantity (amount) of audit evidence. *Appropriateness* is the measure of the quality of audit evidence and its relevance to a particular assertion and its reliability.

Suitably qualified external person – An individual outside the audit firm with the capabilities and competence to act as an engagement partner, for example, a partner of another firm or an employee (with appropriate experience) of either a professional accountancy body whose members may perform audits and reviews of historical financial information, or other assurance or related services engagements, or of an organisation that provides relevant quality control services.

Summarised financial statements – An entity may prepare financial statements summarising its annual audited financial statements for the purpose of informing user groups interested in the highlights only of the entity's financial performance and position.

Summary of procedures description schedule – A schedule which summarises the result of audit procedures performed.

Supreme Audit Institution – The public body of a state which, however designated, constituted, or organised, exercises by virtue of law, the highest public auditing function of that state.

Suspense file – An account used to balance transactions when there is an error, the resolution of which is not possible at that time.

Sustainability – The set of perceptual and analytic abilities, ecological wisdom, and practical wherewithal essential to the meshing of human purposes with the larger patterns and flows of the natural world, and careful study of those patterns and flows to inform human purposes. As a value, it refers to giving equal weight in your decisions to the future as well as the present. Actions are sustainable if:
(a) There is a balance between resources used and resources regenerated.
(b) Resources are as clean or cleaner at end use as at beginning.
(c) The viability, integrity and diversity of natural systems are restored and maintained.
(d) They lead to enhanced local and regional self-reliance.
(e) They help create and maintain community and a culture of place.
(f) Each generation preserves the legacies of future generations.

Swaption – A combination of a swap and an option.

Technical audit quality – The degree to which an audit meets a consumer's expectations with regard to the detection and reporting of errors and irregularities regarding the audited company and its financial statements.

Term structure of interest rates – The relationship between interest rates of different terms. When interest rates of bonds are plotted graphically according to their interest rate terms, this is called the 'yield curve.' Economists and investors believe that the shape of the yield curve reflects the market's future expectation for interest rates and thereby provide predictive information concerning the conditions for monetary policy.

Terms of the engagement – Agreed to conditions or terms to the employment of an auditing firm by a client to provide a specific service for a given period of time which is generally recorded in an engagement letter or other suitable form, such as a contract.

Test of reasonableness schedule – A schedule containing information that enables the auditor to evaluate whether the client's balance appears to include a misstatement considering the circumstances.

Test of controls – An audit procedure designed to evaluate the operating effectiveness of controls in preventing, or detecting and correcting, material misstatements at the assertion level.

Tests of details of balances – Audit tests that substantiate the ending balance of a general ledger or line item in a financial statement.

Tests of details of transactions – Audit procedures related to examining the processing of particular classes of transactions through the accounting system. Tests of transactions are usually performed for major classes of transactions.

Theory of Inspired Confidence – see **Inspired Confidence, theory of.**

Third parties – Someone other than the principals directly involved in a transaction or agreement.

Tick marks – Symbols used by the auditor to indicate the nature and extent of procedures applied in specific circumstances. Tick marks are notations directly on the working paper schedules. Tick marks are generally done by hand with a pen or pencil alongside a specific item.

Timing of audit procedures – Timing concerns the day on which audit procedures occur and in what sequence. For example, are procedures planned at the end of the period or at an earlier (interim) date.

Tolerable misstatement – A monetary amount set by the auditor in respect of which the auditor seeks to obtain an appropriate level of assurance that the monetary amount set by the auditor is not exceeded by the actual misstatement in the population.

Tort – A wrongful act, damage or injury done wilfully, negligently or in circumstances where liability is strictly applied.

Tracing – An audit procedure whereby the auditor selects sample items from basic source documents and proceeds forward through the accounting system to find the final recording of the transaction (e.g. in the ledger).

Trading – The buying and selling of financial instruments for short-term profit.

Transaction logs – Reports that are designed to create an audit trail for each online transaction. Such reports often document the source of a transaction (terminal, time and user) as well as the transaction's details.

Transfer risk – The risk of loss arising when counterparty's obligation is not denominated in the counterparty's home currency. The counterparty may be unable to obtain the currency of the obligation irrespective of the counterparty's particular financial condition.

Transparency – For corporations, practices that make rules, regulations, and accounting methods open and accessible to the public. Transparency includes concepts like openness, reporting and disclosure.

Trend analysis – The analysis of changes in an account balance over time.

Trial balance – A listing of the account balances from the general ledger, prepared at the end of the accounting period.

Triple bottom line – Sustainability reporting in terms of economic, environmental, and social performance based on Global Reporting Initiative.

Type 1 error – see **Audit sampling**.

Type 2 error – see **Audit sampling**.

Unadjusted audit differences – These are proposed adjusting entries with accompanying written justifications suggested by the auditor to bring the account balance on the company financial statements in line with the audited account balance.

Unasserted claim – A potential legal claim against a client where the condition for a claim exists but no claim has been filed.

Uncertainty – An uncertainty is a matter whose outcome depends on future actions or events not under the direct control of the entity but that may affect the financial statements.

Underlying – A specified interest rate, security price, commodity price, foreign exchange rate, index of prices or rates, or other variable. An underlying may be a price or rate of an asset or liability, but it is not the asset or liability itself.

Unqualified opinion – see **Opinion**.

User control procedures – Procedures in audit testing of documentation representing manual checks of the completeness and accuracy of computer output against source documents and other input.

User entity – An entity that uses a service organisation and whose financial statements are being audited.

Valuation assertion – see **Financial statement assertions**.

Valuation risk – The risk that the fair value of the derivative is determined incorrectly.

Valuation services – Involve the valuation of matters material to the financial statements and where the valuation involves a significant degree of subjectivity.

Value at risk (VAR) – A general class of models that provides a probabilistic assessment of the risk of loss in market-risk-sensitive instruments over a period of time, with a selected likelihood of occurrences based upon selected confidence intervals.

Volatility – A measure of the variability of the price of an asset or index.

Vostros – Accounts held by the bank in the name of a correspondent bank.

Vouching – The use of documentation to support recorded transactions or amounts. It is an audit process whereby the auditor starts with an account balance and goes backwards through the accounting system to the source document.

Walk-through test – Involves tracing a few transactions through the accounting system.

Weakness in internal control – The absence of adequate controls which increases the risk of misstatement in the financial statements.

Wide area network (WAN) – A communications network that transmits information across an expanded area such as between plant sites, cities, and nations. WANs allow for online access to applications from remote terminals. Several LANs can be interconnected in a WAN.

Working papers – Also known as *work papers* these are a record of the auditor's planning; nature, timing, and extent of the auditing procedures performed; and results of such procedures and the conclusions drawn from the evidence obtained. Working papers may be in the form of data stored on paper, film, electronic media, or other media.

Write-offs – Costs related to loss in value of an asset (non-collection of accounts receivable, loss in value of equipment, etc.) which are charged to expense or loss.

Written representation – A written statement by management provided to the auditor to confirm certain matters or to support other audit evidence. Written representations in this context do not include financial statements, the assertions therein, or supporting books and records.

Written option – The writing, or sale, of an option contract that obligates the writer to fulfil the contract should the holder choose to exercise the option.

XBRL (Extensible Business Reporting Language) – Based on XML, this is a tagging system for financial data. It provides taxonomy for US Generally Accepted Accounting Principles and International Financial Reporting Standards, and can be used on a transactional basis. An offshoot of **XML**, XBRL is a freely licensed, open technology standard that makes it possible to store and/or transfer data along with the complex hierarchies, data-processing rules and descriptions.

XML (eXtensible Mark-up Language) – A set of rules, guidelines, or conventions for designing text formats for such data, in a way that produces files that are easy to generate and read (by a computer), that are unambiguous, and that avoid common pitfalls, such as lack of extensibility, lack of support for internationalisation/localisation, and platform dependency. XML is an extension of the World Wide Web Consortium's (W3C) Standard Generalised Mark-up Language (SGML) that allows creation of custom (extensible) data tags, provides a universal data format, allows data objects to be serialised into text streams, and can be parsed by all internet browsers.